GLOBAL ISSUES

SELECTIONS FROM CQ RESEARCHER

Los Angeles | London | New Delhi
Singapore | Washington DC

For information:

Pine Forge Press
An Imprint of SAGE Publications, Inc.
2455 Teller Road
Thousand Oaks, California 91320
E-mail: order@sagepub.com

SAGE Publications Ltd.
1 Oliver's Yard
55 City Road
London EC1Y 1SP
United Kingdom

SAGE Publications India Pvt. Ltd.
B 1/I 1 Mohan Cooperative Industrial Area
Mathura Road, New Delhi 110 044
India

SAGE Publications Asia-Pacific Pte. Ltd.
33 Pekin Street #02-01
Far East Square
Singapore 048763

Printed in the United States of America on acid-free paper.

Paperback ISBN: 978-1-4129-8037-1

09 10 11 12 13 10 9 8 7 6 5 4 3 2 1

Acquisitions Editor: David Repetto
Editorial Assistant: Nancy Scrofano
Production Editor: Laureen Gleason
Typesetter: C&M Digitals (P) Ltd.
Cover Designer: Candice Harman
Marketing Manager: Jennifer Reed Banando

Contents

CONFLICT

HUMAN RIGHTS

Annotated Contents

ECONOMIC ISSUES

The Troubled Dollar: Will the World's "Anchor" Currency Be Replaced?

Since World War II, the powerful U.S. dollar has symbolized American economic might and fueled an expanding global economy. Foreign central banks stash dollars in their vaults as secure reserves, and most international financial transactions occur in dollars. But since 2002, America's record-high trade and federal budget deficits have severely weakened the dollar, which has lost 21 percent of its value against other leading currencies. That has helped to push oil and food prices higher around the globe, causing suffering among the poor and painful economic adjustments for others. Foreign investors — who in 2007 held more than half of the U.S. Treasury's $3.5 trillion worth of debt — had begun to lose confidence in the dollar even before the current Wall Street financial crisis and Washington's struggles to craft a rescue plan. Experts now debate whether in the coming decade the dollar could collapse in value against other currencies or even be replaced as the world's currency of choice by the euro — or, eventually, by China's yuan.

The New Latin America: Will Radicals or Moderates Triumph?

Latin America is struggling to re-define its soul. The region's once ubiquitous military dictators in dark glasses have been replaced by a new generation of democratically elected leaders. Under their tutelage Latin America is enjoying steady growth and trying to bridge the notoriously deep chasm between the rich and the poor. Wealth and global trade have brought a new sense of cohesion and an unprecedented regional identity, while newly empowered women and indigenous and mixed-race populations are transforming the political landscape. Amid these positive signs, experts ask whether the future belongs to the more moderate, market-oriented democracies — such as those in Brazil, Chile, Mexico and Argentina — or to the more radical, left-wing populism inspired by Venezuela's bombastic socialist leader Hugo Chávez. Meanwhile, with the United States preoccupied in Iraq and elsewhere, the European Union, the Gulf States and China are increasing their economic presence in the region as U.S. influence declines.

POLITICAL ISSUES

Middle East Peace Prospects: Is There Any Hope for Long-Term Peace?

Three major events reshaped the political landscape of the Middle East during a seven-week period beginning in late 2008. Israel launched a devastating 22-day assault on Gaza to halt ongoing Palestinian rocket and mortar fire, Israeli parliamentary elections displayed growing disenchantment with the peace process and President Barack Obama moved into the White House promising to try to help resolve the Arab-Israeli conflict after more than six decades of violence. Obama's pledge raised hopes in some quarters for a revival of peace talks — in limbo since the controversial Gaza war began on December 27. But Israel's political shift to the right and deep, continuing Palestinian divisions raise the prospect of continued stalemate. Years of talks and several interim agreements have failed to encourage either side that they can eventually get what they want. Israelis, pursuing security, remain the target of militant attacks, while impoverished Palestinians — seeking a state of their own — remain under effective Israeli control.

Future of NATO: Is the Transatlantic Alliance Obsolete?

During the Cold War, the North Atlantic Treaty Organization (NATO) was the West's line of defense against possible Soviet aggression. But the end of the Soviet Union in 1991 and the disappearance of NATO's communist equivalent — the Warsaw Pact — raised doubts about NATO's relevance. Nearly 20 years later, the specter of obsolescence still hangs over the venerable 26-nation alliance. So-called "Atlanticists" in both the United States and Europe say NATO's role in keeping the United States tied strategically to Europe justifies the alliance's continued existence. Moreover, NATO makes Moscow uneasy, and that's a good thing, they say. Others feel NATO should "earn its keep" by assuming new military responsibilities, such as protecting global energy-supply routes. But one thing is certain: It's not your grandfather's alliance. Since the 1990s, nearly a dozen former Soviet states and Soviet-bloc nations have joined NATO, easing their transition to democracy. NATO also has expanded its operations beyond Europe to Afghanistan, which may become the 60-year-old alliance's ultimate testing ground.

RELIGIOUS ISSUES

Religious Fundamentalism: Does It Lead to Intolerance and Violence?

People around the world are embracing fundamentalism, a belief in the literal interpretation of holy texts and, among the more hard-line groups, the desire to replace secular law with religious law. At the same time, deadly attacks by religious extremists in India, Uganda, Somalia and Nigeria are on the rise — and not just among Muslims. Meanwhile, political Islamism — which seeks to install Islamic law via the ballot box — is increasing in places like Morocco and in Muslim communities in Europe. Christian evangelicalism and Pentecostalism — the denominations from which fundamentalism derives — also are flourishing in Latin America, Africa, Central Asia and the United States. Ultra-Orthodox Jewish fundamentalists are blamed for exacerbating instability in the Middle East and beyond by establishing and expanding settlements on Palestinian lands. And intolerance is growing among Hindus in India, leading to deadly attacks against Christians and others. As experts debate what is causing the spread of fundamentalism, others question whether fundamentalists should have a greater voice in government.

Anti-Semitism in Europe: Are Israel's Policies Spurring a New Wave of Hate Crimes?

A wave of anti-Jewish attacks on individuals and synagogues has beset Europe since 2000, when the second

Palestinian uprising against Israel's occupation began. In France anti-Semitic youth gangs recently abducted and tortured two young Jewish men, one of whom was murdered. European soccer fans routinely taunt Jewish teams with Hitler salutes and chants, such as "Hamas, Hamas, Jews to the gas!" And while anti-Semitic attacks overall dipped slightly in some countries, violent assaults on individuals spiked last year, reaching a record high in Britain. Some scholars worry that the "new anti-Semitism" incorporates anti-Zionist language, which has become increasingly acceptable — particularly among Palestinian sympathizers in academia and the media. But Israel's critics — some of whom are Jewish — warn that calling people anti-Semitic because they oppose Israel's treatment of the Palestinians confuses the public. If the charge is made too often, they suggest, people will become cynical and won't recognize genocidal evil when it occurs.

ENVIRONMENTAL ISSUES

Carbon Trading: Will It Reduce Global Warming?

Carbon emissions trading — the buying and selling of permits to emit greenhouse gases caused by burning fossil fuels — is becoming a top strategy for reducing pollution that causes global climate change. Some $60 billion in permits were traded worldwide in 2007, a number expected to grow much larger if the next U.S. administration follows through on pledges to reduce America's carbon emissions. Advocates say carbon trading is the best way to generate big investments in low-carbon energy alternatives and control the cost of cutting emissions. But carbon trading schemes in Europe and developing countries have a mixed record. Some industries are resisting carbon regulations, and programs intended to help developing countries onto a clean energy path have bypassed many poor nations, which are the most vulnerable to the impacts of climate change. Some experts argue that there are simpler, more direct ways to put a price on carbon emissions, such as taxes. Others say curbing climate change will require both taxes and trading, plus massive government investments in low-carbon energy technologies.

Looming Water Crisis: Is the World Running Out of Water?

In the past decade drought has marched across much of the globe, hitting China, the Mediterranean, southeast Australia and the U.S. Sun Belt. The amount of water used by humans has tripled since 1950, and irrigated cropland has doubled. About one-fifth of the world's population lacks sufficient water, a figure that could reach 40 percent by 2025 by some estimates, in part because of growing world economies. In the poorest societies more than a billion people lack access to clean water, and dirty water kills 5,000 children — enough to fill 12 jumbo jets — every day. By century's end drought is expected to spread across half the Earth's land surface due to climate change, causing hunger and higher food prices. The United Nations says it would cost an extra $10 billion or more annually to provide clean water and sanitation for all. Some recommend privatizing water supplies, while others suggest that charging more for water to encourage conservation would help to avoid future crises.

CONFLICT

The Troubled Horn of Africa: Can the War-Torn Region Be Stabilized?

Plagued by conflict, poverty and poor governance, the Horn of Africa is arguably the most troubled corner of the world's poorest continent. In desperately poor Somalia, an 18-year civil war has forced more than a million people from their homes, leaving behind a safe haven for pirates and, possibly, Islamic terrorists. In Ethiopia, an increasingly authoritarian, Western-backed government has jailed opposition leaders and clamped down on the press and human rights activists. In tiny Eritrea, a government that once won the admiration of legions of Western diplomats and journalists for its self-sufficiency and discipline has become an isolated dictatorship. The recent withdrawal of Ethiopian troops from Somalia and the election of a moderate leader to the country's transitional government have raised international hopes that the lawlessness there will be brought under control. But Somalia's new government faces an insurgency from radical Islamists and worldwide pressure to stop the increasingly aggressive pirates who terrorize cargo ship crews off Somalia's coast and find refuge in its seaside villages.

Separatist Movements: Should Nations Have a Right to Self-Determination?

When Kosovo declared its independence on Feb. 17, 2008, thousands of angry Serbs took to the streets to protest the breakaway region's secession from Serbia. Less than a month later, Chinese authorities battled Buddhist monks in Lhasa, the legendary capital of Tibet, where separatist resentments have been simmering since China occupied the Himalayan region more than 50 years ago. The protests were the latest flashpoints in some two dozen separatist "hot spots" — the most active of roughly 70 such movements around the globe. They are part of a post-World War II independence trend that has produced a nearly fourfold jump in the number of countries worldwide, with 26 of those new countries emerging just since 1990. Some nations, like the far-flung Kurds and the Sri Lankan Tamils, are fighting fiercely to establish a homeland, while others — like Canada's Québécois — seem content with local autonomy. A handful have become de facto states that are as-yet-unrecognized by the U.N., including Somaliland, Taiwan, South Ossetia and Nagorno-Karabakh.

HUMAN RIGHTS

Aiding Refugees: Should the U.N. Help More Displaced People?

Some 42 million people worldwide have been uprooted by warfare or other violence, including 16 million refugees who are legally protected because they left their home countries. Most live in refugee camps and receive aid from the United Nations or other agencies but cannot work or leave the camps without special permission. Another 26 million people who fled violence are not protected by international treaties because they remained in their home countries. The number of such "internally displaced persons" (IDPs) has risen in the last decade, largely due to wars in Africa, Iraq, Afghanistan and Colombia. Millions of IDPs live in harsh conditions, and many receive no aid. Some critics say the U.N. High Commissioner for Refugees should do much more for IDPs, but the agency already faces severe budget shortfalls and bleak prospects for more donations from wealthy nations. Meanwhile, scientists warn that the number of people displaced by natural disasters — now about 50 million a year — could rise dramatically in coming years due to climate change.

Child Soldiers: Are More Aggressive Efforts Needed to Protect Children?

Since the mid-1990s, the world has watched in horror as hundreds of thousands of children and young teenagers have participated in nearly 50 wars, mostly in Africa and Asia. Children as young as 5 or 6 have served in combat, and thousands of abducted young girls were forced into sexual slavery. Some terrorist groups even strap explosive-rigged vests onto children and send them off as suicide bombers. Others have been recruited, sometimes forcibly, into the official armed forces or paramilitary units of several dozen countries. U.N. treaties prohibit the use of child soldiers, and the Security Council "names and shames" persistent violators. But only four former guerrilla commanders have been convicted by international tribunals, and some human-rights advocates urge more aggressive prosecution of perpetrators. However, some peace negotiators say threats of prosecution can obstruct cease-fire negotiations and prolong the fighting. In the U.S., where children under 18 serve in the military in non-combat roles, Congress is considering laws to combat the use of child soldiers overseas.

Preface

Are Israel's policies spurring a new wave of hate crimes? Should the U.N. help more displaced people? Is there any hope for long-term peace? These questions and many more are addressed in a unique selection of articles for debate focused on global issues offered exclusively through *CQ Researcher,* CQ Press and SAGE. This collection aims to promote in-depth discussion, facilitate further research and help students formulate their own positions on crucial issues.

This first edition includes twelve up-to-date reports by *CQ Researcher*, an award-winning weekly policy brief that brings complicated issues down to earth. Each report chronicles current core debates within the broad topic globalization and inspires students to think critically and analytically about issues that impact their lives. This reader is distinguished by its particular focus on up-to-date policy concerns and legal implications of the topics discussed. *Global Issues: Selections From CQ Researcher* exposes students to a journalistic approach to controversial sociological topics, inviting them to consider and debate the real-world relevance of course concepts.

CQ RESEARCHER

CQ Researcher was founded in 1923 as *Editorial Research Reports* and was sold primarily to newspapers as a research tool. The magazine was renamed and redesigned in 1991 as *CQ Researcher.* Today, students are its primary audience. While still used by hundreds of journalists and newspapers, many of which reprint portions of the reports, the *Researcher's* main subscribers are now high school, college and public libraries. In 2002, *Researcher* won the American Bar Association's coveted Silver Gavel award for magazine excellence for a series of nine reports on civil liberties and other legal issues.

Researcher staff writers — all highly experienced journalists — sometimes compare the experience of writing a *Researcher* report to drafting a college term paper. Indeed, there are many similarities. Each report is as long as many term papers — about 11,000 words — and is written by one person without any significant outside help. One of the key differences is that writers interview leading experts, scholars and government officials for each issue.

Like students, staff writers begin the creative process by choosing a topic. Working with the *Researcher's* editors, the writer identifies a controversial subject that has important public policy implications. After a topic is selected, the writer embarks on one to two weeks of intense research. Newspaper and magazine articles are clipped or downloaded, books are ordered and information is gathered from a wide variety of sources, including interest groups, universities and the government. Once the writers are well informed, they develop a detailed outline, and begin the interview process. Each report requires a minimum of ten to fifteen interviews with academics, officials, lobbyists and people working in the field. Only after all interviews are completed does the writing begin.

CHAPTER FORMAT

Each issue of *CQ Researcher*, and therefore each selection in this book, is structured in the same way. Each begins with an overview, which briefly summarizes the areas that will be explored in greater detail in the rest of the chapter. The next section chronicles important and current debates on the topic under discussion and is structured around a number of key questions. These questions are usually the subject of much debate among practitioners and scholars in the field. Hence, the answers presented are never conclusive but detail the range of opinion on the topic.

Next, the "Background" section provides a history of the issue being examined. This retrospective covers important legislative measures, executive actions and court decisions that illustrate how current policy has evolved. Then the "Current Situation" section examines contemporary policy issues, legislation under consideration and legal action being taken. Each selection concludes with an "Outlook" section, which addresses possible regulation, court rulings and initiatives from Capitol Hill and the White House over the next five to ten years.

Each report contains features that augment the main text: two to three sidebars that examine issues related to the topic at hand, a pro versus con debate between two experts, a chronology of key dates and events and an annotated bibliography detailing major sources used by the writer.

ACKNOWLEDGMENTS

We wish to thank many people for helping to make this collection a reality. Tom Colin, managing editor of *CQ Researcher*, gave us his enthusiastic support and cooperation as we developed this edition. He and his talented staff of editors and writers have amassed a first-class library of *Researcher* reports, and we are fortunate to have access to that rich cache. We also wish to thank our colleagues at CQ Press, a division of SAGE and a leading publisher of books, directories, research publications and Web products on U.S. government, world affairs and communications. They have forged the way in making these readers a useful resource for instruction across a range of undergraduate and graduate courses.

Some readers may be learning about *CQ Researcher* for the first time. We expect that many readers will want regular access to this excellent weekly research tool. For subscription information or a no-obligation free trial of *CQ Researcher*, please contact CQ Press at www.cqpress.com or toll-free at 1-866-4CQ-PRESS (1-866-427-7737).

We hope that you will be pleased by this edition of *Global Issues: Selections From CQ Researcher.* We welcome your feedback and suggestions for future editions. Please direct comments to David Repetto, Sr. Acquisitions Editor, Pine Forge Press, an Imprint of SAGE Publications, 2455 Teller Road, Thousand Oaks, CA 91320, or david.repetto@sagepub.com.

—The Editors of SAGE

Contributors

Irwin Arieff is a veteran journalist now freelancing in New York City. He served for 23 years as a correspondent for the Reuters news agency in Washington, Paris, New York and the United Nations. During more than four decades as a writer and editor—including five years writing for the *CQ Weekly*—Arieff covered subjects ranging from international affairs, the White House and U.S. politics to science and medicine, the television industry and financial market regulation. He has a masters degree in journalism from Northwestern University's Medill School.

Brian Beary—a freelance journalist based in Washington, D.C.—specializes in European Union (EU) affairs and is the U.S. correspondent for *Europolitics*, the EU-affairs daily newspaper. Originally from Dublin, Ireland, he worked in the European Parliament for Irish MEP Pat "The Cope" Gallagher in 2000 and at the EU Commission's Eurobarometer unit on public opinion analysis. A fluent French speaker, he appears regularly as a guest international-relations expert on television and radio programs. Beary also writes for the *European Parliament Magazine* and the *Irish Examiner* daily newspaper. His last report for *CQ Global Researcher* was "Race for the Arctic."

Peter Behr is a Washington freelance writer who worked for more than 25 years at *The Washington Post*, where he reported on energy issues and served as business editor. A former Nieman Fellow at Harvard University, Behr was a public policy scholar at the Woodrow

Wilson International Center for Scholars and is now writing a book about the U.S. electric power grid. His report on "Water Scarcity" appeared in the February 2008 issue of *CQ Global Researcher.*

John Felton is a freelance journalist who has written about international affairs and U.S. foreign policy for nearly 30 years. He covered foreign affairs for the *Congressional Quarterly Weekly Report* during the 1980s, was deputy foreign editor for National Public Radio in the early 1990s and has been a freelance writer specializing in international topics for the past 15 years. His most recent book, published by CQ Press, is *The Contemporary Middle East: A Documentary History.* He lives in Stockbridge, Massachusetts.

Roland Flamini is a Washington-based correspondent who writes a foreign-affairs column for *CQ Weekly.* Fluent in six languages, he served as *Time* magazine's bureau chief in Rome, Bonn, Beirut, Jerusalem and the European Common Market and later served as international editor at United Press International. He wrote "Afghanistan on the Brink" for *CQ Global Researcher.*

Sarah Glazer, a London-based freelancer, is a regular contributor to the *CQ Researcher.* Her articles on health, education and social-policy issues have appeared in *The New York Times, The Washington Post, The Public Interest* and *Gender and Work*, a book of essays. Her most recent *CQ Global Researcher* report was "Radical Islam in Europe." She graduated from the University of Chicago with a BA in American history.

Jason McLure is a correspondent for Bloomberg News and *Newsweek* based in Addis Ababa, Ethiopia. He previously worked for *Legal Times* in Washington, D.C., and in *Newsweek*'s Boston bureau. His reporting has appeared in *The Economist, Business Week*, the *British Journalism Review* and *National Law Journal.* His work has been honored by the Washington, D.C., chapter of the Society for Professional Journalists, the Maryland-Delaware-District of Columbia Press Association and the Overseas Press Club of America Foundation. He has a master's degree in journalism from the University of Missouri.

Jennifer Weeks is a *CQ Researcher* contributing writer in Watertown, Massachusetts, who specializes in energy and environmental issues. She has written for *The Washington Post, The Boston Globe Magazine* and other publications, and has 15 years' experience as a public-policy analyst, lobbyist and congressional staffer. She has an AB degree from Williams College and master's degrees from the University of North Carolina and Harvard.

1

The Troubled Dollar

Will the World's "Anchor" Currency Be Replaced?

Peter Behr

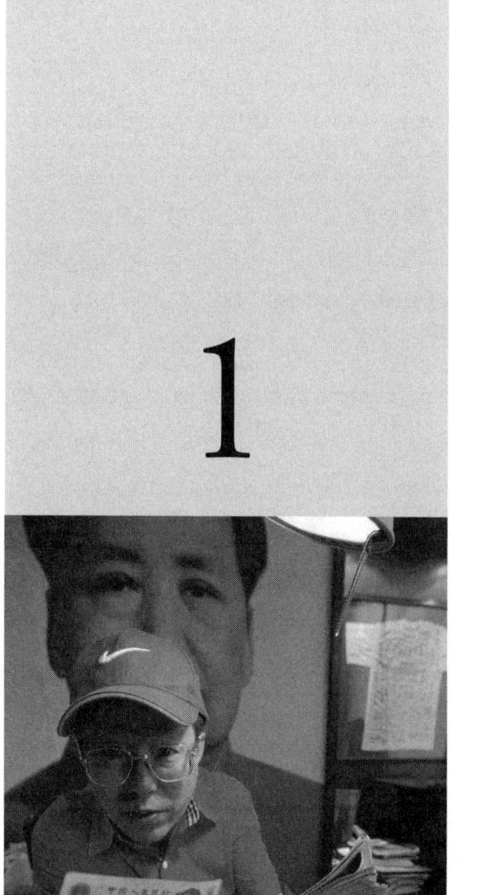
Getty Images/China Photos

Shanghai businessman Chen Haiwen holds a stack of Chinese yuan he exchanged for U.S. greenbacks. Although the yuan has strengthened against the U.S. dollar in the past two years, critics say it still is undervalued, which keeps China's exports unrealistically cheap. The U.S. trade deficit with China and other exporters is partly to blame for the 21 percent decline in the value of the dollar since 2002. The dollar's shakiness is prompting China to consider gradually reducing its reserves of more than $1 trillion in U.S. currency.

From *CQ Global Researcher*, October 2008.

On Sept. 15, 2008 — a Black Monday for financial markets — investors around the world dove for cover following the weekend collapse of legendary Wall Street firms Lehman Brothers and Merrill Lynch.

After dumping their tanking stocks, the stampeding investors — like others before them — began plowing billions of dollars into U.S. Treasury securities.[1]

Once again the dollar had proved to be a safe harbor in a financial storm.

It was a notable, if perhaps momentary comeback for the beleaguered greenback. Since 2002, the dollar has lost 21 percent of its value compared to other leading currencies, marking a profound loss of American economic clout.[2]

With the banking crisis spreading in Europe and Asia, confidence in U.S. economic leadership — and in the dollar — may have suffered an historic blow, some financial experts and government leaders say. Nonetheless, the financial firestorm now raging through Europe and Asia could send foreign investors running back to the dollar as their best option, other experts say.

The risk for the dollar largely stems from the $700 billion rescue package that the U.S. Treasury has been given to buy subprime mortgages and other "toxic" debt that is choking off day-to-day lending in the U.S. economy. Because the United States faces a deep budget deficit already, the federal government will have to borrow those funds, much of it from foreign banks and investors who already hold more than half of the $3.5 trillion in U.S. Treasury debt. But the increasing obligations are likely to

Dollar Has Declined Against Euro and Yen

Since 2002 the dollar's value has fallen about 40 percent against Europe's euro — and about 20 percent versus the Japanese yen — in part because U.S. interest rates have been kept low in order to stimulate the domestic economy. A cheaper dollar makes U.S. exports cheaper but boosts the price of imports. It also triggers increases in worldwide prices for oil, food and other commodities.

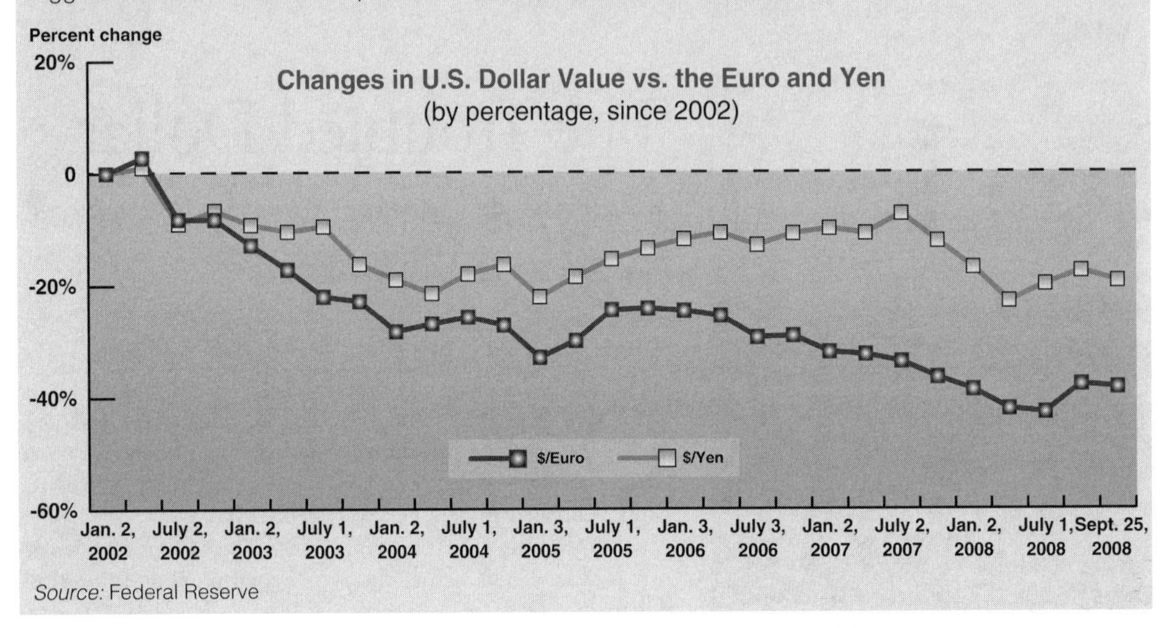

Source: Federal Reserve

further undermine the dollar, making foreigners less willing to increase their dollar investments, some experts say.

"If international investors lose confidence in the ability of the American taxpayer to honor their debts, then the taps will be turned off, the dollar will plunge and interest rates will rocket, destroying demand," wrote Jeremy Warner, business columnist for *The Independent* in London, in early October. "The present crisis in banking would find itself mirrored on a national scale."[3]

"Financing of the losses by the American taxpayer may lead to an American disaster if the cost is simply added to the budget deficit," according to Jacques Attali, former president of the European Bank for Reconstruction and Development.[4]

German Finance Minister Peer Steinbrück is predicting that the crisis will shrink the dollar's role in global trade and finance. The United States will "lose its status as the superpower of the global financial system," he bluntly predicts. The Persian Gulf states, China and Russia will gain influence, in his view. The international financial community "has begun seeking a new world order," says Kazuo Mizuno, the chief economist of Mitsubishi UFJ Securities Co. in Japan.[5]

But other nations and their currencies may fare worse than the dollar. Germany's economy — Europe's strongest — is facing a "pronounced slowdown" that could drag on to 2010, said Deutsche Bank's chief economist Norbert Walter.[6]

"Europe is sitting on a huge financial problem," says David Smick, publisher of *The International Economy* quarterly. "They don't have a European-wide way for handling the collapse of a major financial institution."

The average American may not know the dollar's exchange rate against, the yen, yuan, euro or rupee, but its place in the world economy matters immensely to Americans. Most world trade is conducted in dollars, and the greenback's value on world currency markets affects not only the price U.S. farmers and manufacturers get for their exports but also how much American consumers pay for their favorite Japanese car or high-definition TV set.

Dollar fluctuations also have global implications. Because most commodities are priced in dollars, the currency's slide helped to fuel the 2008 spike in oil prices to nearly $150 a barrel, for instance, triggering strikes, protests and hardships on every continent. A parallel increase in food prices — also sparked in part by the dollar's decline — spread hunger in the world's poorest regions and strained family budgets elsewhere, adding to fears of inflation in many countries.[7]

When the dollar drops in value, it produces both winners and losers. While U.S. buyers of imported products suffer from having to pay higher prices, American manufacturers who sell goods abroad get a break because their products become cheaper for foreign buyers. Conversely, a weaker dollar is handicapping manufacturers in Europe and Asia, making their products less competitive in the United States. Meanwhile, the dollar's slump has triggered a virtual fire sale for foreigners seeking to buy U.S. companies, real estate and other assets. For example, 15 percent of all Florida home sales in early 2008 involved foreign purchasers.[8]

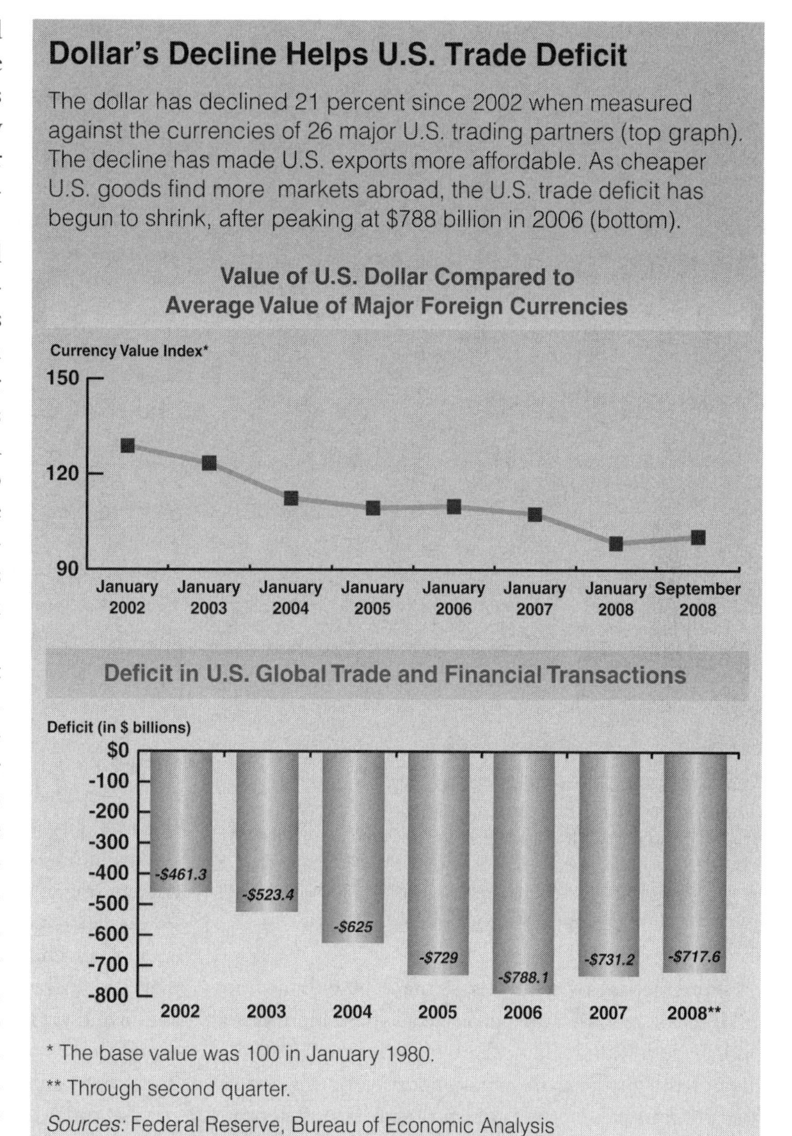

The dollar has been the world's leading currency since 1944, when Allied leaders met in Bretton Woods, N.H., to plan the post-World War II economic order. With much of Europe, Russia, China and Japan prostrate and the British Empire collapsing, the dollar was established as the dominant global currency, and the United States became "the banker to the world." It remained so despite periodic ups and downs during economic booms, oil shocks and recessions. Thus, the dollar became the favored currency held by foreign banks in reserve accounts that back up their lending operations.[9]

The dollar's value compared to other major currencies is tied to fundamental economic conditions. Falling U.S. interest rates make dollar-based investments less appealing to foreigners, while low inflation and strong growth in the United States make them more attractive. Ultimately, the dollar's value is based on investors' confidence in the U.S. economy.

AFP/Getty Images/Toshifumi Kitamura

A currency trader in Tokyo monitors the dollar's value on world currency markets. Because most global trade is conducted in dollars, the greenback's value affects the price of commodities around the world. The dollar's two-year slide helped to fuel the recent spike in oil prices to nearly $150 a barrel, triggering strikes, protests and hardships on every continent.

But America's twin deficits — the $700 billion shortfall in trade in 2007 and a projected $438 billion federal budget deficit in 2009 — have significantly weakened the dollar.[10] As the trade deficit increased in this decade, vast amounts of U.S. currency left the country: Americans spent $5 trillion more buying foreign goods than they earned exporting their own goods. Most of the dollar outflow has ended up in government-controlled banks in the Middle East, Russia, China and other Asian nations. To raise money to cover the budget deficit the U.S. government buys dollars back from foreign banks and investment funds by selling them Treasury securities, making the United States critically dependent on those foreign buyers.

Overall, the volume of worldwide government and private investment has soared in this decade to an estimated $167 trillion, accompanying a burst in global trade in manufactured goods led by the emerging economies of China and India.[11] The dollar figures in more cross-border transactions than any other currency.

But the current U.S. financial crisis — widely viewed as the worst since the Great Depression — has exposed the risks to American financial firms caused by those massive amounts of dollars circulating around the globe. The U.S. government's stunning takeover of the giant mortgage firms Fannie Mae and Freddie Mac three weeks ago exemplifies the risk. Early this year foreign investors, led by China, held $1.3 trillion in housing bonds issued by the two congressionally chartered institutions — up dramatically from the $107 billion they held in 1994.[12] As the U.S. housing market collapse morphed into a global credit crisis last summer, banks in China and elsewhere began an unprecedented sell-off of Fannie and Freddie's bonds, threatening to cripple the two firms whose purchases of mortgages support more than half of the U.S. housing industry.[13] The federal takeover followed.

Ironically, it is precisely the dollar's appeal as a safe currency over the past half-century that has enabled the United States to borrow dollars from international investors at reasonable costs to finance America's budget and trade deficits. Foreigners owned nearly one-fifth of the $49 trillion in overall U.S. government and private debt outstanding in mid-2007, according to official estimates. Foreigners — mainly government-controlled banks in Asia — also held more than half of the $3.5 trillion in marketable Treasury securities.[14] If foreign governments and investors grow doubtful of U.S. economic leadership or anxious about the amount of American debt they hold, they could slow their purchases of Treasury securities and other U.S. assets.

"At some point . . . foreign investors will balk at the growing concentration [of dollars] in their investment portfolios," former Federal Reserve Chairman Alan Greenspan has pointed out. "The well-established principle of not putting all your eggs in one basket holds for global finance as well as for the private household."[15]

A pullback by foreign investors would leave a gap in the budget and trade deficits that would force the government to dramatically cut spending and increase taxes or raise interest rates enough to attract more foreign investment — all of which would slow down the economy.

Until now, foreigners have been willing to accept relatively low returns on Treasury bills and bonds because of their stability, says Kenneth Rogoff, former chief economist of the IMF. He doubts that will continue.[16]

"After so many years of miserable returns on dollar assets, will global investors really be willing to absorb another trillion dollars in U.S. debt at anything near current interest rates and exchange rates?" he asks.

Others aren't so pessimistic, however. "Doomsday predictions about the dollar and interest rates, made year after year, have failed to materialize and are unconvincing," said Miranda Xafa, a member of the International Monetary Fund's (IMF) executive board and a former chief economic adviser to the Greek government.[17]

As economists, policymakers and investors nervously watch the weakened value of the U.S. dollar, here are some of the questions being debated:

Oil Prices Track Dollar-Euro Exchange Rate

Over the past two years, as the dollar lost value and the euro rose in response (top), oil prices rose at about the same rates (bottom). Because oil is priced in dollars, when the dollar drops in value, oil companies raise prices to maintain revenue. The dollar reached its lowest exchange rate — $1.58 per euro — in July, the same time that oil peaked at $132.72 per barrel.

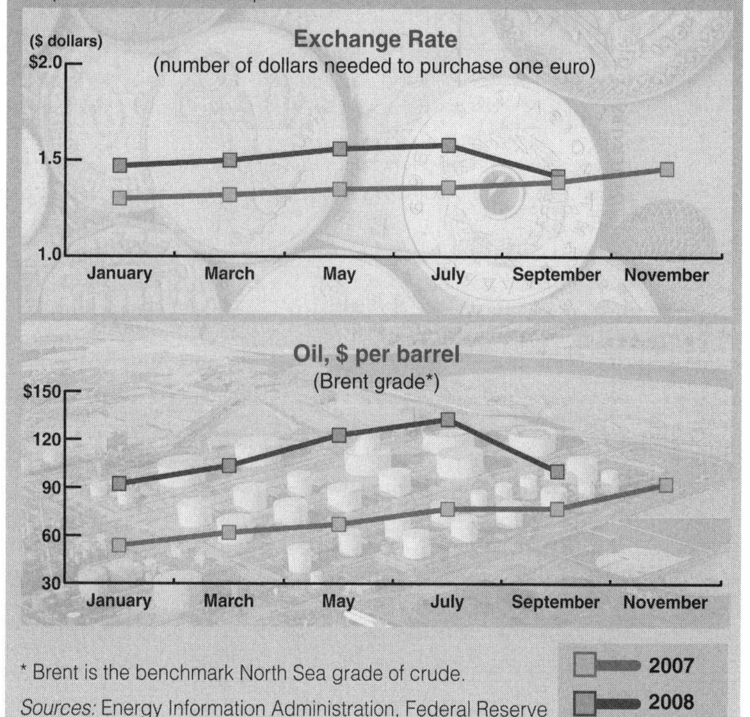

* Brent is the benchmark North Sea grade of crude.

Sources: Energy Information Administration, Federal Reserve

Does the United States need a stronger dollar?

Among the first questions a new U.S. Treasury secretary is asked is whether the dollar's value will remain strong. It is a critical matter for nations in a closely linked global economy, where the dollar's value compared with other currencies can be a decisive competitive factor in each country's ability to sell its products abroad.

For more than half a century, the rote answer by Treasury secretaries was, the dollar will be strong.

Today the world has its doubts. The dollar lost 26 percent of its value between January 2002 and July 2008 compared to a large selection of currencies tracked by the Federal Reserve. (*See graph, p. 2.*) Even with a strong rally since late summer, the dollar was still 21 percent below the 2002 starting point. It has also recovered some ground against the euro, the common currency adopted by 15 members of the 27-nation European Union — a major U.S. competitor.[18] A euro was worth 90 U.S. cents when it went into circulation in January 2002. In early October, the price of a single euro was $1.38, down from $1.59 in July 2008. Under pressure from the Bush administration, China has let its currency, the renminbi, strengthen against the dollar (thus leaving the dollar weaker).*

By the summer of 2008, the dollar's slide and the corresponding rise for European and Asian currencies had begun to alarm financial officials. "European manufacturers are already screeching that the euro is too high,"

* The renminbi, which means "the people's currency," is denominated in yuan units.

Where's the Best Place for a Big Mac Attack?

Undervalued currency makes the burger cheap in Beijing.

If you're going to have a Big Mac attack, have it in China. Last July a Big Mac that would have cost $3.57 in the United States cost only $1.83 in China — largely because the Chinese currency is undervalued by 49 percent, according to a currency benchmark developed by *The Economist* magazine.

The index was designed to answer questions such as: Is the euro overvalued? Is the dollar priced too low? What about Brazil's real or Norway's krona?

An undervalued currency can make a country's exports unrealistically cheap, giving that country an unfair advantage in international trade. With profits, jobs and global political standings at stake, questions about currency values cry for clear answers. But instead, the academic research on currency values is debated by experts, in part because of the difficulties in comparing the costs of living in wealthy and poor nations. Ideological differences about the advantages of strong and weak dollars also color the debate.

The currency exchange rate between two countries reflects many factors, such as interest rates and inflation pressures, investor and speculator hunches about where an economy and its currency rates are headed and sometimes government actions to try to change the rate by buying or selling their own currencies.

In trying to determine what currencies are really worth, *The Economist* created the "Big Mac Index" — a whimsical but seriously regarded benchmark for determining the purchasing power of various countries' national currencies. It compares the price — in each country's currency and in the dollar — for a hamburger in McDonald's franchises around the globe.

"The Big Mac Index is based on the theory of purchasing-power parity (PPP), which says exchange rates should move to make the price of a basket of goods the same in each country. Our basket contains just a single item, a Big Mac hamburger, but one that is sold around the world. The exchange rate that leaves a Big Mac costing the same in dollars everywhere is our fair-value yardstick," *The Economist* said in its latest index update in July 2008.[1]

In July a Big Mac cost $3.57 at a U.S. franchise participating in the survey. At the same time, an American tourist in Reykjavik, Iceland, paid 469 kronur for a Big Mac. Under the actual exchange rate for the two countries

says Richard Koo, chief economist of Tokyo-based Nomura Research Institute.[19] French Finance Minister Christine Lagarde said in May that the euro's surge against the dollar was "a major misalignment."[20]

Mizuno of Mitsubishi Securities predicted at that time "the end of the strong dollar-based currency regime."[21]

The dollar's relative strength versus other major currencies is a critical matter for nations in a closely linked global economy where trade is a vital source of job and wealth creation.

From a U.S. perspective, the "right" value for the dollar can't be determined by looking at past history, says C. Fred Bergsten, director of the Peter G. Peterson Institute for International Economics in Washington. What's important, he said, is that the dollar needs to work as a lever, helping to boost U.S. exports and restrain imports enough to bring the American trade deficit down to an acceptable level. So the right price for the dollar is whatever exchange value with the euro, the yen and other currencies will make that happen, Bergsten and other experts say.

The dollar has settled at a reasonable value versus the euro, he said.[22] But it needs to drop further against leading Asian currencies, including China's yuan and the South Korean won, he adds.

From 2002 into 2008, America's trade deficit widened as imports from China and other nations outstripped U.S. exports, creating a record $788 billion "current account" deficit in 2006 — nearly 7 percent of U.S. gross domestic product (GDP).[23]* A deficit that size is untenable economically and politically, according to the Peterson

* The current account deficit combines the deficit in traded goods with net U.S. financial transactions with the rest of the world.

at the time, $1 was worth only 78.57 kronur, so the tourist had to pay $5.97 to buy enough kronur to buy the burger (469 kronur divided by 78.57 kronur per dollar equals the $5.97).

Thus, according to the index, the kronur is "overvalued," because the burger cost $2.40 more in Iceland than it does in the United States — or 67 percent more. So the "fair value" exchange rate for the kronur should be 67 percent higher, or 131 per dollar.

Conversely, China's currency appears "undervalued" in the Big Mac Index. The $3.57 burger in the United States costs 12.5 yuan in China. At the current exchange rate of 6.83 yuan per dollar, that comes to $1.83. Thus, the yuan is undervalued by the difference between $3.57 and $1.83, or 49 percent, according to the Big Mac Index.

The Economist found that, compared to the dollar, currencies from Britain, Europe, Norway, Brazil and Turkey are overvalued. Undervalued currencies included Saudi Arabia's riyal, the Japanese yen, Thailand's baht and Pakistan's rupee. (*See graph.*)

The results buttress the argument that China and other Asian exporters need to raise their currencies' values to create a fairer trading arena with the rest of the world.

[1] "The Big Mac Index: Sandwiched," *The Economist*, July 24, 2008, www.economist.com/finance/displaystory.cfm?story_id=11793125.

The 'Big Mac Index'

The whimsical but seriously regarded benchmark determines various currencies' purchasing power by comparing the price of a McDonald's hamburger around the world.

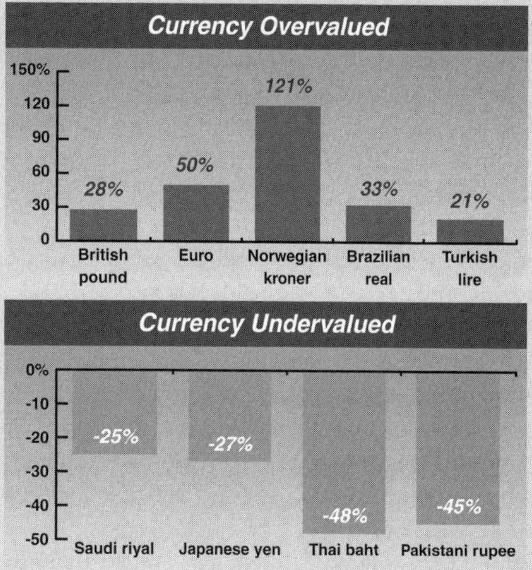

Currency Overvalued

British pound	Euro	Norwegian kroner	Brazilian real	Turkish lire
28%	50%	121%	33%	21%

Currency Undervalued

Saudi riyal	Japanese yen	Thai baht	Pakistani rupee
-25%	-27%	-48%	-45%

Source: The Economist; values are as of July 24, 2008

Institute, because it forces the United States to finance too much of its economy with loans from foreigners.[24]

Bergsten and other economists say the current account deficit must come down to about 3 percent of U.S. GDP to prevent a loss of confidence in the dollar. Such a decline, however, will require a cheaper dollar in order to raise the price of imports and lower the price of U.S. exports.

While a cheaper dollar would help the United States, it burdens other nations, especially Asia's big exporting countries. The dollar has fallen since 2002 against the currencies of Thailand, South Korea, Singapore, India and China (while gaining against Mexico). If the Asian nations agreed to increase their currencies' values against the dollar, their exports would become more expensive in the United States and presumably decline.

The dollar has been on a roller-coaster ride over the past quarter-century, dropping in value in the late 1970s, climbing in the early 1980s, falling again in the early 1990s and then recovering at decade's end. But as long as the United States was the main locomotive for world growth, U.S. policy called for a strong dollar, building wealth in the American economy, which could then afford to purchase more of the world's imports.

Clinton administration Treasury Secretary Robert Rubin made a strong dollar a priority and between 1995 and 2002, when the value of U.S. currency climbed by 40 percent compared with several other leading currencies.[25]

Paul O'Neill, President George W. Bush's first Treasury secretary, caused an international uproar early in 2001 by saying he wanted a "strong economy," not a "strong dollar." O'Neill promptly backpedaled, explaining, "I believe in a strong dollar, and if I decide to shift that stance, I will hire out Yankee Stadium and some rousing brass bands and announce that change in policy to the whole world."[26]

O'Neill did not last long enough in office to keep that promise, but with less fanfare the dollar did turn downward. After the Sept. 11, 2001, terrorist attacks, the Federal Reserve lowered short-term interest rates, which made dollar-denominated bonds less profitable to investors. Currency traders fix on differences in nations' interest rates, and after the Fed's actions the dollar began falling.

The Bush administration has maintained the strong-dollar mantra, but in fact kept hands off. "In reality, of course, the United States does not have a dollar policy — other than letting the market determine its value," said Martin Feldstein, former Council of Economic Advisers chairman under President Ronald Reagan.[27]

The United States has intervened in currency markets in the past to boost the dollar's value and calm volatile or speculative trading in the dollar or other currencies. But it has not done so since Secretary Rubin concluded that the amount of currency trading on foreign exchange markets was growing too large for effective intervention by the U.S. Treasury.[28]

Some experts say the United States must strengthen the dollar to keep its leadership among the world's economies, even if that requires painful decisions on shrinking trade and budget deficits. "The lower the dollar, the poorer we are as a country," says Jeffrey Garten, a professor at the Yale University School of Management and former undersecretary of Commerce for international trade in the Clinton administration.

A stronger dollar increases the value of American-made goods and services, which makes U.S. exports more expensive. But Garten says American firms can compete effectively using new technology, skilled workers and capital to increase the sophistication of products and processes.

"If we want to have influence in the world, we can't have that with a soft currency," Garten says.

Will the euro surpass the dollar as the world's anchor currency?

With President Nicolas Sarkozy on hand to lead the cheering, the French energy company Areva in November 2007 sold two advanced nuclear power reactors to China for a record $12 billion.[29] "In the history of the civilian nuclear industry, there's never been a deal of this magnitude," boasted Areva Chief Executive Anne Lauvergeon.

It was a milestone in another way. The China Guangdong Nuclear Power Corp. (CGNPC), which purchased the reactors, agreed to pay half the price in euros, the official currency of the European Monetary Union. China's policy until then had been to transact international business almost entirely in dollars.[30] Dividing the pie between the dollar and the euro was another visible mark of the European currency's growing prominence.

Much more than national pride in the greenback is a stake in the competition between the dollar and the euro. The United States has long enjoyed an "exorbitant privilege," as former French President Charles de Gaulle tersely put it, because of the dollar's status as the leading global currency. Foreign governments have been eager to hold dollars in their own vaults to support their financial systems — in a crisis a country wants dollars, not Russian rubles.[31] Governments then return those dollars to the United States when they invest them in U.S. Treasury securities. That has helped the United States fund its deficits and live beyond its means, *The Economist* notes. If the dollar ends up sharing that privilege with the euro, the United States could find it significantly more costly to attract the foreign-held dollars it needs to square its trade accounts.[32]

Indeed, Europe's financial markets have nearly caught up with the United States, says the San Francisco-based McKinsey Global Institute. Total financial assets for the 15 euro nations (the "Eurozone"), plus Britain, Switzerland and four Scandinavian countries outside the euro network amounted to $53.2 trillion in 2006 — less than the U.S. total of $56.1 trillion but growing faster — McKinsey said.[33]

"The euro is emerging as a rival to the dollar as the world's global reserve currency, reflecting in part the growing vibrancy and depth of Europe's financial markets," the McKinsey analysts reported. In mid-2007, the value of euro currencies in circulation worldwide passed U.S. dollar currencies for the first time. The euro is also favored for international bond issues.

Whether the euro can overtake the dollar as the favored currency for international transactions is now discussed seriously by currency experts worldwide. (But most say it is less likely that the euro could replace the dollar as the preferred reserve currency held by central banks.)

Tokyo-based author and business consultant Kenichi Ohmae said, "The current weakness of the American economy that has resulted from borrowing abroad to sustain high growth, and of which the subprime crisis is a symptom, is also driving the dollar to historical lows. This is causing China, Japan, the Gulf states and Russia, among others, discreetly, but inexorably, to begin fleeing the declining dollar in favor of the sounder currency of the euro. When all is said and done, the European Union will have the world's largest consumer base and integrated infrastructure."[34]

In a 2008 survey of currency experts, a decided majority predicted either that the dollar would remain the leading currency or would gradually share the distinction with the euro or a basket of international currencies including the euro, and Chinese yuan. *The International Economy*, a Washington-based journal, asked 53 of the world's leading economists, bankers and currency experts to predict what the world's great global currency would be in 10 years. Thirty-one said the dollar would remain on top, although many saw it diminishing.[35]

Tadao Chino, former president of the Asian Development Bank, picked the dollar to hold its premier place. So did Il Sakong, former South Korean finance minister; Boris Fedorov, former Russian finance minister, and Pedto-Pablo Kuczynski, Peru's former top finance official.

Daniel Griswold, director of the conservative Cato Institute's trade policy studies, says the dollar was "still the best bet." Nearly two-thirds of central bank reserves worldwide are held in dollars, and almost 90 percent of all daily currency transactions involve dollars, he noted.

Eight survey responders picked the euro either to match or surpass the dollar within 10 years.

"The euro, for sure," said Maya Bhandari, senior economist at Lombard Street Research in London. About twice as many respondents said the dollar and euro would share leadership, and several said the yuan could eventually rival the dollar and euro, but not within a decade. "The euro is vying with the U.S. dollar for the status of leading global currency," said Chi Lo, a Hong Kong-based investment research director, but the race won't be won in 10 years.

AFP/Getty/Jed Aznar

A vast stockpile of rice sits in a warehouse in Manila last March as the Philippine government prepared for potential rice shortages. A decline in the value of the U.S. dollar helped to trigger a spike in global food prices earlier this year, leading to hoarding and shortages of grain and other commodities in scores of countries.

A dozen respondents said a group of currencies including the dollar, euro and yuan would replace the dollar.

"During the next one or two decades, we will move toward a multilateral currency system with three or four major currencies," predicted Klaus Regling, director general for Economic and Financial Affairs at the European Commission. The dollar will probably be the most important currency, particularly in the Americas, but will no longer be the dominant world currency. The euro will be the currency for at least 25 countries, he added. And the Chinese yuan will gain importance, too.[36]

The euro's position would be significantly boosted if Britain gave up the pound and joined the Eurozone, providing the continent with a financial center in London to rival New York and Shanghai. But Richard H. Clarida, a former assistant Treasury secretary for economic policy, and other experts say that isn't likely in the foreseeable future.[37]

The dollar has remained on top for so long in part because it had no serious rivals. In the 1980s the Japanese yen and the German mark briefly threatened, but those economies stumbled, wrote Menzie D. Chinn, a University of Wisconsin economist, and Jeffrey A. Frankel, a professor of capital formation at Harvard.[38] However, the euro provides a credible option now, they contend.

A Currency Primer

Why a strong dollar is important.

What happens when the dollar's value shifts against other currencies? Consider the dollar and the Japanese yen. In January 2002, $1 would buy about 132 yen. At that exchange rate, a U.S.-made medical device priced at $1,000 would sell for 132,000 yen in Japan.

Fast-forward to March 2008, when the dollar's value against the yen had fallen so that $1 would buy only 100 yen. At that exchange rate, a Japanese hospital could buy the same $1,000 medical device for only 100,000 yen.

From a U.S. business perspective, the dollar's decline made the U.S.-made product a lot more affordable and thus more competitive in international trade.

But the lower dollar puts Japanese manufacturers at a disadvantage. When the dollar was trading for 132 yen in 2002, a Japanese-made television that sold for 150,000 yen in Japan would have cost $1,136 in the United States. But at the lower 2008 exchange rate of 100 yen per dollar, the same television would cost $1,500, potentially putting it out of range for many American consumers.

A weakened dollar has less purchasing power. For example, because of the dollar's slump American tourists in Tokyo would have to pay nearly 25 percent more for the same meal and lodgings in 2008 than their dollars would have bought in 2002.

However, when the dollar's value falls, the United States ends up repaying its debts to foreigners with cheaper — or less valuable — dollars. That's a break for the United States but not for foreigners, who will reconsider investing in U.S. securities.

Could the dollar's value plunge?

As leaders from Saudi Arabia and other oil producers in the Gulf Cooperation Council (GCC) prepared to meet in Qatar last Dec. 3, the dollar began rising and falling against the leading Gulf currencies.

The changes were small but significant all the same, because the dollar and most Persian Gulf currencies are not supposed to vary. Saudi Arabia, Qatar, Bahrain and the United Arab Emirates "peg" their currencies to the dollar in order to piggyback on its stability (and, say some observers, to acknowledge their reliance on U.S. military protection).[39] Thus, while the dollar's price rises and falls on world markets, the Saudi riyal and the other Gulf currencies generally move in sync with the greenback.

These small fluctuations signaled a much deeper uneasiness in world markets about the dollar at the end of last year, as the dimensions of the U.S. mortgage lending crisis became clearer. Worried experts and analysts began to speculate on the possibility the dollar's deep slump would force U.S. trading partners to cut their currencies' values in order to keep prices on their exported goods in line with U.S. competitors' prices. Others warned that the dollar's slide could spin out of control, leading to a free fall in its value and catastrophic losses in dollar-based investments worldwide.

"If we're not careful, monetary disarray could morph into economic war. We would all be its victims," French President Sarkozy said in an address to the U.S. Congress in November 2007.[40]

Those fears were present at the Gulf council meeting. The dollar's fall has reduced the value of Gulf state currencies, raising the prices of imported goods on which the desert kingdoms' breakneck expansion depends and pushing inflation toward economically and politically treacherous levels.

The previous May Kuwait had broken the official link between its dinar currency and the dollar in favor of a linkage to a group of currencies including the dollar. With the U.S. economy reeling from the subprime mortgage and credit crises, a decision by any of the five other states to follow Kuwait's lead could have rocked the dollar.

"This would be seen as a further loss of confidence in the greenback, accelerating its rout," said Gabriel Stein, chief international economist at London's Lombard Street Research.[41]

U.S. Treasury Secretary Henry M. Paulson Jr. said in Saudi Arabia last May that a decision by the Saudis to end the dollar peg is "a sovereign decision," and not for the United States to decide. But he added, "The dollar peg, I think, has served this country and this region well." Saudi Arabia's Finance Minister Ibrahim al-Assaf settled the issue: "We have no intention of de-pegging or revaluation."[42]

Noriel Roubini, an economics professor at New York University, is among the experts who believe confidence in the American currency is seriously undermined by the growing U.S. debt to foreigners. Dubbed "Dr. Doom" in a recent *New York Times* profile, Roubini sounded an early warning that the United States was headed for a cataclysmic housing market bust and credit shock.[43]

Roubini's concern centered on U.S. dependence on foreign investors to channel dollars back into the United States to cover the federal budget deficit and balance the trade gap. An alarming portion of that return investment is coming from about a dozen government central banks, most of them in Asia, he said. "If foreign central banks stopped buying dollar-denominated bonds, the dollar would fall dramatically against their currencies," and U.S. interest rates would be forced sharply higher, pummeling the economy, Roubini wrote.[44]

As the housing and credit crises deepened this year, Roubini said the losses from mortgage foreclosures, bank failures and bad debt would increase America's budget deficit by hundreds of billions of dollars. Will foreigners willingly take on massive, new U.S. debt? he asks. "Our biggest financiers are China, Russia and the Gulf states," he said. "These are rivals, not allies."[45]

But others contend the size, openness and resilience of the U.S. economy — even in hard times — will attract foreigners. And foreign central banks holding large numbers of dollars in their reserves have too much to lose from a free fall in the dollar.

If China tried to sell dollar assets precipitously, the worldwide prices of those assets — especially U.S. Treasury securities and the dollar itself — would likely fall, wrote Donald J. Boudreaux, chairman of the economics department at George Mason University, in Fairfax, Va. "And while Americans would suffer, the Chinese government would suffer even more," he added.[46]

The appeal of the United States to foreign investors goes beyond currency prices, says Adam S. Posen, deputy director of the Peterson Institute. "U.S. political leadership in security, commercial and even cultural affairs globally has a critical impact on the usage of the dollar in the monetary realm," he said. Foreigners invest in the United States in part to gain "insider access" to U.S. government and business decision-making. This desire for membership adds to a kind of unquantifiable "dark matter" that energizes support for the dollar, he adds.[47]

The risk of large, volatile swings in the dollar's value is somewhat lessened by the tremendous volume of dollar trading on world currency exchanges, says Derek Sammann, head of foreign exchange products at CME Group in Chicago, which runs the world's largest currency exchange. More than $3 trillion in currencies are traded on foreign-exchange markets on an average day. So even if China or one of the Gulf states were to sell as much as $1 trillion in dollars over a month, there is sufficient underlying trading activity or liquidity so that it would not overwhelm the dollar market, he says.

"You would see some selling pressure, but the impact on daily dollar trading on foreign exchange markets would be minimal," he says. As long as the U.S. economy holds its underlying strength, a run on the dollar isn't likely, he says.

Nevertheless, the dollar's new volatility worries many experts. The World Bank Commission on Growth and Development warned this year that the United States had been relying too much on foreign capital, which has "financed America's trade deficit, allowing the country to live beyond its means. This American spending has helped keep the world economy growing, but it is unlikely to be sustainable."[48]

BACKGROUND

Untying the Dollar

In 1944 an agreement on postwar international finance and trade forged by world leaders in Bretton Woods, N.H., established the right to convert a U.S. dollar for one-35th of an ounce of gold, a guarantee that anchored a system of stable currency exchange rates for all countries.[49] Gold has been struck into coins since at least the 7th century B.C.[50]

As a result of Bretton Woods, other nations' currencies were linked flexibly to the dollar, permitting countries to devalue or lower their exchange rates with the dollar in extreme economic crises in order to preserve their bank reserves. The goal was a stable, permanent formula for aligning currency values.

But on Aug. 15, 1971, President Richard M. Nixon stunned the world by cutting the historic linkage between

CHRONOLOGY

1700s-Early 1800s *United States adopts a "sound" money policy; struggles over the dollar's role span the century.*

1791 The First Bank of the United States is established, advancing Treasury Secretary Alexander Hamilton's strategy for a sound, centrally managed currency.

1890s-1930s *Several financial crises lead to centralized control by Washington over the nation's money supply.*

1895 Foreign investors exchange U.S. securities for gold, nearly depleting the U.S. government's gold supply. Financier J. P. Morgan heads off a crisis by leading a private syndicate in selling gold bonds in Europe.

1900 United States ties the dollar's value to gold.

1913 Congress creates the Federal Reserve System as the U.S. "lender of last resort" in emergencies.

1933 The 1929 stock market crash is followed by a banking crisis on the eve of Franklin D. Roosevelt's presidential inauguration. He temporarily closes the banks and bans gold hoarding. The New Deal insures bank deposits, but global currency devaluations prolong the Great Depression.

1940s-1995 *United States establishes a stable post-World War II global currency regime based on the dollar.*

1944 World leaders at a meeting in Bretton Woods, N.H., establish the dollar as the world's primary or "anchor" currency, displacing the British pound.

1971 President Richard M. Nixon ends the Bretton Woods policy allowing nations to exchange dollars for U.S. gold, introducing floating currency rates.

1983-85 Dollar soars against the yen, making Japanese imports cheaper. U.S. manufacturers and unions demand a cheaper dollar so they can compete.

1985 Leaders from United States, Japan, West Germany, France and Britain sign the Plaza Accord lowering the dollar's value.

1985-1995 Yen rebounds against the dollar, leading to major Japanese investments in the United States. A massive real estate boom ends in a crash in 1990, triggering an enduring banking crisis in Japan.

1997-Present *Global trade and financial transactions expand rapidly, setting the stage for financial crises that eventually spread to the United States.*

1997-1999 Financial crises erupt in Thailand, Russia, Indonesia, South Korea and Brazil. The Clinton administration and the International Monetary Fund commit billions of dollars in emergency loans to stem the contagion.

1999 European Monetary Union creates a common currency, the euro, which enters circulation in 2002.

2002 The dollar begins a long decline compared to the euro, as higher European interest rates attract investors away from the greenback.

2005 China ends its policy of tying the yuan to the dollar, agreeing to U.S. requests to let the currency float within a controlled range to reduce a huge U.S. trade deficit with China.

2007 A decade-long U.S. housing market bubble bursts following the failure of high-risk, subprime mortgage investments. A chain reaction of financial losses spreads from Wall Street to the banking industry.

2008 Despite domestic inflationary pressures caused by the dollar's decline, Saudi Arabia keeps its currency tied to the dollar. . . . To prevent economic collapse, the Bush administration pledges more than $1 trillion in emergency support, including $700 billion to Wall Street plus loans to banks, mortgage lenders and the nation's leading insurer, American International Group. The rescue lifts the sagging dollar, but may undermine it in the future.

gold and the dollar, blocking foreigners from exchanging dollars for gold from the government's vaults at Fort Knox, Ky.[51] Nixon's decision led to an array of different currency exchange policies that has continued to evolve.

The trend in exchange rate policies is for countries to let their currencies "float," with their value determined by the world's currency exchanges.

Foreign exchange trading is so huge that most governments would be unable to successfully control their currency's value by "intervention" — buying and selling their own currency on the exchanges. (In 2004, for example, the paper value of currencies traded on exchanges in a typical week matched the $9 trillion figure for the total output of the U.S. economy for the entire year.)[52]

Instead, countries with floating rates try to set short-term interest rates at levels that strengthen or weaken their currency values, and in that way hit their goals for exports and imports. Floating currency exchange rates are a cornerstone of economic globalization and a key reason for the huge increase in currency trading.

According to the International Monetary Fund, 23 countries — most of them small, including Bulgaria, Ecuador and Estonia — have adopted a "hard" peg, tying their currencies to various other countries' currencies at fixed rates. Another 63 nations — including Argentina, Nigeria, Pakistan, Saudi Arabia and other oil-producing states — peg their money to a single currency. About half favor the dollar, and a third choose the euro. China's "crawling" peg arrangement allows its foreign exchange rate to be periodically adjusted against the dollar in small steps to meet China's economic goals.[53]

The United States, Britain, Mexico, Brazil, Australia, Israel and Eurozone countries were among 35 nations that let their currencies float freely, the IMF said. Japan allows the yen to float but has intervened at times to keep the yen's exchange value from falling so low that Japanese exports are depressed. Russia, most former Soviet satellite states and smaller Asian, South American and African nations were among the 48 countries that maintained a "managed" float, with their governments intervening to keep their currencies at desired exchange rates.

In general, advanced countries with large exports and imports were most likely to let currencies float. Smaller countries that had suffered from hyper-inflation were likely to peg their currencies to the dollar or euro, seeking protection against inflation.[54] Other countries with

AFP/Getty Images/Jung Yeon-Je

Gold bars are displayed at a bank in Seoul, South Korea. Nations keep gold reserves because their value goes up when inflation increases. After World War II, the gold-backed U.S. dollar was established as the world's "anchor" currency. But in 1971, President Richard M. Nixon stunned the world by cutting the historic linkage between gold and the dollar, blocking foreigners from exchanging dollars for gold from the U.S. government's reserves.

disproportionately large trade and financial flows — such as Saudi Arabia — peg to the dollar for the same reason.[55]

The dollar's long decline beginning in 2002 caused other floating currencies to move in the opposite direction. Moreover, as in the euro's case, the cheap dollar has given U.S. exporters a competitive trade advantage, causing tension between the United States and rival exporting nations. On the other hand, countries whose currencies are pegged to the dollar, such as Saudi Arabia, have suffered with rising prices for oil, food and other commodities. Higher commodity prices have triggered higher inflation and led to calls for a shift from a dollar peg to a linkage with a group, or "basket," of currencies, or ties to a mix of currencies combined with the price of oil itself.[56]

Before Nixon's 1971 move, a government or a foreign investor could switch to gold whenever inflation threatened to undermine a local currency's value (as inflation causes prices to rise, the dollar's purchasing power shrinks). Massive American spending on the Vietnam War, combined with Washington's refusal to cut other spending or raise taxes, meant the United States had to pay for the war by printing more money, causing inflation and lowering the dollar's value.

"When inflation eroded the greenback's purchasing power, gold was the more attractive option. Foreigners traded in their dollars until U.S. gold stocks were close to exhaustion. Higher U.S. interest rates could have lured foreigners back into dollars. But Nixon wouldn't tolerate high rates the year before an election," noted *Washington Post* columnist Sebastian Mallaby.[57]

Rescue Efforts

Concern about the dollar's strength dates from the first years of the republic, when U.S. Treasury Secretary Alexander Hamilton persuaded President George Washington to create a national bank and have the federal government take over the states' heavy Revolutionary War debts. Hamilton's policy enriched speculators who had bought the war debt from investors at cheap prices, infuriating Secretary of State Thomas Jefferson and others who feared concentrated national monetary power.[58]

But Hamilton solidly established the principle of a strong dollar that would be linked to gold for most of the U.S. peacetime history before Nixon's action.

Now the dollar — no longer tethered to gold — depends on the world's confidence in the U.S. economy in relation to other economies. "Money is a belief," writes Jason Goodwin, author of *Greenback, The Almighty Dollar and the Invention of America.* "We accept money because we believe others in turn will accept it, too."[59] It follows, then, that the dollar's position in the world depends on confidence.

In the worst-case scenario, if that confidence eroded and foreign governments abandoned the dollar or reduced the dollars they hold in their central banks, "the dollar could rapidly lose in popularity and value," wrote economists Christopher M. Meissner and Nienke Oomes in an IMF Working Paper. "A similar situation occurred in the early 1970s, when the British pound sterling quite suddenly disappeared as an anchor currency, despite . . . its international status during the preceding 150 years."[60]

Some experts — citing the potential for a sharp plunge in the dollar — call for a coordinated response by the world's leading economies, similar to the action taken by the five largest industrial democracies — in 1985. The finance ministers from France, Germany, Japan, Britain and the United States came together to resolve the problems caused by the large U.S. trade deficit and the dollar's strength against other currencies.

High interest rates engineered by the U.S. Federal Reserve to control inflation in the early 1980s had invited heavy foreign investment in the dollar, driving up its price, particularly against the yen.[61] American manufacturers were being beaten bloody by the high dollar, which penalized U.S. exporters and gave a critical advantage to Japanese exporters of cars, electronics and other products. Democratic Party leaders in Congress were threatening trade sanctions, and U.S. business leaders demanded a change.

The "Plaza" agreement, named for the New York City hotel where the ministers met, pledged to gradually lower the dollar's value and shrink global trade imbalances. (By the time the Plaza conference was held, U.S. interest rates and oil prices were falling, and the dollar had already begun to shift downward from its peak values. Thus, the ministers were able to "lean with the wind," as Japanese journalist Yoichi Funabashi put it.)[62]

The dollar did eventually stabilize, contributing to the economic growth and budget surpluses of the Clinton presidency. Political ferment over trade also eased, helping Clinton win bipartisan approval of the North American Free Trade Agreement (NAFTA) and formation of the World Trade Organization.[63]

The Peterson Institute's Bergsten argues that the current weakness of the dollar and persistent trade deficits require a new round of top-level cooperation among the United States and other economic powers. The major financial powers need an "Asian Plaza Agreement" with China, so that it will allow its currency to gain value against the dollar and the euro, Bergsten and other experts say. That, they say, will shrink the U.S. trade deficit to a sustainable level and head off a new round of congressional demands for trade penalties against China.[64]

Moreover, Bergsten says, any currency move by China must be accompanied by a unified, coordinated increase in foreign currency rates by other leading Asian nations, led by Japan and South Korea. Otherwise, some Asian countries could act independently, he says, suppressing their currency values to gain a competitive advantage and killing the initiative before it could work. Whether China would join such an effort is one of the unknowns in the dollar's future.

CURRENT SITUATION

Oil and the Dollar

The world's investors are viewing the dollar and oil as a linked gauge of anxiety over the ongoing global financial crisis. In a pattern that appeared early in this decade and has been especially pronounced since the credit crisis exploded last year, when the dollar weakens, oil prices rise. The price of Brent crude, the benchmark North Sea crude oil grade, jumped from $50 a barrel in mid-January 2007 to $142 a barrel by early July 2008, while the exchange rate for the euro rose from $1.29 per euro to $1.58.[65] Then the trend reversed. By the third week of August 2008 Brent was $110 a barrel and the dollar had retreated to $1.46 per euro. The linkage was unmistakable, said American oil analyst Philip K. Verleger Jr.[66]

Oil and the dollar had often behaved differently in the past, the Peterson Institute's Bergsten said in congressional testimony in July. In 1985-86, the price of oil sank from nearly $30 a barrel to $10 a barrel while the dollar's value compared to the currencies of the 10 largest industrial nations dropped by 40 percent.[67] Both oil and the dollar rose together again in the late 1990s, Bergsten added.[68]

Normally, oil and the dollar react independently to economic conditions, experts say. Interest rates differ among nations, affecting currency values as investors seek higher returns on bonds. And oil prices respond to shortages or surpluses, wars and political tensions in oil-producing regions or hurricanes that smash into oil fields and refineries.

So what has caused the unusual recent oil-dollar linkage?

Worldwide oil supplies have become increasingly strained since 2000, notes Daniel Yergin, chairman of Cambridge Energy Research Associates in Massachusetts. China's hyper-growth — and accompanying increased demand for oil — plus the Iraq War and violence in Nigeria's oil-producing region all contributed to the scarcity.[69]

The tight balance between oil supply and demand encouraged traders and speculators to sell the dollar on currency exchanges because the oil scarcity stoked higher prices for oil. And because most oil shipments are priced in dollars, a drop in the dollar's value meant lower revenues for producers, who then sought higher oil prices. Meanwhile, European, Chinese and Russian currencies were gaining value against the dollar, so they could afford to pay more for dollar-priced oil.

In addition, major investment and retirement funds rushed into the commodity markets to buy oil and grains instead of increasingly risky stocks, bonds and real estate. At a congressional hearing in June, Yergin called oil "the new gold" — an investment that offers protection against rising inflation, a declining dollar and collapsing real estate values.[70]

As a result, Yergin theorized, instead of the traditional "flight to the dollar" during a time of financial stress, there has been a "flight to commodities." "Although the correlation does not hold week-in and week-out, we believe that this trend — a falling dollar contributing to higher oil prices — is very strong," Yergin said. A Federal Reserve Bank of Dallas study, he said, estimated that about one-third of the $60 increase in oil prices between 2003 through 2007 was caused by the dollar's decline.[71]

"The crisis that started in the subprime mortgage market in the United States has traveled around the world. And through the medium of a weaker dollar it has come back home to Americans [as] higher prices at the pump," he said.

Although members of Congress have trained fire on oil traders and speculators, commodities analyst Peter Beutel, president of a Connecticut-based energy risk-management company, says the entry in 2006 of huge pension and investment funds into speculative commodity trading was a bigger factor in rising oil prices. The trend accelerated after the Federal Reserve cut interest rates repeatedly in 2007, which telegraphed to fund managers that the dollar would decline.

As an example, Beutel cites the California Public Employees' Retirement System (CalPERS) — the nation's largest public retirement fund — which disclosed in September 2006 that it planned to invest in commodities. "There may be serious money to be made by taking advantage of accelerating world demand for commodities and compelling investment opportunities in alternatives to diminishing resources, including cheap oil," said Charles P. Valdes, a CalPERS board member.[72]

Although energy is a relatively minor part of the fund's total capital, profit from energy and other commodity investments ballooned. "CalPERS has racked up a 68 percent return playing the commodities market in the past 12 months," reported the *Sacramento Bee*.[73] Critics in Washington and California say the fund is cashing in on consumers' pain at the gasoline pump.

But CalPERS spokeswoman Pat Macht responded, "Commodities are one small part of a diversification strategy that we . . . and all institutional investors use. We don't think we're causing a problem. There are many, many other factors at play here. Our intentions are honorable."

However, Michael Greenberger, a former U.S. Commodity Futures Trading Commission official, said investments by CalPERS and other pension and endowment funds "are completely distorting the market" and helping to push oil and other commodity prices higher.[74]

The Dollar and Food

A "silent tsunami" of hunger is afflicting the poorest communities in South Africa, where rice prices doubled between May 2007 and May 2008, a government survey reported this month.[75] South Africa's plight is matched throughout the world's poorest regions, all hit by an escalation of food prices connected to the dollar's downward trend in value.

Food has become another important option for investors seeking relief from a falling dollar.

In 2008, developing countries may spend four times what they paid for food imports in 2000, according to a "Food Price Index" study issued by two international agencies.[76] (The increase for developed countries is far less.) The fast-rising track for cereal prices on the index matches the path of crude oil and euros in 2007. And, imitating oil and euro prices on commodity exchanges, the index, covering five food commodities, has flattened out this spring, and sugar and dairy prices have tipped slightly downward, say the Organization for Economic Cooperation and Development (OECD) and the U.N. Food and Agriculture Organization (FAO).

The rising food prices ignited sometimes violent protests in a score of countries, from Haiti to Niger to Uzbekistan. Peruvian farmers blocked rail lines to protest higher fertilizer prices caused by higher oil prices. More than 75,000 protesters filled the streets of Mexico City in January 2007 demanding price controls after a 400-percent jump in the price of tortillas due to rising costs of maize imports.[77] Rice, an essential part of the developing world's diet, shot up from $300 a ton in May 2005 to $900 a ton three years later. A Haitian factory worker earns about $5 a day, so when rice triples to 67 cents a bowl, the worker ends up spending a day's pay for just seven bowls of rice, according to a report by the Progressive Policy Institute, a Washington, D.C., think tank.[78]

As in the case of oil, the escalation in food prices in 2007 followed increased trading in grains and other farm commodities by financial firms, banks, investment funds and other newcomers to these markets. Trading volumes in commodities like maize doubled between February 2005 and February 2008, in large part due to these "new agents."[79]

According to commodities analyst Beutel, the financial industry's move into commodity markets, like its investments in oil contracts, has a decidedly different impact than traditional commodity market activity. Traders and speculators purchase their oil or grain contracts seeking short-term profits and will sell out of their positions when they sense the time is right. The non-commercial newcomers are buying and holding positions in oil and farm commodities as if they were long-term investments in corporate stocks and bonds, says Beutel. "They buy and hold," and that puts upward pressure on oil prices, he adds.

All of that creates upward momentum toward higher prices until events cause a decisive change in investors' outlook. The activities of major funds in commodity markets have become a "key concern," according to a long-term outlook by the OECD and FAO.[80]

The two institutions predict that over the long term food price hikes will level off but remain historically high. The U.S. dollar is expected to regain some strength, they predicted, which will reduce food imports and encourage more local food production, allowing food prices to fall some. But farm commodity markets are expected to remain volatile, and the risk of more food price shocks continues, the agencies concluded.[81]

China's Challenge

The 2008 Olympics delivered to a global television audience the dazzling evidence of China's economic growth.[82] Hundreds of millions of rural Chinese have been lifted out of extreme poverty. China has taken a commanding position in world trade as the world's second-largest exporter — behind Germany and ahead of the United States — and the third-largest importer, trailing the United States and Germany.[83]

AT ISSUE

Could the euro replace the dollar as the globe's anchor currency?

YES

Jeffrey A. Frankel
Professor of Capital Formation and Growth, Harvard Kennedy School

Written for *CQ Global Researcher*, September 2008

The euro is a credible, long-term challenger to the dollar. The Eurozone — the 15 European countries that have adopted the euro currency — is roughly as big as the United States, and the euro has shown itself a better store of value than the dollar. It's true that in the current credit crisis, the dollar has retained its reputation as a safe haven for fearful investors around the world. I might have predicted the crisis would have begun to undermine the dollar's position by now. But U.S. Treasury bills have still been considered the safest thing around.

Taking a longer view, however, the causes of the crisis and the cost to the United States to prevent an economic collapse are negatives for the dollar. Whether measured in terms of a burgeoning federal budget deficit or in damage to New York's reputation as a financial center, the situation certainly appears to significantly undermine confidence in the dollar and in U.S. financial markets.

As the crisis eases, there will be more rethinking of the dollar. We will go back to the more mundane macroeconomic issues, which have been overshadowed by the recent crisis. The rising federal budget deficit could renew downward pressure on the dollar. The current account deficit may grow. Monetary authorities in China and the Persian Gulf have been reluctant to shift out of dollars because they are afraid of setting off a run on the dollar, and they would be the biggest losers. But once the crisis is past, they may see an incentive to quietly reduce dollar holdings.

To be sure, rankings of international currencies change very slowly. The United States surpassed the United Kingdom in economic size in 1872, in exports in 1915 and as a net creditor in 1917, yet the dollar did not surpass the pound as the No. 1 international currency until 1945. In 2005, when University of Wisconsin Professor Menzie Chinn and I created a model to determine the factors that create a dominant global currency, even our pessimistic scenarios had the euro not overtaking the dollar until 2022.

But the dollar has continued to lose ground. We updated our calculations earlier this year, particularly to recognize that London is usurping Frankfurt's role as the financial capital of the euro, even though the U.K. remains outside of the European monetary union. Now we find that the tipping point could come sooner; the euro could overtake the dollar as early as 2015.

For more information: http://papers.ssrn.com/sol3/papers.cfm?abstract_id=1083712

NO

Adam S. Posen
Deputy Director, Peterson Institute for International Economics

Written for *CQ Global Researcher*, September 2008

Financial panics are rarely of lasting significance to the fate of nations or their currencies. Though calm is difficult to maintain while the United States experiences a panic in its many interlocking markets, it would be a mistake to read too much into recent developments. The dollar will continue to benefit from the geopolitical sources of its global role, which the euro cannot yet — or soon, if ever — match.

The euro's ascent to at least comparable status with the dollar has a surface plausibility. Some analysts have argued that the euro's attaining co-dominance simply awaited a significant series of policy mistakes by the United States, similar to how the pound sterling began losing its role in the 1930s. The dollar was spared such a fate during the 1970s only because neither the deutschemark nor the yen were a viable alternative at the time.

It is time for observers to shed excessive doubts about the euro. Yet, the dollar will retain a dominant role in official reserve portfolios, partly because longer-term choices of international currency commitments are driven by both financial and political factors. Moreover, the Eurozone's monetary strengths cannot offset the European Union's economic and political weaknesses in global leadership.

These sources of dollar strength are ignored in a narrow, deterministic focus on why countries choose to hold dollars in official reserves. Other governments' exchange-rate management is influenced by security ties. From Taiwan to Saudi Arabia to Panama, decisions about pegging one's currency to the dollar (and thus to accumulate dollar reserves for intervention) depend as much on foreign policy as on economics. Foreigners' decisions to invest in the United States are influenced by their desire to gain insider access to key U.S. decision-making processes and to membership in transnational elites.

The European Union, let alone the Eurozone, is unable or unwilling to offer these systemic or security benefits beyond a very local area, and thus the euro's global attractiveness is fundamentally limited.

This dependence of the dollar on both political and economic factors, however, suggests that were the dollar no long dominant, the global monetary system would fragment into a multi-currency system, not result in parity between the dollar and the euro.

For more information: The International Economy, spring 2008, pp. 10-11.

But China's remarkable rise has come at a high price. Environmental degradation, income inequality and inflation have accompanied the growth.[84] And China's success has stirred intense criticism over the "people's" currency, the renminbi (RMB).

The complaints are perhaps loudest in the United States, where critics contend China has kept the RMB's value too low against the dollar and other currencies in order to keep China's exports cheap. Although the RMB has risen this year against the dollar, lessening China's currency advantage, the huge U.S. trade deficit with China may yet trigger a political backlash in Congress.

Trade or currency restrictions could ignite a damaging trade conflict between the two countries.[85] Edwin M. Truman, former assistant Treasury secretary for international affairs, notes that China's government-controlled banking and currency policies and actions are deliberately hidden from public view.

"China is subject to multiple suspicions about its political and strategic objectives," he said. Unless China "can demonstrate that it is a good international financial citizen, it risks protectionist reactions."[86]

China contends critics overstate its currency-rate advantage. Low U.S. interest rates engineered by the Federal Reserve are largely responsible for the dollar's weakness, said Jin Zhongxia, chief representative in the United States of the People's Bank of China.[87] "There is no way for Chinese authorities to create a competitive advantage by choosing a specific currency regime," he said, "and they have no intention of doing so."[88]

Despite their differences, China and the United States are lashed together — climbers on a path with many risks. Foreigners owned $9.7 trillion worth of U.S. securities in June 2007, including bonds and stocks issued by government agencies and corporations. China's share — at $922 billion — was second only to Japan's. In fact, China nearly tripled its holdings from 2004 to 2007 as it poured dollars from exports sales back into the United States, primarily by buying Treasury bonds.[89]

"Why are the Chinese monetary authorities so willing to underwrite American profligacy? Not out of altruism," wrote British historian Niall Ferguson.[90] If China doesn't buy U.S. Treasury securities as fast as they are printed, the dollar's value could sink. "The Chinese authorities dread such a dollar slide," he adds. The prices of Chinese goods would climb, exports to the United States would decline and unemployment in China could spike upward when millions of workers from the countryside begin looking for factory jobs in China's cities.

Brad W. Setser, a fellow at the New York-based Council on Foreign Relations, calculates that a one-third decline in the value of the dollar and euro against the renminbi would hit China with a $1 trillion financial loss. "That is a large sum even for a nation of over a billion people," he writes.[91]

The dollar's shakiness is clearly prompting China to consider gradually reducing its dollar holdings, which will tend to depress the dollar against the renminbi, Setser says.[92]

"With China, we have little concept of what is around the bend, yet there is no turning back," writes *International Economy* publisher Smick, in his 2008 book, *The World Is Curved*.[93]

OUTLOOK

Catch-22 Dilemmas

The 2008 global credit crisis has overturned the outlook for the world's leading currencies and sharpened the financial dilemmas facing their governments.

The euro's advantage is the diversity of the economies that make up the 15-nation European Monetary Union, from France and Germany to Slovenia and Greece. That is also its weakness, as Europe's leaders demonstrated in early October as they struggled to find a common response to the threat of bank failures and recession.[94]

"The European financial sector is on trial: We have to support our banks," said French President Sarkozy on Oct. 4 at the start of a European economic summit that brought British Prime Minister Gordon Brown, German Chancellor Angela Merkel and Italian Prime Minister Silvio Berlusconi to Paris. In the previous week, governments in Belgium, Britain, France, Germany, Luxembourg, the Netherlands and Iceland had been forced to shore up the finances of several banks. "We are all staring into the abyss," said German Finance Minister Steinbrück.[95]

But while the leaders expressed solidarity after the Paris meeting, they did not move to create a European emergency fund for banks so normal lending could resume. Prior to the summit, France had suggested Europe create a $415 billion emergency fund to mirror the U.S. financial rescue plan. But Germany and Britain quickly said no, unwilling to pledge their wealth to support other nations' banking systems. A lingering question is whether the fissures within Europe created by the banking crisis will weaken the euro.

Like China, Japan must decide how to handle its huge holdings of dollar-based assets. Japan has more than $1 trillion in foreign currency holdings, most of it in relatively low-yielding U.S. Treasury bills, according to reports from Tokyo.[96] Some financial experts suggest Japan could follow a path taken by China, Norway, Russia, Singapore and the United Arab Emirates in creating a "sovereign wealth fund" empowered to invest government-held dollars in higher-paying foreign securities or real estate. Japan needs improved investment earnings to help fund its rising social security costs.

Financial Services Minister Yuji Yamamoto told *The Japan Times* that with sovereign funds taking a significant role in global finance, "does Japan just sit back as an onlooker and flatly say, 'We don't have to do anything'? That's stubbornly conservative."[97]

But Finance Minister Fukushiro Nukaga rejects the idea, saying Japan's public prefers a safer strategy for investing government-held dollars. "Active management of public wealth involves high risks," he said in February.[98] Analysts note that any significant moves by Japan to reduce its dollar holdings through government investments in non-U.S. assets would undermine the dollar's value — eroding Japan's remaining dollar assets.

China has a similar Catch-22 dilemma, driven home during the current crisis by heavy losses on Wall Street and in U.S. government securities. China's sovereign wealth fund, China Investment Corp. (CIC), "has been bitten several times and is shy" about investing in U.S. financial securities, says Shanghai financial analyst Andy Xie.

"It would be too politically sensitive to buy [more] assets that do not perform well," adds Paul Cavey, chief China economist at Australia's Macquarie Bank in Beijing.[99]

An alternative option for China is to increase purchases in U.S. companies, particularly if the dollar remains weak. The cost of the Bush administration's financial rescue plan and the prospects of higher federal deficits compel the United States to continue borrowing hundreds of billions of dollars a year from foreign governments and banks.

Xie, formerly Morgan Stanley's chief Asia economist, said U.S. political leaders must accept increased foreign investment by China in U.S. companies — a controversial issue for Congress in the past. "If the U.S. is not willing to accept that," he said, "they will have to print money [to fund the deficits], and the dollar will fall. And we will be headed toward a global financial meltdown."[100]

Indeed, German Finance Minister Steinbrück predicted in early October: "One thing is clear: after this crisis, the world will no longer be the same."[101]

NOTES

1. "Five Days That Transformed Wall Street," *The Washington Post*, Sept. 20, 2008, p. A9.
2. Michael M. Grynbaum, "The Fed Holds Rates Steady, and Wall Street Turns a Bad Start Around," *The New York Times*, Sept. 17, 2008, Section C, p. 8.
3. Jeremy Warner, "UK Government may need to guarantee deposits," *The Independent* (London), Oct. 1, 2008, p. 36.
4. Jacques Attali, "Wall Street Meltdown: The First Authentic Global Crisis," *New Perspectives Quarterly*, Sept. 22, 2008.
5. "Subprime woes 'could end dollar regime,'" *The Daily Yomiuri* (Tokyo), March 20, 2008, p. 1.
6. Agence France-Presse, "Germany hit by a 'pronounced slowdown': economist," Aug. 30, 2008.
7. For background, see Marcia Clemmitt, "Global Food Crisis," *CQ Researcher*, June 27, 2008, pp. 553-576.
8. Paul Owers, "Foreign Home Buyers Are Flocking to Florida," *South Florida Sun-Sentinel*, April 12, 2008, p. 1D.
9. Menzi Chinn and Jeffrey Frankel, "Will the Euro Eventually Surpass the Dollar as Leading International Reserve Currency?" http://papers.ssrn.com/sol3/papers.cfm?abstract_id=884261.
10. "U.S. International Trade, Second Quarter 2008," U.S. Bureau of Economic Analysis (BEA), Sept. 11, 2008, Table 2, www.bea.gov/newsreleases/international/trade/2008/trad0708.htm; BEA, "International Transactions Account Data," www.bea.gov/international/bp_web/simple.cfm?anon=78423&table_id=1&area_id=3, and

"The Budget and Economic Outlook: An Update," Congressional Budget Office, Sept. 8, 2008, www.cbo.gov/ftpdocs/97xx/doc9706/09-08-Update.pdf.

11. "Mapping Global Capital Markets, Fourth Annual Report," McKinsey Global Institute, January 2008, p. 10.
12. Jill Treanor and Larry Elliott, "Analysis: Failure of financial heavyweights could have caused markets to implode," *The Guardian* (London), Sept. 9, 2008, p. 9.
13. *Ibid.*
14. "Report on Foreign Portfolio Holdings of U.S. Securities as of June 2007," U.S. Treasury Department, April 2008, pp. 6-8, www.treas.gov/tic/shl2007r.pdf; also "Report to Congress on International Economic and Exchange Rate Policies," U.S. Treasury Department, November 2008, www.treas.gov/offices/international-affairs/economic-exchange-rates/112005_report.pdf.
15. Alan Greenspan, *The Age of Turbulence: Adventures in a New World* (2007), p. 352.
16. Miranda Xafa, "Global Imbalances: Do They Matter?" *Cato Journal*, winter 2007, p. 59.
17. Kenneth Rogoff, "Goodbye to the Dollar," *The International Economy*, spring 2008, p. 51.
18. "Fact Sheet," European Central Bank, www.ecb.int/home/html/index.en.html.
19. "Will dollar lose position as key currency," *The Daily Yomiuri* (Tokyo), April 19, 2008, p. 16.
20. Katrin Bennhold and Steven Erlanger, "French finance minister calls for realignment of currencies," *International Herald Tribune*, May 22, 2008, p. 13.
21. *The Daily Yomiuri*, March 20, 2008, *op. cit.*
22. C. Fred Bergsten, testimony before the House Committee on Financial Services, July 24, 2008, p. 1.
23. "International Economic Accounts," U.S. Bureau of Economic Analysis, June 17, 2008, www.bea.gov/newsreleases/international/transactions/transnewsrelease.htm.
24. "The Current Account Deficit," Peterson Institute of International Economics, www.iie.com/research/topics/hottopic.cfm?HotTopicID=9.
25. Bergsten, *op. cit.*
26. Jonathan Weisman, "Straight-talking Treasury chief stares down critics; O'Neill's remarks don't just ruffle feathers, they rattle markets," *USA Today*, Feb. 21, 2001, p. 1B.
27. Martin Feldstein, "The Dollar Will Fall Further," *The International Economy*, *op. cit.*, p. 16.
28. "Role of Central Banks," Federal Reserve Bank of New York, www.ny.frb.org/education/fx/role.html.
29. Jane Macartney and Robin Pagnamenta, "French seal $12bn Chinese nuclear deal," *The Times* (London), Nov. 27, 2007, p. 55.
30. Joelle Garrus, "Areva announces 8 bln euro nuclear deal with China," Agence France-Presse, Nov. 26, 2006.
31. Brad W. Setser, "Sovereign Wealth and Sovereign Power," Council on Foreign Relations, September 2008, p. 22.
32. "The Falling Dollar," *The Economist*, Nov. 11, 2004, www.economist.com/agenda/displayStory.cfm?Story_id=3372405.
33. McKinsey Global Institute, *op. cit.*, pp. 11-12.
34. Kenichi Ohmae, "The Coming Battle of the Atlantic: Euro vs. the Dollar;" *New Perspectives Quarterly*, April 14, 2008.
35. "The Next Great Global Currency," *The International Economy*, *op. cit.*, pp. 22-37.
36. The International Economy, *op. cit.*, p. 35.
37. Richard H. Clarida, "Reflections on Currency Regimes," *The International Economy*, *op. cit.*, p. 18.
38. Menzie Chinn and Jeffrey A. Frankel, "Will the Euro Eventually Surpass the Dollar as Leading International Reserve Currency?" *G7 Current Account Imbalances* (2007), p. 287.
39. Setser, *op. cit.*
40. "The Dollar in Free Fall," *The New York Times*, Nov. 11, 2007, p. 2.
41. Gary Duncan, "Dollar faces new sell-off if Gulf states end greenback pegs," *The Times* (London), Dec. 3, 2007, p. 45.
42. "Paulson says strong dollar in US interest, Saudi peg 'sovereign decision,' " Thomson Financial

News, May 31, 2008, www.forbes.com/afxnewslimited/feeds/afx/2008/05/31/afx5066473.html.

43. Stephen Mihm, "Dr. Doom," *The New York Times Magazine*, Aug. 17, 2008, p. 26.
44. Brad Setser and Nouriel Roubini, "How Scary is the Deficit?" *Foreign Affairs*, July/August 2005.
45. Mihm, *op. cit.*
46. Donald J. Boudreaux, "A Dollar Dump? Not likely," *Pittsburgh Tribune-Review*, Nov. 30, 2007, www.pittsburghlive.com/x/pittsburghtrib/opinion/columnists/boudreaux/s_540383.html.
47. Adam S. Posen, "It's Not Just About The Money," *The International Economy*, *op. cit.*, p. 10.
48. "The Growth Report — Strategies for Sustained Growth and Inclusive Development," The World Bank Commission on Growth and Development, May 21, 2008, p. 96.
49. "The Role of the U.S. Dollar," Iowa State University, www.econ.iastate.edu/classes/econ355/choi/bre.htm. For background, see F. P. Huddle, "Bretton Woods Agreements," in *Editorial Research Reports*, April 27, 1945, available in *CQ Researcher Plus Archive*, http://library.cqpress.com.
50. Michael D. Bordo, "Gold Standard," *The Concise Encyclopedia of Economics*, www.econlib.org/library/Enc/GoldStandard.html.
51. The right of American citizens to own gold coins and currency ended in 1933 as part of President Franklin D. Roosevelt's emergency measures to end widespread gold hoarding during the nation's banking crisis in the Great Depression. For background, see Lawrence Sullivan, *Prelude to Panic: The Story of the Bank Holiday* (1936), pp. 87-103. For background, see R. C. Deans, "World Money Crisis," in *Editorial Research Reports*, Sept. 8, 1971, available in *CQ Researcher Plus Archive*, http://library.cqpress.com.
52. "Economic Report of the President 2007," p. 150, www.whitehouse.gov/cea/pubs.html.
53. "Review of Exchange Agreements, Restrictions and Controls," International Monetary Fund, Nov. 27, 2007, www.imf.org/External/NP/pp/2007/eng/112707.pdf.
54. Christopher M. Meissner and Nienke Oomes, "Why do Countries Peg the Way They Peg? The Determinants of Anchor Currency Choice," *IMF Working Paper*, May 2008.
55. Brad W. Setser, "The Case for Exchange Rate Flexibility of Oil-Exporting Economies," Peterson Institute for International Economics, November 2007, pp. 1-13.
56. *Ibid.*, p. 4.
57. Sebastian Mallaby, "The Dollar in Danger," *The Washington Post*, Nov. 12, 2007, p. A21.
58. Richard Hofstadter, *The American Political Tradition* (1989), p. 42.
59. Jason Goodwin, *Greenback, The Almighty Dollar and the Invention of America* (2003), p. 5.
60. Meissner and Oomes, *op. cit.*
61. Kent H. Hughes, *Building the Next American Century, The Past and Future of American Economic Competitiveness* (2005), p. 383.
62. *Ibid.*, p. 393.
63. *Ibid.*, p. 340.
64. David M. Smick, *The World Is Curved* (2008), pp. 267-268.
65. "Weekly Europe (UK) Brent Blend Spot Price FOB," *Petroleum Navigator*, Energy Information Administration, http://tonto.eia.doe.gov/dnav/pet/hist/wepcbrentw.htm; and "Foreign Exchange Rates (Daily)," Federal Reserve Statistical Release, www.federalreserve.gov/releases/h10/Hist/.
66. Philip K. Verleger, Jr., "The Oil-Dollar Link," The International Economy, *op. cit.*, p. 48.
67. "Annual Oil Market Chronology," Energy Information Administration, www.eia.doe.gov/cabs/AOMC/Overview.html.
68. Bergsten testimony, *op. cit.*, p. 5.
69. Daniel Yergin, "Oil and the Break Point," testimony to the Joint Economic Committee of Congress, June 25, 2008, pp. 1-5, www2.cera.com/news/DYergin_June2008_Testimony.pdf.
70. *Ibid.*, p. 7.
71. Stephen P.A. Brown, Raghav Virmani and Richard Alm, "Economic Letter — Insights from the Federal Reserve Bank of Dallas," May 2008, p. 6.

72. CalPERS, press release, "CalPERS Explores Natural Resource/Commodities Investing, Sept. 12, 2006, www.calpers.ca.gov/index.jsp?bc=/about/press/pr-2006/sept/natural-resources-commodities.xml, and www.calpers.ca.gov/index.jsp?bc=/investments/home.xml.

73. Dale Kasler, "CalPERS profits as costs surge; While consumers fume over commodity prices, pension fund makes killing in market," *Sacramento Bee*, June 20, 2008, p. A1.

74. *Ibid.*

75. Lyse Comins and David Canning, "Surveys show silent hunger 'tsunami,' " *Pretoria News*, Sept. 1, 2008, p. E2.

76. "The FAO Price Index," Organization for Economic Cooperation and Development and the U.N. Food and Agriculture Organization, www.fao.org/docrep/010/ai466e/ai466e16.htm.

77. Jerome Taylor, "How the rising price of corn made Mexicans take to the street," *The Independent*, June 23, 2007, www.independent.co.uk/news/world/americas/how-the-rising-price-of-corn-made-mexicans-take-to-streets-454260.html.

78. "Trade and Global Markets," Progressive Policy Institute, June 4, 2008, www.ppionline.org/ppi_ci.cfm?contentid=254657&knlgAreaID=108&subsecid=900003.

79. "OECD-FAO Agricultural Outlook 2008-2017," Organization for Economic Cooperation and Development, Food and Agriculture Organization, 2008, pp. 37-38, www.oecd.org/dataoecd/54/15/40715381.pdf.

80. *Ibid.*, pp. 37-38.

81. *Ibid.*, p. 53.

82. Bert Hoffman and Louis Kuijs, "Rebalancing China's Growth," in *Debating China's Exchange Rate Policy* (2008), Peterson Institute for International Economics, p. 110.

83. "Rank Order-Exports," *CIA World Factbook*, August 2008; https://www.cia.gov/library/publications/the-world-factbook/rankorder/2078 rank.html.

84. Rowan Callick, "Communist Party hoping to kick off its 15 millenniums of fame," *The Australian*, Aug. 8, 2008, p. 8; Jim Yardley, "China sees inflation as its top fiscal priority," *The International Herald Tribune*, March 6, 2008, p. 5.

85. Morris Goldstein and Nicholas R. Lardy, "China's Exchange Rate policy: An Overview of Some Key Issues," in *Debating China's Exchange Rate Policy*, *op. cit.*, pp. 17-35, p. 44; Smick, *op. cit.*, p. 119.

86. Edwin M. Truman, "The Management of China's International Reserves: China and a Sovereign Wealth Fund Scoreboard," in *Debating China's Exchange Rate Policy*, *op. cit.*, pp. 182-183.

87. Jin Zhongxia, "The Open Economy Trilemma: An Alternative View from China's Perspective," in *Debating China's Exchange Rate Policy*, *op. cit.*, p. 102.

88. *Ibid.*, p. 105.

89. "Report on Foreign Portfolio Holdings of U.S. Securities, June 2007," *op. cit.*, p. 12.

90. Niall Ferguson, "Our Currency, Your Problem," *The New York Times*, March 13, 2005.

91. Setser, "Sovereign Wealth and Sovereign Power," *op. cit.*, p. 30.

92. "The Case for Exchange Rate Flexibility in Oil-Exporting Economies," Peterson Institute, November 2007, pp. 10-12.

93. Smick, *op. cit.*, p. 127.

94. Philippe Alfroy, "Divided Europe holds financial crisis summit," Agence France-Presse, Oct. 4, 2008.

95. Ambrose Evans-Pritchard, "Now Europe is staring into the abyss; Banks falling like dominoes have led to credit being almost impossible to find," *The Daily Telegraph*, London, Sept. 30, 2008.

96. Shinichi Terada, "LDP studying creation of sovereign wealth fund," *The Japan Times*, April 4, 2008.

97. *Ibid.*

98. "Japan needs to study risks before setting up government investment fund," The Associated Press, Feb. 22, 2008.

99. Ron Scherer, "Wall Street woes: why world's investors sit on sidelines," *The Christian Science Monitor*, Sept. 18, 2008.

100. Blaine Harden and Ariana Eunjung Cha, "Japan, China Locked In by Investments," *The Washington Post*, Sept. 20, 2008, p. D1.

101. Peter Wilson, "Europe wants US power shift," *The Australian*, Oct. 1, 2008, p. 36.

BIBLIOGRAPHY

Books

Goldstein, Morris, and Nicholas R. Lardy, eds., *Debating China's Exchange Rate Policy, Peterson Institute for International Economics*, 2005.
Two China experts present papers from a symposium on China's exchange rate policies and economic outlook.

Greenspan, Alan, *The Age of Turbulence: Adventures in a New World, Penguin Press*, 2008.
The former Federal Reserve chairman recounts a life at the center of economic policy.

Hughes, Kent H., *Building the Next American Century, The Past and Future of American Economic Competitiveness, Woodrow Wilson Center Press*, 2005.
A former Clinton administration official examines the global competitiveness challenges facing the United States.

Smick, M. David, *The World Is Curved, Portfolio*, 2008.
The publisher of *The International Economy* quarterly reviews the pluses and pitfalls of globalization with a warning about the future.

Soros, George, *The New Paradigm for Financial Markets: The Credit Crisis of 2008 and What it Means, Public Affairs*, 2008.
The billionaire investor, speculator and philanthropist describes where he thinks the global credit crisis may lead.

Zandi, Mark, *Financial Shock, FT Press*, 2008.
The founder and chief economist of Moody's economy .com dissects how the subprime mortgage scandal morphed into a global financial crisis.

Articles

Wilson, Peter, "Europe wants US Power shift," *The Australian*, Oct. 1, 2008, p. 36.
The global credit crisis demands a new world order for international finance, says European Union Trade Commissioner Peter Mandelson, with Europe and developing economies — such as China, Brazil and India — having greater regulatory power.

Reports and Studies

"The Dollar Issue," *The International Economy*, Spring 2008, www.international-economy.com/Spring2008archive.htm.
Some 50 experts are surveyed on whether the dollar may be overtaken by the euro and the Chinese yuan as the leading global currency.

"Economic Report of the President 2008," *Council of Economic Advisers*, Feb. 11, 2008, www.whitehouse.gov/cea/pubs.html.
President Bush's economic advisers survey the economy.

"Mapping Global Capital Markets, Fourth Annual Report," *McKinsey Global Institute*, January 2008, www.mckinsey.com/mgi/publications/Mapping_Global/index.asp.
The McKinsey research organization charts worldwide capital flows.

"World Economic Outlook, Housing and the Business Cycle," *The International Monetary Fund*, April 2008, www.imf.org/external/pubs/ft/weo/2008/01/index.htm.
The international lending agency assesses causes of the dollar's decline.

Chinn, Menzie, and Jeffrey Frankel, "The Euro May Over the Next 15 Years Surpass the Dollar as Leading International Currency," *International Finance*, February 2008, http://ksghome.harvard.edu/~jfrankel/EuroVs$-IFdebateFeb2008.pdf.
A professor of economics at the University of Wisconsin (Menzie) and a Harvard professor of capital formation and growth (Frankel) argue that the dollar may be eclipsed as the world's anchor currency.

Meissner, Christopher M., and Nienke Oomes, "Why do Countries Peg the Way They Peg? The Determinants of Anchor Currency Choice," *IMF Working Paper*, May 2008, *Stanford Law School*, http://papers.ssrn.com/sol3/papers.cfm?abstract_id=1154294.

Two international economists examine various foreign exchange policies used by the world's nations. Meissner is at the University of California, Davis, and Oomes is resident representative in Armenia for the International Monetary Fund.

Posen, Adam S., "It's Not Just About the Money," ***Peterson Institute for International Economics*, 2008, http://petersoninstitute.org/publications/papers/posen0408.pdf.**
The Peterson Institute's deputy director argues that the dollar can draw on the political strength and broad economic leadership of the United States.

Setser, Brad W., "Sovereign Wealth and Sovereign Power," ***Council on Foreign Relations*, September 2008, www.cfr.org/publication/17074.**
A former Treasury official now at the Council on Foreign Relations examines the political risks of U.S. foreign indebtedness.

For More Information

American Enterprise Institute, 1150 17th St., N.W., Washington, DC 20036; (202) 862-5800; www.aei.org. A research center devoted to the education and study of government, politics, economics and social welfare issues.

Bank for International Settlements, Centralbahnplatz 2, CH-4002 Basel, Switzerland; (41) 61 280 8080; www.bis.org. Serves as a bank for other banks and works to create global financial cooperation.

Brookings Institution, 1775 Massachusetts Ave., N.W., Washington, DC 20036; (202) 797-6000; www.brookings.edu. A nonpartisan organization dedicated to public policy research.

Competitiveness Institute, Imagina Building, Diagonal Av.177 1st floor, 08018 Barcelona, Spain; (34) 93 309 4834; www.competitiveness.org. An international network of policy makers and leaders working to increase competition in various sectors around the globe.

Economic Report of the President, www.gpoaccess.gov/eop/. Written by the chairman of the president's Council of Economic Advisors, describes the current economic status and progress of the United States.

Federal Reserve Bank of New York, 33 Liberty St., New York, NY 10045; (212) 720-5000; www.ny.frb.org. Helps create financial stability and carry out monetary policy. The New York Fed's president is the only regional Federal Reserve Bank president with a permanent vote on the Federal Open Market Committee, which sets monetary policy.

Federal Reserve Board of Governors, 20th St. and Constitution Ave., N.W., Washington, DC 20551; (202) 452-3000; www.federalreserve.gov. Seven-member panel nominated by the president that sets U.S. monetary policy.

International Monetary Fund, 700 19th St., N.W., Washington, DC 20431; (202) 623-7000; www.imf.org. Monitors economic stability and provides financial and technical assistance to ailing economies.

Peter G. Peterson Institute, 1750 Massachusetts Ave., N.W., Washington, DC 20036-1903; (202) 328-9000; www.iie.com. A nonprofit, nonpartisan think tank that studies international economic policy.

Progressive Policy Institute, 600 Pennsylvania Ave., S.E., Suite 400, Washington, DC 20003; (202) 547-0001; www.ppionline.org. A liberal research and education center.

Tax Policy Center, www.taxpolicycenter.org. A joint project of the Urban Institute and Brookings Institution that provides information and analysis on tax policies.

Woodrow Wilson International Center for Scholars, 1300 Pennsylvania Ave., N.W., Washington, DC 20004-3027; (202) 691-4000; www.wilsoncenter.org. Provides research and a forum for discussions on international affairs.

2

The New Latin America

Will Radicals or Moderates Triumph?

Roland Flamini

AP Photo/Natacha Pisarenko

The changing face of Latin American leaders is reflected in, from left, Brazil's Luiz Inacio Lula da Silva, a former steel worker and an admirer of Cuba's Fidel Castro; Cristina Fernández de Kirchner, Argentina's first female president; and Bolivia's Evo Morales, an Aymara Indian and Latin America's only indigenous head of state.

From *CQ Global Researcher*, March 2008.

When Cuban leader Fidel Castro announced on Feb. 19 that he was stepping down after nearly 50 years in power, the news — though widely reported — had limited impact in other Latin American countries. Once, revolutionary Cuba was an influential force in the region, but Latin America has since moved on.

Of course, the legendary Castro is still an icon of the left. But, while Latin America's current crop of leaders are socialist or left-leaning — like Brazil's President Luiz Inacio Lula da Silva, a life-long admirer of Fidel — their governments are far removed from his dogmatic and ruinous communist system.

Developments in Cuba were quickly overshadowed by tension in the Andes, where Venezuela and Ecuador moved troops to their respective borders with Colombia after Colombian security forces on March 1 killed a top leader of a Colombian Marxist guerrilla group who was hiding in Ecuador's border area. However, an armed confrontation was considered unlikely, and the stand-off failed to dim the good news from the region.

This is Latin America's season of promise. In recent years the 22 countries that make up Latin America have quietly transformed a hemisphere once plagued by civil wars, brutal repression, mass murder, dictatorships and military juntas into functioning democracies focusing increasingly on their daunting social problems.*

* In this report, Latin America refers to South America, Central America, Mexico and Cuba.

Latin Countries Leaning to the Left

The 22 predominantly Spanish-, Portuguese- and French-speaking countries that make up Latin America stretch from Mexico in the north to Chile at the continent's southern tip and have a population of more than 500 million. Four countries, including Cuba, lean decidedly to the left, five are more centrist to right-wing and the rest follow moderate socialist policies.

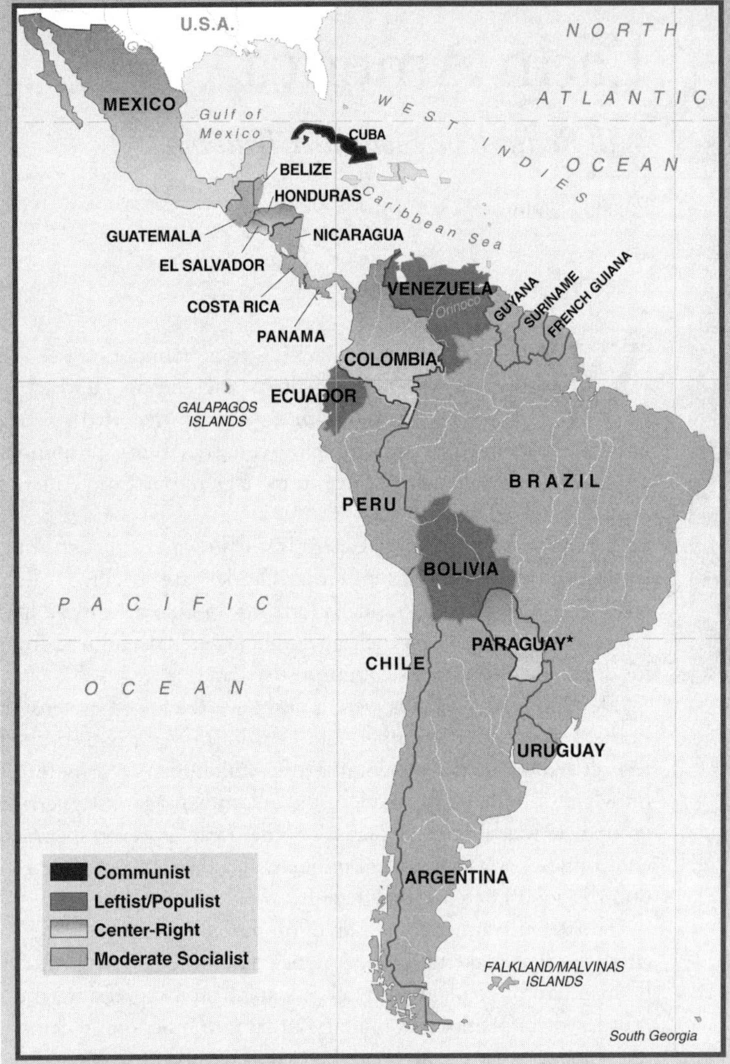

* Having election in April and leftist candidate is expected to win.

Source: The World Bank

Leftist administrations of one sort or another have been elected in Argentina, Brazil, Chile, Uruguay, Nicaragua, Venezuela, Bolivia, Ecuador and, in all likelihood after April elections, in Paraguay. All promised better conditions to the underclass: more employment, better social benefits and a larger share of the country's wealth. Only Colombia, Mexico and Honduras are run by more market-oriented, centrist or right-leaning leaders.

However, pigeon-holing the new generation of leaders is not easy, warns Antonio de Aguilar Patriota, Brazil's ambassador to Washington. "The categories of leftists and rightists don't apply so well to what's happening today in South America," he said recently. "They don't capture the political dynamics of the moment. These days democracy is taking root. All governments in South America are democratically elected."[1] In other words, pragmatism tends to win out over ideology among today's Latin American leaders.

Asked to review a book on the current situation in Latin America, Moisés Naím, a former government minister in Venezuela and now editor-in-chief of Washington-based *Foreign Policy* magazine, headlined his article "Ugly Betty Getting Prettier." His play on the title of the popular U.S. sitcom (itself inspired by a Colombian telenovela, or television soap opera) is, he says, "a good metaphor for what is happening throughout most of the region: Inflation is plummeting, financial debt gone, public financing under control — a fiscal system superior to the that of the United States."

Governments have moved toward open societies and pragmatically embraced the global economy. By carefully managing their economies and benefiting from global trade tailor-made for Latin America's natural resources, the once debt-ridden region has enjoyed five continuous years of respectable growth almost across the board. (*See chart, right.*) Overall, Latin American economies grew an estimated 5.4 percent in 2007, and Mexico and Central America by 4.1 percent.[2]

On the political front, with two elected female presidents, Latinas are emerging as a new political force, as are the region's more than 650 indigenous groups.[3] (*See sidebar, p. 38.*) Mestizo, mixed-race and Indian groups are gaining influence, particularly in some Andean states, where Indians supported socialist Rafael Correa Delgado in Ecuador and Evo Morales — an Aymara Indian and Latin America's only indigenous head of state — in Bolivia.*

As the region tackles its chronic high poverty rates, it has even begun to export its poverty-alleviation systems. Bangladesh and Brazil are among the countries that have adopted Mexico's highly effective *Bolsa Familia* (Family Fund), an initiative that helped cut the number of Mexican families living in extreme poverty by 49 percent between 1998 and 2004.[4] A Venezuelan youth orchestra program that trains at-risk teenagers as musicians has been copied by 23 countries across the hemisphere. A 26-year-old Venezuelan conductor once linked to the program, Gustavo Dudamel, was recently appointed musical director of the Los Angeles Philharmonic.[5]

Latin Incomes on the Rise

Per capita income grew 12.3 percent in Latin America between 1995 and 2005, but incomes fell in Paraguay and oil-rich Venezuela. The biggest increases occurred in Belize and Chile.

Per Capita GDP
(in $US, adjusted for inflation)

Country	1995	2005	% Change
Argentina	$7,199.30	$8,130.80	12.9%
Belize	$2,905.70	$4,024.90	38.5%
Bolivia	$947.70	$1,033.40	9.0%
Brazil	$3,327.10	$3,573.70	7.4%
Chile	$4,261.70	$5,729.20	34.4%
Colombia	$2,076.40	$2,156.90	3.9%
Costa Rica	$3,607.60	$4,504.90	24.9%
Cuba	$2,055.60	n/a	n/a
Ecuador	$1,333.90	$1,550.20	16.2%
El Salvador	$1,993.10	$2,128.60	6.8%
Guatemala	$1,588.50	$1,720.40	8.3%
Guyana	$706.90	$798.60	13.0%
Honduras	$917.80	$977.30	6.5%
Mexico	$4,866.00	$5,993.20	23.2%
Nicaragua	$688.50	$835.10	21.3%
Panama	$3,470.60	$4,433.80	27.8%
Paraguay	$1,483.90	$1,296.20	-12.6%
Peru	$1,978.90	$2,340.40	18.3%
Suriname	$1,727.80	$2,247.40	30.1%
Uruguay	$5,622.20	$6,083.90	8.2%
Venezuela	$5,119.60	$4,939.20	-3.5%
Latin America	**$3,602.20**	**$4,044.10**	**12.3%**

Source: "Statistical Yearbook for Latin America and the Caribbean, 2006," U.N. Economic Commission for Latin America and the Caribbean, 2007

To be sure, corruption, injustice, high crime rates, drug smuggling and dismal social problems still cast a dark shadow over much of Latin America, where the gap between the rich and the poor is the largest in the world.

In his perceptive new book, *Forgotten Continent: The Battle for Latin America's Soul*, British journalist Michael Reid describes the region's struggle as being between durable mass democracies (Brazil, Chile) that follow pragmatic, moderate economic policies while addressing poverty and democratic reform and the autocratic,

---

* In addition to Bolivia and Ecuador, the Andean states — which border on or contain portions of the Andes Mountains — include Peru, Chile, Colombia, Argentina and Venezuela.

Three Economies Dominate the Region

Brazil, Mexico and Argentina generated nearly three-quarters of Latin America's $2.2 trillion gross domestic product (GDP) in 2005, largely thanks to their rich natural resources and extensive agricultural and ranching industries.

Share of Latin America's GDP, 2005

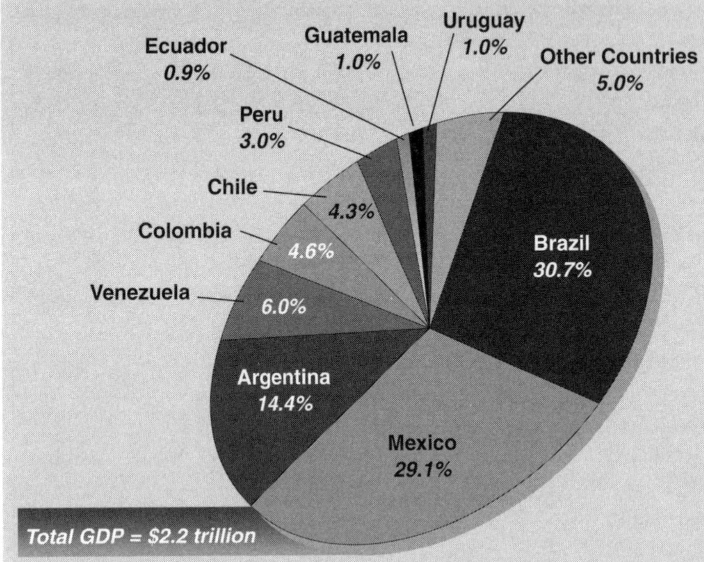

Country	Share
Brazil	30.7%
Mexico	29.1%
Argentina	14.4%
Venezuela	6.0%
Colombia	4.6%
Chile	4.3%
Peru	3.0%
Ecuador	0.9%
Guatemala	1.0%
Uruguay	1.0%
Other Countries	5.0%

Total GDP = $2.2 trillion

Source: "Statistical Yearbook for Latin America and the Caribbean, 2006," U.N. Economic Commission for Latin America and the Caribbean, 2007

left-wing, populist model of Venezuela's flamboyant, radical President Hugo Chávez.[6]

Chávez is Fidel Castro with oil. Like Castro, he is virulently anti-American and embraces revolutionary social policies that he wants to spread beyond his own borders. Using money from Venezuela's vast oil reserves — the largest in the hemisphere — Chávez extends his influence by selling oil at discounted rates to cash-strapped neighbors or lending them billions of dollars.

Domestically, the former paratrooper's tenure has been marked by turbulence largely because of his failure to deliver on promises to improve conditions for the poor. Growing public discontent led to several crippling national strikes — and in 2002 to a coup that removed him from office. Two days later, however, Venezuela's underclass took to the streets to demonstrate in his favor, and he was reinstated. Chávez accused the Bush administration of being behind the coup, and many analysts agreed.

Two years later the opposition engineered a referendum against him, but he emerged unscathed — actually strengthened — by promising more social reforms. But by December 2007 the sense of neglect among his supporters had deepened so dramatically — heightened by massive food shortages in recent months — that his own referendum to amend the constitution and remove presidential term limits was narrowly defeated, his first electoral defeat in nine years.[7]

"I see Chávez traveling and traveling abroad, and the money ends up somewhere else," said Jesus Camacho, 29, a street vendor selling coffee in a Caracas slum who makes about $8 a day. Although he supported Chávez in the past, Camacho says he has lost faith in politics.[8]

Meanwhile, the U.S. government has often appeared indifferent to the problems of Latin America, especially since the terrorist attacks of Sept. 11, 2001. "Has Washington lost Latin America?" asked the December issue of the French foreign affairs monthly *Le Monde Diplomatique.*[9] And former U.S. ambassador to Belize Carolyn Curiel wrote in *The New York Times* recently: "Our mostly Spanish-speaking neighbors have reason to suspect that, except for occasional military and economic interventions, American leaders don't pay them much mind."[10]

Some analysts say that in the post-9/11 world, the United States is primarily concerned about Latin America as it relates to domestic security. The most recent security assessment given to the U.S. Senate by Director of National Intelligence J. Michael McConnell lays out perceived threats posed by Venezuela and Cuba and complains of "sharply anti-U.S. rhetoric" by leftist leaders in Bolivia, Nicaragua and Ecuador. The report alleges that Chávez allows illegal drug shipments by the Colombian guerrilla group known as the FARC (Revolutionary Armed Forces of Colombia) and others to pass through Venezuela en route to the streets of Europe and the

United States. Cocaine exports are a main source of FARC's revenue.[11]

While the United States remains either the first or second largest trading partner of most Latin American countries — including Venezuela — the region has been broadening its ties to the European Union, China, Iran (in the case of Chávez) and others. For example, Brazil is actively lobbying to join the U.N. Security Council's five permanent members — the United States, Britain, France, Russia and China. And Brazil — home to 10 million people of Arab origin — just sent Foreign Minister Celso Amorim on an extended tour of the Middle East to strengthen bilateral relations.[12] A second Latin American-Arab summit — the first was in 2005 — is scheduled for later this year in the Persian Gulf state of Qatar.

A new regional cohesion and cooperation is also taking hold, particularly on the economic front. While the dynamics and mechanisms of change differ from country to country, "there is something that's really Latin American, and it's not only historical," says Peter Hakim, president of Inter-American Dialogue, a Washington-based think tank. "There is a huge circulation of ideas, people and common institutions."

Indeed, if Latin America could ever overcome its perennial internal rivalries and disharmony and act in concert, it could make a formidable bloc. "Our first priority is Latin America," Amorim said recently. Trading within the region itself accounts for about 27 percent of overall trade, he points out, followed by the European Union with 24 percent and the United States with 15 percent. "But like our trade, our foreign relations are also diverse. . . . We have excellent relations with [both] Cuba and with the United States."[13]

As Latin Americans consider how to deal with their economic and political issues, here are some of the questions they are asking:

Are Chávez's days numbered?

Chávez's Dec. 2 referendum defeat — 51 percent to 49 percent — "was a stunning setback . . . and may slow down his movement towards authoritarian rule and implementation of his vision of 21st-century socialism," Intelligence Director McConnell told the Senate Select Committee on Intelligence in February.

But does that mean Chávez's position is seriously threatened? No, says Carlos Malamud, a Latin America specialist at the Real Instituto Elcano, a think tank in Madrid, Spain. Chávez is "very far from being a lame duck" or as unsteady in the saddle as some people think. "He still has significant popular backing and wide-ranging powers." All of the Venezuelan National Assembly seats are held by pro-Chávez parties, thanks to an opposition election boycott in 2005, although one group calling itself *Podemos* ("We can") did break ranks and vote against him in the referendum. The Chávez government also controls the judiciary, the state oil company and all but one provincial government.

"There are problems of inflation, weak investment in the oil sector and food shortages," says Malamud, who also could have added widespread crime to the list. "But internationally, Chávez still has oil as a powerful bargaining tool."

However, Francisco R. Rodríguez, a former economic adviser to the Venezuelan National Assembly and now a professor of political science and Latin American affairs at Wesleyan University in Middletown, Conn., thinks Chávez's days may indeed be numbered. The test, he says, will come in the October provincial elections. Chávez's political machine currently controls 22 of the 23 provinces, but the referendum defeat reflected "growing popular discontent with the regime," he continues, "and Chávez is going to lose badly in the elections, including control of Caracas. Things can deteriorate pretty quickly after that, whether due to a popular revolution, or even the army."

If the opposition gains control of two-thirds of the provincial seats, "a constitutional assembly could unseat Chávez," Rodríguez says. "But there has to be at least a pretext of constitutionality. What you are likely to see is movement in the Venezuelan supreme court." And then there's the worsening economic situation. "It will be difficult for him to hold on to power in the midst of an economic crisis."

Peter DeShazo, director of the Americas program at the Washington-based Center for Strategic and International Studies, said, "Clearly, Chávez's own political agenda in Venezuela is now off track, so that will definitely hurt his overall image."[14]

Chávez himself managed to sound defiant while acknowledging the setback, which he interpreted as a signal that he had moved too far ahead of rank-and-file Venezuelans. "I'm obliged to apply the brakes," the

AP Photo/Gregorio Marrero

Opponents flood Bolivar Avenue in Caracas, Venezuela, on Nov. 27, 2007, to protest the referendum proposed by President Hugo Chávez calling for constitutional changes that would give him more power and eliminate term limits. A week later it was defeated, delivering a stunning setback to Chávez.

president said on his weekly television show "Aló Presidente" ("Hello President"). "The main motor seized up, so we'll have to go by donkey instead." He said he would try again to persuade voters to go along with him. "I haven't been weakened," he told the opposition, "nor have I been pushed back one millimeter. . . . Prepare yourself, because a new offensive will come with a proposed reform," he warned the opposition, either "that one, or transformed or simplified."[15]

"When I was minister of finance in Venezuela, imports ran at a fifth of what they are today, and the population is not five times what it was," observes *Foreign Policy* editor Naím. "Luxury goods are coming in for the new elite, but the country is without milk and very fundamental things like cooking gas." The imported Humvees and other signs of ostentatious wealth flaunted by rich Venezuelans and Chávez's cronies — nicknamed the "Bolivarian bourgeoisie" — contrast sharply with the shortages faced by ordinary citizens, further fueling the unrest.*

"I cannot find beans, rice, coffee or milk," said Mirna de Campos, 56, a nurse's assistant who lives just outside Caracas. "What there is to find is whiskey — lots of it."[16]

The recent food shortages have been caused in part by price controls imposed by Chávez. Food manufacturers and distributors find it more profitable to smuggle their goods into Colombia or Ecuador, where they can make as much as 300 percent profit, rather than sell them in Venezuela at low government-set prices. Milk shortages have been caused in part by dairies converting their price-controlled milk into butter and cheese, which are not subject to price caps. Chávez has recently threatened to nationalize food distribution to discourage hoarding and has beefed up border surveillance to discourage the smuggling — with some success, according to the government.

"Problems of scarcity are being caused by the private sector, which opposes Chávez," says Rodríguez. But the government's actions so far have been a confusing mixture of carrot and stick. "Chávez does not grasp the seriousness of the situation, and does not understand the consequences of what's happening."

Chávez's December defeat gave a boost to the loose alliance of political forces that opposes him because it showed that he was not unbeatable. Malamud believes Chávez's challengers would have even more success if they could find a leader to unite them. Venezuelan students emerged as strong opponents of the referendum, led by Yon Goicoechea, a 23-year-old Caracas law student who is revered as a fearless opponent of Chávez's policies despite the government's relentless harassment of him and his family.

But the anti-Chávez group spans all ages and ideologies, from the Roman Catholic Church to Gabriel Puerta, a former left-wing guerrilla and now leader of the Red Flag opposition organization. Media opponents include 75-year-old Teodoro Petkoff, respected editor of the Venezuelan paper *Tal Cual.* The more conventional

* Chávez calls his socialist program a "Bolivarian Revolution" in honor of the South American hero Simón Bolívar.

resistance comes from middle-class business and professional groups and the Social Christian Party, which Chávez ousted in his first presidential election and is now returning to the political fray after a long boycott.

Whether an ousted Chávez would go quietly is anybody's guess. Malamud points out that while Chávez "talks a lot about revolution, there's been no revolution in Venezuela." Chávez gained his power through the ballot and has repeatedly resorted to the ballot to introduce changes in Venezuela's government.

A report by the Brussels-based International Crisis Group, an independent peace-advocacy organization, said Chávez "is not yet a dictator and for the most part has not tried to act in a dictatorial manner, but the trend towards autocracy is strong." Chávez has been building personal power at the expense of other institutions and militarizing much of the government and political life, risking internal conflicts, the report continued.[17]

Are moderate governments proving more sustainable than Chávez-style radical populism?

When Chávez was first elected in 1998 with 56 percent of the vote, he was the first in a string of successful left-wing candidates across Latin America, each of whom has followed a different course in solving pressing social and economic problems.

Chávez's flashy Bolivarian Revolution programs for reducing poverty caught wide attention, but the populist leader hasn't delivered, according to his critics. His protégés — Morales in Bolivia and Correa in Ecuador — have also faced problems instituting their socialist agendas. Some say the region's more moderate left-wing governments, which have pushed modified macroeconomic programs, retained many liberalizing reforms of the 1990s and instituted gradual social improvements, will have more staying power.

Rather than trying to reform the government's inefficient services, Chávez quickly established social welfare "missions" in the barrios (poor neighborhoods), financed mainly with oil revenues, to address needs ranging from health and education to housing and employment. One mission, for instance, distributed money to enable the poor to buy new homes or repair old ones.

But Wesleyan University's Rodríguez contends the ambitious missions program never lived up to expectations because of understaffing, corruption and underfunding. Writing in *Foreign Affairs* magazine, Rodríguez — who as economic adviser to the National Assembly watched from a ringside seat as Chávez's economy began to crumble — recalls that the government was supposed to ensure that Chávez's social programs benefited from rising oil revenues. "But when oil revenues started to go up [the government] ignored the provision." The fact that the percentage of Venezuelans living in poverty declined from a peak of 54 percent in 2003 to 27.5 percent in 2007, says Rodríguez, was due to the impact on the economy of a tripling of oil prices rather than to Chávez's poverty programs.[18]

By 2006 Venezuela's economy had already begun to unravel, but Chávez was re-elected by an overwhelming margin. Oil revenues were high, and Venezuela had enjoyed three years of double-digit growth. But inflation was also double digit — equivalent to an annual rate of 67.7 percent in 2007, the highest in Latin America.[19]

According to Rodriguez, "Cháveznomics" — which economists Rudiger Dornbusch and Sebastian Edwards have called "the macroeconomics of populism" — is merely a reformulation of "the disastrous experiences of many Latin American countries during the 1970s and 1980s," such as the economic policies followed by Juan Perón in Argentina, Salvador Allende in Chile and Alan García in Peru. Populist macroeconomics usually involves expansionary fiscal and economic policies, coupled with an overvalued currency designed to accelerate growth and income redistribution. Fiscal and foreign exchange constraints are usually disregarded, and price controls are used to control inflation.

"The result is by now well known to Latin American economists: the emergence of production bottlenecks, the accumulation of severe fiscal and balance-of-payments problems, galloping inflation and plummeting real wages," wrote Rodríguez.

Which is what appears to be happening in Venezuela, he asserted. "Chávez's mismanagement of the economy and his failure to live up to his pro-poor rhetoric have finally begun to catch up with him," he wrote. As food shortages spread, Chávez's poll numbers declined. In September 2007 — three months before the referendum — 22 percent of Venezuelans thought the poverty situation had improved under Chávez; 50 percent thought it had gotten worse and the rest said there had been no change.[20]

Brazil Emerging as a Global Power

Pragmatic reliance on trade has helped boost economy.

In the not too distant past, jokesters perennially quipped: "Brazil is the land of the future — and always will be."[1] No longer. "Brazil's future is now," wrote *New York Times* columnist Roger Cohen recently, citing its raw materials, energy, vast and varied ecology and trade with China.[2]

Many would add another reason: Luiz Inacio Lula da Silva, the former metalworker and union leader who has been president since 2002. By electing Lula, voters gave Brazil's political elite its comeuppance. And while Lula's presidency has not been without problems — including charges of corruption in his government — his leadership has played a key role in putting to rest the myth that Brazil would remain unable to live up to its tremendous potential.

Lula's innovative social initiatives have begun making a dent in poverty, notably his *Fome Zero* (Zero Hunger) drive, which distributes money for food to the most needy. In addition, the *Bolsa Familia* (Family Fund) program — which provides aid to families earning less than $100 a month if they keep their children in school and their kids' vaccinations current — is considered highly successful.[3]

Although during the campaign Lula threatened to withdraw Brazil from the International Monetary Fund (IMF) if elected, he ended up complying with previously set IMF fiscal targets and followed his predecessor's macroeconomic policies. Lula has achieved "impressive results in economic stability," writes Jorge G. Castañeda, a former Mexican foreign minister and now Global Distinguished Professor of Politics and Latin American Studies at New York University.[4] Moreover, thanks to a fiscal surplus every year, Lula has paid off Brazil's $3 billion in foreign debt.

Much of Brazil's success is attributed to its aggressive export strategy. Brazil is the world's largest exporter of coffee, beef, sugar and orange juice. It also exported huge amounts of soy beans and $4.2 billion worth of chickens in 2007 — up from $2.9 billion in 2006. The discovery in 2007 of a huge, 5-8-billion-barrel deepwater oil field off Brazil's southeastern coast boosted the country's oil reserves by about 40 percent and narrowed its oil gap with Venezuela. China has invested heavily in Brazil and purchases many of its products, including iron ore.

"For the first time in a generation Brazilians are benefiting from stable economic growth, low inflation rates and improvements in social well-being," the World Bank stated in a recent report on Brazil.[5]

Latin America's largest country also has become a world leader in producing and exporting plant-based fuels, particularly ethanol from sugar cane. In 2007 Brazil signed an ethanol deal with the world's other large producer, the United States, to promote the development of new bio-fuel technologies — a rare example of U.S.-Brazilian cooperation.

"Brazil's independent approach to foreign policy has led to periodic disputes with the United States on trade and political issues, including Brazil's vocal opposition to the war in Iraq," says a U.S. Congressional Research Service report.[6]

"Brazilian foreign policy has recently aimed to strengthen ties with other South American countries, engage in multilateral diplomacy through the United Nations and the Organization of American States (OAS) and act at times as a countervailing force to U.S. political and economic influence in Latin America," the report continues."[7]

Not surprisingly, both Morales and Correa were also planning constitutional changes to introduce their own variations of Chávez's as-yet-undefined "Socialism for the 21st Century." Among other controversial measures, Morales wants to restore Bolivia's indigenous tribal courts, making them available as an alternative to the normal judicial system. But Morales failed to get a majority in the constituent assembly drafting the new laws, so everything depends on a referendum to be scheduled later this year. Correa, whose government is drafting a similar document, is in a stronger position but also needs voter approval in a referendum. Correa is seeking sweeping changes, including increased presidential powers to strengthen his hand in dealing with foreign oil corporations operating in Ecuador — and analysts say he is likely to get them.[21]

Lula also has earned the Bush administration's disapproval with his neighborly dealings with Venezuela's anti-U.S. leader Hugo Chávez and Cuba's recently retired communist dictator Fidel Castro. Now a leftist social democrat, the former union leader has what Castañeda calls "a lingering emotional devotion to Cuba," but "it has not led to subservience to Castro."[8]

The Bush administration also has been less than supportive of Brazil's vigorous campaign to gain a permanent seat on the U.N. Security Council, joining the five original veto-wielding permanent members: China, Russia, the United Kingdom, France and the United States. And, although Brazil has reinforced its military and police presence on its long border with Colombia, Lula has refused Washington's entreaties to become more actively involved in Plan Colombia, the multimillion-dollar U.S. effort to curb Colombia's virulent drug trade.

The darker side of Brazil's emergence as a world player includes its gargantuan social problems and high levels of violent crime. More than 7,000 homicides occurred in Rio de Janeiro alone in 2007, according to Amnesty International, and some of the country's lawless *favelas* — teeming squatter settlements — are considered impenetrable to police.[9]

As a Brazilian commentator put it recently, "The immediate problem that Brazil faces is less to solve these issues — that will take a generation — than to build a consensus on how to solve them. . . . For the country as a whole this is a moral as much as a political challenge."[10]

AP Photo/Dario Lopez-Mills

Workers at a meat-processing plant in Brazil's Sao Paulo state prepare beef for export to Europe, the Middle East and Asia. Brazil has made significant economic strides in recent years, in part because of its heavy reliance on exports.

[1] Clare M. Ribando, "Brazil-U.S. Relations," Congressional Research Service, Feb. 28, 2007, www.wilsoncenter.org/news/docs/RL33456.pdf.

[2] Roger Cohen, "New Day in the Americas," *The New York Times*, Jan. 6, 2008, p. 13, www.nytimes.com/2008/01/06/opinion/06cohen.html; also see Amnesty International, "Brazil: Submission to the UN Universal Periodic Review," April 7-11, 2008, http://archive.amnesty.org/library/pdf/AMR190232007ENGLISH/$File/AMR1902307.pdf.

[3] Gina-Marie Cheeseman, "The Spread of Leftist Politics in Latin America," *American Chronicle*, March 20, 2007, www.americanchronicle.com/articles/22437.

[4] Jorge G. Castañeda, "Latin America's Left Turn," *Foreign Affairs*, May/June 2006, www.foreignaffairs.org/20060501faessay85302/jorge-g-castaneda/latin-america-s-left.html.

[5] "Brazil Country Brief," The World Bank, http://web.worldbank.org/WBSITE/EXTERNAL/COUNTRIES/LACEXT/BRAZILEXTN/0,,contentMDK:20189430~pagePK:141137~piPK:141127~theSitePK:322341,00.html.

[6] Ribando, *op. cit.*

[7] *Ibid.*

[8] Castañeda, *op. cit.*

[9] *Ibid.*

[10] Arthur Ituassu, "Brazil: the moral challenge," openDemocracy, April 18, 2007, www.opendemocracy.net/democracy-protest/brazil_challenge_4544.jsp.

Some in Latin America question whether the outside world isn't giving the Andean neo-populists a disproportionate amount of attention. Norman Gall, executive director of the Fernand Braudel Institute of World Economics in Sao Paolo, Brazil, argues that the more significant trend in Latin America is not what's happening in places like Bolivia and Ecuador — which Gall calls two "marginal and chronically unstable countries" — but the shift "towards domestic stability" among the "more important republics" of Argentina, Brazil, Chile, Peru and Mexico. These more moderate governments have battled poverty and inequality, but not at the expense of their economic growth. In the past four years, for instance, South American economies as a whole have grown on average 4.4 percent.[22]

AP Photo/Kent Gilbert

Costa Ricans protest the Central America-Dominican Republic Free Trade Agreement (CAFTA-DR) in San Jose, the capital, on Feb. 5, 2006. Although the controversial pact went into effect in 2005, Costa Rica didn't ratify it until voters, by a thin margin, approved a referendum on the treaty after a contentious campaign last fall.

As for the populist leaders' social agendas, Venezuela and Ecuador spent 11.7 percent and 6.3 percent of GDP on education, respectively, in 2006 while Chile spent 28.7 percent and Brazil 22 percent — more than any other Latin American countries.[23] Raising education levels is a high priority because Latin America's traditional pool of cheap labor is no longer an asset in an increasingly high-tech world. Rodríguez writes that despite Chávez's claim to have eradicated illiteracy, a recent survey showed that illiteracy is still widespread in Venezuela.[24]

And Chávez hasn't really succeeded in narrowing the income gap between Venezuela's rich and poor — something he has blamed on free-market policies adopted by his predecessors and advocated by rich Western countries. "One would expect pro-poor growth [policies] to be accompanied by a marked decrease in income inequality," Rodríguez argued. "But according to the Venezuelan Central Bank, inequality has actually increased during the Chávez administration."

Other countries across the region, however, are making steady economic progress, including some progress in narrowing the income-inequality gap. The challenge now for the moderate left-wing governments, analysts say, is to convince the public that gradual but reliable improvement is better than unpredictable, flashy bursts of progress that are undermined by setbacks.

In addition, argues former Mexican foreign minister Jorge G. Castañeda, a political science professor at New York University, Latin Americans need to focus on the institutional underpinnings of their new democracies and eradicate "the region's secular plagues: corruption, weak or non-existent rule of law, ineffective governance" and the enduring temptation to concentrate power in the hands of a few.[25]

Can narco-terrorism be eradicated?

On March 1, 2008, Colombian troops crossed into neighboring Ecuador and attacked a FARC camp, killing the Marxist guerrilla group's second-ranking leader, known as Raúl Reyes, along with 22 other guerillas. Taking out Reyes was a major success for Colombia in its long struggle with FARC, which has waged a 40-plus-year insurgency against the Colombian state. But the incident plunged the region into a crisis, as Chávez mobilized 10 armored divisions on the Venezuelan-Colombian border, and Ecuador closed its embassy in Bogotá in protest over the breach of its sovereignty and expelled Colombia's diplomats from Quito.

FARC guerrillas, categorized around the world as terrorists, have long used remote areas of Ecuador and Venezuela along the Colombian border as safe havens.[26] The incursion into Ecuador reflects the growing strength and confidence of the Colombian counter-insurgency forces, largely boosted by Washington's multibillion-dollar Plan Colombia.

The United States has spent $7 billion on the plan, launched in 2000 to halt cocaine production at the source. It was soon broadened to include combating the FARC, which funds its operations by selling drugs and kidnapping the wealthy. According to U.S. military advisers, Colombian security forces have regained control over the country's major cities and large areas of the countryside, long overrun by the narco-terrorists, squeezing the over 10,000-strong group into jungle enclaves.[27]

The U.S. Congress has allotted $545 million to Plan Colombia for 2008, even though the program has yet to succeed in achieving either of its ultimate objectives — eradicating Colombia's cocaine crop and ending the FARC insurgency.

The last vestige of South and Central America's 1980s-era armed struggles, FARC still remains a serious threat to daily life in Colombia. But today it pays only lip service to its Marxist ideology, and its political objective to seize power has long been out of reach.

"Although the FARC has by no means been defeated, it is on the run and has been for the last few years," the *Los Angeles Times* reported from Florencia, Colombia, last month, quoting Colombian and U.S. military analysts.[28]

"The plan has been a success in boosting the Colombian military to contain FARC, but a failure in stopping cocaine production," says former Venezuelan minister Naím. "No assault on drugs will work unless an effort is made to reduce demand. The United States has spent $40 billion on the war on drugs, but very little of it went for demand abatement."

Analysts say eradicating the guerrillas would require an extensive military operation that even the improved and motivated Colombian military cannot launch. A major concern is the fate of the 70 foreigners and more than 700 Colombian citizens being held hostage by FARC. Their lives would be jeopardized by a full-scale military confrontation, and the Colombian government would not take that risk.

That's why many believe the inevitable answer is negotiation. "I don't know how it will work or when it will happen," says Wesleyan University's Rodríguez, "but I think direct talks will happen."[29]

As for cocaine production in Colombia, it is at roughly the same level as in 2000. Eradicating the $2.2-to-$5-billion-a-year cocaine trade — equivalent to 3 percent of the country's GDP — would require a massive operation and an unyielding political will. Both the anti-FARC and anti-cocaine initiatives would require full cooperation from Colombia's neighbors — Brazil, Venezuela and Ecuador — an unlikely prospect since Chávez openly backs FARC, with whom he says he shares some Marxist ideals. Furthermore, the Colombians claim that information gained from two laptop computers captured in the Reyes operation reveals that FARC has the support of top Ecuadorian officials — an allegation denied by the Ecuadorians.

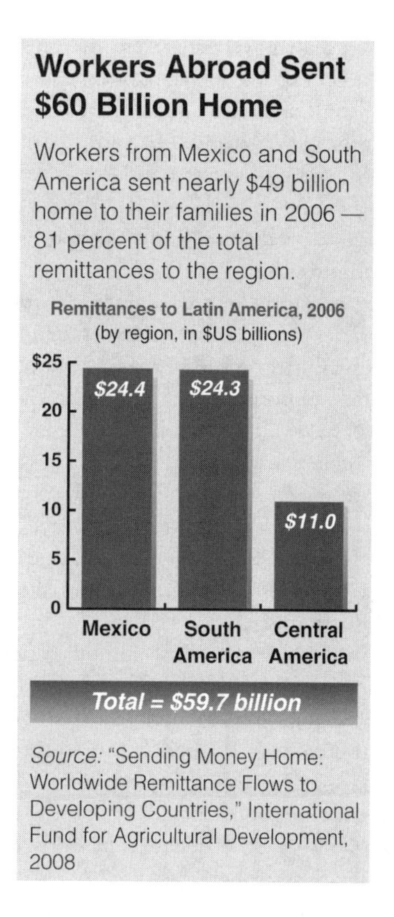

Chávez has urged the European Union nations and others not to classify the Colombian guerrillas as terrorists, arguing that they are freedom fighters, and ordered a two-minute silence in Venezuela for Reyes.

"Drugs and kidnapping finance the FARC, and as long as they have the drug trade and Chávez's support and can count on Venezuela to help them export the drugs, FARC will survive," says Naím. Based on other evidence found in the computers, the Colombian government also alleged that Chávez had given FARC $300 million, but the Venezuelan government has denied the charge.[30]

Meanwhile, U.S.-supported aerial herbicide spraying has not succeeded in destroying Colombia's coca crops. The eradication program is controversial because the weed-killer damages nearby crops and causes breathing difficulties.[31] Spraying coca fields along the border also brought protests from neighboring Ecuador, where chemicals drifted across the boundary and ruined crops.

The Colombian government recently resorted to uprooting the coca bushes by hand, but the farmers simply switched from open fields to smaller, less detectable areas in the jungle. Recent CIA monitoring shows Colombia's cocaine crop is about as large as when aerial spraying began in 2001 — though that doesn't necessarily mean cocaine production hasn't taken a hit, argues the Bush administration.[32]

"The illegal drug trade in Colombia is as robust and as resilient as ever," says John Walsh, a senior associate at the Washington Office on Latin America, a human rights group generally opposed to U.S. policy in the region. "It's business as usual: the trade is regrouping, adapting and coming on in worse form."

Without regional cooperation, the drug trade could move across neighboring borders, or move to other countries like Panama. Brazil, for example, has reinforced its borders with troops and police in an attempt to prevent the FARC from spilling over.

Although Colombia is the Bush administration's most consistent ally in the region, American lawmakers have balked at approving a long-awaited bilateral trade agreement, in part because of Bogotá's failure to suppress the cocaine trade and Democrats' objections that President Álvaro Uribe has not done enough to halt the killing of Colombian labor union officials, apparently by right-wing paramilitary assassins.

"The total economic consequence of the delay is microscopic here in the United States, but very important there," says Naím. "For one thing, it raises the question: What is the point of being a U.S. ally if we can't even get a trade agreement?"

BACKGROUND

Empire to Independence

For three centuries, Latin America — the great colonial empires of Spain and Portugal — stretched from modern-day California to the southernmost tip of the Americas at Cape Horn. The empires collapsed in the early 19th century because of a combination of European power politics and local unrest and rebellion. The newly independent nations of Latin America established governments democratic in form but less so in substance.[33]

In the 1500s Spanish conquistadores destroyed thriving Aztec and Incan civilizations and laid the foundation for colonial rule and economic exploitation. Portugal explored and colonized Brazil under a 1494 papal decree that gave it the lands east of the mouth of the Amazon River. Colonial administration improved in the 1700s, but liberalized trade policies heightened social stratification by benefiting upper-class whites and mixed-race mestizos without helping the indigenous Indian populations or Negro slaves in Brazil. By 1800, professional and business classes were ripe for revolt, as were many of the Indians.

The wars of independence that threw off Spanish and Portuguese rule spanned a little more than a decade, from 1810 to the early 1820s. Spain, distracted by the Napoleonic wars, was unable to counter the revolutions that spread throughout its empire. South America's two great "liberators" — Bolívar and José de San Martín of Argentina — survived repeated reversals to eventually gain decisive military victories in 1821: Bolívar in his native Venezuela, San Martín in Peru. Meanwhile, Brazil won independence from Portugal under a monarchy established in 1822 by Dom Pedro — son of a former regent — with support from British and Brazilian liberals.

In Mexico, a liberal parish priest, Miguel Hidalgo y Costilla, ignited the war for independence in September 1810 but was executed a year later after government forces recovered from initial rebel victories. A guerrilla war succeeded in winning independence in 1821 only after defections by several royal officers and their troops. One of the colonels proclaimed himself emperor, but anti-monarchists succeeded in establishing Mexico's first republic three years later. Similar rebellions won independence in the kingdom of Guatemala, which then broke into separate states in the late 1820s.

Bolívar envisioned a United States of South America, but the nation he established, called Gran Colombia, broke into separate states — Colombia, Venezuela and Ecuador — before his death in 1830. Meanwhile, the colony of Upper Peru had broken away, declared its independence as Bolivia and given Bolívar dictatorial powers as president. Bolívar was no democrat: He favored a system headed by a strong president chosen for life. Shortly before his death, he wrote: "America is ungovernable."

However, South American independence was not accompanied by social or economic reform, according to historian Edwin Williamson. No new classes came to power, and the oligarchic structures of the colonial period remained unchanged. Politically, the era saw the rise of the *caudillos* — strongmen who came to power through

CHRONOLOGY

1930s-1950s *Dictators control most of Latin America. In Cuba, Fidel Castro overthrows Batista regime.*

1932 Brazil and Uruguay become the first Latin American countries to grant women the right to vote.

1936 Dictatorial Somoza dynasty comes to power in Nicaragua.

1939 Fulgencio Batista era begins in Cuba; his regime is a byword for corruption and, wrote historian Hugh Thomas, "formalized gangsterism."

1946 Populist Army Col. Juan Perón is elected president of Argentina.

1948 Organization of American States is formed.

1954 Strongman Gen. Alfredo Stroessner takes over in Paraguay.

1959 Cuban revolutionaries, led by Castro, overthrow Batista.

1960s-1970s *Castro establishes communist regime in Cuba, forms alliance with Soviet Union, triggering long period of tension with the United States. Cuban missile crisis brings world to brink of nuclear war.*

1961 U.S.-backed Cuban exiles unsuccessfully try to overthrow Castro.

1961 Paraguay is last Latin American country to give women the vote.

1962 President John F. Kennedy blockades Cuba after spy photographs reveal bases being built in Cuba for Soviet-controlled nuclear missiles. Soviets agree to withdraw the missiles, and the U.S. agrees to withdraw its missiles from Turkey.

1970 Chile's Salvador Allende is first democratically elected socialist leader in Latin America.

1973 Allende is killed in CIA-supported coup; right-wing Gen. Augusto Pinochet takes over.

1976 Rabidly right-wing military junta takes over Argentina, launches deadly wave of "disappearances."

1980s-1990s *Neo-liberal reforms are short-lived. Former Lt. Col. Hugo Chávez, leader of a failed 1992 coup, wins his first presidential election. Rise of Chávez and Luiz Inacio Lula da Silva in Brazil signals shift to the left in region.*

1983 U.S. invades Grenada to stop alleged Cuban military buildup on the island and, the administration says, to protect Americans there.

1994 North American Free Trade Agreement (NAFTA) takes effect, lowering trade barriers between the United States, Mexico and Canada.

1998 Chávez is elected president of Venezuela.

2000s *Socialists are elected in several key Latin American countries.*

2001 Argentina defaults on its debt.

2002 Left-wing labor leader da Silva wins Brazilian presidential election.

2005 Evo Morales, an indigenous coca grower and labor leader, is elected president in Bolivia, vowing to nationalize the country's gas industry.

2006 Socialist Michelle Bachelet is elected first woman president in Chile. In Venezuela, Chávez is re-elected.

2007 Christina Fernández de Kirchner is elected president in Argentina, succeeding her husband. Chávez suffers setback when his proposed constitutional reforms are defeated. . . . Chávez proposes Bank of the South; seven countries join. . . . U.S. Congress approves U.S.-Peru free trade agreement.

2008 Ailing Castro, 81, retires as president of Cuba and is succeeded by his brother Raúl, 76. . . . On March 1 Colombian troops enter neighboring Ecuador and kill the second-ranking FARC guerrilla leader. In response, FARC supporter Chávez mobilizes 10 armored divisions on the Venezuelan-Colombian border, and Ecuador closes its embassy in Bogotá.

Latin Women Finding Their Political Voices

Gender quotas have helped women get elected.

Women politicians are making dramatic strides in the continent long known for its machismo and ubiquitous military dictators in dark glasses.

Since 2006, two women — Michelle Bachelet and Cristina Fernández de Kirchner — have been elected heads of state of Chile and Argentina, respectively. This spring former education minister Blanca Olevar is running for president of Paraguay, and in Brazil presidential chief of staff and former energy minister Dilma Rousseff is widely expected to run for president when President Luiz Inacio Lula da Silva's term ends in 2010.[1]

While Hillary Rodham Clinton's campaign for the White House is considered groundbreaking in the United States, more than two dozen Latin American women have run for president since 1990. In fact, women have held the chief executive's position in 13 Latin American countries since 1974, although it was usually for brief stints in small countries.[2]

And women's political advancement in Latin America has not been limited to the president's office. Between 2000 and 2006 the percentage of women legislators in the region jumped 39.2 percent. After Cuba's national elections in January, women now make up 43 percent of the National Assembly, making Cuba the third-highest in the world in the proportion of women parliamentarians.[3] Overall, women hold 19.7 percent of Latin America's lower-house legislative seats and 15.8 percent of upper-house seats — compared to 16 percent in the U.S. Congress, which is also the worldwide average.[4]

The sudden prominence of female leaders in influential Latin American countries reflects deep socioeconomic and demographic changes as well as gender quotas adopted by many countries that earmark a certain percentage of legislative seats to women.

The Inter-American Development Bank (IADB) attributes women's progress primarily to strides in education. According to a 2000 IADB study, girls in Latin America today outperform boys in enrollment rates at all levels of schooling — a dramatic reversal from the 1970s.[5] By 2000, close to 60 percent of females were enrolled in secondary schools and 17 percent in higher education — about the same rate as boys.

The rise of women in Latino politics is also linked to the establishment in the 1990s of gender quotas for the parliaments in more than a dozen Latin American countries, effectively turning their legislatures into training grounds for female political leaders.

Number of Female Lawmakers and Ministers Has Surged

Female representation in Latin American senates, or upper houses, more than tripled between 1990 and 2006 — from 5 percent on average to nearly 17 percent. The percentage of female legislators in lower houses and ministers has more than doubled.

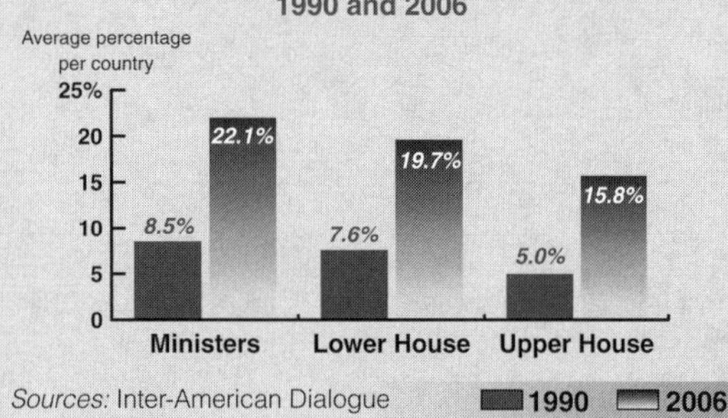

Sources: Inter-American Dialogue

International organizations have advocated gender quotas for parliaments since the 1975 U.N. First World Conference on Women, and some political parties — particularly in the Nordic countries — have had quotas since the 1970s. In Latin America the quotas vary, but most designate a minimum of 30 percent of seats for female delegates; Costa Rica has the highest, at 40 percent.[6]

Argentina's quota law was the first to apply to all political parties, so it offered the greatest opportunity to increase women's representation in the entire legislature. In the 1993 election — the first held after the quota law went into effect — the percentage of women elected to the Chamber of Deputies went from 5 percent to 14.4 percent. Today, Argentina's lower house is 48 percent female, and 31 percent of the senators are women. In Ecuador, women make up 25 percent of the legislature — up from 15 percent before the 2006 election. But in Venezuela, despite President Hugo Chávez's rhetoric about gender equality, only 31 out of 167 deputies — 18.6 percent — in the parliament are women.[7]

As with Clinton's bid for the presidency, there was a "husband factor" in Fernández's campaign: Her husband, President Nestor Kirchner, campaigned strongly for her.

But Latina women haven't all risen to power on their husbands' coattails. In Chile, for instance, pediatrician and single mother Bachelet rose from political obscurity to the presidency in six years without male help.

Moreover, some experts see Latin women's political achievements as a rejection of male politics rather than an extension of it. "We gave men a chance and now it's our turn," says former presidential candidate Ivonne A-Baki of Ecuador. "Traditional political parties failed to give people what they need — stability, education, incorruptible government. Women still enjoyed respect in society; it's automatic that they should go into politics."

AP Photo/Claudio Santana

President Michelle Bachelet of Chile, left, and Argentinean President Cristina Fernández de Kirchner are part of Latin America's new wave of female leaders.

Chilean diplomat and writer Jorge Heine maintains that it's much more than a backlash against males. "As old-fashioned political parties with strong credibility problems struggle to come to terms with this rapidly changing environment, women leaders — often perceived as less corrupt, more task-oriented and with a warmer, more people-friendly leadership style — have moved in and occupied newly emerging political spaces," he wrote in the Indian newspaper *The Hindu* recently, when he was Chile's ambassador in New Delhi.[8]

The IADB report also predicts that the "the trend towards feminization of Latin America's democracy is here to stay." For instance, by the end of the 1990s women made up 53.9 percent of the continent's over-60 population. In this century Latin America will age faster, the report said, and the majority of the elderly will be women, who tend to outlive men. And polls have shown that Latin American women prefer women candidates.[9]

Has the feminization of Latin American politics advanced public policy issues embraced by women leaders? Apparently not yet, the London-based *Economist* pointed out recently. In Argentina, the magazine concluded, "the prominence of women in politics has not led to feminist policies. Proposals for equal pay and [legalizing] abortion have got nowhere."[10] Abortion is still illegal in Venezuela and throughout Latin America, except for Cuba.

But A-Baki says that rather than shifting focus to women's issues, the biggest change has been a change in style. "Women's approach to problems is different from men's," she says. "For example, women are better negotiators than men and tend to get better results."

Still, analysts say the impact across the region is mixed. Brazil, for example, has eliminated adultery from the penal code, but the legal concept of "legitimate defense of honor" — excusing the killing of an adulterous spouse or the spouse's lover — remains on the books.[11] Meanwhile, family issues generally are getting more attention in Brazil, as is income inequality (the gap between the rich and the poor), which is the highest in the world.

Moreover, say critics, a gender quota can be a two-edged sword because it can be manipulated to limit the number of female candidates or the number of women holding parliamentary seats. But few will deny that it has served a useful purpose in raising awareness. Ultimately, however, says Mala Htun, political science professor at New York's New School for Social Research, "advancing women's rights in the region depends on the consolidation of democracy, sustainable development and the promotion of equitable economic growth."[12]

---

[1] See "Women in the Americas: Paths to Political Power, A Report Card on Women in Political Leadership," Inter-American Development Bank, Inter-American Dialogue and League of Women Voters, January 2008; and Monte Reel, "South America Ushers In The Era of La Presidenta; Women Could Soon Lead a Majority of Continent's Population," *The Washington Post*, Oct. 31, 2007, p. A12.

[2] "Women in the Americas: Paths to Political Power," *op. cit.*., p. 7.

[3] According to Leslie Schwindt-Bayer, political science professor at the University of Missouri.

[4] Alexei Barrionuevo, "Political Tango, Women in the Lead," *The New York Times*, Nov. 4, 2007, p. 4; also see Diana Cariboni, "Women — Latin America: Politics, A Territory Still to be Conquered," Inter Press Service, http://ipsnews.net/interna.asp?idnews=27812, and Justin Vogler, "Latin America: woman's hour," Open Democracy Web site, March 17, 2006, www.opendemocracy.net/democracy-protest/womens_hour_3364.jsp.

[5] Mayra Buvinic and Vivian Roza, "Women, Politics, and Democratic Prospects in Latin America," Inter-American Development Bank, www.iadb.org/sds/doc/women.pdf.

[6] Mala N. Htun, "Women in Political Positions in Latin America," Institute for Democracy and Election Assistance, 2002, www.idea.int/publications/wip/upload/Chapter1-Htun-feb03.pdf.

[7] "Women in the Americas: Paths to Political Power," *op. cit.*

[8] Jorge Heine, "Women to the Fore: Feminising Latin Politics," *The Hindu*, Dec. 12, 2007, www.thehindu.com/2007/12/13/stories/2007121356641200.htm.

[9] Buvinic and Roza, *op. cit.*

[10] "Gaucho feminism," *The Economist*, Dec. 13, 2007,www.economist.com/world/la/displaystory.cfm?story_id=10286252.

[11] Cariboni, *op. cit.*

[12] Htun, *op. cit.*

AP Photo/Juan Pablo Toro

AP Photo/El Pais

Combating Coca, By Land And Sea

Colombian police officers beat a hasty retreat after blowing up a cocaine lab in rural Tumaco, along the southern Pacific coast, on June 9, 2005 (top). Colombian sailors unload 13.5 tons of cocaine seized in Tumaco (bottom).

patronage or force and exercised power with scant regard for legal technicalities. Political participation was limited to upper classes that themselves had no tradition of political culture.

Despite such handicaps, a few countries — Chile and Costa Rica, for example — established viable democracies. Historians David Bushnell and Neill Macaulay note that liberalism was advancing in the latter decades of the 19th century. Still, many countries had long periods of authoritarian rule — notably, Mexico under the 34-year dictatorship of Porfirio Diaz that began with his election as president in 1876.

The United States had wielded influence over Latin American affairs since President James Monroe proclaimed his doctrine barring European intervention in hemispheric affairs in 1823. The United States reached the Pacific Coast by wresting half of Mexico's territory in a two-year war, 1846-48. At century's end, the U.S. victory in the Spanish-American War helped Cuba win independence. The United States also sent gunboats to support Panama's secession from Colombia in 1903 in order to secure agreement for construction of the Panama Canal. A year later, President Theodore Roosevelt added his corollary to the Monroe Doctrine, asserting a right to intervene as an "international police power" in any cases of "chronic wrong-doing."

'Men on Horseback'

In the 20th century, democracy continued to compete with the tradition of turning to strongmen — figuratively, if not literally, men on horseback — at times of national crisis. Some of the 20th-century caudillos were military leaders bent on preserving the status quo. Others — notably, Juan Perón in Argentina and Castro in Cuba — challenged the status quo in the name of the dispossessed and disenfranchised masses. The 20th century also saw the formation of mass political parties and revolutionary movements with mixed results for democratic government.

Mexico experienced the hemisphere's first social revolution of the 20th century. A revolution that spanned two decades (1910 to 1929) — and had to overcome two invasions from the United States — led later to the nationalization of foreign-owned companies and widescale land reform for peasants. But democratic procedures — presidential elections every six years, with no right of succession — proved no obstacle to one-party rule by the PRI, Mexico's preeminent political party from 1929 until the early 1990s.

Widely supported leftist parties also formed in Argentina in the 1890s and in Peru in the 1930s. In Argentina, the Radical Civic Union gained the presidency in 1916 and led the country on the road to liberal democracy until a military coup in 1930. Thirteen years later, Perón was among a new generation of nationalist military officers who staged coups. Perón then was elected president in 1946 and gained a devoted following among the urban and rural poor until he was ousted by a conservative military coup in 1955.

In 1959, Cuban revolutionary Castro overthrew the regime of dictator Fulgencio Batista. A powerful speaker and charismatic leader, Castro exercised an almost mystical hold over the Cuban masses. By 1965 he had established the first communist state in the Western hemisphere and become a symbol of socialist revolution for Latin America. The mission of "converting" the region through revolution was entrusted to Ernesto "Che" Guevara, a revolutionary legend in his own time, who was killed in Bolivia in 1967.

In Peru, the American Popular Revolutionary Alliance (APRA) — led by Victor Raúl Haya de la Torre, a charismatic intellectual — drew support from workers and the urban middle class to vie for the presidency in 1931. Haya de la Torre's refusal to accept his apparent defeat touched off violence from both sides. Military governments banned APRA for most of the next three decades. And when Haya came close to winning the presidency in 1962, military rulers nullified the election.

With the exception of Mexico and Costa Rica, every Latin American country has experienced at least one military coup in the 20th century. Colombia's military stepped in to end an undeclared civil war in 1953. In Paraguay, Gen. Alfredo Stroessner seized power in 1954 after years of civil war and political squabbling — and held power until his ouster in 1989. Guatemala's military stood by in 1954 while a U.S. invasion ousted the pro-communist leader Jacobo Arbenz Guzmán. In Brazil, a military coup ousted the left-leaning President Joao Goulart in 1964, instituting two decades of semi-authoritarian rule.

Shock Therapy

Although the region has been called Latin America since the late 19th century — referring both to its predominant Catholicism and its Spanish and Portuguese colonial origins — it has never seemed less Latin or colonial than it does now, during the profound political, social and economic changes that are occurring.

"The region has been transformed in the past 30 years," observes Malamud, the Latin America specialist in Madrid. During the 1970s, he points out, all Latin American nations except Mexico, Costa Rica, Colombia and Venezuela were run by military regimes.

In the aftermath of the 1959 Cuban Revolution, militant left-wing movements proliferated in Latin America, often against a background of faltering economies and weak, inept governments. In response, right-wing military regimes — often secretly aided by the United States — took power in many South American and Central American countries.[34]

AP Photo/ Javier Galeano

Latin America's most stridently anti-U.S. leftist leaders include communist Fidel Castro (center), former president of Cuba, and his socialist protégés, Venezuela's President Hugo Chávez (left) and Bolivia's President Evo Morales (right).

The epidemic of coups d'état — a periodic affliction in Latin American history since independence — lasted until the 1980s, when it ran out of steam, eventually leaving democratically elected governments to deal with the shattered economies and civil institutions.

The Argentine junta, for example, gave up the ghost in 1983, humiliated by its defeat in the war with Britain over the Falkland Islands and burdened by failed fiscal policies. But it left behind a legacy of brutal murders of political opponents and mass arrests — the so-called dirty war. The Chilean military regime lasted until 1990 and eventually laid the foundation for economic recovery. More benign, the Brazilian military junta eased the country into democracy in 1985.

Saddled with skyrocketing foreign debt and hyperinflation, many of the governments turned to a neoliberal economic regime — the so-called Washington Consensus — promulgated by the World Bank and the International Monetary Fund (IMF). It advocated free-market reforms such as privatization of state-owned businesses, free trade, balancing budgets and attracting foreign investment.

It was shock therapy, and it worked — but only for a while, and at a cost. Inflation plummeted, and economies began to recover. But governments were forced to make draconian cuts in public spending — including on social programs — and slash price controls, leaving the majority

Major Trade Agreements Affecting the Western Hemisphere

NAFTA — Implemented on Jan. 1, 1994, the North America Free Trade Agreement eliminates tariff barriers among the United States, Canada and Mexico until 2009. Increases in agricultural trade and investment fostered by NAFTA have made Mexico and Canada the largest and second-largest U.S. markets. From 1993 to 2006, overall trade in goods among the three countries jumped 198 percent — to an estimated $883 billion. During that same period, U.S. exports to Canada and Mexico jumped 157 percent, while imports from those countries increased by 231 percent, according to the International Trade Administration of the U.S. Commerce Department.

CAFTA-DR — The Central America-Dominican Republic-United States Free Trade Agreement went into effect on Aug. 2, 2005. Along with prior agreements, it will eliminate 80 percent of the trade barriers among Costa Rica, the Dominican Republic, El Salvador, Guatemala, Honduras, Nicaragua and the United States. The remaining tariffs are scheduled to be eliminated by 2020. CAFTA-DR also sets guidelines for workers' rights, provides access to sugar markets in the Dominican Republic and Central America and protects patents and trademarks for digital products like U.S. software.

FTAA — The Free Trade Agreement of the Americas, proposed at the First Summit of the Americas in 1994, calls for the gradual abolition of trade and investment barriers among the 34 democracies in the Western Hemisphere. The agreement was to have been signed by Jan. 1, 2005, but numerous countries, including Venezuela and Bolivia, refused to accept the proposed model. At the fourth Summit of the Americas in 2005 in Buenos Aires, 29 countries shelved the agreement until an unspecified future date.

MERCOSUR — Created in March 1991 by Brazil, Argentina, Paraguay and Uruguay, the *Mercado Común del Sur* (the Southern Common Market) is the largest trading bloc in South America, responsible for regulating imports and exports and overseeing trade disagreements among its members. Venezuela is awaiting ratification as the group's fifth member. Associate members include Bolivia, Chile, Colombia, Ecuador and Peru. Although several trade disagreements have arisen between members, MERCOSUR's overall goal is to establish a free-trade area across South America.

of the population worse off than before — and angry. Meanwhile, widespread corruption and mismanagement undermined the system, and the wealthy, European-descended class — which has always controlled a disproportionate share of the region's wealth — was able to further enrich itself, in part by buying up former state enterprises.[35]

Rise of the Left

It was time for a backlash. By the end of the 20th century, it appeared that "a veritable left-wing tsunami" was about to hit the region, observed former Mexican Foreign Minister Castañeda. Beginning with Chávez's election victory in Venezuela in 1998, "a wave of leaders, parties and movements generically labeled 'leftist' swept into power in one Latin American country after another." And, surprisingly, in a region with a history of abusive military dictatorships, support for democracy dropped from 61 percent in 1996 to 57 percent by 2002, according to a U.N. Development Programme poll.[36]

"As a result of neoliberal policies, the continent was severely impoverished," says Francisco Domínguez, head of the Latin American department at Great Britain's Middlesex University. "The level of poverty in the region went from around 25 percent to 44 percent in 2005, or roughly 227 million people." The wealth, he says, "was in the hands of a small elite."

In Venezuela, former Lt. Col. Chávez made his first bid for power in 1992 when he led an unsuccessful coup against President Carlos Andrés Pérez. He spent the next two years in jail but was eventually pardoned. In 1998, he campaigned for president and was elected for his first term.

After Chávez came da Silva and his Workers' Party in Brazil. The small, bearded former metal worker from northeast Brazil, who has a well-earned reputation for lengthy speeches, rose through Brazil's union ranks before making three unsuccessful bids for the presidency. On his fourth attempt, in 2002, he won, and then won re-election in 2006.

In Argentina, President Nestor Kirchner had been the successful governor of Patagonia's oil-rich Santa Cruz province for 12 years when he was elected in 2003 — by default because his rival, former President Carlos Menem, pulled out of the race. Kirchner managed to turn Argentina's deep economic crisis into four years of economic success, but then he declined to stand for a second term so that his wife Cristina, an influential senator, could successfully campaign for the job.[37]

In 2004 Tabaré Vázquez, a 68-year-old cancer specialist and former mayor of Montevideo, was elected president of Uruguay on his third attempt, becoming its first left-wing head of state. The economy was already on the upturn after years in the doldrums, but public resentment had ousted his conservative predecessors because one Uruguayan in three still lived below the poverty line.[38]

In Chile, Michelle Bachelet, a 56-year-old pediatrician and single parent, was elected president in 2006 after serving first as minister of health and then defense. A longtime socialist, she had been active in the underground during the military regime of Gen. Augusto Pinochet and had been arrested along with her mother but allowed to leave the country.

Morales, the Indian coca grower elected president of Bolivia in 2006, played a role in the conflicts between coca farmers and the U.S.-backed drug-eradication program and was involved in clashes with police during political demonstrations. Like his ally Chávez, he is seeking constitutional changes that would give the presidency greater power and increase state control over Bolivia's natural gas industry.[39]

Socialist Daniel Ortega served as Nicaragua's president from 1985 to 1990 after his Soviet-backed Sandinista National Liberation Front overthrew the Somoza dynasty by defeating the U.S.-supported counter-revolutionaries, called the *contras*. He returned to office in January 2007 after winning the 2006 presidential elections.

At the opposite end of the political spectrum, Colombia's Uribe — a conservative lawyer educated at Oxford and Harvard — is an implacable enemy of his country's Marxist guerrillas, whom he has vowed to defeat. Re-elected in 2006 for his second term, he is Washington's staunchest ally in the region and because of his distrust for Chávez tends to be wary of the region's trend towards closer cooperation.[40]

Today's Latin American politicians, Middlesex's Domínguez says, are promising social benefits, employment and a larger share of the country's wealth to the region's hitherto forgotten masses, the 38.5 million indigenous people and other poor, non-whites. Chávez and Morales were elected by mobilizing mestizos and other mixed-race or indigenous voters, many of whom were voting for the first time.

Castañeda identifies two main strains in the Latin American left wing. One, represented by Brazil and Chile, is "modern, open-minded, reformist and internationalist," he says. The other — represented by Venezuela, Bolivia and Ecuador — is "born of the great tradition of Latin American populism" and is "nationalist, strident and close-minded."

U.S. Director of Intelligence McConnell warned a Senate panel in February that "a small group of radical, populist governments continue to project a competing vision that appeals to many of the region's poor."[41] So far, however, that vision is still more a promise than a reality.

The Chávez Factor

Chávez used Venezuela's oil money to become "the only Latin American politician in the past half-century to acquire the type of worldwide name recognition and star power" enjoyed by Guevara, wrote Foreign Policy editor Naím. The Bush administration became Chávez's No. 1 rhetorical target, since he "understood very quickly that the emperor had no clothes and that challenging the American empire and its internationally unpopular leader was a sure bet."[42]

Chávez has been the driving force behind the launching of the seven-nation Bank of the South — a potential regional competitor to the World Bank and the Inter-American Development Bank — with a projected $7 billion in start-up capital. He also pledged billions of dollars to help build oil refineries in Brazil, Nicaragua and Ecuador and has established a strategic alliance with Cuba, at one point importing 20,000 Cuban teachers, doctors and party activists.

"Most of all, he has been attempting, with some success, to split the hemisphere into two camps: one pro-Chávez, and one pro-American," wrote Castañeda.[43] But even as Chávez calls President Bush "the devil," the United States remains Venezuela's main oil customer, buying 1.5 million barrels per day of petroleum products, making Venezuela America's fourth-largest oil supplier.[44] Trade between the two countries totaled $7 billion in 2007.

Meanwhile, as if to poke the U.S. president in the eye, Chávez also has reached out to Iran's President Mahmoud

Ahmadinejad, who is persona non grata in the United States for his refusal to halt Iran's uranium enrichment program. McConnell told the Senate committee that while Chávez and Ahmadinejad have "visited each other seven times since 2005" and have discussed nuclear energy, apparently no "significant developments" have followed these discussions. What causes anxiety among Venezuela's neighbors, McConnell said, is the fact that "military cooperation between Tehran and Caracas is growing." Venezuela has also purchased well over $3 billion in arms from Russia. As regional tensions heightened following the Colombian incursion into Ecuador on March 1, Chávez threatened to deploy his new Russian combat planes against Colombia.

Chávez's saber-rattling, together with Ecuador's decision to follow Venezuela's lead and move troops to the Colombian border, have drawn the Bush administration's attention to a region it has left largely unattended since 9/11.

"We're not using our power very well in general, and certainly not vis-a-vis Latin America," said Col. Lawrence Wilkerson, former chief of staff for Secretary of State Colin Powell and now a professor of government at the College of William and Mary in Williamsburg, Va. "There is very little attention paid to Latin America, and that's a mistake."[45]

Latin Americans, too, have felt the neglect. Ivonne A-Baki, speaker of the Ecuadorian national congress, calls Washington's lack of interest in Latin America since the attacks "patronizing." Terrorism is a global phenomenon, she says, noting, "9/11 could have originated in our region as well as any other part of the world. We need to be strengthening our ties, not weakening them." But, she acknowledges, "We Latin Americans haven't given the problem much attention either."

Inter-American Dialogue's Hakim isn't worried about what some have called Washington's benign neglect of Latin America. "There's nothing urgent we need to do in Latin America," he says. "There's the migration issue with Mexico, but that's really a U.S. border-control issue."[46] And unlike in the 1980s, when "nasty, vicious wars" were compounded by serious economic woes, he says, Latin America is now largely at peace, except for Colombia. And, for all Chávez's bombast, Hakim dismisses him as a "rather peripheral figure" from a second-tier country.

Trade Issues

Virulent anti-Americanism is one thing; commercial interests are another. Chávez may rail against President Bush, but not many other countries besides the United States are equipped to refine Venezuela's low-grade crude. Hence the United States remains the main customer for Venezuela's oil. Similarly, other Latin American leaders may distance themselves from Washington, but in the end they still want access to the U.S. market.

On the U.S. side, successive presidents have hoped to establish a hemisphere-wide free-trade area stretching from Alaska to Tierra del Fuego, but the U.S. Congress has been notoriously skeptical about trade accords.

U.S. lawmakers first and foremost scrutinize trade agreements for their impact on American jobs and exports. Then they often become the political instrument for forcing change abroad — such as improving human rights, intensifying the fight against drug trafficking and cooling relations with Cuba. In 1994, the United States, Canada and Mexico signed the North American Free Trade Agreement (NAFTA). (*See box, p. 42.*) The accord significantly boosted Mexican trade with the United States but has always had its skeptics at home — including, most recently, both the Democratic presidential candidates, Sen. Hillary Rodham Clinton of New York and Sen. Barack Obama of Illinois.

Once NAFTA was approved, the United States switched its focus to regional agreements in Central and South America. But the Central America-Dominican Republic-United States Free Trade Agreement (CAFTA-DR) — approved by Congress in 2005 — is the only one approved so far. It has since been adopted by all the signatories except Costa Rica, where strong public opposition led the government to hold a referendum on the agreement last October. It was approved — but only by a hair — and the national assembly now has until October 1 to ratify the treaty.

Opponents of free-trade agreements include Latin American farmers who fear cheaper, subsidized U.S. agricultural goods flooding their markets, trade unionists afraid of losing jobs to southern lands with cheap, non-unionized labor and others who see such deals as a Trojan horse for "Yanqui" hegemony.

The alternative approach of bilateral trade pacts has had mixed success as a result of conflicting political interests. Congress passed a free-trade agreement with Peru after nearly three years of delays caused by American unions' concerns about jobs and farmers' fears of cheaper Peruvian agricultural imports. Ironically, it was a Democratic majority in Congress that unblocked the deal, on which the Republicans had been stonewalling since

AT ISSUE

Has the United States lost its influence in Latin America?

YES

Janette Habel
Professor, Institute of Latin American Studies, Paris

Written for *CQ Global Researcher*, February 2008

Over the past decade, the United States has suffered a number of setbacks in Latin America. Washington's ambitious plan for a Free Trade Area of the Americas (FTAA) stretching from Alaska to Tierra del Fuego is a dead duck. The demise of neo-liberalism has opened the way for a series of left-wing coalition governments, each anxious to demonstrate in different ways its independence from the United States. Then in 2002, there was the failure of a U.S.-supported coup against Venezuelan President Hugo Chávez.

Finally, the setbacks in Iraq made it unlikely that the United States could contemplate another military action to enforce its will. This state of affairs prompted some observers to ask whether the United States was "losing" Latin America, or had indeed already lost it. To put this loss in perspective, French diplomat Alain Rouquie argued that the collapse of the Soviet Union meant that "Latin America ceased to be of strategic interest to the United States."

The U.S. has regained some lost ground by ratifying a number of new free-trade agreements with Latin America. The failure of the FTAA should not detract from U.S. successes in signing bilateral free-trade accords. Washington also has been trying to beef up military cooperation within the framework of its war on terror and the fight against narco-trafficking.

Furthermore, despite the growing rejection faced by the United States, trade trumps politics. U.S. investments in Latin America and the Caribbean totaled $353 billion in 2005, and U.S. exports to Latin America increased by 12.7 percent in 2006.

As Latin America expands its horizons, the discipline imposed by globalization and world markets tends to reduce the risk of political upheavals. Thus, the old style of Washington arm-twisting would in any case seem less necessary.

Washington also has learned more subtle methods of exerting its influence. By waving the banner of democracy while using more acceptable persuasive measures, the Americans can target different groups and communities and work on their differences to achieve their objectives. North American hegemony over the continent may not be what it was, but its foundations remain solid.

NO

Francisco Rodríguez
Assistant Professor of Economics and Latin American Studies, Wesleyan University
Former chief economist, Venezuelan National Assembly (2000-2004)

Written for *CQ Global Researcher*, February 2008

I don't think the United States has neglected Latin America. The United States does have other priorities, and I think those are also important. If you have to neglect anywhere, it had better not be the Middle East. Policymakers have limited capacities to give priority to different regions.

At the same time, Latin America has been doing relatively well in the last few years, both in terms of economic growth and the consolidation of democracies.

Yes, there has been a surge to the left, but in most of Latin America it's a benign left, with a few exceptions. In Brazil, for instance, voters elected Luiz Inacio Lula da Silva as president, but he has been making good efforts at ensuring Brazil's institutions are compatible with democratic ideals. In Peru, there was the emergence of a radical left, but voters rejected it. Hugo Chávez in Venezuela and Evo Morales in Bolivia — and possibly Manuel Ortega in Nicaragua — are the exceptions, but they are isolated.

There's a broader phenomenon that has occurred in Latin America. In the 1990s the United States and the international financial institutions decided to back very aggressive market reforms. These reforms did not have the results that had been expected, causing a political backlash. The lesson was that it may not be a good idea to try to define Latin American policy with a very active involvement by Washington.

Rather, Latin America is developing home-grown market economies in which moderate, left-wing governments such as Brazil's are respecting the market, but they are also addressing their respective country's social problems, and they are doing it in their own way.

The United States could still help more. It would be a great step for Washington in its relations with Latin America if it lowered agricultural subsidies that hurt the agricultural exports of many countries in the region.

An active initiative to financially support anti-poverty programs could also be very productive in improving the relationship of the United States with Latin America.

2005. Democrats, who have heavy support from unions and environmental groups, voted for the $9 billion agreement after provisions to protect human rights and Peru's environment were added.[47]

In January, faced with strong Democratic resistance to the proposed U.S.-Colombia free-trade accord, Secretary of State Rice took the unusual step of inviting several Democratic lawmakers to accompany her to Colombia in order to assuage their complaints about Colombia's human rights record and failure to protect union leaders from right-wing violence.

In February Ecuadorian legislator A-Baki visited Washington with a group of Andean parliamentarians to lobby for renewal of the special trade preferences enjoyed by Colombia, Peru, Ecuador and Bolivia under the Andean Trade Promotion Agreement, which in February was extended for 10 months for the third time, but not renewed. Congress is balking at renewing the deal because Ecuador and Bolivia have close ties to Chávez. Supporters of extending the agreement argue that denial will drive the two countries even further into Venezuela's orbit, and other Latin American countries will view the cut-off as unjust and high-handed.

But today's Latin Americans have also developed their own approach to trade accords. In 1991, in a push towards greater regional integration, Brazil, Argentina, Uruguay and Paraguay launched Mercosur (*Mercado Comun del Sur* or Common Market of the South). The United States was not invited to join, but Venezuela is awaiting ratification as a full member; Bolivia, Chile, Colombia, Ecuador and Peru are associate members.

Modeled after the European Union and designed to ensure free movement of goods, capital, services and people among its member states, the union has survived internal squabbles to reflect what observers see as a growing interest among Latin American states in cooperating with one another.[48]

CURRENT SITUATION

Tense Times

Two recent events have forced the world — including the United States — to focus its attention on Latin America. The first was Castro's announcement that he would step down from the presidency. The ailing Cuban leader's decision led to intense speculation whether the hand-picked new leadership in Cuba would change the repressively dogmatic communist course that Castro had steered for five decades.

But on March 4, the spotlight shifted to the Andes, where tension mounted as both Venezuela and Ecuador sent troops to their Colombian borders after Colombian forces killed FARC leader Reyes inside Ecuadorian territory. In Bogotá, President Uribe's government did not respond to the implied threat but said computer documents captured in the FARC camp revealed ties to both Venezuelan and Ecuadorian government officials. Both governments denied the allegations.

The Colombians also claimed seized documents showed Chávez had contributed $300 million to FARC — which, if true, raises the question of why the group needs to continue smuggling drugs and kidnapping in order to raise money. But Chávez's alleged contribution can also be seen in the context of another Colombian allegation: that FARC was seeking to buy uranium.[49]

The incident came on the heels of Chávez's high-profile role in getting FARC to release six hostages since Christmas, an intervention that the Colombian government first encouraged then opposed.

Amidst a flurry of negotiations to resolve the border standoff, President Uribe said he is considering action against Chávez in the International Criminal Court for aiding terrorists.[50] But official public reaction in Latin America has tended to criticize Colombia for trespassing across the border. Not so President Bush, who condemned Chávez's "provocative maneuver" in sending troops to the border and called on Congress to pass the stalled U.S.-Colombia Free Trade agreement as a sign of support.

"If we fail to approve this agreement, we will let down our close ally, we will damage our credibility in the region and we will embolden the demagogues in our hemisphere," Bush said. "President [Uribe] told me that the people across the region are watching to see what the United States will do."[51]

The bombastic Venezuelan leader's saber rattling is widely seen as an attempt to distract attention from growing domestic discontent over food shortages and his failure to improve the quality of life for the population. According to the Venezuelan Finance Ministry, food supplies are falling short of demand by "up to 60 percent" despite three consecutive years of production growth. In addition to tightening controls on food distribution and tightening border surveillance, Chávez has lifted restrictions on food imports and says the government is considering reviewing mandated price limits on foodstuffs.

The latest crisis overshadows the good news in Latin America, which is experiencing "a period of economic prosperity that may well continue," says Nora Lustig, a George Washington University professor of international relations specializing in Latin America. In fact, the recent global economic boom plays to the strength of the resource-rich region, where economic growth in the larger commodity-exporting countries, such as Brazil, is spilling over into neighboring countries.

Among the more centrist governments, Mexico is hoping the United States will not follow through with its plan to block illegal border crossings with a wall or electronic "fence." Officials in Mexico City are trying to calculate the impact America's current economic problems will have on bilateral trade, which involves 80 percent of Mexico's business.

The successful Colombian incursion into Ecuador was indicative of the improved effectiveness of the country's U.S.-trained and financed security forces. President Uribe has made progress in "improving security while energetically implementing a comprehensive counternarcotics strategy," Intelligence Director McConnell told the Senate committee. "Bogotá now holds the strategic advantage because of the Colombian military's sustained combat operations in the FARC's rural heartland," McConnell said.

Indeed, ordinary Colombians say the security situation has improved considerably. Military roadblocks have made highway travel between cities safer. According to U.S. statistics (accepted by Colombians as accurate), kidnappings are down 76 percent, homicides by 40 percent. Wealthier Colombians in cities like Cali, for example, can again visit country retreats that had been out of reach for years.[52]

Meanwhile, the Colombian government is negotiating the dismantlement of the right-wing paramilitaries that formed as an antidote to FARC. This is causing congestion in the judicial system and has led to political scandal for Uribe. More than 50 paramilitary commanders have confessed to their involvement, in hopes of obtaining lenient sentences, but some have alleged that several Uribe allies had colluded with the paramilitary.[53] So far, however, investigators have only looked into paramilitary confessions from three of Colombia's 32 provinces.[54]

Skepticism, however, surrounds McConnell's claim that "Bogotá's counterdrug program continues to show impressive results" and that "U.S.-supported aerial eradication has diminished coca cultivation in some areas."[55] But Chávez is undermining counternarcotics operations in the region, McConnell charged, "by giving traffickers access to alternative routes and transit points." The U.S. government recently confirmed earlier press reports that Chávez was allowing Colombian cocaine to be shipped to international markets through Venezuela. McConnell told the Senate panel that Venezuela was "a major departure point for South American — predominantly Colombian — cocaine destined for the U.S. market, and its importance as a transshipment center continues to grow."[56]

But a Feb. 3 *London Observer* report said the cocaine trail from Venezuela leads mainly to Europe, not the United States: "Thirty percent of the 600 tons of cocaine smuggled from Colombia each year goes through Venezuela. Most of that 30 percent ends up in Europe, with Spain and Portugal being the principal ports of entry."

The paper said there was no indication that Chávez himself had a direct role in the trafficking. Nevertheless, the reporter's sources doubted that "Chávez was not aware of the collusion between his armed forces and the leadership of FARC."[57]

Bolivian Discontent

In Bolivia, the government is trying to avert secessionist threats over Morales's efforts to codify his "democratic revolution."

Last year, a constituent assembly approved Morales's draft constitution, which would give Bolivia's 30-plus indigenous groups full citizenship and redistribute natural gas revenues to favor the central government. The proposal drew violent opposition from the eastern provinces, where Bolivians of European descent are concentrated — as are the country's rich natural gas deposits. Some indigenous communities in the area are also part of the opposition movement.

With emotions running high, some provinces threatened outright secession while others declared their autonomy from La Paz. In January, the government and provincial governors began a series of reconciliation talks aimed at reaching a compromise and paving the way for the national referendum on the constitution later in the year.

Although the talks began promisingly with a joint statement stressing the need for unity, in late January they were suspended after Morales suddenly cut gas revenues to the provinces by 30 percent.

OUTLOOK

Uncharted Waters

While analysts don't believe that the Venezuelan-Colombian border face-off will escalate, the residual bad feeling will make the Andes an area of tense relations for some time to come.

Of wider regional concern is the faltering U.S. economy. "Latin Americans don't really know to what extent they are insulated from the economic problems of the United States," says George Washington University's Lustig. "We're sailing in uncharted waters. How will they impact the Latin American macro-economy?" A loss of jobs stateside would reduce the amount of remittances Latin American workers in the United States send home — an amount that totaled $45 billion in 2006.[58]

Meanwhile, says Middlesex University's Domínguez, "the amount of investment from the United States has been almost non-existent, but Europe and China are investing very heavily in raw materials." He also sees the level of collaboration within the region improving. The Mercosur trade agreement and the recently launched Bank of the South (once it is funded) could become useful instruments for creating a closer economic — and, eventually, even political — union of Latin American countries. But other observers feel that such progress requires a greater degree of cooperation and political will than exists at present.

Two Latin American ballots this year could affect the region by potentially leaving the Venezuelan and Bolivian governments in an even more unpredictable state. What will Chávez do if — as seems likely — the growing opposition deals another blow to his prestige by winning a significant number of provincial seats? With his second term ending in 2012, "He'll be focused on concentrating power this year," predicts Daniel Varnagy, a political science professor at Simón Bolívar University in Caracas."[59]

Chávez's ally Morales faces a similar test later this year, when Bolivia holds a national referendum on his proposed constitution. Without some compromises with the opposition, Bolivia could be heading into a dangerous confrontation.

But for all Latin America's considerable — some might say "miraculous" — progress, Inter-American Dialogue's Hakim says its "most daunting challenges" remain "high and persistent rates of poverty; an egregious scale of income and wealth inequality; the dismal performance of public services available to low-income groups; and rampant crime and violence that mainly affect poor people."

Failure to make rapid and significant inroads into these problems, he warns, will deepen the mass discontent already afflicting the region and undermine its gains in other areas.

NOTES

1. Quoted in Larry Luxner, "Despite Some Leftist Leanings, Democracy Takes Root in Latin World," *The Washington Diplomat*, February 2008, p. 14.
2. Eric Green, "Economic Growth Continues in Latin America, Caribbean, U.N. says," america.gov Web site, July 26, 2006, www.america.gov/st/washfile-english/2006/July/20060726164641xeneerg2.906436e-02.html.
3. See "Indigenous peoples of Latin America: old inequities, mixed realities and new obligations for democracies in the twenty-first century," U.N. Economic Mission for Latin America and the Caribbean, www.eclac.org/publicaciones/xml/4/27484/PSI2006_Cap3_IndigenousPeople.pdf.
4. Jorge G. Castañeda, "Latin America's Left Turn," *Foreign Affairs*, May/June 2006, www.foreignaffairs.org/20060501faessay85302/jorge-g-castaneda/latin-america-s-left-turn.html.
5. Jens Erik Gould, "Venezuela youths transformed by music," BBC News, Nov. 28, 2005, http://news.bbc.co.uk/2/hi/americas/4457278.stm.
6. Michael Reid, *Forgotten Continent: The Battle for South America's Soul* (2007).
7. "BBC News Profile: Hugo Chávez," Dec. 3, 2007, http://news.bbc.co.uk/2/hi/americas/3517106.stm.

8. Quoted in Simon Romero and Sandra La Fuente, "In Venezuela, Faith in Chávez Starts to Wane," *The New York Times*, Feb. 9, 2008, p. A1.

9. Janette Habel, "Washington a-t-il perdu l'Amerique Latine?" *Le Monde Diplomatique*, December 2007, p. 1.

10. Carolyn Curiel, "Hello Neighbor," *The New York Times*, Feb. 5, 2008, www.nytimes.com/2008/02/03/books/Curiel-t.html?r=1&ref=review &page.htm.

11. J. Michael McConnell, "Annual Threat Assessment by the Director of National Intelligence for the Senate Select Committee on Intelligence 2008," testimony before Senate Select Committee on Intelligence, Feb. 5, 2008, www.dni.gov/testimonies/20080205_testimony.pdf.

12. Francisco Peregil, "Nuestra prioridad es jugar un gran papel en Suramerica," *El Pais*, Feb. 9, 2008, www.elpais.com/solotexto/articulo.html?xref=2008 0209elpepiint_8&type=Tes& anchor=elpepiint.

13. *Ibid.*

14. Quoted in Pablo Bachelet, "Sunday's defeat likely to hurt Chávez's international standing," *Free Republic*, Dec. 3, 2007, www.freerepublic.com/focus/f-news/1934295/posts.

15. Quoted in Juan Forero, "Chávez Turns Bitter Over His Defeat in Referendum; Foes of Amending Charter Have 'Nothing to Celebrate,' " *The Washington Post*, Dec. 6, 2007, p. A20.

16. Romero and La Fuente, *op. cit.*

17. "Venezuela: Hugo Chávez's Revolution," Executive Summary, International Crisis Group, Feb. 27, 2007, www.crisisgroup.org/home/index.cfm?l=1& id=4674.

18. Francisco R. Rodriguez, "An Empty Revolution: The Unfulfilled Promises of Hugo Chávez," *Foreign Affairs*, March/April 2008, www.foreignaffairs .org/20080301faessay87205/francisco-rodriguez/an-empty-revolution.html.

19. *Ibid.*

20. *Ibid.* Rodríguez is citing pollster Alfredo Kellner Associados.

21. Monte Reel, "Bolivia's Burning question: Who May Dispense Justice?" *The Washington Post*, Feb. 2, 2008, p. 4, www.washingtonpost.com/wp-dyn/content/article/2008/02/01/AR2008020103426 .html. For Ecuador: Brian Wagner, "Ecuador referendum may bring sweeping government changes," Voice of America, April 13, 2007, www.voanews .com/english/archive/2007-04/2007-04-13-voa38. cfm?textmode=0.

22. "Statistical Yearbook for Latin America and the Caribbean, 2006," U.N. Economic Commission for Latin American and the Caribbean, 2007, p. 3 (their p. 85), www.eclac.cl/publicaciones/xml/4/28074/LCG2332B_2.pdf.

23. "Social Panorama of Latin America — 2007," U.N. Economic Mission for Latin America and the Caribbean, www.eclac.org/publicaciones/xme/9/30309/PSI2007_Sintesis_Lanziamento.pdf.

24. Rodríguez, *op. cit.*

25. Castañeda, *op. cit.*

26. Tyler Bridges and Sibylla Bridzinsky, "Latin America On the Brink," *The Miami Herald*, March 3, 2008, p. A1.

27. "FARC frees hostages in deal brokered by Chávez," NPR, Jan. 11, 2008, www.npr.org/templates/story/story.php?storyId=18021246.

28. Chris Kraul, "Colombia's military toughens up," *Los Angeles Times*, Jan. 18, 2008, www/latimes.com/news/nationworld/world/la-fg-colombia18jan18,0,4255537 .story. For background, see Peter Katel, "War on Drugs," *CQ Researcher*, June 2, 2006, pp. 481-504.

29. "FARC frees Colombian hostages," Al Jazeera, Feb. 27, 2008, http://english.aljazeera.net/NR/exeres/88961720-F807-47B8-B93B-0AB5E5C4E D77.htm.

30. "Files in Colombian rebel laptop show Chávez's ties to rebels," Fox News, March 5, 2008, www.foxnews .com/story/0,2933,335128,00.html.

31. PBS OnlineNewsHour, "Colombia's Civil War," www.pbs.org/newshour/bb/latin_america/colombia/trade.html.

32. Juan Forero, "Colombia's low-tech assault," *The Washington Post*, July 7, 2007, p. A1.

33. Early history of Latin America adapted from Kenneth Jost, "Democracy in Latin America," *CQ Researcher*, Nov. 3, 2000, pp. 881-904.

34. For background, see Peter Katel, "Change in Latin America," *CQ Researcher*, July 21, 2006, pp. 601-624.
35. James Surowiecki, "Morales's Mistake," *The New Yorker*, Jan. 23, 2006, www.newyorker.com/archive/2006/01/23/060123ta_talk_surowiecki.
36. "History of Latin America," www.britanica.com.
37. "BBC profile: Kirchner: President by default," May 15, 2003, http://news.bbc.co.uk/2/hi/americas/2981797.stm.
38. "Uruguay elects left wing leader," BBC News, Nov. 1, 2004, http://news.bbc.co.uk/2/hi/americas/3968755.stm.
39. "BBC profile: Evo Morales," Dec. 11, 2005, http://news.bbc.co.uk/2/hi/americas/3203752.stm.
40. "Uribe sworn in amid high security," BBC News, Aug. 7, 2006, http://news.bbc.co.uk/ 2/hi/americas/3214685.stm.
41. McConnell, *op. cit.*
42. Cristina Marcano and Alberto Barrera Tyszka, *Hugo Chávez: The Definitive Biography of Venezuela's Controversial President* (2004), pp. xiii-xiv.
43. Castañeda, *op. cit.*
44. Cesar J. Alvarez, "Council on Foreign Relations Backgrounder — Venezuela's Oil-Based Economy," Council on Foreign Relations, Nov. 27, 2006, p. 2, www.cfr.org/publication/12089/venezuelas_oilbased_economy.html.
45. Luxner, *op. cit.*
46. For background, see Alan Greenblatt, "Immigration Debate," *CQ Researcher*, Feb. 1, 2008, pp. 97-120.
47. David T. Rowlands, "Peru: Free Trade Deal an Andean Tragedy," *Green Left Weekly*, Feb. 6, 2008, http://upsidedownworld.org/main/content/view/1118/68/.
48. "Profile: Mercosur — Common Market of the South," BBC News, Jan. 29, 2008, news.bbc.co.uk/2/hi/americas/5195834.stm.
49. Carin Zissis, "Colombia's Border Crisis," America's Society Web site, March 4, 2008, www.as-coa.org/article.php?id=926.
50. For background, see Kenneth Jost, "International Law," *CQ Researcher*, Dec. 17, 2004, pp. 1049-1072.
51. Quoted in Michael Abramowitz, "Bush Attends to Foreign Policy Issues; President Talks to Medvedev, Pushes Colombian Free-Trade Pact, Discusses Mideast," *The Washington Post*, March 5, 2008, p. A3.
52. "The Case for the U.S.-Colombia Trade Promotion Agreement," U.S. Department of State, December 2007, www.state.gov/e/eeb/tpp/colombia/.
53. Marcela Sanchez, "Rethinking Plan Colombia," *The Washington Post*, March 16, 2007.
54. *Ibid.*
55. McConnell, *op. cit.*
56. *Ibid.*
57. John Carlin, "Revealed: Chávez role in cocaine trail to Europe," *The Observer*, Feb. 3, 2008, www.guardian.co.uk/print/0,,332351756-111259,00.html.
58. "Migrant remittances from the United States to Latin America to reach $45 billion in 2006, says IDB," Inter-American Development Bank, Oct. 18, 2006, www.iadb.org/NEWS/articledetail.cfm?artid=3348&language=En.
59. James Ingham, "Crucial Year for Chávez Revolution," BBC News, Jan. 11, 2008, http://news.bbc.co.uk/2/hi/americas/7179055.stm.

BIBLIOGRAPHY

Books

Chasteen, John Charles, *Americanos: Latin America's Struggle for Independence*, *Oxford University Press*, 2008.

A professor of history at the University of North Carolina offers a compact history of Latin America's revolutions.

Marcano, Cristina, and Alberto Barrera Tyszka, (translated by Kristina Cordero), *Hugo Chávez: The Definitive Biography of Venezuela's Controversial President*, *Random House*, 2004.

Chávez's rise to power is traced by two Venezuelan journalists, who neither extol not attack the Venezuelan president. Based on numerous interviews with enemies as well as those close to him and on documents, the authors emphasize Chávez the man and his quest for power rather than his policies.

Marquez, Gabriel Garcia, *One Hundred Years of Solitude, Harper and Row*, 1967.
This is the Latin American novel and required reading for students of the region. Set in the fictional village of Macondo, Garcia Marquez's family saga is widely seen as an impeccably researched metaphor for the history of Colombia, in particular, and Latin America generally.

Oppenheimer, Andres, *Saving the Americas: The Dangerous Decline of Latin America and What the U.S. Must Do, Random House Mondadori*, 2007.
An acclaimed reporter and columnist at *The Miami Herald* sees Latin America as a commodity-rich but stagnant continent desperately in need of a strategy for survival in the 21st century.

Reid, Michael, *Forgotten Continent: The Battle for Latin America's Soul, Yale University Press*, 2007.
The Economist's Latin America editor says the continent's recent transformation to democracy deserves more attention.

Winn, Peter, *Americas: The changing Face of Latin America and the Caribbean, Berkeley Books*, 2006 edition.
Companion book to the PBS 1992 series of the same name, updated in 2006. Winn, professor of Latin American studies at Tufts University, was the academic director on the series, responsible for its acclaimed historical accuracy.

Articles

Barrionuevo, Alexei, "Political Tango, Women in the Lead," *The New York Times*, Nov. 4, 2007, p. 4WK.
Women in Latin America are rising to top positions in politics as voters seek change.

Phillips, Tom, "Blood on the streets as drug gang and police fight for control of the favelas," *The Guardian*, June 29, 2007, www.guardian.co.uk/world/2007/jun/29/brazil.international.
A British correspondent describes life in Rio de Janeiro's combat zone.

Rodriguez, Francisco, "An Empty Revolution: The Unfulfilled Promises of Hugo Chávez," *Foreign Affairs*, March/April 2008, www.foreignaffairs.org/20080301faessay87205-p0/francisco-rodriguez/an-empty-revolution.html.
A Wesleyan University professor of economics and Latin American studies and former chief economist of the Venezuelan National Assembly says President Hugo Chávez's social reforms have failed because they were underfunded and mismanaged.

Reports and Studies

"Social Panorama of Latin America, 2007," *Economic Council for Latin America and the Caribbean*, www.eclac.org/publicaciones/xml/9/30309/PSI2007Sintesis_Lanziamento.pdf.
The council provides an up-to-date picture of the social and ethnic structure in Latin America and the Caribbean.

Behrman, Jere R., Alejandro Gaviria and Miguel Székely, "Social Exclusion in Latin America: Introduction and Overview," *Inter-American Development Bank*, March, 2002, http://idbdocs.iadb.org/wsdocs/getdocument.aspx?docnum=773155.
The authors blame Latin America's income inequality — the highest in the world — on the absence of opportunities for large segments of the population due to outright or implicit exclusion of people on the basis of gender, ethnicity, place of residence or social status.

McConnell, J. Michael, "Annual Threat Assessment by the Director of National Intelligence for the Senate Select Committee on Intelligence 2008," Feb. 5, 2008, www.dni.gov/testimonies/20080205_testimony.pdf.
This unclassified country-by-country assessment lays out threats to the United States posed by leftist agendas and "sharply anti-U.S. rhetoric" in Venezuela, Cuba and, to some extent, Bolivia, Nicaragua and Ecuador. Especially worrisome are these countries' efforts to undercut checks and balances on presidential power, seek lengthy presidential terms, weaken media and civil liberties and emphasize economic nationalism at the expense of market-based approaches.

***The WWW Virtual Library: International Affairs Resources*, www2.etown.edu/vl/latamer.html.**
The Inter-American Development Bank and other sources provide a huge list of accessible statistics and information about Latin America.

For More Information

Argentine Council for International Relations, Uruguay 1037, Piso Primero, C1016ACA Buenos Aires, República Argentina; 54-11-4811-0071; www.cari.org.ar. Pluralist academic institution that encourages analysis of international affairs from an Argentinian perspective.

Center for Latin American Studies, Edmund Walsh School of Foreign Service, Georgetown University, ICC484, Washington, DC 20057; (202) 687-0140; http://clas.georgetown.edu/index.html. Offers undergraduate and graduate degrees emphasizing democratic governance, economic integration, inter-American affairs and culture and society.

Center for Latin American Studies, University of California, Berkeley, 2334 Bowditch St., Berkeley, CA 94720; (510) 642-2088; www.clas.berkeley.edu. Promotes research and community awareness of issues affecting Latin America.

Council on Foreign Relations, 58 E. 68th St., New York, NY 10065; (212) 434-9400; www.cfr.org. An independent, nonpartisan organization dedicated to improving global understanding and the foreign policy choices facing the United States and other countries.

Council on Hemispheric Affairs, 1250 Connecticut Ave., N.W., Suite 1C, Washington, DC 20036; (202) 223-4975; www.coha.org. Provides research and information promoting the common interests of the hemisphere.

Fernand Braudel School of World Economics, Rua Ceará 2, Sao Paulo, Brazil 01243-010; (5511) 3824-9633; www.braudel.org.br/en/. Conducts research and public debate seeking solutions for the international problems of Brazil and its neighbors.

Institute for International Relations, Rua Marquês de São Vincente, 225, Vila dos Diretórios, Casa 20, Gavea, Rio de Janeiro, RJ, Brasil, 22453-900; (5521) 3527-1557; www.iri.puc-rio.br. Research and graduate-teaching institution dedicated to international affairs.

Inter-American Development Bank, 1300 New York Ave., N.W., Washington, DC 20577; (202) 623-1000; www.iadb.org. Dedicated to accelerating economic and social development in Latin America and the Caribbean.

Inter-American Dialogue, 1211 Connecticut Ave., N.W., Suite 510, Washington, DC 20036; (202) 822-9002; www.thedialogue.org. A center for policy analysis, exchange and communication on issues in the Western Hemisphere.

Latin American and Caribbean Institute for Economic and Social Planning, Avenida Dag Hammarskjöld 3477, Vitacura, Casilla 179-D, Santiago de Chile; (56-2) 206-6104; www.eclac.cl/lipes. Primary training center for the U.N.'s Economic Commission for Latin America and the Caribbean.

Organization of American States, 17th Street and Constitution Ave., N.W., Washington, DC 20006; (202) 458-3000; www.oas.org. Promotes social and economic development in the Western Hemisphere.

U.N. Economic Commission for Latin America and the Caribbean, Avenida Dag Hammarkjold 3477, Vitacura, Casilla de Correo 179-D, Santiago de Chile; (56-2) 210-2380; www.eclac.cl/default.asp?idioma=IN. One of the five regional commissions of the United Nations, founded to contribute to the economic development of Latin America.

3

Middle East Peace Prospects

Is There Any Hope for Long-Term Peace?

Irwin Arieff

AP Photo/Hatem Moussa

Palestinian militants stand guard during an Islamic Jihad rally in Bureij, Gaza, on Dec. 26, 2008 — the day before Israel launched its deadly, three-week assault on the Hamas-governed Palestinian territory. Israel says the invasion was necessary to stop persistent Palestinian shelling of Israeli territory from the Gaza Strip. Despite a six-month cease-fire that began last June, at least 1,750 rockets and 1,520 mortar shells landed in Israeli territory in 2008 — more than double the number in 2007.

From *CQ Global Researcher*, May 2009.

Ezzeldeen Abu al-Aish is a Palestinian physician and media personality well known in Israel. He speaks Hebrew, champions Israeli-Palestinian reconciliation and during Israel's controversial assault on Gaza earlier this year regularly briefed Israeli broadcast audiences on the fighting.

He was at home in Gaza giving a phone interview to Israeli television in mid-January when two Israeli tank shells suddenly struck his house — killing three of his eight children and a niece.

"My daughters, they killed them," sobbed Abu al-Aish on the broadcast. "Oh God. They killed them, Allah. . . . They died on the spot."[1]

The wrenching interview dramatically drove home for Israelis the impact their government's brutal 22-day assault against Gaza was having on innocent Palestinian civilians.

"I cried when I saw this," then-Israeli Prime Minister Ehud Olmert said later. "How could you not? I wept."[2]

The Israeli military later defended the tank-fire as "reasonable" because it was the result of mistaken intelligence that militants were using the doctor's home to fire on Israeli troops.[3]

Israel has justified its deadly Dec. 27 invasion into Hamas-governed Gaza on the grounds that it needed to stop Palestinian militants in the Gaza Strip from firing rockets into Israeli territory. Some 1,750 rockets and 1,520 mortar shells landed in Israel in 2008, killing eight people, according to Israel's nonprofit Intelligence and Terrorism Information Center. That was more than double the number in 2007, the center says, despite a six-month cease-fire that began in mid-June of 2008.[4]

Note: Statistics for Israel include the Golan Heights — a hilly, 444-square-mile strip of land in northeastern Israel occupied during the Six-Day War and unilaterally annexed by Israel in 1981.

Source: The World Factbook, Central Intelligence Agency

Neighbors, But Worlds Apart

Israel's economy is flourishing compared to the territories it occupied after the 1967 Six-Day War. Israel's gross domestic product (GDP) of $28,000 per capita makes it among the world's wealthiest nations, while the West Bank and Gaza Strip are two of the world's poorest areas. Similarly, the unemployment rate in Israel is a relatively low 6 percent compared with 16 in the West Bank — and a staggering 41 percent in Gaza.

Israel

Area: 8,019 square miles (slightly smaller than New Jersey)

Population: 7,233,701 (July 2009 est., including Israeli settlers in the West Bank, Golan Heights and in East Jerusalem

Religion: Jewish 76%, Muslim 16%, Christians 2%, Druze 2%, unspecified 4%

GDP per capita: $28,200 (2008 est.)

Unemployment rate: 6.1% (2008 est.)

West Bank

Area: 2,263 square miles (slightly smaller than Delaware)

Population: 2,461,267 (July 2009 est.)

Religion: Muslim 75%, Jewish 17%, Christian and other 8%

GDP per capita: $2,900 (2008 est.)

Unemployment rate: 16.3% (June 2008)

Gaza Strip

Area: 139 square miles (about twice the size of Washington, D.C.)

Population: 1,551,859 (July 2009 est.)

Religion: Muslim 99%, Christian 1%

GDP per capita: $2,900 (2008 est.)

Unemployment rate: 41.3% (June 2008)

"We wanted to stop the rockets on our cities," says Asaf Shariv, Israel's consul general in New York City. "The goal was to change the security reality on the ground — meaning that they won't shoot without paying a price for that."

During a visit to southern Israel five months before the Gaza war started, then-presidential candidate Barack Obama appeared to support Israel's reasoning. "If somebody was sending rockets into my house where my two daughters sleep at night, I'm going to do everything in my power to stop that. And I would expect Israelis to do the same thing," Obama had said in July 2008.[5]

Palestinian militants say their rockets were fired in retaliation for Israel's continuing stranglehold on Gaza, including regular military raids and tight control over the movement of goods and people in and out of the territory.

But as the deaths of Abu al-Aish's children tragically demonstrated, Middle East violence produces other innocent victims than just Israelis killed by Palestinian rocket fire. According to the Palestinian Centre for Human Rights in Gaza City, of the 1,417 Palestinians killed during Israel's 22-day assault on the densely populated territory, 926 were civilians, including 313 children.[6]

The Israel Defense Forces (IDF) dispute those figures, putting the total at 1,166 Palestinians killed, 709 of them Hamas militants and fewer than 300 of them innocent civilians — including 89 children.[7] The military said it had tried hard to avoid civilian casualties but that the militants often chose to fight in heavily populated areas, effectively using civilians as human shields.

Hamas, one of the two main Palestinian political groups along with Fatah, is a hard-line Islamic organization backed by Iran and Syria that refuses to recognize Israel's right to exist. It also embraces violence — including rocket launches and suicide attacks against Israel — in its fight for what it sees as Palestinian land.

"When we are fired upon, we need to react harshly," then-Foreign Minister Tzipi Livni said on March 9 in Jerusalem after discussing the Gaza war with visiting U.S. Secretary of State Hillary Rodham Clinton.[8]

Ultimately, however, only 13 Israelis died in the conflict — 10 soldiers in combat and three civilians to rocket fire. The disparity in casualties triggered widespread international criticism of Israel's use of fighter jets, tanks and other heavy weapons to target poorly armed urban guerrillas in a densely populated enclosed territory — and accusations of war crimes.[9]

AP Photo/Fadi Adwan

A Palestinian medic rushes an injured child to the hospital during the Israeli invasion of Gaza on Jan. 4, 2009. According to the Palestinian Centre for Human Rights, 926 of the 1,417 Palestinians killed during the three-week assault on the densely populated territory were civilians, including 313 children. Israel Defense Forces estimated that 1,166 Palestinians were killed, fewer than 300 of them civilians, including 89 children.

Israel's initial air campaign unleashed 88 attack aircraft on 100 targets in three minutes and 40 seconds. "It was intense, probably more so than any conflict since the January 1991 start of the Iraq War," said Paul Rogers, an international security expert for the London-based Oxford Research Group. The degree of destruction "far exceeded what Hamas planners had anticipated."[10]

"There is a feeling in the Arab world that this kind of disproportionality has been used in the electoral process — that the [then-governing] Kadima and Labor parties were using [harsh military tactics] to increase their chances in the Israeli election," says Maged Abdelaziz, Egypt's ambassador to the United Nations.

Indeed, Israel's invasion occurred just before a major election on Feb. 10 for Israel's single-chamber parliament, the Knesset. Israeli frustration over the rocket launches and the lack of progress from years of peace efforts resulted in a sharp shift to the right, and the installation of conservative Benjamin Netanyahu as prime minister. (*See sidebar, p. 68.*)

During the several weeks it took for Netanyahu to assemble his governing coalition, former Prime Minister Olmert's caretaker government continued its tight rein on the flow of humanitarian and commercial goods into

Getty Images/Abid Katib

AP Photo/Tsafrir Abayov

Suffering on Both Sides

Israeli air strikes on Jan. 9, 2009, turned entire blocks of the Jabalia refugee camp in the Gaza Strip (top) into piles of rubble. Throughout Gaza, the U.N. estimates that 4,000 Palestinian homes were destroyed and 20,000 severely damaged during the three-week war — about 20 percent of the territory's housing stock. In the Israeli city of Ashdod, a man surveys a house (bottom) damaged by a Palestinian rocket on Jan. 18, 2009.

war-torn Gaza, fueling tensions in the territory just as the international community was trying to calm things down.[11] Although both sides unilaterally agreed to stop fighting in January — and Egypt is mediating long-term cease-fire talks — Palestinian militants quickly resumed their rocket fire, and Israel continued to block full access to Gaza — stirring fresh anguish in southern Israel and Palestinian pleas for international help to rebuild a shattered Gaza. The rocket fire also triggered retaliatory Israeli strikes, leading to more Palestinian casualties.

The developments were only the latest in a seemingly endless cycle of Israeli-Palestinian violence since the Jewish state's creation in May 1948. But a glimmer of hope that change might be in the wind appeared on Jan. 20, when Barack Obama moved into the White House pledging to court global Muslim public opinion and personally strive for a comprehensive Middle East peace. Within days of his inauguration, he named former Sen. George Mitchell, D-Maine, a veteran international mediator, as his special Middle East peace envoy.

"We're not going to wait until the end of my administration to deal with Palestinian and Israeli peace, we're going to start now," Obama said.[12]

His pledge underlined the reality that, despite years of talks and numerous military clashes, Israelis are fed up with years of fruitless peace negotiations while they remain under attack from Palestinian militants, and the Palestinian population bridles at continued Israeli restrictions and sees little hope for a homeland of their own.

Further complicating peace efforts, right-wing fundamentalists are pressuring each side not to accept a two-state solution: Militant Jewish settlers insist that all of the occupied territories rightfully belong to the Jews, while radical Muslims believe Israel itself occupies land wrongfully taken from them.

Moreover, the entire region's geopolitical landscape has been reshaped in recent years by the growing strategic importance of its vast oil reserves, the 2003 U.S. invasion of Iraq, the Muslim world's widening Shiite-Sunni schism and simmering tensions between Syria and Lebanon. In addition, the U.S. toppling of strongman Saddam Hussein's Sunni regime in Iraq unintentionally strengthened predominantly Shiite Iran next door, which worries other Sunni neighbors, such as Saudi Arabia, Jordan and Egypt.

Tehran is also accused by the West of seeking nuclear weapons — a charge it denies — and is openly hostile toward Israel, which is widely presumed to have its own nuclear arsenal. Israel now sees Tehran, not the Palestinians, as its greatest threat, particularly after Iranian President Mahmoud Ahmadinejad repeatedly called for Israel to be "wiped off the map."[13] Iran also supports Hamas as well as Hezbollah, an anti-Israeli militant group that is now a part of the government of Lebanon, Israel's northern neighbor.

In a bold challenge to President Obama's often-stated hopes for swift progress toward Palestinian statehood, a top Israeli official announced in April that Israel's new government would condition entering peace talks with the Palestinians on Washington first making progress in derailing Iran's suspected pursuit of nuclear weapons and curtailing Tehran's regional ambitions.[14]

"It's a crucial condition if we want to move forward," Israeli Deputy Foreign Minister Daniel Ayalon said. "If we want to have a real political process with the Palestinians, then you can't have the Iranians undermining and sabotaging."

Obama has repeatedly warned against delay in addressing the Israeli-Palestinian conflict, and since taking office on Jan. 20 his administration has been simultaneously working to resolve both that crisis and that of Iran — although the global recession has gotten top priority.

Because the United States is Israel's closest ally and arms supplier, the ongoing Israeli-Palestinian conflict continues to fuel anti-American sentiment in the Arab world, perhaps energizing Washington to try harder to resolve the conflict. As part of his post-9/11 war on terror, U.S. President George W. Bush strongly supported Israel's aggressive campaign against Palestinian militants, even though in June 2002 he became the first U.S. leader to publicly embrace the goal of Palestinian statehood.[15]

Nevertheless, the combination of America's pro-Israel stance and its invasion of Iraq have been interpreted by many Muslims as a thinly veiled war on Islam rather than a war on "terrorists." As a result, Islamic militants in Iraq and elsewhere declared holy war against the United States.

After a fruitless year of Middle East diplomacy launched in 2007 in Annapolis, Md., the Bush administration in its final days put the blame squarely on Hamas for the harsh Israeli attack on Gaza, even as many U.S. allies — including moderate Muslim states with normally friendly ties to Israel like Egypt and Turkey — called for Israeli moderation.[16]

In a dramatic moment at this year's World Economic Forum in Davos, Switzerland, Turkish Prime Minister Recep Tayyip Erdogan lashed out at Israeli President Shimon Peres: "When it comes to killing, you know well how to kill."[17]

Some analysts accused Washington of undermining its own interests by blindly supporting Israel.[18] Former President Jimmy Carter drew fire from both U.S. and Israeli officials by meeting with representatives of Hamas, which the United States and Israel shun because it refuses to renounce violence, acknowledge Israel's right to exist and uphold previous Palestinian agreements.[19]

The war, its ratcheting up of regional and international tensions plus the possibility of change have reopened the debate on virtually all aspects of the peace process. Among them: whether Palestinian statehood remains a desirable goal, whether the internationally crafted "roadmap" to peace needs revising and whether the so-called Quartet of international mediators can help the parties along the path to peace.

The Quartet — representing the United States, the United Nations, the European Union and Russia — was pulled together in 2002 by former U.N. Secretary-General Kofi Annan and Spanish Foreign Minister Miguel Angel Moratinos, former European Union (EU) special envoy for the Middle East. The next year the Quartet published its "roadmap" to peace, aimed at Palestinian statehood by the end of 2005.[20]

The roadmap was meant to build on the landmark 1993 Oslo Accords. In those agreements and in accompanying letters, Palestinian leaders recognized Israel's right to exist, Israel recognized the Palestinians' right to eventual self-government and they both agreed to negotiate a final, comprehensive peace agreement gradually over a five-year period.[21]

As it turned out, neither plan did the trick. Six years after the roadmap and 16 years after Oslo, Arab-Israeli peace and Palestinian statehood appear as elusive as ever.

As the search for a peaceful solution in the Middle East continues, here are some questions being debated:

Is a two-state solution still a viable possibility?

Palestinian statehood was not widely accepted as a central focus of the Middle East peace process until recently. The 1993 Oslo Accords did not even mention statehood. (*See box, p. 62.*) And although the idea was central to the failed 2000 Camp David Two peace talks, President Bill Clinton — the host of the summit — didn't publically acknowledge that fact until January 2001, his final month in office.

Palestinian statehood was formally affirmed as a U.S. goal in June 2002, when President Bush declared in a White House speech, "My vision is two states, living side by side, in peace and security."[22] Since then, both sides

Expanding Israeli Settlements Undermine Peace Efforts

The continuing growth of Israeli settlements in Palestinian territories occupied by Israel during the 1967 Six-Day War poses a major barrier to Middle East peace. Although Israel has evacuated its Gaza Strip settlements and repeatedly promised to cap growth in West Bank and East Jerusalem settlements, they have grown steadily. Israel has also been walling off many settlements to bar suicide bombers but also blocking Palestinian access to the land. The Israelis also have built more than two dozen settlements in the Golan Heights, which was abandoned by the Syrian population when the Israelis invaded in 1967.

Source: Foundation For Middle East Peace

have endorsed the idea, and the U.N. Security Council has incorporated it in several resolutions. But the lack of progress over the last seven years has prompted questions about the viability and desirability of statehood.

In fact, in a reflection of growing Arab impatience with the peace process, Libyan leader Muammar Qaddafi recently has called for a single state, on the grounds that a two-state solution would neither satisfy Israeli security concerns nor give Palestinians the borders they desire. "In absolute terms, the two movements must remain in perpetual war or a compromise must be reached. The compromise is one state for all, an 'Isratine' that would allow the people in each party to feel that they live in all of the disputed land, and they are not deprived of any one part of it," he argued.[23]

In time, he predicted, "these two peoples will come to realize, I hope sooner rather than later, that living under one roof is the only option for a lasting peace." Years before Qaddafi's article, the idea had caught on with some Palestinians and liberal Israelis, who argue that Israel will never actually allow a separate Palestinian state — despite past commitments.

But Israeli leaders say the one-state idea is a nonstarter due to changing demographics. Within about a decade Jews will comprise a minority in "Greater Israel" — the original state plus the lands it acquired in the 1967 Six-Day War — because its Arab population is growing faster than the Jewish population. Thus, a single state would be run, eventually, by Arabs rather than by Jews.

The demographic trend leaves Israel precious little time to negotiate Palestinian statehood, Prime Minister Olmert warned a Knesset committee in September. "Ever-growing segments of the international community are adopting the idea of a binational state," he said. "[But] I see a Jewish state as a condition for our existence."[24]

Israeli concerns about a single state strengthened during the Gaza invasion, after many Israeli Arabs participated in anti-Israel demonstrations.

And while some Palestinians may dream of controlling a greater Israel, the idea that "Israel would give equal rights to Palestinians in such a model is a bit of an illusion," says Dutch diplomat Robert H. Serry, the U.N. special coordinator for the Middle East peace process.

For the Palestinian Authority, the internationally acknowledged administrator of the Palestinian territories, the two-state plan remains the best option, but the two sides cannot close a deal on their own, says Riyad Mansour, Palestine's non-voting observer at the United Nations. "They need a third party that they know and trust, and if that third party could act decisively, then the deal could be closed," he says. "And we hope that President Obama is the third party that will help us to reach that conclusion."

Since taking office, the Obama administration has repeatedly reaffirmed the two-state model. "The inevitability of working toward a two-state solution seems inescapable," Secretary of State Clinton said during a visit to Israel in March. "We happen to believe that moving toward the two-state solution, step by step, is in Israel's best interest."[25]

But following the Israeli elections, many diplomats and analysts began wondering whether the parties might instead end up with what some call the "non-state" solution — a continuation of the status quo in which the peace process is indefinitely frozen. Netanyahu, Israel's new prime, has consistently refused to express support for Palestinian statehood, preferring instead to focus on Palestinian economic development and security issues and giving a higher priority to the potential nuclear threat from Iran.

Moreover, despite Palestinian efforts to form a national unity government that could include Hamas, Netanyahu insists he would not negotiate with a Palestinian government that includes Hamas — a movement he sees as an enemy of the Jewish state that must be defeated. "We won't negotiate with Hamas, because we won't negotiate with people who only want to negotiate our funeral arrangements," says Israeli Consul General Shariv.

But, he adds, if Hamas agrees to the three key principles set out by the Quartet as a prerequisite for Hamas to be accepted by the international community, "we negotiate with Hamas. It's as simple as that."

A Quartet statement issued after Hamas won the 2006 Palestinian election advised all world governments against dealing with any new Palestinian administration that did not reject violence, recognize Israel and accept all prior Palestinian commitments and obligations — including the roadmap.[26]

Hamas has so far refused to honor those principles, leaving it and Gaza increasingly isolated. After the 2006 elections, the isolation fueled a fierce rivalry between Hamas and Fatah, the other main Palestinian political

Israeli Settlements Continue to Grow

Despite repeated calls for Israel to withdraw its settlers from the West Bank and East Jerusalem and freeze further settlement expansion, the population in West Bank settlements rose 61 percent from 1999 to 2008. The Israeli population in East Jerusalem in 2006, the latest year for which data are available, was 8 percent more than in 2000. Israel withdrew all settlers from Gaza in 2005.

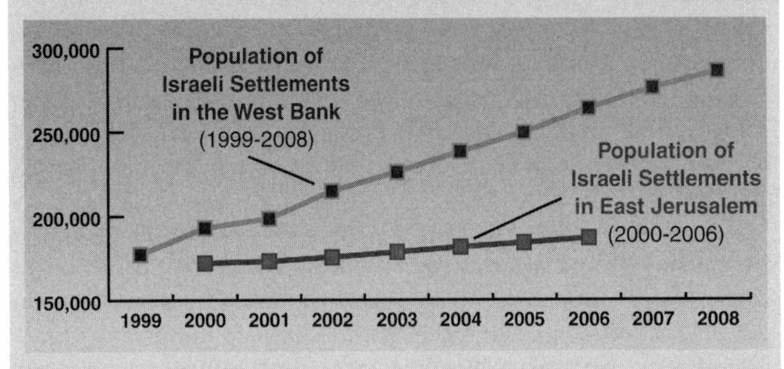

Source: Foundation for Middle East Peace, based on data from Israel's Central Bureau of Statistics and The Jerusalem Institute for Israel Studies.

organization, leading to a civil war that left Hamas in control of the Gaza Strip and Fatah running the West Bank.

Hamas believes Israel was established on land belonging to the Palestinians, regardless of what this or any other Israel government believes about an eventual Palestinian state. But Palestinian President Mahmoud Abbas, whose Fatah party is more moderate than Hamas, said the shared goal of Palestinian statehood — as embraced by past Israeli governments — should not be affected by elections. "We respect the choice of the Israeli people, and we respect the elections that took place in Israel," he said when Secretary Clinton visited the West Bank on March 4. "But we demand that the Israeli government also commits itself to the roadmap plan and the two-state vision."[27]

But Shariv says it is not Netanyahu who is blocking Palestinian statehood but the deep divisions between Hamas and Fatah. "The Palestinians understand that they cannot go to a Palestinian state without Gaza," he says. "They don't want to have a three-state solution."

Has the "roadmap for peace" become a fig leaf for inaction?

The idea of an international overseer — the Quartet — that would push Israelis and Palestinians toward peace grew out of the lack of progress that followed the Oslo Accords. The Quartet was set up in 2002 when its members concluded the Israelis and Palestinians could not work together on their own to reach a final peace agreement. The Quartet then gave them a "roadmap" to follow.

"They saw that the parties were not capable of producing any peace agreement. You needed the U.S. and the Quartet to hold the hand of both parties," says Norwegian diplomat Terje Roed-Larsen, a former U.N. special coordinator for the Middle East peace process and an architect of the Quartet. "So the roadmap was negotiated between the European Union, the United Nations, the United States and Russia, and then presented to the parties."

The roadmap set out parallel paths for each side to pursue simultaneously, in three phases, culminating in a permanent and comprehensive peace agreement in 2005. "Both parties accept this vision. But we can reach it only if we move rapidly and in parallel on all fronts. The so-called 'sequential' approach has failed," U.N. chief Annan explained at the time.[28] (*See box, p. 62.*)

But in practice the roadmap didn't work. While the Quartet monitored the process and met on an irregular basis to comment on developments and appeal to the parties, there was no mechanism to enforce or even document the parties' performance. And Israel quickly announced that it viewed its obligations under the plan as conditioned on an immediate end to Palestinian violence.

"Full performance will be a condition for progress between phases and for progress within phases," the Israeli cabinet said in attaching 14 reservations to its acceptance of the plan.[29]

The roadmap made its debut during one of the lowest points of the peace process. The 2000 Camp David Two summit — attended by Palestinian leader Yasser Arafat and Israeli leader Barak — had failed to produce a peace agreement, instead triggering a Second Intifada, or Palestinian uprising against Israeli occupation. The violence lasted more than four years and caused the deaths of more than 4,000 people, three-quarters of them Palestinians.[30]

With the Intifada raging, President Clinton asked former Sen. Mitchell to look for ways to bring the violence to an end. Mitchell's first foray into high-stakes Middle East diplomacy called for a freeze on Israeli settlements in occupied territories and a Palestinian crackdown on terrorism. The roadmap later built on Mitchell's 2001 recommendations.[31]

But progress stalled when each side argued that its actions should be contingent on the other side's performance, rather than occur simultaneously. Israel insisted that Palestinian attacks end before Israel would take such required political steps as dismantling settlements erected since March 2001 and easing restrictions on the movements of people and goods; the Palestinians have said the attacks would not end until Israel honors its commitments.

While the Quartet called on both sides to take specific steps, some analysts and diplomats say the Quartet has been softer on Israel overall, due to the United States' close ties to the Jewish state.

"Even though there has developed a generally agreed approach on some aspects of what should be demanded of the Palestinian side, this is not the case as regards Israel," wrote Peruvian diplomat Alvaro de Soto, who served as the chief U.N. Middle East peace envoy from 2005 to 2007, in his confidential end-of-mission report. The report, which cited Washington's "very serious qualms about exerting pressure on Israel," was quickly leaked and ended up on the Internet.[32]

Harvard University professor Stephen Walt, a critic of Israel's outsized political influence in the United States, has argued that, because the roadmap is unevenly enforced, "defending the two-state solution has become a recipe for inaction, a fig leaf that leaders can utter at press conferences while ignoring the expanding settlements and road networks on the West Bank that are rendering it impossible."[33]

Egypt's U.N. ambassador Abdelaziz agrees. "There was a period of calm for about two years immediately after the roadmap was introduced, but during this entire time settlement activities continued, roadblocks continued, confiscation of land continued."

According to the most recent statistics, the number of Israeli settlers living in the Palestinian West Bank grew from 223,954 in 2003 — the year the roadmap was issued — to 276,462 in 2007.[34]

"The Israelis argue that calm is required before steps along the roadmap can be taken," Abdelaziz says. "We need to prove the contrary: If there is to be calm, we want the political process to move forward."

U.N special Middle East coordinator Serry hopes Sen. Mitchell's appointment will be just one part of Obama's strategy. "I very much hope also that the Americans will be using the Quartet a bit more, and a bit more effectively, in a determined international role here," he says.

"Quartet meetings have so far been very much ad hoc. They need to be more structured. And top envoys need to be present more on the ground [in the region] rather than just meeting in capitals," adds Serry, who is based in Jerusalem. Other Quartet members agree the group should be more effective and not be abandoned.

The Obama administration believes "the Quartet remains the most effective instrument for advancing the international community's engagement in the effort to bring lasting peace to the Middle East," Susan Rice, Washington's new U.N. ambassador, told the Security Council in February.[35]

"This is one of the best things we have," says Russia's U.N. ambassador, Vitaly Churkin.

"It is easy to blame the Quartet for not having made peace in the Middle East in so many years. But nobody else has, or has even tried," adds the EU ambassador to the Middle East, Marc Otte, a Belgian. "The Quartet has been useful in harmonizing and coordinating action and has been a plus for EU-U.S. cooperation."

Can the Palestinians form a national unity government?

Hamas's 2006 election victory, its takeover of Gaza in 2007 and the recent Israeli assault on Gaza have left Palestinians deeply divided at a time when they face enormous domestic and international challenges.

To restore its economy, for instance, postwar Gaza must obtain basic food, medicine and commercial goods and rebuild its institutions and shattered housing. The U.N. estimates that 4,000 Palestinian homes were destroyed and 20,000 severely damaged during the three-week war — about 20 percent of the housing stock.[36] In March, at a conference in the Egyptian resort town of

Major Milestones in Israeli-Palestinian Peace Process

The Israeli-Palestinian conflict began immediately after Israel declared itself a state in May 1948, but progress toward peace has been painfully slow and elusive. The U.S.-mediated Camp David Accords led to the first peace treaty between Israel and an Arab state. The Oslo Accords, negotiated secretly between Israeli and Palestinian officials in Norway, set out a plan for a Palestinian Authority to gradually take over administration of lands seized by Israel in the 1967 Six-Day War. The 2003 Roadmap for Peace was drafted by the United States, the United Nations, the European Union and Russia — a self-proclaimed Quartet of international mediators — to guide Israelis and Palestinians to establishment of a Palestinian state as part of a comprehensive peace agreement. While Israel and Egypt remain at peace today, the Oslo Accords and the Roadmap were never carried out.

Here are three major milestones reached along the way:

Camp David Accords (1978)

- Negotiated in secret at the Camp David, Md., U.S. presidential retreat under the guidance of then-President Jimmy Carter.
- Signed at the White House by Egyptian President Anwar El Sadat and Israeli Prime Minister Menachem Begin.
- Led to the Israel-Egypt Peace Treaty of 1979, in which both countries agreed to mutual recognition.
- Established a framework for Egyptian-Israeli relations and for an autonomous, self-governing authority in the West Bank and Gaza Strip.
- Deliberately excluded the fate of Jerusalem.
- Established U.S. economic and military aid packages for each country that over the past 30 years have totaled $142 billion.
- Led to Sadat and Begin winning 1978 Nobel Peace Prize.

Oslo Accords (1993)

- Signed by Israeli Prime Minister Yitzhak Rabin and PLO Chairman Yasser Arafat on Sept. 13, 1993, in the White House Rose Garden with President Bill Clinton. Highlight of the ceremony was the first public handshake between Israeli and Palestinian leaders.
- Called for withdrawal of Israeli forces from certain parts of West Bank and Gaza Strip; creation of a transitional Palestinian Authority to administer the territories under its control, and democratic election of a transitional representative council.
- Called for the two sides to negotiate a comprehensive and permanent peace agreement within five years,

Sharm el-Sheikh, international donors pledged nearly $4.5 billion in aid for the Palestinians.

But Israel and Egypt tightly control all access to Gaza, including financial flows. And under the Quartet principles, none of the aid can pass through Hamas. Since the Palestinian Authority is not present on the ground in Gaza, that effectively leaves only international agencies in charge of reconstruction.

To address the problem, Egypt has pressed Fatah and Hamas to try to form a government of national unity. If the talks succeed, some U.N. and European diplomats have said such a government might also be accepted by Israel and the international community as a negotiating partner in peace talks.

"If we succeed in having a national unity govt., the U.S. and the Quartet should accept that," says Palestinian U.N. envoy Mansour.

To U.N. Secretary-General Ban Ki-moon, unity is crucial. "For any sustainable political progress to occur, and for Gaza to properly recover and rebuild, Palestinians must engage in reconciliation," Ban told a Feb. 10 news conference.[37] He appealed to Palestinians to "overcome divisions and to work toward one Palestinian government within the framework of the legitimate Palestinian Authority."

But how can a unity government include Hamas, which has refused to accept the Quartet principles that all Palestinian factions must renounce violence, recognize Israel and accept past Palestinian peace deals?

Looking back, it was a mistake for the international community to isolate Hamas after its 2006 election victory, argued de Soto, who was the U.N. Middle East envoy at that time. Hamas "has become a formidable political player. They cannot be ignored in the search

based on principles previously established by the U.N. Security Council.

- Divided the West Bank and Gaza into three zones, pending a final agreement: Areas under complete control of the Palestinian Authority; areas under Palestinian civil control and Israeli security control and areas under complete Israeli control.
- Established a framework for future relations between the two parties, with particular emphasis on regional development and economic cooperation. In side letters (agreements) to the accords, Arafat said the Palestine Liberation Organization (PLO) recognized Israel's right to exist in peace and security and renounced the use of terrorism and other acts of violence, and Rabin said Israel recognized the PLO as the representative of the Palestinian people and would begin negotiations with the PLO within the Middle East peace process.

AFP/Getty Images/J. David Ake

President Bill Clinton gleams with pride as Palestinian Liberation Organization leader Yasser Arafat (right) and Israeli Prime Minister Yitzhak Rabin (left) shake hands in the White House Rose Garden on Sept. 13, 1993. It was the first direct, face-to-face meeting between Israeli and Palestinian political representatives.

Roadmap for Peace (2003)

Set out a performance-based and goal-driven roadmap to a comprehensive and final settlement of the Israeli-Palestinian conflict by 2005, in three phases:

- **Phase I** (to be completed by May 2003): end Palestinian violence; implement Palestinian political reform; Israeli withdrawal and freeze on expansion of settlements in the West Bank and Gaza Strip; Palestinian elections.
- **Phase II** (to be completed by December 2003): hold international conference on Palestinian economic recovery; establish a process leading to an independent Palestinian state.
- **Phase III** (to be completed by the end of 2005): Israel and Palestinians conclude a permanent agreement that ends their conflict, ends the Israeli occupation that began in 1967, defines Palestinian refugees' right to return to their former homes, establishes Jerusalem's borders and status and fulfills the vision of two states — Israel and Palestine — living side by side in peace and security. Arab states agree to establish full diplomatic relations and make peace with Israel.

for peace with Israel," he wrote recently. "And yet ignore them, and beyond, undermine them and sidestep them, is precisely what the international community has done since their election to a majority in the Palestinian legislature. . . . It should not surprise us that many in Hamas have interpreted this as meaning that there is no interest in a move by them toward democracy and peace, leaving no other recourse but continued armed struggle."[38]

For the time being, however, Israel and most of the key international players, including most Arab donors, appear to be sticking with the three principles and ensuring their aid bypasses Hamas. The three principles are "not the United States talking. That is the Quartet and the Arab League," Secretary of State Clinton said in March during a tour of the region. "Everyone knows what Hamas must do, and it is up to Hamas."[39]

While Egypt has said the unity talks show that Hamas and Fatah want a unity deal, Israeli Consul General Shariv says: "They have been saying that for approximately two years now." The talks will drag on, he says, because "the hate between Fatah and Hamas is bigger than the hate between the Palestinians and Israelis."

Egypt has an uneasy relationship with Hamas, due in part to its repression of the Muslim Brotherhood in Egypt, with which Hamas is allied. But Egypt argues that isolating Hamas unfairly harms all Gazans, most of whom are not Hamas supporters. "We deal with Hamas as part of the Palestinian population. Whether we believe that this national unity government is going to be successful or not, we must first achieve some kind of reconciliation among the Palestinian people themselves," says Egypt's U.N. envoy Abdelaziz.

Obama's Middle East Troubleshooter Gets Mixed Reception

Arab-American George Mitchell is expected to take an even-handed approach.

President Barack Obama's appointment of George Mitchell as his special envoy to the Middle East was widely greeted as a potential game-changer in one of the world's most enduring trouble spots. But he is certainly not the first special envoy to be dispatched to the region.

Former British Prime Minister Tony Blair currently fills that bill for the Quartet — the "pressure group" of diplomats from the United States, Russia, the European Union and the United Nations — with a mandate to focus on beefing up the Palestinian economy. Veteran U.S. diplomat Dennis Ross spent years shuttling between Washington and the region and remains a special envoy to the Obama administration, although this time for Iran.

Mitchell, a 14-year veteran of the U.S. Senate representing Maine, has gained a global reputation as a skilled international troubleshooter for helping tame violence in Northern Ireland and expose steroid use among U.S. Major League Baseball players. His mother migrated to the United States from Lebanon at 18 and he identifies himself as an Arab-American.

After a previous stint in the Middle East at the request of President Clinton, Mitchell in 2001 called on Palestinians to reform their security forces and end violence and for Israel to halt the expansion of settlements on land seized in the 1967 Six-Day War. Clinton had asked Mitchell to investigate the causes of the Second Intifada, or Palestinian uprising, which began in mid-2000 after a Clinton-hosted peace initiative failed.

Mitchell's recommendations had little impact, however, and the Intifada raged on for years, resulting in thousands of Palestinian and Israeli deaths. Palestinian rockets and mortars remain a top international concern, as do Israel's ever-expanding West Bank settlements. Israel withdrew its settlers from Gaza when it pulled out of the territory in 2005.

Obama's appointment of Mitchell was greeted warmly in the Arab world while Israel has reacted more coolly. "George Mitchell has rich experience in solving conflicts — in Northern Ireland, for example — and he has a lot of respect among parties in the region," says Palestinian U.N. Ambassador Riyad Mansour.

But Asaf Shariv, Israel's consul general in New York, stopped short of praising the former senator. Asked if Mitchell made Israel nervous, he responded: "If Sen. Mitchell can help us reach a peace agreement, we would be the most happy people in the world. That is what we want. We know who our friends are, and the United States is the best friend we have, and we want to have peace."

The Mitchell appointment is significant for three reasons, said Paul Rogers, a global security expert with the Oxford Research Group in London. "Mitchell has family knowledge of the Middle East combined with a reputation for evenness in his work in Northern Ireland," Rogers said. "He is not regarded as close to the Israel lobby in Washington, and . . . President Obama made it clear that this was his [personal] initiative" rather than the action of an underling.[1]

However, many Israelis warn that even if the Palestinian Authority led the unity government initially, Hamas could soon end up in control, because President Abbas's four-year term expired in January. He is calling for new presidential and legislative elections by Jan. 24, 2010.[40]

A recent poll showed Hamas gaining popularity after the Gaza war, the opposite of what Israel had hoped. The survey of 1,270 people in the West Bank and Gaza, conducted March 5-7 by the Palestinian Center for Policy and Survey Research, showed Hamas leader Ismail Haniyeh defeating Abbas in a hypothetical election for Palestinian president, which could give Hamas a political foothold in the West Bank and East Jerusalem as well as Gaza.[41] The Fatah leadership has been plagued for years by criticism that the party is corrupt and resists needed financial and security reforms, and this is undoubtedly hurting Fatah among Palestinian voters.

"According to Palestinian public-opinion experts, Hamas emerged from the recent Gaza war stronger than

"For the Arabs, the Americans are the only ones who can actually deliver the Israelis," says a U.N. Middle East analyst, who spoke on condition of anonymity because he is not authorized to speak for the world body. During the George W. Bush administration, "the U.S. appeared to them to be more and more wedded to the Israeli side. So the Arab world is so enthralled with Obama because they see him as a change."

But Egyptian U.N. Ambassador Maged Abdelaziz warns that, while he is "cautiously optimistic" about the role Sen. Mitchell can play, it will take him a while to learn the terrain and identify openings to a solution. "The Americans are still learning to drive, and for them, it is a new car," he says.

He adds, however, "We don't want to repeat the experience of those other envoys, who come every month and have the same round of discussions with everybody, and then go back to Washington, and then come back the next month, and nothing moves forward. We need a time-bound plan, that we are going to do this now, and then that the next month."

EU Middle East envoy Mark Otte also advises caution. "Mitchell is held in very high regard in the region, and also in Europe, due to his involvement in resolving the Northern Ireland conflict. And true statesmanship actually occasionally happens, even in the Middle East," he says. "But I think there is a delusion that just because we — the U.S., the Europeans — want a problem to be solved, that people are ready to solve it.

"There is a new opportunity in that the U.S. government is willing to deal up-front with the problem," he continues. "But there is also a negative side, in that time is running out for a number of strategic problems of the region, including the confrontation with Iran on the nuclear issue and its regional ambitions that are scaring off the Arab governments. There is a potential for a deal between Arabs and Israelis. But the opportunity should not be lost before something else maybe more radical or catastrophic happens."

AFP/Getty Images/Menahem Kahana

President Barack Obama's envoy to the Middle East, former Democratic Sen. George Mitchell (left), has a global reputation as a skilled international troubleshooter. A Lebanese-American, Mitchell is expected to take an even-handed approach to discussions with both sides, including hard-line Israeli Foreign Minister Avigdor Lieberman (right).

[1] Paul Rogers, "Gaza — The Aftermath," Oxford Research Group, January 2009, www.oxfordresearchgroup.org.uk/publications/monthly_briefings/index.html.

ever, especially in the West Bank, where the Fatah party has been neither reformed nor rebuilt," said Yossi Alpher, an Israeli blogger and former director of the Jaffee Center for Strategic Studies at Tel Aviv University. "This means a unity government could quickly confront Israel with the challenge of Hamas rule rather than 'unity' rule in the West Bank as well as Gaza."[42]

"Then Hamas takes over, and then we will see rockets landing on Tel Aviv, certainly on Ben Gurion Airport, and of course where I live in the center of Jerusalem," adds Amnon Lord, an Israeli writer and former editor of the *Makor Rishon* newspaper.

International diplomats say that unity could be achieved without Hamas by establishing a government of technocrats — skilled administrators without political affiliations — such as the current Palestinian Authority cabinet.

That may be the only way to keep Israel on board, predicts a veteran European diplomat with long experience in the Middle East. To include Hamas in a unity government "would be the perfect cover for those in Israel who do not want a two-state solution, who want a non-state solution," he says, speaking on condition of anonymity due to his continued involvement in the matter.

"They will never agree to a Hamas role," he continues. "Given that thousands of rockets have flown into Israel, given that those rockets continue to fly, public opinion in Israel is so strong on these issues that there is no government in Israel that could engage with a Palestinian government like that and survive."

BACKGROUND

Decades of Deadlock

While the Israeli-Palestinian conflict has continued for years, the broad outlines of a plan for ending the conflict have long been known to the parties. At one time or another, both sides have endorsed most of the major elements of an agreement.[43]

"All the issues have been negotiated so many times before that we know what the solutions will be," says Palestinian U.N. Ambassador Mansour.

Yet a final resolution remains elusive, say Middle East peacemakers, in part because the two sides view virtually every issue and every development in a fundamentally different way, and thus discussions tend to proceed in endless circles of blame and retribution.

Outside mediators say they try to steer the parties to focus on the future and avoid eternal debate over events long past. But the two sides seem to prefer to dwell on past wrongs: on how to interpret them and how to correct them.

The result has been decades of deadlock.

"It is a conflict over a very small piece of land, and it is a conflict between two rival nationalist movements, with all the rancor and violence that can come with nationalism," says U.N. Middle East specialist Markus Bouillon, a German. "The divergent points of view are fueled by historical experience: For the Jewish people, there is the Holocaust, having no home, the diaspora. And that completely clashes with the Palestinian perspective — that 'this is our land, we have always been here, everybody else has their state, why did you come and steal our land?' These arguments are driven by morality and emotion, making for a powerful argument on both sides."

So the parties in effect end up pitting the Arab grandmother living in a Palestinian refugee camp and still clutching the keys to the family home abandoned in 1948 against the Jewish grandmother with the concentration camp number tattooed on her arm, Bouillon says.

In search of the roots of the conflict, a convenient starting point is the surge in Jewish immigration to the Middle East shortly after the start of the 20th century. Starting in 1904, Jews escaping Russia's anti-Semitic massacres — called pogroms — began creating a state-within-a-state in a region of the Ottoman Empire known as Palestine, where an Arab population was already long established.

Earlier, in the 19th century, Austro-Hungarian journalist Theodor Herzl, considered the father of Zionism, and other Jews began calling for Jews to settle in "Zion," their historic homeland. They argued that Europe had never accepted their presence and never would. The Zionists based their claim to Palestine on the Jews' ancient presence there, which had ended when the Romans destroyed Jerusalem and dispersed most of the Jews in 70 A.D.

The nascent state grew even stronger after a fresh wave of immigration following World War I, when Great Britain took over Palestine under a mandate from the League of Nations, the predecessor of the United Nations. The new arrivals further stoked tensions with the longtime Arab population. Under the so-called Balfour Declaration of 1917, Britain committed itself to allowing the establishment of a Jewish "national home" in Palestine, with the proviso that "nothing shall be done which may prejudice the civil and religious rights of existing non-Jewish communities in Palestine." The measure was endorsed by France, Italy, Japan and, in principle, by the U.S. Congress in 1922.[44]

After the genocide of 6 million Jews by the Nazis in World War II, thousands of Holocaust survivors flooded into Palestine, many joining the ranks of a determined and effective underground army called the Haganah and other similar militias. Their guerrilla-style attacks on British and Arab targets and Palestinian Arab violent resistance to growing Zionist strength prompted the United Nations General Assembly to vote in November 1947 to partition the Palestinian territory into separate countries for Arabs and Jews — Israel and Palestine.

CHRONOLOGY

1948-1977 *Israel becomes a nation, opening new era regularly punctuated by war with its Arab neighbors.*

1948 Israel declares statehood on May 14; Arab armies attack a day later. Israel emerges as victor within months, but 750,000 Palestinians are uprooted.

1965 Exiled Fatah leader Yasser Arafat, now heading new Palestine Liberation Organization (PLO), declares armed struggle against Israel to reclaim former Arab lands.

1967 In Six-Day War, Israeli troops repulse Arab attack, enter Jerusalem and occupy west bank of Jordan River, Gaza Strip along Mediterranean.

1973 Egypt and Syria launch initially successful surprise attack on Israel on Oct. 6, the Jewish holiday of Yom Kippur. Israel makes major territorial gains in the Golan Heights and in the Sinai desert before a U.N.-sponsored cease-fire takes effect, just weeks after the conflict started.

1978-2000 *Peace attempts alternate with periods of heightened violence.*

1978 After secret talks hosted by President Jimmy Carter at Camp David, Egyptian President Anwar Al-Sadat and Israeli Prime Minister Menachem Begin sign agreement leading to 1979 peace treaty, the first between Israel and an Arab neighbor.

1987 Palestinians rise up against Israeli occupation in first Intifada ("uprising"); violence continues for six years.

1993 In secretly negotiated Oslo Accords, Israel agrees to gradually transfer administration of West Bank and Gaza to Palestinians; PLO, in accompanying letter, recognizes Israel's right to exist.

2000 President Bill Clinton fails in push for final Palestinian-Israeli peace deal at second Camp David summit. Second Intifada erupts. Clinton appoints former Sen. George Mitchell, D-Maine, to lead an international inquiry into how to end it.

2001-2007 *Bush administration initially steers clear of involvement in Middle East peace efforts.*

2001 Mitchell tells President George W. Bush Israel should freeze its settlements and the Palestinians end terrorism. Arab terrorists attack United States on Sept. 11, prompting Bush's global war on terror and increasing Muslim-Western tensions.

2002 U.S., European Union, Russia and U.N. form Quartet of global mediators to help resolve Arab-Israeli differences. Bush endorses Palestinian statehood.

2003 United States and allies topple Saddam Hussein in a move widely seen as a grab for Iraqi oil. Quartet's two-year plan (roadmap) calls for Palestinian state.

2005 Israel abandons its Gaza settlements and withdraws from the area.

2006 Hamas wins Palestinian elections. Arab guerrillas capture Israeli soldier Gilad Shalit and demand release of imprisoned Palestinians. Israel invades southern Lebanon on July 12 after Hezbollah guerrillas capture two Israeli soldiers.

2007 Hamas defeats Fatah in Palestinian civil war and takes full control of Gaza on June 15. Bush convenes conference in Annapolis, Md., to seek Israeli-Palestinian peace deal.

2008-Present *Israelis elect new conservative government after controversial invasion of Gaza.*

2008 Palestinian militants in Gaza fire thousands of rockets and mortars into southern Israel. Mid-year truce ends on Nov. 4 after Israeli and Hamas forces clash along Gaza border. On Dec. 27 Israel launches 22-day invasion of Gaza. Annapolis conference ends without a deal.

2009 Barack Obama becomes U.S. president, says time is ripe for new Middle East negotiations and names Mitchell his special Middle East envoy. In Feb. 10 elections, Israel elects Likud Party leader Benjamin Netanyahu to head new right-leaning government. Obama plans to meet with Netanyahu on May 18 and later with Palestinian and Egyptian leaders.

Israel's New Government Could Block Quick Peace

Netanyahu: No peace talks until progress is made on Iran.

While the Palestinian Authority, President Barack Obama and most world governments are calling for a quick, new push for Palestinian statehood, Israel has signaled through its votes in Feb. 10 parliamentary elections that it is not in any hurry.

What's more, even as critics express concern over Israel's aggressive tactics in Gaza, some Israeli officials are warning of fresh military action over the rocket fire still raining down on southern Israel from Gaza. Sporadic rocket attacks resumed within days of the end of the Gaza operation in January, undermining initial Israeli boasts about the success of its initial assault, launched mainly to stop the attacks.

Continuing rocket fire "will be answered with a painful, harsh, strong and uncompromising response from the security forces," caretaker Prime Minister Ehud Olmert warned on March 1, a month before turning power over to his successor, conservative Likud Party leader Benjamin Netanyahu.[1]

But Hamas — the militant political party that governs Gaza and refuses to recognize Israel's right to exist — was not firing the rockets launched in the months after the Gaza operation, Israeli government and private experts say. "It is only independents — very small and extreme groups — that are shooting. It is not Hamas. We can tell by the rocket and who manufactured it who is shooting," Asaf Shariv, the Israeli consul general in New York and one-time media spokesman for former Prime Minister Ariel Sharon, said in late March. Should Hamas later resume fire, Israel could "go back in" to Gaza, he added.

But the lull continued in April, says Reuven Erlich, head of the Intelligence and Terrorism Information Center, a private organization in Ramat Hasharon, Israel. "It is in Hamas' interest to keep a low profile and calm down the situation at this time. But this won't necessarily continue for the long run," he continues, speculating that Hamas may be using the lull to rebuild its military or enable the reconstruction of Gaza to get under way.

The threat of renewed military action in Gaza is just one sign of Israelis' unhappiness with the peace process. Judging by the election results, "Israel realizes that the so-called peace process has led it to the brink of great peril for its own existence," says Amnon Lord, an Israeli writer and former newspaper editor.

Netanyahu argues that now is not the time for a Palestinian state. He wants to focus instead on Palestinian economic development and security issues. He also champions Israeli settlements in the West Bank and East Jerusalem, despite multiple U.N. Security Council demands to freeze all settlement activity.

Netanyahu also wants to focus above all on the threat from Iran. Israel's deputy foreign minister, Daniel Ayalon, said in April that his country's new government would not begin peace talks with the Palestinians until Washington first made progress in ensuring that Tehran does not develop nuclear weapons.[2]

But the Obama administration has been pushing for a comprehensive approach that aims for progress on the

But borders were never established for the two separate states, and Palestine's Arabs and Jews engaged in a spiral of deadly clashes in the months following the U.N. vote. When Britain's mandate to administer Palestine ran out, Israel simply declared itself an independent nation on May 14, 1948. Immediately, the Arab League went to war to reclaim the land. But Israel defeated the league — made up of Egypt, Syria, Lebanon, Transjordan (now Jordan), Iraq, Saudi Arabia and Yemen — in what Israelis call the "War of Independence." Palestinians call it "the catastrophe" ("al-Naqba") because it led to the departure or expulsion of hundreds of thousands of Arabs from the new country of Israel — creating the root of today's conflict. Debate over whether the Palestinians were forced out or fled on their own has since become part of the two sides' divergent historical narratives.[45]

Israel's founding triggered a succession of Middle Eastern wars that essentially continues to this day. The 1948 War of Independence was followed by the Six-Day War of 1967 against the region's major Arab countries — led by Syria and Egypt — and the Yom Kippur War of 1973. After the Six-Day War Israel occupied lands now known as the Palestinian territories — the West Bank (of the Jordan River) and the Gaza Strip, which runs along the Mediterranean.

Palestinian and Syrian peace tracks as well as Iran. "The United States is committed to a comprehensive peace between Israel and its Arab neighbors, and we will pursue it on many fronts," Secretary of State Hillary Rodham Clinton said during a March Middle East visit that included trips to Jerusalem, the West Bank city of Ramallah and the Egyptian resort town of Sharm el-Sheikh.[3]

During her tour of the region, Clinton made it clear that, unlike the previous U.S. administration, Washington would press Israel on its commitments to freeze settlement activities and speak out when it disagreed with Israeli leaders.[4]

In elections for the 120 seats in Israel's single-chamber parliament, the Knesset, Likud won 15 additional seats — for a total of 27 — but still finished in second place behind the centrist Kadima Party's 28 seats, despite months of polls suggesting Likud would end up leading the pack. The biggest surprise was the right-wing Yisrael Beitenu Party of Avigdor Lieberman, which captured four new seats — for a total of 15 — putting it in third place.

While Kadima normally would have been tasked with assembling a coalition government supported by more than half of Knesset members, the job in this case went to Netanyahu because right-wing and religious parties enjoyed an overall strong majority.

As coalition talks dragged on, Netanyahu managed to cut deals with the center-left Labor Party as well as with Yisrael Beitenu that assigned the post of foreign minister to Lieberman, whose campaign was widely seen by Israelis as extremist, racist or advocating ethnic cleansing of the Palestinians.[5]

Netanyahu's new government took power on March 31.

Analysts saw the agreement with Labor as helping to shield Netanyahu from U.S. criticism that the government was too right-wing and too opposed to the peace process.

But Lieberman has called for all Israeli citizens — including Israeli Arabs, who make up a fifth of the population — to swear an oath of loyalty to the state in order to retain their rights. Critics said the proposal was aimed at driving Israeli Arabs out of the country. Others, however, have painted Lieberman as more difficult to categorize.

"Lieberman is an enigma for me," says one international diplomat, speaking on condition he not be identified because he will have to work with the Israeli politician. "If you look at what he is saying, it is very, very dangerous to talk of an ethnic Jewish state with no place at all for Israeli Arabs. But on the other hand, Lieberman is for a two-state solution, he wants a Palestinian state. He even wants to think about parts of Jerusalem being part of it."

Adds Israel's Shariv: "It is true that he had a very interesting campaign that made everyone in the world raise some questions about him, but he is a very practical person."

---

[1] Matti Friedman, "Israeli leader vows 'painful' response to rockets," The Associated Press, March 1, 2009, http://news.yahoo.com/s/ap/20090301/ap_on_re_mi_ea/ml_israel_palestinians;_ylt=Aizxs6J4fCD8EJDs_WfT2RRI2ocA.

[2] Howard Schneider and Glenn Kessler, "Israel Puts Iran Issue Ahead of Palestinians," *The Washington Post*, April 22, 2009, www.washingtonpost.com/wp-dyn/content/article/2009/04/21/AR2009042103998.html?hpid=topnews.

[3] Hillary Rodham Clinton, "Intervention at the International Conference in Support of the Palestinian Economy for the Reconstruction of Gaza," Sharm el-Sheikh, Egypt, March 2, 2009, www.state.gov/secretary/rm/2009a/03/119900.htm.

[4] "Secretary Clinton, Palestinian President Abbas in Ramallah," March 4, 2009, www.america.gov/st/texttransEnglish/2009/March/20090304125709eaifas0.3768885.html?CP.rss=true.

[5] See for example, Lily Galili, "Avigdor Lieberman said to be ex-member of banned radical Kach movement," *Haaretz.com*, Feb. 3, 2009, www.haaretz.com/hasen/spages/1061172.html.

During the second half of the 20th century, nationalism grew among Palestinian Arabs, who demanded the return of their homeland. By 1964, a group of exiles that included Fatah leader Arafat founded the Palestine Liberation Organization (PLO), which brought together religiously oriented political activists and left-wing Arab nationalists. The following year, they declared an armed struggle against Israel to reclaim the formerly Arab lands.

Peace Accords

Just as there was a series of Arab-Israeli wars, there has been a series of peace summits to settle the intractable conflict.

The first Camp David summit, hosted by President Carter in 1978, led to a formal peace treaty between Israel and Egypt in 1979. As part of the deal, the United States agreed to provide $7.5 billion in economic and military aid to the two countries that year, with the lion's share going to Israel. Over the following three decades, seeking to encourage continued friendly ties, Washington has funneled an average of $4.3 billion a year in aid (three-quarters of it to Israel) to the two Middle East neighbors — a costly arrangement that could well be repeated in future Middle East agreements mediated by the United States.[46]

Support for the Palestinian cause eroded, however, with the collapse of the Eastern European bloc — a strong financial and political backer of the Arab world — as the Cold War began to wind down in the late 1980s. Palestinians, frustrated by the continued Israeli occupation of their lands, rose up in 1987 in what is now called the First Intifada, an uprising that lasted until 1993.

In response to the violence, a secret peace initiative was launched in Oslo with the help of Norwegian diplomat Roed-Larsen, leading to the first face-to-face negotiations between Israel and the PLO and ultimately to the so-called 1993 Oslo Accords.[47] The agreements were signed on Sept. 13, 1993, in an historic White House Rose Garden ceremony in which Arafat and Israeli Prime Minister Yitzhak Rabin shook hands as a beaming President Clinton looked on.

Under the accords, the parties committed themselves to negotiate the final details of a comprehensive peace agreement by 1999. The final details — concerning such crucial issues as borders, the disposition of Jerusalem and Palestinian refugees' "right of return" to their former home — became known as the "final status" or "permanent status" issues and remain unresolved today.

The accords also provided for Israel to gradually transfer power and responsibility for the West Bank and Gaza to the Palestinians, and to recognize Arafat's Palestine Liberation Organization as the representative of the Palestinian people and as a negotiating partner.

For its part, the PLO in a letter accompanying the accords formally recognized Israel's right to exist and renounced the use of "terrorism and other acts of violence." The agreement also divided up security responsibilities among the two parties.

But extremists on both sides were unhappy with the accords and in 1995 essentially sabotaged the negotiations toward a comprehensive peace: Palestinian militants stepped up their attacks against Israel, and a Jewish extremist assassinated Rabin.

Five years after that, in May 2000, Israel withdrew its forces from southern Lebanon, which it had first invaded in 1978 in hopes of ending cross-border guerrilla attacks on civilians in northern Israel. Years of occupation and low-intensity warfare between the Israeli occupiers and Hezbollah militia had taken a political toll on Israel, and most Israelis saw the conflict with Palestinians in the West Bank and Gaza as a more pressing concern.[48]

Two months later, the Clinton administration came the closest ever to a broad agreement ending the Israeli-Palestinian conflict by luring Arafat and then-Israeli Prime Minister Barak to the Camp David presidential retreat near Washington.

Their talks, known as Camp David Two, convened on July 11, 2000, and at first made significant progress. But they ran out of steam and ended after two weeks without a deal.[49]

Blame for the failure of Camp David Two has since been hotly debated, with each side blaming the other for failure to go the final mile.[50] Following the talks' collapse, Palestinian frustration boiled over, leading to the popular uprising in September 2000 that became known as the Second Intifada. Dismayed by the deadly violence, Clinton asked former Sen. Mitchell to chair a commission to identify its causes and recommend how to end the uprising.

Clinton left office in January 2001, and Mitchell turned over his findings to President George W. Bush, whose administration avoided direct involvement in the conflict even as it offered strong support for Israeli policies. Mitchell's May 4, 2001, report split the blame, calling for an end to Palestinian violence and a freeze on Israeli settlements. Mitchell saw the settlements as undermining Israel's earlier commitments to the general principle of "land for peace," under which Israel would cede land gained in the Six-Day War in exchange for peace with the Palestinians.[51]

But both sides largely ignored Mitchell's recommendations.

War on Terror

Less than four months after Mitchell's report was published, Islamic extremists hijacked airliners and crashed them into the World Trade Center and the Pentagon, radically altering Washington's relationship with the Middle East and greatly complicating peace efforts while drawing the United States more deeply into the region's political woes.

Bush declared a global war on terror in which the United States vowed to use all its power against radical Islamists. The campaign started with a coalition-led invasion of Afghanistan to oust the ultraconservative Taliban regime, which was harboring al Qaeda leader Osama bin Laden, the architect of the 9/11 attacks. At the same time, Israel adapted Washington's war on terror to its own ends, citing it to defend a crackdown on Palestinian militants.

Following a deadly suicide bombing in the northern town of Netanya during the Jewish Passover holiday in 2002, Prime Minister Ariel Sharon sent the military into the West Bank to reoccupy towns evacuated as part of the Oslo Accords. Israeli forces surrounded Arafat, confining him to his Ramallah offices.[52]

As Middle East violence picked up, U.N. Secretary-General Annan convened a meeting of top diplomats from the United States, the European Union and Russia, urging them to join the United Nations in a pressure group of four, which they dubbed the Quartet. The group began drafting a roadmap to peace to present to the Israelis and Palestinians.

To counter accusations that he was biased against the Arab world, Bush in a June 24, 2002, White House address became the first U.S. president to publicly embrace the so-called two-state solution — separate Palestinian and Israeli states, existing side by side within secure borders.[53] Palestinian statehood was included as a provision of the roadmap, which became international law upon adoption by the U.N. Security Council on Nov. 19, 2003.[54]

But Bush inflamed the Arab world anew with his March 2003 invasion of Iraq to rid it of alleged chemical, biological and nuclear weapons. The weapons were never found, and Washington ended up occupying the oil-rich country. The invasion, building on Bush's war on terror and his unwavering support for Israel, prompted fresh Arab accusations that Washington was waging a war on Islam.[55]

With violence persisting in Gaza, Sharon pushed through a domestically unpopular plan to shut down Israeli settlements there and withdrew from the territory in September 2005. The pull-out initially was widely hailed as a fulfillment of Israeli commitments to end its occupation of Palestinian areas.

But Israel, worried that weapons and fighters would enter Gaza through Egypt, continued to clamp down on border crossings into Gaza from Israel and Egypt. That severely limited the commerce on which Gaza's economic future depended.[56]

Within months, Israel was attacking militants inside Gaza with artillery and air strikes. Militants in Gaza in turn continued their attacks on the Jewish state, arguing they remained under occupation despite the withdrawal.[57]

Getty Images/Yoray Liberman

A Jewish settler cries out in despair when Israeli policemen tell her she must abandon her home in the Atzmona settlement in Gaza Strip on Aug. 21, 2005. All Israeli settlers were forced to leave Gaza under an unpopular plan engineered by Prime Minister Ariel Sharon. Although the pull-out was widely hailed as a fulfillment of Israeli commitments to end its occupation of Palestinian areas, Israel has continued to expand its settlements in other occupied areas.

In the January 2006 elections, the militant Gaza-based Hamas movement defeated long-dominant Fatah to win a majority of the seats in the Palestinian Legislative Council. Bush had been promoting Middle East democracy, but when Hamas won power, Israel and the Quartet refused to deal with it or recognize its authority. To gain recognition, the Quartet declared, Hamas would have to recognize Israel's right to exist, foreswear violence and honor all agreements reached by previous Palestinian administrations.[58] The Quartet principles, presented as recommended policy to all world governments, ended up isolating the Gazan population as well as Hamas from the international community.

Growing tension between Hamas and Fatah soon led to intermittent civil war that ended in the seizure of Gaza by Hamas fighters in mid-2007. That left the Palestinian Authority effectively in charge only of the West Bank, although in international eyes it remains the leader of both territories.[59]

To the north, meanwhile, Lebanon's Hezbollah paramilitary forces resumed targeting Israel from a second front, launching rockets at northern Israeli towns and then kidnapping two Israeli soldiers in a daring cross-border raid. In July 2006 Israel responded by sending troops back into southern Lebanon with orders to wipe out Hezbollah forces. Like Sharon's 2002 reoccupation of the West Bank and the December 2008 incursion into Gaza, the 34-day operation started out with great fanfare but soon began rolling up heavy civilian casualties even as it fell short of its goals, triggering international criticism of the Israeli military's tactics.[60]

Although Hezbollah ended up suffering militarily, it was politically strengthened by the Israeli assault in Lebanon. Within a year, a new Lebanese government had been formed in which the group and its allies held effective veto power over government actions.[61]

With time running out on his presidency, Bush in November 2007 gave a final try to advancing the Israeli-Palestinian peace process from Washington, convening an international peace conference in Annapolis, Md. But even as the conference began, participants played down expectations of a dramatic result, and Bush — shying from specifics — called on the parties only to try to finish whatever they chose to accomplish by the end of 2008.[62]

In line with expectations, the Annapolis initiative produced no agreement before time ran out 13 months later. The U.N. Security Council on Dec. 16, 2008, adopted a resolution supporting the failed initiative's attempt at peace and welcoming the idea of another international conference, as yet unscheduled, in Moscow in 2009.[63] On Dec. 27, four days before the deadline for an Annapolis deal, Israel sent its troops into Gaza.

CURRENT SITUATION

U.S. Role

With new U.S. and Israeli governments settling in, and Palestinian leaders crippled by internal divisions, the Middle East peace process seems on hold for now. In the region and around the world, interested governments are standing on the sidelines, putting off any initiatives until they hear what the Obama administration has in mind.

Meanwhile, Israel, the Palestinians and outsiders involved with the region all agree on at least one thing: The United States must continue to play a central role in Middle East diplomacy.

Washington's key role, of course, can cut both ways. Washington's disinterest has nipped some initiatives in the bud, while U.S. support has breathed life into other proposals. Washington is Israel's closest and most trusted ally and the world's lone superpower. International diplomats say Washington alone has the power to influence — although not necessarily alter — Israeli policy, and Washington's deep pockets will make it a necessary partner in any agreement.

"U.S. commitment to the resolution of this conflict is indispensable," says Otte, the EU's Middle East ambassador.

For his part, President Obama appears eager to get involved but cautious about the outcome. "I am a strong supporter of a two-state solution, and I think that there are a lot of Israelis who also believe in a two-state solution," he told reporters on April 21 during a visit to Washington by King Abdullah of Jordan. "Unfortunately, right now what we've seen not just in Israel but within the Palestinian territories, among the Arab states, worldwide, is a profound cynicism about the possibility of any progress being made whatsoever.

"What we want to do is to step back from the abyss," he continued, "to say, as hard as it is, as difficult as it may be, the prospect of peace still exists, but it's going to require some hard choices, it's going to require resolution on the part of all the actors involved, and it's going to require that we create some concrete steps that all parties can take that are evidence of that resolution. And the United States is going to deeply engage in this process to see if we can make progress."[64]

Obama's caution is understandable. Months of Palestinian negotiations on a national unity government have gone nowhere. Because of Hamas's pariah status with the Quartet, most international donors refuse to provide it with direct funding, and it can only participate indirectly in the multibillion-dollar international program to rebuild Gaza.

Meanwhile, Egyptian-led talks between Israel and the Palestinians seeking a long-term Gaza cease-fire are at an impasse. Hamas's refusal to release kidnapped Israeli soldier Gilad Shalit, held by Gaza militants since June 2006, has been a major stumbling block. And Israel, furious over continued rocket fire from Gaza, has maintained a tight rein on the movement of people and goods in and out of the area. Despite Israel's insistence that it is not slowing the shipment of food and medicine into Gaza, U.N. officials say otherwise.[65]

Since the 2007 Hamas takeover of Gaza, both before and after its invasion of the territory, Israel has pursued a policy "of near-total closure of the Gaza Strip," Lynn Pascoe, the U.N. undersecretary-general for political affairs, told the Security Council on April 20.[66] Israeli officials say vital supplies are not being blocked. But Pascoe pointed out that while basic emergency needs such as food and blankets have been met, broader humanitarian and reconstruction aid has been "impossible" due to restrictions on the flow of fuel, cash and construction materials.

"The lack of access to Gaza is deeply frustrating," he continued. "Without the materials for recovery and reconstruction, the process cannot begin, and that requires a substantial easing by Israel of its policy of closure of the Gaza Strip."

Besides promoting negotiations between Israel and the Palestinians, the Obama administration also hopes to revive the so-called Syrian track of the Middle East peace process, which centers on the Golan Heights. Israel captured the tract of Syrian land in the 1967 Six-Day War, and Syria wants it back.

Despite being neighbors, Syria and Israel have no diplomatic relations. They held secret, indirect peace talks under Turkish mediation in 2008, but Damascus put the talks on hold after Israel invaded Gaza in December. But in February President Bashar al-Assad told a visiting U.S. official that an agreement with Israel was still possible and that Syria was prepared to resume the talks if Washington joined them.[67]

Syria — a close ally of Iran and a backer of Hamas and Hezbollah — has been listed as a state sponsor of terrorism by the United States since 1979.[68] But Secretary of State Clinton in March dispatched two U.S. envoys to Damascus to explore bilateral and regional issues. "We have no way to predict what the future with our relations concerning Syria might be," she said. "But I think it is a worthwhile effort to go and begin these preliminary conversations."[69]

AFP/Getty Images/Adem Altan

Global Reaction

Israel's harsh three-week campaign against Hamas militants in the Gaza Strip sparked demonstrations around the world, both in support of the assault and in condemnation. Demonstrators outside the Israeli embassy in Madrid (top) show their support for Israel on Jan. 18, 2009, while protesters in Ankara, Turkey, on Jan. 3, 2009, show their outrage (bottom).

Israel's Role

The new coalition government formed by Israeli Prime Minister Netanyahu teams right-wing parties cool to Palestinian statehood and the peace process with the Labor Party, which supports negotiations for a Palestinian state. Netanyahu assembled a cabinet after his Likud Party finished first in the Feb. 10 parliamentary elections.

Netanyahu said during the campaign that he would continue negotiating with the Palestinians, but not about statehood. Instead, he would grant the Palestinians some degree of sovereignty over any territory they govern while maintaining Israeli control over their borders and airspace.

"Netanyahu has already announced that he will continue the negotiations, especially in the West Bank, about these issues, and to strengthen what he calls the economic peace — to make the Palestinian economy much stronger, to build infrastructure, to encourage companies to work there, to make life better," says Shariv, the Israeli consul general.

Under its coalition agreement with the Labor Party, Likud agreed to respect all of Israel's international agreements — which presumably would include the roadmap to Palestinian statehood.

But Netanyahu thus far has avoided the word "statehood," seemingly seeking to divert international attention from peace talks with the Palestinians and keep it focused instead on containing Iran. While some observers worry that Tehran may be just months away from being able to make nuclear weapons, the timetable on Palestinian statehood "is open-ended," Israeli Deputy Foreign Minister Daniel Ayalon said in April, defying President Obama's insistence that ending the Israeli-Palestinian conflict is an urgent global priority.[70]

"The Palestinians should understand that they have in our government a partner for peace, for security and for rapid economic development of the Palestinian economy," Netanyahu said in late March. "If we have a strong Palestinian economy, that's a strong foundation for peace."[71]

Israelis are also heatedly debating whether a second military thrust into Gaza might be needed to halt the renewed rocket fire into southern Israel. While the continued attacks on Israeli civilians show the 22-day military campaign fell short of its goals, the invasion also prompted a flood of international criticism of aggressive Israeli tactics in Gaza's densely populated urban area as well as of Hamas's rocket fire at Israeli civilians.

Within days after the war ended, New York-based Human Rights Watch called for an international investigation into allegations of war crimes by both Hamas and Israel.[72] A U.N. human rights investigator issued a similar appeal several weeks later. Gaza's civilian population was subjected to "an inhumane form of warfare that kills, maims and inflicts mental harm," said Richard Falk, the U.N. special rapporteur on human rights in the Palestinian territories. "As all borders were sealed, civilians could not escape from the orbit of harm." Israel has prevented Falk — who is a professor emeritus on international law at Princeton — from visiting Gaza, so he based his findings on "preliminary evidence" that was available.[73]

The Geneva-based U.N. Human Rights Council announced in April that famed South African judge Richard Goldstone, who has been involved in human-rights investigations and prosecutions in South Africa, Yugoslavia and Rwanda, would lead an investigation into the allegations on both sides.[74]

International efforts to promote peace in the region will also focus in the coming months on the steady growth of Israeli settlements, diplomats said. All settlements in Gaza were dismantled in 2005, when Israel withdrew from the area. But despite repeated Israeli commitments to freeze them, settlements in the West Bank and East Jerusalem have grown steadily, reaching a combined population of at least 472,657 by the end of 2008, according to the latest available Israeli figures.[75]

"Illegal settlement activity continues, prejudicing final status negotiations and undermining Palestinians who seek a negotiated peace," U.N. envoy Serry told the Security Council in February. "The approach taken since Annapolis to secure implementation of roadmap commitments to freeze settlement activity, including natural growth, and remove outposts, has not worked. This is a clear challenge that must be addressed," Serry said, adding that in 2008, there were 69 percent more new structures built in settlements than in 2007.[76]

"When the Quartet repeatedly states that Israel must freeze all settlement activity and dismantle all outposts, and the Quartet does not do anything, then the Quartet is marginalizing itself," says Mansour, the Palestinian U.N. observer.

But Israel's Shariv dismisses the settlement concerns as overwrought. "When the Palestinians completely stop the terror, we are going to take a few bulldozers or tractors and soldiers, and we are going to evacuate according to the agreement," he says. Israel "should do a better job" of meeting its commitments on settlements, "but you cannot compare terror to settlements."

Discussion of the future of the settlements almost certainly will be on the agenda in May, when Obama meets for the first time with Netanyahu, Abbas and Egyptian President Hosni Mubarak to discuss new U.S. priorities for the region. Obama and Netanyahu are scheduled to meet May 18.[77]

Palestinians' Role

While Israel's political divisions represent an enormous challenge to international peacemakers, Palestinian disunity — specifically the intense hatred between Fatah and Hamas — seems far more untenable.

International donors have offered to pour billions of dollars into Gaza's reconstruction, but tight Israeli border controls and Quartet restrictions on Hamas prevent the people of Gaza from reaping the benefits. Palestinian leaders demand evidence of good faith from the Israelis on fulfilling their commitments, including freezing settlement activities, easing access to Gaza and pursuit of a Palestinian state. But the Israelis say the Palestinians must prevent militants from firing rockets into Israel.

Talks among Palestinians on a national unity government drag on in a fitful way without result. Palestinian Authority bureaucrats scramble to clean up the West Bank's finances and reform their security forces, only to come under fire from hardliners who either question their competence or say they don't deserve to govern because they are cozying up to Israel. Talks aimed at ensuring a lasting cease-fire between Gaza and Israel have stalled over a Hamas plea for the release of some of the 11,000 Palestinian prisoners — a mix of criminals, alleged terrorists and political prisoners — held in Israeli jails in exchange for the freeing of kidnapped Israeli soldier Shalit.

In early April, nearly two weeks passed without violence in Gaza and southern Israel. But during the previous four-week period, 30 rockets and mortar rounds were launched into southern Israel by Palestinian militants, according to Pascoe, the U.N. undersecretary-general for political affairs. The Israeli military retaliated by carrying out two air strikes on the Gaza Strip.[78]

In addition, the Israeli army reported that a Palestinian ship loaded with explosives had blown up in the vicinity of an Israeli naval vessel in mid-April, though without causing injury to the Israeli ship. Egyptian police seeking to prevent the smuggling of arms into Gaza — whether by underground tunnel, the sea or donkey cart — found nearly 2,000 pounds of explosives along Egypt's border with Gaza, Pascoe reported.

While Palestinian Authority security forces stepped up their activity in the West Bank in April — bearing down on criminal gangs and shutting down a suspected explosives manufacturing lab in the West Bank city of Qalqilia — a Palestinian wielding an axe killed a 13-year-old boy and injured a 7-year-old in the Israeli settlement of Bat Ayin, triggering clashes between Israeli settlers and Palestinians that ultimately was halted only after Israeli military intervention, Pascoe told the U.N. council.

Getty Images/David Silverman

The sprawling Ramot housing development in East Jerusalem is built on land Israel captured from Jordan during the 1967 Six-Day War. Despite repeated Israeli commitments to freeze expansion of such settlements in the West Bank and East Jerusalem, they have continued to grow in recent years — undermining peace talks.

Such violence makes a durable end to the war in Gaza just one of peacemakers' many priorities, Secretary of State Clinton said during her early March visit to the region.

"That can only be achieved if Hamas ceases the rocket attacks. No nation should be expected to sit idly by and allow rockets to assault its people and its territories," she said. "These attacks must stop and so must the smuggling of weapons into Gaza."

There have been recent indications that Hamas leaders may be softening their refusal to participate in the peace process, although probably not enough to fully satisfy the Quartet principles. Hamas leader Khaled Meshal said in early May that the group had made a conscious decision to curtail militants' rocket fire into southern Israel.

"Not firing the rockets currently is part of an evaluation from the movement which serves the Palestinians' interest," he said. "After all, the firing is a method, not a goal."[79]

OUTLOOK

'Mammoth Job'

With so little progress in the Middle East peace process, how can the search for peace emerge headed in the right direction? Much will depend on Sen. Mitchell's recommendations and President Obama's resolve to carry them out, say international diplomats.

AT ISSUE

Did Israel's military action in Gaza make Israel more secure?

YES

Yoaz Hendel
Security and Military Affairs Analyst and Research fellow, Begin-Sadat Center for Strategic Studies Bar-Ilan University, Israel

Written for *CQ Global Researcher*, April 2009

The Israeli operation in Gaza started too late and ended too early. For the past eight years, southern Israeli citizens have been under a continuous rain of rockets from Gaza. Repeated threats of military action have done nothing to deter Gaza terror organizations from strikes on Israeli civilians.

The fighting between the Israel Defense Forces (IDF) and Gaza terrorist groups is different from other conflicts pitting conventional armies against guerrilla groups. Intelligence reports show deep Iranian involvement in Gaza. Right under Israel's nose, Iran has established a foothold with the potential to threaten most IDF southern bases, including major air force facilities.

When the IDF withdrew from Gaza in summer 2005, then-Prime Minister Ariel Sharon warned of a strong reaction to any violation of Israeli sovereignty. But Palestinian groups including Hamas only intensified their attacks.

Last summer, the Israeli government — then led by Ehud Olmert — approved a six-month cease-fire with Gaza despite continued attacks on Israeli civilians. During the cease-fire, intelligence reports warned that the terrorists intended to use new weapons from Iran to alter the power balance in the area. The rockets kept falling, even as Hamas prepared for renewed war with Israel.

Part of any state's responsibility is to protect its citizens. But the IDF, established to provide this protection, was not deployed for this purpose until last December.

The basic assumption for Israel in fighting terror across borders is that its forces will pay a heavy price for attacking. The IDF had assumed since its 2005 withdrawal from Gaza that it risked significant casualties by sending its forces back across the border to fight terror. This assumption had been upheld in the 2006 war between Israel and Hezbollah, when 119 Israeli soldiers and 44 Israeli civilians were killed.

But the decisive military tactics in Gaza forced the terrorists to retreat and go into hiding, with just one Israeli soldier killed by a direct Hamas attack. The IDF was just a step short of absolute victory when the fighting was halted. The Israeli military was on the verge of a historic opportunity to alter the basic conditions that had allowed Hamas to steadily increase its military might.

The Israeli government decision to end the operation was a mistake that will lead us in the near future to another war in Gaza — but this time with a higher price in lives for both Israelis and Palestinians.

NO

Paul Rogers
Global Security Consultant, Oxford Research Group, and Professor of Peace Studies, University of Bradford, United Kingdom

Written for *CQ Global Researcher*, April 2009

Israel's military assault on Gaza had the stated aim of so weakening Hamas' paramilitary capabilities that it could no longer fire unguided rockets into Israeli territory.

As the war began, senior Israeli sources made it clear that the aim extended beyond this, toward destroying Hamas' political and administrative infrastructure in order to weaken and possibly destroy the movement as a functioning entity. The actual conduct of the war suggests that this more extensive operation was indeed being implemented.

Indeed, the war started with a remarkably intensive and sudden air assault in which 88 aircraft attacked 100 targets in under four minutes. The initial assault included an attack on a police graduation ceremony in which 60 people reportedly were killed.

Four hundred more targets were hit during the first week, including numerous police stations and agricultural facilities, government offices and the main campus of the Islamic University.

At the end of the three-week war, the United Nations estimated that 1,300 Gazans had been killed, including 412 children. More than 5,000 people were injured, 4,000 homes were destroyed and 20,000 severely damaged — about 20 percent of the entire housing stock.

Although Hamas' paramilitary was undoubtedly caught by surprise in the initial assault, it reacted very quickly, and most of the personnel went to ground. There was some limited engagement with Israeli ground troops, but for the most part Hamas' military wing recognized the futility of engaging the vastly superior Israeli firepower and escaped with little damage. Rockets continued to be fired into Israel throughout the war. Afterward, Hamas quickly resumed control, returning police and security personnel to the streets and repairing smuggling tunnels to Egypt.

Claims of Israeli attacks on civilians were persistently rebutted by the Israeli Defense Force, but sources within the Israeli Army have recently provided evidence to support the claims. Israel might have expected a strong Arab public reaction to the war, but what was much less expected was considerable antagonism across much of Europe. With Hamas still in control of Gaza and substantially more popular among Palestinians, with rockets still being fired and with Israel losing public support in the wider world, the end result has been counterproductive to Israel's long-term security interests. It may, however, have some impact in persuading Israelis that a state of permanent war is not the best way to ensure the country's long-term survival.

"In spite of all the wars and the difficulties and the rise of extremists on both sides, I still believe that, if there is a decisive political will in Washington, D.C. — and potentially there is one — then . . . a peace deal could be reached between the two sides in a relatively short period of time," says Palestinian U.N. envoy Mansour.

"Honestly I really don't know if it is five minutes before 12, or five past," adds U.N. envoy Serry. "An early engagement of the Americans will be very much needed."

But even then, a deal is likely to remain out of reach for now, diplomats caution. "We face serious difficulties," says EU envoy Otte. "Nobody has really concentrated on the ability of the parties to implement such an agreement."

For example, any deal likely would require the Palestinians to give up the right of refugees to return home to what is now Israel. Its two feuding factions would have to agree to work closely together in governing their new state. At the same time, given the current realities, such a state's economy and security likely would remain heavily dependent on Israel.

Meanwhile, Israel would have to evacuate as many as hundreds of thousands of settlers from the West Bank and East Jerusalem and find a place for them to live and work. It also would have to accept the reality of the Palestinians, former foes, as permanent neighbors and friends.

"It's not something that is done easily," Otte says. "It's not impossible, but it would take years to implement."

Each side also must have the confidence that what it offers will be politically acceptable to its people. Is a new Israeli government capable of delivering on the two-state solution? Is the institutional chaos on the Palestinian side capable of accepting it?

"Both are highly unlikely," laments a veteran Middle East mediator, speaking on condition of anonymity on grounds that his grim view could damage future negotiations. "That is why any kind of significant diplomatic breakthrough at this time — I wish it had happened yesterday — is totally unrealistic." Doing the necessary groundwork, he continues, "is a mammoth job, and it will take time."

With those difficulties in mind, the Israeli approach during the year-long Annapolis discussions was to consider peace talks as only theoretical. The process was aimed at reaching what was referred to as a "shelf agreement" because it would, if reached, be put aside until conditions were right for it to take effect.

Since nothing was changing on the ground, "Prime Minister Olmert said, 'Let's change the sequence. Let's start with negotiation on a final status agreement,' " explains Israel's Shariv. "If we reach an agreement, we'll put it on a shelf. . . . This will show the Palestinians something they can wish for."

But Rashid Khalidi, a prominent U.S. scholar of Arab descent at Columbia University's Middle East Institute, sounds a more urgent note. "Current discussions of whether [to seek] a one-state or a two-state solution . . . have an unrealistic quality at the present moment," says Khalidi. "What has to be devised is how to reverse — very rapidly — the current dynamic, which is a highly inequitable, de facto, one-state solution that looks more and more entrenched — and will become more and more untenable as time goes on."

NOTES

1. "Israeli TV airs Gaza doctor's pleas after children killed," Israel's Channel 10 via YouTube, www.youtube.com/watch?v=OLUJ4fF2HN4.
2. " 'I wept,' Olmert says of death of Gaza children," Reuters, Jan. 23, 2009, www.reuters.com/article/latestCrisis/idUSLN571480.
3. "Agency Says Hamas Took Aid Intended for Needy," *The New York Times*, Feb. 5, 2009, www.nytimes.com/2009/02/05/world/middleeast/05mideast.html?ref=world.
4. "Summary of Rocket Fire and Mortar Shelling in 2008," Intelligence and Terrorism Information Center, Jan. 1, 2009, www.terrorism-info.org.il/malam_multimedia/English/eng_n/pdf/ipc_e007.pdf.
5. "Obama's Speech in Sderot, Israel," *The New York Times*, July 23, 2008, www.nytimes.com/2008/07/23/us/politics/23text-obama.html?ref= politics.
6. "PCHR Contests Distortion of Gaza Strip Death Toll," Palestinian Centre for Human Rights, press release 44/2009, March 26, 2009, www.pchrgaza.org/files/PressR/English/2008/44-2009.html.
7. "Israel challenges Palestinian claims on Gaza death toll," Ynetnews, March 26, 2009, www.ynetnews.com/articles/0,7340,L-3692950,00.html.

8. "Remarks With Israeli Foreign Minister Tzipi Livni: Hillary Rodham Clinton, Secretary of State," Jerusalem, March 3, 2009, U.S. Department of State transcript, www.state.gov/secre tary/rm/2009a/03/119956.htm.

9. Dan Williams, "Israel fends off censure over Gaza civilian deaths," Reuters, Jan. 19, 2009, http://uk.reuters.com/article/usTopNews/idUKTRE50I2LU20090119.

10. Paul Rogers, "Gaza — The Aftermath," Oxford Research Group, January 2009, www.oxfordresearchgroup.org.uk/publications/monthly_briefings/2009/02/gaza-aftermath.html.

11. "Gaza: situation at border crossings 'intolerable,' Ban says," U.N. Department of Public Information, March 10, 2009, www.un.org/apps/news/story.asp?NewsID=30138&Cr=gaza&Cr1=.

12. "Transcript: Obama's interview with Al Arabiya," Al Arabiya News Channel, Jan. 27, 2009, www.alarabiya.net/articles/2009/01/27/65096.html.

13. "Iranian President Stands by Call to Wipe Israel Off Map," *The New York Times*, Oct. 29, 2005, www.nytimes.com/2005/10/29/international/middleeast/29iran.html.

14. Howard Schneider and Glenn Kessler, "Israel Puts Iran Issue Ahead of Palestinians," *The Washington Post*, April 22, 2009, www.washingtonpost.com/wp-dyn/content/article/2009/04/21/AR2009042103998.html?hpid=topnews.

15. "Text of U.S. President George W. Bush's Middle East speech," June 24, 2002, www.bitterlemons.org/docs/bush.html.

16. Robert Pear, "White House Puts Onus on Hamas to End Violence," *The New York Times*, Dec. 28, 2008, www.nytimes.com/2008/12/28/world/middleeast/28diplo.html.

17. Katrin Bennhold, "Leaders of Turkey and Israel Clash at Davos Panel," *The New York Times*, Jan. 29, 2009, www.nytimes.com/2009/01/30/world/europe/30clash.html.

18. See, for example, John J. Mearsheimer and Stephen M. Walt, *The Israel Lobby and U.S. Foreign Policy* (2007).

19. "Israel's U.N. envoy calls Jimmy Carter 'bigot,' " Reuters, April 24, 2008, www.reuters.com/article/politicsNews/idUSN2448131520080425.

20. "A Performance-Based Road Map to a Permanent Two-State Solution to the Israeli-Palestinian Conflict," the Quartet (of the United States, the European Union, the United Nations and Russia), April 30, 2003, www.bitterlemons.org/docs/roadmap3.html.

21. "Declaration of Principles on Interim Self-Government Arrangements," Government of the State of Israel and the P.L.O. Team, Sept. 13, 1993, www.bitterlemons.org/docs/dop.html. Also see "Israel-PLO Recognition: Exchange of Letters between PM Rabin and Chairman Arafat — Sept. 9, 1993," Israel Ministry of Foreign Affairs, www.mfa.gov.il/MFA/Peace+Process/Guide+to+the+Peace+Process/Israel-PLO+Recognition+-+Exchange+of+Letters+betwe.htm.

22. "Text of U.S. President George W. Bush's Middle East speech," *op. cit.*

23. Muammar Qaddafi, "The One-State Solution," *The New York Times*, Jan. 22, 2009, www.nytimes.com/2009/01/22/opinion/22qaddafi.html.

24. Shahar Ilan and Barak Ravid, "Olmert warns of binational state if no peace deal reached," *Haaretz.com*, Sept. 16, 2008, *Haaretz.com*, www.haaretz.com/hasen/spages/1021689.html.

25. "Remarks With Israeli Foreign Minister Tzipi Livni: Hillary Rodham Clinton, Secretary of State," *op. cit.*

26. "Quartet Statement," *London*, Jan. 30, 2006, www.un.org/news/dh/infocus/middle_east/quartet-30jan2006.htm.

27. "Secretary Clinton, Palestinian President Abbas in Ramallah," transcript of joint press conference, March 4, 2009, www.america.gov/st/texttrans-english/2009/March/20090304125709eaifas0.3768885.html?CP.rss=true.

28. "Kofi Annan's speech to the General Assembly," *The Guardian*, Sept. 13, 2002, www.guardian.co.uk/world/2002/sep/13/iraq.united nations1.

29. "Israel's road map reservations," *Haaretz.com*, May 27, 2003, www.haaretz.com/hasen/pages/ShArt.jhtml?itemNo=297230.

30. "Intifada toll 2000-2005," BBC News, Feb. 8, 2005, http://news.bbc.co.uk/2/hi/middle_east/3694350.stm.

31. "The Sharm el-Sheikh Fact-Finding Committee," April 30, 2001, www.al-bab.com/arab/docs/pal/mitchell1.htm.

32. "Secret UN report condemns US for Middle East failures," *The Guardian*, June 13, 2007, www.guardian.co.uk/world/2007/jun/13/usa.israel.

33. Stephen Walt, "What do we do if the 'two-state' solution collapses?" *ForeignPolicy.com*, Feb. 10, 2009, http://walt.foreignpolicy.com/posts/2009/02/10/what_do_we_do_if_the_two_state_solution_collapses.

34. "Settlement population," based on figures obtained from Israel's Central Bureau of Statistics and the Jerusalem Statistical Yearbook, *B'tselem*, www.btselem.org/English/Settlements/Settlement_population.xls.

35. "Statement by Ambassador Susan E. Rice, U.S. Permanent Representative, Middle East Consultations in the Security Council," Feb. 18, 2009, www.usunnewyork.usmission.gov/press_releases/20090218_031.html.

36. See Rogers, *op. cit.*

37. Transcript of press conference by Secretary-General Ban Ki-moon, U.N. headquarters, Feb. 10, 2009, www.un.org/News/Press/docs/2009/sgsm12092.doc.htm.

38. Alvaro de Soto, "Few will thank UN when this war ends," *The Independent*, Jan. 16, 2009, www.independent.co.uk/opinion/commentators/alvaro-de-soto-few-will-thank-un-when-this-war-ends-1380408.html.

39. Hillary Rodham Clinton, "Press Availability at the End of the Gaza Reconstruction Conference," Sharm el-Sheik, Egypt, March 2, 2009, www.state.gov/secretary/rm/2009a/03/119929.htm.

40. "Secretary Clinton, Palestinian President Abbas in Ramallah," *op. cit.*

41. "Hamas's popularity rises after Israel's Gaza war," Reuters, March 9, 2009, www.reuters.com/article/worldNews/idUSTRE52841Q20090309.

42. Yossi Alpher, "Not now," bitterlemons.org, March 2, 2009, www.bitterlemons.org/previous/bl020309ed9.html#isr1.

43. For background, see the following *CQ Researchers*: Peter Katel, "Middle East Tensions," Oct. 27, 2006, pp. 889-912; Nicole Gaouette, "Middle East Peace," Jan. 21, 2005, pp. 53-76; and David Masci, "Prospects for Mideast Peace," Aug. 30, 2002, pp. 673-696.

44. This section is drawn from Reinhard Schulze, *A Modern History of the Islamic World* (2002); Thomas L. Friedman, *From Beirut to Jerusalem* (1989); Ali M. Ansari, *Confronting Iran: The Failure of American Foreign Policy and the Next Great Conflict in the Middle East* (2006); and Walter Laqueur, *A History of Zionism* (2003).

45. See, for example, Daniel Williams, "New Conflicts of Historic Interest Rack the Heart of the Holy Land," *Los Angeles Times*, May 14, 1989, Part 5, p. 2; Joel Greenberg, "Israel's History, Viewed Candidly, Starts a Storm," *The New York Times*, April 10, 1998, p. A8.

46. Figures from Jeremy M. Sharp, author of two Congressional Research Service reports: "Egypt: Background and U.S. Relations," March 26, 2009, and "U.S. Foreign Aid to Israel," Feb. 3, 2009.

47. "Declaration of Principles on Interim Self-Government Arrangements," *op. cit.*

48. "Q & A: Leaving Lebanon," BBC, May 23, 2000, http://news.bbc.co.uk/1/hi/world/middle_east/636594.stm.

49. Jane Perlez and Elaine Sciolino, "High Drama and Hard Talks at Camp David, Against Backdrop of History," *The New York Times*, July 29, 2000, www.nytimes.com/2000/07/29/world/high-drama-and-hard-talks-at-camp-david-against-backdrop-of-history.html.

50. See, for example, Hussein Agha and Robert Malley, "Camp David: The Tragedy of Errors," *The New York Review of Books*, Aug. 9, 2001, www.nybooks.com/articles/14380.

51. "The Mitchell Report," May 4, 2001, www.jewishvirtuallibrary.org/jsource/Peace/Mitchellrep.html.

52. Yoav Peled, "Dual War: The Legacy of Ariel Sharon," *Middle East Report Online*, March 22, 2006, www.merip.org/mero/mero032206.html.

53. Text of U.S. President George W. Bush's Middle East speech, *op. cit.*

54. "Security Council Adopts Resolution Endorsing Road Map Leading Towards Two-State Resolution

of Israeli-Palestinian Conflict," U.N. Security Council press release SC/7924, Nov. 19, 2003, www.un.org/News/Press/docs/2003/sc7924.doc.htm.

55. See, for example, "Bush Says US Not At War With Islam," *Sky News*, Sept. 20, 2006, http://news.sky.com/skynews/Home/Sky-News-Archive/Article/20080641234424.

56. See, for example, Greg Myre, "Envoy in Mideast Peace Effort Says Israel Is Keeping Too Tight a Lid on Palestinians in Gaza," *The New York Times*, Oct. 25, 2005, www.nytimes.com/2005/10/25/international/middleeast/25mideast.html.

57. Greg Myre, "Because of Attacks, Israel Declares Part of Gaza Off Limits," *The New York Times*, Dec. 29, 2005, www.nytimes.com/2005/12/29/international/middleeast/29mideast.html.

58. "Quartet Statement," *op. cit.*

59. "Hamas takes full control of Gaza," BBC, June 15, 2007, http://news.bbc.co.uk/2/hi/middle_east/6755299.stm.

60. "Why They Died: Civilian Casualties in Lebanon during the 2006 War," Human Rights Watch, Sept. 5, 2007, www.hrw.org/en/reports/2007/09/05/why-they-died-0.

61. Laila Bassam, "Lebanon forms unity government with Hezbollah," Reuters, July 11, 2008, www.reuters.com/article/homepageCrisis/idUSL1159875._CH_.2400.

62. Sheryl Gay Stolberg, "Peace? Sure, I'll See What I Can Do," *The New York Times*, Dec. 2, 2007, http://query.nytimes.com/gst/fullpage.html?res=9802E5D61638F931A35751C1A9619C8B63.

63. "Adopting Text on Middle East Conflict, Security Council Reaffirms Support for Annapolis Outcomes, Declares Negotiations 'Irreversible,' " press release SC/9539, U.N. Department of Public Information, Dec. 16, 2008, www.un.org/News/Press/docs/2008/sc9539.doc.htm.

64. "President Obama Discusses Mideast During Visit of Jordan's King Abdullah," CQ Transcriptswire, April 21, 2009, www.cqpolitics.com/wmspage.cfm?parm1=5&docID=news-000003099340.

65. "Efforts to end current Gaza 'impasse' imperative — UN political chief," U.N. News Centre, March 25, 2009, www.un.org/apps/news/story.asp?NewsID=30290&Cr=gaza&Cr1=.

66. U.N. Undersecretary-General for Political Affairs Lynn Pascoe, "Briefing to the Security Council on the Situation in the Middle East," April 20, 2009, http://domino.un.org/UNISPAL.NSF/e872be638a09135185256ed100546ae4/b24712e38d4c2a0a8525759f004bc662!OpenDocument.

67. "Peace with Israel possible, says Syria's Assad," Reuters, March 9, 2009, www.reuters.com/article/worldNews/idUSTRE5281NL20090309.

68. "Background Note: Syria," U.S. Department of State Web site, www.state.gov/r/pa/ei/bgn/3580.htm. Also see "State Sponsors of Terrorism Overview," U.S. Department of State, April 30, 2008, www.state.gov/s/ct/rls/crt/2007/103711.htm.

69. "Remarks With Israeli Foreign Minister Tzipi Livni: Hillary Rodham Clinton, Secretary of State," *op. cit.*

70. Schneider and Kessler, *op. cit.*

71. Jeffrey Heller, "Netanyahu says will negotiate peace with the Palestinians," Reuters, March 25, 2009, www.reuters.com/article/middleeastCrisis/idUSLP254174.

72. "Israel/Gaza: International Investigation Essential," Human Rights Watch, Jan. 27, 2009, www.hrw.org/en/news/2009/01/27/israelgaza-international-investigation-essential.

73. Stephanie Nebehay, "U.N. rights envoy sees Israeli war crimes in Gaza," Reuters, March 20, 2009, www.reuters.com/article/middleeastCrisis/idUSLJ155314.

74. "Richard J. Goldstone Appointed to Lead Human Rights Council Fact-Finding Mission on Gaza Conflict," U.N. Human Rights Council, press release, April 3, 2009, www.unhchr.ch/huricane/huricane.nsf/view01/2796E2CA43CA4D94C125758D002F8D25?opendocument.

75. "Settlement Population," *op. cit.*

76. "The situation in the Middle East, including the Palestinian question," U.N. Security Council, Feb. 18, 2009, http://domino.un.org/UNISPAL.NSF/e872be638a09135185256ed100546ae4/44906205538f760085257562004be029!OpenDocument.

77. See Barak Ravid, "Netanyahu aides fear 'surprise' demands from Obama," *Haaretz.com*, May 2,

2009, www.haaretz.com/hasen/spages/1082144.html.

78. "Briefing to the Security Council on the situation in the Middle East," April 20, 2009, http://domino.un.org/UNISPAL.NSF/e872be638a09135185256ed100546ae4/b24712e38d4c2a0a8525759f004bc662!OpenDocument.
79. Quoted in Taghreed El-Khodary and Ethan Bronner, "Addressing U.S., Hamas says it Grounded Rockets," *The New York Times*, May 5, 2009, p. A5, www.nytimes.com/2009/05/05/world/middleeast/05meshal.html?_r=1&ref=world.

BIBLIOGRAPHY

Books

Hirst, David, *The Gun and the Olive Branch: The Roots of Violence in the Middle East, Nation Books,* 2003.
The Middle East correspondent for the *Manchester Guardian* traces the history of the Israeli-Palestinian conflict from the 1880s through the Sept. 11, 2001, terrorist attacks in the United States.

Indyk, Martin, *Innocent Abroad: An Intimate Account of American Peace Diplomacy in the Middle East, Simon & Schuster,* 2009.
A former U.S. ambassador to Israel dissects the successes and failures of President Bill Clinton's intensive and highly personal pursuit of a peace deal.

Khalidi, Rashid, *Sowing Crisis: The Cold War and American Dominance in the Middle East, Beacon Press,* 2009.
The director of Columbia University's Middle East Institute explores how George W. Bush's global war on terror spilled over into the Middle East.

Kurtzer, Daniel, and Scott Lasensky, *Negotiating Arab-Israeli Peace, United States Institute of Peace Press,* 2008.
A veteran U.S. diplomat and lecturer in Middle Eastern policy at Princeton University's Woodrow Wilson School of Public and International Affairs (Kurtzer) and a researcher at the U.S. Institute of Peace analyze two decades of U.S. peace efforts in the Middle East.

Miller, Aaron David, *The Much Too Promised Land: America's Elusive Search for Arab-Israeli Peace, Bantam,* 2008.
A former adviser on Middle East negotiations to six U.S. secretaries of state (1978-2003) provides a frank, insightful walk through decades of diplomacy in the region.

Oz, Amos, *A Tale of Love and Darkness, Harcourt,* 2004.
An Israeli writer traces his family history from 19th-century Ukraine to the Palestine of the 1930s to Jerusalem in the 1940s and '50s, illuminating some of the human drama leading to Israel's birth.

Tolan, Sandy, *The Lemon Tree: An Arab, A Jew, and the Heart of the Middle East, Bloomsbury,* 2007.
A journalist and producer of radio documentaries views the Middle East crisis through the eyes of two families — one Arab and one Jewish — that lived at different times in a house near Tel Aviv with a lemon tree in its garden.

Articles

"Timeline: Israel, the Gaza Strip and Hamas," *The New York Times*, Jan. 4, 2009, www.nytimes.com/interactive/2009/01/04/world/20090104_ISRAEL-HAMAS_TIMELINE.html.
This interactive Web-based timeline traces the history of Israel and the Gaza Strip from Israel's statehood to the withdrawal of Israeli troops from Gaza on Jan. 21, 2009.

Qaddafi, Muammar, "The One-State Solution," *The New York Times*, Jan. 22, 2009, www.nytimes.com/2009/01/22/opinion/22qaddafi.html.
The Libyan leader argues that Israelis and Palestinians will never find peace until they band together in a single state he calls "Isratine."

Walt, Stephen, "What do we do if the 'two-state' solution collapses?" *ForeignPolicy.com*, Feb. 10, 2009.
A professor of international relations at Harvard University argues that U.S. support for Palestinian statehood makes it sound reasonable and moderate without actually having to do anything to bring about that goal.

Reports and Studies

"Israeli settlements in the Occupied Palestinian Territory, including Jerusalem, and the occupied

Syrian Golan: Report of the Secretary-General," *U.N. General Assembly*, Nov. 5, 2008.
This annual report documents Israeli settlement activity through mid-2008 and recommends steps for both Israel and the Palestinians to comply with international law.

"The Middle East Quartet: A Progress Report," *CARE, Christian Aid, Oxfam, Save the Children Alliance, World Vision, et al.*, Sept. 25, 2008, www.reliefweb.int/rw/rwb.nsf/db900sid/VDUX-7JSSZD.
This report by a consortium of nongovernmental relief organizations finds that the Quartet of international Middle East mediators falls short in addressing an ongoing humanitarian crisis in Palestinian areas.

"The Six Months of the Lull Arrangement," *Intelligence and Terrorism Information Center*, December 2008, www.terrorism-info.org.il/malam_multimedia/English/eng_n/pdf/hamas_e017.pdf.
This report by an Israeli nongovernmental organization documents Palestinian rocket and mortar fire into southern Israel from Gaza during 2008. Includes many color photos and charts.

Migdalovitz, Carol, "Israeli-Arab Negotiations: Background, Conflicts, and U.S. Policy," *Congressional Research Service*, updated March 9, 2009.
A Middle East expert documents decades of efforts to find a peaceful solution to the region's longest-running conflict.

For More Information

American Israel Public Affairs Committee, 440 First St., N.W., Suite 600, Washington, DC 20001; (202) 639-5200; www.aipac.org. Widely known as AIPAC, the leading lobbying group for Israel in the United States.

Bitterlemons.org; www.bitterlemons.org. Presents weekly commentary from both the Palestinian and Israeli point of view on key developments in the Middle East conflict; features a helpful archive of key historic documents dating back to 1947.

B'Tselem, 8 HaTa'asiya St. (4th Floor), P.O. Box 53132, Jerusalem 91531, Israel; (972-2) 673-5599; www.btselem.org/English. Leading Israeli human-rights organization that seeks to document human-rights violations in the occupied territories and to promote the protection of Palestinians' human rights.

Intelligence and Terrorism Information Center, Maj. General Aharon Yariv Blvd., P.O. Box 3555, Ramat Hasharon 47134, Israel; (972-3) 760-3579; www.terrorism-info.org.il/. A private organization focuses on issues linked to terrorism and intelligence; reports available on its Web site on a broad range of related topics including Palestinian policies concerning terrorism, Palestinian groups it considers terrorist groups, terrorism-related activities in other countries including Syria and Iran and global terrorism financing mechanisms.

J Street, Washington, D.C.; (202) 248-5870; http://jstreet.org/. Launched in April 2008; a nongovernmental organization that represents Americans who support both a secure Jewish homeland and a sovereign Palestinian state; advocates strong U.S. leadership to end the Arab-Israeli and Israeli-Palestinian conflicts through diplomatic rather than military means.

Jerusalem Center for Public Affairs, Beit Milken, 13 Tel Hai St., Jerusalem 92107, Israel; (972-2) 561-9281; http://jcpa.org. A private, nonprofit Israeli think tank that focuses on analysis of various global challenges facing Israel, including Islamic extremism and global anti-Semitism. The group's president, Dore Gold, is a close associate of Israel's new prime minister, Benjamin Netanyahu.

Oxford Research Group, Development House, 56-64 Leonard St., London EC2A 4LT; (44-20) 7549-0298; www.oxfordresearchgroup.org.uk. Independent British think tank that promotes nonviolent resolution of international conflicts, with a special focus on the Middle East.

Palestinian Centre for Human Rights, P.O. Box 1328, Gaza City; (972-8) 282-4776 or (972-8) 282-5893; www.pchrgaza.org. Private nonprofit organization dedicated to protecting human rights and promoting the rule of law and democratic principles in the occupied Palestinian territories. It has branch offices in the West Bank town of Ramallah and three in the Gaza Strip.

United Nations, First Avenue at 46th St., New York, NY 10017; (212) 963-1234; www.un.org/english. Supports Middle East programs ranging from economic development and humanitarian aid to human rights, peacekeeping and diplomacy. Its Web site has two main sections devoted to the region, on U.N.-related Middle East news (www.un.org/apps/news/infocusRel.asp?infocusID=22&Body=middle&Body1=east) and on Palestinian programs (http://un.org/Depts/dpa/qpal/).

4

Future of NATO

Is the Transatlantic Alliance Obsolete?

Roland Flamini

AFP/Getty Images/Katja Buchholz

With global energy resources heavily concentrated in countries with unstable or unpredictable governments and terrorism on the rise, protecting energy supplies has become a legitimate security issue. NATO is debating whether its 21st-century mandate should include protecting oil pipelines — like these transporting Russian oil to Germany — and global energy-supply routes, including ocean shipping lanes.

From *CQ Global Researcher*, January 2009.

For weeks, Germany's special forces and Afghan intelligence had been secretly spying on a notorious Taliban commander known only as the Baghlan bomber. They had pieced together his behavior patterns and followed him whenever he left his safe house in northern Afghanistan.

The insurgent leader was linked to a long list of terrorist acts, including the shocking November 2007 raid on the ceremonial reopening of a new sugar factory in Baghlan province, which killed 79 people, including dozens of children and several high-ranking officials and politicians.

Last March, German and Afghan commandos moved in to arrest him. Clad in black and wearing night-vision goggles, they came within a few hundred yards of the house when lookouts raised the alarm. In the ensuing confusion, their quarry got away, though several marksmen had him in their sights.

In fact, said *Der Spiegel*, Germany's most popular news magazine, "It would have been possible for the Germans to kill him," but the notorious terrorist was allowed to escape — and subsequently returned to carry out further attacks.[1] He got away because German troops are among the national contingents serving in Afghanistan with North Atlantic Treaty Organization (NATO) forces who are not allowed to shoot unless they are being fired upon. Troops from France, Italy, Spain, Portugal and several other countries are similarly restricted. Because the Baghlan bomber was fleeing instead of attacking, he could not be shot.

As a result of these "selective participation" policies, most of the casualties among the 50,000 troops serving in the alliance's International Security and Assistance Force (ISAF) in Afghanistan

NATO in Europe Has Doubled in Size

The North Atlantic Treaty Organization (NATO) — the postwar defense alliance that originally linked the United States and Western Europe — now has 26 members, with additional participants from the fragments of the collapsed Soviet Union, including most of Eastern Europe and the Baltic states, making it twice its original size within Europe. In North America, the United States, Canada and Greenland — a self-governing Danish province — are part of NATO. Croatia and Albania are expected to join in April — and possibly Macedonia. Ukraine and Georgia are involved in intense talks with NATO about joining the alliance someday, as are Bosnia and Herzegovina and Montenegro. Although Turkey — on the southern border of the former Soviet Union — had joined the alliance in 1952, NATO's inclusion of Romania, Bulgaria and the three former Baltic states (Lithuania, Latvia, and Estonia) in 2004 brought the alliance smack up against Russia's northern and eastern borders, stirring Kremlin objections.

* West Germany was admitted to NATO prior to German reunification in 1990.

Source: North Atlantic Treaty Organization

are being suffered by U.S., British and Canadian soldiers, who are fully engaged in combat operations against insurgents. The United States has lost 630 troops in its NATO contingent in Afghanistan since 2001, Britain 138 and Canada 106; but Italy had only 13 deaths, Germany 28 and Portugal 2.[2]

The restrictive rules of engagement for some NATO participants reflect the widely divergent views about the alliance's goals in Afghanistan. But the dispute is only one of the many contentious issues plaguing NATO as it celebrates its 60th year at a summit in April. Others include:

• **How best to help Afghanistan** — The United States and Britain see NATO as being engaged in a full-scale conflict against the Taliban insurgency. But most Europeans eschew the idea of achieving a military victory and focus more on helping the Afghan people become self-sufficient in security and democratic governance. The ongoing debate has stymied ISAF's efforts to formulate a unified strategy in Afghanistan and has allowed the Taliban to continue its attacks from within safe havens in Pakistan's largely uncontrolled frontier territory.[3]

• **How to deal with global terrorism** — After the Sept. 11, 2001, terrorist attacks in the United States, NATO responded to President George W. Bush's appeal for support in invading Afghanistan and hunting down 9/11 mastermind Osama bin Laden and his al Qaeda terrorist organization. The Bush administration at first opted to go it alone, but once the Taliban were driven out of Afghanistan, the alliance deployed the ISAF. But European governments generally view terrorists as criminals — rather than as jihadist fighters — and disagree with the Bush administration's declaration of a global "war on terror."[4]

"Europe is not at war," European Union foreign policy chief Javier Solana famously declared dismissively,

U.S. Provides Most Funds, Troops

NATO's 24 European members contributed about half of the alliance's $1.2 trillion budget for military operations in 2007, while the United States alone contributed 45 percent. Most of the money was used for the war in Afghanistan and to maintain NATO troops in Kosovo. NATO doesn't maintain a standing force. Its troops come from the armies of member nations, and all 3.8 million troops in NATO's member countries are considered potentially available for a NATO deployment. The United States maintained 1.3 million troops in its armed forces in 2007, more than twice the amount maintained by Turkey, the NATO member with the second-largest army. Iceland does not maintain an army or contribute to NATO's military budget.

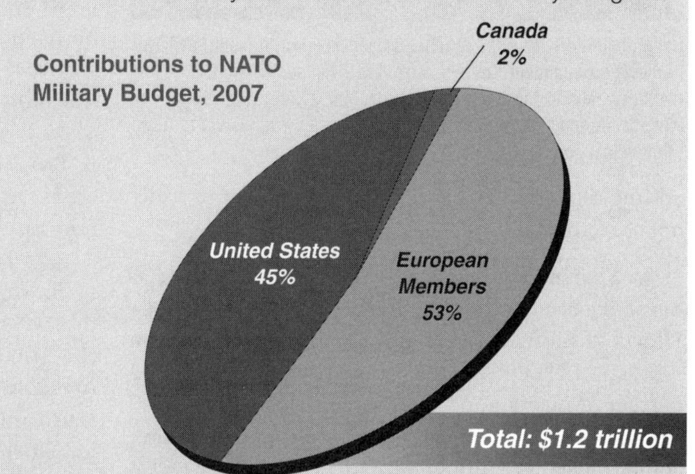

Number of Troops Maintained by NATO Members, 2007
(in thousands)

Country	Troops	Country	Troops	Country	Troops
Belgium	39	Hungary	20	Portugal	41
Bulgaria	41	Iceland	0	Romania	76
Canada	65	Italy	298	Slovakia	18
Czech Republic	25	Latvia	6	Slovenia	7
Denmark	18	Lithuania	10	Spain	132
Estonia	5	Luxembourg	1.6	Turkey	496
France	354	Netherlands	51	United Kingdom	190
Germany	247	Norway	20	United States	1,346
Greece	142	Poland	150	Total:	3,799

Source: North Atlantic Treaty Organization

AFP/Getty Images/Elvis Barukcic

Belgian soldiers from the NATO-led peacekeeping mission (KFOR) in newly independent Kosovo patrol Mitrovica last March. NATO has been monitoring the area since the late 1990s, when the alliance launched air strikes against the former Yugoslavia to halt ethnic cleansing in Kosovo.

adding that Europeans do, however, "energetically oppose terrorism."[5]

• **Sharing the burden** — The United States has borne the brunt of funding and arming NATO, despite efforts to persuade the Europeans to invest more in defense. NATO members promise to earmark at least 2 percent of their annual gross domestic product (GDP) for defense, but over the years many members have come to regard that minimum as a ceiling. (*See graph, p. 85.*)

In fact, while the United States spends 4 percent of its GDP on defense, only five European members — Bulgaria, Britain, France, Greece and Turkey — allocate even 2 percent for defense. Other European governments spend less, in part because of peacetime complacency and the high cost of their social programs. France and Britain accounted for 48 percent of Europe's defense spending in 2008, while Germany — NATO's largest European member — spent only 1.2 percent of its GDP on defense in 2008 (scheduled to increase to 1.4 percent this year through 2012). Overall, NATO's 24 European members have budgeted $280 billion in military expenditures in 2009, but the impact of those expenditures is dissipated since they are spread out over dozens of separate national programs.[6]

The gap between the United States and its European allies in military technology is also widening, making it increasingly difficult for forces to work together. When NATO intervened to prevent ethnic strife in the Balkans in 1998, for instance, only the United States could conduct precision strikes and airborne refueling and had high-tech surveillance and command-and-control systems. And the situation hasn't changed much since then. (*See sidebar, p. 92.*)

• **Selective participation** — During the Cold War, members of the alliance agreed on the threat NATO faced from the Soviet Union and how to address it. While consensus remains the cornerstone of the alliance, in today's more complex, post-Cold War world agreeing on strategy is more difficult, which puts a constant strain on relations. It is generally agreed that if NATO is to survive it must be willing to act "out of area" — or outside of members' territories. Indeed, "out of area or out of business" is a popular refrain at NATO headquarters in Brussels, Belgium, nowadays. Yet European nations are increasingly cautious about committing forces to non-self-defense missions.

As a result, the "coalition of the willing" approach — in which individual members decide which missions they will participate in — has become the norm. Though the alliance dutifully closed ranks in the case of Afghanistan, NATO refused to become involved in the Iraq conflict, even though several alliance members joined the U.S.-initiated attack. And in April 2009, when incoming President Barack Obama is expected to ask U.S. allies to match projected U.S. troop increases in Afghanistan, Europe will probably balk. With both military and civilian deaths rising in Afghanistan, opposition to what Europeans once regarded as the "good" war — as opposed to the "bad" one in Iraq — is increasing in some European countries.

• **NATO enlargement** — After the fall of the Soviet Union, NATO survived — and even grew from 15 members to 26 — because it became "a great tool to transform Cold War countries into democracies," observes Henning Riecke, a security specialist at the German Foreign Policy Institute in Berlin. Former communist states in Eastern Europe and the Baltics were offered membership in the alliance if they became more democratic. Countries like the Czech Republic, Poland and Lithuania eagerly complied, attracted by the implied promise — through NATO — of American protection from their old nemesis Russia.

Too battered economically and politically to protest, the Russians were allowed to participate in the alliance by joining the specially created NATO-Russia Permanent Joint Council, in which Russia has military-observer status in Brussels. But when in 2007 the Bush administration began pressing the alliance to extend membership to Georgia and Ukraine, a newly prosperous, oil-rich Russia began to raise strong objections.

"The emergence of the powerful military bloc at our borders will be seen as a direct threat to Russia's security," Russian Prime Minister Vladimir Putin declared in October 2008, referring to NATO. "I heard them saying . . . that the expansion is not directed against Russia. But it's the potential, not the intention that matters."[7] Led by France and Germany — both heavily dependent on Russian energy supplies — NATO has stalled on admitting Russia's two southern neighbors.

Then last August, Russia's massive incursion into Georgia in response to a botched Georgian bid to invade its separatist province of South Ossetia stirred new fears in Eastern Europe that Moscow might overrun its democratic neighbors in an effort to reclaim the old Soviet empire.[8] President Bush has continued to push for NATO membership for Georgia and Ukraine despite Europe's coolness to the idea, and President-elect Obama supported Georgia's membership during the election campaign.

But perhaps the biggest arguments within NATO today focus on the alliance's future. "The end of the USSR . . . destroyed any rationale for the United States to continue defending Europe," argued Doug Bandow, a former Reagan administration senior policy analyst.[9]

Moreover, Europeans have "a growing lack of enthusiasm for defense spending and far-flung military commitments," says Elizabeth Sherwood-Randall, an expert on alliance relations at the New York-based Council on Foreign Relations think tank.

Allied leaders must do some "careful bricklaying" if NATO is to stay in business for another 60 years — or even 10 more years, says Sherwood-Randall. Until now, they have based their commitments "on past understandings but now need to renew the effort to reach a joint threat assessment, set allied expectations for behavior and prepare militarily for future scenarios."

The problem may be that NATO has too many roles in the 21st century. "Today, three NATOs co-exist," says Riecke. "There's the NATO of the Cold War, there's the exporter of stability to ex-Soviet countries and there's the NATO directed against new threats. East Europeans favor the first NATO because it offers protection from Russia; Western Europeans want the second because it has brought democratic stability; the United States favors the third because of its commitment to the war on terrorism. But which is the real NATO? It's hard to reconcile the three."

To mark its 60th anniversary this April, NATO is updating its strategic concept — a document second in importance only to the alliance's 1949 founding treaty. Alliance officials hope the end product will become the basis for NATO's post-Cold War strategic role — a discussion many believe is long overdue.

With little likelihood of a new war in Europe, the alliance's political and military objectives are expected to continue to concentrate on scenarios that involve NATO action outside of members' territory. Officials also may decide that NATO's goals include protecting the global energy infrastructure, responding to the rise of China and fighting global terrorism.

As NATO member states discuss the future of the alliance, here are some of the questions being debated:

Is NATO obsolete?

"NATO is an interesting paradox because normally alliances disappear when they win the war," says Josef Joffe, publisher-editor of the German intellectual weekly *Die Zeit* and a highly respected specialist on defense issues. "Yet this one is still alive for all the old reasons. You want to be allied to the United States because the United States is a kind of security lender of last resort. You never know what might happen, especially with Russia coming back, point No. 1.

"Point No. 2, NATO is the most important thing that stands between us and the renationalization of our defense policies" — that is, the return to nationalism in Europe, which he argues has historically led to weapons escalations and eventually to conflict.[10]

The debate over whether the North Atlantic Alliance should remain in existence has been going on since the Soviet Union — the threat that sparked NATO's creation — collapsed in 1991.

American critics of the alliance argue that NATO no longer serves any strategic purpose yet ties up U.S. troops, financially burdens the United States and alarms and alienates Russia. In addition, some Americans say that

AFP/Getty Images

AP Photo/Allauddin Khan

Death and Rebuilding

Residents of Afghanistan's Helmand province display the bodies of some of the 17 civilians they say were killed by misguided U.S. or NATO air strikes on Oct. 16, 2008. NATO's International Security Assistance Force (ISAF) said reports of enemy air strikes in the region that day make it difficult to determine what happened. At least 321 Afghan civilians were killed in air strikes in 2007 — three times as many as in the previous year — feeding Afghan resentment toward U.S. and NATO forces. To avoid such unintended consequences, some European governments promote non-military "soft" power, such as the work provided by NATO's Provincial Reconstruction Teams (PRTs). An Afghan military official, (below, left) and a Canadian ISAF member (right) inaugurate a road-building project funded by the Canadian Provincial Reconstruction Team in Kandahar province, in April 2008.

reliance on the U.S.-led organization discourages Europe from assuming responsibility for its own defense.

"NATO has become absurd in the post-Cold War world, with global warming and food shortages transcending the antiquated security notions associated with armies," Saul Landau, a fellow at the Institute for Policy Studies, a liberal Washington think tank, wrote recently.[11]

With Albania and Croatia about to join NATO, "It's not clear against whom these countries need to be defended. It's even less clear why America should do the defending," says Bandow, the former Reagan analyst.[12]

A conservative American critic of NATO, E. Wayne Merry, said U.S. domination of the North Atlantic Alliance, with the Europeans relegated to junior partner roles, has stunted Europe's growth by preventing "the evolution of European integration to include full responsibility for continental security." Merry, a former senior U.S. State Department and Pentagon official and now a senior associate at the American Foreign Policy Council in Washington, contends that, "The growth of European identity and European integration makes this approach obsolete."[13]

Advocates of preserving NATO point out that it embodies multilateralism in an increasingly interdependent world. "Bush quickly discovered [in Iraq] that unilateralism didn't work, and when NATO let him down, he had to create an ad hoc NATO of his own," observes Massimo Franco, a leading political commentator and columnist at the Italian paper *Corriere della Sera.* Bush's so-called coalition of the willing in Iraq fell apart, he says, "because it didn't have the underpinnings of a true alliance."

Or, as Riecke of the German Foreign Policy Institute points out, "Only NATO is capable of mustering the forces for a very complex operation; no other organization can do it. NATO is the stability actor in Europe."

Responding to a proposal by Russian President Dmitry A. Medvedev that NATO consider a new "security architecture" for Europe, NATO Secretary General Jaap de Hoop Scheffer of the Netherlands said in early December that NATO members are "quite happy" with the existing security structure in Europe and that there is "not a shimmer of a chance that . . . NATO could or would be negotiated away."[14]

NATO is also a built-in customer for the multibillion-dollar U.S. weapons industry, and American arms manufacturers are avid supporters of NATO expansion. NATO expansion into Eastern Europe and the Baltic nations has been a boon for weapons sales.[15] The boom began in the 1990s, when former Soviet states wishing to join the alliance were required to modernize their armed forces. Many replaced their dated Soviet arms with new Western weapons.[16]

As the number of new NATO countries has increased, arms sales have kept pace. In 2006, U.S.

government-to-government arms sales were valued at $16.9 billion, including $6.6 billion with NATO countries and Japan and the balance to developing countries. By 2008, the overall amount of such transactions had almost doubled, to $32 billion, with the United States capturing 52 percent of the world arms market.[17] These numbers do not include private arms sales to different countries by U.S. companies without government involvement — rare in the case of major sales of combat hardware. Such sales are impossible to calculate with any accuracy.

Polish Foreign Minister Radek Sikorsky says the downside of dismantling NATO far outweighs any advantages. He identifies five reasons for keeping NATO in existence:

- The transition costs "would be problematic," he says. U.S. withdrawal from NATO would deprive the European economy of billions of dollars, not counting the cost of extracting and relocating the U.S. troops.
- With no power to check them, Germany and France would dominate Europe, which other countries would dread — especially Eastern and Central European countries like Poland.
- As a full-fledged power with a bigger population and economy than the United States, Europe would begin to see itself more as a competitor with America, especially with the U.S. arms industry. And once "divorced" from the United States, Europe could align itself with other powers. "A Europe with its own independent military capability will more frequently say 'no' to America" on a wide range of international issues, Sikorsky says.
- If the United States and Europe subsequently had to fight alongside each other, "they would no longer be a workable coalition," he says. "Pretty soon, they would be working to reinvent NATO."

Should energy security become a new NATO responsibility?

European members of NATO import 50 percent of their energy needs — 25 percent of it from Russia. Thus, as demand rises for oil and gas, and with much of the world's energy resources in countries with unstable or unpredictable governments, energy has become a legitimate security issue.[18]

In 2006, a NATO forum on energy-security technology was told that the global oil market loses a million barrels a day to politically motivated sabotage.[19] Later that year at a NATO summit in Riga, Latvia, alliance leaders decided to add energy security to its agenda.

"Alliance security interests can also be affected by the disruption of the flow of vital resources," said the summit's final declaration. "We support a coordinated, international effort to assess risk to energy infrastructure and to promote energy infrastructure security." Member states were charged to "consult on the most immediate risks in the field of energy security."[20]

Precedents for protecting member states' energy supplies date back to the Cold War, when NATO created and maintained 10 storage and distribution facilities across Europe, primarily for military use. During the Iran-Iraq War in the 1980s, NATO ships protected Saudi Arabian and Gulf state oil tankers from attack by either side in case they tried to cut off supplies to the West. And in 1990, although NATO did not participate as an organization in the first Gulf War, France, Italy, Britain and the Netherlands joined the United States in liberating Kuwait from Iraqi occupation — thus ensuring that Kuwait retained its oil fields.

The alliance has yet to make public any plan of action, but analysts say NATO could help protect energy sources, including oil fields, pipelines and sea routes used for transporting unrefined oil — especially vital sea routes like the Panama and Suez canals and the straits of Hormuz in the Persian Gulf and Malacca between Malaysia and Indonesia. Terrorist attacks on these strategic routes would have drastic consequences for energy supplies. Moreover, pipelines deliver 40 percent of the oil and gas to world markets and are even more susceptible to terrorist action.[21]

The idea of expanding NATO's tasks to include protecting global energy supplies has its problems. For example, guarding the thousands of miles of pipelines carrying Russian oil and gas across Central Asia and the Caucasus, if it were even possible, could lead to tension with the Russians.

The size of the undertaking is daunting. "NATO cannot really protect pipelines, but it can control the maritime 'choke' points where traffic is heavy, such as the Gulf, and key drilling points," observes Riecke at the German Foreign Policy Institute. The involvement of an

NATO Troop Levels in Afghanistan Jumped Sixfold

Over 51,000 NATO troops are serving in the war in Afghanistan — more than a sixfold jump over 2004 levels. About 40 percent of the NATO troops are Americans. Another 12,000 Americans are serving in the U.S.-led coalition in Afghanistan. President-elect Barack Obama has vowed to send additional U.S. troops and is expected to ask NATO countries to deploy more troops as well.

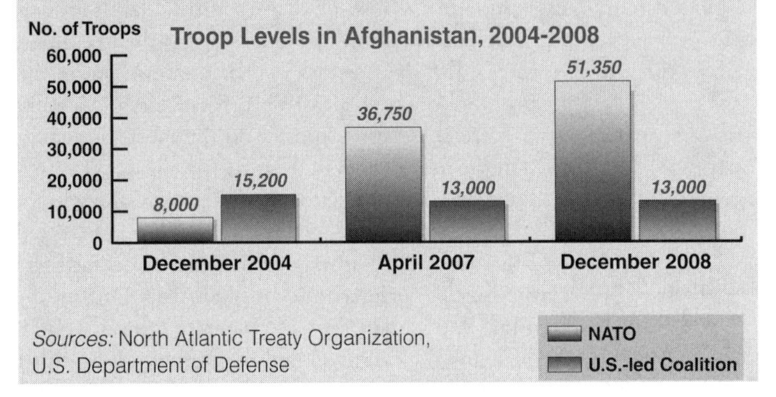

Sources: North Atlantic Treaty Organization, U.S. Department of Defense

essentially Western alliance in global energy security could make other countries feel uneasy as well. For example, an energy role would extend NATO's reach into Asia, and the Chinese will almost certainly object, he says.

In addition, argues Turkish commentator and oil executive Sohbet Karbuz, if NATO deploys in Gulf waters, non-NATO countries might decide to do the same, adding to regional tensions. "What if China now wants to patrol the Strait of Hormuz?" asks Karbuz. "After all, China imports more oil from the region than the United States or the European Union."

Can NATO effectively address international terrorism?

On Sept. 12, 2001, less than 24 hours after terrorists attacked the World Trade Center and the Pentagon, NATO invoked Article 5 of the alliance charter, which commits all members to aid any member that is attacked. Thus the first time the article came into play was not against the Soviet Union — for whom it was originally intended — but against jihadist terrorists.

In 2002, at a summit in Prague, Czech Republic, NATO retroactively included antiterrorism as "a permanent agenda item and priority for the alliance," according to NATO.[22] Leaders recognized the challenge of international terrorism as a new role for the alliance, even though there was no consensus among members about the nature of the threat and how to deal with it.

Former Spanish Prime Minister José María Aznar even calls on NATO to break out of its transatlantic mold and become a global antiterrorist force. NATO needs what he calls a "bold transformation . . . to build a "strategic [antiterrorist] partnership," he says. He would like to see the alliance open its doors to Japan, Australia and Israel in order "to better reflect the nations that are willing and able to cooperate in eliminating the threat of Islamist terror."[23]

Although the alliance has not taken Aznar's advice, it did launch a major antiterrorist program, including developing expertise in detecting chemical, biological and nuclear weapons and establishing specialist teams to deal with the after-effects of such attacks. An alliance-wide, fail-safe cyber system to protect the NATO computer network from terrorist hackers has also been implemented. And in 2004, NATO agreed to establish a Terrorism Threat Intelligence Unit to analyze and distribute terrorist intelligence throughout the alliance.[24]

Since 9/11, NATO has also carried out Operation Active Endeavour to "detect and deter" terrorist activity in the Mediterranean, through which 65 percent of Europe's oil and gas imports pass.[25] The continuous maritime surveillance operation escorts oil supertankers and other ships and inspects ships on the high seas, looking for illegally transported nuclear materials. The operation was initially limited to the eastern Mediterranean but in 2004 was extended to cover the entire Mediterranean.

In 2004, NATO provided Greece with a massive, protective blanket — in the form of navy patrols and air surveillance — around Athens and other Summer Olympics venues to protect the games from terrorists. In 2006, NATO did the same for the Soccer World Cup in Germany. But militarily NATO's biggest antiterrorist engagement to date has clearly been Afghanistan, where nearly all member states are deployed.

"NATO has brought essential value to the fight against terrorism, and Afghanistan is the best example of this," says Secretary General de Hoop Scheffer.

It is widely agreed that NATO needs to succeed in Afghanistan if its role in the fight against terrorism is to have credibility. "The mission is vital for NATO," says Bastian Giegerich, a research fellow on European Security at the London-based International Institute of Security Studies. "If the alliance fails in Afghanistan, its appetite to engage in that kind of operation will become very limited."

But the strong differences that persist over how the International Security and Assistance Force should approach its mission in Afghanistan are seen as fundamental flaws in NATO's commitment. Rather than defeating the Taliban and al Qaeda, Europeans generally perceive ISAF's role as "counterinsurgency coupled with helping to improve governance," says Giegerich. Europeans focus on beefing up the effectiveness of Afghan troops and police and strengthening democratic institutions.

Germany's Gen. Egon Ramms, until recently overall commander of ISAF operations in Afghanistan, defined NATO's role in Afghanistan as "to help the people of the country . . . protect the Afghan people" against insurgents.[26]

Britain, Canada and the Netherlands — on the other hand — follow the U.S. approach, which entails armed engagement with the insurgents. The result of this double standard, as an unnamed Pentagon consultant told the *London Daily Telegraph*, is "frustration [and] irritation. . . . The mistake was handing it over to NATO in the first place. For many countries being in Afghanistan seems about keeping up appearances, rather than actually fighting a war that needs to be won."[27]

What does not seem in dispute throughout the alliance is that NATO should be involved in the war on terror. But as U.S. Army Gen. Bantz John Craddock, NATO's supreme commander, says, "Each NATO nation has its own internal issues that it must address."

On the other hand, he added, "a completely resourced force sends a clear message to our adversary . . . that NATO is committed to achieving success."

AFP/Getty Images/Bill Pugliano

A military funeral is held for U.S. Army Pfc. Joseph A. Miracle, 22, on July 14, 2007, in Waterford, Mich. He was one of the 630 Americans killed during NATO operations in Afghanistan since 2001. About 60 percent of the NATO's casualties in Afghanistan have been Americans, followed by British and Canadian forces. German, French, Italian and other NATO troops are only allowed to shoot in self-defense, so their troops are not stationed in heavy combat areas.

BACKGROUND

Internal Differences

Differences over Afghanistan are hardly the first time NATO members have run into internal dissent. In fact, the alliance's 60-year history is full of spirited debates, but all of them have been peacefully overcome — a testament to the institution's resilience and adaptability. Meanwhile, the fact that the Soviet Union never attacked defines NATO's success as a mutual defense alliance between the United States and Western Europe.

At the start of the alliance's often querulous existence, NATO's first secretary general, Britain's Lord Ismay, said the alliance was designed "to keep Russia out, the Germans down and the Americans in."

Technology Gap Separates U.S. and NATO Forces

Combat interoperability is still a long way off.

Working together effectively in combat has always been a key objective of the North Atlantic Treaty Organization (NATO). So far, however, so-called interoperational cooperation among NATO allies remains more an earnest desire than military reality.

A wide technology gap exists not only between the United States and Eastern Europe's armed forces, which for the most part are still switching from Soviet-era arms to Western versions, but also with its more modern Western European allies.

The gap is partly a legacy of the Cold War, when Europeans were forced to concentrate on defensive equipment against a possible invasion, such as armor and heavy artillery, while the United States — worried more about a long-distance war on another continent — devoted more resources to long-range air transport and missile development.

During the Balkan conflict in the 1990s, the Europeans suddenly realized that without U.S. support they could never have sustained their participation in the conflict. The Americans carried out 75 percent of the combat and support sorties and fired 95 percent of the cruise missiles and other precision-guided devices. Americans also had the only satellite-supported system that guides so-called "smart" bombs and tactical missiles. The U.S. Air Force also had several hundred aircraft equipped with electronic systems that protect planes from enemy air-defense systems and can perform in-flight refueling.[1]

In recent years Europe's aircraft industry has been closing the technology gap. NATO forces began using German-made in-flight refueling aircraft in 2004. But completion of a European-made equivalent of the U.S. C-17 Globemaster military transport, originally due for delivery in late 2008, has been delayed more than a year due to production hold-ups.

As for high-tech combat, Europeans are far from becoming interoperational with their U.S. counterparts because they lag behind in technology. In Iraq and Afghanistan U.S. forces use spy satellites, airborne intelligence-gathering units and software that analyzes combat options — all linked via satellite to troops on the ground.

However, all this precision technology hasn't always been able to avoid killing Afghan civilians, and NATO's image has suffered badly as a result. Yet, without U.S. involvement, the Europeans could not conduct such modern warfare. Experts also say Europe's annual $150 billion defense expenditures would be more effective if they were pooled. But Europeans find collective decision-making difficult.

Once Russia was out and Germany was no longer regarded as a threat to European peace, many predicted NATO would dissolve. The alliance has done just the opposite, evolving into an expanded security and peacekeeping organization. And its aggressive recruitment effort across Central and Eastern Europe has resulted in a doubling in the alliance's size in Europe.

When NATO was formed in 1949, a shattered, vulnerable postwar Europe still sought a continued U.S. presence, both out of fear of a possibly resurgent Germany and as protection from the often unpredictable Soviet Union. The Soviets had at least 700,000 troops capable of overrunning Western Europe. European poverty made Moscow-backed communist parties attractive — posing a viable political threat to take power democratically. Fearing that if Moscow somehow took control of industrial Europe it could threaten U.S. interests and even the United States itself, Washington pumped billions of dollars into shattered European economies (through the massive Marshall Plan), and committed itself to the defense of Europe through NATO.[28]

The original signatories of the NATO treaty were Belgium, Denmark, France, Iceland, Luxembourg, the Netherlands, Norway, Canada, Portugal, Italy, the United Kingdom and, of course, the United States. (*See map, p. 84.*) The French, seeking greater influence, were difficult partners from the start. "The French attitude seems pretty hopeless: they still fear the Germans and still want our money, but not our advice," U.S. Navy Adm. Forrest Sherman complained in his diary in 1950.[29]

But there were other strains as well. In 1950 Sherman warned British negotiators that the United States might

European NATO members also spend a smaller percentage of their income on defense than the United States. Although under NATO rules all members vow to spend at least 2 percent of their gross domestic product (GDP) on defense, most European members now treat the 2 percent minimum as a ceiling instead, spending about 1.4 percent of their GDPs on defense. The United States spends about 4 percent of its GDP on defense.

American critics of NATO say that with a productive population of 445 million and a combined GDP of about $11 trillion, Europeans can afford to look after themselves militarily. But by spending less on defense — and refusing to pool their resources on most joint projects — the Europeans create resentment across the Atlantic about the unfair financial burden borne by the United States. The situation also undermines efforts to create a common defense policy within the military organization.

Aside from technological coordination issues, basic cooperation also needs to improve among the allies. "Considerations of competition and security, proliferation fears and numerous laws, especially on the U.S. side, often still obstruct the path toward a joint allied 'plug and fight' architecture," wrote German security specialist Henrik Enderlein.[2]

Coordinating the alliance's military efforts bogs down for two other key reasons, according to Dag Wilhelmsen, manager of NATO's Consultation and Command and Control Agency, which strives to increase interoperability. The greatest challenge, he said, "is the desire of individual nations to safeguard information and technology from their allies." It is also difficult to bring together systems "designed to address national needs, which often differ widely among member nations."[3]

AP Photo/Sr. Airman Julianne Showalter

A helicopter is loaded aboard a huge U.S. C-17 Globemaster military transport plane. Europe's NATO members rely on U.S. cargo planes as they try to close the military technology gap between U.S. and other NATO forces.

[1] Hendrik Enderlein, "Military Interoperability," *IP Internationale Politik*, www.ip-global.org/archiv/2002/winter2002/military-interoperability.html.

[2] *Ibid.*

[3] Quoted in Robert Ackerman, "In NATO, technology challenges yield to political interpolarity handles," *Signal Communications*, Jan. 17, 2006, www.imakenews.com/signal/e_article000509437.cfm?x=b11,0,w.

change its mind about joining NATO if London didn't withdraw its insistence on appointing a British supreme commander over the U.S. fleet in the Mediterranean. The British "demanded exclusive control in the Mediterranean of our fleet plus their odds and ends," Sherman fumed.[30]

By 1952, the alliance had expanded to include Greece and Turkey. In 1955, after a long debate, West Germany was allowed to re-arm and was brought into the pact. The Soviets responded by forming the Warsaw Pact alliance with seven Eastern and Central European satellite states.

Guarding the Gap

NATO's anti-Soviet line of defense extended from the Turkish border with Russia in the south to Norway in the north. But the major threat was in divided Germany, where watchful U.S. and European forces were concentrated along the Fulda Gap in the Bavarian mountains, which created a natural divide between communist East Germany and the West German Federation. In the event of hostilities, it was there on the broad, flat plain that a potential Soviet tank invasion was most likely.

In 1952, NATO members agreed to deploy 100 divisions within two years. But by 1954 it was obvious that the alliance didn't have the economic strength or the political will to achieve that target. In any case, by 1953 the United States had begun deploying strategic nuclear weapons at friendly bases in Europe, and Washington — and eventually NATO — opted for a strategy of massive retaliation in defense of Europe, which entailed the almost exclusive use of nuclear weapons regardless of the size and nature of the attack. By the late 1950s, Moscow also

CHRONOLOGY

1940s *The North Atlantic Treaty Organization (NATO) emerges as an alliance of democracies in Europe and North America.*

1945 World War II ends.

1949 Twelve Western countries sign the North Atlantic Treaty, promising mutual defense.

1950s-1960s *NATO deploys forces along Iron Curtain to prevent Soviet attack on Western Europe*

1950 U.S. Gen. Dwight D. Eisenhower becomes first NATO commander.

1952 Greece and Turkey join NATO.

1955 West Germany joins NATO; Soviet Union and seven Eastern European states form the Warsaw Pact.

1966 France withdraws from NATO's military structure, evicts NATO troops.

1967 NATO headquarters moves from Paris to Brussels. NATO agrees to work to improve East-West relations.

1970s-1980s *U.S. and Soviet Union negotiate on nuclear arms control. Soviets invade Afghanistan.*

1972 Interim arms limitation and anti-ballistic missile treaties are signed.

1979 NATO deploys medium-range missiles — but continues arms-control diplomacy — after Moscow deploys intermediate-range nuclear missiles aimed at Western Europe. . . . Soviets invade Afghanistan.

1982 Spain joins NATO.

1990s *Soviet Union collapses; Warsaw Pact dissolves. East European nations begin joining NATO. Alliance launches its first military operation.*

1991 Soviet Union collapses; Warsaw Pact dissolves.

1995 NATO flies 3,515 missions to defend civilians in Bosnia from Serb attacks and . . . deploys troops to enforce cease-fire in Bosnia.

1999 Hungary, Czech Republic, Poland become first former Soviet-bloc states to join NATO. . . . Alliance launches air strikes against Yugoslavia to halt ethnic cleansing in Kosovo.

2000-Present *NATO continues eastward expansion, deploys troops in Afghanistan. Members debate NATO's 21st-century role.*

2001 NATO declares the Sept. 11 terrorist attack on the United States an attack on all NATO members. U.S.-led coalition — including some NATO members — attacks Taliban and al Qaeda in Afghanistan.

2002 NATO-Russia Council is launched, allowing joint consultations.

2003 NATO deploys forces to Kabul, its first major operation outside Europe.

2004 Estonia, Latvia, Lithuania, Bulgaria, Romania and Slovakia join NATO.

2005 NATO enlarges its force in Afghanistan.

2006 NATO takes over from U.S.-led coalition in southern Afghanistan.

2007 Many European governments limit their troops in Afghanistan to self-defensive actions.

2008 At summit in Bucharest, Romania, NATO puts off U.S. request for immediate membership for Georgia and Ukraine but endorses American plan to deploy missile shield in Poland and Czech Republic. In August, Russia invades Georgia after surprise Georgian attack on separatist South Ossetia. NATO condemns Russia's "disproportionate" use of force. In December, NATO agrees to delay Georgia and Ukraine membership. To counter U.S. missile plan, Russian President Dmitry A. Medvedev vows to deploy intermediate-range missiles in Kaliningrad in 2009.

April 2009 NATO holds 60th-anniversary summit in Strasbourg, France.

had developed intercontinental ballistic missiles, making the United States itself vulnerable to nuclear attack.[31]

It took NATO nearly a decade of debate to develop and adopt a new, more rational, defensive approach — so-called flexible response. President John F. Kennedy outlined the strategy in 1962, but it didn't become official NATO policy until five years later. It relied on a sequence of three escalating responses: conventional, tactical nuclear and strategic nuclear. The first involved conventional defense against attack, also called direct defense. If that failed, tactical nuclear weapons (short-range missiles for use on the battlefield) were to be used to force the attacker to stop the conflict and withdraw from NATO territory. The third line of defense was a strategic nuclear response using intercontinental rockets, which shifted the focus of the conflict from the European battlefield to a direct U.S.-Soviet nuclear confrontation.

Flexible response worried Washington's European allies because it "decoupled" the United States from the conflict until the third option. They felt the United States would be prepared to brave Soviet retaliation as a last resort, after Europe had taken a lot of punishment. In fact, U.S. strategists did envision a long conventional war before moving to the second option.[32] Meanwhile, several efforts were made to integrate U.S. and European forces, such as the U.S.-proposed Multilateral Force of the early 1960s. The 25-ship seaborne force was to be equipped with 200 Polaris ballistic missiles, manned by European sailors from NATO powers under U.S. control. But NATO member states had no enthusiasm for mixed crews, and the project was quietly dropped.

France Pulls Out

In 1966, French President Charles de Gaulle pulled France out of NATO's military command structure, complaining that France had been relegated to a secondary role in the alliance. At de Gaulle's insistence, NATO's headquarters moved from Paris to Brussels.

France's departure reflected internal uncertainties about NATO's continued role, especially given that the Soviets had never invaded. East-West tension began to relax, and the alliance began to broaden its political role. In 1967, NATO adopted recommendations from a report by Belgian Foreign Minister Pierre Harmel that its future military posture combine defense and détente. In other words, defense programs were to be combined with efforts to establish better relations with the Soviet Union and its Eastern European satellites.

The decision would greatly influence NATO in subsequent years.[33] At the time, some member states were improving their bilateral relations with Moscow. The Harmel Report helped reconcile the different diplomatic approaches of the American and European leaders in the face of the Soviet challenge. It also eventually led to NATO-Soviet negotiations beginning in 1973 to reduce ground forces in Central Europe — the Mutual and Balanced Force Reduction talks, and to the Conference on Security and Cooperation in Europe in 1975.

In the late 1970s the Soviet Union introduced the medium-range SS-20 missile, capable of carrying nuclear warheads to European cities. NATO responded in the early 1980s with a "dual track" strategy: plans to deploy 108 U.S.-supplied Pershing II missiles and 462 ground-launched cruise missiles in Europe while pressuring Moscow to negotiate the mutual removal of medium-range arsenals from Europe.

What quickly became known as Euromissiles stirred strong public opposition, with violent protests breaking out in West Germany and Italy. Meanwhile, Moscow worked hard to open a rift between the United States and its European allies. Ailing Soviet leader Leonid Brezhnev flew to Bonn in an attempt to persuade Chancellor Helmut Schmidt to reject the American missiles. However, faced with a critical test of the alliance's political resolve and cohesion, European governments stood firm.

Enlarging NATO

After the collapse of the Soviet Union in 1991, NATO began expanding its membership to include former Soviet satellite countries, starting with Poland, Hungary and the Czech Republic in March 1999, followed by Bulgaria, Romania, Estonia, Lithuania, Latvia, Slovakia and Slovenia in 2004.

Aspiring nations were required to show progress towards democratization and improve their military effectiveness. NATO enlargement thus became a catalyst for quick change in the former communist states, under close Western guidance. Eastern Europeans and the Baltic nations, still nervous about the intentions of their Russian neighbor, welcomed NATO's (i.e. America's) protective shield.

"What we're doing here is hoping for the best and creating the conditions for the best but also being prepared for the possibility of Russia's reasserting itself," President Bill Clinton told members of Congress on

NATO-Russia Relations Are Strained

Alliance enlargement and U.S. missile defense system alarm Russia.

When the Russian missile frigate *Pytlivy* steamed into the Mediterranean in the summer of 2006, it was reversing history. Twenty years earlier, the presence of a Soviet vessel in the area would have triggered alarm bells at NATO's Sixth Fleet headquarters in Naples, Italy.

But that was then. The *Pytlivy* was reporting for duty as the first unit of the Russian Navy to take part in Operation Active Endeavour, NATO's permanent, post-9/11 counterterrorist patrol in the Mediterranean.[1]

Russian participation in Active Endeavour is one of the initiatives of the NATO-Russia Permanent Joint Council, an outgrowth of the cooperation agreement signed in 1997 by President Bill Clinton and President Boris Yeltsin to deepen and widen the scope of bilateral relations and — not incidentally — to offset the largely negative impact of NATO's decision to admit former Soviet republics and satellites into the alliance.[2] By participating in the council, Moscow has maintained a permanent presence at NATO headquarters and a military office at the alliance's military command headquarters since 2002. The council normally consists of military and diplomatic representatives from Russia and all 26 NATO members, but if the occasion calls for it, higher-ranking officials — up to heads of government — can participate in meetings.

Since creation of the council, NATO and Russia have initiated a slew of wide-ranging bilateral programs, including improvements in military-to-military interoperability (designed to enable respective armed forces to work together in joint military operations), cooperation in submarine-crew search and rescue and Active Endeavour. The Russians have also cooperated with NATO on counternarcotics operations, such as anti-drug training for Central Asian and Afghan personnel.[3]

In the 1990s, an economically weak Russia had been in no position to effectively oppose the earlier enlargements, but by 2000, enriched and emboldened by oil and gas exports, Russia began to draw the line. President — more recently Prime Minister — Vladimir Putin has raised strong objections, and President Dmitry A. Medvedev told the *Financial Times*, "No state can be pleased about having representatives of a military bloc to which it does not belong coming close to its borders."[4]

Col.-Gen. Nikolai Pishchev, first deputy-chief of the Russian general staff, took the same approach in the military newspaper *Krasnaya Zvezda*: "How would the public and government of any self-respecting state react to the expansion in the immediate proximity of its borders of what is already the world's biggest politico-military alliance? I believe that both the leadership and the citizens of that country would be quite skeptical of any assurances of the purely peaceful character of such an alliance, and Russia in this sense is certainly no exception from the general rule."[5]

The NATO-Russian relationship survived and developed "even though Moscow's foreign policy from 2003 onward became more independent and assertive, and Russian relations with NATO began to sour," wrote Dmitri Trenin, senior associate at the Carnegie Institute for Peace in Moscow.[6]

But despite Russian protests, NATO continued to expand. In 2003 the three remaining Soviet satellites — Romania, Bulgaria and Slovakia — and the former Soviet republics of Latvia, Lithuania and Estonia joined NATO. The Bush administration was also pushing the candidacy of Georgia and Ukraine on Russia's southern border.

The Russians call their immediate neighbors the "near abroad" and consider them part of their sphere of influence. Indeed, Russia has been meddling in the politics of both Georgia and Ukraine ever since their independence in 1992. In the case of Georgia, Russia has backed militarily the separatist provinces of Abkhazia and South Ossetia. In Ukraine, Moscow backed candidates acceptable to the large Russian-speaking minority and even allegedly tried to fix the elections.

At a security conference in Munich in 2007, then-President Putin famously suggested that NATO's eastward expansion was directed against Russia. "NATO's expansion does not have any relation with the modernization of the alliance itself or ensuring security in Europe," Putin told an audience of defense officials and specialists that included U.S. Defense Secretary Robert Gates. "On the contrary, it represents a serious provocation that reduces the level of natural trust. And we have the right to ask: Against whom is this expansion intended?"[7]

NATO was divided over admitting Georgia, with Germany and France questioning the wisdom of accepting into the alliance a country with an unresolved territorial dispute. Then in August 2008 Russian troops invaded Georgia, sweeping aside the Georgian army and advancing across the country to the Black Sea port of Poti.[8] The Russians said they were reacting to a pre-emptive strike by Georgia on South Ossetia — which Georgian President Mikheil Saakashvili acknowledged in December. He said he had ordered the August attack in self-defense because of a build-up of Russian armor and troops on the Georgian border, which he believed could only mean that Moscow planned to invade his country.[9]

On Aug. 13, five days after Russian troops invaded, a cease-fire was brokered by French President Nicolas Sarkozy, then president of the European Union. NATO denounced Russia's "disproportionate" incursion and declared that while it was not breaking off all contact with Russia, it would not be "business as usual" in the NATO-Russia council. In December 2008, NATO foreign ministers agreed to resume what Secretary General Jaap de Hoop Scheffer called a "conditional and graduated re-engagement" with Russia.[10]

The Bush administration was not happy with the resumption of contact, but Secretary of State Condoleezza Rice went along with it to avoid a confrontation. Moreover, NATO remained adamant about withholding fast-track membership for Georgia and Ukraine, which the United States had sought. The two former Soviet states would join "some day," the alliance stated.[11]

The decision on Georgia and Ukraine sends a message to incoming President Barack Obama, who has publicly supported NATO membership for the two nations. Obama will also have to deal with the other major divisive issue in the complex relationship between Moscow and NATO: Washington's plan to deploy a missile defense shield in Poland and the Czech Republic. Although the Bush administration has insisted that the shield is intended to defend Europe from possible nuclear attack by Iran or North Korea, Russia is skeptical.

Russian officials say their country is the obvious target. "Since there aren't and won't be any [Iranian or North Korean] missiles, then against whom, against whom, is this [U.S.] system directed?" asked Russian Foreign Minister Sergei Lavrov. "Only against us!"[12]

As a result of the planned U.S. missile deployment and Russia's robust incursion into Georgia, Obama will inherit strained bilateral relations with Moscow. "Most analysts agree that relations between Washington and Moscow are not good," the Voice of America reported in November. "Some experts use 'poor,' 'tense,' and 'at a very low point,' to describe the relationship."[13] The Bush administration is blamed for pushing the missile shield and a hard line on the Georgia conflict.

For example, in September the administration insisted NATO cancel participation of the Russian ship *Ladno* in the Operation Active Endeavour anti-terrorism patrol. The *Ladno* was already off the coast of Turkey when the cancellation was transmitted to the Russians. Washington also blocked a request by the Russians for an emergency meeting of the NATO-Russia council to discuss the situation.[14]

Meanwhile, the Kremlin's level of protest also has been criticized within Russia as being too strident. Alexander Khramchikhin of the Institute of Political and Military Analysis in Moscow suggests the Kremlin is overstating the threat because the American ground-based interceptors "can hardly be said to exist, because many tests have failed. On top of that the bulky radar and launch pads are highly vulnerable to conventional tactical weapons."[15]

President-elect Obama appears to share this skepticism: He has said a case can be made for deploying the missile shield — if it works.

AFP/Getty Images/Dmitry Kostyukov

Russian troops invade South Ossetia in August 2008, shortly after Georgian forces entered the breakaway province. Georgian President Mikheil Saakashvili later said he invaded the province because he feared a Russian invasion. NATO quickly denounced Russia's "disproportionate" incursion.

---

[1] "Russian ship to join NATO exercise," *Eaglespeak*, May 19, 2006, www.eaglespeak.us/2006/05/russian-ship-to-join-nato-exercise.html.

[2] Jack Mendelsohn, "The NATO-Russian Founding Act," Arms Control Association, May 1997, http://legacy.armscontrol.org/act/1997_05/jm.asp.

[3] "NATO-Russia Relations," Topics Web page, North Atlantic Treaty Organization, Dec. 4, 2008, www.nato.int/issues/nato-russia/index.html.

[4] Newser.com, "Medvedev warns against NATO plans," March 28, 2008, www.newser.com/story/22487/medvedev-warns-against-nato-plans.html.

[5] Col. Gen. Nikolai Pishchev, "NATO Myths and Reality," *Krasnaya Zvezda*, Jan. 5, 2008, www.fas.org/man/nato/national/msg00006c.htm.

[6] Dmitri Trenin, "Partnerships Old and New," *NATO Review*, summer 2007, www.nato.int/docu/review/2007/issue2/english/art1.html.

[7] Yaroslav Butakov, "NATO against whom?" *Rpmonitor*, Feb. 12, 2007, www.rpmonitor.ru/en/en/detail.php?ID=3220.

[8] "Russian troops to patrol Georgian port — Gen. Staff," Novosti (Russian News and Information Agency), Aug. 23, 2008, http://en.rian.ru/russia/20080823/116235138.html.

[9] Mikheil Saakashvili, "Georgia Acted in Self-Defense," *The Wall Street Journal*, Dec. 2, 2008, http://online.wsj.com/article/SB122817723737570713.html?mod=googlenews_wsj.

[10] Reuters, "NATO, Russia to resume high-level contacts Friday," Dec 18, 2008, http://uk.reuters.com/article/latestCrisis/idUKLI401387.

[11] "NATO to resume Russian contacts," *Sky News*, Dec. 2, 2008, http://news.sky.com/skynews/Home/World-News/Nato-Agrees-To-Gradually-Resume-Contacts-With-Russia-In-Wake-Of-War-With-Georgia/Article/200812115171101?f=rss.

[12] M. K. Bhadrakumar, "In the Trenches of the New Cold War," *Asia Times*, April, 28, 2007, www.atimes.com/atimes/central_asia/ID28Ag01.html.

[13] Andre De Nesnera, "Obama to face strained U.S.-Russian relations after taking office," VOAonline, Nov. 20, 2008, www.voanews.com/english/archive/2008-11/2008-11-20-voa61.cfm?CFID=82992383&CFTOKEN=88186048.

[14] "NATO bars Russian ship from anti-terror patrol," *Javno*, Sept. 3, 2008, www.javno.com/en/world/clanak.php?id=172085.

[15] Alexander Khramchikhin, "Anti-ballistic missiles: menace or myth," *Space War*, www.spacewar.com/reports/Mutual_Destruction_Danger_In_US_Anti_Missile_Plan_Says_Putin_999.html.

Americans Suffer Most Casualties

Most of the 1,045 NATO troops killed in Afghanistan since 2001 have been American, British and Canadian, who are fully engaged in combat operations against Taliban and al Qaeda insurgents. Germany, France, Italy and other NATO governments only allow their soldiers to shoot at the enemy in self-defense, so their troops are not stationed in areas with heavy combat.

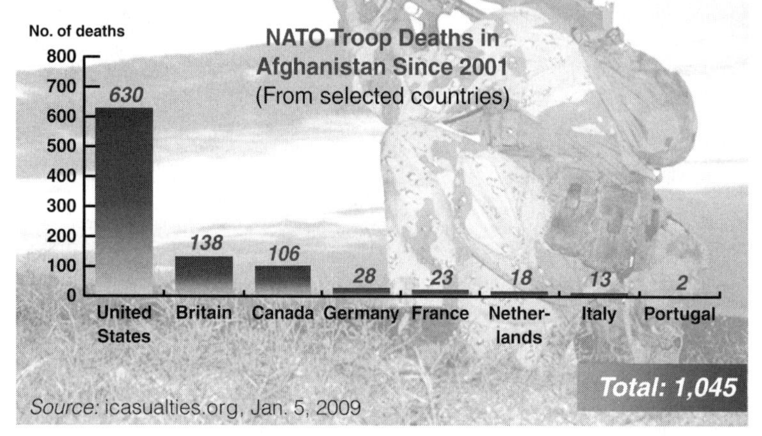

the day of the first NATO enlargement. "We're walking a tightrope."[34]

As NATO's borders edged closer to Russia, the alliance tried to reassure Moscow by establishing the NATO-Russia council, with permanent military representation in Brussels, and — as Clinton said — "holding open a place for Russia in some future, evolved version of NATO."[35]

But Moscow's discomfort with NATO expansion grew as additional countries — including Croatia, Macedonia, Azerbaijan, Georgia and Ukraine — stood in line to join the alliance. Since 2006, Putin — first as president and more recently as prime minister — has issued several strong protests against NATO's continued enlargement into the "near abroad," as Moscow calls its closest neighbors.

The latest threat to NATO's survival, however, comes not from Russia but from a wild, rugged country where — ironically — 20 years ago, the Russians themselves learned the lesson of bitter defeat.

CURRENT SITUATION

Slowing Expansion

The war in Afghanistan, however, is not the only challenge facing NATO today.

At a NATO summit in Bucharest, Romania, in April 2008 — in the first known instance of NATO turning down a personal request by a U.S. president — the alliance rebuffed Bush's proposal that Georgia and Ukraine be given so-called Membership Action Plan (MAP) status, a period of preparation designed to improve an aspiring member's democratic credentials and military effectiveness. The alliance put the plan on the back burner and then reaffirmed its decision in early December at a meeting of the NATO foreign ministers in Brussels. Faced with strong protests from Prime Minister Putin, Germany and France led other member states in a maneuver acknowledging that the two Caucasian nations would become NATO members eventually but stopping short of giving them MAPs, saying further negotiations would be necessary.

The decision came after months of tense confrontation and rhetoric over the issue. In what many saw as a quid pro quo, NATO backed the Bush administration's plan to deploy interceptor missiles in Poland linked to a missile defense radar system in the Czech Republic. The United States says the system is intended to defend Europe from possible ballistic missile attacks by rogue states, such as Iran and North Korea, but Russia views it as a potential threat. Agreements on the deployment have since been signed with both NATO countries.

In retaliation, Moscow announced in November 2008 that it would begin installing its own intercontinental, nuclear-capable missiles within a year.[36] President Medvedev said newly developed RS24 missiles — with a range of 4,000 miles — would be sited in Kaliningrad, a Russian enclave awkwardly perched between NATO members Poland and Lithuania.[37]

The brief conflict between Russian and Georgian forces last August chilled relations between NATO and Russia. It also split the alliance, with the Bush administration continuing to champion Georgian President Mikheil Saakashvili despite his rash attempt to annex the breakaway province of South Ossetia — which Washington officials say they repeatedly warned him not to try — and the Europeans' more measured inclination to give Moscow at least some benefit of the doubt.[38]

The American position was complicated by the fact that a hotly contested presidential election was in full swing. Republican candidate Sen. John McCain of Arizona exploded in hawkish anti-Russian comments. Democratic candidate Sen. Obama of Illinois took a tough stance as well, saying Georgia's NATO aspirations should not be undermined by the August fighting.

South Ossetia (birthplace of Soviet dictator Josef Stalin) and the nearby region of Abkhazia have long sought to separate from Georgia and are supported by Russia.[39] Given the opportunity, the Russians retaliated in force, advancing across Georgia like a knife through butter as far as the Baltic port of Poti. NATO quickly censured Moscow's "disproportionate use of force" and expressed support for Tblisi, putting its relations with Moscow on hold. As Secretary General de Hoop Scheffer put it in August, there would be "no business as usual" in the NATO-Russia council for a while.[40]

The "while" lasted three months. At its December meeting NATO announced it was resuming a "conditional and graduated re-engagement" with Russia, which it said did not signify approval of Russia's incursion into Georgian territory or its continued presence in, and recognition of, the breakaway province of South Ossetia.[41] The decision represented a defeat for the tough line with Moscow that Washington wanted to maintain and a success for the European argument that NATO needed to engage the Russians rather than isolate them.

In fact, NATO support for either Georgian or Ukrainian membership has dwindled. "Even the position of friends of Georgia and Ukraine within the alliance has evolved," said Slawomir Debski, director of the Polish Institute of International Affairs in Warsaw, who believes no decision is likely until after the 60th-anniversary summit in April.[42] In Ukraine, he pointed out, the government had collapsed, and public opinion is deeply divided over NATO membership, with 60 percent of the population opposing joining the alliance.

"The political upheavals in Ukraine mean that there is no partner reliable enough to talk to," he said. "NATO should wait until the territorial conflict with Russia is resolved" before making a decision on Georgia's application. For instance, if Georgia had been able to invoke Article 5 as a NATO member in August, the alliance would have been pulled into war with Russia, he pointed out.

AP Photo/Michal Dolezal

"Yankees, Leave Your Radar At Home," say Czech communists to protest a radar base the United States wants to build in the Czech Republic as part of a global missile defense shield against a potential threat from Iran or North Korea. NATO's endorsement of the plan — which includes installing 10 interceptor missiles in neighboring Poland — has caused tension between the alliance and the Kremlin.

Extending NATO membership to Ukraine and Georgia "borders on insanity," says Benjamin Friedman, a research fellow on security at Washington's Cato Institute, a libertarian think tank. "These countries are security consumers, not producers, and can provide little military benefit to the alliance. Both countries come with pre-existing conflicts with their stronger neighbor, Russia. . . . If you designed a country to be an uncomfortable ally, it would look something like Georgia — a weak nation with a territorial conflict with a nuclear-armed neighbor, led by a leader with a demonstrated capacity for recklessness."

That view is increasingly shared even in Washington, which has backed away somewhat from its position earlier in the summer, when outgoing Secretary of State Condoleezza Rice proposed that NATO consider dropping the MAP requirement and fast-tracking Georgia's and Ukraine's membership.

By December, faced with alliance opposition to circumventing the system, Rice had backtracked: "There should be no shortcuts," she declared, admitting that membership was "a long road ahead" for both countries.

'A Beast with 100 Heads'

The past year has been the deadliest yet for NATO forces in Afghanistan since the U.S.-led invasion. Financed by a flourishing opium trade, Taliban insurgents and al Qaeda

AT ISSUE

Has NATO become irrelevant?

YES

Fyodor Lukyanov
Editor, Russia in Global Affairs,
a Moscow-Based Foreign-Policy Quarterly

Written for *CQ Global Researcher*, January 2009

It is difficult to find any institution besides the North Atlantic Treaty Organization (NATO) that would manifest such a wide gap between progress in form and lack of success in substance. Its public image is great: The alliance outlived its main enemy, the Warsaw Pact, and won the Cold War. The number of members has more than doubled, and other countries are queuing to join the most powerful and prestigious club in the world.

But this historic triumph brought a few existential challenges to which NATO can't respond — at least not yet. First, what, after all, is the new strategic mission of NATO? Twenty years after the end of the Cold War, it is still unclear what kind of tasks this alliance should address: The Euro-Atlantic area doesn't need protection from a Soviet threat any more. Attempts to turn NATO into a global alliance and main international security institution — which would be a natural continuation of post-Cold War logic — haven't been realized. European allies are far from enthusiastic to fulfill missions in distant parts of the world, where they don't see their clear interests. Afghanistan is evidence enough.

Second, why is transatlantic unity still necessary in the 21st century? Tradition? Sure. Common values? Yes, but Europe and the United States differ on how those should be implemented. Common threats? Unlikely. Neither China nor international terrorism provides a consolidating threat, while Russia is simply unable to pose it. Strategic horizons? Not at all. The United States, as a global superpower and Europe as a regional entity with a unique political culture have different views on world affairs.

Third, is NATO still able to spread stability and security? In the 1990s the West could transform the security system according to its own ideas. Russia was unable and unwilling to resist; China was completely focused on internal development.

Now, however, in an effort to export security NATO expansion has become a catalyst for serious conflict, provoking Russia by intruding into its historical domain. Since NATO is rooted in the previous Cold War epoch, it is unrealistic to expect Moscow to change its attitude *vis-à-vis* enlargement.

Conceptually, NATO is obsolete and unfit to address real threats, but political and bureaucratic inertia will keep it going and provoking new strategic misunderstandings.

NO

Bastien Giegerich
Research Fellow on European Security,
International Institute of Security Studies,
London

Written for *CQ Global Researcher*, January 2009

Since the end of the Cold War NATO has confounded regular predictions of its demise by demonstrating an impressive adaptive ability.

NATO's transformation is by no means complete, but it has mutated to reflect the myriad security threats posed in today's security environment, including international terrorism. Yet, at the same time, it has maintained its core capacity for collective defence, even though this latter capacity is no longer directed against a particular enemy.

The alliance provides a vital forum for transatlantic dialogue on security issues. It is also an invaluable tool to influence third countries through cooperation — a quick browse through NATO's various partnership programmes underlines this point.

The degree of pre-crisis military coordination among its member states remains unrivalled: NATO's defence planning system, commonly agreed goals and efforts to standardize procedures and equipment mean NATO member forces are much more interoperable than they would be otherwise. When NATO does deploy forces, there is a functional multilateral framework for doing so in which its members understand each other's strengths and weaknesses.

Being a coalition of democracies makes it necessary to build and maintain political consensus as a prerequisite for action, which is always time-consuming and sometimes tedious. However, the upside provided by being a genuine coalition of democracies means that once consensus exists, the international legitimacy of NATO's actions is high.

NATO remains the most promising tool for the United States to influence the security and defence policies of European countries, and thus an important instrument of leadership.

The United States does not have the capacity to deal with global security threats on its own. In eight out of 10 cases her NATO allies will remain the most capable and most reliable partners around.

This is not an argument for nostalgia: NATO must continue to adapt to stay relevant. The last two decades suggest that it can do both.

fighters have regrouped in Pakistan's lawless territories bordering Afghanistan, where fellow Pashtun tribes give them shelter and protection between their raids across the border.[43] The 294 allied military deaths in 2008 are the most ever in the seven years of the war. Reporters in Afghanistan say the conflict is "stalemated, at best."[44]

All 26 NATO countries and 13 non-NATO allies — which have small contingents, such as Sweden (with 85 personnel) and Austria (3) — have contributed troops to NATO's 50,000-strong International Security and Assistance Force (ISAF). The United States has 20,000 American troops serving under NATO command, plus another 12,000 in the U.S.-run Operation Enduring Freedom, which originally hunted for bin Laden — who is still at large — and his al Qaeda terrorists.

But terrorists are just one aspect of the challenge facing NATO forces. "We now have a country that's infested with everything from the Taliban and al Qaeda on the insurgency side, to bandits, warlords and narcotics traffickers," said former CIA officer Michael Scheuer in a recent PBS documentary. "We're really fighting a beast with 100 heads."[45]

U.S. Defense Secretary Robert Gates has called Afghanistan, "NATO's first ground war."[46] But that's not really true for troops from Germany, France and Italy, whose governments have imposed rules of engagement — so-called "caveats" — specifically prohibiting them from engaging in combat unless they come under attack.

The caveats are not just the result of domestic political pressure generated by the unpopularity of the Afghanistan mission. They also reflect differences in approach within NATO. While the United States plans to send in more troops for an Iraq-type "surge," the French attitude is more typical of the European position. France believes "the focus must be on transferring more power and responsibility to the Afghan authorities," says Shada Islam, senior program executive at the European Policy Centre think tank in Brussels. That's a tall order in a country where large areas have yet to be brought under the control of President Hamid Karzai's not-very-effective government.

French Foreign Minister Bernard Kouchner, Islam points out, has said he does not believe there will be a "military solution in Afghanistan." Instead, he and many European leaders say efforts should be focused on helping to develop Afghanistan's armed forces so the country can ultimately provide its own security.

Getty Images/Michael Kappeler

A German military policeman (left) trains Afghan police officers in northern Afghanistan in September 2008. Many Europeans contend that rather than seeking a military solution in Afghanistan, NATO should focus on helping Afghan police and armed forces provide the country's own security. The army has improved in combat capability under NATO's guidance, but the police reportedly remain largely inefficient and corrupt.

So far, the 70,000-man Afghan army has improved in combat capability, say NATO leaders. But it's a small force in a country with a population of more than 32 million, and current plans are to expand it to 134,000 over the next five years. By contrast, the Afghan police, who are also being trained by ISAF, remain largely inefficient and corrupt.[47]

Provincial Reconstruction Teams (PRTs) — another non-combat project, made up of NATO military personnel and civilian aid workers — have had an uneven record of success, according to a 2008 report by specialists from the Woodrow Wilson School of International Affairs in Washington.[48] The German PRT operating in the northern province of Kunduz is the largest and one of the more successful, but its role was typical, albeit on a larger scale than most. Working with the provincial authorities, the report says, the PRT helped to restore drinking water to 850,000 inhabitants, constructed hundreds of elementary schools and clinics, conducted training for teachers, police and judges and provided security. But it has failed to convince the Afghans that the state had contributed to the effort.

"Kabul's authority continues to be regarded as more or less nonexistent," the report says. "Citizens are disappointed in the performance of the province's institutions."[49]

Meanwhile, the Pentagon is planning to deploy another 20,000-30,000 troops in Afghanistan this year, and incoming President Obama is expected to ask the NATO partners to send additional troops. But "European governments are likely to ignore Obama's demands that they assume greater responsibility by sending more troops," says Islam, which is expected to cast a pall over Obama's first official dealings with his NATO allies next April.

Many Europeans question whether a troop surge will work in Afghanistan's rugged terrain, which makes a heavy ground war nearly impossible, and air strikes mean heightened civilian casualties. In 2007, 321 Afghan civilians were killed in U.S. and NATO air strikes — three times as many as in the previous year — which has corroded Afghan views of U.S. and NATO forces as "liberators."

As an American soldier put it in the PBS documentary, "I don't think that even the little kids like us."[50]

OUTLOOK

New Strategic Concept

The upcoming NATO summit in April to celebrate the alliance's 60th anniversary would seem an obvious platform to begin reshaping its future. The French city of Strasbourg was chosen as the summit venue to mark the return of France to NATO's military command 40 years after President de Gaulle's withdrawal.

Former NATO Supreme Commander Gen. James L. Jones, who has been tapped to head President Obama's National Security Council, pinpoints one pressing change. "Most [NATO nations] understand that for NATO to survive as an institution in the 21st century, they need to start thinking about a new strategic concept," the former Marine commandant told *The New York Times* recently. "Unfortunately, NATO's mission is still rooted in the 20th-century, Cold War model of a defensive, static, reactive alliance instead of an agile, flexible and proactive 21st-century reality."[51]

But Poland's Debski doubts that the alliance will be able to produce a new strategic concept at the April summit. "The thinking about a new strategic concept is in progress; the machinery of consultation is moving," he says. But the summit will probably not discuss it in any depth in order "to give the Obama administration time to elaborate its own strategy towards NATO.

"The summit will be Obama's first NATO meeting, and . . . such a postponement seems likely," Debski continues. "With a new president in the White House we are at a point of departure." With a former NATO commander as national security adviser, however, the Obama administration might be in a position to articulate an alliance policy sooner than Europeans expect.

Equally important, say observers, NATO will want to see how U.S.-Kremlin relations develop with Obama in the Oval Office.

Oil-rich Russia's new determination to reshape its place in world affairs makes NATO members that are former Soviet satellites nervous. They want reassurance that NATO's security blanket is more than just rhetoric. If, for example, Russia attacks Latvia, will NATO come to its rescue under Article 5?

"Today, three NATOs co-exist. There's the NATO of the Cold War, there's the exporter of stability to ex-Soviet countries and there's the NATO directed against new threats. . . . But which is the real NATO? It's hard to reconcile the three."

— Henning Riecke, security specialist German Foreign Policy Institute

The 60th-anniversary summit is likely to reaffirm alliance guarantees because, as Giegerich of London's International Institute for Security Studies points out, "If there's an attack on a NATO member and the alliance doesn't respond to Article 5, then the alliance is dead." Debski calls the article "the essential fundament of the Alliance. If Article 5 is weakened, the whole institution may die very soon."

Developing NATO's role in protecting energy resources and transportation routes is also likely to be on the summit agenda. And it's not clear whether the new U.S. administration will continue President Bush's push for membership for Georgia and Ukraine. Giegerich foresees "a strategic pause" in the push for enlargement. "As long as the situation in Georgia is unsettled, it's not in NATO's interest to admit it."

However, Albania and Croatia are expected to be admitted.

Despite its problems, the alliance keeps the United States engaged in European security affairs. NATO enlargement has helped to unify a continent divided by 60 years of conflict and ease the entry of Eastern and Central European countries into the European Union. NATO has brought peace to the Balkans — and maintains that peace by keeping troops there. Through its Partnership for Peace, the alliance has established links with countries in other regions, such as Central Asia. Military cooperation between the allies promotes military interoperability and develops professional bonds and habits of cooperation that endure beyond an immediate deployment.[52]

Most observers say that if NATO is to remain an instrument for transatlantic security, it must be ready to take on more so-called out-of-area operations like the war in Afghanistan. But the alliance must establish parameters for such a commitment.

"In a world of 'globalized insecurity,' a regional Eurocentric approach simply no longer works," Secretary General de Hoop Scheffer declared recently. "We have to address security challenges where and when they emerge, or they will show up on our doorstep."[53]

NOTES

1. Suzanne Koelbl and Alexander Szander, "German Special Forces in Afghanistan Let Taliban Commander Escape," *Spiegel OnLine*, May 19, 2008, www.spiegel.de/international/world/0,1518,554033,00.html.
2. See http://icasualties.org/oef/.
3. For background, see Robert Kiener, "Crisis in Pakistan," *CQ Global Researcher*, December 2008, pp. 321-324.
4. Howard De Franchi, "US vs. Europe: two views of terror," *The Christian Science Monitor*, March 18, 2004, www.csmonitor.com/2004/0318/p01s01-usfp.html.
5. Tom Regan, "EU, U.S., differ on how to fight terrorism," *The Christian Science Monitor*, Feb. 2, 2004, www.csmonitor.com/2004/0329/dailyUpdate.html?s=entt.
6. "Forecast International Inc. News — Category Defence: A Frugal Pax Europa," Aerospace and Defence Network, Nov. 12, 2008, www.asd-network.com/press_detail/18416/A_Frugal_Pax_Europa.htm.
7. Terence Hunt, "Bush, Putin at odds over NATO plans," *Oakland Tribune*, April 5, 2008, http://findarticles.com/p/articles/mi_qn4176/is_/ai_n25144063.
8. Vanessa Gera, "Polish Support for Missile Deal Soars," *Topix*, Aug. 18, 2008, www.topix.com/forum/world/czech-republic/T1DPMN6G522MV45HV.
9. Doug Bandow, "The NATO Alliance: Dangerous Anachronism," AntiWar.com, Oct. 17, 2008, www.antiwar.com/bandow/?articleid=13603.
10. Koelbl and Szander, *op. cit.*
11. Saul Landau, "The NATO Axiom: 2+2=5," *ukwatch*, May 22, 2008, www.ukwatch.net/article/the_nato_axiom_2_2_5.
12. Bandow, *op. cit.*
13. E. Wayne Merry, "Therapy's End: thinking beyond NATO," *The National Interest*, Winter 2003, http://findarticles.com/p/articles/mi_m2751/is_74/ai_112411717/pg_8?tag=outBody;col4.
14. Steven Erlanger, "NATO Chief Defends Opening to Russia," *The New York Times*, Dec. 4, 2008, www.nytimes.com/2008/12/04/world/europe/04nato.html?partner=rss&emc=rss.
15. Jeff Gerth and Tom Weiner, "Arms Makers See Bonanza in Selling NATO Expansion," *The New York Times*, June 29, 1999, http://query.nytimes.com/gst/fullpage.html?res=9A06E4D81131F93AA15755C0A961958260&sec=&spon=&pagewanted=2; see also Tom Lipton, "With White House Push, U.S. Arms Sales Jump," *The New York Times*, Sept. 18, 2008, www.nytimes.com/2008/09/14/washington/14arms.html?pagewanted=1&_r=1&hp.
16. Hendrik Enderlein, "Military Interoperability," *IP Internationale Politik*, www.ip-global.org/archiv/2002/winter2002/military-interoperability.html.
17. Congressional Research Service reports to Congress for 2006 and 2008, respectively, www.fas.org/sgp/crs/weapons/RL34187.pdf; and www.scribd.com/doz/7788295/Arms-Sales-Transfers-2000-2007.
18. Federico Bordonaro, quoted from "Power and Interest News Report" in *ASAM Foreign Press Review*, May 19-20, 2005, www.avsam.org/fpr/rcs.htm, and Steve Clemons, "After Bucharest: Energy Security and Russia," *The Washington Note*, April 11, 2008, www.thewashingtonnote.com/archives/2008/04/after_bucharest/.
19. "NATO Forum on Energy Security Technology," Institute for the Analysis of Global Security, Feb. 22, 2006, www.iags.org/natoforum.htm.

20. Sohbet Karbuz, "NATO and energy security," *Energy Bulletin*, Nov. 3, 2007, www.energybulletin.net/node/36716.

21. Johannes Varwick, "NATO's Role in Energy Security," *SpiegelOnline*, Jan. 7, 2008, www.spiegel.de/international/0,1518,563210,00.html.

22. "NATO and the fight against terrorism," NATO, www.nato.int/issues/terrorism/index.html.

23. Jose Maria Aznar, "Reforming NATO: The focus must be terrorism," *Europe's World*, spring 2006, www.europesworld.org/EWSettings/Article/tabid/191/ArticleType/ArticleView/ArticleID/21005/Default.aspx.

24. NATO, *op. cit.*

25. See "Operation Active Endeavour," www.nato.int/issues/active_endeavour/practice.html.

26. Alexander Kudascheff, "German NATO General: Most Afghans Back ISAF Mission," *Deutsche Welle*, Sept. 27, 2008, www.dw-world.de/dw/article/0,2144,3675301,00.html.

27. Tim Shipman, "US officials 'despair' at NATO allies' failings in Afghanistan," *Telegraph News*, June 22, 2008, www.telegraph.co.uk/news/worldnews/northamerica/usa/2170135/US-officials-%27despair%27-at-Nato-allies%27-failings-in-Afghanistan.html.

28. Benjamin Friedman and Justin Logan, "Don't Expand NATO: The Case Against Membership for Georgia and Ukraine," Cato Institute, Oct. 22, 2008, www.cato.org/pub_display.php?pub_id= 9738. For background on the Marshall Plan, see "Marshall Plan Home Page," U.S. Agency for International Development, www.usaid.gov/multimedia/video/marshall/.

29. Forrest P. Sherman, unpublished diary, Sept. 25, 1950 (quoted by permission of the Fitzpatrick family).

30. *Ibid.*, March 4, 1951.

31. "NATO's Strategy of Flexible Response and the Twenty-first Century," GlobalSecurity.org, www.globalsecurity.org/wmd/library/report/1986/LLE.htm.

32. *Ibid.*

33. For an analysis of the Harmel Report, see "NATO Strategy in 1967," www.db.niss.gov.ua/docs/nato/nato/sco32.html.

34. Strobe Talbott, *The Russia Hand: A Memoir of Presidential Diplomacy* (2002), p. 248.

35. *Ibid.*

36. "Russia Slams U.S., threatens missile deployment," CNN.com, Nov. 5, 2008, www.cnn/2008/WORLD/Europe/11/05/russia.missiles.

37. "Russia to deploy missile to counter US missile shield next year," *Daily Telegraph*, Nov. 28, 2008, www.telegraph.co.uk/news/worldnews/europe/russia/3533320/Russia-to-deploy-missile-to-counter-US-missile-shield-next-year.html. For background on Kaliningrad, see Brian Beary, "A Sliver of Russia Trapped in Europe," pp. 194-195, in "The New Europe," *CQ Global Researcher*, August 2007.

38. Lanny Davis, "Are we all Georgians? Not so fast," *Fox Forum*, Aug. 25, 2008, http://foxforum.blogs.foxnews.com/2008/08/25/are-we-all-georgians-not-so-fast/.

39. For background, see Brian Beary, "Separatist Movements," *CQ Global Researcher*, April 2008, pp. 85-114.

40. "NATO Agrees to Thaw in Contacts with Russia," *VOAnews*, Dec. 2, 2008, www.voanews.com/english/2008-12-02-voa58.cfm.

41. "NATO reopens talks with Russia, hold off on Ukraine and Georgia," *Deutsche Welle*, Dec. 2, 2008, www.dw-world.de/dw/article/0,2144,3843756.00.html.

42. Judy Dempsey, "U.S. presses NATO on Georgia and Ukraine," *The New York Times*, Nov. 25, 2008, www.nytimes.com/2008/11/26/world/europe/26nato.html?_r=1&ref=world.

43. See Kiener, *op. cit.*

44. Michael Gordon, "Strategy Shift for Afghan War Poses Stiff Challenge for Obama," *The New York Times*, Dec. 2, 2008, p. A1.

45. Marcela Gaviria and Martin Smith, "Frontline: The War Briefing," PBS, Oct. 28, 2008, www.pbs.org/wgbh/pages/frontline/warbriefing/view/.

46. Carol Bowers, "NATO grows with Afghanistan experience," U.S. Dept. of Defense, April 2, 2008, www.defenselink.mil/news/newsarticle.aspx?id=49433.

47. Gordon, *op. cit.*
48. Nima Abbaszadeh, *et al.*, "Provincial Reconstruction Teams: Lessons and Recommendations," January 2008, http://wws.princeton.edu/research/pwreports_f07/wws591b.pdf.
49. *Ibid.*
50. Gaviria and Smith, *op. cit.*
51. Helene Cooper and Scott L. Malcomson, "Welcome to My World, Barack," *The New York Times Magazine*, Nov. 16, 2008, www.nytimes.com/2008/11/16/magazine/16rice-t.html?ref=magazine&pagewanted=all.
52. Elizabeth Sherwood-Randall, "Is NATO Dead or Alive?" *The Huffington Post*, April 1, 2008, www.huffingtonpost.com/elizabeth-sherwoodrandall/is-nato-dead-or-alive_b_94469.html.
53. See NATO Online Library, April 4, 2005, www.nato.int/docu/speech/2005/s050401b.htm.

BIBLIOGRAPHY

Books

Asmus, Ronald D., *Opening NATO's Door: How the Alliance Remade Itself for a New Era, Columbia University Press*, 2004.
The executive director of the Brussels-based Transatlantic Center provides an insider's account of the fierce divisions within the alliance over the Yugoslav wars and NATO enlargement.

Henricksen, Dag, *NATO'S Gamble: Combining Diplomacy and Airpower in the Kosovo Crisis, 1998-1999, Naval Institute Press*, 2007.
A Norwegian Air Force captain and military strategist who participated in NATO'S 78-day aerial-bombing campaign during the Kosovo conflict examines what happened.

Howorth, Jolyon, and John T. S. Keeler, (eds.), *Defending Europe: The EU, NATO, and the Quest for European Autonomy, Palgrave Macmillan*, 2003.
A professor of European politics at England's University of Bath (Howorth) and the dean of the School of Public and International Affairs at the University of Pittsburgh (Keeler) have compiled a variety of commentaries on the complex relationship between NATO and the European Union.

Kaplan, Lawrence S., *NATO 1948: The Birth of the Transatlantic Alliance*, 2007.
In his fourth book on NATO, a Georgetown University history professor examines the often-contentious 1948 negotiations about whether the United States should join the proposed alliance.

Kaplan, Lawrence S., *NATO Divided, NATO United: The Evolution of an Alliance*, 2004.
A leading NATO historian explores persistent differences between the United States and its European partners that quickly re-emerged after NATO rushed to support the United States following the Sept. 11, 2001, terrorist attacks.

Articles

Daalder, Ivo, and James Goldgeier, "Global NATO," *Foreign Affairs*, spring, 2006.
A senior fellow at the Brookings Institution (Daalder) and a professor of political science at The George Washington University (Goldgeier) argue that NATO must expand its membership beyond Europe in order to meet new security challenges.

Hulsman, John C., *et al.*, "Can NATO Survive Europe?" *The National Interest*, March 22, 2004.
Four distinguished scholars debate whether NATO can co-exist with the European Union.

Myers, Stephen Lee, and Thom Shanker, "NATO Expansion and a Bush Legacy Are in Doubt," *The New York Times*, March 18, 2008.
Disparities of might and will exist among NATO members.

Reports and Studies

Archick, Kristin, "The United States and Europe: Possible Options for U.S. Policy," *Congressional Research Service*, March 8, 2005, http://fpc.state.gov/documents/organization/41324.pdf.
An analyst of European affairs offers options for improving U.S.-European relations.

Gordon, Philip H., "NATO and the War on Terrorism: A Changing Alliance," *Brookings Institution*, Dec.

12, 2008, www.brookings.edu/articles/2002/summer_globalgovernance_gordon.aspx.
A leading analyst wonders if NATO has an enduring role but says writing off NATO would be "perverse and mistaken."

Hunter, Robert E., Edward Gnehm and George Joulwan, "Integrating Instruments of Power and Influence: Lessons Learned and Best Practices," ***National Security Research Division, RAND Corporation*****, 2008, www.rand.org/pubs/conf_proceedings/2008/RAND_CF251.pdf.**
A former U.S. ambassador to NATO (Hunter) leads a prestigious group of "senior practitioners" in developing a blueprint for post-conflict operations.

Hunter, Robert E., Sergei M. Rogov and Olga Oliker, "NATO and Russia: Bridge-building for the 21st century, Report of the Working Group on NATO," ***RAND Corporation*****, 2002, www.rand.org/pubs/white_papers/WP128/.**
A former U.S. ambassador to NATO (Hunter) and director of the Institute for U.S. and Canadian Studies at the Russian Academy of Sciences (Rogov) — a Moscow-based independent research organization — argue for closer cooperation between NATO and post-communist Russia.

Phillips, David, "Post-Conflict Georgia," ***The Atlantic Council of the United States*****, Oct. 3, 2008, www.acus.org/publication/post-conflict-georgia.**
A visiting scholar at Columbia University's Center for the Study of Human Rights examines the impact of the Georgia conflict on U.S.-European relations within NATO.

Rupp, Richard E., "NATO after 9/11: An Alliance in Decline," March 2006, www.allacademic.com//meta/p_mla_apa_research_citation/0/9/9/2/4/pages99241/p99241-1.php.
A Purdue University history professor argues that NATO is increasingly ineffective and cannot be reformed.

For More Information

Atlantic Council of the United States, 1101 15th St., N.W., 11th Floor, Washington, DC 20005; (202) 463-7226; www.acus.org. Promotes constructive American leadership in helping the Atlantic community meet the challenges of the 21st century.

Brookings Institution, 1775 Massachusetts Ave., N.W., Washington, DC 20036; (202) 797-6000; www.brookings.edu. A think tank that studies how to strengthen U.S. democracy and promote a more cooperative international system.

Cato Institute, 1000 Massachusetts Ave., N.W., Washington, DC 20001; (202) 842-0200; www.cato.org. Seeks to increase understanding of public policies based on the libertarian principles of limited government, free markets, individual liberty and peace.

Council on Foreign Relations, 58 East 68th St., New York, N.Y. 10021; (212) 434-9400; www.cfr.org. Promotes a better understanding of the foreign policy choices facing the United States and other governments.

French Institute of International Affairs (IFRI), 27 rue des Processions, Paris 75740, France; 33(0)1 40-61-60-00; www.ifri@ifri.org. A leading European center for research, meetings and debates on international issues.

International Institute for Strategic Studies, 13-15 Arundel St. Temple Place, London WC2R 3DX, England; 44(0)20 7379-7676; www.iiss.org. Think tank focusing on international security with an emphasis on political-military conflict.

North Atlantic Treaty Organization, Blvd. Leopold III, 1110 Brussels, Belgium; 32(0)2 707-50-41; www.nato.int. Headquarters of the North American-European mutual defense alliance.

Polish Institute for International Affairs, 1a Warecka Slwe, P.O. Box 1010, 00-950 Warsaw, Poland. Established in 1996 to conduct research and provide unbiased expertise in international relations.

RAND Corporation, 1776 Main St., Santa Monica, CA 90401; (310) 393-0411; www.rand.org. Nonprofit organization that focuses on national security issues.

Russian Academy of Sciences, Leninskii Avenue, 14, Moscow, Russia 119991; (495) 938-0309; www.ras.ru. Nonprofit organization researching policies that promote economic, social, technological and cultural development in Russia.

Transatlantic Center, German Marshall Fund, Résidence Palace, Rue de la Loi 155 Wetstraat, Brussels, Belgium 1040; +32-2-238-5270; www.gmfus.org. Promotes a more integrated Europe and studies the impact on NATO.

5

Religious Fundamentalism

Does It Lead to Intolerance and Violence?

Brian Beary

AFP/Getty Images/Shah Marai

Burqas enshroud women in Kabul, Afghanistan's capital, reflecting life under strict Islamic regimes like the Taliban. Overthrown in 2001, the radically fundamentalist Taliban has regained control in some parts of the country. In addition to requiring the burqa, it restricts women's movements, prevents men from shaving or girls from being educated and prohibits singing and dancing.

From *CQ Global Researcher*, February 2009.

Life is far from idyllic in Swat, a lush valley once known as "the Switzerland of Pakistan." Far from Islamabad, the capital, a local leader of the Taliban — the extremist Islamic group that controls parts of the country — uses radio broadcasts to coerce residents into adhering to the Taliban's strict edicts.

"Un-Islamic" activities that are now forbidden — on pain of a lashing or public execution — range from singing and dancing to watching television or sending girls to school. "They control everything through the radio," said one frightened Swat resident who would not give his name. "Everyone waits for the broadcast." And in case any listeners in the once-secular region are considering ignoring Shah Duran's harsh dictates, periodic public assassinations — 70 police officers beheaded in 2008 alone — provide a bone-chilling deterrent.[1]

While the vast majority of the world's religious fundamentalists do not espouse violence as a means of imposing their beliefs, religious fundamentalism — in both its benign and more violent forms — is growing throughout much of the world. Scholars attribute the rise to various factors, including a backlash against perceived Western consumerism and permissiveness. And fundamentalism — the belief in a literal interpretation of holy texts and the rejection of modernism — is rising not only in Muslim societies but also among Christians, Hindus and Jews in certain countries. (*See graph, p. 108.*)

Religious Fundamentalism Spans the Globe

Fundamentalists from a variety of world religions are playing an increasingly important role in political and social life in countries on nearly every continent. Generally defined as the belief in a literal interpretation of holy texts and a rejection of modernism, fundamentalism is strongest in the Middle East and in the overwhelmingly Christian United States.

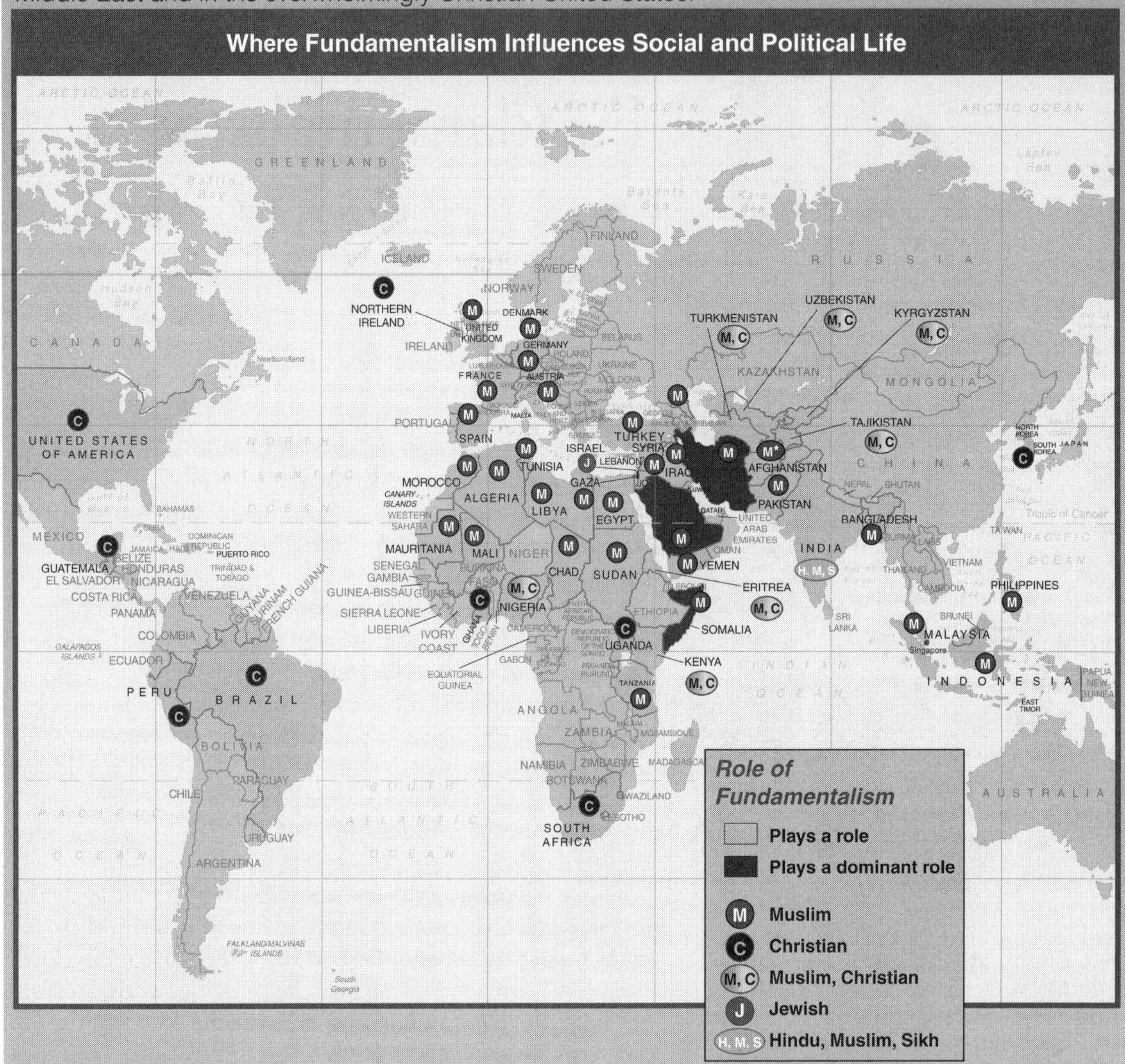

* The ultra-conservative Taliban ruled from 1996-2001 and are fighting to regain control.

Sources: U.S. National Counter Terrorism Center, Worldwide Incidents Tracking System, http://wits.nctc.gov; David Cingranelli and David Richards, Cingranelli-Richards (CIRI) Human Rights Dataset, CIRI Human Rights Project, 2007, www.humanrightsdata.org; The Association of Religious Data Archives at Pennsylvania State University, www.thearda.com; Office of the Coordinator for Counterterrorism, Country Reports on Terrorism, United States Department of State, April 2008, www.state.gov/documents/organization/105904.pdf; Peter Katel, "Global Jihad," *CQ Researcher,* Oct. 14, 2005

Islamic fundamentalism is on the rise in Pakistan, Afghanistan, the Palestinian territories and European nations with large, often discontented Muslim immigrant populations — notably the United Kingdom, Germany, Denmark, Spain and France, according to Maajid Nawaz, director of the London-based Quilliam Foundation think tank.

In the United States — the birthplace of Christian fundamentalism and the world's most populous predominantly Christian nation — 90 percent of Americans say they believe in God, and a third believe in a literal interpretation of the Bible.[2] Perhaps the most extreme wing of U.S. Christian fundamentalism are the Christian nationalists, who believe the scriptures "must govern every aspect of public and private life," including government, science, history, culture and relationships, according to author Michelle Goldberg, who has studied the splinter group.[3] She says Christian nationalists are "a significant and highly mobilized minority" of U.S. evangelicals that is gaining influence.[4] TV evangelist Pat Robertson is a leading Christian nationalist and "helped put dominionism — the idea that Christians have a God-given right to rule — at the center of the movement to bring evangelicals into politics," she says.[5]

Although the number of the world's Christians who are fundamentalists is not known, about 20 percent of the 2 billion Christians are conservative evangelicals, according to the World Evangelical Alliance (WEA).[6] Evangelicals reject the "fundamentalist" label, and most do not advocate creating a Christian theocracy, but they are the socially conservative wing of the Christian community, championing "family values" and opposing abortion and gay marriage. In recent decades they have exercised considerable political power on social issues in the United States.

Many Religions Have Fundamentalist Groups

Religious fundamentalism comes in many forms around the globe, and many different groups have emerged to push their own type of fundamentalism — a handful through violence. The term "Islamist" is often used to describe fundamentalist Muslims who believe in a literal interpretation of the Koran and want to implement a strict form of Islam in all aspects of life. Some also want to have Islamic law, or sharia, imposed on their societies.

Christian Fundamentalists

- Lord's Resistance Army (LRA), a rebel group in Uganda that wants to establish a Christian nation — **violent**
- Various strands within the evangelical movement worldwide, including the U.S.-based Christian nationalists, who insist the United States was founded as a Christian nation and believe that all aspects of life (including family, religion, education, government, media, entertainment and business) should be taken over by fundamentalist Christians — **rarely violent**
- Society of St. Pius X, followers of Catholic Archbishop Marcel Lefebvre, who reject the Vatican II modernizing reforms — **nonviolent**

Islamic Fundamentalists

- Jihadists, like al Qaeda and its allies across the Muslim world — **violent***
- Locally focused Islamist groups Hezbollah (Lebanon) and Hamas (Gaza) — **violent**
- Revolutionary Islamists, like Hizb-ut-Tahrir (HT), a pan-Islamic Sunni political movement that wants all Muslim countries combined into a unitary Islamic state or caliphate, ruled by Islamic law; has been involved in some coup attempts in Muslim countries and is banned in some states — **sometimes violent**
- Political Islamists, dedicated to the "social and political revivification of Islam" through nonviolent, democratic means. Some factions of the Muslim Brotherhood — the world's largest and oldest international Islamist movement — espouse using peaceful political and educational means to convert Muslim countries into sharia-ruled states, re-establishing the Muslim caliphate. Other factions of the group have endorsed violence from time to time.
- Post-Islamists, such as the AKP, the ruling party in Turkey, which has Islamist roots but has moderated its fundamentalist impulses — **nonviolent**

Judaism

- Haredi, ultra-orthodox Jews — **mostly nonviolent**
- Gush Emunim, aim to reoccupy the biblical Jewish land including Palestinian territories — **sometimes violent**
- Chabad missionaries, who support Jewish communities across the globe — **nonviolent**

Indian subcontinent

- Sikh separatists — **sometimes violent**
- Hindu extremists, anti-Christian/Muslim — **sometimes violent**

* For an extensive list of global jihadist groups, see "Inside the Global Jihadist Network," pp. 860-861, in Peter Katel, "Global Jihad," *CQ Researcher*, Oct. 14, 2005, pp. 857-880.

Sources: Encyclopedia of Fundamentalism; "Foreign Terrorist Organizations," U.S. Department of State

Christians Are a Third of the World's Population

About 20 percent of the world's 2 billion Christians are evangelicals or Pentecostals — many of whom are fundamentalists. But statistics on the number of other fundamentalists are not available. Christians and Muslims together make up more than half the world's population.

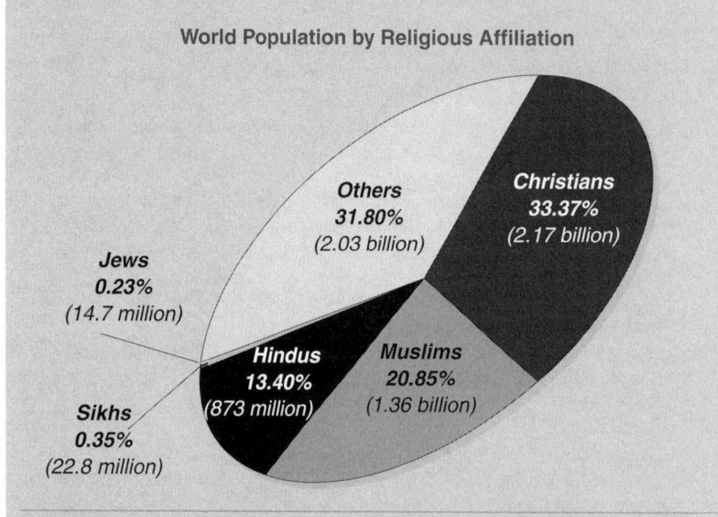

Major Concentrations of Religious Denominations

(in millions)

Christians	
United States	247
Brazil	170
Russia	115
China	101
Mexico	100

Muslims	
Indonesia	178
India	155
Pakistan	152
Bangladesh	136
Turkey	71

Hindus	
India	817
Nepal	19
Bangladesh	15
Indonesia	7
Sri Lanka	2.5

Sikhs	
India	21
United Kingdom	0.4
Canada	0.3
United States	0.3
Thailand	0.05

Jews	
United States	5.3
Israel/Palestine	5.3
France	0.6
Argentina	0.5
Canada	0.4

Sources: World Christian Database, Center for the Study of Global Christianity, Gordon-Conwell Theological Seminary, www.worldchristiandatabase.org/wcd/home.asp; John L. Allen Jr., "McCain's choice a nod not only to women, but post-denominationalists," National Catholic Reporter, Aug. 30, 2008, http://ncrcafe.org/node/2073

Christian evangelicalism is booming in Africa — especially in Anglophone countries like Kenya, Uganda, Nigeria, Ghana and South Africa.[7] "We are all — Pentecostals, Anglicans and Baptists — very active in evangelizing," says James Nkansah, a Ghanaian-born Baptist minister who teaches at the Nairobi Evangelical Graduate School of Theology in Kenya. "Even the Catholics are doing it, although they do not call themselves evangelists." A similar trend is occurring in Latin America, especially in Brazil, Guatemala and Peru among the Pentecostals, who stress the importance of the Holy Spirit, faith healing and "speak in tongues" during services.

Both evangelicals and Catholics in Latin America have adopted the basic tenets of U.S.-style evangelicalism, according to Valdir Steuernagel, a Brazilian evangelical Lutheran pastor who is vice president at World Vision International, a Christian humanitarian agency. Like U.S. evangelicals, South American evangelicals passionately oppose gay marriage and abortion, but they do not use the term "fundamentalist," says Steuernagel, because the word "does not help us to reach out to the grassroots."

South Korea also has a thriving evangelical community. A visiting U.S. journalist describes a recent service for about 1,000 people at a popular Korean evangelical church: "It was part rock concert and part revival meeting," with the lead guitarist, "sometimes jumping up and down on the altar platform" like Mick Jagger, recalls Michael Mosettig.[8] Elsewhere in Asia — the world's most religiously diverse continent — Christian missionaries in China have grown their flocks from fewer than 2 million Christians in 1979 to more than 16 million Protestants alone in 2008.[9] It is unknown how many of those are fundamentalists.

Among the world's 15 million Jews, about 750,000 are ultra-Orthodox "Haredi" Jews who live in strict accordance with Jewish law. Half of them live in Israel, most of the rest in the United States, while there are small pockets in France, Belgium, the United Kingdom, Canada and Australia. About 80,000 live in the Palestinian territories on Israel's West Bank because they believe it is God's will.[10] The flourishing fundamentalist Chabad movement — whose adherents would prefer to live in a Jewish theocracy governed by religious laws — sends missionaries to support isolated Jewish communities in 80 countries.

"We accept the Israeli state, but we would have liked the Torah to be its constitution," says Belgian-based Rabbi Avi Tawil, an Argentine Chabad missionary. "But we are not Zionists, because we do not encourage every Jew to go to Israel. Our philosophy is, 'Don't run away from your own place — make it better.' "

In India, Hindu fundamentalists insist their vast country should be for Hindus only. In late 2008, a sudden upsurge in fundamentalist Hindu attacks against Christian minorities in the state of Orissa in eastern India ended with 60 Christians killed and 50,000 driven from their homes.[11] (*See p. 131.*)

Besides their rejection of Western culture, the faithful embrace fundamentalism out of fear of globalization and consumerism and anger about U.S. action — or inaction — in the Middle East, experts say. Some also believe a strict, religiously oriented government will provide better services than the corrupt, unstable, secular regimes governing their countries. Religious fundamentalism also thrives in societies formerly run by repressive governments. Both Christian and Muslim fundamentalism are spreading in Central Asian republics — particularly Uzbekistan, Kyrgyzstan and Tajikistan — that were once part of the repressive, anti-religious Soviet Union. (*See sidebar, p. 122.*)

Many fundamentalists — such as the Quakers, Amish and Jehovah's Witnesses — oppose violence for any reason. And fundamentalists who call themselves "political Islamists" pursue their goal of the "social and political revivification of Islam" through nonviolent, democratic means, according to Loren Lybarger, an assistant professor of classics and world religions at Ohio University and author of a recent book on Islamism in the Palestinian territories.[12]

In recent years radical Islamic extremists have perpetrated most violence committed by fundamentalists. From January 2004 to July 2008, for instance, Muslim militants killed 20,182 people, while Christian, Jewish and Hindu extremists together killed only 925, according to a U.S. government database.[13] Most of the Muslim attacks were between Sunni and Shia Muslims fighting for political control of Iraq. (*See chart, p. 113.*)[14]

Asmaa Abdol-Hamiz, a Muslim Danish politician and social worker, questions the State Department's statistics. "When Muslims are violent, you always see them identified as Muslims," she points out. "When Christians are violent, you look at the social and psychological reasons."

In addition, according to Radwan Masmoudi, president of the Center for the study of Islam and Democracy, such statistics do not address the "more than one million innocent people" killed in the U.S.-led wars in Iraq and Afghanistan, which, in his view, were instigated due to pressure from Christian fundamentalists in the United States. (*See "At Issue," p. 129.*)

Nevertheless, some radical Islamists see violence as the only way to replace secular governments with theocracies. The world's only Muslim theocracy is in Iran. While conservative Shia clerics exert ultimate control, Iranians do have some political voice, electing a parliament and president. In neighboring Saudi Arabia, the ruling royal family is not clerical but supports the ultraconservative Sunni Wahhabi sect as the state-sponsored religion. Meanwhile, in the Palestinian territories, "there has been a striking migration from more nationalist groups to more self-consciously religious-nationalist groups," wrote Lybarger.[15]

Experts say Muslim militants recently have set their sights on troubled countries like Somalia and nuclear-armed Pakistan as fertile ground for establishing other Islamic states. Some extremist groups, such as Hizb-ut-Tahrir, want to establish a single Islamic theocracy — or caliphate — across the Muslim world, stretching from Indonesia to Morocco.

Still other Muslim fundamentalists living in secular countries such as Britain want their governments to allow Muslims to settle legal disputes in Islamic courts. Islamic law, called sharia, already has been introduced in some areas in Africa, such as northern Nigeria's predominantly Muslim Kano region.[16]

AP Photo/Sunday Alamba

AP Photo/Gurinder Osan

In the Wake of Fundamentalist Violence

Two days of fighting between Christians and fundamentalist Muslims in December destroyed numerous buildings in Jos, Nigeria, (top) and killed more than 300 people. In India's Orissa state, a Christian woman (bottom) searches through the remains of her house, destroyed during attacks by fundamentalist Hindus last October. Sixty Christians were killed and 50,000 driven from their homes.

Muslim extremists are not the only fundamentalists wanting to establish theocracies in their countries. The Jewish Israeli group Kach, for instance, seeks to restore the biblical state of Israel, according to the U.S. State Department's list of foreign terrorist organizations. Hindu fundamentalists want to make India — a secular country with a majority Hindu population that also has many Muslims and Christians — more "Hindu" by promoting traditional Hindu beliefs and customs.

While militant Christian fundamentalist groups are relatively rare, the Lord's Resistance Army (LRA) has led a 20-year campaign to establish a theocracy based on the Ten Commandments in Uganda. The group has abducted hundreds of children and forced them to commit atrocities as soldiers. The group has been blamed for killing hundreds of Ugandans and displacing 2 million people.[17]

In the United States, most Christian fundamentalists are nonviolent, although some have been responsible for sporadic incidents, primarily bombings of abortion clinics. "The irony," says John Green, a senior fellow at the Washington-based Pew Forum on Religion and Public Policy, "is that America is a very violent country where the 'regular' crime rates are actually higher than they are in countries where global jihad is being waged."

Support for violence by Islamic extremists has been declining in the Muslim world in the wake of al Qaeda's bloody anti-Western campaigns, which have killed more Muslims than non-Muslims. U.S. intelligence agencies concluded in November 2008 that al Qaeda "may decay sooner" than previously assumed because of "undeliverable strategic objectives, inability to attract broad-based support and self-destructive actions."[18]

But fundamentalist violence, especially Islamist-inspired, remains a serious threat to world peace. In Iraq, fighting between Sunni and Shia Muslims has killed tens of thousands since 2003 and forced more than 4 million Iraqis to flee their homes. And 20 of the 42 groups on the State Department's list of terrorist organizations are Islamic fundamentalist groups.[19] No Christian or Hindu fundamentalists are included on the terrorist list.

However, Somali-born writer Ayaan Hirsi Ali — herself a target of threats from Islamic fundamentalists — says that while "Christian and Jewish fundamentalists are just as crazy as the Islamists . . . the Islamists are more violent because 99 percent of Muslims think Mohammad is perfect. Christians do not see Jesus in as absolute a way."

As religious fundamentalism continues to thrive around the world, here are some of the key questions experts are grappling with:

Is religious fundamentalism on the rise?

Religious fundamentalism has been on the rise worldwide for 30 years and "remains strong," says Pew's Green.

Fundamentalism is growing throughout the Muslim and Hindu worlds but not in the United States, where its growth has slowed down in recent years, says Martin Marty, a religious history professor at the University of Chicago, who authored a multivolume series on fundamentalism.[20] Christian fundamentalism is strong in Africa and Latin America and is even being exported to industrialized countries. Brazilian Pastor Steuernagel says "evangelical missionaries are going from Brazil, Colombia and Argentina to Northern Hemisphere countries like Spain, Portugal and the United Kingdom. They are going to Asia and Africa too, but there they must combine their missionary activities with aid work."

Islamic fundamentalism, meanwhile, has been growing for decades in the Middle East and Africa. For example, in Egypt the Muslim Brotherhood — which seeks to make all aspects of life in Muslim countries more Islamic, such as by applying sharia law — won 20 percent of the seats in 2005 parliamentary elections — 10 times more than it got in the early 1980s.[21] In Somalia, the Islamist al-Shabaab militia threatens the fragile government.

More moderate Muslims who want to "reform" Islam into a more tolerant, modern religion face an uphill battle, says Iranian-born Shireen Hunter, author of a recent book on reformist voices within Islam. Reformers' Achilles' heel is the fact that "they are often secular and do not understand the Islamic texts as well as the fundamentalists so they cannot compete on the same level," she says.

In Europe, secularism is growing in countries like France and the Netherlands as Christian worship rates plummet, but Turkey has been ruled since 2002 by the Justice and Development Party, which is rooted in political Islam. Though it has vowed to uphold the country's secular constitution, critics say the party harbors a secret fundamentalist agenda, citing as evidence the government's recent relaxation of restrictions on women wearing headscarves at universities.[22]

In Israel, the ultra-Orthodox Jewish population is growing thanks to an extremely high birthrate. Haredi Jews average 7.6 children per woman compared to an average Israeli woman's 2.5 children.[23] And ultra-Orthodox political parties have gained 15 seats in the 120-member Knesset (parliament) since the 1980s, when they had only five.[24] Secularists in the United States saw Christian fundamentalists grow increasingly powerful during the presidency of George W. Bush (2001-2009). Government policies limited access to birth control and abortions, and conservative religious elements in the military began to engage in coercive proselytizing. "From about 2005, I noticed a lot of religious activity: Bible study weeks, a multitude of religious services linked to public holidays that I felt were excessive," says U.S. Army Reserve intelligence officer Laure Williams. In February 2008, she

Radical Muslims Caused Most Terror Attacks

More than 6,000 religiously motivated terrorist attacks in recent years were perpetrated by radical Muslims — far more than any other group. The attacks by Christians were mostly carried out by the Lord's Resistance Army (LRA) in Uganda.

Religious Attacks, Jan. 1, 2004-June 30, 2008

	Killed	Injured	Incidents
Christian	917	371	101
Muslim*	20,182	43,852	6,180
Jewish	5	28	5
Hindu**	3	7	6
Total	**21,107**	**44,258**	**6,292**

* More than 90 percent of the reported attacks on civilians by Sunni and Shia terrorists were by Sunnis. Does not include the Muslim attacks in Mumbai, India, in December 2008, allegedly carried out by Muslim extremists from Pakistan.

** Uncounted are the Hindu extremist attacks on Christian minorities in late 2008 in India, which left more than 60 Christians dead.

Note: Perpetrators do not always claim responsibility, so attributing blame is sometimes impossible. Also, it is often unclear whether the attackers' motivation is purely political or is, in part, the result of criminality.

Sources: National Counter Terrorism Center's Worldwide Incidents Tracking System, http://wits.nctc.gov; Human Security Research Center, School for International Studies, Simon Fraser University, Vancouver, www.hsrgroup.org.

AFP/Getty Images/Simon Maina

Moderate Islamist cleric Sheik Sharif Ahmed became Somalia's new president on Jan. 31, raising hope that the country's long war between religious extremists and moderates would soon end. But the hard-line Islamist al-Shabaab militia later took over the central Somali town of Baidoa and began imposing its harsh brand of Islamic law.

recalls, she was sent by her superiors to a religious conference called "Strong Bonds," where fundamentalist books advocating sexual abstinence, including one called *Thrill of the Chaste*, were distributed. Williams complained to her superiors but did not get a satisfactory response, she says.

In the battle for believers among Christian denominations, "Conservative evangelicals are doing better than denominations like Methodists and Lutherans, whose liberal ideology is poisonous and causing them to implode," says Tennessee-based Southern Baptist preacher Richard Land. "When you make the Ten Commandments the 'Ten Suggestions,' you've got a problem."

However, the tide may be turning, at least in some quarters, in part because the next generation appears to be less religious than its elders. Some see the November 2008 election of President Barack Obama — who got a lot of his support from young voters in states with large evangelical populations where the leaders had endorsed Obama's opponent — as evidence that the reign of the Christian right is over in the United States.

"The sun may be setting on the political influence of fundamentalist churches," wrote *Salon.com* journalist Mike Madden.[25] In fact, the fastest-growing demographic group in the United States is those who claim no religious affiliation; they make up 16 percent of Americans today, compared to 8 percent in the 1980s.[26]

And in Iran, while the Islamic theocracy is still in charge, "the younger generation is far less religious than the older," says Ahmad Dallal, a professor of Arab and Islamic studies at Georgetown University in Washington, D.C.

Moreover, support for fundamentalist violence — specifically by al Qaeda's global terrorist network — has been declining since 2004.[27] For example, 40 percent of Pakistanis supported suicide bombings in 2004 compared to 5 percent in 2007.[28] Nigeria is an exception: 58 percent of Nigerians in 2007 said they still had confidence in al Qaeda leader Osama bin Laden, who ordered the Sept. 11, 2001, terrorist attacks on the United States. Notably, al Qaeda has not carried out any terrorist attacks in Nigeria. Support for al Qaeda has plummeted in virtually all countries affected by its attacks.[29]

And while the Muslim terrorist group Jemaah Islamiyah remains active in Indonesia — the world's most populous Muslim-majority country — claims of rampant fundamentalism there are overstated, according to a report by the Australian Strategic Policy Institute. The study found that 85 percent of Indonesians oppose the idea of their country becoming an Islamic republic.[30]

Although there has been a "conspicuous cultural flowering of Islam in Indonesia," the report continued, other religions are booming, too. In September 2008, for example, authorities overrode Muslim objections and approved an application for a Christian megachurch that seats more than 4,500 people.[31]

Is religious fundamentalism a reaction to Western permissiveness?

Religious experts disagree about what attracts people to religious fundamentalism, but many say it is a response to rapid modernization and the spread of Western multiculturalism and permissiveness.

"Fundamentalism is a modern reaction against modernity," says Jerusalem-based journalist Gershom Gorenberg. "They react against the idea that the truth is not certain. It's like a new bottle of wine with a label saying 'ancient bottle of wine.' "

Peter Berger, director of the Institute on Culture, Religion and World Affairs at Boston University, says fundamentalism is "an attempt to restore the taken-for-grantedness that has been lost as a result of modernization. We are constantly surrounded by people with other views, other norms, other lifestyles. . . . Some people live with this quite well, but others find it oppressive, and they want to be liberated from the liberation."[32]

Sayyid Qutb, founder of Egypt's Muslim Brotherhood, was repulsed by the sexual permissiveness and consumerism he found in the United States during a visit in 1948.[33] He railed against "this behavior, like animals, which you call 'Free mixing of the sexes'; at this vulgarity which you call 'emancipation of women'; at these unfair and cumbersome laws of marriage and divorce, which are contrary to the demands of practical life. . . . These were the realities of Western life which we encountered."[34]

A similar sentiment was felt by Mujahida, a Palestinian Islamic jihadist who told author Lybarger she worried that her people were losing their soul after the 1993 peace agreement with Israel. "There were bars, nightclubs, loud restaurants serving alcohol, satellite TV beaming American sitcoms, steamy Latin American soap operas [and] casinos in Jericho" to generate tax and employment.[35]

And opposition to abortion and gay rights remain the primary rallying call for U.S. evangelicals. In fact, the late American fundamentalist Baptist preacher Jerry Falwell blamed the 9/11 Islamic terrorist attacks in the United States on pagans, abortionists, feminists and homosexuals who promote an "alternative lifestyle" and want to "secularize America."[36]

In her account of the rise of Christian nationalism, journalist Goldberg said the things Islamic fundamentalists hate most about the West — "its sexual openness, its art, the possibilities for escaping the bonds of family and religion, for inventing one's own life — are what Christian nationalists hate as well."[37]

Pew's Green agrees fundamentalists are irritated by permissive Western culture. "There has always been sin in the world," he says, "but now it seems glorified."

But others say the U.S.-led invasion of Iraq in March 2003 triggered the global surge in violent Islamic militancy. The average annual global death toll between March 2003 to September 2006 from Muslim terrorist attacks jumped 237 percent from the toll between September 2001 to March 2003, according to a study published by Simon Fraser University in Canada.[38]

Moreover, when bin Laden declared war on the United States in a 1998 fatwa, he never mentioned Western culture. Instead, he objected to U.S. military bases in Saudi Arabia, the site of some of Islam's holiest shrines. "The Arabian Peninsula has never — since God made it flat, created its desert and encircled it with seas — been stormed by any forces like the crusader armies now spreading in it like locusts, consuming its riches and destroying its plantations." Bin Laden also railed against Israel — "the Jew's petty state" — and "its occupation of Jerusalem and murder of Muslims there."[39]

Some believe former President George W. Bush's habit of couching the "war on terror" in religious terms helped radical Islamic groups recruit jihadists. *An-Nuur* — a Tanzanian weekly Islamic magazine — noted: "Let us remember President Bush is a saved Christian. He is one of those who believe Islam should be destroyed."[40]

Nawaz, a former member of the revolutionary Islamist Hizb ut-Tahrir political movement, says fundamentalists' motivation varies depending on where they come from. "Some political Islamists are relatively liberal," says the English-born Nawaz. "It's the Saudis that are religiously conservative. The problem is their vision is being exported elsewhere."

Indeed, since oil prices first skyrocketed in the 1970s, the Saudi regime has used its growing oil wealth to build conservative Islamic schools (madrassas) and mosques around the world. As *New York Times* reporter Barbara Crossette noted, "from the austere Faisal mosque in Islamabad, Pakistan — a gift of the Saudis — to the stark Istiqlal mosque of Jakarta, Indonesia, silhouettes of domes and minarets reminiscent of Arab architecture are replacing Asia's once-eclectic mosques, which came in all shapes and sizes."[41]

Pew Forum surveys have found no single, predominant factor motivating people to turn to Islamic fundamentalism. Thirty five percent of Indonesians blame immorality for the growth in Islamic extremism; 40 percent of Lebanese blame U.S. policies and

What Is a Fundamentalist?

Few claim the tarnished label

With the word fundamentalism today conjuring up images of cold-blooded suicide bombers as well as anti-abortion zealots, it is hardly surprising that many religious people don't want to be tarred with the fundamentalist brush.

Yet there was a time when traditionalist-minded Christianity wore it as a badge of honor. Baptist clergyman Curtis Lee Laws coined the term in 1910 in his weekly newspaper *Watchman-Examiner*, when he said fundamentalists were those "who still cling to the great fundamentals and who mean to do battle royal for the faith."[1] Several years earlier, Christian theologians had published a series of pamphlets called "The Fundamentals," which defended traditional belief in the Bible's literal truth against modern ideas such as Charles Darwin's theory of evolution.

Essentially a branch within the larger evangelical movement, the fundamentalists felt that the Christian faith would be strengthened if its fundamental tenets were clearly spelled out. Today, while one in three U.S. Christians considers himself an evangelical, "a small and declining percentage would describe themselves as fundamentalist," says Southern Baptist minister Richard Land of Nashville, Tenn. "While most evangelicals support fundamentalist principles, it is unfair to compare them to the Islamists who take up arms and kill people," he says.

Although some may see the label "fundamentalist" as synonymous with radical Islamic extremists, Ahmad Dallal, a professor of Arab and Islamic Studies at Georgetown University in Washington, D.C., notes that the Arabic word for fundamental — *usul* — was never used in this context historically. "There is some logic to applying the word 'fundamental' in an Islamic context, however," he says, because "both the Muslim and Christian fundamentalists emphasize a literal interpretation of the holy texts."

Traditionalist Catholics do not call themselves fundamentalists either. But Professor Martin Marty, a religious history professor at the University of Chicago and author of a multivolume series on fundamentalism, says Catholic followers of French Archbishop Marcel Lefebvre are fundamentalists because they refuse to accept reforms introduced by the Second Vatican Council in 1965. But "theocons" — a group of conservative U.S. Catholic intellectuals — are

influence; 39 percent of Moroccans blame poverty and 34 percent of Turks blame a lack of education.[42]

Then there are those who just want to regain their lost power, notes Iranian-born author Hunter. "In Iran, Turkey, Tunisia and Egypt, there was a forced secularization of society," she says. "Religious people lost power — sometimes their jobs, too. They had to develop a new discourse to restore their standing."

Religious fundamentalists in Nigeria are largely motivated by anger at the government for frittering away the country's vast oil supplies through corruption and mismanagement. "When a government fails its people, they turn elsewhere to safeguard themselves and their futures, and in Nigeria . . . they have turned to religion," asserted American religion writer Eliza Griswold.[43]

Many Christian and Muslim leaders preach the "Gospel of prosperity," which encourages Nigerians to better themselves economically. But Kenyan-based Baptist preacher Nkansah says that "while the Gospel brings good health and prosperity," the message can be taken too far. "There are some people in the Christian movement who are too materialistic."

Nkansah argues that evangelism is growing in Africa because "as human beings we all have needs. When people hear Christ came onto this planet to save them, they tend to respond."

But a journalist in Tajikistan says poverty drives Central Asians to radical groups like the Hizb ut-Tahrir (HT). "In the poor regions, especially the Ferghana Valley on the Kyrgyz-Tajik-Uzbek border, HT is very active," says the journalist, who asks to remain unnamed for fear of reprisals. "Unemployment pushes people to find consolation in something else, and they find it in religion."

Should religious fundamentalists have a greater voice in government?

Religious fundamentalists who have taken the reins of government — in Iran (since 1979), Afghanistan

not fundamentalists, he says, because they accept the so-called Vatican II changes. Theocon George Weigel, a fellow at the Ethics and Public Policy Center in Washington, eschews the word "fundamentalist" because he says it is "a term used by secular people with prejudices, which doesn't illuminate very much."

Neither are religious Jews keen on the term. Rabbi Avi Tawil, director of the Brussels office of the Chabad Jewish missionary movement, says "fundamentalism is about forcing people. We don't do that. We strictly respect Jewish law, which says if someone would like to convert then you have to help them."

AFP/Getty Images/MBC

Al Qaeda leader Osama bin Laden hails the economic losses suffered by the United States after the Sept. 11, 2001, terrorist attacks. "God ordered us to terrorize the infidels, and we terrorized the infidels," bin Laden's spokesman Suleiman Abu Ghaith said in the same video, which was broadcast soon after the attacks that killed nearly 3,000 people.

Jerusalem-based writer Gershom Gorenberg notes that unlike Christians and Muslims, fundamentalist Jews do not typically advocate reading holy texts literally because their tradition has always been to have multiple interpretations. The term is even harder to apply to Hinduism because — unlike Christianity, Judaism and Islam — whose "fundaments" are their holy texts, Hinduism's origins are shrouded in ancient history, and its core elements are difficult to define.[2]

Yet fundamentalists are united in their aversion to modernism.

As Seyyed Hossein Nasr, an Islamic studies professor at George Washington University, noted: "When I was a young boy in Iran, 50 or 60 years ago . . . the word fundamentalism hadn't been invented. Modernism was just coming into the country."[3]

[1] Brenda E. Brasher, *Encyclopedia of Fundamentalism* (2001), p. 50.

[2] *Ibid.*, p. 222.

[3] His comments were made at a Pew Forum discussion, "Between Relativism and Fundamentalism: Is There a Middle Ground?" March 4, 2008, in Washington, D.C., http://pewforum.org/events/?EventID=172.

(1996-2001) and the Gaza Strip (since 2007) — have either supported terrorism or have instituted repressive regimes. Grave human rights abuses have been documented, dissenters tortured, homosexuals hanged, adulterers stoned, music banned and education denied for girls.

Ayaan Hirsi Ali — a Somali-born feminist writer, a former Dutch politician and a fellow at the conservative American Enterprise Institute who has denounced her family's Muslim faith — says fundamentalists should be able to compete for the chance to govern. "But we must tell them a system based on Islamic theology is bad," she says. "The problem is that Muslims cannot criticize their moral guide. Mohammad is more than a pope, he is a king. As a classical liberal, I say not even God is beyond criticism."

However, Danish politician Abdol-Hamid, whose parents are Palestinian, argues that because most countries won't talk to Hamas, the ruling party in the Gaza Strip, because of its terrorist activities, "we failed the Palestinians by never giving Hamas a chance." In Denmark, she continues, "We have Christian extremists, and I have to accept them." For instance, she explains, the far-right Danish Peoples Party (DPP) wants to ban the wearing of Muslim headscarves in the Danish parliament, and DPP member of parliament Soren Krarup, a Lutheran priest, says the hijab and the Nazi swastika are both symbols of totalitarianism. Abdol-Hamid hopes to become the first hijab-wearing woman elected to the parliament.

After interviewing Hamas' founding father, Sheikh Ahmed Yassin, Lebanese-born journalist Zaki Chebab wrote that Yassin "was confident that . . . Israel would disappear off the map within three decades," a belief he said came from the Koran.[44]

A Christian fundamentalist came to power in Northern Ireland without dire consequences after the Rev. Ian Paisley — the longtime leader of Ulster's Protestants, who established his own church stressing biblical literalism and once called the pope the "antichrist" — ultimately

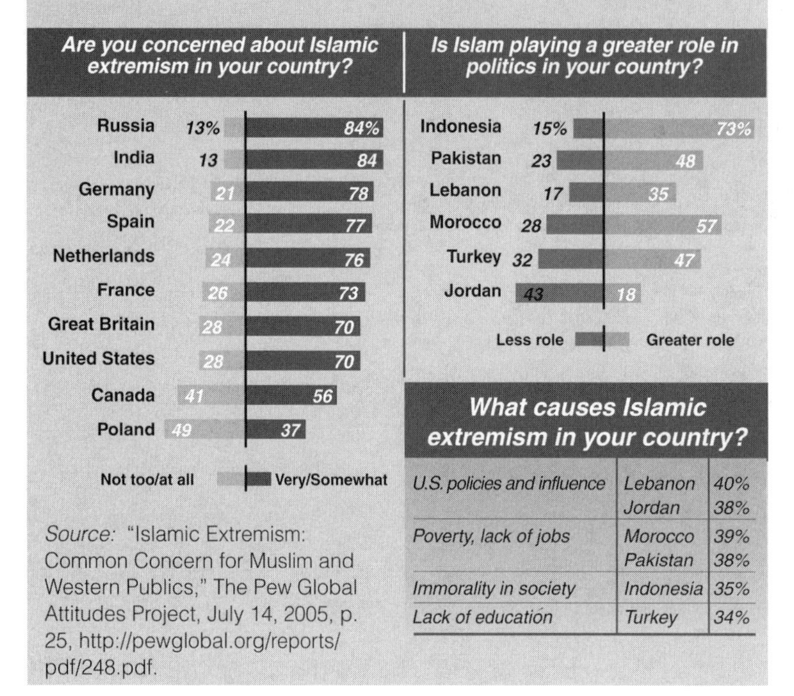

U.S. policies and influence	Lebanon	40%
	Jordan	38%
Poverty, lack of jobs	Morocco	39%
	Pakistan	38%
Immorality in society	Indonesia	35%
Lack of education	Turkey	34%

Source: "Islamic Extremism: Common Concern for Muslim and Western Publics," The Pew Global Attitudes Project, July 14, 2005, p. 25, http://pewglobal.org/reports/pdf/248.pdf.

reconciled his lifelong differences with Northern Irish Catholic leaders and has served amicably with them in government after they offered him political power.[45]

Kenyan-based evangelical Nkansah says "politics is part of life." If a religious person is called into politics in Kenya, he explains, "they should go because that is their vocation." He supports Kenya's model, in which many clergy members, including bishops, enter politics, even though the constitution bans parties based on religion. But evangelical pastor Steuernagel says that in Brazil, religious leaders are increasingly going into politics. "I do not think it is healthy," he says, "but it is happening."

In Central Asia, Islamic parties are only allowed in Tajikistan. But while the Islamic Revival Party has become a significant force there, the party "is neither dangerous nor radical," according to the Tajik journalist, and "does not dream about having a state like Iran."

"It is a delicate game," says fundamentalism expert Marty. "If you have a republican system with a secular constitution, then, yes [fundamentalists must be allowed to have a voice], because they have to respect that constitution. But it's very much a case of 'handle with care.' "

Conservative Catholic theologian George Weigel, a senior fellow at the Ethics and Public Policy Center in Washington, says religious people are entitled to be involved in politics, but "they should translate their religiously informed moral convictions into concepts and words that those who don't share their theological commitments can engage and debate. This is called 'democratic courtesy.' It's also political common sense."

Indeed, religious Muslims not only have the right but also the duty to participate in government, according to Rachid Ghannouchi, a Tunisian-born Islamic thinker. Denouncing countries like Tunisia and Algeria that repress Islamic fundamentalism, Ghannouchi said, "the real problem lies in convincing the ruling regimes... of the right of Islamists — just like other political groups — to form political parties, engage in political activities and compete for power or share in power through democratic means."[46]

But ex-Islamist Nawaz warns: "We should not be encouraging Islamists, because every terrorist group has grown out of a nonviolent Islamist group."

Israeli journalist Gorenberg also notes that radical Jewish fundamentalists have repeatedly resorted to violence, citing the case of Baruch Goldstein, a U.S.-born Israeli doctor and supporter of the Kach party who killed 29 Muslims at the tomb of Abraham in Hebron in 1994.

Washington-based Turkish journalist Tulin Daloglu is anxious about her country's future under the ruling Justice and Development Party. "Women are starting to cover their hair in order to get jobs in government," she claims. "The case is not at all proven that Islam and democracy can live in harmony. Turkey is a swing state" in that regard.

Meanwhile, in some Asian and African countries where the rule of law is weak — Pakistan and Somalia for example — many are clamoring for Islamic law. Often the existing government is so dysfunctional that the quick, decisive administration of Islamic law, or sharia, is attractive. In Pakistan, says British journalist Jason Burke, "the choice between slow, corrupt and expensive state legal systems and the religious alternative — rough and ready though it may be — is not hard." Even educated, relatively wealthy women are demanding sharia, he said.[47]

For example, the Taliban has been able to seize control in Pakistan's Swat region because of "an ineffectual and unresponsive civilian government, coupled with military and security forces that, in the view of furious residents, have willingly allowed the militants to spread terror deep into Pakistan."[48]

BACKGROUND

'Great Awakening'

Christian fundamentalist movements trace their origins to the emergence of Protestantism in 16th-century Europe, when the German monk Martin Luther (1483-1546) urged people to return to the basics of studying the Bible.[49] In 1620 a group of fundamentalist Protestants known as the Pilgrims fleeing persecution in England settled in North America and, along with the Puritans who arrived shortly afterwards, greatly influenced the course of Christianity in New England.

In the 1700s, as science began to threaten religion's preeminence, North Americans launched a Protestant revival known as the "Great Awakening," from which the evangelical movement was born. Revivals held throughout the American colonies between 1739 and 1743, offered evangelical, emotionally charged sermons — often in open-air services before large groups — that stressed the need to forge a personal relationship with Jesus Christ. Leaders in the movement included preachers George Whitfield, Gilbert Tennent and Jonathan Edwards.[50]

A similar revival movement — the Sunday school movement — began in the late 18th century, becoming a

AFP/Getty Images/Walter Astrada

Evangelicals from Uganda's Born Again Church are spiritually moved last August while listening to a sermon by Pastor Robert Kayanja, one of Uganda's most prominent evangelical preachers. While Uganda has long been heavily Christian, many churchgoers have switched from mainstream to Pentecostal sects in recent years.

primary vehicle for evangelism.[51] The term "fundamentalist" originated in the United States when the first of a 12-volume collection of essays called *The Fundamentals* was published in 1910, outlining the core tenets of Christianity.[52] In 1925 fundamentalists were the driving force in the trial of Tennessee schoolteacher John Scopes, who was convicted of breaking a Tennessee law that forbade the teaching of evolution instead of the Bible's version of how the world was created. Even though the fundamentalists won the case, they were lampooned in the popular press, and their credibility and esteem suffered. They withdrew from the limelight and formed their own subculture of churches, Bible colleges, camps and seminaries.

By 1950, the charismatic American Baptist preacher Billy Graham had begun to broaden the fundamentalists' base, and they became masters at harnessing the mass media, especially radio and television. The 1973 U.S. Supreme Court's *Roe v. Wade* ruling legalizing abortion further galvanized evangelicals, leading Baptist preacher Falwell in 1979 to establish the Moral Majority — a conservative political advocacy group.

After his unsuccessful run for president of the United States in 1988, television evangelist and Christian nationalist Robertson formed the Christian Coalition to fight for "family-friendly" policies — specifically policies against homosexuality and abortion. By the mid-1990s

CHRONOLOGY

A.D. 70-1700s *The three great, monotheistic, text-based religions — Christianity, Islam and Judaism — spread worldwide.*

70 Romans destroy the second Jewish temple in Jerusalem, causing Jews to scatter across the globe.

319 Christianity becomes the official religion of the Roman Empire; pagan sacrifices are outlawed.

632 Mohammad dies in Medina, Arabia. . . . Islam begins to spread to the Middle East, Africa, India, Indonesia and Southern Europe.

1730s-40s Evangelical movement is born in the United States in a religious revival known as the "Great Awakening."

1800s-1920s *Fundamentalist impulses are triggered in reaction to scientific developments, modernization and — in the case of Islam — Western colonization.*

1859 British biologist Charles Darwin presents theory of evolution in *On the Origin of Species*, casting doubt on the Bible's account of creation.

1906 African-American evangelist William J. Seymour launches the Azusa Street revival in Los Angeles, sparking the worldwide Pentecostal movement.

1910 American Christian oil magnates Lyman and Milton Stewart commission The Fundamentals, promoting fundamentalist Protestant beliefs that the Bible contains no errors.

1921 Jailed Hindu nationalist Vinayak Damodar Savarkar writes *Hindutva: Who is a Hindu?* — laying the foundation for movements promoting Hindu identity, including the radical Bajrang Dal.

1928 Hasan al-Banna, a schoolteacher in Cairo, Egypt, establishes the Muslim Brotherhood, which calls for all Muslims to make their societies more Islamic.

1940s-1970s *Fundamentalism becomes a significant force in politics and society.*

1948 Israel declares independence, causing millions of Jews — both secular and religious — to return to their spiritual homeland.

1967 Fundamentalist Jews settle in Palestinian territories occupied after the Six-Day War, triggering an explosion in Islamic fundamentalism among disgruntled Arabs.

1973 U.S. Supreme Court's *Roe v. Wade* ruling legalizes abortion, galvanizing Christian fundamentalists into political activism.

1979 Islamists overthrow the Shah of Iran and install the world's first Islamic theocracy in modern times.

1980s-2000s *Fundamentalists increasingly endorse violence to further their goals — especially in the Muslim world.*

1984 Indian government storms a Sikh temple, which Sikh militants had occupied, leading two of Prime Minister Indira Gandhi's Sikh bodyguards to murder her.

1994 American Jewish fundamentalist Baruch Goldstein kills 29 Muslims praying at a mosque in the Palestinian city of Hebron.

Sept. 11, 2001 Al Qaeda Islamists kill nearly 3,000 people by flying hijacked planes into the World Trade Center and Pentagon; a third hijacked plane crashes in Pennsylvania.

2002 Sectarian fighting between Hindus and Muslims in Gujarat, India, kills more than 800 people — mostly Muslims.

2006 Palestinians elect Hamas, a radical Islamic party, to lead the government.

2008 Sixty Christians die after outbreak of fundamentalist Hindu violence against Christians in India. . . . Pakistan-based Islamists launch coordinated attacks in Mumbai, India, killing 164 people. . . . Troops from Congo, Uganda and South Sudan launch ongoing joint offensive to crush Uganda's fundamentalist Lord's Resistance Army. . . . Israel launches major attack on Gaza in effort to weaken Hamas, resulting in 1,300 Palestinian deaths.

the coalition became the most prominent voice in the Christian movement, largely by publishing voter guides on how local politicians voted on specific social issues important to Christian fundamentalists. Many credit the coalition with helping the Republican Party, which had embraced their platform on social issues, to take majority control of the U.S. Congress in the 1994 midterm elections.[53]

Some U.S. fundamentalists segregated themselves from mainstream society — which they saw as immoral — and educated their children at home.[54] A strand of race-based fundamentalism also emerged, called the Christian Identity movement, which claimed the Bible was the history of the white race and that Jews were the biological descendants of Satan. A Christian Reconstructionist movement, led by preacher Mark Rushdoony, emerged as well, advocating local theocracies that would impose biblical law.[55] The reconstructionists oppose government schools and demand that civil disputes be settled in church courts and that taxes be limited to 10 percent of income (based on the tithe). Through its books, the movement has had a significant influence on other Christian political organizations.[56]

Meanwhile, a fundamentalist Catholic movement emerged in Europe after French Archbishop Marcel Lefebvre refused to accept changes introduced by the Vatican in the 1960s, notably saying Mass in languages other than Latin.[57] Other conservative Catholic movements include Opus Dei, founded by Spanish priest Josemaria Escriva in 1928. Today it is based in Rome, has 75,000 members in 50 countries and appeals to well-educated lay Catholics.[58] In the United States, a group of Catholic intellectuals — including Michael Novak, Weigel and Richard John Neuhaus — became known as the "theocons" and allied themselves with Protestant evangelicals in opposing abortion and gay rights.[59]

Bush's presidency was a high point for U.S. evangelicals. Bush announced during the 2000 campaign that he was a "born again" Christian whose favorite philosopher was Jesus Christ — "because he changed my heart." He also told a Texas evangelist that he felt God had chosen him to run for president, and he was accused of "creeping Christianization" of the federal government by establishing an Office for Faith-Based Initiatives, which critics claimed was just a vehicle for channeling tax dollars to conservative Christian groups.[60]

Bush liberally used religious rhetoric — declaring, for example, after the 9/11 attacks that his mission was "to rid the world of evil."[61] He named Missouri Sen. John Ashcroft, a fellow evangelist, as attorney general and filled his administration with Christian conservatives, such as Monica Goodling, a young Justice Department official who vetted candidates for executive appointments by checking their views on moral issues like abortion.[62]

Christian missionaries have been evangelizing — spreading their faith — since the 16th century, but fundamentalist strands have grown increasingly prominent in recent decades. Pentecostalism — which began in 1901 when a Kansas Bible studies student, Agnes Ozman, began "speaking in tongues" — is the dominant form of Protestantism in Latin America.[63] In Guatemala, evangelicalism began to overtake the Roman Catholic Church in the 1980s after Catholicism was seen as too European and elitist.[64] Although Pentecostals usually distinguish themselves from run-of-the-mill fundamentalists, both are part of the evangelical family.

In Africa, Christian fundamentalism developed its strongest base in sub-Saharan regions — particularly Nigeria, triggering rising tensions and sporadic violence between the country's Christian and Muslim populations. U.S. Christian fundamentalists have helped to spread an extreme brand of Christianity to Africa, according to Cedric Mayson, director of the African National Congress' Commission for Religious Affairs, in South Africa. "We are extremely concerned about the support given by the U.S. to the proliferation of right-wing Christian fundamentalist groups in Africa," Mayson wrote, as "they are the major threat to peace and stability in Africa."[65]

Uganda became home to the militant Christian fundamentalist Lord's Resistance Army. Its leader Joseph Kony — known as the "altar boy who grew up to be a guerrilla leader" — has transformed an internal Ugandan power struggle into an international conflict by roaming across Sudan and the Democratic Republic of Congo, kidnapping children en route for use as soldiers after slaughtering their parents.[66]

Patrick Makasi, the LRA's former director of operations, called Kony "a religious man" who "all the time . . . is talking about God. Every time he keeps calling many people to teach them about the legends and about God. That is how he leads people."[67]

Officials in the 'Stans' Uneasy About Islamization

Education is a key battleground

"The crowd in the airport parking lot was jubilant despite the cold, with squealing children, busy concession stands and a tangle of idling cars giving the impression of an eager audience before a rock concert," wrote journalist Sabrina Tavernise of a scene in Dushanbe, the capital of Tajikistan.[1]

"But it was religion, not rock 'n roll, that had drawn so many people," she wrote. The families were there to meet relatives returning from the Hajj — the pilgrimage to Mecca that Muslims strive to undertake at least once in their lifetime. Last year, 5,200 Tajiks participated — 10 times more than in 2000.

Getty Images/Uriel Sinai

The refurbished Juma Mosque in Tashkent, Uzbekistan, reflects Islam's resurgence in Central Asia, where 18 years after the breakup of the former Soviet Union neighboring Iran and Saudi Arabia are exerting their influence on the vast region.

Since gaining independence from the anti-religious Soviet Union, Tajikistan has been re-embracing its Islamic roots, and a Westerner in the country — who asked to remain unnamed — worries the nation of 7.2 million people may adopt an extreme form of Islam. "Every day you can see on our streets more women wearing the veil and more men with beards," he says.

But while many women in Central Asia today do cover themselves from head to toe, it is "extremely rare" for them to cover their faces as well, which was not unusual in pre-Soviet Tajikistan and Uzbekistan, says Martha Brill Olcott, a senior associate at the Carnegie Endowment for International Peace in Washington, who has traveled there frequently since 1975.

The region is undergoing a wide mix of outside influences, not all of them Islamic, Olcott notes. For example, some women have begun wearing the hijab (a headscarf pinned tightly around the face so as to cover the hair) worn by modern Islamic women in the West, while others, notably in Uzbekistan, imitate secular Western fashions such as short skirts and visible belly piercing.

The Westerner in Tajikistan fears that the government's efforts to block the growing Islamization may be having the opposite effect. Government policies "are too severe," he says. "They give long prison sentences to young men and shut down unregistered mosques. This just strengthens people's resolution to resist an unfair system."

Further, he suggests, "If they developed local economies more, people would not think about radical Islam." Without economic development, "Tajikistan could become another Afghanistan or Iran."

Tajikistan, one of the poorer countries in the region, is in the midst of reverse urbanization due to economic decline, with 77 percent of the population now living in rural areas compared to 63 percent in the mid-1980s.[2] A million Tajiks work in Russia.

In neighboring Uzbekistan, the picture is similar. Olcott likens the California-sized nation of 27 million people to an "ineffective police state. There are restrictions, but people can get around them and — more important — they are not afraid to get around them." She says the government's response is erratic: "If you do not draw attention to yourself, you can be an Islamist. But if you preach and open schools or wear very Islamic dress, you can get into trouble."

Christian missionaries are also active in Central Asia. Russian-dubbed broadcasts from U.S. televangelist Pat Robertson are aired throughout the region. According to the Tajikistan-based Westerner, after the 1991 fall of the Soviet Union "Jehovah's Witnesses, Baptists and Adventists came from Russia, Western Europe, South Korea and the United States. The locals were friendly to them because they provided humanitarian aid to poor people." However, authorities in the region have recently clamped down — especially on the Jehovah's Witnesses, he says.[3]

In Kazakhstan authorities have cracked down on Protestants and repressed the Hindu-based Hare Krishnas, while in Kyrgyzstan a new law makes it harder to register religious organizations.[4]

In Kyrgyzstan, the authorities are in a quandary about whether to allow a new political movement, the Union of Muslims, to be set up because bringing Islam into politics violates the constitution. Yet union co-founder Tursunbay Bakir Uulu argues that a moderately Islamic party would help stabilize the country. "Currently Hizb-ut-Tahrir is conquering the Issyk-Kul region," he warned. "Religious sects are stepping up their activities. We want moderate Islam, which has nothing to do with anti-religious teaching and which respects values of other world religions, to fill this niche."[5]

The Islamization began in the 1980s, when Soviet President Mikhail Gorbachev eased restrictions on religious worship that had been enforced by the communists for decades. After the Soviet Union's collapse, the relaxation accelerated as the Central Asian republics became independent nations. Muslim missionaries flocked to the region, and conservative Islamic schools, universities and mosques quickly sprang up, many financed by foundations in oil-rich Arab states like Saudi Arabia, where the ultra-fundamentalist Wahhabi Muslim sect is the state-sponsored religion.[6]

Many Central Asians see embracing conservative Islam as a way to define themselves and reject their Russian-dominated communist past. Curiously, their increasing exposure to secular culture through Russia-based migrant Tajik workers appears to be having a Westernizing influence on the society even as Islam is growing: "Five years ago, I could not wear shorts on the street," said the Westerner in Tajikistan. "Now in summer you can see a lot of Tajik men and even girls wearing shorts in the cities, although not in the villages."

The rise of Islam is strongest in Uzbekistan, Tajikistan and Kyrgyzstan, while Turkmenistan and Kazakhstan have stronger secular traditions. Uzbek authorities initially encouraged Islamization, believing it would help strengthen national identity. But by the late 1990s, they were afraid of losing control to radical elements and began repressing militant groups like the Islamic Movement of Uzbekistan and Hizb-ut-Tahrir.[7] A jailbreak by Islamists in Andijan, the Uzbek capital, in May 2005 triggered violent clashes between government forces and anti-corruption protesters — whom the government claimed were Islamic extremists — resulting in 187 deaths.[8]

Meanwhile, the Saudis are sending Islamic textbooks that promote their own conservative brand of Islam to schools in the region.[9] Saudi-Uzbek ties stretch back to the 1920s, when some Uzbeks fled to Saudi Arabia, according to Olcott.

But Saudi-inspired fundamentalism "is not a major factor" in Turkmenistan yet, says Victoria Clement, an assistant professor of Islamic world history at Western Carolina University, who has lived in Turkmenistan. "There are maybe a few individuals, but the government has not allowed madrasas [Islamic religious schools] since 2003." Even so, she notes, "when I went to the mosques, I saw clerics instructing the kids in the Koran, which technically they should not have been doing [under Turkmen law], but I do not think it was harmful."

Nevertheless, the Turkmen education system is growing more Islamic, Clement says, as new schools follow the model devised by Turkish preacher Fethullah Gulen. "They do not have classes in religion, but they teach a conservative moral code — no drinking, smoking, staying out late at night. I think it is a great alternative to the Islamic madrasas," she says.

Olcott says while the quality of education in the Gulen schools may be good, it is "still very Islamic." Gulen himself now lives in the United States, having left Turkey after being accused of undermining secularism.

The Westerner in Tajikistan notes, however, that in their efforts to stem the growth of radical Islam authorities have a bit of a blind spot when it comes to education. "In most Tajik villages, the children's only teacher is the person who can read the Koran in Arabic, and that is dangerous. The government makes demands about how students look — ties and suits for example — but does not care about what they have in their minds."

Islam Booming in the "Stans"

Several of the nations in Central Asia dubbed "the Stans" are rediscovering their Islamic roots, including Tajikistan and Uzbekistan. The Islamization began in the 1980s, when then Soviet President Mikhail Gorbachev eased restrictions on religious worship.

[1] Sabrina Tavernise, "Independent, Tajiks Revel in Their Faith," *The New York Times*, Jan. 3, 2009, www.nytimes.com/2009/01/04/world/asia/04tajik.html?emc=tnt&tntemail0=y.

[2] *Ibid.*

[3] Felix Corley, "Tajikistan: Jehovah's Witnesses Banned," Forum 18 News Service (Oslo, Norway), Oct. 18, 2007, www.forum18.org/Archive.php?article_id=1036; Felix Corley, "Turkmenistan: Fines, beatings, threats of rape and psychiatric incarceration," Forum 18 News Service (Oslo, Norway), Nov. 25, 2008, www.forum18.org/Archive.php?article_id=1221.

[4] Mushfig Bayram, "Kazakhstan: Police Struggle against Extremism, Separatism and Terrorism — and restaurant meals," Forum 18 News Service, Nov. 21, 2008, www.forum18.org/Archive.php?article_id=1220; and Mushfig Bayram, "Kyrgyzstan: Restrictive Religion Law passes Parliament Unanimously," Forum 18 News Service (Oslo, Norway), Nov. 6, 2008, www.forum18.org/Archive.php?article_id=1215.

[5] "Kyrgyz Experts Say Newly Set Up Union of Muslims Aims for Power," *Delo No* (Kyrgyzstan), BBC Monitoring International Reports, Dec. 9, 2008.

[6] See Martha Brill Olcott and Diora Ziyaeva, "Islam in Uzbekistan: Religious Education and State Ideology," Carnegie Endowment for International Peace, July 2008, www.carnegieendowment.org/publications/index.cfm?fa=view&id=21980&prog=zru.

[7] *Ibid.*, p. 2.

[8] For background, see Kenneth Jost, "Russia and the Former Soviet Republics," *CQ Researcher*, June 17, 2005, pp. 541-564.

[9] *Ibid.*, p. 19.

Getty Images/Chip Somodevilla

Anti-abortion demonstrators carry a statue of the Virgin Mary during the March for Life in Washington, D.C., on Jan. 22, 2009. The rally marked the 35th anniversary of the Supreme Court's landmark Roe v. Wade decision legalizing abortion in the United States. Fundamentalist Christians continue to exert significant influence on U.S. policies governing abortion, birth control and gay rights.

Islamic Fundamentalism

Originating in the 7th century with the Prophet Mohammad, Islam considers the Koran sacred both in content and form — meaning it should be read in the original language, Arabic. Muslims also follow the Hadith, Mohammad's more specific instructions on how to live, which were written down after he died. Though Islamic scholars have interpreted both texts for centuries, fundamentalists use the original texts.

The concept of a militant Islamic struggle was developed by scholar Taqi ad-Din Ahmad Ibn Taymiyyah (1263-1328), who called for "holy war" against the conquering, non-Muslim Mongols.[68] The Saudi-born Islamic scholar Muhammed Ibn Abd-al-Wahhab (1703-1792) criticized the Ottoman Empire for corrupting the purity of Islam. The descendants of one of Wahhab's followers, Muhammed Ibn Saud, rule Saudi Arabia today.[69]

Responding to the dominating influence of Western powers that were colonizing the Islamic world at the time, Egyptian schoolteacher Hasan Al-Banna set up the Muslim Brotherhood in 1928 to re-Islamize Egypt. The organization later expanded to other Arab countries and to Sudan.[70] "They copied what the Christian missionaries were doing in Africa by doing social work," notes Islamic studies Professor Dallal. "But they had no vision for 'the state,' and they paid a price for this because the state ultimately suppressed them."

In the 1950s the extremist group Hizb-ut-Tahrir, which advocates a single Islamic state encompassing all predominantly Muslim countries, emerged and spread across the Islamic world. In the mid-1950s, while imprisoned in Egypt by the secular government, the U.S.-educated Egyptian scholar and social reformer Qutb (1906-1966) wrote *Milestones*, his diatribe against the permissiveness of the West, which persuaded many Muslims they needed to get more involved in politics in order to get their governments to make their societies more Islamic. In Pakistan, the politician Sayyid Abul A'la Mawdudi (1903-1979) urged Islamists to restore Islamic law by forming political parties and getting elected to political office, according to Dallal.

The 1973 oil crisis helped to spread conservative Islam by further enriching Saudi Arabia, which set up schools, universities and charities around the world advocating ultraconservative wahhabi Islam. And the 1979 Iranian Revolution — in which the pro-Western Shah Mohammad Reza Pahlavi was deposed in a conservative Shia Muslim revolt led by Ayatollah Ruhollah Khomeini — installed the first Islamic theocracy in the modern era.

In 1991 Islamists were voted into power in Algeria, but the military refused to let them govern, triggering a bloody civil war that the secularists eventually won. In Afghanistan, the ultraconservative Pakistan-sponsored Taliban seized power in 1996 and imposed their strict version of Islamic law — outlawing music, forbidding girls from going to school or leaving their homes without a male relative, forcing women to completely cover their bodies — even their eyes — in public, requiring men to grow beards and destroying all books except the Koran.[71] After the al Qaeda terrorist attacks of 9/11, the United States ousted the Taliban, which had been sheltering bin Laden.

Al Qaeda, a Sunni Muslim group that originated in Saudi Arabia, had been based in Afghanistan since the 1980s, when it helped eject Soviet occupiers, with U.S. aid. But in the 1990s bin Laden redirected his energies against the United States after American troops were stationed in his native Saudi Arabia, home to several sacred Muslim shrines.

After the U.S.-led invasion of Iraq in 2003, al Qaeda urged its followers to switch their attentions to Iraq, which became a magnet for Islamist jihadists. In 2007 al Qaeda attacks in Iraq escalated to such a level of violence — including attacking Shia mosques and repressing local Sunnis — that other Islamic groups like the Muslim Brotherhood repudiated them.[72]

In Europe, meanwhile, beginning in the 1980s the growing Muslim immigrant population began to attach greater importance to its religious identity, and some turned to violence. Algerian extremists set off bombs in Paris subways and trains in 1995-1996; Moroccan-born Islamic terrorists killed 191 people in train bombings in Madrid in 2004; and British-based al Qaeda operatives of mainly Pakistani origin killed 52 people in suicide train and bus bombings in London in 2005.[73] And an al Qaeda cell based in Hamburg, Germany, plotted the 9/11 attacks on the World Trade Center towers and the Pentagon.

The estimated 5 million Muslims in the United States — who are a mix of immigrants and African-Americans — are more moderate than their Western European counterparts.[74] Poverty is likely to have played a role in making European Muslims more radical: Whereas the average income of American Muslims is close to the national average, Muslims' average income lags well behind the national average in Spain, France, Britain and Germany.[75]

Meanwhile, the creation of Israel in 1948 — fiercely opposed by all of its Arab neighbors — and its successive expansions in the Gaza Strip and West Bank have helped to spur Islamic fundamentalism in the region. To Israel's north, the Shia-Muslim Hezbollah group emerged in the 1980s in Lebanon with the goal of destroying Israel and making Lebanon an Islamic state. The Sunni-Muslim group Hamas — an offshoot of the Muslim Brotherhood — won elections in the Palestinian territories in 2006. Hamas, which was launched during the Palestinian uprising against Israel of 1987, has forged strong links with Islamic fundamentalists in Iran and Saudi Arabia.[76]

Fundamentalist Jews

Predating both Islam and Christianity, Judaism takes the Torah and Talmud as its two holy texts and believes that the Prophet Moses received the Ten Commandments — inscribed on stone tablets — from God on Mount Sinai.[77] Fundamentalist Jews believe they are God's chosen people and that God gave them modern-day Israel as their homeland. A defining moment in this narrative is the destruction of the second Jewish Temple in Jerusalem in 70 A.D., which triggered the scattering of Jews throughout the world for nearly 2,000 years.

AFP/Getty Images/Jack Guez

Members of the ultra-Orthodox Chabad-Lubavitch Jewish fundamentalist movement attend the funeral in Israel of two members of the missionary sect killed last fall during Islamist militant attacks in Mumbai, India.

Jews began returning to their spiritual homeland in significant numbers in the early 1900s with the advent of Zionism — a predominantly secular political movement to establish a Jewish homeland, founded by the Austro-Hungarian journalist Theodor Herzl in the late 19th century in response to rising anti-Semitism in Europe. The migration was accelerated after Nazi Germany began persecuting the Jewish people in the 1930s in a racially motivated campaign that resulted in the Holocaust and the murder of 6 million Jews and millions of others.[78] Today, a third the world's 15 million Jews live in Israel; most of the rest live in the United States, with substantial Jewish communities in France, Argentina and Canada.

Fundamentalist Jews regret that Israel was established as a secular democracy rather than a theocracy. While most Israelis support the secular model, there is a growing minority of ultra-Orthodox (Haredi) Jews for whom the Torah and Talmud form the core of their identity. They try to observe 613 commandments and wear distinctive garb: long black caftans, side curls and hats for men and long-sleeve dresses, hats, wigs and scarves for women.[79] The Haredim dream of building a new Jewish temple in Jerusalem where the old ones stood, which also happens to be the site of the Dome on the Rock — one of Islam's most revered shrines. The fundamentalist

Islamic Fundamentalism Limits Women's Rights

But Muslim women disagree on the religion's impact

As a high official in Saudi Arabia, Ahmed Zaki Yamani crafted many of the kingdom's laws, basing them on Wahhabism, the strict form of Islam that is Saudi Arabia's state religion. Under those laws, Muslim judges "have affirmed women's competence in all civil matters," he has written, but "many of them have reservations regarding her political competence." In fact, he added, one of Islam's holiest texts, the Hadith, "considered deficiency a corollary of femaleness."[1]

Since the 1970s, the Saudis have used their vast oil wealth to spread their ultra-conservative form of Islam throughout the Middle East, North Africa and South and Central Asia, including its controversial view of women as unequal to men. Under Saudi Wahhabism, women cannot vote, drive cars or mix freely with men. They also must have a male guardian make many critical decisions on their behalf, which Human Rights Watch called "the most significant impediment to the realization of women's rights in the kingdom."[2]

The advocacy group added that "the religious establishment has consistently paralyzed any efforts to advance women's rights by applying only the most restrictive provisions of Islamic law, while disregarding more progressive interpretations."[3]

In her autobiography, *Infidel*, Somali-born writer and former Dutch politician Ayaan Hirsi Ali writes about how shocked she was as a young girl when her family moved from Somalia's less conservative Islamic society to Saudi Arabia, where females' lives were much more restricted. "Any girl who goes out unaccompanied is up for grabs," she says.

Raised a Muslim but today an outspoken critic of Islam, Hirsi Ali says Saudi Arabia has had a "horrific" influence on the Muslim world — especially on women. In Africa, she says, religious strictures against women going out in public can have dire consequences, because many women must work outside the home for economic reasons.

While Wahhabism is perhaps the most extreme form of Islam, Hirsi Ali doubts any form of Islam is compatible with women's rights. "Islamic feminism is a contradiction in terms," she says. "Islam means 'submission.' This is double for women: She must appeal to God before anyone else. Yet this same God tells your man he can beat you."

In 2004, Dutch filmmaker Theo Van Gogh was murdered by a Muslim man angered by a film he made portraying violence against women in Islamic societies. Hirsi Ali, then a member of the Dutch parliament, had written the script for the movie, and the assassin left a note on Van Gogh's body threatening her.

She believes the entire philosophical underpinnings of Islam are flawed. For example, she says, she had been taught that Muslim women must wear the veil so they will not corrupt men, yet, "when I came to Europe I could not understand how women were not covered, and yet the men were not jumping on them. Then I saw all it took was to educate boys to exercise self-control. They don't do that in Saudi Arabia, Iran and Pakistan."

But forcing women to cover themselves is not the only way conservative Muslim societies infringe on women's rights. Until recently in Pakistan, rape cases could not be prosecuted unless four pious Muslim men were willing to testify that they had witnessed the attack. Without their testimony the victim could be prosecuted for fornication and alleging a false crime, punishable by stoning, lashing or prison.[4]

Ali's views are not shared by Asmaa Abdol-Hamid, a young, Danish Muslim politician of Palestinian parentage who lived in the United Arab Emirates before moving to Denmark at age 6. Covering oneself, she says, "makes women more equal because there is less focus on her body. . . . When you watch an ad on television, it is always women in bikinis selling the car."

A social worker, local council member representing a left-wing party and former television-show host, Abdol-Hamid is a controversial figure in Denmark. She wears a hijab and refuses to shake hands with men. "I prefer to put my hand on my heart," she explains. "That's just my way of greeting them. It's not that shaking hands is un-Islamic."

She has her own view of Islam's emphasis on female submission. "If women want to obey their husbands, it's up to them." However, "I could not live the Arab lifestyle, where the men beat the women. That's not Islam — it's Arab." In a global study of women's rights, Arab states accounted for 10 of the 19 countries with the lowest ranking for women's equality.[5]

Many fundamentalist Muslims say the freedoms advocated by secular women's-rights advocates disrupt the complementary nature of male and female roles that have been the basis of social unity since the rise of Islam. A Palestinian Islamic jihadist, known only as Mujahida, said women should "return to their natural and [Koran-based] functions as child-bearers, home-keepers and educators of the next generation." She rejects women's-rights advocates who urge women to take their abusive husbands to secular courts.

Muslim "family mediators," she said, were best placed to resolve such disputes.[6]

According to the Washington-based Pew Research Center, more than a third of Jordanians and Egyptians oppose allowing women to choose whether or not to veil, although the percentage is falling.[7] Also on the decline: the number of those who support restrictions prohibiting men and women from working in the same workplace.[8] In Saudi Arabia, such restrictions limit women's employment, because employers must provide separate offices for women.[9]

AFP/Getty Images/Kristian Brasen/Martin Bureau

Ayaan Hirsi Ali (right), a Somali-born former member of the Dutch parliament, has been threatened with death for her outspoken criticism of Islam's treatment of women in Islam. But Danish Muslim politician and social worker Asmaa Abdol-Hamid (left) attributes repressive gender-based policies in Muslim countries to local culture, not the Koran.

In Iran, an Islamic theocracy since 1979, a debate is raging over whether to allow women to inherit real estate, notes Shireen Hunter, an Iranian-born author and visiting scholar at Georgetown University in Washington. "Reformers are also trying to have the age of [marriage] consent raised from 9 to 16 years. This will take time," she says, because "trying to blend Islam and modernity is hard. It is easier to just say, 'Let's go back to fundamentalism.' "

Yet Abdol-Hamid argues that "fundamentalism does not have to be a bad thing. In Islam, going back to the Koran and Hadith would be good."

However, Pew found considerable support in Muslim nations for restricting a woman's right to choose her husband. For example, 55 percent of Pakistanis felt the family, not the woman, should decide.[10]

In Nigeria, Islamic fundamentalism has hurt women's rights, according to Nigerian activist Husseini Abdu. "Although it is difficult separating the Hausa [Nigerian tribe] and Islam patriarchal structure, the reintroduction or politicization of sharia [Islamic law] in northern Nigeria has contributed in reinforcing traditional, religious and cultural prejudices against women," Abdu says.[11] This includes, among other things, the absence of women in the judiciary, discrimination in the standards of evidence in court cases (especially involving adultery) and restrictions in the freedom of association.[12]

Christian countries are not immune from criticism for limiting women's rights. Human Rights Watch found that in Argentina the Catholic Church has had a hand in establishing government policies that restrict women's access to modern contraception, sex education and abortion.[13] And fundamentalist Christian groups have played a significant role in restricting sex education and the availability of birth control and abortion services in the United States.

But while Islamic countries are often criticized for their treatment of women, the world's two most populous Muslim nations, Pakistan and Indonesia, have both elected female leaders in the past — the late Benazir Bhutto in Pakistan and Megawati Sukarnoputri in Indonesia. The world's largest Christian country, the United States, has never had a female president.

Does Hirsi Ali see anything positive about a woman's life in Islamic societies? "I have never seen Muslim women doubt their femininity or sensuality," she says. "Western women question this more. They are less secure. They are always thinking, 'Am I really equal?' "

---

[1] Ahmed Zaki Yamani, "The Political Competence of Women in Islamic Law," pp. 170-177, in John J. Donohue and John L. Esposito, *Islam in Transition: Muslim Perspectives* (2007).

[2] "Perpetual Minors — Human Rights Abuses Stemming from Male Guardianship and Sex Segregation in Saudi Arabia," Human Rights Watch, April 19, 2008, p. 2, www.hrw.org/en/node/62251/section/1.

[3] *Ibid.*

[4] Karen Foerstel, "Women's Rights," *CQ Global Researcher*, May 2008, p. 118.

[5] *Ibid.*

[6] Loren D. Lybarger, *Identity and Religion in Palestine: The Struggle between Islamism and Secularism in the Occupied Territories* (2007), p. 105.

[7] In Jordan, 37 percent of respondents opposed women being allowed to choose whether to veil, compared to 33 percent in Egypt.

[8] The Pew Global Attitudes Project, "World Publics Welcome Global Trade — But Not Immigration," Pew Research Center, Oct. 4, 2007, p. 51, http://pewglobal.org/reports/pdf/258.pdf.

[9] "Perpetual Minors — Human Rights Abuses Stemming from Male Guardianship and Sex Segregation in Saudi Arabia," *op. cit.*, p. 3.

[10] Pew, *op. cit.*, p. 50.

[11] Carina Tertsakian, "Political Shari'a? Human Rights and Islamic Law in Northern Nigeria," Human Rights Watch, Sept. 21, 2004, p. 63, www.hrw.org/en/reports/2004/09/21/political-shari.

[12] *Ibid.*

[13] See Marianne Mollmann, "Decisions Denied: Women's Access to Contraceptives and Abortion in Argentina," Human Rights Watch, June 14, 2005, www.hrw.org/en/node/11694/section/1.

Haredim are represented by several different political parties in Israel — each with a distinct ideology.

A newer strain of Jewish fundamentalism, the Gush Eminum movement, grew out of the 1967 Israeli-Arab War, in which Israel captured large swathes of Syrian, Egyptian and Jordanian territory. Founded by Rabbi Zvi Yehuda Kook, it believes Israel's victory in that war was a sign that God wanted Jews to settle the captured territories. Israeli authorities initially opposed such actions but did a U-turn in 1977, setting up settlements to create a buffer to protect Israel from hostile Arab neighbors. There now are some 500,000 settlers, and they have become a security headache for the Israeli government, which protects them from attacks from Palestinians who believe they have stolen their land.[80]

Meanwhile the Chabad movement — founded in the 18th century in Lubavitch, Russia, by Rabbi Schoeur Zalman — operates outside of Israel.[81] "They are very religious communities that have become missionaries, even though Jews are not supposed to convert non-Jews, and conversion is very difficult and mostly refused," says Anne Eckstein, a Belgian Jewish journalist. "They are especially active in ex-Soviet countries where the Holocaust and Soviet power wiped out the Jewish community or reduced it to a bare minimum."

Fundamentalism in India

Unlike Christianity, Islam and Judaism, which are monotheistic, Hinduism has thousands of deities representing an absolute power. In addition, it is based not on a single text but the belief that the universe is impersonal and dominated by cosmic energy.[82] Hindu fundamentalism emerged in the early 20th century, partly in reaction to proselytizing by Muslim and Christian missionaries. Some Hindus came to believe that their country needed to be made more Hindu, and that only Hindus could be loyal Indians.

Indian politician Vinayak Damodar Savarkar wrote the book *Hindutva*, the philosophical basis for Hindu fundamentalism.[83] Its cultural pillar is an organization called Vishva Hindu Parishad, founded in 1964, which has had a political wing since the 1980 establishment of the Bharatiya Janata Party, whose leader, Atal Bihari Vajpayee, was prime minister from 1998-2004.

The assertion of Hindu religious identity provoked unease among some of India's 20 million Sikhs, who worship one God and revere the *Adi Granth*, their holy book.[84] Indian Prime Minister Indira Gandhi was murdered in 1984 by two of her Sikh bodyguards in revenge for sending troops to storm the Sikhs' holiest shrine, the Golden Temple, which had been occupied by militant Sikh separatists. Hundreds of people were killed in the botched government operation.[85]

CURRENT SITUATION

Political Battles

Christian conservatives remain a potent force in American political life, even though they appear to have lost some of their political clout with the election of a liberal, pro-choice president and a decidedly more liberal Congress.

In the 2008 U.S. presidential election, evangelicals were briefly buoyed by the nomination of a Christian conservative, Alaska Gov. Sarah Palin, as the Republican vice presidential candidate. But their hopes of having another evangelical in high office were dashed when Palin and her running mate, Sen. John McCain, R-Ariz., were comfortably beaten by their Democratic rivals in November.

Palin was raised as a Pentecostal and regularly attended the Assemblies of God church in Wasilla, Alaska. In a Republican National Convention speech, she stressed the need to govern with a "servant's heart" — which in the evangelical world means Christian humility.[86]

But as details of her religious and political views were revealed, secular Americans began to question her candidacy. Video footage surfaced of her being blessed by a Kenyan pastor in 2005 who prayed for her to be protected from "every form of witchcraft" and for God to "bring finances her way" and to "use her to turn this nation the other way around."[87] Palin was also videotaped speaking at the same church in June 2008, calling a $30 billion gas pipeline project in Alaska "God's will" and the war in Iraq "a task that is from God."[88]

While Palin ultimately may have hurt the Republican ticket more than helping, the passage on Election Day of referenda banning gay marriage in several states — including California — shows that Christian conservatism remains a significant force. And across the American South and heartland, religious conservatives have pressured state and local governments to pass a variety of "family" and faith-based measures, ranging from

AT ISSUE

Is Islamic fundamentalism more dangerous than Christian fundamentalism?

YES

Maajid Nawaz
Director, Quilliam Foundation, London, England

Written for *CQ Global Researcher*, February 2009

While not all Muslim fundamentalists are a threat, certain strands of Muslim fundamentalism are more dangerous than Christian fundamentalism. This is simply a truth we must face up to as Muslims. The first stage of healing is to accept and recognize the sickness within. Until such recognition comes, we are lost.

But if Muslim fundamentalism is only a problem in certain contexts, this is not true of political Islam, or Islamism. Often confused with fundamentalism, political Islamism is a modernist project to politicize religion, rooted in the totalitarian political climate of post-World War I Egypt. But this ideology didn't restrict itself to political goals. Instead, its adherents aspired to create a modern, totalitarian state that was illiberal but not necessarily fundamentalist.

In the 1960s, the Muslim Brotherhood — Egypt's largest Islamist group — failed to impose their non-fundamentalist brand of Islam in Egypt. Instead, they fled to religiously ultra-conservative Saudi Arabia. Here they allied with reactionary fundamentalists. It is from this mix of modernist Islamism and fundamentalism that al Qaeda and jihadist terrorism emerged. It was in Saudi Arabia that Osama bin Laden was taught by Muslim Brotherhood exiles. It was from Saudi Arabia that streams of Muslim fundamentalists traveled to Afghanistan and Pakistan where they fell under the spell of the Egyptian Islamist Abdullah Azzam, another inspiration for bin Laden. The root of the present terrorist danger is the alliance between modernist political Islamists and Muslim fundamentalists.

This global jihadist terrorism — modern in its political ideals and tactics yet medieval in both its religious jurisprudence and justification for violence — is more dangerous than Christian fundamentalism. I believe that such terrorism, far from representing the fundamentals of Islam, is actually un-Islamic. However, a Christian may similarly argue that attacking abortion clinics is un-Christian. We both need to acknowledge the role that religion plays in motivating such individuals.

So, having recognized this problem, how can Muslims tackle it? It is not enough for Muslims to merely take a stand against terrorism and the killing of innocent civilians. This is the very least that should be expected of any decent human being. Muslims must also challenge both conservative fundamentalism and the modern Islamist ideology behind jihadist terrorism. Islamism is to blame, alongside Western support for dictatorships, for the situation we face today.

NO

Radwan Masmoudi
President, Center for the Study of Islam and Democracy, Washington, D.C.

Written for *CQ Global Researcher*, February 2009

The term "fundamentalism" can be misleading, because the overwhelming majority of Muslims believe the Koran is the literal word of God and a guide for the individual, the family and society to follow on everything social, political and economic. In a recent Gallup Poll, more than 75 percent of Muslims — from Morocco to Indonesia — said they believe Islamic laws should be either the only source or one of the main sources of laws in their countries. Under a U.S. definition of "fundamentalism," these people would all be considered "fundamentalists."

However, the overwhelming majority of Muslims are peaceful and reject violence and extremism. In the same poll, more than 85 percent of Muslims surveyed said they believe democracy is the best form of government. Thus, they are not interested in imposing their views on others but wish to live according to the teachings of their religion while respecting people of other religions or opinions. Democracy and respect for human rights — including minority rights and women's rights — are essential in any society that respects and practices Islamic values.

It would be a terrible mistake to consider all fundamentalist Muslims a threat to the United States or to mankind. Radical and violent Muslim extremist groups such as al Qaeda and the Taliban represent a tiny minority of all Muslims and a fringe minority of religious (or fundamentalist) Muslims. These extremist groups are a threat both to their own societies and to the West. But they do not represent the majority opinion among religious-based groups that are struggling to build more Islamic societies through peaceful means.

Many Christian fundamentalist groups have resorted to violence, specifically attacks against abortion clinics in the United States. In addition, prominent Christian fundamentalist leaders, such as John Hagee, Pat Robertson and others say Islam is the enemy and have called for the United States to invade Muslim countries like Iraq, Afghanistan and even Iran. These wars have cost the lives of more than 1 million innocent people in these countries and could still cause further deaths and destruction around the world. The devout of all faiths should condemn the killing of innocents and the self-serving labeling of any religion as the "enemy" against which war should be waged. Surely, one — whether Muslim or Christian — can be extremely devout and religious without calling for violence or hoping for Armageddon.

AFP/Getty Images/Yehuda Raizner

AFP/Getty Images/Gali Tibbon

Jewish Settlements Stir Outrage and Support

Left-wing Israelis criticize Israel last December for allowing fundamentalist Jews to build settlements in the Palestinian territories (top). Evangelicals from the U.S.-based Christians United for Israel movement (bottom) support the settlements during a rally in Jerusalem last April. Many analysts say pressure from American fundamentalist Christians led former President George W. Bush, a born-again Christian, to offer unqualified support for Israel and to invade Iraq — policies that have exacerbated U.S.-Muslim relations.

restrictions on access to birth control and abortion to requirements that "intelligent design" be taught in place of or alongside evolution in schools. The laws have triggered ire — and a slew of lawsuits — on the part of groups intent on retaining the Constitution's separation of church and state.[89]

Meanwhile, thousands of conservative Episcopalians in the United States have abandoned their church because of the hierarchy's tolerance of homosexuality and are teaming up with Anglican Protestants in Africa who share their conservative views.[90]

In Latin America, evangelical television preachers are using their fame to launch themselves into politics, notes Dennis Smith, a U.S.-born Presbyterian mission worker who has lived in Guatemala since 1977. He says that in Brazil, Pentecostal preacher Edir Macedo cut a deal with President Luiz Inacio Lula de Silva in which Macedo got to hand-pick the country's vice president. In Guatemala Harold Caballeros, a Pentecostal who preaches that the Mayan Indians there have made a pact with the devil by clinging to their traditional beliefs, is trying to become president, Smith adds.

In Africa, the Somali parliament on Jan. 31 elected a moderate Islamist cleric, Sheik Sharif Ahmed, as the country's new president. The election occurred just as the hard-line Islamist al-Shabaab militia took control of the central Somali town of Baidoa and began imposing its harsh brand of Islamic law there.[91]

Rising Violence

Attacks on Christian minorities in Iraq and India — and efforts to forcibly convert them — have escalated in recent months.

In November militants said to be from the Pakistan-based Lashkar-e-Taiba carried out a meticulously planned attack in Mumbai, India, killing 164 people in a shooting spree that targeted hotels frequented by Western tourists.[92] Ex-Islamist Nawaz says of the group: "I know them well. They want to reconquer India. They see it as being under Hindu occupation now because it was once ruled by Muslim emperors of Turko-Mongol descent. They use the territorial dispute between India and Pakistan over the sovereignty of Kashmir as a pretext for pursuing their global jihad agenda."

Lisa Curtis, a research fellow for South Asia at the Heritage Foundation in Washington, believes that Pakistan is playing a sinister role here. "The Pakistan military's years of support for jihadist groups fighting in Afghanistan and India," she says, is "intensifying linkages between Pakistani homegrown terrorists and al Qaeda."

India's suspicion that forces within the Pakistani government have given Lashkar-e-Taiba a free rein is further straining an already tense relationship between the two nations.

The Lashkar attackers also killed two young Jewish missionaries, Rabbi Gavriel Holtzberg and his wife Rivkah, in an assault on the Chabad center in Mumbai, where they had been based since 2003. While some accuse the Chabad of proselytizing, Rabbi Avi Tawil, who studied with U.S.-born Gavriel Holtzberg for two years in Argentina, insists, "He did not force anyone to accept his philosophy. He was doing social work — working with prisoners for example."

But the Mumbai attacks were not the only violence perpetrated by religious extremists in India last year. Between August and December, members of the paramilitary, right-wing Hindu group Bajrang Dal — using the rallying cry "kill Christians and destroy their institutions" — murdered dozens of Christians, including missionaries and priests, burned 3,000 homes and destroyed more than 130 churches in Orissa state.[93] The attackers were angered at proselytizing by Pentecostal missionaries in the region and tried to force Christians to convert back to Hinduism.[94]

Martha Nussbaum, a professor of law and ethics at the University of Chicago and author of the recent book *The Clash Within: Democracy, Religious Violence and India's Future*, writes that no one should be surprised right-wing Hindus "have embraced ethno-religious cleansing." Since the 1930s, "their movement has insisted that India is for Hindus, and that both Muslims and Christians are foreigners who should have second-class status in the nation."[95]

India's bloodiest religiously based violence in recent years was the slaughter of up to 2,000 Muslim civilians by Hindu mobs in Gujarat state in 2002.[96] A Bajrang Dal leader boasted: "There was this pregnant woman, I slit her open. . . . They shouldn't even be allowed to breed. . . . Whoever they are, women, children, whoever . . . thrash them, slash them, burn the bastards. . . . The idea is, don't keep them alive at all; after that, everything is ours."[97]

In Iraq last fall, in the northern city of Mosul, some 400 Christian families were forced to flee their homes after attacks by Sunni Muslim extremists.[98]

In Nigeria, sectarian violence between Christians and Muslims in the city of Jos spiked again in late November, leaving at least 300 dead in the worst clashes since 2004, when 700 people died. Religious violence in Nigeria tends to break out in the "middle belt" between the Muslim north and the predominantly Christian south.[99]

Then in December Israel launched a massive offensive against the Islamist Hamas government in the Gaza Strip, in response to Hamas' continuous rocket attacks into Israel; at least 1,300 Palestinians died during the 22-day assault. An uneasy truce now exists, but Hamas remains defiant, refusing to accept Israel's right to exist and vowing to fight for the creation of an Islamic Palestinian state in its place.[100]

While most commentators focus on the political dimension of the conflict, Belgian Jewish journalist Anne Eckstein is as concerned about Hamas' religious extremism. "I see nothing in them apart from hatred and death to all who are not Muslims. . . . Jews first but then Christians and everybody else. And those who believe that this is not a war of civilization are very mistaken."

Also in December, troops from, Uganda, southern Sudan and the Democratic Republic of Congo launched a joint offensive to catch Lord's Resistance Army (LRA) leader Kony.[101] The LRA retaliated, massacring hundreds. Kenya-based evangelical Professor Nkansah insists the LRA is "not really religious — no one has ever seen them praying. They are just playing to the Christian communities in Uganda. If they were true Christians, they would not be destroying human life like they are."

Even in areas where religious violence has not broken out, a certain fundamentalist-secular tension exists. In the United Kingdom, for example, a debate has broken out over whether Muslim communities should be allowed to handle family matters — such as divorce and domestic violence cases — in Muslim courts that apply Islamic law. These increasingly common tribunals, despite having no standing under British law, have "become magnets for Muslim women seeking to escape loveless marriages."[102] In Africa, the Tanzanian parliament is having a similar debate, with proponents noting that Kenya, Rwanda and Uganda have had such courts for decades.[103]

In Israel, the majority-secular Jewish population has begun to resent ultra-Orthodox Jewish men who subsist on welfare while immersing themselves in perpetual study of the holy texts. "They claim this is what Jews did in the past, but this is nonsense," says Jerusalem-based journalist Gorenberg, who notes that ultra-Orthodox wives often work outside the home in order to support their very large families. The Haredim are trying to restore ancient Judaism by weaving priestly garments in the traditional way, producing a red heifer using genetic engineering and raising boys in a special compound kept ritually pure for 13 years, says Gorenberg, a fierce critic of fundamentalist Jews.[104]

Many secular Israelis also resent the religious Jews that have settled in the Palestinian territories, arguing they make Muslims hate Israel even more and thus threaten Israel's very security.

OUTLOOK

More of the Same?

Al Qaeda's Egyptian-born chief strategist, Ayman Al-Zawihiri, is very clear about his goal. "The victory of Islam will never take place until a Muslim state is established in the heart of the Islamic world, specifically in the Levant [Eastern Mediterranean], Egypt and the neighboring states of the [Arabian] Peninsula and Iraq."[105]

Former-Islamist Nawaz says such a state would not, as fundamentalists claim, be a return to the past but a modernist creation, having more in common with the totalitarian regimes of 20th-century Europe than with the tolerant Islamic caliphates in the Middle Ages. He thinks Islamists have the greatest chance of seizing power in Egypt and Uzbekistan.

Given the Islamization that she has observed on numerous visits to Uzbekistan, Martha Brill Olcott, a senior associate at the Carnegie Endowment for International Peace in Washington, predicts the country will not remain secular. Because the Muslims there are Sunni, she thinks they will follow an Egyptian or Pakistani model of government.

Georgetown Professor Dallal predicts Iran will remain the world's only theocracy. "I do not think the Iranian model will be replicated," he says. "The religious elite is more institutionalized and entrenched there than elsewhere."

And although young Iranians are more secular than their parents and have been disenchanted with the religious rulers, "We should not assume this is a deep-rooted trend," warns Iranian-born author Hunter. "Look at Arab countries: Forty years ago we thought they were going secular, but not now."

As for Islamist militancy, the signs are mixed. While a Pew survey showed a drop in support for global jihad among Muslims overall, it also found that young Muslims in the United States were more likely to support radical Islam than their parents. Fifteen percent of 18-29-year-olds thought suicide bombing could be justified compared to just 6 percent of those over 30.[106]

And even if, as some analysts suggest, al Qaeda is faltering, other Islamist groups may thrive, such as Hezbollah in Lebanon, Hamas in Gaza and Pakistan's Lashkar-e-Taiba. They attract popular support because they also provide social services, unlike al Qaeda, whose bloody campaigns have alienated most Muslims.[107]

The Israel-Palestine conflict, intractable as ever, will continue to be grist for the Islamist mill. Bin Laden has urged Muslims to "kill the Americans and their allies [and] to liberate the Al-Aqsa Mosque," which is located on the Temple Mount in Jerusalem that Israel has controlled since 1967.[108]

In the Palestinian territories, "Islamist symbols, discourses and practices have become widely disseminated across the factional spectrum," according to Ohio State's Lybarger, but whether it continues depends on the actions of Israel, the United States and other Arab states toward Palestine, he says.[109] Many observers hope President Obama and his newly-appointed Middle East envoy George Mitchell will be able to broker a peace deal, given Obama's aggressive outreach to the Muslim world.

In the United States, the Christian right is likely to remain strong, even as Obama moves to overhaul Bush's faith-based initiatives. Secularists may ask Obama to prohibit groups receiving government funds from discriminating in hiring based on religious beliefs. "Hiring based on religious affiliation is justified," says Stanley Carlson-Thies, director of the Center for Public Justice in Washington, D.C. "Would you ask a senator not to ask about political ideology when selecting staff? A ban would [be] a sweeping change."[110]

Looking farther afield, Baptist minister Land says "by 2025 the majority of Christians . . . will be African, Latin American and Asian. That is where evangelical Christianity is growing fastest." The fastest-growing Christian denominations are in Nigeria, Sudan, Angola, South Africa, India, China and the Philippines, according to the World Christian Database.[111]

But Kenya's Nkansah doubts that Christian-based political parties will emerge in sub-Saharan Africa. "In North Africa almost everyone is Muslim, so it is easier to have Islamic parties. But here, there is more of a mix, and politicians do not want to create unnecessary tensions."

In Guatemala, American Presbyterian missionary Smith says, "Since neither modernity nor democracy has been able to bring security, the rule of law, social tolerance or broad-based economic development" evangelical television preachers will "continue to have great power for the foreseeable future."

Meanwhile, a glimpse of Asia's future might be found in South Korea. "As dusk turns to dark in this capital city," journalist Mosettig wrote, "the skyline glitters with more than the urban lights of office towers and apartment blocks. From the hills that define Seoul's topography and neighborhoods, it is easy to spot lighted electric crosses. They are among the most visible reminders of just how deeply Christianity shapes South Korea."[112]

NOTES

1. Richard A. Oppel Jr. and Pir Zubair Shah, "In Pakistan, Radio Amplifies Terror of Taliban," *The New York Times*, Jan. 24, 2009, www.nytimes.com/2009/01/25/world/asia/25swat.html?_r=1&scp=1&sq=Taliban%20Pakistan&st=cse.
2. "The U.S. Religious Landscape Survey," Pew Forum on Religion and Public Life, Feb. 25, 2008, p. 170, http://religions.pewforum.org.
3. Michelle Goldberg, *Kingdom Coming: The Rise of Christian Nationalism* (2007), p. 7.
4. *Ibid.*, p. 8.
5. Dominionism, Goldberg notes, is derived from a theocratic sect called Christian Reconstructionism, which advocates replacing American civil law with Old Testament biblical law.
6. See World Evangelical Alliance Web site, www.worldevangelicals.org. For background, see David Masci, "Evangelical Christians," *CQ Researcher*, Sept. 14, 2001, pp. 713-736.
7. Quoted in Eliza Griswold, "God's Country," *The Atlantic*, March 2008, www.theatlantic.com/doc/200803/nigeria.
8. Michael Mossetig, "Among Sea of Glittery Crosses, Christianity Makes Its Mark in South Korea," PBS, Nov. 5, 2007, www.pbs.org/newshour/indepth_coverage/asia/koreas/2007/report_11-05.html. For background, see Alan Greenblatt and Tracey Powell, "Rise of Megachurches," *CQ Researcher*, Sept. 21, 2007, pp. 769-792.
9. Presentation by Wang Zuoan, China's deputy administrator of religious affairs, Sept. 11, 2008, at the Brookings Institution, Washington, D.C.
10. Estimates provided by Samuel Heilman, Sociology Professor and expert on Jewish fundamentalism at City University of New York.
11. "Christians Attacked in Two States of India" World Evangelical Alliance Web site, Dec. 15, 2008, www.worldevangelicals.org/news/view.htm?id=2277.
12. Loren D. Lybarger, *Identity and Religion in Palestine: The Struggle between Islamism and Secularism in the Occupied Territories* (2007), p. 73.
13. See National Counter Terrorism Center's Worldwide Incidents Tracking System, http://wits.nctc.gov.
14. The Shia, who make up 15 percent of the world's 1.4 billion Muslims, believe only the prophet Mohammad's family and descendants should serve as Muslim leaders (imams). Sunnis — who make up the other 85 percent — believe any Muslim can be an imam. Iran is the world's most Shia-dominated country, while there are also significant Shia communities in Iraq, Turkey, Lebanon, Syria, Kuwait, Bahrain, Saudi Arabia, Yemen, Pakistan and Azerbaijan.
15. Lybarger, *op. cit.*
16. "Sharia stoning for Nigeria man," BBC News, May 17, 2007, http://news.bbc.co.uk/2/hi/africa/6666673.stm.
17. For background, see John Felton, "Child Soldiers," *CQ Global Researcher*, July, 2008.
18. Scott Shane, "Global Forecast by American Intelligence Expects Al Qaeda's Appeal to Falter," *The New York Times*, Nov. 20, 2008, www.nytimes.com/2008/11/21/world/21intel.html?_r=1&emc=tnt&tntemail0=y.
19. "Country Reports on Terrorism," Office of the Coordinator for Counterterrorism, U.S. Department of State, April 2008, www.state.gov/documents/organization/105904.pdf.
20. Martin Marty and R. Scott Appleby, eds., *Fundamentalisms Comprehended* (The Fundamentalism Project), 2004, University of Chicago Press.

21. Source: Talk by Egyptian scholar and human rights activist Saad Eddin Ibrahim, at Woodrow Wilson International Center for Scholars, Washington, D.C., Sept. 8, 2008.
22. For background, see Brian Beary, "Future of Turkey," *CQ Global Researcher*, December 2007.
23. Raja Kamal, "Israel's fundamentalist Jews are multiplying," *The Japan Times*, Aug. 21, 2008, http://search.japantimes.co.jp/cgi-bin/eo20080821a1.html.
24. *Ibid.*
25. Mike Madden, "Sundown on Colorado fundamentalists," *Salon.com*, Nov. 2, 2008, www.salon.com/news/feature/2008/11/03/newlifechurch/index.html?source=rss&aim=/news/feature.
26. Susan Jacoby, "Religion remains fundamental to US politics," *The Times* (London), Oct. 31, 2008, www.timesonline.co.uk/tol/comment/columnists/guest_contributors/article5050685.ece.
27. "Human Security Brief 2007," Human Security Report Project, Simon Fraser University, Canada, May 21, 2008, www.humansecuritybrief.info.
28. "Unfavorable views of Jews and Muslims on the Increase in Europe," Pew Research Center, Sept. 17, 2008, p. 4, http://pewglobal.org/reports/pdf/262.pdf.
29. *Ibid.*
30. Andrew MacIntyre and Douglas E. Ramage, "Seeing Indonesia as a normal country: Implications for Australia," Australian Strategic Policy Institute, May 2008, www.aspi.org.au/publications/publication_details.aspx?ContentID=169&pubtype=5.
31. Michael Sullivan, "Megachurch Symbolizes Indonesia's Tolerance," National Public Radio, Oct. 19, 2008, www.npr.org/templates/story/story.php?storyId=95847081.
32. Comments from Pew Forum on Religion and Public Life discussion, "Between Relativism and Fundamentalism: Is There a Middle Ground?" March 4, 2008, Washington, D.C., http://pewforum.org/events/?EventID=172.
33. Sarah Glazer, "Radical Islam in Europe," *CQ Global Researcher*, November 2007.
34. Sayyid Qutb, *Milestones*, *SIME* (Studies in Islam and the Middle East) *Journal*, 2005, p. 125, http://majalla.org/books/2005/qutb-nilestone.pdf.
35. Lybarger, *op. cit.*
36. See Goldberg, *op. cit.*, p. 8.
37. *Ibid.*, p. 208.
38. "Human Security Brief 2007," *op. cit.*, p. 19.
39. Osama Bin Laden, "Text of Fatwa Urging Jihad Against Americans," Feb. 23, 1998, in John J. Donohue and John L. Esposito, *Islam in Transition: Muslim Perspectives* (2007), pp. 430-432.
40. "Tanzania: Muslim paper says war on terror guise to fight Islam," BBC Worldwide Monitoring, Aug. 24, 2008 (translation from Swahili of article in Tanzanian weekly Islamic newspaper *An-Nuur*, Aug. 15, 2008).
41. Barbara Crossette, "The World: (Mid) East Meets (Far) East; A Challenge to Asia's Own Style of Islam," *The New York Times*, Dec. 30, 2001.
42. Pew Global Attitudes Project, "Islamic Extremism: Common Concern for Muslim and Western Publics," July 14, 2005, p. 25, http://pewglobal.org/reports/pdf/248.pdf.
43. Griswold, *op. cit.*
44. Zaki Chehab, *Inside Hamas — The Untold Story of the Militant Islamic Movement* (2007), p. 104.
45. Gabriel Almond, Scott Appleby and Emmanuel Sivan, *Strong Religion: The Rise of Fundamentalisms Around the World* (The Fundamentalism Project), The University of Chicago Press, 2003, p. 110.
46. Rachid Ghannouchi, "The Participation of Islamists in a Non-Islamic Government," in Donohue and Esposito, *op. cit.*, pp. 271-278.
47. Jason Burke, "Don't believe myths about sharia law," *The Guardian* (United Kingdom), Feb. 10, 2008, www.guardian.co.uk/world/2008/feb/10/religion.law1. For background, see Robert Kiener, "Crisis in Pakistan" *CQ Global Researcher*, December 2008, pp. 321-348.
48. Oppel and Shah, *op. cit.*
49. Brenda E. Brasher, *Encyclopedia of Fundamentalism* (2001), p. 397.
50. *Ibid.*, pp. 202-204.
51. *Ibid.*, pp. 465-467.
52. *Ibid.*, p. 186.
53. For background, see the following *CQ Researchers*: Kenneth Jost, "Religion and Politics," Oct. 14, 1994,

pp. 889-912; and David Masci, "Religion and Politics," July 30, 2004, pp. 637-660.

54. For background, see Rachel S. Cox, "Home Schooling Debate," *CQ Researcher*, Jan. 17, 2003, pp. 25-48.
55. David Holthouse, "Casting Stones: An Army of radical Christian Reconstructionists is preparing a campaign to convert conservative fundamentalist churches," Southern Law Poverty Center, winter 2005, www.splcenter.org/intel/intelreport/article.jsp?aid=591.
56. Brasher, *op. cit.*, pp. 407-409.
57. *Ibid.*, p. 86.
58. *Ibid.*
59. Adrian Wooldridge, "The Theocons: Secular America Under Siege," *International Herald Tribune*, Sept. 26, 2006, www.iht.com/articles/2006/09/25/opinion/booktue.php.
60. See Paul Harris, "Bush says God chose him to lead his nation," *The Guardian*, Nov. 2, 2003, www.guardian.co.uk/world/2003/nov/02/usa.religion; and Melissa Rogers and E. J. Dionne Jr., "Serving People in Need, Safeguarding Religious Freedom: Recommendations for the New Administration on Partnerships with Faith-Based Organizations," The Brookings Institution, December 2008, www.brookings.edu/papers/2008/12_religion_dionne.aspx. For background, see Sarah Glazer, "Faith-based Initiatives," *CQ Researcher*, May 4, 2001, pp. 377-400.
61. James Carroll, "Religious comfort for bin Laden," *The Boston Globe*, Sept. 15, 2008, www.boston.com/news/nation/articles/2008/09/15/religious_comfort_for_bin_laden.
62. For background, see Dan Eggen and Paul Kane, "Goodling Says She 'Crossed the Line'; Ex-Justice Aide Criticizes Gonzales While Admitting to Basing Hires on Politics," *The Washington Post*, May 24, 2007, p. A1.
63. Brasher, *op. cit.*, p. 154.
64. Almond, Appleby and Sivan, *op. cit.*, p. 171.
65. Cedric Mayson, "Religious Fundamentalism in South Africa," African National Congress Commission for Religious Affairs, January 2007, http://thebrenthurstfoundation.co.za/Files/terror_talks/Religious%20Fundamentalism%20in%20SA.pdf.
66. Rob Crilly, "Lord's Resistance Army uses truce to rearm and spread its gospel of fear," *The Times* (London), Dec. 16, 2008, www.timesonline.co.uk/tol/news/world/africa/article5348890.ece.
67. *Ibid.*
68. Brasher, *op. cit.*, p. 37.
69. For background, see Peter Katel, "Global Jihad," *CQ Researcher*, Oct. 14, 2005, pp. 857-880.
70. Almond, Appleby and Sivan, *op. cit.*, pp. 177-79.
71. Brasher, *op. cit.*, p. 37.
72. "Human Security Brief 2007," *op. cit.*
73. For background, see Glazer, "Radical Islam in Europe," *op. cit.*
74. "World Christian Database," Center for the Study of Global Christianity, Gordon-Conwell Theological Seminary, www.worldchristiandatabase.org/wcd/home.asp.
75. "Muslim Americans: Middle Class and Mostly Mainstream," Pew Forum on Religion and Public Life, May 22, 2007, p. 4, http://pewforum.org/surveys/muslim-american.
76. Chehab, *op. cit.*, pp. 134-150.
77. Brasher, *op. cit.*, p. 255.
78. "World Christian Database," *op. cit.*
79. Brasher, *op. cit.*, p. 255.
80. *Ibid.*, p. 204.
81. See American Friends of Lubavitch Washington, D.C., www.afldc.org.
82. Brasher, *op. cit.*, p. 222.
83. Almond, Appleby and Sivan, *op. cit.*, pp. 136-139.
84. *Ibid.*, pp. 157-159.
85. *Ibid.*
86. John L. Allen Jr., "McCain's choice a nod not only to women, but post-denominationalists," *National Catholic Reporter*, Aug. 30, 2008, http://ncrcafe.org/node/2073.
87. Garance Burke, "Palin once blessed to be free from witchcraft," The Associated Press, Sept. 25, 2008, http://abcnews.go.com/Politics/wireStory?id=5881256. Video footage at www.youtube.com/watch?v=QIOD5X68lIs.

88. Alexander Schwabe, "Sarah Palin's Religion: God and the Vice-Presidential Candidate," *Spiegel* online, Sept. 10, 2008, www.spiegel.de/international/world/0,1518,577440,00.html. Video footage at www.youtube.com/watch?v=QG1vPYbRB7k.
89. For background see the following *CQ Researchers*: Marcia Clemmitt, "Intelligent Design," July 29, 2005, pp. 637-660; Kenneth Jost and Kathy Koch, "Abortion Showdowns," Sept. 22, 2006, pp. 769-792; Kenneth Jost, "Abortion Debates," March 21, 2003, pp. 249-272; and Marcia Clemmitt, "Birth-control Debate," June 24, 2005, pp. 565-588.
90. See Karla Adam, "Gay Bishop Dispute Dominates Conference; Anglican Event Ends With Leader's Plea," *The Washington Post*, Aug. 4, 2008, p. A8.
91. Jeffrey Gettleman and Mohammed Ibrahim, "Somalis cheer the selection of a moderate Islamist cleric as President," *The New York Times*, Feb. 1, 2009, www.nytimes.com/2009/02/01/world/africa/01somalia.html.
92. Ramola Talwar Badam, "Official: India received intel on Mumbai attacks," The Associated Press, *Denver Post*, Dec. 1, 2008, www.denverpost.com/business/ci_11111305.
93. Somini Sengupta, "Hindu Threat to Christians: Convert or Flee," *The New York Times*, Oct. 12, 2008, www.nytimes.com/2008/10/13/world/asia/13india.html?pagewanted=1&_r=1&sq=Christians percent20India&st=cse&scp=1.
94. "Indian Christians Petition PM for Peace in Orissa at Christmas," World Evangelical Alliance Web site, Dec. 14, 2008, www.worldevangelicals.org/news/view.htm?id=2276.
95. Martha Nussbaum, "Terrorism in India has many faces," *Los Angeles Times*, Nov. 30, 2008, p. A35.
96. For background, see David Masci, "Emerging India," *CQ Researcher*, April 19, 2002, pp. 329-360.
97. Quoted in Nussbaum, *op. cit.*
98. "Iraq: Christians trickling back to their homes in Mosul," IRIN (humanitarian news and analysis service of the U.N. Office for the Coordination of Humanitarian Affairs), Nov. 6, 2008, www.irinnews.org/Report.aspx?ReportId=81317.
99. Ahmed Saka, "Death toll over 300 in Nigerian sectarian violence, The Associated Press, Nov. 29, 2008," www.denverpost.com/breakingnews/ci_11101598.
100. Gilad Shalit, "Hamas rejects Israel's Gaza cease-fire conditions," *Haaretz*, Jan. 28, 2009, www.haaretz.com/hasen/spages/1059593.html.
101. Scott Baldauf, "Africans join forces to fight the LRA," *The Christian Science Monitor*, Dec. 16, 2008, www.csmonitor.com/2008/1217/p06s01-woaf.html.
102. Elaine Sciolino, "Britain Grapples With Role for Islamic Justice," *The New York Times*, Nov. 18, 2008, www.nytimes.com/2008/11/19/world/europe/19shariah.html?_r=1&emc=tnt&tntemail0=y.
103. "Tanzania: Islamic Courts Debate Splits Legislators," *The Citizen* (newsletter, source: Africa News), Aug. 14, 2008.
104. Gershom Gorenberg, "The Temple Institute of Doom, or Hegel Unzipped," *South Jerusalem* (Blog), July 8, 2008, http://southjerusalem.com/2008/07/the-temple-institute-of-doom-or-hegel-unzipped.
105. See Katel, *op. cit.*, p. 859.
106. "Muslim Americans: Middle Class and Mostly Mainstream," *op. cit.*
107. Scott Shane, "Global Forecast by American Intelligence Expects Al Qaeda's Appeal to Falter," *The New York Times*, Nov. 20, 2008, www.nytimes.com/2008/11/21/world/21intel.html?_r1&emc=tnt&tntemail0=y.
108. Bin Laden, *op. cit.*
109. Lybarger, *op. cit.*, p. 244.
110. Carlson-Thies was speaking at a discussion on faith-based initiatives organized by the Brookings Institution in Washington, D.C. on Dec. 5, 2008.
111. See 'fastest growing denominations' category in "World Christian Database," *op. cit.*
112. Michael Mosettig, "Among Sea of Glittery Crosses, Christianity Makes its Mark in South Korea," Nov. 5, 2007, Public Broadcasting Service, www.pbs.org/newshour/indepth_coverage/asia/koreas/2007/report_11-05.html.

BIBLIOGRAPHY

Books

Almond, Gabriel A., Scott Appleby and Emmanuel Sivan, *Strong Religion: The Rise of Fundamentalisms Around the World, University of Chicago Press*, 2003.
Three history professors synthesize the findings of a five-volume project that looks at 75 forms of religious fundamentalism around the world.

Brasher, Brenda E., ed., *Encyclopedia of Fundamentalism, Routledge*, 2001.
Academics provide an A-Z on Christian fundamentalism — from its origins in the United States to its spread to other countries and religions.

Donohue, John J., and John L. Esposito, *Islam in Transition: Muslim Perspectives, Oxford University Press*, 2007.
Essays by Muslim thinkers address key questions, such as the role of women in Islam, the relationship between Islam and democracy and the clash between Islam and the West.

Lybarger, Loren D., *Identity and Religion in Palestine: The Struggle between Islamism and Secularism in the Occupied Territories, Princeton University Press*, 2007.
A U.S. sociologist who spent several years in the Palestinian territories explores how groups promoting fundamentalist Islam have gradually eclipsed secular nationalism as the dominant political force.

Thomas, Pradip Ninan, *Strong Religion, Zealous Media: Christian Fundamentalism and Communication in India, SAGE Publications*, 2008.
An associate professor of journalism at the University of Queensland, Australia, examines the influence of U.S televangelists in India and the battle for cultural power between Hindu, Muslim and Christian fundamentalists. SAGE is the publisher of *CQ Global Researcher.*

Articles

"The Palestinians: Split by geography and by politics," *The Economist*, Feb. 23, 2008, www.economist.com/world/mideast-africa/displaystory.cfm?story_id=10740648.
The secular organization Fatah controls the West Bank while the Islamist group Hamas is in charge in Gaza.

Crilly, Rob, "Lord's Resistance Army uses truce to rearm and spread its gospel of fear," *The Times* (London), Dec. 16, 2008, www.timesonline.co.uk/tol/news/world/africa/article5348890.ece.
A violent military campaign led by Ugandan Christian fundamentalists threatens to destabilize the neighboring region.

Griswold, Eliza, "God's Country," *The Atlantic*, March 2008, pp. 40-56, www.theatlantic.com/doc/200803/nigeria.
An author recounts her visit to Nigeria, a deeply religious country where Christian and Muslim clerics compete to grow their flocks, and religious tensions often spill over into violence.

Tavernise, Sabrina, "Independent, Tajiks Revel in Their Faith," *The New York Times*, Jan. 3, 2009, www.nytimes.com/2009/01/04/world/asia/04tajik.html?emc=tnt&tntemail0=y.
The Central Asian republic has become increasingly Islamic since its independence from the Soviet Union, with strong influence from Saudi Arabia.

Traynor, Ian, "Denmark's political provocateur: Feminist, socialist, Muslim?" *The Guardian*, May 16, 2008, www.guardian.co.uk/world/2007/may/16/religion.uk.
The controversial Danish politician Asmaa Abdol-Hamid, a devout Muslim, hopes to become the first person elected to the Danish parliament to wear the Islamic headscarf.

Reports and Studies

"Islamic Extremism: Common Concern for Muslim and Western Publics," *The Pew Global Attitudes Project*, July 14, 2005, http://pewglobal.org/reports/pdf/248.pdf.
A U.S.-based research center surveys public opinion in 17 countries on why Islamic extremism is growing.

MacIntyre, Andrew and Douglas E. Ramage, "Seeing Indonesia as a normal country: Implications for Australia," *Australian Strategic Policy Institute*, May 2008, www.aspi.org.au/publications/publication_details.aspx?ContentID=169&pubtype=5.
Two Australian academics argue that claims of rampant Islamic fundamentalism in Indonesia — the world's most populous Muslim country — are exaggerated.

Mayson, Cedric, "Religious Fundamentalism in South Africa," ***African National Congress, Commission for Religious Affairs*****, January 2007, http://thebrenthurstfoundation.co.za/Files/terror_talks/Religious%20Fundamentalism%20in%20SA.pdf.**
A South African activist blames growing fundamentalism in South Africa on U.S. Christian fundamentalists.

Olcott, Martha Brill and Diora Ziyaeva, "Islam in Uzbekistan: Religious Education and State Ideology," ***Carnegie Endowment for International Peace*****, July 2008, www.carnegieendowment.org/publications/index.cfm?fa=view&id=21980&prog=zru.**
Two academics chart the growth of Islam in the Central Asian republic.

For More Information

Association of Evangelicals in Africa, www.aeafrica.org. A continent-wide coalition of 33 national evangelical alliances and 34 mission agencies that aims to "mobilize and unite" evangelicals in Africa for a "total transformation of our communities."

European Jewish Community Centre, 109 Rue Froissart, 1040 Brussels, Belgium; (32) 2-233-1828; www.ejcc.eu. Office of the Chabad Jewish missionary movement's delegation to the European Union.

Evangelical Graduate School of Theology, N.E.G.S.T., P.O. Box 24686, Karen 00502, Nairobi, Kenya; (254) 020-3002415; www.negst.edu. An Evangelical Christian institution devoted to the study of religion in Africa.

Forum 18 News Service, Postboks 6603, Rodeløkka, N-0502 Oslo, Norway; www.forum18.org. News agency reporting on government-sponsored repression of religion in Central Asia.

Organisation of the Islamic Conference, P.O. Box 178, Jeddah 21411, Saudi Arabia; (966) 690-0001; www.oic-oci.org. Intergovernmental organization with 57 member states, which promotes the interests of the Muslim world.

The Oxford Centre for Hindu Studies, 15 Magdalen St., Oxford OX1 3AE, United Kingdom; (44) (0)1865-304-300; www.ochs.org.uk. Experts in Hindu culture, religion, languages, literature, philosophy, history, arts and society.

Pew Forum on Religion and Public Life, 1615 L St., N.W., Suite 700, Washington, DC 20036-5610; (202) 202-419-4550; http://pewforum.org. Publishes surveys on religiosity, including fundamentalist beliefs, conducted around the world.

World Christian Database, BRILL, P.O. Box 9000, 2300 PA Leiden, The Netherlands; (31) (0)71-53-53-566; www.worldchristiandatabase.org. Provides detailed statistical data on numbers of believers, by religious affiliation; linked to U.S.-based Center for the Study of Global Christianity, Gordon-Conwell Theological Seminary.

World Evangelical Alliance, Suite 1153, 13351 Commerce Parkway, Richmond, BC V6V 2X7 Canada; (1) 604-214-8620; www.worldevangelicals.org. Network for evangelical Christian churches around the world.

Worldwide Incidents Tracking System, National Counter Terrorism Center, University of Maryland, College Park, MD 20742; (301) 405-1000; http://wits.nctc.gov. Provides detailed statistics on religiously inspired terrorist attacks across the world from 2004-2008.

6

Anti-Semitism in Europe

Are Israel's Policies Spurring a New Wave of Hate Crimes?

Sarah Glazer

AP Photo/Benoit Tessier

Ilan Halimi, a French Jew, was kidnapped and killed by a gang in Paris. He was found naked, handcuffed and covered with burn marks and died on the way to a hospital. The case spurred national outrage and huge marches protesting the rise of anti-Semitism in France.

From *CQ Global Researcher*, June 2008.

On Feb. 22, Mathieu Roumi, a 19-year-old French Jew, was tortured for nine hours in a basement in a Paris suburb by a group of young men, including several Muslims, who wrote "dirty Jew" on his face and forced him to eat cigarette butts and suck on a condom-covered stick.[1]

The incident bore eerie parallels to the 2006 murder of Ilan Halimi, a 23-year-old Jewish cell phone salesman who was kidnapped and killed by a gang in Paris after three weeks of torture. Halimi was found naked, covered in bruises, knife slashes and burns; he died on the way to the hospital.[2]

Both Halimi and Roumi were abducted in their own neighborhoods in Paris' low-income Bagneux quarter. Halimi had been abducted by a gang calling itself the Barbarians, which had tried unsuccessfully to extort a ransom of 3 million Euros ($4.5 million) from Halimi's family. Unlike Halimi, however, Roumi knew his attackers and was ultimately released.

When police raided the apartments of gang leader Youssouf Fofana and other gang members charged with Halimi's killing, they discovered anti-Semitic, neo-Nazi and radical Muslim, or Islamist, literature. Fofana continued to send anti-Semitic letters to the judge overseeing the case.

Gang members later admitted they selected Halimi assuming he was "one of these rich Jews" — although Halimi's family actually was of only modest means, defying the stereotype.[3]

The Halimi case spurred a storm of controversy about the state of anti-Semitism in France and was seen by the Jewish community as the culmination of a wave of anti-Jewish attacks on individuals and synagogues that has surged since 2000 — just after the start of

Individuals Targeted in Many Incidents

Forty percent of the 632 major attacks and violent incidents against Jews worldwide in 2007 targeted specific individuals, while 22 percent targeted cemeteries and memorials. More than half of the incidents were nonviolent — involving vandalism, graffiti or slogans.

Anti-Semitic Attacks and Incidents Worldwide, 2007

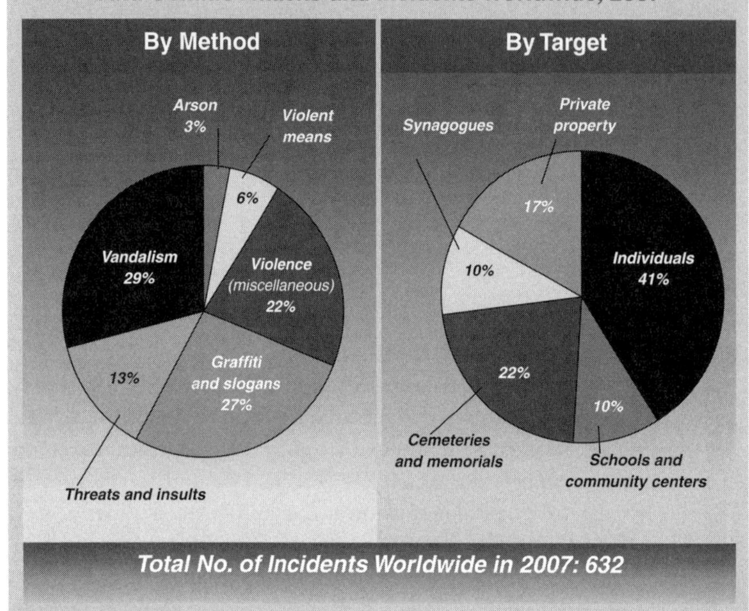

Source: Stephen Roth Institute, 2007

the second Palestinian intifada, or uprising, against Israel's occupation — according to the Stephen Roth Institute for the Study of Contemporary Anti-Semitism and Racism in Tel Aviv.[4] It also raised questions about a new source of anti-Semitism in Europe — radical, anti-Zionist Muslims.

In fact, the institute's latest report on global anti-Semitism found mixed trends in 2007: Anti-Jewish incidents of all kinds slowed and even declined a bit from the previous year in a handful of countries, and it was the quietest year the French Jewish community has known since the rise in attacks began in 2000.[5] But violent attacks on individuals continued to rise, causing some Jewish groups and experts to worry that Europe appears to be adjusting to a new, high level of violent hate incidents and blatant anti-Jewish rhetoric.

Although anti-Semitic incidents overall declined last year in Britain,[6] Belgium and Germany,[7] major attacks and violent incidents against Jews in Western Europe — including attacks on individuals and vandalizing of Jewish property — reached a new high — 352 incidents, or more than quadruple the number in 1999, according to the institute.[8] For instance, while France experienced a 33 percent drop in anti-Semitic acts of all kinds, major violent attacks on French individuals and property quadrupled from 2 to 8; violent, anti-Semitic offenses in Germany jumped more than 50 percent.[9]

A British parliamentary inquiry raised concern in 2006 about a "widespread change in mood and tone when Jews are discussed" in the media, at universities and in other public settings.

"We are concerned that anti-Jewish themes and remarks are gaining acceptability in some quarters in public and private discourse in Britain, and there is a danger that this trend will become more and more mainstream," the report warned.[10]

Many young people in the Jewish community tolerated living with verbal and physical assaults — so much so, the report found, that many incidents weren't even reported, particularly in orthodox Jewish neighborhoods. "The routineness of anti-Semitism was most shocking — how it became accepted as a normal part of life," says John Mann, chair of the Parliamentary Committee Against Anti-Semitism.

A month before the report's release on Aug. 9, 2006, Jasmine Kranat — a 13-year-old Jewish girl riding home from school on a bus — was asked by teenagers demanding money whether she was Jewish. The teenagers punched her in the face until she lost consciousness, and no one on the bus offered her assistance.[11]

Middle East or Muslim-related news events — such as the 9/11 terrorist attacks in the United States or the 2006 Lebanon war between Israel and Hezbollah — appear to trigger anti-Jewish violence in Europe, notes Mark Gardner, a spokesman for the Community Security Trust, a London-based group that tracks anti-Semitic incidents in Britain.

"Our fear is that since 2000 there have been so many trigger events that the net effect is a considerable increase in underlying anti-Semitic incidents," contributing to a high, ongoing base level, says Gardner. "In 2007 there were no trigger events, yet it was still the second-worst year on record" since his organization began recording them in 1984. Even with the slight drop in anti-Jewish incidents in Britain last year, the 547 incidents that did occur — which included assaults, hate mail, anti-Semitic graffiti and verbal abuse — amounted to twice as many as in 1999. And, disturbingly, 114 of the 2007 incidents were violent assaults — the highest number since 1984.[12]

Most Anti-Semitic Attacks Occur in Europe

Major anti-Semitic attacks and violent incidents worldwide jumped more than fourfold between 1999 and 2007. North America saw more than a fivefold increase — from 25 in 1999 to 140 in 2007 — but more than half of the 632 major attacks worldwide last year occurred in Europe.

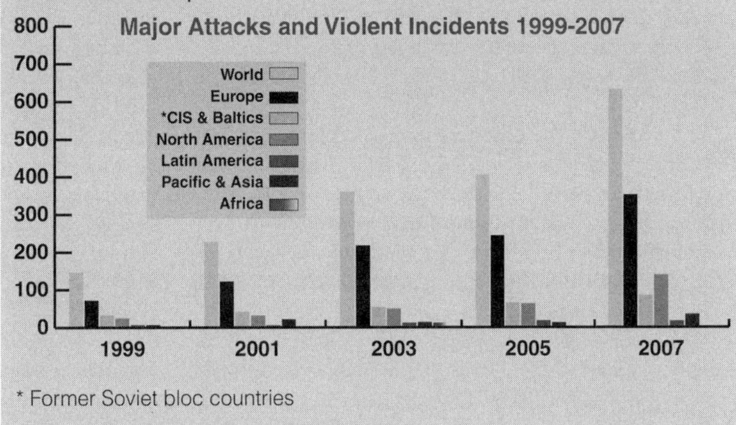

* Former Soviet bloc countries

Source: Stephen Roth Institute, 2007

Last year many religious Jews, identifiable by their dress, were attacked and injured by Arabs or North Africans, according to the Roth Institute. For example, on Sept. 7, Rabbi Zalman Gurevitch was stabbed in the stomach in Frankfurt am Main, Germany, by someone he described as an Arab speaker who shouted "[Pig] Jew, I will kill you."[13]

A great deal of this violence apparently is stimulated by opposition to the existence of Israel, or anti-Zionism, which is shared both by Muslims and by much of Europe's intellectual elite, according to the Roth Institute's latest report on anti-Semitism worldwide. "The fact that anti-Zionism has become politically correct in some sectors encourages not only anti-Semitic activists of the left and right but also young, second- or third-generation Muslims who have been exposed (via satellite TV and the Internet) to hate preachers from the Arab world," the report says.[14]

Franco Frattini, the European Union (EU) commissioner responsible for combating racism and anti-Semitism in Europe, has attributed half of all documented anti-Semitic incidents in Europe to "radical Islamic elements."[15]

The U.S. State Department calls anti-Zionist political cartoons and news commentary that appear after Israeli-Palestinian flareups the "new anti-Semitism," a term adopted by critics of the European left and even included in a working definition of anti-Semitism agreed to by EU states in January 2005.[16] These critics have savaged the liberal European media and leftist activists for what they consider their one-sided sympathizing with the Palestinians.

"Zionism is now a dirty word in Britain, and opposition to Israel has become a fig leaf for a resurgence of the oldest hatred," Melanie Phillips, a commentator for the British *Daily Mail*, recently charged.[17]

Some find this new type of anti-Semitism particularly disturbing because they fear it arouses European racial canards that existed before and during World War II. Political cartoons in newspapers and on the Internet have revived caricatures reminiscent of medieval beliefs in the Jew as child-killer and employed Nazi-like imagery to portray Jewish Israelis as cruel and bloodthirsty in countries as varied as Norway, Greece and England.[18]

So many familiar anti-Jewish stereotypes appeared in the mainstream media during the Lebanon war in 2006 that British scholar David Hirsch described the period as "the summer in which anti-Semitism entered the mainstream."[19]

Hate rhetoric coming out of the Middle East is often beamed into Europe via Syrian and Egyptian satellite TV

Who Are Israel's Harshest Critics?

Liberal British Jews oppose Palestinian occupation.

At a March meeting in London of activists opposed to Israel's occupation of Palestinian territories, attendees could buy fair-trade, organic Palestinian olive oil soap, with revenues going to widows in Ramallah.

But this was not a meeting directed at London's large Muslim population. It featured a panel of Israeli protesters who have come to view their nation's treatment of the Palestinians as incompatible with a democratic, racially equitable society. And it was organized primarily by liberal-left British Jewish groups critical of Israel, such as Jews for Justice for Palestinians.

About 200 mostly middle-aged Jews crowded into the room, the kind of rumpled, intellectual audience one might expect at a talk at New York's famous 92nd Street Y. Palestinian psychiatrist Eyad El-Sarraj, director of the Gaza Community Mental Health Program, described on a live phone line how Israel's blockade had left Gazans so short of bottled water and water filters that they were forced to drink salty, polluted tap water.

"Imagine living in a prison that you're not allowed to leave, and the prison is bombed," he told the hushed room. As for the violence, he said, "I cry for the children killed in Gaza," but also "I cry when my people celebrated in the streets" over the killing of children in Jerusalem.

Parallels to apartheid South Africa were frequently drawn by the speakers as photos flashed across a screen of impoverished Palestinians confronting armed soldiers at checkpoints and standing dwarfed by Israel's security wall dividing it from Palestinian villages. The overwhelmingly sympathetic crowd applauded calls for a boycott of Israeli academics and of companies that benefit from the occupation of Palestinian territories.

Michael Kustow, a British writer and organizer of the event, anticipated criticism from the British Jewish community. "Those of us who criticize Israel do not think we're disloyal or self-hating," he maintained. "We're trying to return Israel to . . . its own values."

Harsh criticism of Israel is common on campuses in Great Britain, which often comes as a shock to visiting American Jewish students. "I've been very surprised at the amount of anti-Israel programming at the institutional level," says Naomi Berlin, a student at Tufts University in Medford, Mass., spending her junior year at Oxford. "When you say Israel, you get words like 'occupation,' 'apartheid,' 'racist.' "

Berlin cited two highly controversial debates organized this academic year by the eminent Oxford Union Debating Society. One, a November forum on free speech featuring Holocaust denier David Irving, was picketed by Jewish students. Another, a debate on whether Israel should exist, invited two prominent critics of Israel to argue in favor of Israel's existence. One of them actually switched sides during the debate and argued against Israel's right to exist.

stations and the Internet, but it has been getting less attention from the liberal press than it once did, says Charles Small, director of the Yale Initiative for the Interdisciplinary Study of Antisemitism. As an example, Small cites the lack of coverage for a recent speech by Iranian President Mahmoud Ahmadinejad calling Israel "filthy bacteria," in language reminiscent of Nazi demands for eradication of Jews.[20]

"On the one hand, you have a genocidal movement" coming out of the Muslim world, says Small, "and on the other you have acquiescence in Europe. . . . I think increasingly because of anti-Semitism among the elite in Europe, particularly in the U.K. and France, you have this dual-loyalty issue coming in. As Israel becomes more and more tarnished as an apartheid, Nazi-like state, you also have the accusation that Jews are loyal to this entity."

In England, the majority of perpetrators identified in connection with anti-Semitic incidents are not disaffected Muslims but white youths, according to criminologist Paul Iganski of Britain's Lancaster University. Although he agrees the Middle East conflicts serve as trigger events, incidents often start with a mundane irritation such as road rage or a dispute over a parking spot — which "becomes aggravated by deep-seated anti-Semitic feeling," he says. "There is a reservoir of anti-Semitic bigotry there simmering below the surface."

Adam Parker, a first-year student from Manchester who co-founded the Israeli Cultural Society at Oxford this year, helped organize a protest against the Irving event. "I think it was a disgrace," he says.

Yair Zivan, campaigns director for the Union of Jewish Students, claims anti-Zionism on campus "often spills over into anti-Semitism." According to Zivan, three anti-Semitic incidents were reported at Manchester University when Jewish students protested a resolution to "twin" their student union with Palestinian An-Najah University, where some students have become suicide bombers, Zivan says.

The harshest critics of Israel at places like Oxford are Jewish professors, notably Israeli Professor of International Relations Avi Shlaim, who charges that Israel's aim in its current blockade of Gaza is "to starve the people of Gaza into submission."[1]

Seth Anziska, an American Oxford graduate student in Middle Eastern studies, says, "Europeans — and the British in particular — have a much more pessimistic outlook" about the peace process between Israel and the Palestinians than Americans. But he adds, "In some ways, it's more realistic."

Yet some prominent British Jews aren't buying it. Shalom Lappin, a professor of computational linguistics at King's College, London, who has written on the history of British Jews, dismisses groups like Jews for Justice for Palestinians. He sees them as part of a long tradition of what he calls "a survival strategy" among British Jews to gain acceptance from the British establishment by not provoking anger.

"I don't doubt their sincerity," he says, "but they're celebrated with open access to *The Guardian* and the *London*

Max Nash/Press Association via AP Images

Demonstrators outside England's famed Oxford Union Debating Society protest the presence of British writer David Irving, a notorious Holocaust denier, at a debate on freedom of speech.

Review of Books and paraded across campuses as 'the good Jews,' not the 'tribal and bad Jews.' "

"I'm proud to be Jewish," responds the organization's chair, Dan Judelson, who said he became active after his daughter was born. "That sense of Jewish injustice and treating people equitably was something I wanted to pass on to my daughter."

[1] Avi Shlaim, "Free Speech? Not for Critics of Israel," *The Jewish Chronicle*, Feb. 29, 2008.

For example, anti-Semitic taunts now ring out at soccer stadiums throughout Europe, where so-called soccer hooligans have traditionally sympathized with the extreme right, according to two recent reports. In the Netherlands, supporters of the traditionally Jewish soccer team Ajax Amsterdam are regularly taunted by fans of opposing teams with Hitler salutes and chants of "Hamas, Hamas, Jews to the gas!"[21]

In a recent report, British MP Mann found that anti-Semitic cheers and paraphernalia are proliferating at Europe's soccer stadiums in part because of the increasing tendency of fans to travel across borders and share anti-Jewish attitudes on the Internet. "We're not prepared to tolerate that; we're meeting with football authorities to take action to stamp this out," Mann says.

However, some experts downplay such concerns, noting that Jews no longer face discriminatory laws in Europe, while Muslims and other minorities are far more likely to face prejudice in employment and housing.

And liberal critics of Israel are leery of what they see as a tendency to equate criticism of Israel's policies with anti-Semitism. "This redefining devalues the word [anti-Semitism] itself. You desensitize people — they become confused," objects Antony Lerman, executive director of the Institute for Jewish Policy Research, a London-based think tank.[22] *(See "At Issue," p. 161.)*

CQ Press/Sarah Glazer

Vandals spray-painted a star of David hanging from a gallows on this gravestone at the only remaining Jewish cemetery in Bialystok, Poland. Defacing Jewish gravestones is a frequent outlet for expressions of anti-Semitism.

"I'm critical of what is done [by Israel] in the occupied territories, but I've never seen myself as an anti-Semite," says Lerman. "I feel as if I'm being bracketed in with anti-Semites."

Here are some of the questions about anti-Semitism and other forms of prejudice being debated across Europe:

Is anti-Semitism on the rise in Europe?

Some Jewish groups and experts point to the surge in reported anti-Semitic incidents since 2000, particularly violent attacks on individuals and anti-Jewish imagery in the press, as a sign that anti-Semitism is growing.[23]

In addition, the European Union's Agency for Fundamental Rights (FRA) and other Europe-wide groups have documented increases in anti-Semitism.[24]

In June 2007, the Parliamentary Assembly of the Council of Europe issued a resolution noting "the persistence and escalation of anti-Semitic phenomena. . . . [F]ar from having been eliminated, anti-Semitism is today on the rise in Europe. It appears in a variety of forms and is becoming commonplace."[25]

The data are somewhat problematic, however, because Jewish communities that are best organized and living in open, democratic societies tend to report the highest number of incidents. Assiduous reporting by Jewish groups in Britain, for instance, makes that country look worse than nations that are less transparent, such as those in Eastern Europe with a long tradition of anti-Semitism in both the church and government. For example, in Belarus, government enterprises produce and distribute anti-Semitic material, but the nation does not rank high on comparative international charts. In addition, figures compiled by law-enforcement agencies or community groups often do not measure anti-Semitic attitudes, such as those captured in political cartoons.[26] (*See graph, p. 140.*)

A recent State Department report makes a distinction between traditional anti-Semitism — which draws on older ideas of Jews as racially inferior, bloodthirsty or Christ killers — and the "new anti-Semitism," which relies primarily on anti-Zionist language but sometimes also incorporates older stereotypes such as Jews as world conspirators.

Eastern European countries tend to specialize in older forms of anti-Semitism. According to a June 2007 report by Human Rights First, extreme, nationalist political groups in Eastern Europe recently have adopted 19th-century anti-Semitic language. The group singled out Poland, Ukraine and Hungary as countries where certain Orthodox and Roman Catholic institutions have encouraged anti-Semitism.[27] (*See "Background" and sidebar, p. 148, for more detail on Poland.*)

In Poland, recent attention has focused on anti-Semitic remarks broadcast on Catholic Radio Maryja, part of the Polish media empire run by the Rev. Tadeusz Rydzyk of the Catholic missionary order Redemptorists. Rydzyk was quoted most recently calling Jews greedy and responsible for lobbies that control the Polish president.[28]

The Rydzyk empire's audience is estimated to be approaching 3 million mostly elderly Poles. Polls show Polish seniors are more likely than young people to hold anti-Semitic views, such as the belief that Jews killed Christ, observes Michal Bilewicz, a social psychologist at Warsaw University's Centre for Research on Prejudice. "We have demography on our side," he says.

Polls also suggest that many traditional stereotypes are commonly held in both Western and Eastern Europe. Anti-Defamation League polls show substantial percentages in many countries believe traditional conspiracy theories about Jews, such as that they have too much power in the business world or in international financial markets.[29]

The most heated debate in Europe, however, has focused on the new anti-Semitism, which often emanates from radical Muslims, relies on anti-Zionism and is concentrated in Western European countries like Great Britain and France, according to advocates of the term.

These experts say they are most concerned about the type of anti-Semitism promoted by radical Muslims known as Islamists, who often appeal to left-leaning European intellectuals for support of the Palestinian liberation movement.

In a 2005 interview, French philosopher and political scientist Pierre-André Taguieff, who helped coin the term "the new anti-Semitism," said all Jews have come to be seen as "more or less hidden Zionists; Zionism equals colonialism, imperialism and racism; therefore the Jews are colonialists, imperialists and racists, openly or not." Zionism, says Taguieff, "became the incarnation of absolute evil."[30]

AP Photo/Francois Mori

Demonstrators in Paris protest racism and anti-Semitism in February 2006. The sign says "Anti-Semitic barbarism. Our child murdered." The photograph is of Ilan Halimi, the Jewish Frenchman murdered in Paris.

Like Taguieff, critics in England and Germany have charged that anti-Semitic comments by Muslim groups are often ignored by the liberal media and by leftist academics who support the Palestinians' liberation movement.

For example, in a recent book, *Jihad and Jew-Hatred*, political scientist Matthias Küntzel reports trial testimony showing that 9/11 leader Mohammed Atta and fellow plotters were convinced that "the Jews" sought world domination. The plotters saw New York City as the center of world Jewry, making it their obvious target.[31]

Yet that testimony was widely ignored in the German and international media, according to Küntzel. "If we had the same quotes by the Oklahoma [City] bomber — by far-right white perpetrators — I think it would have made headlines. But if the very same anti-Semitism is displayed by Muslims, people think perhaps this is Israel's fault, and we just have to tackle the Middle East problem and it will vanish again," says Küntzel, a research associate at the Vidal Sassoon International Center for the Study of Antisemitism at Hebrew University in Jerusalem.

It's no accident, he says, that al Qaeda leader Osama bin Laden quotes left-leaning American intellectual Noam Chomsky, a strong critic of Israel's Palestinian politics. "This is the most dangerous aspect of this Islamism ideology," Küntzel says. In an effort to appeal to the European left, he maintains, Islamist leaders "put themselves in the same role as communism [once played] — as the only potent force against global capitalism. They want to build a broad alliance in order to fight against America and Israel."

Leftist criticism of Israelis as powerful oppressors with Nazi-like characteristics can spur anti-Semitic violence, suggests British journalist Phillips. For example, in a widely reported incident in 2005, when a Jewish reporter approached London's former far-left Mayor Ken Livingstone with a question, the mayor snapped, "What did you do before? Were you a German war criminal?" When the reporter said he was Jewish, Livingstone compared him to a "concentration camp guard."

Later, several perpetrators of anti-Semitic attacks mentioned those comments, according to the Community Security Trust, which tracks anti-Semitic incidents in Britain and provides security advice to Jewish schools and other institutions.[32]

"The Jewish organizations — particularly Jewish-defense organizations — are highlighting how these themes on campuses, Web sites and classrooms have physical manifestations: That can be a swastika on a wall or a physical attack like the one in Paris," says Ben Cohen, the American Jewish Committee's associate director for tackling anti-Semitism and extremism and the editor of a new Web site, www.z-word.com, focusing on anti-Zionism.

However, some observers think the significance of anti-Semitic acts counted by Jewish groups is often overplayed. "Every time someone smears anti-Semitic graffiti on a synagogue wall in France we are warned that 'the unique evil' is with us once more, that it is 1938 all over again," New York University historian Tony Judt recently wrote. "We are losing the capacity to distinguish between the normal sins and follies of mankind — stupidity, prejudice, opportunism, demagogy and fanaticism — and genuine evil. . . . After all, if we see evil everywhere, how can we be expected to recognize the real thing?"[33]

In a similar vein, a prominent French historian, Patrick D. Weil, of the National Center for Scientific Research (CNRS) at the University of Paris, downplays the significance of the recent kidnapping in Paris and paints a positive picture of the general climate in France. "It is in France that you have the most open society with respect to Jews," he says, citing surveys that find French Muslims and French people generally rate at the top of European countries when asked if they have a favorable view of Jews. "But it doesn't mean at the local individual level or at the margin you won't have activist anti-Semitism from some very small segments of the population," he adds.

Bagneux, the poor suburb where Roumi lived and was kidnapped, is integrated, with Jews living alongside Arabs, and Roumi apparently knew his attackers. News reports indicate he was "not a saint," Weil points out, but was involved in some petty criminality like his attackers. "The fact that people [of different ethnic origin] live all together is perhaps good for the integration of society, but it can also produce these extreme attitudes and acts," says Weil. Such assaults may stem as much from the rising tendency of people in France to identify with their own ethnic group, he suggests, which affects other minorities as well.

Experts critical of Israel downplay the levels of anti-Semitism in Europe. "I don't think the evidence is there to suggest that the growth is as bad as many people do claim," says Lerman, at the Institute for Jewish Policy Research. "Quite a few research institutions in Europe and the U.S. have spoken of anti-Semitism as being so extreme it's like being back at *Kristallnacht* on the eve of the Holocaust — which I find unnecessary. I personally would say in the last year or so it's reached a plateau."

Is anti-Zionism a cover-up for anti-Semitism?

Increasingly, groups such as the American Jewish Committee charge that inflammatory anti-Zionist language is being used in Europe as a pretext for anti-Semitism. Anti-Defamation League Director Abraham Foxman has charged that in Britain, hostility towards Jews often "is camouflaged as criticism of Israel."[34]

"The canard," in Foxman's words, that Israel resembles apartheid-era South Africa — reflected in February's "Israel Apartheid Week" organized on British campuses by Muslim students — is "fueling dislike, distrust, hatred of Jews," Foxman has written.[35]

Critics in Britain and France have charged that members of the liberal intelligentsia, in their eagerness to make common cause with the Palestinians, have turned a blind eye to the anti-Semitism that is part of Islamist rhetoric.

"Essentially, you see the movement into the mainstream of ideas that until 10 years ago were confined to the far left and the far right," says Shalom Lappin, a professor at King's College in London and one of the founders of a group of academics, the Euston Manifesto, which has protested against British anti-Semitism. "They place Israel and Jews at the center of the Jewish conspiracy, part of the lobby used to subvert foreign policy. . . . It's sweeping campuses; it lends toxicity to public debate."

French philosopher and political scientist Taguieff contends that anti-Jewish stereotypes and accusatory themes originally drawn from Palestinian nationalism "have become more and more widespread since the 1970s in the French public arena . . . as well as in the West more generally." This new anti-Semitism, he said, often relies on anti-Zionist themes, using metaphors like "cancer" to describe Israel and creating what he called the most recent form of "eliminationist" anti-Semitism.[36]

Weil of CNRS is skeptical of the concept. "I think what we call a new anti-Semitism resembles the old one — the same kind of theory of the plot of the *Protocols of the Learned Elders of Zion*," says Weil, referring to the infamous anti-Semitic literary hoax alleging a Jewish plot to achieve world domination. "Some people call it new because it comes from Arabs."

British journalist Phillips has charged that "Language straight out of the lexicon of medieval and Nazi Jew-hatred has become commonplace in acceptable British discourse, particularly in the media." For her, "the most striking evidence that hatred of Israel is the latest mutation of anti-Semitism is that it resurrects the libel of the world Jewish conspiracy, a defining anti-Semitic motif that went underground after the Holocaust."[37]

For example, she cites the left-leaning *New Statesman* magazine's investigation into the "Zionist" lobby in Britain, which it headlined the "Kosher Conspiracy" and illustrated on its Jan. 14, 2002, cover with a gold Star of David piercing the Union Jack.[38] *The Guardian*, Britain's leading liberal daily, published a cartoon on July 19, 2006, depicting a huge fist, armed with brass knuckles shaped like Stars of David, hammering a bloody child.[39] A cartoon in *The Independent* in 2003 showing former Israeli leader Ariel Sharon biting the head off a Palestinian baby won first prize in the British Political Cartoon Society's annual competition for that year.[40]

Some critics say such drawings of Jews killing children are reminiscent of the imagery of the "blood libel," the medieval European belief that Jews murdered Gentile children to obtain their blood for religious rituals — sparking massacres of Jews throughout history.

But not all Jews see these media images as intentionally ill-motivated. "What that proves is there's a great deal of criticism of Israel, some of which spills over into odious anti-Semitism," says Dan Judelson, chair of Jews for Justice for Palestinians, a British group. "It's not a type of deep-seated, visceral hatred of the Jews; it's just intellectual laziness."

Judelson's is one of several groups of generally left-leaning Jews who have been active in criticizing Israel's actions towards the Palestinians. He says Israel's defenders equate criticism of Israel with anti-Semitism as a way of "de-legitimizing" sincere criticism. And he takes issue with a commonly used definition of anti-Semitism from the European Union's monitoring arm, which encompasses "denying the Jewish people their right to self-determination, e.g. by claiming that the existence of a State of Israel is a racist endeavor."[41] Not all Jews define self-determination as having a Jewish state, he points out. (*See sidebar, p. 142.*)

Groups like Judelson's have been criticized for marching for Palestinian liberation with Muslim activists who carried placards linking a swastika to a Star of David with an equal sign. Judelson says whenever he's confronted Muslim marchers about this kind of imagery, they have responded by changing their symbols.

But other observers, including a former Islamist, say liberal Jewish groups are naïve about the ultimate motives of such Muslim activists. Rashad Ali, a former director in the command structure of the radical Islamist group Hizb-ut-Tahrir Britain, says the group would capitalize on sentiments against Israel for its own political ends.

During the conflict between Israel and Lebanon, he says, "We'd always know we can get a Jewish rabbi to talk about the atrocities in Israel; then we'd take over and say what we need is the Caliphate" — which Ali describes as a dictatorship in which laws would be based on Islamic religious interpretation. (When asked which groups such a rabbi would come from, Ali mentioned Neturei Karta, an orthodox Jewish group that opposes the establishment of the state of Israel before the coming of the Messiah.)

At least one radical Islamist group has been careful to replace the word "Jew" with "Zionist" in its leaflets and Web sites in order to appeal to more mainstream critics of Israel, says Ali, now head of research and policy at the Quilliam Foundation, a new London-based group aimed at fighting extremist forms of Islam. He has printed out an online leaflet that he said Hizb had recently removed from its Web site following wide distribution. Entitled "The Muslim Ummah will never submit to the Jews," the leaflet is replete with anti-Semitic stereotypes such as "The Jews are cowards, they are a people of money and not a people of fighting."

Formerly, anti-Semitic language was used heavily "because it has a lot of currency in Islamist crowds," Ali says. But after then-Prime Minister Tony Blair declared he wanted to ban Hizb, the group underwent a public re-imaging. "They didn't change any of their ideas, but they realized the need to re-brand themselves for public media consumption. They started to tailor their language to say the 'Zionist state,' not 'the Jewish state.' "

But is anti-Zionism always anti-Semitism? NYU historian Judt, a British Jew and an outspoken critic of Israel, recently argued that by "shouting anti-Semitism every time someone attacks Israel or defends the Palestinians, we are breeding cynics" and risk losing the attention of those who need to recognize genuine genocidal evil.

"When people chide me and others for criticizing Israel too forcefully, lest we rouse the ghosts of prejudice,

Confronting the Past in Poland

Accounts of pogroms rouse anti-Semitic ghosts.

Anti-Semitism in Poland today is almost entirely about history. Unlike France and England, where Israel's treatment of the Palestinians is often the source of anti-Jewish feeling, the most recent debates in Poland have centered on Poles' responsibility for the deadly fate of their Jewish neighbors during and after the Holocaust.

In Poland today, "The problem of the Jews is the problem of the past," says Anna Bikont, a Polish journalist with the leading daily newspaper *Gazeta Wyborcza*, who has written about Polish reactions to the revelations that Poles in the town of Jedwabne killed Jewish neighbors during the war.

The most prominent Jewish issue in the Polish media since the fall of communism in 1989 has been the infamous massacre. On July 10, 1941, about 400 people were forced into a barn on the town's outskirts and burned alive by their Polish neighbors. During the communist era, the incident was blamed on the Nazis; even the monument at the site made no mention of Poles' part in the massacre.

But in 2001, the publication of the book *Neighbors*, by Jan T. Gross, a Polish Jewish historian now at Princeton University, revealed documentary evidence that residents of the town were primarily to blame for the deaths of up to 1,600 of their Jewish neighbors.[1] When news reports made clear that Poles had carried out the deadly pogrom, with only a little encouragement from the Nazis, the "bombshell" shocked the Polish public, according to Hanna Kwiatkowska, who has analyzed anti-Semitism in the right-wing Polish press for her doctoral thesis at University College, London.

The ensuing discussion encouraged the press, which denied that Poles ever participated in the crime, to launch a full-blown anti-Semitic campaign. Seven years later Jedwabne continues to serve as an anti-Semitic tool and litmus test of "real Poles," according to Kwiatkowska.[2]

The newspaper *Nasz Dziennik*, which is part of a conservative Catholic media empire in Poland, charged that Jews were using "lies" about the massacre to blackmail Poland into paying them "billions of dollars" in restitution. The theme of "Jewish profiteers" has persisted several years later in the paper's coverage.[3] While such views were confined mainly to the right-wing press, skepticism about Poles' guilt in the event was surprisingly widespread in Poland. In 2002, 35 percent of respondents said the Germans had murdered the Jews in Jedwabne, while 38 percent believed the townspeople had been forced by the Germans to launch the pogrom.[4]

"We have an old and strong tradition of anti-Semitism," which Poles use to define their national identity, says Bikont. "To be very Polish you have to be different from the Jew." She cites typical stereotypes: "The Jews are so intelligent, they like to manipulate other people; the Polish people are honest and supported one another. The Jews didn't fight in the diaspora; the Poles were always very brave."

But Bikont says views about responsibility for the past seem to be changing among young people. In a recent poll, *Gazeta Wyborcza* asked if Poles should examine their conscience in connection with actions against Jews in the past. Only 14 percent of respondents old enough to have been alive in World War II answered yes, but 37 percent of 18- to 24-year-olds answered in the affirmative, Bikont reports. (The audience for the most anti-Semitic newspapers and radio programs is composed largely of elderly pensioners, who have been forced into reduced circumstances since the fall of communism.)

Shortly after the revelations about Jedwabne, residents in their forties, most with family links to the original murderers, clung angrily to the town's innocence and blamed the new account on Jewish journalists or Jews seeking money or political power, Bikont reported.

When Bikont questioned residents about Jews who had lived on their street, a typical response was, "Now, don't you try to threaten us. We have all the papers proving our ownership of this house."[5] (Gross suggests that Poles' attacks on Jews during and after the war were partly motivated by Poles' coveting and subsequent confiscation of Jewish property.)

The family of a resident who revealed more details to the press about the residents' part in the massacre was forced to move away after they were ostracized, called "Jewish lapdogs" and received death threats, according to Bikont. Some elderly residents who concurred in Gross's account were told by the local priest they would not be buried in the Catholic cemetery, she adds.[6]

Gross's latest historic revelation describes how a few Jewish survivors of the Holocaust, destitute and emaciated, returned to their Polish hometowns after the war, only to be attacked and sometimes murdered by residents, who often had occupied former Jewish homes.[7] In the most horrifying instance, an estimated 42 people, including a mother with her baby and a pregnant woman, were shot or stoned to death by residents of Kielce in 1946. Until the release of Gross' account in January, many people in Poland believed the Kielce massacre had been provoked by the communists.

At a recent meeting in Kielce to discuss Gross's book, Bikont said only a few people spoke in virulently anti-Semitic tones. "Many people talked about feelings of guilt about things in Kielce" — a contrast from her interviews in Jedwabne several years ago, where she met mainly denial.

"I think Jedwabne opened up something in Poland," she says. "It's really changed."

Poland's chief rabbi, Michael Schudrich, has a different take on Kielce. "People forget that in the postwar period the Nazis had so succeeded in destroying morality in society that one of the normal options to resolve a conflict was killing the other person."

In a recent U.S. State Department report, Poland is criticized for desecrations last year at one of the country's largest Jewish cemeteries. Vandals in Czestochowa spray-painted about 100 gravestones with swastikas, "SS" and "Jews out."[8]

The report doesn't say, Schudrich notes, that "the mayor of the town was out there with me and teens scrubbing off the swastikas" shortly afterwards. "Yeah, bad things happen," but the question is, "How does the rest of society react?" Harking back to the Holocaust, he observes, "Genocide happens when the good are silent."

Neglect, rather than vandalism, is the main threat to Jewish cemeteries in communities where no Jews remain, says Bikont. Some have been used to dump garbage, while others have been dug up for building sites. In a few towns, Polish Jews are trying to restore crumbling cemeteries. Bikont also points out that it's no longer dangerous to be a Jew in Poland.

At the same time, however, Kwiatkowska finds it "a worrying sign" that Poland's second-most-popular daily newspaper, *Rzeczpospolita*, gave a platform to right-wing voices in response to Gross's recent revelations about Kielce. It could be a nod towards the current, conservative government, which partially owns the paper.[9]

But Schudrich has a more optimistic outlook. In May 2006, he was attacked in the most serious anti-Semitic incident in Poland in years. Schudrich, who wears a kepah (Jewish skullcap), was walking on the street after Sabbath prayers when a man, later identified with right-wing causes,

AP Photo/Czarek Sokolowski

Then-Polish President Aleksander Kwasniewski lays a wreath at a new monument to mark the place where Poles massacred Jews from the town of Jedwabne, Poland, in 1941. Kwasniewski addressed relatives of the victims and apologized in the name of Poland.

yelled "Poland for Poles," a well-known anti-Semitic slogan from before the war, historically followed by "Jews to Palestine!"

When Schudrich confronted the man and asked why he had yelled that, the rabbi was punched and pepper-sprayed. After the incident, Schudrich received a call from the prime minister and an invitation to the presidential palace, where government officials condemned the incident before the Polish media. His attacker served two months in jail.

"It did happen," but "much more important was the response — universal condemnation," Schudrich said in an interview last year.[10]

Asked about the incident recently, he added, "And no such attack has happened again. If anti-Semitism is rampant, it should be happening every other day."

---

[1] Jan T. Gross, *Neighbors: The Destruction of the Jewish Community in Jedwabne, Poland* (2002). In 2002, the Institute of National Memory (IPN) in Poland disputed Gross's figure of 1,600 deaths (the pre-war Jewish population in Jedwabne) after an investigation, suggesting it was only in the hundreds, but concluded the real figure would never be known. See "'Fear'": An Exchange," *The New York Times*, Aug. 20, 2006. For an estimate that half of adult men, plus some women and children, witnessed or participated in the massacre and an estimate that some 400 were killed in the barn, see, Peter S. Green, "Polish Town Still Tries to Forget its Dark Past," *The New York Times*, Feb. 8, 2003.

[2] Hanna Kwiatkowska, "Conflict of Images. Conflict of Memories. Jewish Themes in the Polish Right-Wing Nationalistic Press in the Light of Articles from Nasz Dziennik 1998-2007," unpublished doctoral thesis.

[3] *Ibid.*

[4] *Ibid.*

[5] Anna Bikont, "Seen from Jedwabne," www1.yadvashem.org/download/about_holocaust/studies/bikont.pdf.

[6] *Ibid.*

[7] Jan T. Gross, *Fear: Anti-Semitism in Poland after Auschwitz* (2007).

[8] "Contemporary Global Anti-Semitism: A Report Provided to the United States Congress," U.S. State Department, March 2008, p. 17, www.state.gov/g/drl/rls/102406.htm.

[9] Hanna Kwiatkowska, "Book Reviews: Jan T. Gross, *Fear,*" East European Jewish Affairs, April 1, 2007, pp. 119-121, www.informaworld.com.

[10] "Insight: Interview with Michael Schudrich, chief rabbi of Poland," *San Francisco Chronicle* podcast, May 4, 2007, www.sfgate.com/cgi-bin/blogs/sfgate/detail?blogid=5&entry_id=16203.

Young Poles Turn to Judaism

"People treat it like something exotic."

If you walked into the only active synagogue in Warsaw during morning prayers, many of those praying would probably have been brought up as Catholics. Most would have discovered only as adults that they had Jewish family roots.

In a country where over 90 percent of its more than 3 million Jews perished under the Nazis, where Jewish concentration camp survivors who returned to their villages were murdered by their Polish neighbors and where communist oppression reigned for decades, it was for many years dangerous to reveal one's Jewish heritage.[1]

But since 1989, as the collapse of communism in Poland made it safe for families to reveal their Jewish ties to their children and as interest in their lost culture has grown, a growing number of young Poles have been drawn to Judaism, even some with no known Jewish heritage.

"It's a fun thing . . . oriental. People treat it like something exotic with a secret language no one understands," says Krzystof Izdebski, 27, a lawyer and secretary of Zoom, a Warsaw cultural group aimed at bringing young Jewish Poles together. "Also, there are people who have empathy for the Jews; they are taught about the *Shoah* [Holocaust] in school and want to pay tribute. The majority of Zoom's 126 members, ages 16-35, only discovered their Jewish heritage in their teens, or even later, according to Izdebski.

Of an estimated 5,000-10,000 Jews who participate in Jewish religious life in Poland today, more than 60 percent did not discover they were Jewish until adulthood, estimates Michael Bilewicz, a social psychologist at Warsaw University who studies Polish Jewish identity. (Some estimates place the number of Jews in Poland much higher, around 20,000, as a result of the growing number discovering they have Jewish roots.[2])

The discovery of Jewish roots is often problematic, especially if it breaches a deeply held family secret. Anna Bikont, a 54-year-old Warsaw journalist, was 35 when she discovered that her mother was Jewish but had survived the war on "the Aryan side" in Poland, married to a Christian.

When Bikont decided to raise her children as Jews and send them to a Jewish school, her mother at first refused to have any contact with her. "She was anxious and furious," Bikont recalls. "All her life she did all she could [to make sure] that my sister and I wouldn't be Jews." Today, Bikont's 19-year-old daughter Ola identifies strongly with Judaism, is a member of Zoom and has applied for Israeli citizenship.

The variety of reasons for this enduring secrecy reflects the historical difficulty of being Jewish in Poland. During the war, many Jewish children were given to Christian families by parents who would not survive the Holocaust. Some Jewish families passed as Christians with false identity papers and after the war were still afraid to reveal their true identity. Those Jewish families who stayed after the war or returned as communists from the Soviet Union were more likely to be secular or atheistic in a Catholic country known for its hostility toward Jews. And some children of Jewish communists rebelled against their parents' generation by participating in the Catholic opposition that gave rise to the Solidarity anticommunist movement. (Adam Michnik, editor of Warsaw's *Gazeta Wyborcza*, a leading Polish newspaper, is the most famous Solidarity leader with Jewish roots.)

In an attempt to curry favor with the Soviet Union, the communist government in Poland responded to the 1967 Six-Day Israeli war with an anti-Semitic campaign in 1967-68, accusing Jews of loyalty to the Zionist state, blaming Jews for student protests against the regime, firing Jewish workers and confiscating property. Of Poland's 30,000 remaining Jews, about 20,000 emigrated in 1968-69.[3]

What's driving young Poles to reconnect with Jewish culture or religion — especially if their link is as tenuous as a grandparent they never knew? "The need to belong to a defined and exotic ethnic group is very common," Bilewicz found in an ongoing study of young Polish Jews.[4] Poland's homogeneous population is 90 percent ethnically Polish, white and Christian, he points out, so "being Jewish gives a sense of being distinctive."

I tell them that they have the problem exactly the wrong way around. It is just such a taboo that may itself stimulate anti-Semitism," Judt recently asserted.[42]

But British MP Mann argues that anti-Zionism in the press and public discussion stirs up deeper hatred than criticism of other countries because it is fundamentally racist, not just making a political point.

"Why are young Jewish kids abused in the streets when there's conflict in Lebanon?" he asks. "Young Chinese kids are not abused when there's conflict in Tibet. People feel free

The desire to get in touch with a family tradition broken during the Holocaust is also important, he says. Ironically, it's often religious Catholics who feel most comfortable making the switch to religious Judaism, he notes, because they already believe in God. Indeed, Zoom has some members who consider themselves Jews but also attend Catholic church, according to Izdebski.

Courtesy Czulent

Members of Czulent, a group for young Polish Jews in Krakow, pose in front of graffiti referring to "Jude Gang" (literally "Jewish Gang"), the name taken by fans of Krakow's soccer team. The team's fan club protected Jews during the Nazi era and represents a positive link with Jews in Poland. "We decided to take the photo here to show we are not afraid to tell people we are Jewish," says Czulent's Anna Makowka.

Chief Rabbi of Poland Michael Schudrich says he knows of a handful of Poles with no Jewish family heritage who have converted to Judaism. "They simply believe Judaism helps them find God and brings morality into their lives."

The movement may also reflect a growing curiosity among Poles generally about a people that virtually disappeared. Many Poles have never laid eyes on a Jew, notes Bikont. "In Poland, many young people are now interested in Jewish history," she says. "It's very new, and it's very strong. We have five or six new plays about Jews written by young people this year." A Jewish cultural festival attracts thousands to Krakow every year.

The recent Jewish revival dates back to the early 1990s, when young Poles who had just discovered their Jewish family connections found the elderly regulars at Polish synagogues less than welcoming toward people who knew nothing about the faith, according to Bilewicz.

Schudrich, then a dynamic young American rabbi, started to offer "a new way of being Jewish," Bilewicz says — organizing Shabbat dinners, translating prayers into Polish and introducing guitar music to services.

Today, Rabbi Schudrich estimates that thousands of Jews have discovered they have Jewish roots since the fall of communism. "The question is, what are they going to do about it? That's what we do: Try to create programming and an environment that will empower them to look into their Jewish heritage."

In this vein, cultural associations like Zoom in Warsaw and Czulent* in Krakow — organized by young Poles who returned from Israel wanting to know more about their new-found Judaism — organize Jewish holiday parties, seminars on Judaism and multicultural dialogues. These gatherings offer a way for young Poles to connect to Judaism as a culture — not necessarily by conversion. They also offer companionship for new entrants to a tiny minority group that has lost most of its communal memory.

Young people who suddenly discover their Jewish background often have to overcome a feeling of alienation from Poles around them, Czulent's Web site acknowledges. "Sometimes it's better to have a beer together than to go to lectures," says Izdebski. "Or go for Shabbat dinner to someone's home, so you don't feel so alone in Polish society."

* Czulent is the name of a traditional Sabbath dish of slow-cooking meat and beans, http://czulent.org.

[1] See Tony Judt, *Postwar* (2007), p. 804. According to Judt, 97.5 percent of Poland's Jews were exterminated.

[2] See Stephen Roth Institute for the Study of Antisemitism and Racism, "Poland 2006," p. 1, and "Poland" 1997, p. 1, at www.tau.ac.il/Anti-Semitism/asw2006/poland.htm. The 2006 report estimates 5,000-10,000 Jews in Poland.

[3] Judt, *op. cit.*, pp. 434-435.

[4] Cohen Center for Modern Jewish Studies, Brandeis University, "Taglit-Birthright Israel International," http://cmjs.org/Project.cfm?idProject=18.

to criticize China or Israel, but the consequences are very different. That is because of the language used. . . . There is a difference: It's stoked by anti-Semitic discourse, and the language used in attacking Israel is a big part of that," he says. "It creates this legitimacy for racist abuse."

Recently, Small at Yale's Initiative for the Interdisciplinary Study of Antisemitism and a colleague decided to test whether there is a statistical correlation between Israel-bashing and anti-Semitic attitudes in a survey of 500 people in 10 European countries.[43] The results,

CHRONOLOGY

Middle Ages *Ritual-murder rumors incite pogroms; Jew are persecuted during Spanish Inquisition.*

1144 Blood-libel charge emerges in England.

1218 English Church requires Jews to wear special badges to identify them as non-Christians.

1247 Pope declares ritual-murder allegations fraudulent.

1290 Jews expelled from England.

1492-1498 Jews expelled from Spain, then Portugal and France.

18th Century *Some European Jews are emancipated during Enlightenment.*

1791 France gives Jews equal rights.

19th Century *Ottoman Empire declares religious tolerance; Russian pogroms scatter Jews to Western Europe; "Dreyfus affair" spurs Zionism.*

1839 Ottoman sultan decrees equality for Jews, Christians.

1879 German journalist Wilhelm Marr coins term "anti-Semitic."

1880 First wave of Russian Jews arrives in England.

1894-99 Capt. Alfred Dreyfus, a French Jew, is falsely accused of treason. Affair radicalizes Austrian Jewish journalist Theodor Herzl, who later leads Zionist movement.

Early 20th Century *Britain restricts Jewish immigration, declares support for Jewish homeland.*

1903 "Protocols of the Learned Elders of Zion" — an anti-Semitic literary hoax — appears in Russia.

1906 Britain's Aliens Act of 1905 limits Jewish refugees.

1917 Balfour Declaration states British support for Jewish homeland in Palestine.

1930s *Nazis begin persecuting Jews, followed by systematic eradication.*

1933 Nazis begin restricting Jews' rights; Dachau concentration camp opens.

Nov. 9-10, 1938 A night of mob attacks on German Jews, known as *Kristallnacht* ("Night of Broken Glass") destroys Jewish businesses and synagogues. Some 30,000 Jews are sent to concentration camps, launching the Nazi plan to eradicate Europe's Jews.

1940s *Six million Jews die in Nazi concentration camps; Vichy French hand over Jews to Nazis; Allied propaganda and press barely mention Jews.*

July 1940 Vichy regime initiates anti-Jewish laws.

July 10, 1941 Poles kill Jewish neighbors in Jedwabne.

1942 Mass gassings begin at Auschwitz-Birkenau camp; Polish Jews are deported to concentration camps; Vichy government deports 13,000 French Jews to Auschwitz.

Postwar 1940s *Anti-Semitism continues.*

1945 Soviet troops liberate Auschwitz-Birkenau; Nuremberg war trials begin.

1946 Jews returning to Poland are murdered by former neighbors.

1960s-1980s *Holocaust enters public consciousness; fall of communism opens door for Eastern European Jews to reveal family roots.*

1962 Israel kidnaps former Nazi official Adolf Eichmann in Argentina, prosecutes and later hangs him for his role in killing Jews.

1968-1969 Polish communist regime invokes anti-Semitism to suppress student protests.

January 1979 "Holocaust" TV series raises awareness of war-time atrocities among millions of West Germans.

1985 Documentary "Shoah" raises awareness in France.

1989 Communist regimes fall in Eastern Europe.

1990s-2000s *Anti-Jewish crimes surge in Europe as Arab-Israeli tensions escalate; anti-Israel resolutions are debated in international, national arenas.*

1991 U.N. General Assembly overturns 1975 resolution declaring Zionism "racism."

1995 President Jacques Chirac acknowledges French responsibility in sending Jews to concentration camps.

2000 Second Palestinian uprising spurs anti-Semitic crimes; European Union begins tracking anti-Jewish incidents.

2004 Organization for Security and Co-operation in Europe declares that events in the Middle East do not justify anti-Semitism.

Feb. 13, 2006 Kidnapped French Jew Ilan Halimi dies after being found tortured in Paris suburb; national outrage ensues.

Sept. 7, 2006 British report finds anti-Semitism increasing.

Feb. 14, 2008 Report shows anti-Semitic incidents in Britain dropped slightly in 2007.

Feb. 22, 2008 French Jew Mathieu Roumi is kidnapped and tortured in Paris.

May 2008 British professors' union revives debate over boycotting Israel.

published in the *Journal of Conflict Resolution*, showed an "off-the-charts" correlation with beliefs that Israel purposely kills children or that Israel is an apartheid state, he says. "In many countries, people who hold such beliefs are 13 times more likely to be anti-Semitic than the average population," reports Small.

Is anti-Semitism as severe as racial discrimination against other minorities in Europe?

"Would you feel safe, accepted [and] welcome today as a 'Paki' in parts of England? A black in Switzerland? Or would you not feel safer more integrated, more accepted as a Jew?" historian Judt recently asked.[44]

Although attacks like the recent kidnappings of two young French Jews are disturbing, young Arabs and Africans frequently face harassment in France — often several times a day — including interference from police, according to Weil of CNRS. Most people concede that European Jews — largely assimilated, educated and middle class — do not face the kinds of job, housing or personal discrimination faced by darker-skinned immigrants.

Those most concerned about the state of anti-Semitism today concede it does not approach the social discrimination faced by other minorities. But some experts contend that anti-Semitism has always been different in nature from other kinds of racial discrimination. Since the 19th century, anti-Semitism has not just been about looking down on Jews as an inferior race, notes Ruth Wisse, a professor of Yiddish and comparative literature at Harvard University and author of the 2007 book *Jews and Power*. It's also been the polar opposite: attributing great power to Jews as a global conspiracy controlling government, banks and the media. As such, Jews often served as a convenient scapegoat for a society's social ills, she says.

Following this logic, the Nazis called for killing all Jews as a way of cleansing society of all evil, something Iran's Ahmadinejad has repeatedly called for, notes historian Küntzel. By contrast, no head of state today calls for the killing of all blacks as a way to solve society's ills, he notes. "Therefore anti-Semitism is the most dangerous" of these phenomena and the threats of Ahmadinejad are to be taken seriously, he says.

Yet, while assaults on individual Jews have clearly risen in recent years in Britain, the Institute for Jewish Policy Research's Lerman says the attacks against other groups, especially Muslims, are far worse. They are rarely captured in statistics, however, because other ethnic communities are less organized in collecting the data, according to Lerman.

In London, a Jewish person is three times as likely to be the subject of racial attack as a non-Jewish white person, but Arabs, blacks and Asians are 9 to 12 times more

Some Poles Hid Jews From the Nazis

More than 70 people are alive today thanks to Jerzy Kozminski.

Editor's note: During a recent trip to Poland, CQ Global Researcher *contributing writer Sarah Glazer interviewed 83-year-old Jerzy Kozminski, whose family in Warsaw had helped hide several members of her own family during the Nazi occupation.*

In the winter of 1942, a gas company meter reader — a member of the underground Council for Aid to Jews — approached a Christian Polish family living in a small house in German-occupied Warsaw and asked if they would be willing to hide three Jews.

The family agreed, even though it was widely known that Poles who hid Jews would be executed by the Nazis — along with their entire families. The Kozminskis had just enough room to house the two men, watchmakers, and one of their wives, recalls 83-year-old Jerzy Kozminski — then a 17-year-old living with his father, stepmother and 2-year-old stepbrother. But the family could not afford to feed three more people.

So when the two watchmakers ran short of watch parts — essential for buying their food on the black market — they asked young Jerzy to seek help from an acquaintance in the Jewish ghetto, Samuel Glazer — a cousin of mine — who had owned a shirt factory in Lodz before the war.

Donning a yellow Jewish armband, which the Nazis required all Jews to wear, Jerzy crept into the Jewish ghetto for the first of numerous trips as a courier. Once, a guard sprayed him with submachine fire as he began scaling the ghetto wall; another time, as he emerged on the "Aryan" side of the wall, he was grabbed by an undercover officer, whom he paid off with a small bribe.

Samuel asked if Jerzy's family would hide his large extended family of seven. Jerzy's father agreed, and the Kozminskis rented a larger house on the outskirts of Warsaw and dug a basement bunker where the family could hide.

The Glazers paid smugglers to get them out of the ghetto on April 19, 1943, the day the Warsaw ghetto uprising began, just as residents were being ordered to gather for the fateful transfer to the Treblinka death camp. Only one family member didn't make it out: Samuel's sister-in-law, Anda Herling, the mother of a 10-year-old daughter, was caught by guards while escaping, and the family never saw her again.

Later, Jerzy led another four members of the Glazer family to a safe hiding place in Warsaw, where he continued to look after them. The Kozminskis also took in other groups of Jews for varying periods of time.

Eleven members of the Glazer family survived the war hidden in the Kozminski house and their Warsaw hiding place until liberation by the Russians. All told, Kozminski is credited with saving more than 20 Jews.[1] He has been honored by the Yad Vashem Institute in Jerusalem as one of the Righteous Among the Nations — non-Jews who risked life or liberty to rescue Jews during the Holocaust.

Today, the retired engineer with a keen, blue-eyed gaze and a smile playing around his lips remembers many of his close calls with a sense of humor. After three residents of the Warsaw apartment where Samuel's elderly father was hiding were arrested on the street, the Glazers feared he was in danger of being discovered by police. It was vital to move the old man to a new hiding place. But his long beard would instantly identify him as an Orthodox Jew. Kozminski remembers with a chuckle that the old man's son Sewek shaved off the beard over his father's vigorous protests. Then, disguised as a peasant with a handlebar mustache in an old-fashioned cap and boots, the old man followed Kozminski to his home through the streets of Warsaw without being discovered.

It was difficult to hide the fact that so many people were living in the house, especially since large amounts of food had to be purchased. On at least one occasion, Kozminski remembers his little brother blurting out cheerfully at the local store, "There is no one living in our basement."

"The neighbors knew someone was there, but they didn't know who," Kozminski believes. If those hidden had been Polish underground partisans, he points out, the neighbors knew that denouncing the family would put them at risk of being killed by the Polish resistance.

Kozminski says he does not like the word "hero" and tends to brush off the idea that he did anything out of the ordinary. Indeed, in his view, "This rescue was a patriotic act" at a time when Poles were suffering under Nazi occupation. "Many people in Poland did things against the Germans."

In his modesty, Kozminski is typical of other Poles who saved Jews, of whom more than 6,000 have received the Righteous award.[2] In their insistence that they did nothing unusual, "I sense a stubborn belief in human decency being not the exception but the rule," suggests Konstanty Gebert, founder of the Polish-Jewish monthly *Midrasz*. "[A]nd were the Righteous to be considered exceptional, this belief would fail."[3]

Simple humanity may be another explanation. Kozminski's father had many Jewish friends while a student in Switzerland, the son recalls, and had once been in love with a Jewish girl — or so his wife used to tease him.

Moreover, Kozminski's stepmother, "was a woman who couldn't say 'No' " if someone came to her door seeking help, recalls Gita Baigelman, 86, of New York City, one of Samuel's surviving sisters, who met the Kozminski family after the war.[4]

When asked about the Poles who murdered their Jewish neighbors in notorious pogroms during and after the war, Kozminski displayed his only flare of anger during a recent interview, declaring, "The pope said that a Christian, if an anti-Semite, is not a Christian."

After joining the Polish resistance, Kozminski was caught by the Nazis in October 1943 while on a gun-buying run. When he failed to return home, the Glazers feared their hiding place would be revealed, Baigelman recalls. What they didn't know was that Jerzy had been questioned by the Gestapo but had kept their secret.

After his interrogation, Kozminski was sent to Auschwitz and then to the Mauthausen concentration camp. Upon the camp's liberation by the Americans in May 1945, he emerged emaciated, unable to eat, his health broken by starvation. By happy coincidence, he located Samuel, who was once again running a clothing factory in Lodz. The Glazers sent him to a doctor, who gradually restored his health.

One theme that is often overlooked in rescue accounts is the extent to which Jewish families aided those who hid them. As Kozminski remembers it, the Glazers "promised to help me recover; they delivered on their word."[5]

In 1964, Samuel and his family, who had moved to Israel, invited Jerzy's stepmother Theresa to stay with them. Then a widow, she took them up on their invitation, married a Jewish man, converted to Judaism and lived out the rest of her life in the Jewish homeland. She was made an honorary citizen of Tel Aviv and buried in a cemetery for distinguished citizens.

In 1996, when the Anti-Defamation League honored Kozminski for the rescue, it estimated that more than 70 people around the world — the descendants of those he saved — were alive because of his efforts.[6]

Halinka Herling, the 10-year-old whose mother did not survive the escape from the ghetto, is now a grandmother living in Israel.

CQ Press/Sarah Glazer

Jerzy Kozminski, now 83, helped hide several members of the author's family in Warsaw during the Nazi occupation.

Kozminski proudly displays a photograph of Halinka surrounded by her smiling grandchildren, which he received after he was reunited with her two years ago. This, he declares, is his reward. "God gave me the present of the grandchildren of Halinka on my 81st birthday," he says, adding he could not imagine a better gift.

— ***Sarah Glazer***

[1] Jerzy Kozminski, "The Memories of a Righteous Man" (unpublished memoir, undated). Those rescued include 11 members of the extended Glazer family, the three-member Seifman family and eight Jews housed for three weeks.

[2] A total of 6,066 people from Poland were honored with the award, more than any other nation. However, Poland also had the largest number of Jews of any country in Europe before the Holocaust, www1.yadvashem.org/righteous_new/statistics.html.

[3] "Recalling Forgotten History: For Poles Who Rescued Jews During the Holocaust," album prepared to accompany a ceremony honoring the Righteous at the Polish National Opera in cooperation with the Museum of History of Polish Jews, Oct. 10, 2007, published by the Chancellery of the President of the Republic of Poland.

[4] Gita Baigelman was living in the Lodz ghetto, from where she was transferred to Ravensbrück concentration camp and a labor camp in Germany. She met the Kozminskis after the war.

[5] Kozminski, *op. cit.*

[6] Anti-Defamation League, press release, "ADL Honors Christian Rescuers of Jews During the Holocaust Who Had the Courage to Care," Nov. 22, 1996, www.adl.org/PresRele/ChJew_31/2857_31.asp.

likely to be attacked, according to police authorities cited by Lerman. A recent speech by the Archbishop of Canterbury proposing adoption of sharia law for Muslims in England for personal matters like marriage was followed by a storm of hostile protest, including some 500 incidents against Muslims in Britain ranging from verbal abuse to attacks on mosques, according to Lerman.

Lerman sees these attacks, like anti-Semitic crimes, as part of "the rise of racism generally. More has to be done to combat racism."

But some scholars of anti-Semitism think there's something unique that distinguishes it from other forms of racism. Hitler, of course, spoke of the inferior racial nature of Jews and their need to be eliminated in his quest for Aryan racial purity. "People love to talk about that form of anti-Semitism — that was the only form that was defeated," says Wisse.

It's more important, she suggests, to defend against the tendency to use Jews as a scapegoat for everything that's wrong with capitalism and modernity.

"It's an anti-modernist ideology that says, 'You think emancipation, democracy, is such a terrific force, but it's only a vehicle for the Jews to take us over.' " In Wisse's view, "The horror is that this organization of politics against the Jews is much more important to the Arabs than it ever was to Europe" because anti-Semitism has become the "glue" that ties disparate Muslim countries together.

Meanwhile, discrimination against Muslims — dubbed "Islamophobia" — has been garnering growing government and press attention. A 2006 report by the EU's European Monitoring Centre on Racism and Xenophobia said that while discrimination and incidents against European Muslims remain underdocumented and underreported, Muslims in the European Union "frequently suffer different forms of discrimination which reduce their employment opportunities and affect their educational achievement."[45]

Indeed, several columnists have recently described Muslims as "the new Jews" of Britain in connection with events seen as discriminatory against Muslims. After several Muslims were arrested in connection with an alleged terrorist plot, Mohammad Naseem, chairman of the Birmingham Central Mosque, told the press that Britain was becoming a "police state" and compared the police raids to the persecution of Jews in Germany.[46]

But when the EU's racism-monitoring arm investigated incidents of Islamophobia following 9/11, it found very few incidents of physical assaults on Muslims in most countries. (Only in the U.K. was a significant rise in attacks on Muslims reported.)[47] Historian David Cesarani of Royal Holloway, University of London, says this is a significant contrast from the spikes in attacks on Jews following events like the invasion of Afghanistan and Israeli incursions into the West Bank and Gaza Strip.

In addition, while Muslim immigrants may experience poverty and social discrimination, as Jewish immigrants once did, Muslims today are often connected to powerful foreign governments, while diaspora Jews historically had no homeland. When Muslims in Denmark were offended in September 2005 by cartoons depicting the Prophet Mohammed, for example, they could appeal to governments of Muslim countries, triggering an international wave of protests.

In addition, Cesarani notes, Jews historically never constituted a rival military or economic force to Europe, whereas Europeans rightfully feared Muslim power during the Ottoman Empire. Today, European reactions to Muslims are to some degree accurate perceptions of the real menace of Islamic terrorism, according to Cesarani.

"Islamophobia is incommensurable with anti-Semitism because Jews as Jews never espoused the attitudes ascribed to them by anti-Semites" or threatened a state in the name of Judaism, he argues. "Islamophobia may be an inappropriate . . . reaction to a grossly inflated 'threat,' but the danger of terrorism by Islamists is real, and there are several conflicts in the world in which Islamic militants are at war in the name of Islam."[48]

BACKGROUND

'Blood Libel' Slander

The accusation that Jews killed Christians, usually children, to obtain their blood for religious rituals originated in England in 1144, when Jews were accused of a ritual murder during the Passover period. This fabricated slander would become one of the most common incitements to anti-Jewish riots and killings throughout Europe during the Middle Ages, despite a papal bull in 1247 that declared such accusations false.[49]

The blood libel accusation lasted well into the 20th century, providing the ostensible cause for a pogrom as late as 1946 against Jewish survivors returning to their homes in Kielce, Poland. The accusation: The Jews planned to use the blood from the murder of a small boy to bake matzo for Passover.

In England and other European countries these seemingly spontaneous riots occurred as Jews were being denied equal rights with Christians. Restrictions imposed on Jews owning land and their exclusion from craft guilds made them dependent upon money lending and other forms of commerce, providing a historical basis for the stereotype of the Jew as greedy money-lender, notably the character of Shylock in Shakespeare's "Merchant of Venice."[50]

In 1218 England became the first European country to implement a church decree that Jews wear a badge to distinguish them from Christians, a directive the Nazis revived when they required all Jews to wear a yellow Jewish star.[51]

In 1290, King Edward expelled all Jews from England, ending their official presence in Britain for the next 400 years — the first large-scale deportation of Jews from a country in Europe. In 1656, British political leader Oliver Cromwell achieved limited recognition for Jews in England, many of whom were descended from Spanish and Portuguese Jews, known as "Conversos," who had fled the Inquisition and been converted to Christianity to prevent discovery.

In a recent paper delivered at Yale, Lappin of Kings College argues that Britain mistakenly perceives itself as a society tolerant of Jews. While the year 1492 is infamous in history for Spain's expulsion of the Jews, notes Lappin, Britain's own expulsion is generally not mentioned in British school curriculum.

History, he says, reveals a "deeply rooted view of Jews as fundamentally alien to British life." For decades, if not centuries, Jews' social acceptability has been "conditional upon suppression of one's Jewish associations and cultural properties," Lappin argues.[52]

With each new influx of Jews, the British government imposed further legal restrictions, such as banning land ownership or citizenship — notably in 1753 and again in 1768 after pogroms in Poland and the Ukraine brought waves of impoverished East European Jews to London.

In the 19th century, while British reformers crusaded for abolition of the slave trade, giving women the vote and establishing workers' rights, no political movement supported Jewish emancipation, according to Lappin. Rather, Anglo-Jewish leaders pursued a strategy of "quiet diplomatic engagement."[53]

AFP/Getty Images/Ralf Succo

Exactly 68 years after a Nazi mob destroyed Munich's main synagogue, members of the city's Jewish community and Israeli Rabbi Mei Lau, left, deliver Torahs to a new Munich synagogue in 2006. Germany's growing Jewish community opened the synagogue amid a resurgent debate about rising anti-Semitism in Germany.

For example, between 1847 and 1852, banker Lionel Rothschild was prevented three times from taking the House of Commons seat to which he was elected. Rothschild was only allowed to enter the House 11 years after his first election and only after the Commons made an exception — suspending the required Christian oath for members of Parliament. Then, from 1880 to 1905 a large wave of Jewish immigrants escaping pogroms in Russia stimulated a strong anti-immigrant sentiment. The Aliens Act of 1905 was the first of several 20th-century measures aimed at limiting entry into the country.

Restricting Jewish Refugees

Britain's attitude towards Jewish refugees during the Nazi regime was more hostile than sympathetic, Lappin argues, in contrast to the country's reputation as a welcoming refuge. After the Nazis took power in Germany in 1933, British officials, like other Western governments, were flooded with requests from German Jews seeking to escape the regime. However, throughout the pre-war period, Britain maintained its system of rigorous controls on immigration, keeping Jewish immigration to a minimum except for those who could fill jobs in which labor was needed — notably female servants.

Nazis Exported Anti-Semitism to the Middle East

Hitler repackaged anti-Semitism as anti-Zionism.

On Nov. 2, 1917, Britain's foreign minister, Lord Balfour, announced Britain's support for the establishment in Palestine of a national home for the Jewish people.

The Balfour Declaration is often cited as the start of the Jewish-Arab conflict — and some would say it was the original source of anti-Israel sentiment in Europe.[1] But as political scientist Matthias Küntzel points out in his recent book, *Jihad and Jew-Hatred*, it wasn't clear that it would turn out that way. Some Arab leaders initially supported Zionist settlements, hoping Jewish immigration would bring economic development.

Before 1937, when the German government first decided it needed to turn the Arabs against the Jews, Jews held prominent positions in business and government in Egypt.[2] Indeed, in 1839 the sultan of the Ottoman Empire had decreed equality for Jews and Christians, and in 1856 such equality was established in law, motivated partly by the Ottoman elite's desire to draw closer to European civilization and to modernize.[3]

But some Arab leaders violently opposed Jewish immigration and the prospect of a Jewish homeland. In the decade leading up to 1936, the mufti of Jerusalem, Amin al-Husseini, the highest religious authority in Palestine, incited Palestinian Arabs to violence against Jews with the aim of ending Jewish immigration and destroying the prospect of a Jewish majority ruling the area. This movement culminated in the 1936-39 Arab revolt, which included anti-Semitic demonstrations, riots, bombings and raids on Jewish villages.[4]

As perhaps the leading inciter of hatred against Jews in the Arab world, the mufti became the region's most committed supporter of Nazism and "a local henchman of the Nazis," according to Küntzel, a research associate at the Vidal Sassoon International Center for the Study of Antisemitism at Hebrew University, Jerusalem.[5]

By 1938, amid mounting tension in Europe, the continuing flight of Jews from Germany to Palestine was provoking renewed Arab violence, including attacks against British fortifications, attacks on Jews and Jewish reprisals. The mufti fled Palestine in 1938 to avoid arrest by the British for his part in the Arab revolt. He spent most of the war in Berlin, recruiting Bosnian Muslims for the SS, the semi-military Nazi organization that oversaw Hitler's extermination of the Jews. From 1939 to 1945, the mufti's Arabic radio broadcasts, which mixed anti-Semitic propaganda with quotes from the *Koran*, made his station the most popular in the Arab world.[6]

The mufti also agreed with the Nazi policy of exterminating the Jews. In 1943, as a propaganda stunt, SS leader Heinrich Himmler wanted to permit 5,000 Jewish children to emigrate to Palestine, in exchange for 20,000 German prisoners. The mufti fought against the plan, and the children were sent to the gas chambers.[7]

The Nazis funded the burgeoning growth of Muslim fundamentalism, helping the radical Muslim Brotherhood distribute Arabic translations of *Mein Kampf*, Hitler's autobiographical political treatise, and the forged *Protocols of the Learned Elders of Zion* and helped fan anti-Zionist flames in the Arab world.[8]

In Germany, a mutual-admiration society appeared to have developed between the mufti and Hitler, who described the mufti inaccurately as having blond hair and blue eyes, to emphasize that he was not a member of an inferior race. Hitler had also expressed his antagonism to Zionism in *Mein Kampf*.

Küntzel argues that the idea of Jews as an all-powerful, dominating world force was essentially a Western idea exported to the Middle East by the Nazis in an effort to turn Muslims against Jews and Zionism. After all, the *Koran* portrays Jews primarily as a defeated force, and for centuries

In 1938, the "Kindertransports" brought about 10,000 Jewish children from Germany and Austria to Britain. These efforts often are cited as proof of British efforts to help the Jews. However, because of British immigration rules — not German restrictions — the children were forced to come without their parents, according to Lappin. As a result, many of these children became orphans at the end of the war.

Jews were treated as second-class citizens in most Arab countries.

But in a recent review of Küntzel's book, Jeffrey Goldberg, a journalist who writes about the region for *The Atlantic*, disagrees, arguing that plenty of anti-Jewish ideas were organic to Muslim thought. And he doesn't buy Küntzel's view that this history explains much Arab hostility towards Israel today. "Jews today have actual power in the Middle East, and Israel is not innocent of excess and cruelty," he writes.[9]

In Europe, Hitler's propaganda machine didn't begin waging a public war on Zionism until 1944, according to Michael Berkowitz, a professor of modern Jewish history at University College, London. In his 2007 book *The Crime of My Very Existence*, Berkowitz argues that Nazi leaders refashioned anti-Semitism as anti-Zionism as part of a broader tactic of painting Jews as criminals. Zionism was painted as the guise for a criminal conspiracy to create a Jewish world government. The Nazis often concocted specific charges against Jews based on technical aspects of tax laws and currency-exchange regulations in addition to charges of petty criminality.[10]

The criminality charges, Berkowitz argues, were chosen because Nazis feared their project of wiping out the Jews for racial reasons would not be universally compelling among German citizens who might be friendly with Mr. Stern the baker or Mrs. Morgen the neighbor. By contrast, the "law and order" motive for assailing an ethnic group was much more persuasive and survives today in stereotypical attitudes toward other ethnic groups, like blacks in the United States or West Indians in Britain, Berkowitz observes.

By 1944, as Nazis feared they were losing the war and would face international outrage at the genocide of the Jews, Zionism "was reconfigured as the apex of Jewish evil and organized criminality to rationalize the decimation of 6 million" Jews, he writes.[11]

Toward the end of the war, when the Nazis had nearly annihilated European Jews, they were searching for new enemies. As a Nazi propagandist put it at the time, once the Jews were all gone, momentum and sympathy for anti-Semitism would be lost: "When asked, young 20-year-old officers say that they have never yet knowingly seen a Jew. Therefore they find no interest . . . in the Jewish problem as it has been presented to them up to now."[12]

Keystone/Getty Images

Adolf Hitler meets with Grand Mufti Amin el-Husseini.

Most significantly for today, the Nazis' anti-Zionism represented "a new form of anti-Jewish discourse," Berkowitz writes, one that "contributed to the evil brew of post-1948 Arab anti-Semitism."[13]

[1] See www.yale.edu/lawweb/avalon/mideast/balfour.htm.

[2] The stimulus for Nazi support of Arabs was the British Peel Commission's 1937 partition plan, providing for a Jewish state, which the Germans feared would increase power for world Jewry. See Matthias Küntzel, *Jihad and Jew-Hatred* (2007), p. 29.

[3] *Ibid.*, p. 33.

[4] Martin Gilbert, *Churchill and Jews* (2007), p. 102.

[5] Küntzel, *op. cit.*, p. 101.

[6] *Ibid.*, pp. 34-35.

[7] *Ibid.*, p. 36.

[8] See www.hitler.org/writings/Mein_Kampf/.

[9] Jeffrey Goldberg, "Seeds of Hate," *New York Times Book Review*, Jan. 6, 2008, www.nytimes.com/2008/01/06/books/review/Goldberg-t.html?_r=1&oref=slogin.

[10] Michael Berkowitz, *The Crime of My Very Existence: Nazism and the Myth of Jewish Criminality* (2007), p. xviii.

[11] Berkowitz, *op. cit.*, pp. 112-113, xix.

[12] *Ibid.*, p. 133.

[13] *Ibid.*, p. 113.

By then, approximately 60,000 Jewish refugees remained in Britain, while another 10,000-20,000 had entered and then re-emigrated or were deported. Lappin notes that while the U.S. government's attitude towards aiding Jews shifted in early 1944 due in part to public pressure from American Jewish groups, the British Jewish community consistently refrained from publicly challenging the government on its handling of refugees.

AP Photo

In a dramatic gesture that helped to raise Europe's consciousness about the Holocaust, West Germany's Chancellor Willy Brandt kneels before the Jewish Heroes' monument in Warsaw, Poland, on Dec. 6, 1970.

In addition, the postwar Labor government refused to accept survivors beyond token numbers. Fewer than 5,000 survivors were admitted from 1945-50 under a family-reunification program, even as Britain was admitting 365,000 non-Jewish immigrants to solve its severe labor shortage. Foreign Secretary Ernest Bevin insisted Jews would not be easily assimilated into British life and that admitting large numbers would aggravate anti-Jewish sentiment stemming from Britain's conflict with Zionists in Palestine.[54]

Ironically, many of the most vocal anti-Zionists among today's British leftists insist that a solution to the Jewish refugee problem during the Holocaust should have been found in European countries rather than in Palestine — "obtuse to the fact that their own political precursors" helped to block Jewish immigration to Britain, Lappin observes.[55]

Forged 'Protocols'

The forgery known as the "Protocols of the Learned Elders of Zion" is the most famous document to libel the Jews. The tract purportedly comprises the minutes from 24 sessions of a conference supposedly held by representatives from the 12 tribes of Israel and led by a Grand Rabbi, whose apparent purpose is to lay out a plan for Jewish world conquest.

It first appeared in Russia in 1903 and again in 1905, inspired partly by the first Zionist congress, held in 1897 under the leadership of Theodor Herzl, an Austro-Hungarian Jewish journalist considered the father of Zionism. The protocols initially were used to blame the Jews for the 1905 Russian Revolution, but the tract soon proved adaptable to other situations where Jews were the target of blame.

"The Nazis saw its value immediately," writes Stephen Eric Bronner, a professor of political science at Rutgers University. The document provides a glimpse into what makes anti-Semitism unique by presenting the Jew as a kind of "chameleon," in Bronner's words. "The Jew is not simply a capitalist or a communist revolutionary, but the Jew is now any enemy required by the anti-Semite."[56]

Herzl, Paris correspondent for the liberal Viennese daily newspaper *Neue Frei Presse*, covered the notorious 1894 trial of Capt. Alfred Dreyfus, a French Jew falsely accused of spying for the Germans. During the trial Herzl witnessed anti-Jewish demonstrations in which cries of "Death to the Jews" were common. The Dreyfus Affair, as it is known, became a watershed event for Jews in France, who felt increasingly vulnerable to anti-Semitism — even though Dreyfus was pardoned in 1899 and his innocence officially recognized in 1906.

A secular Jew, Herzl decided that if anti-Semitism was so entrenched in the capitals of the European Enlightenment, Jews had no hope of assimilating in Europe. In 1896, he published *Der Judenstaat* (The Jewish State), in which he argued that Jews needed to create their own state. In 1897 he organized the First Zionist Congress in Basel, Switzerland, which voted to establish a "publicly and legally secured home" for the Jews in Palestine.[57]

Herzl had a utopian vision of the future homeland, imagining in his 1902 novel *Altneuland* (Old-New Land) an Israel much like his home city of Vienna, an intellectual café society of opera-going, German-speaking Jews. He also imagined that Arabs in Palestine would welcome the gifts of science and improved hygiene brought by the Jews.[58] But Arab opposition to the influx of Jews only hardened over time, leading to the development of the Palestine national liberation movement. (*See sidebar, p. 158.*)

Numerous theories have been put forward in trying to explain the success of anti-Semitism during the Nazi period, some reaching back to much earlier historical

AT ISSUE

Is anti-Zionism a cover-up for anti-Semitism?

YES

Ben Cohen
Associate Director, Department on Anti-Semitism and Extremism, American Jewish Committee; editor, www. z-word.com

Written for *CQ Global Researcher*, June 2008

Anti-Zionism has gained greater visibility over the last decade, but it is not an unknown phenomenon historically. In communist Europe, remnants of Jewish communities that perished during the Nazi Holocaust were frequently persecuted in the name of anti-Zionism.

These days, anti-Zionist views are heavily concentrated among the educated elite. If you regard anti-Zionism as one more expression of hatred towards Jews, this is somewhat puzzling, because anti-Semitism — particularly after the Holocaust — is widely perceived to be more beer hall than bistro.

Anti-Semites regard Jews as a malign social force that controls the banks, media and governments. But most of Zionism's mainstream critics say they are only concerned with the Jewish state, not demented fantasies about what Jews are up to.

So can we construct an unbreachable partition between anti-Semitism and anti-Zionism? The answer is "No," and here is why:

- You can't disavow anti-Semitism as a vulgar form of bigotry and then invoke the age-old themes of anti-Semitic conspiracy theory. After assuring us their arguments were not anti-Semitic, U.S. academics John Mearsheimer and Stephen Walt upended decades of political science research by advancing a monocausal theory of U.S. foreign policy in the Middle East: The powerful "Israel Lobby" cajoles the United States into doing things it otherwise wouldn't do.
- Anti-Zionism is founded upon a caricature of Israel as the apartheid-like child of a colonial enterprise. But Zionism's goal is to guarantee, after centuries of horrendous persecution, the freedom and security of Jews, not the subjugation of non-Jews.
- Before Israel's creation in 1948, there was a vibrant debate about the desirability of a Jewish state. But to be an anti-Zionist now is to question the legitimacy of only Israel, out of nearly 200 states worldwide. In a world of disintegrating polities from Iraq to the Democratic Republic of Congo, why should only Israel's existence be subject to debate?

No serious supporter of Israel claims that mere criticism is anti-Semitism. There is, however, a vital distinction between a rational critique of Israeli policies and demonization, which too often is stimulated by or evokes anti-Semitism.

NO

Antony Lerman
Director, Institute for Jewish Policy Research

Written for *CQ Global Researcher*, June 2008

Anti-Zionism and hostility to Israel can be anti-Semitic if they are expressed using the symbols of the anti-Semitic figure of the Jew or of Jewry as a whole. For example, if Zionism is characterized as a worldwide Jewish conspiracy, or a plan straight out of the forged, anti-Semitic "Protocols of the Learned Elders of Zion," that is anti-Semitism.

But to believe that anti-Zionism and anti-Semitism are one and the same ignores the history of Zionism.

For decades Zionism was supported only by a minority of Jews. The rest were either indifferent or manifestly opposed to the whole idea of the establishment of a Jewish state. Anti-Zionism was therefore a perfectly respectable position to hold, and one that continues to be held today by hundreds of thousands of strictly orthodox Jews and many secular Jews with left-liberal perspectives.

Equating anti-Zionism and anti-Semitism — what has become known as the "new anti-Semitism" — fundamentally subverts the shared understanding of what anti-Semitism is, built up painstakingly through research and study by scholars over many years: It drains the word anti-Semitism of any useful meaning. The advocates of the concept of a new anti-Semitism argue that it is anti-Semitic to either criticize Israeli policies or deny Israel's right to exist, even if one does not hold beliefs historians have traditionally regarded as an anti-Semitic view: hatred of Jews per se, belief in a worldwide Jewish conspiracy, belief that Jews created communism and control capitalism, belief that Jews are racially inferior and so on.

Those who argue that anti-Zionism and anti-Semitism are one claim they don't say criticism of Israeli policies is illegitimate. However, in practice this view virtually proscribes any such thing.

As the Oxford academic Brian Klug has written, anti-Zionism and hostility to Israel — if based on a political cause or moral code that is not anti-Jewish per se — is not anti-Semitic. And arguing that it is harms the all-important struggle to combat anti-Semitism. If people feel unfairly stigmatized as anti-Semitic simply for speaking out about the plight of the Palestinians and the Israeli government's role in causing their suffering, they could become cynical and alienated whenever the problem of anti-Semitism is raised.

roots. Austrian-born American historian Raul Hilberg contends the Germans greeted Nazi anti-Semitism without suspicion as to its ultimate goal because it drew on old forms of anti-Semitism that had been part of Christian writings since the 16th century, when Martin Luther railed against what he saw as recalcitrant Jews because of their resistance to Christianity.[59]

The term "anti-Semitism" was coined in 1879 by German journalist and Jew-hater Wilhelm Marr, who wished to emphasize the "scientific," ethnic character of his opposition to Jews. Like the Nazis that followed him, Marr saw the Jews as a threatening race, incapable of assimilating, that had seized control of the German economy and society. "Semite" was his preferred term for Jews because it sounded scientific, neutral and modern.[60]

The Nazis, drawing on these ideas, believed exterminating Jews would cleanse humanity and save the world from a lethal threat to European morality and culture. Jews were allegedly a satanic race involved in a conspiracy for world domination that would lead to extinction of so-called "Aryan" civilization.

Holocaust Denial

By the end of 1942, Allied governments were aware of concentration camps holding thousands of Jewish prisoners across Europe and that six camps were devoted exclusively to killing. But in 1943, Jews were barely mentioned in Allied propaganda.[61]

Nor were Jews discussed much in the press. In Britain, where the photo of British troops liberating the Nazi camp Bergen-Belsen became a familiar image, the skeleton-like survivors shown on cinema newsreels were not generally identified as Jews.[62]

Not until Israel captured and tried Nazi official Adolf Eichmann in the early 1960s did the horrifying nature of European Jewry's fate enter public consciousness. For example, there is no mention of genocide in the charter under which the major Nazi war criminals were tried at Nuremberg. The term Holocaust did not come into use to describe the extermination of the Jews until several years after the war.

"Today we find this difficult to understand, but the fact is that the Shoah — the attempted genocide of the Jews of Europe — was for many years by no means the fundamental question of postwar intellectual life in Europe. . . . Indeed most people — intellectuals and others — ignored it as much as they could," writes historian Judt.[63]

However, it was no mystery that 6 million Jews had been put to death during World War II — a fact widely accepted within a few months of the war, Judt notes in *Postwar: A History of Europe Since 1945.*[64]

In France, less than 3 percent of the 76,000 Jews deported in 1940-44 survived. In the Netherlands, which had 140,000 Jews before the war, fewer than 5,000 returned. In Germany, just over 21,000 of the country's 600,000 Jews remained after the war.[65]

But even the remnants of returning Jews were "not much welcomed," Judt notes. "After years of anti-Semitic propaganda, local populations everywhere were not only disposed to blame 'Jews' in the abstract for their own suffering but were distinctly sorry to see the return of men and women whose jobs, possessions and apartments they had purloined."[66]

In Paris in 1945, hundreds of people protested when a returning Jewish deportee tried to reclaim his occupied apartment, screaming "France for the French!"[67]

Postwar Poland's Anti-Semitism

Poland was perhaps the most dangerous country for returning Jews. Although it had the largest concentration of Jews before the war — more than 3 million — 97.5 percent of them had been exterminated under the Nazis.[68]

In his recent book, *Fear*, Princeton historian Jan T. Gross estimates that after the war, 500-1,600 Jews returning to their hometowns in Poland — sick, traumatized and destitute, often from concentration camps — were killed by Poles upon their arrival.[69] (*See sidebar, p. 148.*)

Why did Poles attack their returning neighbors after the war? During the Nazi persecution and following the Jews' deportation to concentration camps, many Poles benefited materially, moving into Jewish homes and seizing their possessions. (Sometimes the property was pitiful: Gross describes a 1945 letter from a surviving Polish Jew asking a Polish court to make his neighbor return the two eiderdown quilts and pillows he had left in his safekeeping.[70])

As Jews returned, Poles often feared this property would be reclaimed. The Poles' "widespread collusion" in Nazi plunder and murder of the Jews — and suppressed guilt about it — generated virulent anti-Semitism after the war, in Gross' view.[71] "Jews were perceived as a threat to the material status quo, security and peaceful conscience of their Christian fellow-citizens," he writes.[72]

More people witnessed the death of Jews in Poland than in any other country, since it was the site of Auschwitz and other major concentration camps. But in some cases, Poles also participated in the killings.

During the Soviet occupation of Poland, many Poles believed the Jews had betrayed Poland, collaborating with the Russians while the Poles were fighting and being deported to Siberia. In recent years, some Poles cited this version of history, which Gross discredits, as the reason behind the massacres.[73]

In addition, Polish national identity depended to some extent on stories Poles told about their own suffering during the war, and "comparative victimhood" continued to poison relationships with the few remaining Jews after the war.[74]

In fact, the communist period became yet another period in which the memory of the Jews' suffering was suppressed in official accounts, and many Jews were afraid to reveal their origins. In the 1960s, a student uprising against the communist regime was denounced as being perpetrated by Zionist agents. The 1968 campaign also drew on the myth of "Judeo-communism," in which Jews were believed to have cooperated with the Stalinists. By the end of 1968, two-thirds of Poland's Jews had been driven away.[75]

Facing the Holocaust

The trials of Eichmann and of Auschwitz guards in the early 1960s triggered renewed interest in the Holocaust in countries like Germany and the Netherlands, where silence had reigned. The postwar baby boomers were curious about recent history and skeptical of the story told by the "silent generation" of their parents, Judt notes.

During the 1960s and '70s, several events helped to put the Jews' suffering in the German spotlight, according to Judt: The Six-Day Arab-Israeli War of 1967, Chancellor Willy Brandt dropping to his knees at the Warsaw Ghetto memorial and the telecast in Germany in 1979 of an American miniseries, "Holocaust."[76]

Twenty million German viewers saw the series — well over half the population. From then on, writes Judt,

AFP/Getty Images/Gali Tibbon

English Football Association Chief Executive Brian Barwick (left) and Noel White (2nd-left), chairman of the association's International Committee, and representatives of fans lay wreaths on March 23, 2007, at the "Hall of Remembrance" at the Yad Vashem Holocaust Memorial in Jerusalem commemorating the 6 million Jews killed by the Nazis during World War II. The association says it is committed to reducing anti-Semitism at soccer matches.

"Germans would be among the best-informed Europeans on the subject of the Shoah and at the forefront of all efforts to maintain public awareness of their country's singular crime." Compared to 1968, when a little over 400 school groups visited Dachau, by the 1970s more than 5,000 a year were visiting the former concentration camp, located 10 miles outside of Munich.[77]

As Judt notes, some major European countries — the Netherlands, Belgium, Norway, Italy — could claim that their orders to deport and execute Jews came from the Germans. The exception was France. Marshal Philippe Petain's Vichy regime, elected in July 1940 by the French parliament, initiated its own anti-Jewish laws in 1940 and 1941. French authorities rounded up the country's Jewish population; most Jewish deportees from France never saw a foreign uniform until they were handed over to Germans for the final shipment to Auschwitz.

Not until 1995 did President Jacques Chirac break a 50-year silence and acknowledge for the first time that the French were responsible for rounding up nearly 13,000 Jews — more than 4,000 of them children — for deportation to Auschwitz in July 1942.[78]

Chirac's acknowledgement followed publication in the late 1960s and mid-'70s of several books by foreign historians demonstrating that the Vichy crimes were French, not German initiatives.

President Charles de Gaulle's 1967 press conference after Israel's victory in the Six-Day War, when he referred to Jews as "a people sure of themselves and domineering" provoked outrage among French Jews and contributed to a new level of awareness of French Jews.[79] Marcel Ophuls's film "The Sorrow and the Pity," about the trials of high-ranking French officials, and a 1985 documentary film, "Shoah," by the French director Claude Lanzmann, also had a dramatic impact.

Anti-Semitism Re-emerges

Immediately after World War II, Austria and West Germany, led by anti-Nazi parties, barred Nazis from political participation and banned overt support of Nazi ideology. On May 8, 1948, the Austrian government banned Nazi activities. West Germany prohibited public expression of Nazi beliefs, banned Nazis from the political process and outlawed swastikas.

In the 1960s, however, extremist, neo-Nazi groups re-emerged in both countries. After German reunification in the 1990s, the groups gained followers among disaffected teenagers from the former East Germany. Such groups tended to merge with skinheads, a far-right youth subculture that developed in Britain during the "rude boy" music scene of the 1960s.[80] Skinheads re-surfaced in the late 1970s with white-power, racist, anti-Semitic overtones. The term "skinhead" described the close-cropped hairdo adopted by its adherents, sometimes accompanied by leather boots and tattoos. Skinheads were known for creating violent confrontations with non-whites, Muslims, Jews and gays — a movement that soon spread to the rest of Europe and North America.

The German National Democratic Party (NPD) is Germany's oldest and most influential right-wing party. In 2006, after receiving 7.3 percent of the vote in the regional parliamentary elections for Mecklenburg-Western Pomerania, the party launched an online news show on its Web site featuring videos, for example, of a memorial march in honor of Hitler's deputy Rudolf Hess.[81] The party holds weekly demonstrations and meetings of extreme-right sympathizers, including neo-Nazis and skinheads, according to the Stephen Roth Institute. To get around the legal bans on Nazi activity, the groups recruit East German youth using music — including music videos and far-right music portals on the Web — sponsoring trips to concerts and offering free beer. At a 2006 NPD event, an Iranian flag was hoisted to demonstrate the party's solidarity with the Iranian government's denial of the Holocaust — a way to express that view without violating German law against Holocaust denial.[82]

Between 2001 and 2005 anti-Semitic incidents increased in eight European countries — Austria, Belgium, Denmark, France, Germany, Netherlands, Sweden and Britain. At the same time, anti-Jewish crimes increased significantly in France between 2001 and 2006, but only slightly in Germany and Sweden.[83]

Although many perceive that today's anti-Semitic hate crimes are perpetrated by disaffected Muslims instead of right-wing skinheads, the European Union's monitoring agency says the shift is "difficult to substantiate," noting that several countries prohibit investigating ethnic or religious backgrounds of criminal suspects.[84]

According to the EU Agency for Fundamental Rights, the most troubling development in European attitudes has been the increase since 2005 in the number of respondents questioning the loyalty of Jewish citizens, as recorded in surveys by the Anti-Defamation League. Last year, the percentage of those believing Jews are "more loyal to Israel than to this country" rose in the United Kingdom, Austria, Belgium, Hungary, the Netherlands and Switzerland.[85]

Today there is no single hand directing anti-Semitic propaganda worldwide, as there was under the Nazis or under the Soviet Union in the 1970s or '80s. Anti-Semitism today generally does not have the power of the state behind it, except for governments in the Muslim world like Iran with its official discrimination against Jews.

International Action

Since the beginning of its upsurge in 2000, anti-Semitism in Europe has been monitored and surveyed continually, and analyzed at international conferences and by Europe-wide organizations. Since 2003, the 56-nation Organization for Security and Co-operation in Europe (OSCE) has held six major conferences on anti-Semitism. A conference in April 2004 produced the "Berlin Declaration," which stated that "international developments . . . including those in Israel or elsewhere in the Middle East, never justify anti-Semitism."[86]

In 2003 the OSCE recommended that member states actively collect data on hate crimes, including anti-Semitic incidents, and it has established a special envoy to combat anti-Semitism.

On March 1, 2007, the EU established the Agency for Fundamental Rights, to collect reliable and comparable data on racism and anti-Semitism. In 2000, its forerunner agency, the European Monitoring Centre on Racism and Xenophobia, established a system to help states collect and analyze data. However, only four out of 27 member states — Germany, France, the Netherlands and Great Britain — have mechanisms for accurate data collection on anti-Semitic incidents, the agency reported last year.[87]

In April 2007, the Council of the European Union agreed that member states should harmonize their minimal criminal provisions against racist agitation, including Holocaust denial. The final document, if adopted, would give countries two years to incorporate these provisions into their national laws.[88]

On June 27, 2007, the Parliamentary Assembly of the Council of Europe issued a resolution noting that it "remains deeply concerned about the persistence and escalation of anti-Semitic phenomena."[89]

In response to the Iranian government's sponsorship of an international conference aimed at denying the Holocaust, the U.N. General Assembly in January 2007 declared Holocaust denial "tantamount to approval of genocide in all its forms."[90]

In 1991, the General Assembly had overturned a 1975 resolution declaring Zionism "a form of racism." However, according to a recent State Department report, the assembly has established bureaucracies "with the sole mandate of singling out Israel as a violator of the human rights of others." In its first 16 months, which ended on Sept. 30, 2007, the U.N. Human Rights Commission adopted 15 anti-Israel decisions but has taken little action against notorious human-rights violators like Myanmar, complains the State Department. The report also charges that Muslim countries have used the U.N. system to "demonize Israelis implicitly, and Jews generally," an approach, the department warns, which may be "fueling anti-Semitism."[91]

In response to rising anti-Semitism worldwide, the U.S. Congress passed the Global Anti-Semitism Review Act of 2004, which requires the State Department to document and combat anti-Semitic acts internationally. The act also established a special envoy to combat anti-Semitism.

CURRENT SITUATION

Britain Reacts

Countries today vary widely in their legal approaches to combating anti-Semitism. Six European countries, including France and Germany, impose criminal penalties on certain forms of anti-Semitic expression, such as denial of the Holocaust. British MP Mann, chair of the committee on anti-Semitism in Parliament, says he wants to shut down Web sites spewing anti-Semitic ideas, several of which originate in the United States. So far, the U.S. government has resisted these efforts because they would conflict with constitutional protection for freedom of speech.

A British parliamentary inquiry produced a report in September 2006 finding that "violence, desecration of property and intimidation directed towards Jews is on the rise."

The report found that only a minority of police forces in Britain can record anti-Semitic incidents. According to Mann, a new national data-gathering and reporting system will shortly be in place to correct this.[92]

The panel also complained that only a few anti-Semitic incidents are being prosecuted as racial harassment, which carries increased penalties, and called on the Crown Prosecution Service to address the problem. The Service released an investigation in May that found the low number of prosecutions resulted from the inability to identify suspects and the unwillingness of victims to pursue prosecution. To reverse the trend, the Service is encouraging the Jewish community and police to pursue these crimes.[93]

Noting that anti-Semitic incidents in Britain declined by 8 percent in 2007 from the previous year, Mann says, "We're bringing the problem down to more reasonable levels, where it can be dealt with more routinely."

A campaign for an academic boycott of Israel, the focus of much campus-based anti-Zionism in Britain, died last year after a legal opinion found that the movement would violate discrimination laws. The proposed boycott by the University and College Union — which would have barred Israeli academics from coming to British universities and prevented British academics from participating in Israeli conferences — provoked international outrage and charges of anti-Semitism.

However, it appears the debate is being re-ignited. In May, delegates to the union's annual congress passed a motion asking members "to consider the moral and political implications of educational links" with Israel in light of Israel's policies towards the Palestinians.[94] Union leaders said the motion's goal was "to provide solidarity with Palestinians," not to boycott Israel.[95] But Stop the Boycott Coalition, formed of academics and Jewish and non-Jewish groups, fought the motion, saying it constituted a thinly veiled illegal boycott.

Whatever the motion's impact, observers say boycott proposals are likely to come back in the form of "divestment" resolutions on campuses vowing not to purchase Israeli products. In February, the student union of the London School of Economics was one of the first to pass such a resolution, which called for students to lobby the school to divest from Israel and from companies that "provide military support for the occupation."[96]

In February, a report on the continued presence of anti-Semitic soccer chants came out just as Avram Grant, the Israeli manager of the Chelsea soccer team, received a package said to contain a lethal white powder and a threatening note describing him as "a backstabbing Jewish bastard" who would die "a very slow and painful death."[97]

French Anti-Semitism?

While overall anti-Semitic incidents in France decreased 32 percent for the first eight months of 2007 compared to the same period the previous year, several troubling developments have led to government action.

The 2006 kidnapping and death of the 23-year-old Halimi led to a government report to then-Prime Minister Dominique de Villepin stressing the gravity of anti-Semitic propaganda. The Education Department also ratified inclusion of Holocaust studies, anti-Semitism and Jewish-Arab relations in the 2007 school curriculum.[98]

In February President Nicolas Sarkozy proposed making every 10-year-old French student honor one of the 11,000 Jewish children from France killed in the Holocaust, by learning about the selected child's background and fate. The proposal provoked a storm of protests from experts, including some prominent Jews, who said it would be too traumatic for young children. France's education minister later softened the proposal so that entire classes would adopt one child.

But Sarkozy defended the plan, saying "We must tell a child the truth."[99]

Sarkozy had been toying with this idea since serving as interior minister under President Chirac, when he was astonished by the high number of anti-Semitic incidents.[100]

Many are particularly disturbed by the growing popularity of French comedian Dieudonné M'bala M'bala, who claims the African slave trade was a Jewish enterprise and that France is ruled by Zionists and neo-Zionists.

After Halimi's death, French groups monitoring anti-Semitism said the words of the comedian, who made an abortive bid for the presidency, had influenced the killers. Dieudonné (as he is known), is of Afro-Caribbean descent and is a folk hero among black and Arab immigrants. A great many attacks against Jews occur in their neighborhoods.[101]

Jean-Marie Le Pen, leader of the right-wing National Front Party, wooed Muslim immigrants by receiving Dieudonné at his party convention in 2006. (In February, Le Pen, widely known for his anti-Semitism, received a suspended prison sentence for saying that the Nazi occupation of France was "not particularly inhumane.")[102] Last March, a Paris court fined Dieudonné 5,000 euros for saying Jews had been slave traders and were now bankers and terrorists.[103]

However, in the presidential balloting in May, Le Pen won only 10 percent of the vote — his worst showing since 1974 — and failed to qualify for a second round. In June, his party failed to win a single seat in the legislative elections.[104]

In February, 21 people were charged in Halimi's kidnapping and murder, including Muslim immigrants from North Africa and immigrants from Congo and the Ivory Coast. The gang's self-proclaimed leader, Fofana, who was eventually found and arrested in the Ivory Coast, told police he organized Halimi's kidnapping but has denied killing him. No trial date has been set.[105]

Meanwhile, six people are being held in connection with Roumi's February kidnapping and torture, also in the Bagneux quarter.[106] In both cases, money appears to have been a substantial part of the motive.

In Bagneux, following Halimi's murder, a social worker said the belief that "all Jews are rich is an anti-Semitic prejudice that didn't exist in the neighborhood 20 years ago."[107]

OUTLOOK

Growing Discomfort

By many measures, life for Jews in Europe has never been better. They no longer fear any political party agitating for discrimination against them or for their deportation, as in past centuries.

But Jews also maintain a historical consciousness that a comfortable middle-class life can suddenly become a mirage, as it did in Germany, France and Poland in the late 1930s. To one another, Jews often speak of having, at least metaphorically, a bag packed under the bed, "just in case." Indeed, Jews increasingly are emigrating from France to Israel — 2,400 in 2004; 3,000 in 2005 — indicating a growing sense of discomfort as attacks on Jews and religious property have risen.[108]

As the Middle East conflict continues, anti-Jewish and anti-Zionist attitudes are likely to gain even more force. A conference last month in Jerusalem marking the 60th anniversary of Israel's creation treated global threats like terrorism and Iran as especially harmful to Israel and Jews.

"Cataclysms always seem to affect Jews first," said Stuart E. Eizenstat, a senior official in the Clinton and Carter administrations and author of an essay that formed the basis for the conference. "Go back to the Black Plague. It was not a Jewish issue, but it had particular impact on Jews because they were blamed for it."[109]

Some fear that European leftists will continue to court the growing population of young Muslims — who are often hostile to Jews — as the new working class, contributing to the new anti-Semitism. By contrast, the French Jewish population is small and aging, and many French Jews adhere to the traditional stance of "being Jewish at home and a citizen outside," making them a less strident political faction.

Nevertheless, the French left appears to be "turning away from the unholy alliance with Islamic fundamentalism," especially as the anti-Semitic content of Islamic ideology is exposed, noted a 2005 analysis from the Stephen Roth Institute.[110] Indeed, French historian Weil suggests this alliance is no longer a problem, though it's understandable how it happened.

"There was a cognitive impossibility for some people, especially some Jews who fought against racism and colonialism in the past, to suddenly acknowledge that anti-Semitism could come from the people they were defending for so many years," who themselves suffered from racism, he observes. "It took time for some people on the left. It was, 'Oh my God, how can this happen?'"

In Eastern Europe, notably Poland, while the older generation continues to do battle with its Jewish ghosts, the younger generation is showing greater curiosity and openness toward Jewish culture, and some are even returning to Jewish roots. (*See sidebar, p. 150.*) Many hope that will change the overall climate for the better.

Meanwhile, in Central and Eastern Europe left-wing anti-Semites are joining right-wing nationalists to protest globalization, which they blame on Jewish financiers.[111]

Officials in Europe and in international bodies have become more conscious of anti-Semitism, arguing that where it is tolerated other forms of racism will follow. "We're making it less acceptable by challenging it and doing things about it," says British MP Mann. But he adds, "We're not complacent."

NOTES

1. Brett Kline, "Echoes of Halimi in French Suburb," *JTA*, March 6, 2008, www.jta.org.

2. "The Terrible Tale of Ilan Halimi," *The Economist*, March 4, 2006.

3. Stephen Roth Institute for the Study of Contemporary Antisemitism and Racism, "Antisemitism Worldwide 2006," p. 6, www.tau.ac.il/Anti-Semitism/asw2006/gen-analysis.pdf.

4. Stephen Roth Institute, "France 2006," p. 12, www.tau.ac.il/Anti-Semitism/asw2006/france.htm.

5. Daniel Ben Simon, "Anti-Semitism in France/Calm Interrupted," *Haaretz*, March 6, 2008, www.haaretz.com/hasen/spages/961302.html.

6. Community Security Trust, press release, "Antisemitic hate incidents remain at unacceptably high level," Feb. 14, 2008, www.thecst.org.uk.

7. Stephen Roth Institute, "Antisemitism Worldwide 2007," 2008, p. 1.

8. *Ibid.*, Appendices: "Major Attacks and Violent Incidents 1999-2007." Major attacks are defined as attacks and attempted attacks by violent means such as shooting, arson, or firebombing. Major violent incidents include harassment of individuals,

vandalizing Jewish property and street violence not involving a weapon.

9. *Ibid.*, pp. 1, 7.
10. All-Party Parliamentary Group Against Antisemitism, "Report of the All-Party Parliamentary Inquiry into Antisemitism," September 2006, www.thepcaa.org/report.pdf.
11. Office of the Special Envoy to Monitor and Combat Anti-Semitism, U.S. Department of State, "Contemporary Global Anti-Semitism: A Report Provided to the United States Congress," March 2008, p. 77. See "Action Heroes," *Telegraph Magazine*, June 2, 2007, www.telegraph.co.uk.
12. Community Security Trust, "Antisemitic Incidents Report 2007," 2008, www.thecst.org.uk.
13. Stephen Roth Institute, "Antisemitism Worldwide, 2007," *op. cit.*, p. 6.
14. *Ibid.*, p. 6.
15. *Ibid.*, p. 6. Frattini is EU Commissioner for Justice, Freedom and Security.
16. Stephen Roth Institute, *op. cit.*, p. 12.
17. Melanie Phillips, "Britain's Anti-Semitic Turn," *City Journal*, autumn 2007, www.city-journal.org/html/17_4_anti-semitism.html.
18. U.S. Department of State, *op. cit.*, pp. 28-35. See p. 35 for cartoons in *Guardian* and Norwegian press.
19. Stephen Roth Institute, "Antisemitism Worldwide 2006," *op. cit.*, p. 5.
20. *Jerusalem Post* staff and Michael Lando, "Amadinejad: Israel Filthy Bacteria," *Jerusalem Post*, Feb. 20, 20008, www.jpost.com/servlet/Satellite?pagename=JPost%2FJPArticle%2FShowFull&cid=1203343707673.
21. Yves Pallade, *et al.*, "Antisemitism and Racism in European Soccer," American Jewish Committee Berlin Office, May 2007, p. 10.
22. www.jpr.org.uk.
23. U.S. Department of State, *op. cit.*, p. 3.
24. European Agency for Fundamental Rights, "Anti-Semitism: Summary Overview of the Situation in the European Union 2001-2007," January 2008, *FRA Working Paper*, http://fra.europa.eu.
25. U.S. Department of State, *op. cit.*, p. 3.
26. *Ibid.*, p. 3.
27. *Ibid.*, p. 31.
28. Vanessa Gera, "Israel Urges Poland, Catholic Church to Condemn Polish Priest for Anti-Semitic Comments," The Associated Press, July 30, 2007.
29. U.S. Department of State, *op. cit.*, pp. 22, 28.
30. "Pierre-André Taguieff on the New Anti-Zionism," interview in *Observatoire du Communautarisme*, Sept. 7, 2005, www.zionism-israel.com/ezine/New_Antizionism.htm. Taguieff's 2002 book published in France *La nouvelle judeophobie* (The New Judephobia) was published in English translation in 2004 under the title *Rising from the Muck: The New Anti-Semitism in France.*
31. Matthias Küntzel, *Jihad and Jew Hatred: Islamism, Nazism and the Roots of 9/11* (2007), p. 129.
32. Phillips, *op. cit.*
33. Tony Judt, "On the 'Problem of Evil' in Postwar Europe," *New York Review of Books*, Feb. 14, 2008, pp. 33-36, www.nybooks.com/articles/21031.
34. Abraham H. Foxman, "Britain's Jewish Problem," *New York Sun*, May 18, 2005, at www.adl.org/ADL_Opinions/Anti_Semitism_Global/20050518-NY+Sun.htm.
35. *Ibid.*
36. Pierre-André Taguieff, *Rising from the Muck: The New Anti-Semitism in Europe* (2004), pp. 12-17.
37. Phillips, *op. cit.*
38. See Dennis Sewell, "A Kosher Conspiracy," newstatesman.com, Jan. 14, 2002, www.newstatesman.com/200201140009.
39. U.S. Department of State, *op. cit.*, p. 35.
40. "Report of the All-Party Parliamentary Inquiry into Antisemitism," *op. cit.*, p. 35.
41. "EUMC Working Definition of Anti-Semitism," *ibid.*, p. 6.
42. Judt, *op. cit.*, pp. 33-36.
43. Edward H. Kaplan and Charles A. Small, "Anti-Israel Sentiment Predicts Anti-Semitism in Europe," *Journal of Conflict Resolution*, August 2006, www.h-net.org/~antis/papers/jcr_antisemitism.pdf.
44. Judt, *op. cit.*

45. "EUMC Presents Reports on Discrimination and Islamophobia in the EU," European Monitoring Centre on Racism and Xenophobia, Dec. 18, 2006, www.fra.europa.eu/fra/index.php?fuseaction=content.dsp_cat_content&catid=43d8bc25bc89d&contentid=4582ddc822d41. The report found only one member state, the United Kingdom, publishes criminal justice data that specifically identify Muslims as victims of hate crimes.

46. "Cameron to Meet Mosque Leaders," *Birmingham Daily Mail*, Feb. 5, 2007, www.birminghammail.net/news/tm_headline=cameron-to-meet-city-mosque-leaders&method=full&objectid=18577092&siteid=50002-name_page.html.

47. David Cesarani, "Are Muslims the New Jews? Comparing Islamophobia and Anti-Semitism in Britain and Europe," draft discussion paper delivered to the Yale Initiative for the Interdisciplinary Study of Antisemitism, March 27, 2008, www.yale.edu/yiisa/Cesarani_Paper.pdf.

48. *Ibid.*, p. 12.

49. Jan T. Gross, *Fear* (2007), p. 149.

50. Shalom Lappin, "This Green and Pleasant Land: Britain and the Jews," delivered to the Yale Initiative for the Interdisciplinary Study of Anti-Semitism, Nov. 29, 2007, p. 7, at www.yale.edu/yiisa/lappin_yiisa072.pdf.

51. *Ibid.*, p. 6.

52. *Ibid.*, p. 12.

53. *Ibid.*

54. Lappin, *op. cit.*, p. 18. In the period immediately following the war, the British government kept legal restrictions on the 60,000 refugees still in the country — as aliens without full rights to seek employment until 1948. This group included people who had served in the British army or worked for the war effort in other ways.

55. *Ibid.*, p. 19.

56. Stephen Eric Bronner, "Libeling the Jews: Truth Claims, Trials and the Protocols of Zion," in Debra Kaufman, *et al.*, eds., *From the Protocols of the Learned Elders of Zion to Holocaust Denial Trials* (2007), pp. 15-17.

57. David Remnick, "Blood and Sand," *The New Yorker*, May 5, 2008, p. 72.

58. Jeffrey Goldberg, "Unforgiven: Israel Confronts its Existential Fears," *The Atlantic*, May 2008, pp. 34-51, p. 42. Also See Martin Gilbert, *Churchill and the Jews* (2007).

59. Michael Berkowitz, *The Crime of My Very Existence: Nazism and the Myth of Jewish Criminality* (2007), p. xvii.

60. Robert S. Wistrich, "European Anti-Semitism Reinvents Itself," American Jewish Committee, May 2005, www.ajc.org. Originally, the term Semite referred to peoples from ancient southwestern Asia who spoke Hebrew, Aramaic, Arabic or Amharic.

61. Henry Feingold, "The Surprising Historic Roots of Holocaust Denial," in Debra Kaufman, *et al.*, *op. cit.*, pp. 66-79.

62. Tony Judt, *Postwar: A History of Europe since 1945* (2007), p. 807. Also see B. W. Patch, "Anti-Semitism in Germany," in *Editorial Research Reports*, Aug. 2, 1935, available in *CQ Researcher Plus Archive*, www.library.cqpress.com.

63. Judt, *New York Review of Books*, *op. cit.*, p. 33.

64. Judt, *Postwar*, *op. cit.*, p. 804.

65. *Ibid.*

66. *Ibid.*

67. *Ibid.*, p. 805.

68. *Ibid.*, p. 804.

69. Gross, *op. cit.*, p. 35.

70 *Ibid.*, p. 42.

71. *Ibid.*, p. xiv.

72. *Ibid.*, p. 247.

73. See Gross, *op. cit.*, and Peter S. Green, "Polish Town Still Tries to Forget its Dark Past," *The New York Times*, Feb. 8, 2003.

74. Judt, *op. cit.*, p. 823.

75. *Ibid.*

76. *Ibid.*, p. 811.

77. *Ibid.*

78. Tom Reiss, "Letter from Paris: Laugh Riots," *The New Yorker*, Nov. 19, 2007, pp. 44-50, www.newyorker.com/reporting/2007/11/19/071119fa_fact_reiss.

79. Judt, *Postwar*, *op. cit.*, p. 817.

80. For background, see R. L. Worsnop, "Neo-Nazism in West Germany," *Editorial Research Reports*, April

12, 1967, available at *CQ Researcher Plus Archives*, www.library.cqpress.com. See "Neo-Nazi Skinheads," Anti-Defamation League, www.adl.org/hate-patrol/njs/neonazi.asp.

81. Stephen Roth Institute, "Germany 2006," at www.tauc.il/Anti-Semitism, p. 2.
82. *Ibid.*, pp. 4, 6, 7.
83. European Agency for Fundamental Rights, *op. cit.*, p. 18. The report specifies that only these three countries collect sufficient criminal data to analyze a trend, www.libertysecurity.org/IMG/pdf_Antisemitism_Overview_Jan_2008_en.pdf.
84. *Ibid.*, p. 21.
85. *bid.*, p. 17.
86. U.S. Department of State, *op. cit.*, p. 3.
87. Stephen Roth Institute, *op. cit.*, 2007, p. 18.
88. *Ibid.*, p. 16.
89. U.S. Department of State, *op. cit.*, p. 68.
90. *Ibid.*, p. 69.
91. *Ibid.*, pp. 47, 48-50.
92. All-Parliamentary Group against Anti-Semitism, *op. cit.*
93. The Crown Prosecution Service, press release, "CPS Publishes Response to All-Party Parliamentary Inquiry into Antisemitism," May 6, 2008, www.cps.gov.uk/news/pressreleases/134_08.html.
94. Francis Beckett, "Israel, administration or pay?" *The Guardian*, May 27, 2008, http://education.guardian.co.uk.
95. University and College Union, press release, "UCU Delegates vote for International Solidarity," May 28, 2008, www.ucu.org.uk.
96. Simon Rocker, "LSE Student Union in New Drive to Encourage Divestment from Israel," *The Jewish Chronicle*, Feb. 22, 2008, p. 5, http://education.guardian.co.uk/higher/worldwide/story/0,2268513,00.html.
97. Dana Gloger and Simon Griver, "Racist Death Threats Don't Scare Us, Say Avram's Family," *The Jewish Chronicle*, Feb. 22, 2008, p. 2, www.thejc.com/home.aspx?ParentId=m11&SecId=11&AId=58231&ATypeId=1.
98. European Agency for Fundamental Rights, *op. cit.*
99. The Associated Press, "French Government Softens Sarkozy Plan to Honor Holocaust Victims," *Haaretz*, Feb. 18, 2008, www.Haaretz.com.
100. Daniel Ben-Simon, "Analysis: Sarkozy's Holocaust Education Plan Baffles Jews," *Haaretz*, Feb. 19, 2008, www.Haaretz.com.
101. Reiss, *op. cit.*
102. Reuters, "France's Le Pen Gets Suspended Jail Term for Comments on Nazi Occupation," *Haaretz*, Feb. 20, 2008, www.haaretz.com/hasen/spages/952527.html.
103. Stephen Roth Institute, "France 2006," *op. cit.*
104. *Ibid.*
105. Daniel Ben-Simon, "21 Charged with Kidnap, Murder of Jewish Man," *Haaretz*, Feb. 20, 2008, www.haaretz.com/hasen/spages/955962.html.
106. Ingrid Rousseau, "6 Held in Anti-Semitic Attack in France," *USA Today*, March 5, 2008, www.usatoday.com/news/world/2008-03-05-2346559257_x.htm.
107. Reiss, *op. cit.*
108. Stephen Roth Institute, "France 2006," *op. cit.*
109. Ethan Bronner, "At 60, Israel Redefines Roles for Itself and for Jews Elsewhere," *The New York Times*, May 8, 2008, p. A23.
110. Jean-Yves Camus, "The French Left and Political Islam: Secularism Versus the Temptation of an Alliance," Stephen Roth Institute, 2005, p. 13, www.tau.ac.il/Anti-Semitism/asw2005/camus.html.
111. Stephen Roth Institute, 2007, *op. cit.*, p. 35.

BIBLIOGRAPHY

Books

Berkowitz, Michael, *The Crime of My Very Existence: Nazism and the Myth of Jewish Criminality, University of California Press*, 2007.
A professor of modern Jewish history at University College, London, traces how the Nazis used accusations of criminality and a Zionist conspiracy to justify murdering the Jews.

Gross, Jan T., *Fear: Anti-Semitism in Poland after Auschwitz, Random House Trade Paperbacks*, 2007.
A Princeton University historian analyzes why Poles killed their Jewish neighbors returning to Poland after the war.

Judt, Tony, *Postwar: A History of Europe Since 1945, Pimlico*, 2007.

This history of postwar Europe by a New York University historian contains an excellent epilogue cataloguing the hostility to Jews who remained in Europe after the war.

Kaufman, Debra, *et al.*, *From the Protocols of the Learned Elders of Zion to Holocaust Denial Trials: Challenging the Media, Law and the Academy*, *Valentine Mitchell*, 2007.
This collection of essays on Holocaust denial and anti-Semitism grew out of a conference at Northeastern University in 2001.

Küntzel, Matthias, *Jihad and Jew-Hatred: Islamism, Nazism and the Roots of 9/11*, *Telos Press Publishing*, 2007.
Anti-Semitism in today's jihadist movement and its Nazi roots are discussed in this account by a German political scientist.

Taguieff, Pierre André, *Rising from the Muck: The New Anti-Semitism in Europe*, *Ivan R. Dee*, 2004.
A French philosopher and historian of ideas at France's Center for Scientific Research (CNRS) charges that anti-Zionist rhetoric in France has become the "New Anti-Semitism."

Articles

Judt, Tony, "The 'Problem of Evil' in Postwar Europe," *New York Review of Books*, Feb. 14, 2008, pp. 33-35.
Historian Judt asks whether the threat of anti-Semitism today is exaggerated, especially when linked to criticism of Israel.

Kline, Brett, "Echoes of Halimi in a French Suburb," *JTA* (Jewish Telegraphic Agency), March 6, 2008, www.jta.org.
Jews in Paris respond to the torture of a young Jewish man in the Paris suburbs in February.

Phillips, Melanie, "Britain's Anti-Semitic Turn," *City Journal*, autumn 2007, www.city-journal.org.
A British journalist claims that anti-Semitism is growing and that anti-Israel actions like the proposed academic boycott of Israel are inherently anti-Semitic.

Reiss, Tom, "Letter from Paris: Laugh Riots," *The New Yorker*, Nov. 19, 2007, pp. 44-50.
Some experts fear that the popularity of French comedian Dieudonné M'Bala M'Bala, whose routines have become increasingly anti-Jewish, may be tapping a reservoir of anti-Semitic feeling in France.

Reports and Studies

***All-Party Parliamentary Group against Antisemitism*, "Report of the All-Party Parliamentary Inquiry into Antisemitism," September 2006, www.thepcaa.org/report.html.**
A parliamentary investigation calls on the British government to tackle a disturbing rise in anti-Semitism.

***European Union Agency for Fundamental Rights*, "Anti-Semitism: Summary Overview of the Situation in the European Union 2001-2007," updated version January 2008, http://fra.europa.eu/fra/material/pub/AS/Antisemitism_Overview_Jan_2008_en.pdf.**
The arm of the European Union responsible for monitoring racism and anti-Semitism compiled data on anti-Semitic incidents from government and community organizations within EU countries. The most recent data for most countries were from 2006.

Mann, John, and Johnny Cohen, "Antisemitism in European Football: A Scar on the Beautiful Game," *The Parliamentary Committee Against Antisemitism*, 2008, www.johnmannmp.com/publications.
A report lists examples of anti-Jewish behavior at soccer stadiums as well as "good practices" aimed at curbing the behavior.

Pallade, Yves, *et al.*, "Antisemitism and Racism in European Soccer," *American Jewish Committee Berlin Office*, May 2007.
The problem of anti-Semitic incidents and chanting continues in soccer stadiums, according to this report, which also describes some initiatives to counteract them.

***Stephen Roth Institute for the Study of Contemporary Antisemitism and Racism*, "Antisemitism Worldwide."**
The institute's annual report contains statistics and analysis on anti-Jewish incidents around the world.

***U.S. Department of State*, "Contemporary Global Anti-Semitism: A Report Provided to the United States Congress," March 2008, www.state.gov/documents/organization/102301.pdf.**
The State Department's mandated report on anti-Semitism worldwide shows anti-Jewish incidents are increasing.

For More Information

American Jewish Committee, 165 E. 56th St., New York, NY 10022; (212) 751-4000; www.ajc.org. Monitors anti-Semitism in Europe through offices in Berlin, Brussels, Geneva and Paris.

Anti-Defamation League, 605 Third Ave., New York, NY 10158; (212) 692-3900; www.adl.org. Monitors anti-Semitism around the world.

Community Security Trust; 020-8457-9999; www.thecst.org.uk. A U.K.-based group that provides physical security for British Jews and monitors anti-Semitism in Britain.

Engage; www.EngageOnline.org.uk. A British group that challenges anti-Semitism in unions and universities and opposes an academic boycott of Israeli academics.

European Jewish Congress, 78 Avenue des Champs-Elysées, 75008 Paris, France; 33-1-43-59-94-63; www.eurojewcong.org/ejc. A Paris-based group that coordinates 40 elected Jewish leaders in Europe to represent their concerns, including anti-Semitism.

Institute for Jewish Policy Research, 79 Wimpole St., London W1G 9RY, United Kingdom; +44-20-7935-8266; www.jpr.org.uk. A think tank promoting multiculturalism and the role of Jews in Europe.

Jews for Justice for Palestinians, P.O. Box 46081, London W9 2ZF, United Kingdom; www.jfjfp.org. Opposes the Israeli occupation.

Middle East Media Research Institute, P.O. Box 27837, Washington, DC 20038; (202) 955-9070; www.memri.org. A Washington-based group with offices in London and Rome that translates messages coming from the Middle East in Arabic, Persian and Turkish.

Office of Special Envoy to Monitor and Combat Anti-Semitism, U.S. Department of State, 2201 C St., N.W., Washington, DC 20520; (202) 647-4000; www.state.gov/g/drl/seas. Advocates for U.S. policy on global anti-Semitism.

Parliamentary Committee Against Antisemitism, P.O. Box 4015, London W1A 6NH, United Kingdom; 020-7935-8078; www.thepcaa.org. A committee of the British Parliament that monitors anti-Semitism in Britain and issues annual reports on the subject.

Quilliam Foundation; 020-7193-1204; www.quilliamfoundation.org. London-based think tank created by former activists of radical Islamic organizations that aims to counter extremism among Muslims in the West.

Stephen Roth Institute, Tel Aviv University, P.O. Box 39040, Ramat Aviv, Tel Aviv 69978, Israel; 972-3-6408779; www.tau.ac.il/Anti-Semitism. Publishes annual reports on anti-Semitism worldwide.

Yale Institute for the Interdisciplinary Study of Anti-semitism, Yale University, 77 Prospect St., New Haven, CT 06520; (203) 432-5239; www.yale.edu/yiisa. A center for research on anti-Semitism that presents papers on European anti-Semitism by prominent experts.

The Z-word, 165 E. 56th St., New York, NY 10022; (212) 751-4000; www.z-word.com. Independent online journal created by the American Jewish Committee focusing on the link between anti-Zionism and anti-Semitism.

AP Photo/Mustafa Quraishi

A worker pours chemicals into a vat of molasses used to make ethanol in Simbhaoli, Uttar Pradeshi, India. Replacing gasoline with ethanol in cars can reduce emissions of carbon-based "greenhouse gases" (GHGs), created by burning fossil fuels, which contribute to climate change. Projects in developing countries that produce such alternative fuels are part of an international carbon trading scheme that allows polluters in industrialized countries to "offset" some of their GHG emissions by buying pollution credits from companies in developing countries.

From *CQ Global Researcher*, November 2008.

7

Carbon Trading

Will It Reduce Global Warming?

Jennifer Weeks

It's little wonder that Tirumala temple in Tirupati, in the south Indian state of Andhra Pradesh, prepares 30,000 meals for visiting Hindu pilgrims daily. The shrine is among the busiest religious pilgrimage sites in the world. In years past, cooks fired up pollution-spewing diesel generators to power their stoves to boil water in massive cauldrons. But today there's a new, clean energy source: the sun. Curved solar collectors heat water up to 280 degrees Centigrade, creating steam to cook foods such as rice, lentils and vegetables.[1]

"With most businesses, the first question is of economics," says engineer Deepak Gadhia, whose company built the system. "But spiritual organizations look at larger issues. They want energy that is spiritually positive."[2]

In fact, the temple does quite well financially, too, and so do many other temples, schools and government offices throughout India that use energy-saving systems built by Gadhia and his wife. The energy they save enables them to amass credits that can be used in a process called "carbon trading" — buying and selling rights to emit greenhouse gases.

Two years ago, the energy-saving systems at those sites were approved as carbon credit sources under the Kyoto Protocol.[3] The international agreement is designed to stem global warming, and — among other things — allows some developing countries to profit from projects that reduce emissions of greenhouse gases (GHGs) that cause climate change. (*See sidebar, p. 178.*)

Under the protocol, most of the world's wealthy countries agreed to reduce their GHG emissions by fixed percentages between 2008 and 2012, mainly by reducing energy use and switching to

Which Countries Emit the Most Carbon Dioxide?

Australia and major oil producing countries like the United States, Norway, Russia, Canada, Saudi Arabia, Kuwait and other Gulf states emit the most carbon dioxide (CO_2) per capita. Carbon dioxide is the most abundant greenhouse gas — one of several blamed for causing global warming.

Carbon Dioxide Emissions Per Capita, 2004 (in metric tons*)

Metric Tons Per Capita:

- 10.0 or more
- 5.0-9.9
- 2.5-4.9
- 1.0-2.4
- Less than 1.0
- No data

* *A metric ton is 2,204.6 pounds.*

Source: Human Development Report 2007/2008, World Bank, 2008

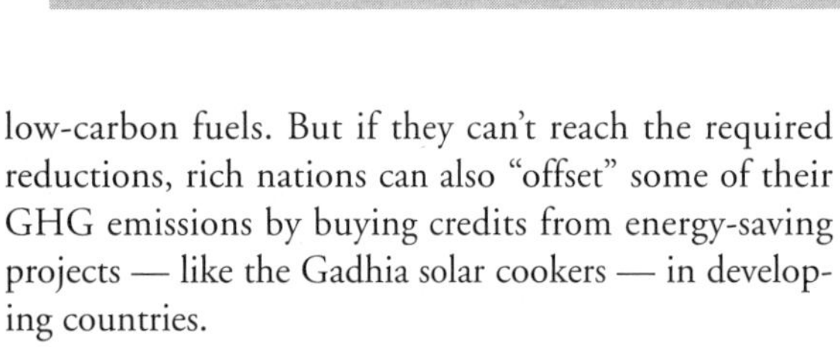

low-carbon fuels. But if they can't reach the required reductions, rich nations can also "offset" some of their GHG emissions by buying credits from energy-saving projects — like the Gadhia solar cookers — in developing countries.

If U.N. officials certify that those projects reduce GHG emissions beyond levels that would have occurred otherwise, they can sell "certified emission reductions," each representing one avoided metric ton of carbon dioxide (CO_2). Companies in industrialized nations buy these credits to help reach their GHG reduction targets.

Virtually all scientists agree that human use of carbon-based fossil fuels such as oil, coal and natural gas is raising concentrations of heat-trapping gases in the atmosphere to the highest levels in at least 650,000 years.[4] The gases are called "greenhouse" gases because their heat-trapping properties warm the Earth's surface, much as the glass walls of a greenhouse retain the sun's heat. Unless countries sharply reduce their GHG emissions by mid-century, the buildup of greenhouse gases — often referred to as "carbon" emissions since carbon dioxide (CO_2) is by far the most abundant GHG in Earth's atmosphere — could cause dramatic planetary warming. Climate scientists predict that higher temperatures will cause melting of the polar ice caps, rising sea levels and more intense droughts, floods and hurricanes.[5]

The Kyoto Protocol, which was signed in 1997 and went into effect in 2005, requires major industrialized countries (except for the United States, which failed to ratify the agreement) to reduce their GHG emissions, on average, by 5.2 percent below 1990 levels.[6] Members of the European Union vowed to reduce their emissions even farther — to 8 percent below 1990 levels by 2012. At the same time, the EU launched the world's largest mandatory carbon emissions trading system, in which governments cap national emissions and allow polluters to buy and sell permits to emit carbon dioxide. Australia, Canada and Japan are developing their own emission reduction systems, which will likely include some form of carbon trading.

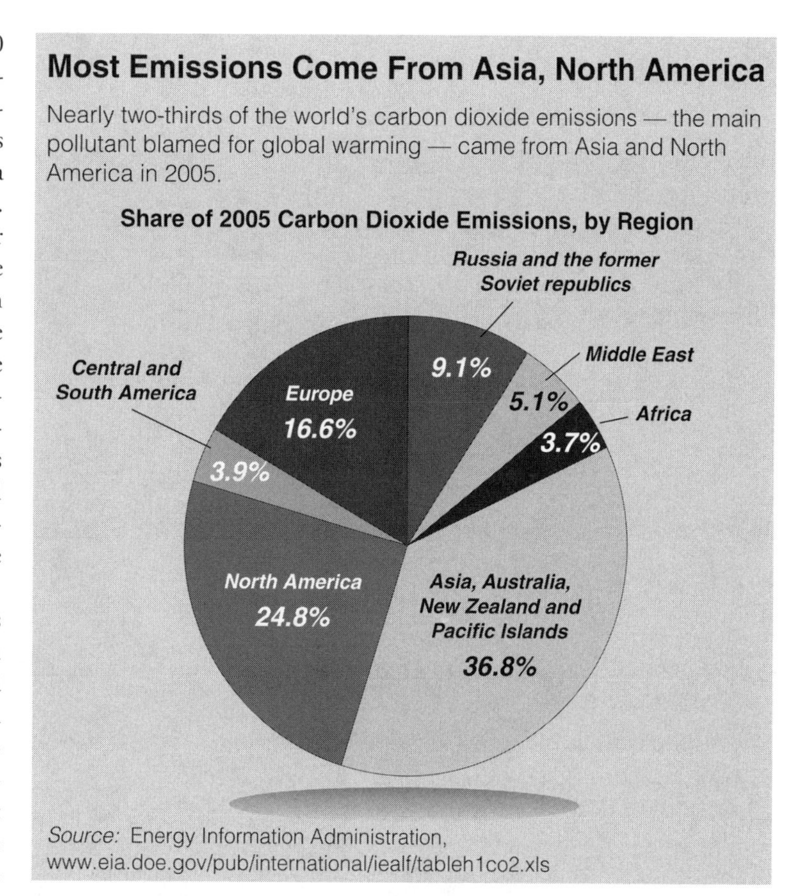

Global interest in carbon trading is part of a gradual movement toward market-based environmental policies — strategies that give polluters economic incentives to clean up instead of simply telling them how much pollution they can release and what kinds of controls to install. The approach makes sense because climate change is what scholars refer to as a "commons problem" — in which a resource (in this case, Earth's atmosphere) is held in common by everyone. Individual polluters profit more by using and degrading a common resource than by cleaning it up while their competitors continue polluting.

"The rational man finds that his share of the cost of the wastes he discharges into the commons is less than the cost of purifying his wastes before releasing them," wrote biologist Garrett Hardin in a famous 1968 essay that identified commons problems as a central challenge for modern societies. "Since this is true for everyone, we are locked into a system of 'fouling our own nest,' so long as we behave only as independent, rational, free-enterprisers."[7]

Climate experts agree that one of the best ways around the commons problem is to "put a price on carbon" by making factories, power plants and other large GHG sources pay for their emissions. Hitting them in the pocketbook gives them more incentive to clean up — for example, by imposing a tax so that every source pays for its own GHG emissions at some set rate per ton.

However, an alternative approach — trading emission allotments — has become increasingly popular in

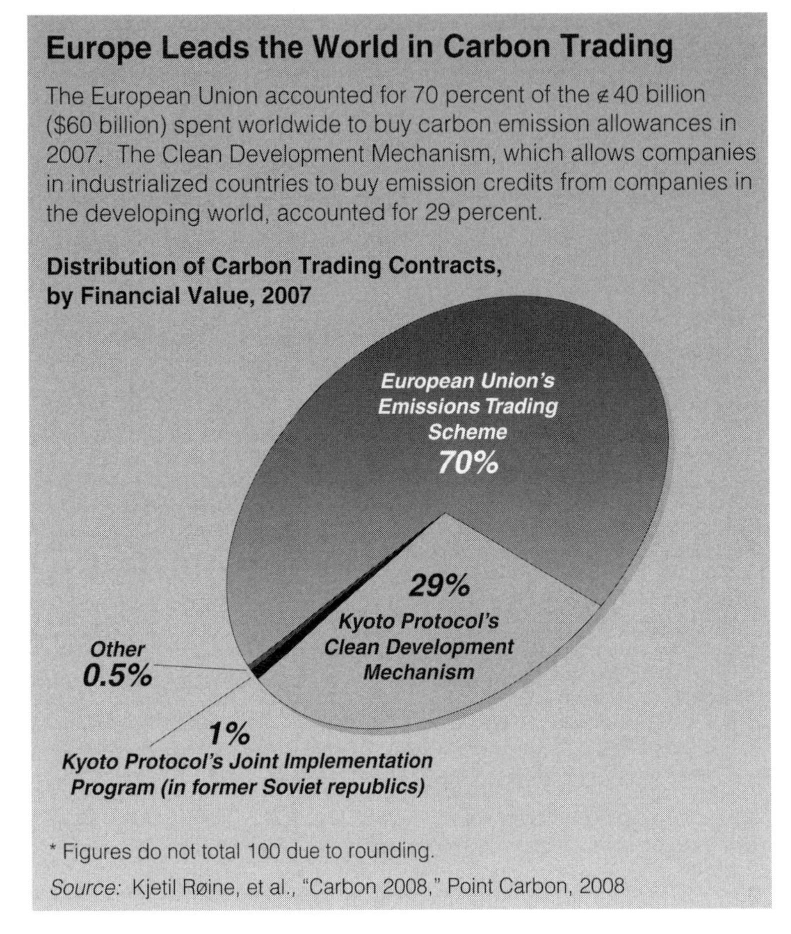

recent decades. It is usually enacted through so-called cap-and-trade policies, in which regulators set an overall cap on emissions and then issue quotas that limit how much pollution each company can release. If a company wants or needs to emit more than its allowance, it must buy permits from cleaner companies that don't need all their allotments. Over time, regulators can lower a country's cap to further reduce total pollution.

Advocates say carbon emissions trading encourages companies to use clean fuels and technologies because firms that reduce their own emissions can then sell their unneeded allowances. "The carbon market gives companies an incentive to reduce emissions so they can make money," says Henrik Hasselknippe, global carbon services director for Point Carbon, an international market research firm in Oslo, Norway. Moreover, he predicts, since carbon trading tells companies to limit their emissions but lets them decide how, it will stimulate research and development into a wide range of new, clean technologies. "It puts an infrastructure in place that releases capital for long-term investments," Hasselknippe explains.

Global carbon markets have grown quickly since the Kyoto Protocol entered into force in 2005. The total value of international carbon trades increased more than 80 percent between 2006 and 2007, from €22 billion ($33 billion) to €40 billion ($60 billion).[8] The market is expected to grow still larger as Europe lowers its cap on GHG emissions, and new trading systems gear up in some U.S. states and in other countries.[9]

Moreover, public support is growing for the U.S. government to act on climate change. President George W. Bush rejected the Kyoto treaty shortly after taking office in 2001, claiming that capping GHG emissions would harm the U.S. economy. But since then 23 states have joined regional carbon trading schemes, and the United States is widely expected to participate in a post-Kyoto agreement to limit GHG emissions after 2012.[10] Many U.S. political leaders, including both major presidential candidates, say the United States should create a cap-and-trade system similar to Europe's to cut GHG emissions in the United States far below 1990 levels by 2050.[11]

Ironically, several market-based elements were included in the Kyoto agreement at U.S. insistence in hope of convincing the United States to sign on to the treaty. They included two programs that let companies in industrialized countries offset some emissions by investing in carbon reduction projects elsewhere. The Clean Development Mechanism (CDM) paves the way for projects in developing countries, such as Gadhia's steam cookers at the temples in India, while Joint Implementation (JI) supports projects in other industrialized countries, mainly former Soviet satellite countries that are transitioning to market economies.

However, offset projects are controversial for several reasons. First, companies in industrialized countries can emit more carbon than is allowed under their countries' total allowable levels under the Kyoto Protocol by buying credits from developing countries, which have no emission caps. In effect, offsets allow industrialized countries to outsource reductions to places where they can be done more cheaply.

Supporters say offsets are primarily designed to lower the cost of meeting Kyoto targets, and that it shouldn't matter where reductions take place because a ton of CO_2 causes the same amount of warming whether it's released in Germany or Malaysia. But others worry that if rich countries rely on offsets too heavily, they will have little incentive to reduce fossil fuel use or develop cleaner technologies. Ultimately, they argue, developing countries will refuse to make deep cuts in their own emissions if they see little change in rich countries.

"The developed world is responsible for the majority of greenhouse gas emissions," the World Wildlife Fund warned in 2007. "If the [European Union] is to maintain its status as a major player in global climate change negotiations, then it must put its own back yard in order first and ensure that Europe is placed firmly on a path towards a low carbon economy."[12]

Moreover, say critics, offset projects sometimes credit "anyway tons" — reductions from projects that would have gone forward anyway, even without extra revenue from selling emission reductions. Reductions are supposed to be "additional" to business as usual, but that concept can be hard to prove.

As governments, corporations and advocacy groups weigh the pros and cons of carbon trading, here are some issues they are debating:

Are current trading systems working?

Global carbon markets are booming, but some experts question whether carbon trading systems are making emission reductions affordable or reducing GHG emissions at all.

Two markets dominated world carbon trading through 2007. The European Union's Emissions Trading Scheme (EU ETS) accounted for 70 percent of trades by value, followed by the Clean Development Mechanism, which accounted for 29 percent. Joint Implementation projects and all other carbon trading forums generated less than 2 percent.

Carbon Trading Tripled

Nearly 3 billion metric tons worth of greenhouse gas emission allowances were traded in 2007, more than triple the amount sold in 2005.

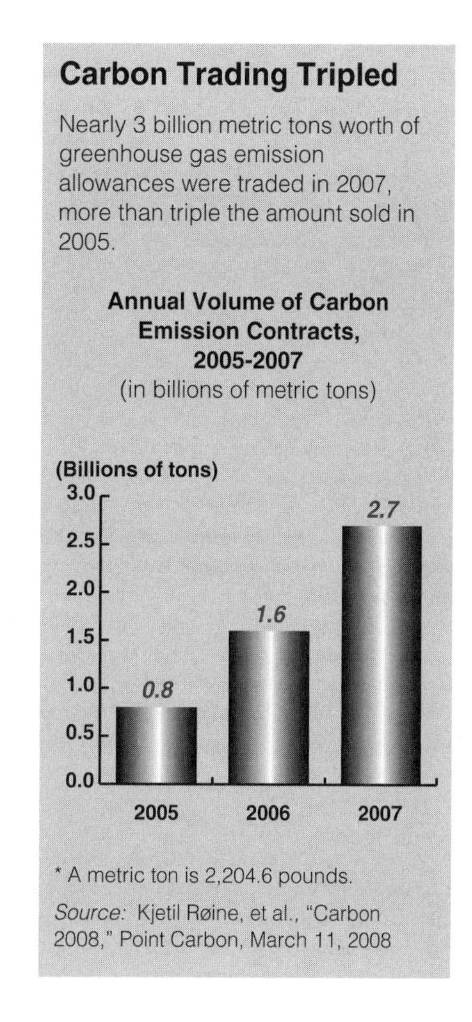

* A metric ton is 2,204.6 pounds.

Source: Kjetil Røine, et al., "Carbon 2008," Point Carbon, March 11, 2008

During its trial phase from 2005 through 2007, the EU ETS produced mixed results. Carbon allowances initially traded for €20-30 (about $30-$45) per ton of CO_2, but in April 2006 the Czech Republic, Estonia, the Netherlands, Switzerland and France announced that their 2005 GHG emissions had been lower than expected. Demand for allowances fell sharply. Share prices plunged to €10-15 ($15-23) within a few days. And prices for allowances that were valid only for the trial period — and hence not usable after 2007 — fell to almost zero in early 2007. Allowances then stabilized at €15-25 ($23-38) for the second trading period.[13]

Some observers called the price gyrations a sign that the ETS was failing. Open Europe, a London think tank, charged that ETS had failed to provide either a "workable

How Greenhouse Gases Are Measured

When discussing greenhouse gas (GHG) emissions, businesses and government agencies often use shorthand terms, like "carbon" or "carbon dioxide," to refer to the various gases emitted when carbon-based fuels are burned.

The Kyoto Protocol and other schemes to regulate greenhouse gases cover six major types of emissions that remain in the atmosphere for a significant time, trapping heat that is reflected back to Earth, which warms the planet's surface. Most are caused by various human activities.

Climate scientists have assigned each gas a global warming potential (GWP), based on its heat-trapping properties. A GWP value measures the impact a gas has on the climate over a given time period (usually 100 years) compared to the heat-producing impact of a ton of carbon dioxide (CO_2) — the most abundant greenhouse gas. For example, methane's GWP value is 25, which means that a ton of methane released into the atmosphere will cause as much warming as 25 tons of CO_2 over a 100-year period.[1] Thus, the higher the GWP, the more global warming the gas causes.

Carbon trading schemes allow emitters to trade allowances to release some or all of the six types of gases, whichever are covered by a particular system. For example, under the Kyoto Protocol, so-called Clean Development Mechanism (CDM) projects in developing countries can generate credits that they can then sell abroad by reducing their own emissions from any of the six GHG categories. Each credit certifies that the project has reduced greenhouse gas emissions by the equivalent of one metric ton (2,205 pounds) of carbon dioxide per year.

Under the European Union's Emissions Trading System (EU ETS), an electric power company in Italy might buy credits to cover excess CO_2 emissions created by its coal- or oil-fired power plants. These credits could come from CDM projects that reduced other GHG emissions through such actions as collecting methane emissions from landfills or reducing hydrofluorocarbon leakage at aluminum-smelting plants. Using the GWP values for these gases, project owners can calculate how many tons of CO_2 equivalent the project releases or avoids, and then sell the reduction credits easily across international borders.

Types of Greenhouse Gases

GHG Categories	GWP Value*	Major Sources
Carbon dioxide (CO_2)	1	Fossil fuel combustion, deforestation
Methane (CH_4)	25	Landfills, rice paddies, digestive tracts of cattle and sheep
Nitrous oxide (N_2O)	298	Fertilizer, animal waste
Hydrofluorocarbons (HFCs)	Varies (up to 14,800)	Semiconductor manufacturing and other industrial processes
Perfluorocarbons (PFCs)	Varies (up to 12,200)	Same as HFCs, plus aluminum smelting
Sulfur hexafluoride (SF_6)	22,800	Electrical transmission systems, magnesium and aluminum production

* Global warming potential

Source: U.S. Environmental Protection Agency

[1] U.S. Environmental Protection Agency, "Inventory of U.S. Greenhouse Gas Emissions and Sinks: Fast Facts," April 2008.

market in carbon" or reduced emissions.[14] Others said market volatility was not surprising for the trial phase of a new system without historical data to guide it.

"Since companies had not previously been required to track and disclose emissions, there were no hard numbers on which to base allocations," wrote Annie Petsonk, an attorney for the New York-based Environmental Defense Fund. "So companies were asked how much they'd need to emit, and naturally they said, 'A lot!' When emissions data became available and companies saw that cutting emissions was easier than they anticipated, the price of allowances plummeted."[15]

In a detailed assessment, Massachusetts Institute of Technology (MIT) economists A. Denny Ellerman and Paul Joskow pointed out that ETS was not intended to deliver big emissions cuts during its trial run, and that estimating emissions for any given year is difficult because weather patterns and fuel prices affect fossil fuel use.

Similar fluctuations occurred when the United States launched a trading program for sulfur dioxide (SO_2) allowances in the late 1990s, they noted, and as in the SO_2 program, ETS allowance prices settled down once policy makers had some real emissions data to work with.[16]

In its second trading period, which runs from 2008 through 2012, the EU's total emissions cap is 6.5 percent below the 2005 level. "Leaders learned their lesson after they over-allocated allowances in Phase I, and the cap is more stringent now. They have definitely done a better job in Phase 2," says Anja Kollmuss, an analyst at the Stockholm Environment Institute (SEI).

EU leaders now are grappling with new challenges for Phase 3, which starts in 2013, including bringing more emitters under the pollution cap. Currently the ETS only covers six sectors — energy, iron and steel, cement, glass, ceramics and pulp and paper — which produce about 45 percent of EU emissions. The European Parliament voted in July 2008 to include aviation emissions, beginning in 2012, and EU government ministers formally approved the policy in October over industry resistance.[17] Airlines assert that their industry has been hit hard by high oil prices and that the EU does not have legal authority to regulate emissions from flights, regardless of where airlines are based. (*See "At Issue," p. 191.*) European leaders also propose to include emissions from petrochemicals, aluminum and ammonia production in Phase 3.

Another critique points up flaws in both the ETS and CDM systems. In a 2007 report, the World Wildlife Fund warned that many EU countries might allow emitters to use offset credits from CDM and JI projects to meet most or all of their Phase 2 EU emission limits. Because they are not buying allowances from other EU sources, that would mean they aren't really cutting carbon among EU emitters.[18]

That prospect raises two problems, says Kollmuss. First, the Kyoto Protocol and EU directives say offsets should be "supplemental" to direct reductions. "When emitters can use a high fraction of offset credits, some sectors may not have to actually cut their emissions at all," she says.

Second, some offsets fail the "additionality" test, critics say, which occurs when the GHG reductions they produce are not additional to what would have happened anyway. For example, if local law already requires landfill owners to collect methane emissions instead of venting them into the air, they should not be able to market that action as a CDM project and sell the emission credits to a company in an industrialized country. Conversely, they say, if there is no clear financial reason to carry out a project unless it can produce CDM credits that can be sold, then the project is probably additional.

"Additionality is a simple concept, but it often comes down to subjective decisions," says Kollmuss. "And it's very easily fudged."

As one example, Stanford University law professors Michael Wara and David Victor pointed out in a 2008 paper that nearly all new renewable and gas-fired power plants in China are applying for CDM credits, even though China's energy sector is growing rapidly and the Chinese government has asked companies to invest in non-coal energy sources. Given these trends, they contend, China would probably be moving toward lower-carbon fuels even without CDM credits for new power plants. "[I]n practice, much of the current CDM market does not reflect actual reductions in emissions, and that trend is poised to get worse," the authors argued.[19]

Such controversies have spurred development of an entirely new industry of consultants and third-party certifiers who screen and verify claims from "green" development projects and help buyers find high-quality offset sources. (*See sidebar, p. 186.*)

U.N. officials acknowledge that additionality is a key challenge but argue that the CDM has effective rules for measuring it. They also point out that that the CDM has generated three times more funding for climate-friendly technology transfers to developing countries than direct foreign aid programs.

"Has the Kyoto Protocol's Clean Development Mechanism met the goal for which it was designed?" Yvo de Boer, executive secretary of the U.N. Framework Convention on Climate Change, asked in October. "In my view, the answer is yes."[20]

The EU has barred using reforestation projects in developing countries as offsets because regulators say reductions from these projects are hard to measure and can be quickly reversed (for example, if a forest plantation burns down). Ironically, developing countries without large industrial sectors would have a better chance of earning money through the CDM if the EU accepted forestry credits, since farming and forestry projects are among their best options for slowing climate change.

Carbon marketers generally see the CDM as an important tool despite its flaws. "CDM has the strictest review and approval process for emission reduction projects in the world," says Point Carbon's Hasselknippe. "Some offset projects in North America [where companies are experimenting with emission reductions and trading] are even more questionable than CDM projects. Without a regulated market, anything goes."

Are there better ways to cut emissions?

Creating carbon markets and trading carbon emission allowances is the best way to speed the transition to a low-carbon world, say proponents, because it puts a limit on carbon pollution and creates big profit incentives for cutting emissions. But critics see it as a complicated scheme that isn't guaranteed to deliver innovative energy solutions. Instead, some say, carbon taxes would be a simpler and more direct way to slow climate change.

Both approaches make polluters pay for carbon emissions, which spurs investments in cleaner technologies — with one important difference. In cap-and-trade schemes regulators specify how much pollution can be emitted, but they can't predict exactly how much allowances will cost once trading starts. Many factors, including weather, economic conditions and the discovery of new technologies influence fossil fuel use, which can drive demand for carbon allowances either up or down.

Economists can model what allowance prices may look like, but experience can be quite different from predictions, as the U.S. acid rain trading program of the 1990s (*see p. 188*) and the trial phase of EU ETS both showed.

Carbon taxes, on the other hand, charge polluters a set rate for each ton of greenhouse gases released, so there are no surprises about compliance costs. Regulators can't be sure, however, how taxes will affect pollution levels because they don't know how businesses will handle those costs. Some companies may pay taxes on their emissions and pass the expense on to consumers, while others clean up their operations to avoid the extra charge. In other words, carbon taxes offer more certainty for businesses, but cap-and-trade systems provide more certainty that the environment will improve.

"A tax doesn't put any legal limits on how much pollution can be released, so it's like a blind bet," says Fred Krupp, president of the Environmental Defense Fund (EDF). "You know what the ante is, but not what the payoff will be. Only a cap guarantees results."

Norway has achieved mixed results since it imposed a $65-per-ton carbon tax on oil and gas companies in 1991. The tax prompted StatoilHydro, one of Norway's largest energy companies, to sharply cut its carbon emissions, largely by pumping them into an undersea reservoir. Today the firm is one of the world's few companies doing large-scale geologic storage of CO_2 emissions.[21]

But StatoilHydro also has expanded drilling operations since the tax was levied. So, even though the company is more carbon efficient than many other big energy producers, its net emissions have increased as world demand for oil has grown. Today Norway's total GHG emissions are 15 percent higher than in 1991. Norway still has the tax in place, but it also has joined the EU ETS, even though it is not an EU member.

Cap-and-trade supporters also argue that carbon trading generates larger investments in new technologies than taxes do, because polluters can turn emissions into income by cleaning them up and selling their unneeded allowances. "A tax creates no such market and, so, fails to enlist the full range of human potential in a struggle where every bit of creativity is needed," writes Krupp.[22] But many energy experts say a whole suite of measures is needed to commercialize new energy technologies and that the process shouldn't be left up to market forces. Rather, they argue, a combination of big governmental investments and other measures like tax credits and clean energy targets are needed to help ensure that clean technologies are put to use.

"Emissions trading won't do much to stimulate investment in research and development of technologies that may be able to deliver deep cuts in emissions in the future," says Chris Riedy, research director at the CAP Institute for Sustainable Futures at the University of Technology in Sydney, Australia. "Markets are very good at meeting short-term goals but not so good at looking many years ahead."

Australia is developing a national carbon trading plan, Riedy notes, but it also has established a national target to generate 20 percent of its energy from renewable fuels by 2020. "That will ensure that renewable energy is developed over time until it can establish itself in the market," says Riedy. "We need to give the industry some long-term certainty."

The challenge is even larger in fast-growing countries like China, India and Brazil, which are just now industrializing and have not yet accepted binding caps on GHG emissions. As those countries raise their living standards over the next several decades, they will account for a rising share of world energy consumption. It is crucial to help those countries move onto clean energy pathways in order to slow climate change.

For instance, carbon trading could become an important option for China at some point, says Yang Fuqiang, chief representative in Beijing for the U.S.-based Energy Foundation. "China is now the top CO_2 emitter in the world, and we expect that its emissions will be much larger by 2030, perhaps as much as 20 percent of world emissions," he says. "If carbon becomes a commodity that is traded in the market, and China is the biggest source, trading can help China make more cuts because businesses will see value in carbon."

But several things must happen before carbon trading becomes a useful tool for cutting Chinese GHG emissions, Yang continues. First, Beijing must make a political commitment to reducing emissions. Then the Chinese government must fund development of clean energy sources. Carbon trading will not work, however, without a strong legal system to ensure trades are protected and penalties enforced if partners violate the rules.

"China's legal systems aren't strong enough for carbon trading yet," says Yang.

AFP/Getty Images/Frederic J. Brown

China's booming growth has made it one of the world's top emitters of carbon dioxide, the most abundant greenhouse gas (GHG). Advocates of carbon trading say that if China were to set formal limits on its GHG emissions, polluters would have an incentive to cut emissions in order to trade their allowances for cash.

Does carbon trading help developing countries?

Global climate change policy has been complicated by the need to create strategies that enable countries to share the burdens fairly. Because developed nations got rich from fossil-fueled growth and produced most of the human-driven warming that has occurred to date, the framers of the Kyoto Protocol decided that developed countries should make the deepest GHG emissions cuts. However, large developing countries like China and India are rapidly becoming the world's biggest carbon sources, so it is also crucial to limit their emissions while allowing their citizens to enjoy rising standards of living, say climate experts.

"[W]e need to provide resources to see that the developing countries don't get hooked onto the same path of development that we have," said Rajendra K. Pachauri, chairman of the Intergovernmental Panel on Climate Change (IPCC), which advises governments on climate science.[23]

The Clean Development Mechanism was designed as a first step to help poor countries grow while reducing their emissions. But critics argue that CDM projects primarily benefit the rich nations that sponsor them and that some actually damage the environment in the host countries.

For instance, the environmental advocacy group International Rivers charged in a 2007 report that awarding carbon reduction credits to numerous hydropower projects resulted in "blindly subsidizing the destruction of rivers, while the dams it supports are helping destroy the environmental integrity of the CDM." The study contended that the CDM has few standards to block projects that harm nearby ecosystems and that many hydropower projects applying for CDM credit would clearly be built in any case. As examples it cited a 60-megawatt dam in Kenya that started construction in 1999 (before the CDM was established) and an 880-megawatt dam in Brazil that applied for CDM validation six months after it began generating power in May 2007.[24]

Funding is not the only yardstick, replies U.N. spokesman David Abbass. "A company might have the ability to undertake an emission-reduction improvement, but not the incentive," he says. "If CDM was a motivating factor, then the project could potentially qualify, regardless of when construction was begun. In most hydro projects, CDM is providing incentives for efficiency improvements such as installing more efficient turbines. Such a decision could be undertaken after dam construction has begun or even after the dam has entered operation."

Forest carbon credits are also controversial. Under the CDM program, carbon credits can be granted for planting trees on formerly forested land that is either being reforested or used for other purposes. Many early CDM forestry projects were commercial tree plantations that were popular because planting swathes of fast-growing tree species absorbs large quantities of carbon. But opponents complained that such projects sometimes ended up clearing large areas of native forest, expelling local populations and damaging the environment.

"The fact that eucalyptus absorbs carbon dioxide to grow . . . can never be used to justify the environmental, social, economic and cultural damage that has occurred in places where large-scale monoculture tree plantations have been implemented in our country," wrote 53 unions and nonprofits in 2003 opposing a tree plantation proposed by a company called Plantar in the Brazilian state of Minas Gerais. The project ultimately was approved by the CDM board after three tries, not for absorbing carbon into the trees but for using a low-carbon process to turn those trees into charcoal.[25]

"The CDM is riven with fraud, just like other government-to-government aid programs, and it doesn't save any carbon," says Michael Northcott, a divinity professor at Scotland's Edinburgh University who views carbon trading as a route by which governments can avoid imposing hard limits on GHG emissions. Citing projects like the Plantar venture, Northcott writes, "The new global carbon market is not incentivizing real reductions in emissions. But it has created tremendous, new trading opportunities and new opportunities for fraud and injustice."[26]

Now, however, awarding credits for forest protection is gaining new support from tropical countries and conservation experts, who say forests can soak up carbon emissions, protect biodiversity and provide economic benefits to developing nations. Advocates are proposing some new approaches to make this method more rigorous. For example, avoided emissions would be measured at the national level instead of project by project, so it would be harder for a host country to claim credit for saving one forest while it cut down others.[27]

Advocates say the new approach would reward countries that preserve their forests instead of cutting them down and then seeking carbon credits for new tree plantations. "Central African countries consider that their efforts made in managing forests deserve to be recognized and supported, because they are positive for climate," the 15-member Coalition of Rainforest Nations contended in 2007.[28] More than 300 national leaders, research institutes and conservation groups have signed a policy statement urging governments to include tropical forests in global carbon markets.[29]

As negotiations on a post-Kyoto climate treaty proceed, CDM officials say the program needs to be scaled up. "Carbon markets and market-based mechanisms, like the [CDM], are essential for achieving the large shifts in investment required . . . to put the world on a clean path to development," said the U.N.'s de Boer.[30]

For the long term, some experts are thinking beyond the CDM model. "The CDM only lets developing countries trade credits if they prove additionality project-by-project, which is a nightmare. It's cumbersome, it leads to endless arguments and small countries have been squeezed out by big projects in China, India and Brazil," says EDF's Krupp. "We should . . . offer all developing nations technical assistance and more generous emissions targets if they agree to cap their emissions quickly. We need a global system where everyone agrees to a cap that's fair, given their level of development."

Even CDM advocates agree that benefits have been spread unequally up to now. About three-quarters of all CDM projects to date are located in China, Brazil, India and South Korea.[31] Many poor regions like sub-Saharan Africa, which are extremely vulnerable to the negative impacts of climate change, have seen little benefit from carbon trading.

"So far, the poorest developing countries have been bypassed — and there have been limited benefits for broad-based sustainable development" from carbon trading, the U.N. Development Programme observed in its 2007/2008 *Human Development Report.* "Marginal women farmers in Burkina Faso or Ethiopia are not well placed to negotiate with carbon brokers in the City of London."

However, the report noted, new approaches, such as "bundling" many small, rural projects together for CDM credit, could help poor countries participate.[32] Under a 2006 initiative called the Nairobi Framework, the U.N. is working to channel CDM projects to countries in sub-Saharan Africa. In 2008 the U.N. Environment Programme estimated that CDM projects in Africa could generate nearly $1 billion worth of credits by 2012.[33]

AP Photo/Firdia Lisnawati

Indonesian environmental activists at the U.N. climate change conference in Bali, Indonesia, last December demonstrate against a proposal to award carbon credits to tropical countries that join the Reducing Emissions From Deforestation and Degradation (REDD) program. The protesters say the Indonesian government can't handle the delicate and complicated carbon trading scheme and that the program will benefit developed countries and large corporations at the expense of indigenous communities. Delegates agreed to include forest conservation in future discussions on a new global warming treaty.

BACKGROUND

Who Pays for Pollution?

The fledgling global carbon trading industry represents the intersection of two complex debates that stretch back for more than a century. Scientists have worked since the early 1800s to understand how Earth's climate systems function and whether human actions affect them. And for nearly as long, economists who study the environment have sought cost-effective ways to control pollution.

Climate science has been international from its earliest days. In 1859 Irish physicist John Tyndall showed that certain gases in the atmosphere absorbed heat. Svante Arrhenius, a Swedish chemist, built on this idea with his calculation in 1896 that doubling the quantity of CO_2 in the atmosphere would raise Earth's average by 5 to 6 degrees Centigrade. Other researchers have shown that natural processes also influence climate cycles. For example, in 1860, Scottish physicist James Croll theorized that regular variations in Earth's orbit could trigger ice ages. Eighty years later Milutin Milankovic, a Serbian geophysicist, calculated these variations more precisely and developed a theory of glacial periods, now known as Milankovic cycles.

Other environmental issues were more urgent in the early 1900s. Air and water in industrialized countries were already heavily polluted from factory operations and urban growth, but governments had little power to respond. In Britain and the United States the nuisance doctrine — an historic concept of English common law — held that people should not use their property in ways that infringed heavily on their neighbors and that injured parties could sue those responsible for noise, odors and toxic discharges. Noxious facilities such as metal smelters were frequent early targets for nuisance lawsuits in the United States.

However, nuisance law was ineffective at controlling harmful discharges and emissions from large-scale industrial production. With pollution coming from many sources, it was hard to prove direct connections between discharges and impacts. Moreover, by the early 1900s, U.S. courts had come to view pollution as an unavoidable result of economic activity. Rather than shutting down dirty factories, they generally weighed harms against benefits and compensated plaintiffs for serious damages while allowing polluters to keep operating.[34]

Governments then developed new approaches, like zoning, which established rules for using large areas of land. City and state agencies enforced a growing body of public health laws barring practices such as dumping untreated waste into waterways. In 1920, British economist Arthur Pigou proposed a new option: pollution taxes. Pollution, he argued, was a "negative externality" — a production cost that polluters did not have to pay for. If

CHRONOLOGY

1900s-1960s *As scientists study Earth's climate, experts debate controlling pollution efficiently.*

1920 British economist Arthur Pigou suggests taxing polluters for the indirect costs of their emissions.

1945 Researchers start developing models to test atmospheric behavior.

1957 American geochemist Charles David Keeling begins measuring atmospheric carbon dioxide (CO_2) levels in Hawaii, where readings are not skewed by pollution.

1960 British economist Ronald Coase proposes tradable emission allowances.

1970s-1980s *Scientists warn that humans may be causing global warming. Stricter pollution controls are enacted.*

1970 Congress creates Environmental Protection Agency, expands Clean Air Act.

1972 First major global environmental conference — held in Stockholm, Sweden — spurs creation of United Nations Environment Programme.

1976 Scientists identify deforestation as a major cause of climate change.

1980 U.S. President Ronald Reagan's election signals a backlash against technology-specific regulations.

1987 Montreal Protocol sets international limits on ozone-destroying gases.

1988 U.N. creates Intergovernmental Panel on Climate Change (IPCC) to provide expert views on global warming.

1990 IPCC says global temperatures are rising and likely to keep increasing. . . . U.S. adopts emissions trading to reduce acid rain.

1990s *Governments pledge to tackle climate change, but worry about costs.*

1992 The United States and over 150 nations pledge to cut greenhouse gas (GHG) emissions below 1990 levels by 2000.

1995 IPCC finds that global warming has a "human-driven" signature.

1997 Kyoto Protocol is adopted after intense negotiations, requiring developed countries to cut GHG emissions 5.2 percent, on average, below 1990 levels by 2012. U.S. Senate refuses to ratify it until developing nations also are required to make cuts.

2000s-Present *Carbon emissions trading begins, primarily in Europe. Support grows in United States for action to reduce GHGs.*

2001 IPCC says major global warming is "very likely."

2002 Clean Development Mechanism (CDM) — which allows industrialized countries to partly fulfill their carbon-reduction commitments by purchasing GHG reductions in developing countries — begins.

2003 Chicago Climate Exchange launches voluntary GHG trading system for selected U.S. companies and nonprofits.

2005 Kyoto Protocol enters into force with only the United States and Australia as non-participating developed countries. . . . EU Emissions Trading Scheme begins trials. . . . Seven Northeastern states agree to form GHG cap-and-trade system for electric power plants.

2006 EU carbon allowance prices plummet after emissions are lower than expected. . . . Global carbon trading reaches $30 billion, triple the previous year's level. . . . California promises to cut CO_2 emissions 25 percent by 2020 and to start trading emissions in 2012.

2007 IPCC says climate warming is mostly due to human activities. . . . Australia joins Kyoto Protocol. . . . Three more states join Northeastern cap-and-trade system. . . . 180 countries agree to negotiate a post-Kyoto climate change treaty.

2008 EU emissions trading scheme enters Phase 2, with tighter caps. . . . U.N. proposes stricter standards for CDM projects.

manufacturers were taxed for their pollution they would have an incentive to pollute less, according to the theory.

Economists generally agreed with Pigou's approach, but environmental regulation did not gain a serious foothold until after World War II. Economic growth expanded worldwide in the 1950s and '60s, first in the United States and then in post-war Western Europe and Japan. Governments began to limit industrial pollution, but instead of taxing it they applied so-called command-and-control standards, which told polluters how much pollution they could release and often specified what kind of technologies had to be used to clean up their operations. The same standards applied to all producers, whether their operations were relatively clean or dirty. As a result, these laws imposed much larger costs on some sources than on others.

In 1960 University of Chicago economist Ronald Coase proposed a way to control pollution with lower total costs to society. If rights to pollute could be bought and sold, he argued, polluters could bargain and find an efficient way to distribute those rights. Other economists took up his idea and called for government regulators to limit total quantities of pollutants and then create markets for pollution rights.

"[N]o person, or agency, has to set the price — it is set by the competition among buyers and sellers of rights," wrote Canadian economist John Dales in 1968.[35] This approach was more effective, proponents contended, because producers (who knew more about their own costs and production methods than regulators) could decide who would clean up and find the best ways to do it.

International Cooperation

By the 1960s, protecting the environment was a national political issue in many industrialized countries. Social Democrat Willy Brandt campaigned for chancellor in West German in 1961 with a promise to clean up air pollution. Japanese activists began suing large polluters in the mid-1960s, pressuring regulators and industrialists into adopting tighter controls. In 1970 two versions of Earth Day were launched: an international celebration on the date of the spring equinox, formally endorsed by the United Nations, and a U.S. observance on April 22 that drew millions of Americans to rallies and teach-ins.

National governments began setting standards for air and water quality, waste management and land conservation. Then a 1972 international conference on the environment, held in Stockholm, set lofty goals for international cooperation and led to the formation of the United Nations Environment Programme. The conferees declared that most environmental problems in the developing world were caused by poverty and underdevelopment, and that rich countries should try to reduce the gap between rich and poor countries.[36]

Meanwhile, international cooperation was growing in the field of climate science. In the 1950s and '60s, international research groups in the United States, England, Mexico and elsewhere developed circulation models to simulate climate processes and began testing theories about how the system might change in response to natural or manmade events. French, Danish, Swiss, Russian and U.S. scientists drilled into ice sheets in Greenland and Antarctica and analyzed air bubbles trapped thousands of years earlier to determine how the atmosphere's composition had changed over time. A growing body of climate studies showed that many processes shaped global climate patterns, and that human actions could disrupt the system.

In 1976, frustrated with the slow pace of pollution reductions under the Clean Air Act, U.S. policymakers began experimenting with market-based measures. As a first step, companies were permitted to build new factories in polluted areas if they bought credits from nearby sources that had reduced emissions below legal limits. In 1977 Congress amended the act to allow policies like banking credits (saving them for use or sale in the future). In 1982 the Environmental Protection Agency (EPA) used a trading program to phase out lead from gasoline. Refiners were issued tradable lead credits that they could sell if they were already blending unleaded gasoline or use while retooling their plants. Lead, which had been outlawed from U.S. gasoline, was finally eliminated by 1987.

Other nations also tried market-based environmental policies, primarily pollution taxes. Many European countries — including West Germany, the Netherlands, Czechoslovakia and Hungary — taxed water pollution discharges to help fund sewage treatment and bring water quality up to healthy standards.[37] France and Japan imposed charges for air pollution emissions. China also

Nonprofit Auditors Keep Projects 'Honest'

Gold Standard projects provide jobs, help the environment.

Power outages and voltage fluctuations once plagued the Honduran city of La Esperanza, and many rural residents in the surrounding countryside had no electricity at all.

Now a small hydroelectric project on the nearby Intibuca River reliably produces 13.5 megawatts of electricity — enough to power 11,000 households for a year — while avoiding 37,000 tons of annual carbon dioxide emissions from diesel generators previously used to produce electricity. And because it is a so-called run-of-river project, it generates electricity without damming the river.

The La Esperanza Hydroelectric Project is the first to be certified as reducing greenhouse gas (GHG) emissions under the Kyoto Protocol's Clean Development Mechanism (CDM). The CDM allows Third World developers whose projects reduce carbon emissions to sell "emission credits" — equal to the emissions they avoid — to polluting companies in industrialized countries.

The project also will provide a variety of other sustainable benefits in the community, such as reducing local residents' use of carbon-consuming trees for fuel, encouraging reforestation and providing reliable jobs and technical skills for the dam construction, maintenance and operating staffs, providing running water for households near the project and engaging more women in work and community life.

How can La Esperanza's developers prove their facility will provide all those benefits? The project is being evaluated by Gold Standard, an independent, nonprofit organization in Basel, Switzerland. Founded by the World Wildlife Fund and other nongovernmental organizations and funded by public and private donors, Gold Standard accredits high-quality CDM projects that benefit the local community and cut carbon emissions. Gold Standard approval gives carbon-credit buyers extra assurance that the carbon credits they are purchasing come from measurable GHG reductions that have clearly benefited the host countries where they were carried out.

Nonprofits like Gold Standard have emerged to provide extra certification for carbon offset projects because of concerns that private verification companies, which are paid by project developers, have a financial incentive to certify that the projects they are auditing reduce carbon emissions just to get them approved. And the CDM Executive Board, which reviews CDM applications, does not have enough staff to verify all of the information submitted by auditors.

"Right now, good auditors get their projects approved, but that shouldn't be the only incentive," says Stanford University law professor Michael Wara. The CDM board has "done the best it can, but it's in an untenable situation," he contends, because it is understaffed and facing a growing demand for offset credits.

adopted air and water pollution taxes in the early 1980s, although these levies were quite low, and a large share of the funds were distributed back to pollution sources as subsidies.[38]

Then, in an important milestone for global environmental cooperation, 23 nations signed the Montreal Protocol in 1987, agreeing to restrict production and use of industrial chemicals that were damaging Earth's protective ozone layer. Over the next decade, as science showed that damage was still occurring, more nations joined, and members amended the agreement to eliminate the substances completely. Several nations used allowance trading systems to phase out domestic use of ozone-depleting chemicals, including the United States, Canada, Mexico and Singapore.

The protocol established some other important precedents: It relied on expert advice from scientists, forced governments to act in time to prevent serious environmental harm and required developed nations to help developing countries adjust to the ban without harming their living standards.[39]

Confronting the Evidence

By the late 1980s many environmentalists and scientists believed human activities were affecting Earth's climate and that policy makers needed to act. In 1988 the United Nations established the Intergovernmental Panel on Climate Change (IPCC) to advise national governments about climate science and potential impacts from global warming. But critics, including large

Some critics have claimed that as a result of these conflicts of interest and other problems, carbon markets, in effect, are generating "rights to pollute."

"We require project developers to make positive contributions to local communities in two out of three categories — economic, social and environmental — and our screening process gives them numbers they can use to rate what they're delivering in each area," says Caitlin Sparks, U.S. marketing director for Gold Standard. "We monitor those promises through the full life of the project. U.N.-accredited auditors validate and verify all of the documents, and the information is re-verified after the project starts."

For instance, all CDM projects are supposed to promote "sustainable development," but it's usually left up to the host country to define what that means. However, Gold Standard makes its own judgment.

"They are doing the sorts of things that should be applied wholesale to CDM," says Wara. "They dig in and do better verification, which costs more and makes the process more time-consuming, but that needs to happen. We need more scrutiny of these projects."

Gold Standard projects have three key features: They must focus on renewable energy or energy efficiency to help promote a transition to a clean-energy economy; developers must prove that the carbon reductions will be "additional" to business as usual (this test is optional when projects go through CDM review but is required by Gold Standard); and they must show that their projects will make measurable economic contributions to sustainable development in host communities.

"A free market for credits will tend to focus on quantities of tons," says Sparks. "The Gold Standard is meant to focus on quality" of emission reductions.

Gold Standard projects in India and South Africa reflect the program's diversity and focus on quality:

- The Shri Chamundi biomass co-generation power plant in Karnataka, India, will generate 16 megawatts of electricity from biomass fuels such as eucalyptus branches, coconut fronds, rice husks and cashew shells. It will also use waste heat to produce steam for manufacturing, replacing boilers that run on heavy fuel oil. The plant will create more than 800 jobs, including collecting and preparing biomass, converting previously useless crop residues into fuel. It also will reduce open burning of crop wastes in fields, which pollutes the atmosphere and local water supplies.
- In Cape Town, South Africa, the Kuyasa housing service upgrade project installed ceiling insulation, solar hot water heaters and energy-efficient lighting in a low-income housing development and will install similar improvements in future developments. Making homes more energy-efficient will reduce CO_2 emissions, local air pollution and the danger of household fires.[1]

[1] Information about these projects comes from validation reports in the Gold Standard Registry, http://goldstandard.apx.com; and "Reducing the Carbon Footprint of the UN: High-Level Event on Climate Change," U.N. Headquarters, Sept. 24, 2007, www.un.org/climatechange/2007highlevel/climatefriendly.shtml.

corporations and President George H. W. Bush, argued that the scientific evidence was uncertain and that reducing GHG emissions would seriously harm economic growth.

Other nations, led by Western European countries with strong Green parties, wanted a binding agreement to limit greenhouse emissions. The Framework Convention on Climate Change (FCCC), signed at the 1992 Earth Summit in Rio de Janeiro, Brazil, amounted to a compromise: It called only for voluntary reductions in greenhouse gases to 1990 levels but laid out a path for further action. Some countries — including the Netherlands, Sweden, Finland, Norway and Denmark — passed domestic carbon taxes to reduce their emissions. But total GHG emissions from industrialized nations kept rising, making it clear that mandatory targets and timetables would be needed.

In 1997 FCCC members adopted the Kyoto Protocol, which required signatories to make specific reductions (averaging 5.2 percent below 1990 levels) by 2012. U.S. President Bill Clinton supported the goal, but his administration was worried about costs. A U.S. carbon tax was not an option: The administration had suffered an embarrassing defeat in 1993 when it proposed a BTU tax (a levy on the energy content of fuels), only to be blocked by fellow Democrats in Congress. Instead, U.S. negotiators at Kyoto pushed to include emissions trading and credits for funding offset projects in developing countries and former Eastern Bloc nations.

Although the final agreement included these policies and the Clinton administration signed the treaty, the Senate voted 95-0 for a resolution against ratifying it unless developing countries also had to make binding reduction pledges. President George W. Bush, who had promised during his campaign to limit carbon dioxide emissions, repudiated the Kyoto agreement shortly after taking office, arguing that mandatory GHG reductions (even through market-based mechanisms) would harm the U.S. economy.

Nonetheless, President Bush embraced the idea of emissions trading to address domestic air pollution issues and sought to build on a successful program initiated a decade earlier under the first Bush administration. In 1990 Congress had amended the Clean Air Act to create an emissions trading program for sulfur dioxide (SO_2) and nitrogen oxide (NO_x), two pollutants from fossil fuel-fired power plants. These emissions formed acids in the atmosphere that fell back to Earth in rain and snow, damaging forests, soils and buildings. The so-called acid rain trading program, which began in 1995, capped emissions of SO_2 (with looser limits for NO_x) and set up a trading market for emission allowances.

The program was widely viewed as a success. EPA reported in 2004 that a decade of emissions trading had reduced the power sector's SO_2 and NO_x emissions 34 and 38 percent, respectively, below 1990 levels.[40] Economists estimated trading had saved $1 billion or more per year over command-and-control approaches.[41] Touting these results, President Bush proposed emissions trading initiatives to cut U.S. SO_2 and NO_x emissions even further and suggested using a trading scheme to control mercury emissions. But congressional critics argued that these measures did not cut far or fast enough and that emissions trading was the wrong way to reduce toxic pollutants like mercury.[42]

As the Bush administration continued to oppose cutting GHG emissions, other U.S. leaders grew increasingly worried about climate change. Sens. John McCain, R-Ariz., and Joseph Lieberman, D-Conn., offered carbon cap-and-trade legislation in 2003 and 2005 and reintroduced the bill in 2007. Seeing the political handwriting on the wall, large U.S. corporations began to endorse carbon controls.

"We know enough to act on climate change," said the U.S. Climate Action Partnership, an alliance of major corporations including Alcoa, Dupont and General Motors. The group called on Congress to pass mandatory GHG limits and create a cap-and-trade system to attain them.[43]

"Marginal women farmers in Burkina Faso or Ethiopia are not well placed to negotiate with carbon brokers in the City of London."

— U.N. Human Development Report 2007/2008

CURRENT SITUATION

A New Player?

As Americans increasingly worry about climate change, many observers expect the United States to limit its greenhouse gas emissions and create a domestic carbon trading system after the 2008 elections. Multiple cap-and-trade bills were introduced in both houses of Congress in 2007 and 2008, including several with bipartisan support.[44] And the two major-party presidential candidates, Sens. McCain and Barack Obama, D-Ill., both pledged to set up a cap-and-trade system and to pursue deep cuts in U.S. GHG emissions.

Since the United States is one of the world's largest GHG emitters, U.S. entry into carbon trading would dramatically expand global carbon markets. New Carbon Finance, a market research firm in London, estimated in October that the total value of world carbon trading would reach $550 billion by 2012 and just over $2 trillion by 2020, even without U.S. participation. If the United States introduces a federal cap-and-trade system, however, those figures would increase to $680 billion by 2012 and more than $3 trillion by 2020.[45] By way of comparison, $3 trillion is roughly the size of the combined world markets for oil, coal, natural gas and electricity today.[46]

Two legislative proposals — one debated by the Senate in mid-2008 and a House Energy and Commerce committee proposal released on Oct. 7 — offer some indication of what national cap-and-trade legislation might look like. Both bills would cap U.S. greenhouse gas emissions and set up a trading system to reduce them. The House bill would require a 6 percent cut below 2005 levels by 2020, and the Senate bill calls for a 19 percent cut. By 2050, however, the House measure would reduce emissions by 80 percent below 2005 levels, compared to 71 percent under the Senate bill.

Along with public concern and growing scientific evidence that human activities are warming the planet, another factor pushing U.S. policy makers to act is a 2007 Supreme Court ruling which held — contrary to the Bush administration's position — that carbon dioxide was a pollutant under the Clean Air Act and that the EPA had authority to regulate it.[47] "CO_2 controls are clearly coming. The only remaining questions are when and who is going to do the controlling," said Rep. Rick Boucher, D-Va., chair of the House Energy and Commerce Committee's Subcommittee on Energy and Air Quality, in late 2008. A coauthor of the committee's cap-and-trade proposal, Boucher said he thought Congress rather than the EPA should lead on regulating carbon and that he planned to hold hearings on cap-and-trade legislation early in 2009.[48]

If Congress does pass such legislation, its effectiveness will depend on which sectors it covers, how quickly it cuts emissions and whether it compensates businesses and consumers for higher costs. Carbon marketers will watch closely to see how strictly the U.S. limits the use of offset credits from foreign sources such as CDM projects.

Some states are launching regional cap-and-trade schemes to show the approach can work and to build support for national action. In September, 10 Northeastern states, stretching from Maryland to Maine, launched the Regional Greenhouse Gas Initiative (RGGI) — the first mandatory U.S. carbon cap-and-trade system. RGGI is designed to reduce GHG emissions from electric power plants 10 percent below current levels by 2018. Unlike systems that have given polluters emission allowances for free, RGGI auctioned off its first batch of allowances and will invest the proceeds — $38.5 million, at a final price of $3.07 per ton of CO_2 — in energy efficiency and renewable energy programs.

State officials called the first RGGI auction a success. "Demand was high, and fears of low-ball bidding did not come to pass," said Democratic New York Gov. David Paterson. "Instead, RGGI has used market forces to set a price on carbon."[49]

AP Photo/Somnuk Attipanyo

River waters crash into a Buddhist temple during high tide on the outskirts of Bangkok, Thailand. Climatologists say higher global temperatures are causing polar ice caps to melt, raising sea and river levels in low-lying coastal areas. Carbon trading schemes are the world's current answer to the question of how to control global warming.

At nearly the same time, seven Western states and four Canadian provinces agreed on the basics of a broader regional cap-and-trade program that would cover emissions from electricity generation, industry, transportation and residential and commercial energy use. The initiative would cut members' GHG emissions to 15 percent below 2005 levels by 2020. Trading is scheduled to start in 2012, with a second phase beginning in 2015.[50]

"The Western Climate Initiative is increasingly the system that many observers see as a possible precursor to a U.S. federal system because of its size and design features. They've received input from some key experts who were involved in setting up the EU system," says Hasselknippe of the Point Carbon research firm. However, if Congress enacts national GHG controls, that system would almost certainly replace regional cap-and-trade programs.

Beyond Kyoto

Global negotiators are working on a follow-on agreement to the Kyoto Protocol, which only limits signatories' emissions through 2012, although some countries have made longer-term commitments. For example, in 2007 EU countries pledged to cut their total GHG emissions 20 percent by 2020 and to increase this target to 30 percent if other nations sign a post-Kyoto treaty.

Getty Images/Jeff J. Mitchell

Thousands of planes will be required to cut their carbon emissions now that the European Union has decided that airliners should be included in EU carbon emission caps under Phase 3 of the Kyoto Protocol climate change treaty, beginning in 2012. Airlines are resisting, saying that their industry has been hit hard by high oil prices and that the EU does not have legal authority to regulate emissions from flights that originate in other countries. Above, planes in Glasgow, Scotland.

At a contentious international conference in 2007 in Bali, Indonesia, negotiators agreed on basic principles for crafting a post-Kyoto agreement. The plan calls for finalizing a new treaty in 2009 (to take effect in 2013) that includes deep cuts in developed countries' greenhouse emissions and unspecified "mitigation actions" by developing countries. It also pledges to develop policies that reward tropical countries for protecting their forests and creates a fund using a surcharge on CDM projects to help poor countries adapt to climate change impacts.[51]

Many developed countries wanted emissions cuts of 25 to 40 percent in rich countries by 2020, but the United States refused to approve an agenda with specific targets. U.S. representatives were booed during the talks, and at one point Papua New Guinea's representative was cheered when he told them, "If you're not going to lead, get out of the way." Ultimately, however, the U.S. supported the principles — the first time that the Bush administration had agreed to negotiate climate targets with other nations.[52]

It is not yet clear what shape a post-Kyoto agreement may take. It could set binding national emissions targets, like the Kyoto treaty, or build on pledges by individual countries or groups of countries. Some nations have already made significant commitments outside the Kyoto framework. The European Parliament, for example, is already setting emissions caps and planning to auction some carbon allowances in the third phase of EU ETS, to start in 2013.[53]

Some developing countries have also pledged to reduce their contribution to climate change. China's current five-year plan, which runs through 2010, calls for reducing the energy intensity of gross domestic product (the amount of energy used to produce each unit of income) 20 percent below 2005 levels by 2010. Beijing is also working to generate 10 percent of national energy demand with renewable sources by 2010 and 15 percent by 2020; by contrast, the U.S. currently gets about 7 percent of its energy from renewables. And Costa Rica has pledged to become carbon-neutral, as have New Zealand, Monaco, Norway and Iceland.[54]

Beyond these steps, however, experts warn that unless large developing countries like China, India, Indonesia and Brazil accept binding carbon caps soon, it will be impossible to avoid disastrous climate change. "If China and India keep doing what they're doing, their emissions will be tremendous," says Kollmuss of the Stockholm Environment Institute. "At the same time, these countries need to develop, so we need to find a just and equitable climate solution that will get them to buy in."

The U.N. Development Programme seconded this view in its 2007/2008 *Human Development Report*, which urged large developing countries to accept emissions targets proportional to what they could accomplish. "Any multilateral agreement without quantitative commitments from developing countries will lack credibility," the report asserted. However, it also argued that it would be impossible to negotiate such an agreement unless wealthy countries provided money and technology to help poorer nations adopt low-carbon strategies.[55]

Some advocates in developing countries worry that they will be asked to take on GHG reduction commitments when many rich nations have not cut their emissions significantly (or, in the case of the United States, at all).

"The message from Bali is that the fight against climate change will be brutal and selfish," says Sunita Narain, director of the Centre for Science and Environment in New Delhi. She agrees that India is "devastatingly vulnerable" to climate change impacts like floods and heat waves. By signing an action plan in Bali without hard reduction targets or timetables, she argues,

AT ISSUE

Should the European Union cap aviation carbon emissions?

YES

Joao Vieira
Policy Officer, European Federation for Transport and Environment

From *T&E Bulletin*, July 22, 2008

After years of us and others highlighting the environmental damage caused by aviation, the [European Union] has finally done something to try and counteract its impact. It has shown courage, in particular, in standing up to threats from the USA and against a background of abysmal inaction from the International Civil Aviation Organisation, the body charged with regulating emissions from aircraft under the Kyoto Protocol. . . .

So why are we at *T&E* so reluctant to be happy about this? There are two reasons. The terms on which aviation has entered the ETS [Emissions Trading Scheme] will mean very limited reductions in emissions from aircraft [which] might create the illusion that other measures that would do much more to reduce emissions . . . are no longer needed. And . . . the ETS might now be seen as a "silver bullet" solution for emissions from transport. . . .

Airlines will be allowed to buy permits from other sectors without restrictions, so their emissions will continue to grow. Instead of changing to greener technologies and operations, the aviation sector is likely to limit its climate efforts to buying permits in the carbon market. In addition, this directive only addresses CO_2 [carbon dioxide] emissions, ignoring the fact that NO_x [nitrogen oxides] is emitted from aircraft . . . and aviation-induced clouds also have climatic impact. It will mean aviation remains the least-efficient and most climate-intensive mode of transport.

The limitations of a cap-and-trade system's ability to effectively reduce emissions from transport should be a lesson for EU decision-makers, some of whom seem tempted by the idea of emissions trading for road transport.

The ETS is . . . for large, fixed-emission facilities. Transport . . . has numerous operators of mobile emissions sources, which do not face international competition [since] transport is a geographically bound activity.

T&E has said all along that including aviation in the ETS can only be a first step. If the transport sector is to reduce its emissions, other measures to address the climatic impacts of all modes of transport will be needed.

Without the courage to apply fuel taxation, fair and efficient infrastructure charging and strict emission standards, applying emissions trading to transport will simply allow transport to keep growing its emissions. . . . That is unfair to [other] industries, and irresponsible to future generations.

NO

Giovanni Bisignani
Director General and CEO, International Air Transport Association (IATA)

From remarks at the Farnborough [England] International Air Show, July 18, 2008

Today, airlines are in crisis. Oil is above $140. Jet fuel is over $180. In five years fuel went from 14 percent of operating costs to over 34 percent. If oil averages $135 for the rest of the year, the industry bill will be $190 billion. And next year it could be over $250 billion. . . .

IATA's environment leadership is delivering results. We worked with our members to implement best practices in fuel management. In 2007 this saved 6.7 million tonnes of CO_2 and $1.3 billion in cost.

We also worked with governments and air navigation service providers. Optimising 395 routes and procedures in 81 airports saved 3.8 million tonnes of CO_2 and $831 million in costs.

We could save up to 73 million tonnes of CO_2 with better air traffic management, but, while painting themselves green to win votes, governments are slow to deliver results. . . .

IATA supports emissions trading, but it must be global, fair and effective. Europe's approach could not be more wrong.

First, it's not an effective incentive. Developed when oil was $55 per barrel, it was meant to be an economic stick to force airlines to become more fuel-efficient. Europe's politicians had not foreseen the giant club of $140 oil.

It has beaten the life out of 25 airlines already this year, and we expect many more to follow into bankruptcy protection if they can afford it or straight into liquidation if they cannot. To survive, airlines are doing everything possible to reduce fuel burn. The [Emissions Trading Scheme] will add costs but will not improve the results. . . .

Second, the timing is wrong. Why make long-range policy decisions in the moment of a crisis when the future is completely uncertain — even five years out. And why make fuel more expensive when it is at its highest level ever — an 87 percent increase in the last year? Clearly, green politics has got in the way of good policy. . . .

How can Europe expect to charge an Australian airline for emissions over the Middle East on a flight from Asia to Europe? This will be challenged at [the International Civil Aviation Organisation] and in the International Court of Justice. And a responsible industry could easily be caught in a trade war of a layering of punitive economic measures.

Instead of cleaning up the environment, Europe is creating an international legal mess.

AP Photo/Ed Wray

Growers burned down a dense forest in Sumber, Kalimantan, Indonesia, to make way for a palm oil plantation. Deforestation accounts for about 20 percent of human-generated greenhouse gas emissions worldwide. Environmentalists point out that forest preservation is one of the most cost-effective ways to address climate change.

"The world powers have reneged on all of us. Now developing countries will be even more reluctant to engage. Hardliners will say, 'We told you so.' "

In September U.N. Secretary-General Ban Ki-moon announced a cooperative program to test ways of managing tropical forests to keep them healthy and store large amounts of carbon. Norway donated $35 million for the first phase, which will involve at least nine countries in Africa, Asia and Latin America. The program seeks to pave the way for including forest conservation in a post-Kyoto treaty.

"This initiative will not only demonstrate how forests can have an important role as part of a post-2012 climate regime," said Ban, "it will also help build much needed confidence that the world community is ready to support the implementation of an inclusive, ambitious and comprehensive climate regime, once it is ratified."[56]

OUTLOOK

Cost of Inaction

As world leaders struggle to address this fall's global financial meltdown, some policy makers say now is the wrong time to impose further limits on greenhouse gas emissions. Putting a price on carbon, they worry, will raise energy costs when economies are already sputtering.

In October, for example, some East European countries tried unsuccessfully to delay the auctioning of EU ETS emission allowances, and conservative U.S. legislators questioned whether the economy could handle the added impact of cap-and-trade legislation.[57] If the world goes through a prolonged recession, energy prices are likely to fall, which would ease the financial crunch somewhat but would also reduce some of the imperative to shift away from fossil fuels.

Indeed, controlling carbon emissions won't be cheap. The total cost of controlling global warming could cost 1-2 percent of world gross domestic product — or roughly $350 to $700 billion — per year over the next few decades, according to several prominent economists, including Nicholas Stern of Great Britain and Jeffery Sachs of the United States.[58]

But advocates say it's more urgent than ever to act on climate change. Since renewable fuels like wind, solar and geothermal energy are free or low-cost, investing in them now will not only reduce GHG emissions but also make nations less dependent on oil and gas. And, they argue, green technologies can generate thousands of new, high-paying jobs.

Supporting this view, a 2008 study by David Roland-Holst, an economist at the University of California, calculated that energy efficiency policies in California from 1976 through 2006 had saved households some $56 billion and created about 1.5 million jobs.[59]

"The longer we wait to cap our emissions, the farther we fall behind in the remaking of a $6 trillion economy," says Environmental Defense Fund President Krupp.

Moreover, the cost of inaction is likely to be much higher than those of cutting emissions. Climate change will have major impacts worldwide, especially in poor countries that have few resources to protect people or move them out of harm's way. Global policy experts warn that recent progress against poverty in developing countries could be wiped out by climate change impacts like crop failures, water shortages and catastrophic flooding in river deltas that could leave millions hungry and homeless.

"If we are to avoid the catastrophic reversals in human development that will follow in the wake of climate change, we need to more than halve emissions of greenhouse gases," wrote Kevin Watkins, lead author of the U.N.'s *Human Development Report*, during the Bali climate conference. "That will not happen without a global accord that decarbonises growth and extends access to affordable energy in the developing world: a shake-up in energy policy backed by a programme similar to the post-Second World War Marshall Plan."[60] Under that initiative, the United States spent about $13 billion from 1947 through 1951 to rebuild war-torn Western Europe. The price tag for a program on the same scale, measured in 2007 dollars, would be roughly $740 billion.[61]

Rising concerns about costs make it increasingly likely that carbon trading will be a central part of the climate change solution, since it offers the opportunity to make cuts where they are most affordable. But cap-and-trade programs alone will not be enough. Government also must fund energy research and development; tighten energy efficiency standards and create markets for new technologies by setting national renewable energy targets. The overall goal, says IPCC Chair Pachauri, is to create a cleaner, less resource-intensive development path.

Pachauri often recalls Mahatma Gandhi's quip when asked whether India's people should have the same standard of living as the British. "It took Britain half the resources of the planet to achieve this prosperity," Gandhi replied. "How many planets will a country like India require?"[62]

NOTES

1. Mamuni Das, "Germany To Buy Carbon Credits From TTD Solar Kitchen," *The Hindu Business Line.com*, Aug. 24, 2005, www.thehindubusinessline.com/2005/08/24/stories/2005082402960100.htm; "Solar Amenities Way Above Sea Level," *The Statesman*, Oct. 15, 2006, www.thestatesman.net/page.arcview.php?clid=30&id=161337&usrsess=1; Madhur Singh, "India's Temples Go Green," *Time*, July 7, 2008, www.time.com/time/world/article/0,8599,1820844,00.html.
2. Singh, *ibid.*
3. http://cdm.unfccc.int/UserManagement/File Storage/4WZXEVUUTRCJDV4AC6SY7VSL0KBFC5.
4. David Adam, "World Carbon Dioxide Levels Highest for 650,000 Years, Says U.S. Report," *The Guardian*, May 13, 2008, www.guardian.co.uk/environment/2008/may/13/carbonemissions.climatechange.
5. For background, see Colin Woodard, "Curbing Climate Change," *CQ Global Researcher*, February 2007, pp. 27-52.
6. For background, see Mary H. Cooper, "Global Warming Treaty," *CQ Researcher*, Jan. 26, 2001, pp. 41-64.
7. Garrett Hardin, "The Tragedy of the Commons," *Science*, Dec. 13, 1968, pp. 1243-1248.
8. "Carbon 2008" Point Carbon, March 11, 2008, p. 3.
9. Fiona Harvey, "World Carbon Trading Value Doubles," *Financial Times*, May 7, 2008, http://us.ft.com/ftgateway/superpage.ft?news_id=fto050720082214562909.
10. "Regional Initiatives," Pew Center on Global Climate Change, www.pewclimate.org/what_s_being_done/in_the_states/regional_initiatives.cfm.
11. Sen. Barack Obama (D-Ill.) endorsed cutting U.S. emissions 80 percent below 1990 levels by 2050, while Sen. John McCain (R-Ariz.) called for reducing at least 60 percent below 1990 levels on the same timetable. "Science Debate 2008," www.sciencedebate2008.com.
12. "Emission Impossible: Access to JI/CDM Credits in Phase II of the EU Emissions Trading Scheme," World Wildlife Fund-UK, June 2007, p. 10, http://assets.panda.org/downloads/emission_impossible__final_.pdf.
13. A. Denny Ellerman and Paul Joskow, "The European Union's Emissions Trading System in Perspective," Pew Climate Center, May 2008, figure 1, p. 13, www.pewclimate.org/docUploads/EU-ETS-In-Perspective-Report.pdf.
14. "Europe's Dirty Secret: Why the EU Emissions Trading Scheme Isn't Working," *Open Europe*, 2007, p. 16, www.openeurope.org.uk/research/etsp2.pdf.
15. "What's Really Going On in the European Carbon Market," Environmental Defense Fund, June 27, 2007, http://blogs.edf.org/climate411/2007/06/27/eu_carbon_market/.
16. Ellerman and Joskow, *op. cit.*, pp. 12-15.

17. James Kanter, "Europe Forcing Airlines to Buy Emissions Permits," *The New York Times*, Oct. 25, 2008, p. B2.
18. "Emission Impossible . . . ," *op. cit.*, pp. 3-4.
19. Michael W. Wara and David G. Victor, "A Realistic Policy on International Carbon Offsets," *Working Paper #74*, Program on Energy and Sustainable Development, Stanford University, April 2008, p. 5, http://pesd.stanford.edu/publications/a_realistic_policy_on_international_carbon_offsets/.
20. Yvo de Boer, "Prepared Remarks for Public Debate on the Kyoto Mechanisms," New York, Oct. 9, 2008.
21. Leila Abboud, "An Exhausting War On Emissions," *The Wall Street Journal*, Sept. 30, 2008, p. A15.
22. Fred Krupp and Miriam Horn, *Earth: The Sequel: The Race to Reinvent Energy and Stop Global Warming* (2008), p. 247.
23. "A Conversation with Nobel Prize Winner Rajendra Pachauri," *Yale Environment 360*, June 3, 2008, http://e360.yale.edu/content/print.msp?id=2006.
24. Barbara Haya, "Failed Mechanism: How the CDM is Subsidizing Hydro Developers and Harming the Kyoto Protocol," *International Rivers*, November 2007, http://internationalrivers.org/files/Failed_Mechanism_3.pdf.
25. Oliver Balch, "Forests: A Carbon Trader's Gold Mine?" ClimateChangeCorp.com, May 7, 2008, www.climatechangecorp.com/content.asp?ContentID=5305; for project details and review documents, see "Project 1051: Mitigation of Methane Emissions in the Charcoal Production of Plantar, Brazil," United Nations Framework Convention on Climate Change, http://cdm.unfccc.int/Projects/DB/DNV-CUK1175235824.92/view.
26. Michael S. Northcott, *A Moral Climate: The Ethics of Global Warming* (2007), p. 136.
27. William F. Laurance, "A New Initiative to Use Carbon Trading for Tropical Forest Conservation," *Biotropica*, vol. 39, no. 1 (2007), pp. 20-24, www.globalcanopy.org/themedia/NewCarbonTrading.pdf.
28. Keya Acharya, "Rainforest Coalition Proposes Rewards for 'Avoided Deforestation,'" Environmental News Network, Aug. 15, 2007, www.enn.com/ecosystems/article/21854.
29. "Forests in the Fight Against Climate Change," www.forestsnow.org.
30. De Boer, *op. cit.*
31. "CDM Experiences and Lessons" (presentation), slide 5, U.N. Development Programme, April 1, 2008, http://unfccc.meta-fusion.com/kongresse/AWG_08/downl/0401_1500_p2/Krause%20UNDP%20JI_CDM1.pdf.
32. "Fighting Climate Change: Human Solidarity in a Developed World, *Human Development Report 2007/2008* (2008), United Nations Development Programme, p. 155.
33. " 'Global Green Deal' — Environmentally-Focused Investment Historic Opportunity for 21st Century Prosperity and Job Generation," United Nations Environment Programme, press release, Oct. 22, 2008.
34. Richard N. L. Andrews, *Managing the Environment, Managing Ourselves: A History of American Environmental Policy* (1999), pp. 127-128.
35. J. H. Dales, *Pollution, Property and Prices* (1968), p. 801.
36. The final conference declaration is online at www.unep.org/Documents.Multilingual/Default.asp?DocumentID=97&ArticleID=1503.
37. See Thomas H. Tietenberg, *Environmental and Natural Resource Economics*, 5th ed. (2000), pp. 454-455.
38. Randall A. Bluffstone, "Environmental Taxes in Developing and Transition Economies," *Public Finance and Management*, vol. 3, no. 1 (2003), pp. 152-55.
39. Richard Elliot Benedick, *Ozone Diplomacy: New Directions in Safeguarding the Planet* (1998), pp. 314-320.
40. "Acid Rain Trading Program, 2004 Progress Report," U.S. Environmental Protection Agency, October 2005, pp. 2, 10, www.epa.gov/airmarkt/progress/docs/2004report.pdf.
41. Robert N. Stavins, "Lessons Learned from SO2 Allowance Trading," *Choices*, 2005, p. 53, www.choicesmagazine.org/2005-1/environment/2005-1-11.htm; Nathaniel O. Keohane and Sheila M. Olmstead, *Markets and the Environment* (2007), p. 184.

42. For background see Jennifer Weeks, "Coal's Comeback," *CQ Researcher*, Oct. 5, 2007, pp. 817-840. The Bush administration then issued regulations through EPA to promote emissions trading, but in 2007 the D.C. Circuit Court held that the EPA did not have authority under the Clean Air Act to develop such broad trading programs.
43. "A Call for Action," Jan. 22, 2007, U.S. Climate Action Partnership, p. 2, www.us-cap.org/ClimateReport.pdf.
44. For a summary of bills pending in September 2008, see "Comparison of Legislative Climate Change Targets," World Resources Institute, Sept. 9, 2008, www.wri.org/publication/usclimatetargets.
45. "Carbon Market Round-Up Q3 2008," *New Carbon Finance*, Oct. 10, 2008; www.newcarbonfinance.com/download.php?n=2008-10-10_PR_Carbon_Markets_Q3_20082.pdf&f=fileName&t=NCF_downloads.
46. Simon Kennedy, " 'Carbon Trading' Enriches the World's Energy Desks," *Marketwatch*, May 16, 2007.
47. *Massachusetts v. Environmental Protection Agency*, 549 U.S. 497 (2007).
48. Rep. Rick Boucher, remarks at the Society of Environmental Journalists annual conference, Roanoke, Va., Oct. 17, 2008.
49. "Governor Paterson Hails Nation's First Global Warming Cap and Trade Auction A Success," Sept. 29, 2008, www.ny.gov/governor/press/press_0929083.html.
50. For details see www.westernclimateinitiative.org/.
51. Robert N. Stavins and Joseph Aldy, "Bali Climate Change Conference: Key Takeaways," Harvard Project on International Climate Agreements, Dec. 18, 2007, http://belfercenter.ksg.harvard.edu/publication/17781/bali_climate_change_conference.html.
52. Daniel Howden and Geoffrey Lean, "Bali Conference: World Unity Forces U.S. to Back Climate Deal," *The Independent*, Dec. 16, 2007, www.independent.co.uk/environment/climate-change/bali-conference-world-unity-forces-us-to-back-climate-deal-765583.html; Gary LaMoshi, "Bumpy Ride Ahead for Bali Road Map," *Asia Times*, Dec. 18, 2007, www.atimes.com/atimes/Southeast_Asia/IL18Ae01.html.
53. Ian Traynor and David Gow, "EU Promises 20% Reduction in Carbon Emissions by 2020," *The Guardian*, Feb. 21, 2007, www.guardian.co.uk/environment/2007/feb/21/climatechange.climatechangeenvironment; Pete Harrison and Gerard Wynn, "EU Lawmakers Watch Credit Crisis in Climate Fight," Reuters, Oct. 7, 2008.
54. Stefan Lovgren, "Costa Rica Aims to Be 1st Carbon-Neutral Country," *National Geographic News*, March 7, 2008, http://news.nationalgeographic.com/news/2008/03/080307-costa-rica.html.
55. "Fighting Climate Change, . . ." *op. cit.*, pp. 27-28.
56. " 'Redd'-Letter Day for Forests: United Nations, Norway United to Combat Climate Change from Deforestation, Spearheading New Programme," U.N. press release, Sept. 24, 2008.
57. Pete Harrison and Gerard Wynn, "EU Lawmakers Watch Credit Crisis in Climate Fight," Reuters, Oct. 7, 2008, www.reuters.com/article/rbssIndustryMaterialsUtilitiesNews/idUSL711408420081007?sp=true; Dina Cappiello, "Economic Woes Chill Effort to Stop Global Warming," The Associated Press, Oct. 12, 2008, http://ap.google.com/article/ALeqM5jFaQmoLWbpKq8HH1AAQ5GoGZjz0gD93OTVC00; James Kanter, "Europe's Leadership in Carbon Control at Risk in Credit Crisis," *The New York Times*, Oct. 21, 2008, p. B10.
58. Juliette Jowit and Patrick Wintour, "Cost of Tackling Global Climate Change Has Doubled, Warns Stern," *The Guardian*, June 26, 2008, www.guardian.co.uk/environment/2008/jun/26/climatechange.scienceofclimatechange; Jeffrey D. Sachs, *Common Wealth: Economics for a Crowded Planet* (2008), pp. 308-311.
59. David Roland-Holst, "Energy Efficiency, Innovation, and Job Creation in California," Center for Energy, Resources and Economic Sustainability, University of California, Berkeley, October 2008.
60. Kevin Watkins, "Bali's Double Standards," *The Guardian*, Dec. 14, 2007, www.guardian.co.uk/commentisfree/2007/dec/14/comment.bali.
61. Niall Ferguson, "Dollar Diplomacy: How Much Did the Marshall Plan Really Matter?" *The New Yorker*, Aug. 27, 2007, p. 81.
62. "A Conversation with Nobel Prize Winner Rajendra Pachauri," *op. cit.*

BIBLIOGRAPHY

Books

Krupp, Fred, and Miriam Horn, *Earth: The Sequel*, *Norton*, 2008.
The president and senior staff writer, respectively, at the U.S.-based Environmental Defense Fund describe innovators who are leading a clean-energy revolution and argue that the United States should adopt a carbon cap-and-trade system to boost investments in innovative energy technologies.

Northcott, Michael S., *A Moral Climate: The Ethics of Global Warming*, *Orbis*, 2007.
An Episcopal priest and divinity professor at the University of Edinburgh views climate change as an ethical issue and criticizes carbon trading as biased toward rich countries and large greenhouse gas emitters.

Tietenberg, Thomas H., *Emissions Trading: Principles and Practice*, 2nd edition, *Resources for the Future*, 2006.
An environmental economist shows how emissions trading became popular as an alternative to command-and-control regulation and assesses successes, failures and lessons learned in 25 years of application.

Zedillo, Ernesto, ed., *Global Warming: Looking Beyond Kyoto*, *Brookings*, 2008.
Authors from around the globe examine how to structure a post-Kyoto climate change agreement that can reduce emissions quickly enough to avert disastrous warming.

Articles

"C is for Unclean," *Down to Earth*, Dec. 15, 2007.
A critique of the Clean Development Mechanism (CDM) by India's Centre for Science and Environment argues that the program has been taken over by carbon entrepreneurs and turned into a financial tool instead of fighting climate change.

"First Africa Carbon Forum Fosters Clean Climate Projects," *Environment News Service*, Sept. 4, 2008.
Only a fraction of CDM projects are in Africa, but African leaders and international development officials want to increase the continent's share.

Arrandale, Tom, "Carbon Goes to Market," *Governing*, September 2008, p. 26.
As Congress debates cap-and-trade policies, nearly half the states are working on their own carbon trading schemes.

Scott, Mark, "Giant Steps for Carbon Trading in Europe," *Business Week*, Jan. 23, 2008.
The EU Emissions Trading Scheme is setting stringent, new targets, which will make carbon credits more valuable.

Szabo, Michael, "Problems Plague Canada's Emissions Trading Plans," *Reuters*, May 8, 2008.
Canada wants to start carbon trading, but some of its provinces have already adopted their own schemes, and emissions from the Canadian oil industry are rising.

Turner, Chris, "The Carbon Cleansers," *Canadian Geographic Magazine*, October 2008, p. 3.
Norway's carbon tax on the oil and gas industry, adopted in 1992, has spurred research into cleaner energy technologies, as well as carbon capture and storage.

Reports and Studies

"Carbon 2008," *Point Carbon*, March 11, 2008, www.pointcarbon.com/polopoly_fs/1.912721!Carbon_2008_dfgrt.pdf.
An international market research firm focusing on carbon markets provides an overview of global carbon trading and major carbon policy trends.

"Fighting Climate Change: Human Solidarity in a Developed World," *Human Development Report 2007/2008*, 2008, *United Nations Development Programme*, http://hdr.undp.org/en/media/hdr_20072008_en_complete.pdf.
Climate change is a major threat to human development and is already undercutting global efforts to reduce poverty in some parts of the world. This report calls for urgent action on a post-Kyoto agreement and policies to help poor countries adapt to unavoidable climate change impacts.

Ellerman, A. Denny, and Paul Joskow, "The European Union's Emissions Trading System in Perspective," *Pew Center on Global Climate Change*, May 2008,

www.pewclimate.org/docUploads/EU-ETS-In-Perspective-Report.pdf.
Two economists from the Massachusetts Institute of Technology conclude that the EU ETS is still a work in progress but has successfully set a European price for carbon emissions and offers important lessons for U.S. leaders as they debate cap-and-trade policies.

Wara, Michael W., and David G. Victor, "A Realistic Policy on International Carbon Offsets," ***Working Paper #74, Program on Energy and Sustainable Development, Stanford University*****, April 2008, http://iis-db.stanford.edu/pubs/22157/WP74_final_final.pdf.**
Two Stanford University law professors recommend major reforms to the Kyoto Protocol's Clean Development Mechanism, which they say awards credits for projects that don't really reduce emissions, and argue the United States should not rely on offsets to lower the cost of reducing carbon emissions.

For More Information

Centre for Science and Environment, 41 Tughlakabad Institutional Area, New Delhi, India; (+91)-11-29955124; www.cseindia.org. An independent public interest organization that works to increase awareness of science, technology, environment and development issues.

China Sustainable Energy Program, The Energy Foundation, CITIC Building, Room 2403, No. 19, Jianguomenwai Dajie, Beijing, 100004, P.R. China; (+86)-10-8526-2422; www.efchina.org. A joint initiative funded by U.S. foundations to support China's policy efforts to promote energy efficiency and renewable energy.

The Gold Standard, 22 Baumleingasse, CH-4051, Basel, Switzerland; (+41)-0-61-283-0916; www.cdmgoldstandard.org. A nonprofit that screens carbon offset projects and certifies initiatives that provide measurable economic, environmental and social benefits.

Institute for Sustainable Futures, University of Technology, L11, 235 Jones St., Broadway, Sydney, Australia; (+61)-2-9514-4590; www.isf.uts.edu.au. Research institute that works with Australian businesses and communities to promote sustainable environmental and design policies.

Intergovernmental Panel on Climate Change, 7bis Ave. de la Paix, C.P. 2300, CH-1211 Geneva 2, Switzerland; (+41)-22-730-8208; www.ipcc.ch. A U.N.-sponsored organization created to advise national governments on climate change science.

Regional Greenhouse Gas Initiative, 90 Church St., 4th Floor, New York, NY 10007; (212) 417-7327; www.rggi.org. A joint venture launched in 2008 by 10 Northeastern states to reduce greenhouse gas emissions from the electric power sector through carbon emissions trading.

U.N. Development Programme, One United Nations Plaza, New York, NY 10017; (212) 906-5000; www.undp.org. Works to cut poverty and use aid effectively.

World Wildlife Fund — UK, Panda House, Weyside Park, Godalming, Surrey GU7 1XR, United Kingdom; (+01)-483-426444; www.wwf.org.uk. The British arm of an international conservation organization.

8

Looming Water Crisis

Is the World Running Out of Water?

Peter Behr

AFP/Getty Images/Simon Maina

Kenyan children play in raw sewage in Kibera, Nairobi's largest slum. Each year 1.8 million children — 5,000 a day — die from waterborne illnesses due to a lack of access to sanitation and clean water.

From *CQ Global Researcher*, February 2008.

As 2007 came to a close, the steady drumbeat of headlines about China's worst drought in a half-century affirmed Prime Minister Wen Jiabao's earlier warning that the crisis threatens "the survival of the Chinese nation."[1]

The alarming developments included:

- The drying up of 133 reservoirs in burgeoning Guangdong Province, leaving a quarter of a million people facing water shortages.[2]
- The lowest levels since 1866 on portions of the Yangtze River, restricting barge and ship traffic and reducing hydroelectric output on China's largest river, even as pollution from 9,000 industrial plants along its course jeopardizes drinking water supplies.[3]
- Near-record low levels in vast Lake Poyang, restricting water supplies for 100,000 people.[4]

"My house used to be by the side of the lake," villager Yu Wenchang told the Xinhua News Agency. "Now I have to go over a dozen kilometers away to get to the lake water."[5]

Similar woes are being reported across the globe, as one of the worst decades of drought on record afflicts rich and poor nations alike. While scientists hedge their conclusions about whether long-term climate change is causing the dry spell, many warn that Earth's gradual warming trend unquestionably poses a growing threat to water supplies and food production in arid regions. Already, population growth and economic expansion are straining water supplies in many places, particularly in the poorest nations. But despite an unending series of

Serious Shortages Projected for Many Regions

Water shortages are expected to afflict much of the Earth by 2025, as growing populations use vastly more water for daily life and farming. Areas likely to be hardest hit include China, Western Europe, the United States, Mexico and a wide swath of the globe's midsection from India to North Africa. In the most severe cases, humans are expected to use up to 40 percent of the available water, compared with the current average withdrawal, or use, rate of 10 percent.

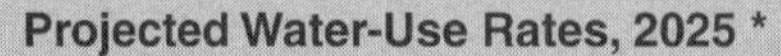

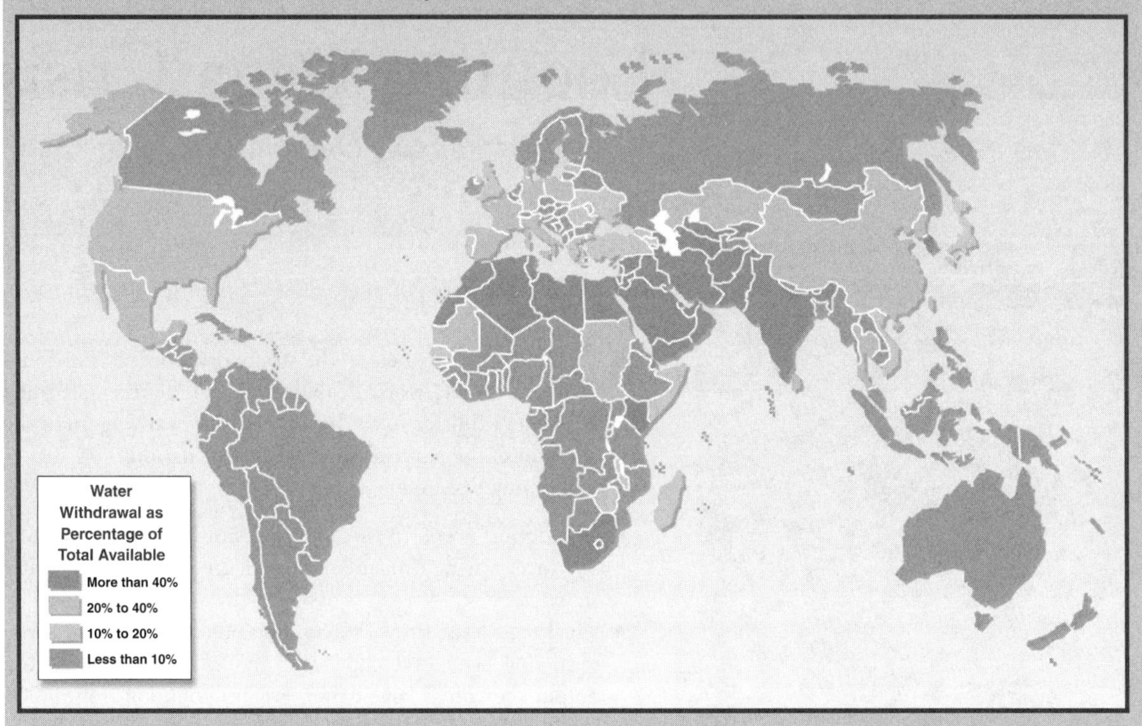

* Based on data from 1996-2000

Source: World Meteorological Organisation, Global Environment Outlook, U.N. Environment Programme, Earthscan, www.unep.org/dewa/assessments/ecosystems/water/vitalwater/21.htm#21b

international water conferences — attended by thousands of experts — no consensus has emerged on how to make adequate clean water available to all people in affordable, environmentally sustainable ways.[6]

A fifth of the world's population — 1.2 billion people — live in areas experiencing "physical water scarcity," or insufficient supplies for everyone's demands, according to a 2006 study by the International Water Management Institute that draws on the work of 700 scientists and experts. Another 1 billion face "economic scarcity," in which "human capacity or financial resources" cannot provide adequate water, the report found.[7]

While drought and expanding populations visibly affect the world's lakes and rivers, a less-visible problem also threatens water supplies. Accelerated pumping of groundwater for irrigation is depleting underground aquifers faster than they can be refreshed in densely populated areas of North China, India and Mexico. And land and water resources there and beyond are being degraded through erosion, pollution, salination, nutrient depletion and seawater intrusion, according to the institute.

A United Nations task force on water predicted that by 2025, 3 billion people will face "water stress" conditions, lacking enough water to meet all human and environmental needs.[8] By that time, there will be 63 major river basins with populations of at least 10 million, of which 47 are either already water-stressed, will become stressed or will experience a significant deterioration in water supply, according to a separate study by the World Resources Institute incorporating the U.N. data.[9] (*See map, p. 200.*)*

As water depletion accelerates, drought is undermining nature's capacity to replenish this essential resource, punishing the planet's midsection — from eastern Australia and northern China through the Middle East and sub-Saharan Africa to the U.S. Sun Belt, the Great Plains and northern Mexico.

In the United States, chronic alarms over depleted water resources in the Southwestern states have spread to the Southeast. The water level in giant Lake Sidney Lanier outside Atlanta has dropped about a dozen feet in this decade, causing an intense struggle among Georgia and neighboring Alabama and Florida over rights to the lake's diminished flows.[10]

And drought conditions worldwide are likely to worsen as the effects of climate change are felt, many scientists warn.[11] Climate change is expected to expand and intensify drought in traditionally dry regions and disrupt water flows from the world's mountain snowcaps and glaciers.

Finally, a new threat to global water supplies has emerged: terrorism. "The chance that terrorists will strike at water systems is real," said Peter H. Gleick, president of the Pacific Institute for Studies in Development, Environment and Security in Oakland, Calif.[12] Modern public water systems are designed to protect users from biological agents and toxins, but deliberate contamination by terrorists could kill or sicken thousands, he said. Since the Sept. 11, 2001, terrorist attacks most major U.S. cities have sent the federal government confidential reports on the vulnerability of local water supplies, and the Environmental Protection Agency's (EPA) Water Sentinel Initiative is designing a water-contamination warning system.[13]

Perhaps the grimmest long-range prediction on water availability was issued by the Met Office Hadley Centre for Climate Prediction and Research in London. Using

* "Water stress" occurs when less than 1,700 cubic meters (448,000 gallons) per person of new fresh water is available annually from rainfall or aquifers for human use, making populations vulnerable to frequent interruptions in water supply.

World Water Consumption Varies

The average American uses nearly 160 gallons of water per day for drinking, cooking, bathing and sanitation — more than any other nationality and more than twice the amount used by many Europeans. People in sub-Saharan Africa use only about a quarter of the 13 gallons the United Nations sets as a minimum basic standard.

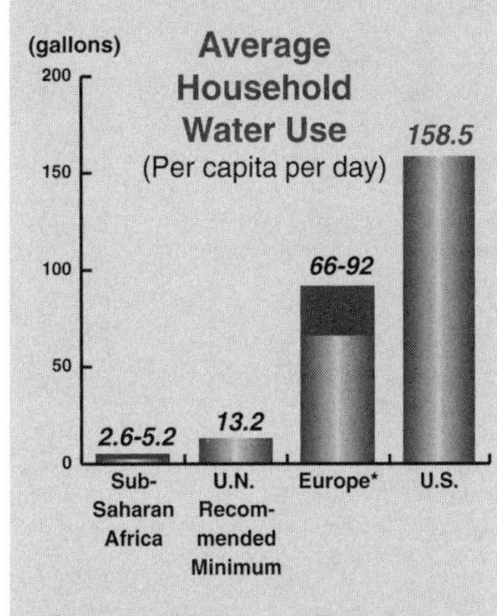

* Consumption among European countries ranges from 66-92 gallons

Source: World Water Council

supercomputer modeling, the center projected that if current trends continue, by this century's end drought will have spread across half the Earth's land surface due to climate change, threatening millions of lives. Moreover, "extreme drought" — which makes traditional agriculture virtually impossible — will affect about a third of the planet, according to the group's November 2006 report.

"Even though (globally) total rainfall will increase as the climate warms, the proportion of land in drought is projected to rise throughout the 21st century," the report said.[14]

"There's almost no aspect of life in the developing countries that these predictions don't undermine — the ability to grow food, the ability to have a safe sanitation system, the availability of water," said Andrew Simms, policy director of the liberal London-based New Economics Foundation.[15] The consequences will be most

Poorest Lag Far Behind in Access

Although progress has been made since 1990, only 37 percent of the residents in sub-Saharan Africa and South Asia had access to sanitation services in 2004. Sub-Saharan Africa lags behind the rest of the world in access to reliable sources of clean water. Meanwhile, more than 90 percent of those living in the industrialized countries, Central and Eastern Europe, Latin America, the Caribbean and the former Soviet republics had access to water in 2004.

Percentage of Population with Access to:
(1990-2004)

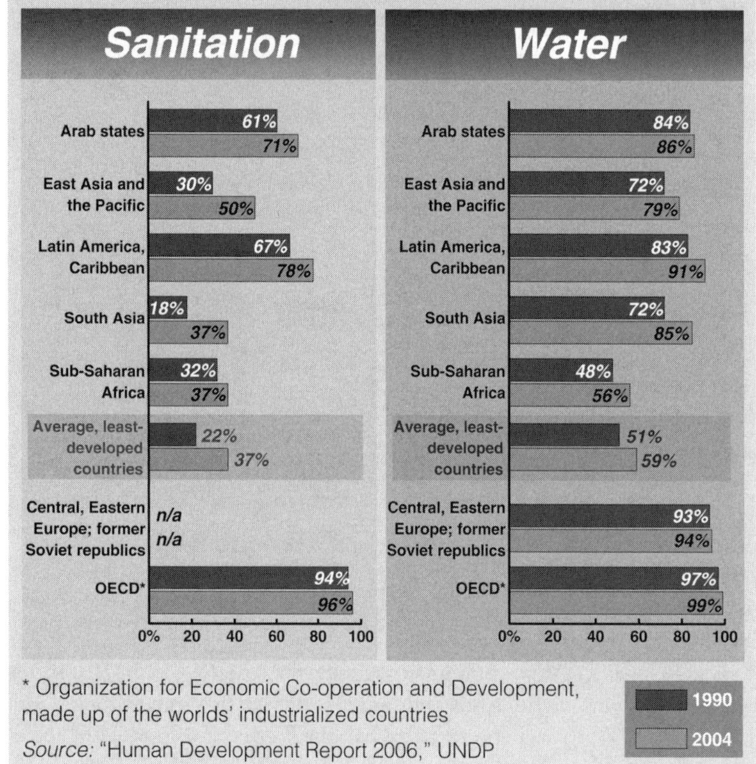

* Organization for Economic Co-operation and Development, made up of the worlds' industrialized countries

Source: "Human Development Report 2006," UNDP

dire for the planet's poorest inhabitants, he added. "For hundreds of millions of people for whom getting through the day is already a struggle, this is going to push them over the precipice."

Access to safe, fresh water separates the well-off — who can treat water as if it were air — from the world's poorest, who hoard it like gold. In the United States, the average consumer uses nearly 160 gallons of water per day, summoned by the twist of a faucet. In much of Africa, women often trudge for hours to and from wells, carrying the two to five gallons per person used by the typical person in sub-Saharan Africa. (*See graph, p. 201.*)[16]

But the lack of clean water is not only inconvenient. It can also be deadly. Each year 1.8 million children — 5,000 per day — die from waterborne illnesses such as diarrhea, according to the United Nations. "That's equivalent to 12 full jumbo jets crashing every day," said U.N. water expert Brian Appleton. "If 12 full jumbo jets were crashing every day, the world would want to do something about it — they would want to find out why it was happening."[17]

Policymakers are trying various ways to solve the global water challenge, including contracting with private firms to operate urban water and sanitary systems, adopting new conservation technologies, enacting multination pacts to manage regional watersheds and increasing funds for water projects in the world's poorest regions. Water experts advocate "environmental flow" policies — the release of enough water from dams to sustain the environment of rivers, wetlands and underground aquifers.[18]

And their efforts seem to be paying off — at least in some areas. Between 1990 and 2002, more than 1 billion people in the developing world gained access to fresh water and basic sanitation. But because of population growth, the total number of people still lacking safe water remained more than a billion, and there was no change in the number lacking basic sanitation.[19]

In 2003, the U.N. General Assembly designated the period from 2005 to 2015 as the International Decade for Action on "Water for Life." And the U.N.'s new Millennium Development Goals include a campaign to cut in half by 2015 the proportion of people without sustainable access to safe drinking water and basic sanitation — at a cost of more than $10 billion per year.[20] Currently, governments and international agencies like the U.N. and World Bank provide only $4 billion a year in aid for water and sanitation projects.[21]

"We will see these issues play out silently: dry rivers, dead deltas, destocked fisheries, depleted springs and wells," wrote Margaret Carley-Carlson, chairwoman of the Global Water Partnership in Stockholm, and M. S. Swaminathan, president of the Pugwash Conferences on Science and World Affairs in Chennai, India.[22] "We will also see famine; increased and sometimes violent competition for water, especially within states; more migration; and environmental devastation with fires, dust, and new plagues and blights."

Averting that future will require fundamental changes in governmental policies and human practices governing the use, conservation and value of water, experts agree.

As water experts and policymakers discuss how to conserve and protect future water supplies, here are some of the questions they are debating:

Are we running out of water?

Amid the growing alarm about water shortages, water expert Frank Rijsberman offers a contrarian perspective. "The world is far from running out of water," he says. "There is land and human resources and water enough to grow food and provide drinking water for everyone."[23]

The issue is how efficiently water is used, says Rijsberman, former director of the International Water Management Institute in Colombo, Sri Lanka. Every year, about 110,000 cubic kilometers* of rain falls on Earth's surface, of which humans withdraw just over 3 percent — about 3,700 cubic kilometers — from rivers and groundwater to use in cities, industries and farming. About 40,000 cubic kilometers flows into rivers and is absorbed into groundwater, and the rest evaporates.

Much of the water used by humans is returned to watersheds as wastewater, farm runoff or discharges from energy and industrial plants, with only a small fraction used for drinking and cooking.[24] Irrigation claims 70 percent of total water withdrawals, 22 percent is used by industry and the rest goes for homes, personal and municipal uses.[25]

AP Photo/Xinhua, He Fenglun

Dead plants in a parched field attest to the ravages of the worldwide drought in Liujiang, a county of southwest China's Guangxi Zhuang Autonomous Region, in November 2006. Nearly all of the region's 84 counties were affected by the drought, which was caused by unseasonably warm temperatures, according to the Xinhua News Agency.

Water isn't running out everywhere, said Canadian journalist Marq de Villiers, author of *Water: The Fate of Our Most Precious Resource.* "It's only running out in places where it's needed most. It's an allocation, supply and management problem."[26]

It's also a demand problem: Over the past half-century, millions of people have migrated from colder, wetter, northern climates to warmer, drier, southern locales such as the American Southwest or southern France, putting new pressure on those expanding "Sun Belt" communities to build irrigation systems, tap into groundwater supplies or rechannel large amounts of river water.

Experts agree that the world should not be facing an overall water-scarcity crisis. But water supplies in much of Africa, parts of China, southern Europe, northern Mexico and the American Southwest and high plains aren't meeting demand, and climate change may be accelerating the problem, the experts say.[27] The issues

---

* 1 cubic kilometer would cover an area of about 810,000 acres with one foot of water.

Is Access to Clean Water a Human Right?

The question is at the heart of a global debate.

Should all humans have guaranteed access to clean water, or is water an increasingly scarce commodity that should be priced according to its value?

The question stands at the center of a global debate over threats to the world's water resources, as competition for water increases among industry, farming and households. It is also critical in efforts to protect the long-term environmental viability of rivers, lakes and aquifers.

The debate goes back at least to 1992, when an international commission on water and the environment meeting in Ireland issued the "Dublin Principles," which were later adopted by a U.N. panel. The commission concluded: "Water has an economic value . . . and should be recognized as an economic good." Only by recognizing that economic value can water "be properly conserved and allocated to its most important uses."[1]

But the principle also declared it a "basic right of all human beings to have access to clean water and sanitation at an affordable price." Poor households cannot compete with industry for scarce water supplies. Nor could most farmers, who typically receive subsidized prices for irrigation water.

The U.N. Committee on Economic, Social, and Cultural Rights declared in 2002 that all people are entitled to an essential minimum amount of clean water. "Water is fundamental for life and health," it said. "The human right to water is indispensable for leading a healthy life in human dignity."[2]

Canadian activist Maude Barlow says, "You can't really charge for a human right; you can't trade it or deny it to someone because they don't have money." Barlow is co-author of *Blue Gold: The Battle Against Corporate Theft of the World's Water.*[3]

The other side in the debate argues that until water is priced and valued as a scarce resource it will be wasted and billions of dollars required annually to extend water service to the poor and fix leaking water systems will not be forthcoming. Two years before the U.N. declared clean water a human right, the World Water Council — which reflects the views of international lenders and the water-supply industry — called for "full pricing" of water to reflect its "economic, social, environmental and cultural values."[4]

Farmers in dry regions throughout the world get water at preferential rates — or at no charge at all — as a matter of government policy. But if farmers were required to pay the full price for water, they could not compete with industry, which would be willing and able to pay market price.

In industrial countries, 60 percent of the water withdrawn from freshwater sources is used by industry, mainly to generate electricity. The developing world is moving rapidly in the same direction. China's industrial water use, for example, is projected to grow fivefold by 2030.[5]

add up to what the World Commission on Water calls the "gloomy arithmetic of water."[28]

In addition, man has transformed most of the world's great rivers. For example, the Danube — Central Europe's "lifeline" — has been dredged, deepened, straightened, channelized and obstructed by dams and fishing weirs. It is now "a manufactured waterway," says de Villiers, with more than a third of its volume withdrawn for human use, compared to an average of about 10 percent for other rivers.[29]

Pollution is also reducing the world's supply of potable water. In Asia, many rivers "are dead or dying," according to Rijsberman. The Musi River near India's Hyderabad technology center has become "a dwindling black wastewater stream," he writes. "[Y]et the cows that produce the curd and the dairy products for Hyderabad are bathing in that black and stinking water."[30] In China, 265 billion gallons of raw sewage is dumped into the Yangtze River every year.[31]

The depletion and despoiling of the world's reservoirs, rivers and watersheds also contribute to the problem. During the 20th century, more than half the wetlands in parts of Australia, Europe, New Zealand and North America were destroyed by population growth and development. The loss of wetlands increases water runoff, which exacerbates flooding, reduces the replenishment of aquifers and leaves rivers and lakes more vulnerable to pollution.[32]

Aquifers — the immense storehouses of water found beneath the Earth's surface — are the largest and fastest-growing source of irrigation water. Depleting those

"As urban centers and industry increase their demand for water, agriculture is losing out," said the U.N. "Human Development Report 2006."[6]

And the world's poor cannot compete with either farmers or business for water at market prices, said the report. About a third of those without access to clean water live on less than $1 a day. Twice that many live on less than $2 a day. "These figures imply that 660 million people lacking access to [safe] water have, at best, a limited capacity to pay more than a small amount for a connection to water service," the report said. "People might lack water because they are poor, or they might be poor because they lack water." The end result is the same: a limited ability to pay for water.[7]

American water expert Peter H. Gleick calls for a truce in the water rights dispute in favor of problem-solving. Workshops on privatization standards and principles for implementing a human right to water "would be far more likely to produce progress," he writes.[8]

AP Photo/Julie Plasencia

A man protesting the privatization of water in Cochabamba, Bolivia, waves a sign saying "what is ours is ours and it cannot be taken away."

---

1 "Dublin Statements and Principles," Global Water Partnership; www.gwpforum.org/servlet/PSP?iNodeID=1345.

2 Meena Palaniappan, *et al.*, "Environmental Justice and Water," *The World's Water 2006-2007*, p. 117.

3 Jeff Fleischer, "Interview with Maude Barlow," *Mother Jones*, Jan. 14, 2005, www.motherjones.com/news/qa/2005/01/maude_barlow.html.

4 "Ministerial Declaration of The Hague," World Water Forum, March 22, 2000.

5 Palaniappan, *op. cit.*, p. 125.

6 See "Summary, Human Development Report 2006: Beyond scarcity: Power, poverty and the global water crisis," United Nations Development Programme, p. 17, http://hdr.undp.org/en/media/hdr2006_english_summary.pdf.

7 *Ibid.*, pp. 49-52.

8 Peter Gleick, "Time to Rethink Large International Water Meetings," *The World's Water 2006-2007*, p. 182.

---

underground rivers will have deleterious effects on the 40 percent of the planet's agricultural output that relies on irrigation from groundwater.[33] Experts say some of that water — which dates back to past ice ages — would take eons to refresh but is being consumed in less than a century.

"Large areas of China, South Asia and the Middle East are now maintaining irrigation through unsustainable mining of groundwater or over-extraction from rivers," said the U.N. "Human Development Report 2006."[34] The problem is widespread in Mexico, India and Russia, as well, although precise data are not available for many countries.[35]

In his seminal 1986 book *Cadillac Desert*, the late Marc Reisner warned about the long-term effects of water policies in the Western United States, including the depletion of the giant Ogallala Aquifer, which runs southward from South Dakota to Texas. It has two distinctions, he wrote, "one of being the largest discrete aquifer in the world, the other of being the fastest-disappearing aquifer in the world."[36]

In the 1930s a farmer on the Great Plains could raise a few gallons per minute from the Ogallala, using a windmill-driven pump. After the New Deal brought electricity to the region and oil and gas discoveries provided plenty of cheap fuel, electric pumps raised 800 gallons per minute.

"All of a sudden, irrigation became very energy- and labor-efficient. You turn on the switch and let it run," says Robert M. Hirsch, associate director for water at the

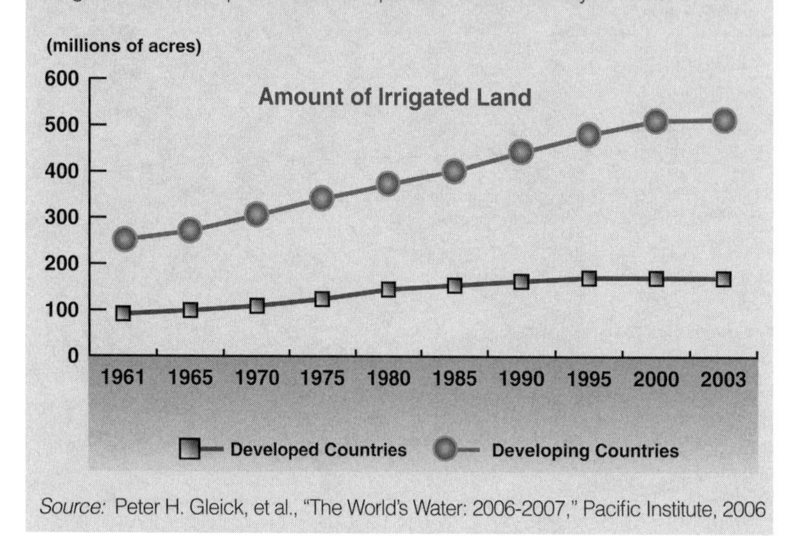

Source: Peter H. Gleick, et al., "The World's Water: 2006-2007," Pacific Institute, 2006

U.S. Geological Survey. "There was an explosion of irrigated agriculture, particularly on the high plains, and in California."

In 1937, West Texas had 1,116 irrigation wells. Thirty years later it had 27,983. By 1977, Texas was withdrawing 11 billion gallons of groundwater a day to grow corn, cotton and other crops in what once had been part of the Great American Desert, Reisner wrote.[37]

Now, experts say the Ogallala — a resource that could have lasted hundreds of years — will be virtually depleted within the lifetimes of today's farmers.

Yet during the optimism and opportunism that characterized development of the modern American West, worries about future water supplies evaporated. "What are you going to do with all that water?" the late Felix Sparks, former head of the Colorado Water Conservation Board, asked in the mid-1980s. "When we use it up, we'll just have to get water from somewhere else." But today, "somewhere else" is not an answer, say authors Robin Clarke, editor of climate publications for the United Nations and World Meteorologal Organization, and environmental author Jannet King. The co-authors of *The Water Atlas* insist water must be considered a finite resource.[38]

Should water be privatized?

In 2000, street fighting broke out between government forces and political activists, rural cocoa farmers and residents of shantytowns on the hilly outskirts of Cochabamba — Bolivia's third-largest city. The dispute was over privatization of the city's water supplies.

The year before, Cochabamba had turned its water and sanitation system over to Aguas del Tunari, a coalition of multinational and Bolivian water and engineering corporations whose biggest stakeholder was Bechtel Corp., based in San Francisco.[39] This was the high-water mark of a global, pro-market movement toward deregulation and privatization of state-owned monopolies in water, electricity and other services.[40] The World Bank and other international lenders had been supporting privatization strategies in hopes that investments and better management by private industry would help bring water and sanitation to more than a billion poor people whose governments couldn't or wouldn't do the job.

But Cochabamba's privatization included a costly dam and pipeline to import more water, which required sharp rate increases starting at 35 percent. Some customers' water bills doubled. Farmers outside the city, who had enjoyed free water, suddenly had to pay. The city erupted in protest, the water company's officials fled and their contract was rescinded.[41] The government reclaimed the water operations, and Cochabamba became a rallying cry against privatization and globalization for the political left.

Elsewhere, however, corporate involvement in water and sanitation system operations has not ceased. Veolia Water, a subsidiary of the French firm Veolia Environment SA — the world's largest water-services firm —signed a $3.8 billion, 30-year contract in 2007 to supply drinking water to 3 million residents of the Chinese river port city of Tianjin. Since 1997, Veolia has signed more than 20 water and sanitation contracts in China, and supplies more than 110 million people in 57 countries worldwide.[42]

These projects, and smaller-scale versions in poorer nations, suggest that while the inflamed debate over water privatization continues, threats of water scarcity and climate change may help accelerate the search for private-sector support.

The percentage of the world's population served at some level by private firms has grown from 5 percent in 1999 to 11 percent — or 707 million people — in 2007, according to *Pinsent Masons Water Yearbook*, a widely consulted summary of private-sector water projects.[43]

Opponents of privatization argue that safe drinking water and adequate sanitation are essential human rights, obligating governments to provide them at affordable rates or free if necessary. "If it's a human need, it can be delivered by the private sector on a for-profit basis. If it's a human right, that's different," says Canadian anti-globalization activist Maude Barlow, co-author of *Blue Gold: The Battle Against Corporate Theft of the World's Water.* "You can't really charge for a human right; you can't trade it or deny it to someone because they don't have money."[44]

Bringing in private firms to run water and sewer operations does not make the services more efficient or affordable, opponents also argue, but forces the poor to pay for corporate profits, shareholder dividends and high executive salaries. "The efficiencies don't happen," asserts Wenonah Hauter, executive director of Food and Water Watch, a Washington anti-globalization group. "The companies simply lay off staff members until they don't have enough people to take care of the infrastructure. And they raise rates. We've seen this all over the world." Last year Hauter's organization issued a study claiming privatized water operations in California, Illinois, Wisconsin and New York charged more for water than comparable publicly owned systems.[45]

Privatization advocates dispute Hauter's claims, and facts to settle the issue are illusive. A 2005 survey by the AEI-Brookings Center for Regulatory Studies found "no systematic empirical evidence comparing public and private water systems in the United States."[46]

A study by the Inter-American Development Bank of water rates in Colombia said prices charged by privatized systems were not significantly different from those charged by public systems.[47] And privatization appears to have improved water quality in urban areas but not in rural communities, said the study. After privatization began, water bills for the poor rose about 10 percent but declined for the wealthy, reflecting a scaling back in government subsidies to poorer consumers. Similar shifts occurred in both privatized and non-privatized cities.[48]

In central cities, water-rate subsidies tend to favor the wealthy and middle classes, who are usually connected to municipal water systems, while the poor often are not, says American journalist Diane Raines Ward, author of *Water Wars: Drought, Flood, Folly, and the Politics of Thirst.* And by keeping water rates artificially low, utilities typically collect only about a third of their actual costs, so they don't raise enough money to expand pipelines to unserved poor neighborhoods, she says.[49]

The rural poor or those living in urban slums often must haul water home from public wells or buy it from independent merchants — delivered by truck or burro — at much higher prices. In Cairo, Egypt, for instance, the poor pay 40 times the real cost of delivery; in Karachi, Pakistan, the figure is 83 times; and in parts of Haiti, 100 times, Ward says.

In the years since Cochabamba galvanized the left against privatizing water, privatization has declined in Latin America and sub-Saharan Africa but increased in Europe and Asia, according to the *Water Yearbook.*[50] The average contract size also has diminished since the 1990s, it said, due to a trend away from mega-contracts with multinational water companies in favor of "local and possibly less contentious contracts."[51]

A U.N.-sponsored analysis cites Chile and parts of Colombia among the successful examples of collaborative water and sanitation services. In Cartagena, Colombia's fifth-largest city, the local government retains control of the pipes and facilities and raises investment capital, but a private firm runs the service. Today, nearly all the city's residents have water in their homes, up from only one-quarter in 1995.[52] Chile's water program offers subsidies to the poorest households, guaranteeing an essential minimum of supply of up to 4,000 gallons per month. Deliveries are monitored to limit cheating, and every household must have a water meter to verify usage.[53]

Experts say the political problems of water privatization cannot be managed without effective government regulation and consumer involvement at all levels. Both elements were missing in Cochabamba but are present in Chile, the U.N. report says.[54]

AP Photo/Peter Lorimer

The outlook is bleak for rancher Andrew Higham's parched land in Gunnedah, in northwestern New South Wales, Australia, in October 2006. Scarce winter rains caused drought across much of the continent last fall and led to severely reduced wheat and barley harvests.

Will water scarcity lead to conflicts?

In 1995 Ismail Serageldin, a World Bank vice president, predicted that "the wars of the next century will be over water."[55]

The reality has been different thus far. "Water resources are rarely the sole source of conflict, and indeed, water is frequently a source of cooperation," writes Gleick, of the Pacific Institute for Studies in Development, Environment and Security, in the new edition of *The World's Water 2006-2007.* [56] The survey of reported conflicts over water in the past 50 years, compiled by Oregon State University researchers, found 37 cases of violence between nations, all but seven in the Middle East.[57]

In 1964, Israel opened its massive National Water Carrier canal to carry water from the Sea of Galilee and the Jordan River to its farms and cities. Syria retaliated to maintain its access to the Jordan by starting two canals to divert Jordan flows for its uses. Skirmishes by military units and raids by the newly established al-Fatah forces escalated until Israeli air strikes halted the diversion projects. By then, Israel and the Arab League were on the road to the Six-Day War of 1967.[58]

"The attacks by Syria, Egypt, and Jordan that eventually followed had many causes, but water remained a priority for both sides," says author Ward.[59]

Still, more than 200 water treaties have been negotiated peacefully over the past half-century. The Partition of India in 1947, for instance, could have led to war between India and newly created Pakistan over control of the mighty Indus River basin. Instead, the two nations were brought together with World Bank support over a perilous decade of negotiations, signing the Indus Water Treaty in 1960. Three rivers were given to Pakistan, and three to India, with a stream of international financial support for dams and canals in both countries. Even when war raged between the two nations in later years, they never attacked water infrastructure.[60]

"Most peoples and even nations are hesitant to deny life's most basic necessity to others," Ward wrote. Two modern exceptions occurred during the Bosnian War (1992-1996), when Serbs "lay waiting to shoot men, women and children arriving at riverbanks or taps around Sarajevo carrying buckets or bottles," and during Saddam Hussein's regime in Iraq, when he diverted the lower waters of the Tigris and Euphrates rivers to destroy the homes and livelihood of the Marsh Arabs.[61]

Except for such instances, cooperation over water resources is common today, even if sometimes grudging and incomplete, says Undala Alam, a professor and specialist in water diplomacy at Britain's Cranfield University. "Turkey was releasing water for Syria and Iraq; the Nile countries are preparing projects jointly to develop the river; the Niger countries have a shared vision for the basin's development, and the Zambezi countries are working within the Southern African Development Community," she notes.[62]

But analysts warn that growing stress on water supplies, coupled with the impact of climate change, will create combustible conditions in the coming years that will undermine collaboration over water.

There is plenty of precedence for the concern, notes Gleick, who describes the history of violence over fresh water as "long and distressing."[63] The latest volume of *The World's Water* lists 22 pages of historical water conflicts — beginning in about 1700 B.C. with the Sumerians' efforts to dam the Tigris River to block retreating rebels.

In the future, climate change is expected to extend and intensify drought in Earth's driest regions and disrupt normal water flows from mountain snowcaps in Europe, North America and Central Asia. "Climate change has the potential to exacerbate tensions over water as precipitation patterns change, declining by as much as 60 percent in some areas," warned a recent report by a panel of retired U.S. generals and admirals convened by CNA, a think tank with longstanding ties to the military. "The potential for escalating tensions, economic disruption and armed conflict is great," said the report, "National Security and the Threat of Climate Change."[64]

On the simplest level, the report said, climate change "has the potential to create sustained natural and humanitarian disasters on a scale far beyond those we see today." Already, it said, Darfur, Ethiopia, Eritrea, Somalia, Angola, Nigeria, Cameroon and Western Sahara have all been hit hard by tensions that can be traced in part to environmental causes.[65] If the drought continues, the report said, more people will leave their homelands, increasing migration pressures within Africa and into Europe.[66]

The impact will be especially acute in the Middle East, where about two-thirds of the inhabitants depend on water sources outside their borders. Water remains a potential flashpoint between the Israelis and Palestinians, who lack established rights to the Jordan River and receive only about 10 percent of the water used by Israel's West Bank settlers.[67] "Only Egypt, Iran and Turkey have abundant fresh water resources," the CNA report said.

Mountain Snowpack Is Shrinking

The amount of snow covering the globe's highest mountains has been shrinking over the past half-century, upsetting crucial seasonal water flows that restock rivers, lakes, reservoirs and aquifers. Scientists think short-term climate conditions like El Niño and long-term warming caused by climate change are to blame. By century's end, only 16 percent of New Zealand's current snowpack will remain.

Snowpack Now and Projected in 2100

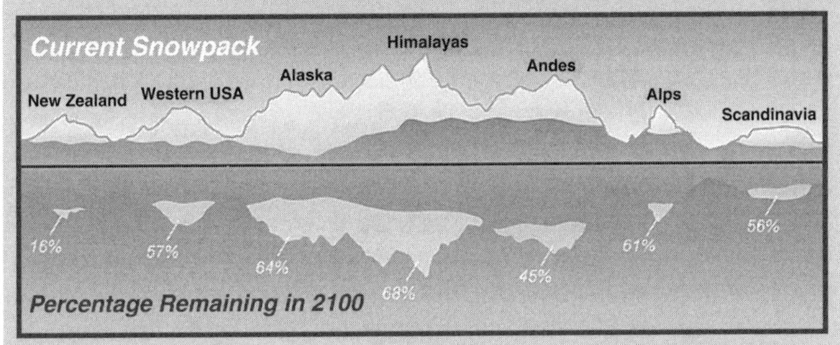

Source: Pacific Northwest National Laboratory, http://picturethis.pnl.gov/picturet.nsf/by+id/AMER-6PWV.V?opendocument.

The military advisers urged the United States to take a stronger national and international role in stabilizing climate change and to create global partnerships to help less-developed nations confront climate impacts.[68]

Currently, there is only a weak international foundation for water collaboration, according to the U.N. Human Development report. While a 1997 U.N. convention lays out principles for cooperation, only 14 nations have signed it, and it has no workable enforcement mechanism. In 55 years, the International Court of Justice has decided only one case involving international rivers.[69]

It is possible, however, that as the awareness of climate impacts on water supplies deepens, so will the urgency for governments to respond. "Unlike the challenges that we are used to dealing with, these will come upon us extremely slowly, but come they will, and they will be grinding and inexorable," said former Vice Adm. Richard H. Truly, a former astronaut who headed the U.S. National Aeronautics and Space Administration (NASA) and served as a CNA consultant.[70] "They will affect every nation, and all simultaneously."

BACKGROUND

Taming Water

The ruins of irrigation canals 8,000 years old have been found in Mesopotamia.[71] Remains of water-storage dams 5,000 years old survive in Egypt and Jordan. Humans have been using waterwheels for milling and threshing since the 1st century B.C., and by 1291 China had completed its Grand Canal running nearly 1,800 kilometers between Beijing and Hangzhou.[72] Water power drove mining, metal drilling, textile and milling industries at the dawn of the Industrial Age.[73] In the United States, the opening of the Niagara Falls hydroelectric power station in 1896 — built by American entrepreneur and inventor George Westinghouse and backed by financier J. P. Morgan and others — inaugurated water's use to generate electric power.[74]

But these early accomplishments were dwarfed in the 20th century by nearly 100 years of massive dam projects that have transformed most of the world's major rivers. Between 1950 and 2000, the number of dams higher than 50 feet increased sevenfold — to more than 41,000

China Leads World in Dam Building

China has three times as many dams as the United States and more than all the next 11 countries combined. Dams typically generate electricity, control flooding and provide water for irrigation.

Countries with the Most Dams

	Country	Dams
1.	*China*	*22,000*
2.	*United States*	*6,575*
3.	*India*	*4,291*
4.	*Japan*	*2,675*
5.	*Spain*	*1,196*
6.	*Canada*	*793*
7.	*South Korea*	*765*
8.	*Turkey*	*625*
9.	*Brazil*	*594*
10.	*France*	*569*
11.	*South Africa*	*539*
12.	*Mexico*	*537*

Source: Peter H. Gleick, et al., "The World's Water: 2002-2003," Pacific Institute, 2002

structures impounding 14 percent of the world's average river runoff.[75] By 2000, large dams were supplying nearly a fifth of all electrical power worldwide.

Dams also have been critical in the rapid expansion of irrigated farming. "Half of the world's large dams are built exclusively for irrigation, supporting about 12 to 16 percent of world food production, according to the World Commission on Dams."[76]

About 12 percent of large dams were constructed specifically to provide drinking water and sanitation (and a similar percentage were built to control flooding), and many have multiple uses. Whether used for energy, community water, flood control or agriculture, dams have been a key tool of economic growth, according to the commission. Typically, however, the full consequences of such giant projects were not taken into consideration, the commission said. In the past century, the world built, on average, one large dam per day without asking whether it was getting a fair return from the $2 trillion investment, said South African Minister of Education Kader Asmal, who chaired the commission.[77]

The dam-building blitz was enabled by political bias in favor of dams. From the Aswan High Dam in Egypt to the Hoover Dam on the Colorado River, big dams have stood as preeminent symbols of governments' engineering prowess and the use of state power to control devastating floodwaters and feed economic expansion. "Colossal engineering works bestow big contracts and big benefits, divide up waters, hold them fast, channel them away from some and give them to others," says author Ward. "It has always been politics that start the bulldozers moving."[78]

While dams helped expand supplies of drinking water, hydropower and irrigation water, they also attract population expansion that eventually strains the new resources. And until recently, the commission said, policymakers have not fairly considered the damaging impact dams have on downstream rivers and aquifers and the populations that are forced to move to make room for reservoirs.

Resistance to major new dam projects emerged with the rise of the environmental movement in the 1970s, particularly in Europe and the United States, as advocates pointed to the harm caused by dam construction. In the industrial world, "it is now more likely that a dam will be torn down than a new one will go up," says Ward.

But in China, South Asia and South America, dams are "multiplying like mushrooms," she writes.[79] If China's new Three Gorges Dam — the world's largest hydroelectric project — had been built midway through the past century, it might have been considered one of the world's great engineering feats. The main wall of the massive, 60-story structure spanning the Yangtze River was completed in 2006, and by the end of 2008 it is expected to deliver up to 18 million kilowatts per hour — nearly a tenth of the electricity needs of China's surging economy.[80] But in today's perspective, the monumental structure symbolizes the threat of environmental destruction caused by major dam construction.

The gargantuan project's human and environmental costs have alarmed opponents. According to the Chinese government, more than a million riverside residents were forced to move as the water rose behind the dam. The rising water levels have triggered some massive landslides on the riverbanks, and a senior government official warned last September that if such ecological and environmental dangers are not dealt with, "the project could lead to a catastrophe."[81] But more recently, Chinese officials have insisted the project will be operated safely.[82]

CHRONOLOGY

19th Century *The industrial age and urbanization create critical need for municipal water treatment and sanitation services.*

1848 The Public Health Act, followed in 1852 by the Metropolitan Water Act, lead to investments in water treatment and sanitation that dramatically reduce waterborne illnesses in Britain by the end of the century.

1876 Berlin city planner James Hobrecht starts work on drainage system and waterworks that channels sewage to fields as fertilizer. He designs similar systems for Moscow, Cairo and Tokyo.

1900-1980 *Governments around the globe launch major dam construction.*

1902 The Aswan Dam on the Nile River in Egypt is completed to control flooding and regulate water flow for agriculture.

1910 Chlorination begins in the United States. Typhoid fever from polluted drinking water falls from 25 deaths per 100,000 people to almost zero.

1936 Hoover Dam on the Colorado River is opened, fulfilling an agreement among Southwestern states and cities to share the river's flow.

1945 Large-scale groundwater irrigation begins expanding in the Western United States, aided by rural electrification and innovations in pumping and irrigating technology.

1986 Major dam construction has largely stopped in the U.S. but continues in Asia.

1990s *Britain's public utilities are sold to private firms in the late 1980s, triggering a wave of water-system privatization worldwide.*

1994 Construction begins on the Three Gorges Dam on China's Yangtze River, designed to be the largest in the world. More than 1 million people will have to be relocated as the river rises.

2000s *Drought spreads worldwide, heightening concern about climate change's impact on water scarcity. Privatization strategies shift.*

2000 Violent public protests against higher water rates force cancellation of a water-privatization plan in Cochabamba, Bolivia. But privatization continues in China, India and other parts of the world. . . . U.N. adopts the Millennium Development Goals calling for halving the number of people without access to safe water and adequate sanitation by 2015.

2002 China approves massive South-to-North Water Diversion Project, which will eventually link the country's four major rivers to bring water from the south to the arid north.

2005 Group of Eight industrialized nations pledge to double their aid for water, sanitation and other development projects in poorer nations by 2010.

2006 Waterborne-disease epidemics strike Karachi, Lahore and other Pakistani cities, caused by the leakage of sewage and industrial wastes into damaged water-distribution pipelines. . . . U.N. Human Development Report warns that without a major increase in investment, improvements in water and sanitation services will fall far short of the Millennium Development Goals.

2007 Multi-year drought afflicts China, the Horn of Africa, Turkey, Australia, Spain and the U.S. Sun Belt. . . . A director of the Three Gorges Project warns that rising waters behind the dam could cause "water pollution, landslides and other geological disasters," but other officials later say environmental problems will be ameliorated. . . . The Intergovernmental Panel on Climate Change predicts that freshwater resources will decrease in large river basins over the next decade due to drought. . . . Drought prompts several Australian cities to commission new desalination plants. Algeria also has a major plant in construction.

2008 The scarcity of water in key agricultural areas has contributed to soaring world prices for wheat, soybeans, corn, rice and poultry, and the trend is likely to continue this year, say agricultural forecasters.

Empowering Women May Quench Thirst

'Should girls be kept home from school to collect water?'

For millennia, the nomadic Tuareg people have lived by herding, migrating across vast rangelands south of the Sahara Desert to water and graze their animals. But decades of drought are destroying the traditional Tuareg way of life — killing herds, drying up grazing lands and forcing many to settle in villages.

"We used to saddle the camel and put all the nice things on its back and put on our nice clothes and go," Tuareg chief Mohamed Ag Mata told a reporter last year. "We were afraid of nothing."[1]

But the changes, paradoxically, offer hope for a better existence to women and children in the male-dominated Tuareg culture — giving them access to the employment, education and social rights that will give them a greater say in community water policy.

Increasingly, educating and empowering women is seen as an effective way to expand access to clean water across the developing world. Virtually every major international organization dealing with water scarcity is calling for change in women's decision-making roles, including The World Bank, the U.N. Human Development Programme, the World Health Organization, the World Water Forum, the World Commission on Dams and the Stockholm-based Global Water Partnership.

In the developing world, the job of hauling water rests, literally, almost entirely on women's shoulders. A UNICEF study in 23 sub-Saharan countries found that a quarter of women spent 30 minutes to an hour each day collecting and carrying water, and 19 percent spent an hour or more. In Mile Gully, an impoverished rural area of Jamaica, hauling the family's water can take a woman two to five hours a day.[2]

The high incidence of waterborne disease caused by the lack of clean water further burdens women in poor, rural communities, because they are the primary caregivers for the sick. "Should a woman care for a sick child or spend two hours collecting water?" asks the latest U.N. human development report. "Should girls be kept home from school to collect water, freeing time for mothers to grow food or generate income? Or should they be sent to school to gain the skills and assets to escape poverty?"[3]

But despite having to bear the greatest burden caused by a lack of water, women "play no role in the decision making for their communities," said Margaret Mwangi, a specialist in forestry and environmental issues who has worked for UNESCO.[4]

Women's lack of property rights prevents them from having a say in how water is distributed in their provinces. Women own less than 15 percent of the world's land and in many countries cannot legally own property separately from their husbands. "Lacking rights to land, millions of women in South Asia and sub-Saharan Africa are denied formal membership rights to participate in water-user association meetings," according to the U.N. "Human Development Report 2006."[5] And even those who are welcomed at irrigation-association meetings often cannot find the time. "Meetings are on Friday nights. At that time, after cooking for my husband and the kids, I still have a lot of work to do around the house," said a woman in Ecuador. "Even if I go to the meeting, it's only to hear what the men have to say. Men are the ones who talk and discuss."[6]

Unless both water and gender policies are reformed, water scarcity threatens to worsen women's plight, says the Sri Lanka-based International Water Management

Some water experts still advocate new, smaller dams in developing countries to control flooding, store irrigation water and generate electricity. For instance, most of India's rainfall occurs in about 100 hours during the monsoon season. While reservoirs capture some of these torrents, most escape to the sea.[83]

The 4th World Water Forum in Mexico City in 2006 cited Norway as a role model for the value of dams. "Electricity from hydropower was the key factor in transforming Norway from one of the poorest countries in Europe a century ago to the industrialized and wealthy nation of today," said Anita Utseth, Norway's deputy minister for petroleum and energy.[84]

As Ward notes, "In some places, if no reservoirs are built, poor people will be denied the means to improve their lives."[85]

Institute.[7] Studies recommend a wide range of strategies to strengthen women's roles in gaining access to water and sanitation services, including micro-credit and micro-insurance programs that target women; training programs in rural irrigation and sanitation processes; creating rural women's councils and broadcasting radio programs on women's issues.[8]

But gender traditions can prove hard to change. Along the Bay of Bengal coast, decision-making and financial control over irrigation systems in the Indian state of Andhra Pradesh, has been decentralized, giving more authority to local communities. Nevertheless, only 4 to 5 percent of the women surveyed in two districts believed they could influence decisions in village meetings. "Women, and particularly poor women, rarely participate," the human development report concluded.[9]

Experts say progress for women requires a push from the bottom and pressure from the top. Legislation in Uganda, for instance, requires that all agencies — from national to village levels — include at least 30 percent female representation.

"Affirmative action may not remove cultural barriers," the U.N. report said, "but it does challenge their legitimacy."[10]

That may even be happening among the Tuaregs, says Hadijatou, describing her new life in a village near Timbuktu in Mali. "Before, everything was given to us by the men. When you are given what you need by other people, you are dependent on them. But when you are producing what you need, you depend on nobody. So life is far better now."[11]

AP Photo/Shakil Adil

Women and girls in poor countries, like these in Pakistan, bear the greatest burden from a lack of potable water.

[1] Richard Harris, "Drought Forces Desert Nomads to Settle Down," National Public Radio, July 2, 2007.

[2] Polioptro Martinez Austria and Paul van Hofwegen, "Synthesis of the 4th World Water Forum," Mexico City, 2006 p. 4, www.worldwaterforum4.org.mx/files/report/SynthesisoftheForum.pdf.

[3] "Human Development Report 2006 — Beyond Scarcity: Power, Poverty and the Global Water Crisis," U.N. Development Programme, 2006, p. 87; http://hdr.undp.org/en/reports/global/hdr2006/.

[4] Margaret Mwangi, "Gender and Drought Hazards in the Rangelands of the Great Horn of Africa," *Women & Environments International Magazine,* Spring 2007, p. 21.

[5] "Human Development Report," *op. cit.*, p. 194.

[6] *Ibid.*

[7] David Molden, ed., "Summary," *Water for Food, Water for Life: A Comprehensive Assessment of Water Management in Agriculture*, International Water Management Institute, p. 10, www.iwmi.cgiar.org/assessment/files_new/synthesis/Summary_SynthesisBook.pdf.

[8] Austria and Hofwegen, *op. cit.*, pp. 43, 63, 96.

[9] "Human Development Report," *op. cit.*, p 193.

[10] *Ibid.*, p. 194.

[11] Harris, *op. cit.*

Regulating Water

Who owns water? What rights do water users have? How should conflicts be resolved?

The globe's oldest recorded societies were formed not only for defense but also to try to control the flow of water in rivers that were crucial to farming. Under Roman law, water resources were the property of the state, which was responsible for their development and protection. Islamic water law in the parched Middle East followed a similar path — irrigation canals and ditches had to be adequately planned and spaced to prevent infringement on others' water sources.[86]

But ancient codes also recognized that landowners did not have to share well water in times of scarcity, and people living closest to rivers and lakes had first claim on their waters. "The cistern nearest to a water channel is

Imaginechina via AP Images

China's 60-story Three Gorges Dam — the world's largest hydroelectric project — is expected to deliver up to 18 million kilowatts per hour by the end of 2008, nearly a tenth of China's electricity needs. Critics say the Yangtze River structure symbolizes environmental destruction that can be caused by major dam construction. More than a million riverside residents were forced to move as the water rose behind the dam.

filled first, in the interests of peace," said the 12th-century Jewish theologian and philosopher Maimonides.[87]

Eventually, the doctrine of "riparian" rights — giving those living closest to water the first claim on its use — became merged with a "public trust" doctrine, holding that water was a common resource to be managed by the state for the common benefit. One person's use of water could not infringe on a neighbor's reasonable needs. The doctrine was embraced by many countries in Europe — including Britain, France and Spain — which then exported the principle to their colonies abroad.[88]

But in the Western United States, Chile and Mexico, private water rights were recognized, particularly after the 1848 gold rush in the United States. A miner finding a gold seam would claim water from the nearest creek to wash dirt away from precious nuggets. His claim established a "first-in-time, first-in-use" priority allowing him to take as much as he needed.[89] This "prior appropriation" doctrine was a starter's gun for unchecked diversion and exploitation of water resources to create farms and cities in the arid West.[90]

Of course, in most legal debates about water, individual rights are submerged by political elites, rulers and dominant factions. For instance, Senegalese law provides for a democratic distribution of irrigated lands. But in practice, tribal nobles' descendants still claim the lion's share of the land and allocate rights to powerful outsiders, including military leaders, politicians and judges.[91]

In Central Asia during Soviet rule, for instance, Kyrgyzstan, Tajikistan and Uzbekistan — which abut the Syr Darya and Amu Darya river basins — shared the reservoir and hydropower output from Kyrgyzstan's largest reservoir. Now, as separate states, their cooperation has virtually ended, according to a U.N. report. Kyrgyzstan is holding on to more of its reservoir volume in order to increase its hydropower exports, severely reducing irrigation flows in the other two countries. A constructive dialogue "has been conspicuously absent," according to the U.N. Human Development Report.[92]

Two international treaties — the Helsinki Rules of 1966, adopted by the International Law Association, and articles adopted by the U.N. International Law Commission — specify how cross-border water disputes should be resolved. Rivers that divide nations, according to the treaties — must be considered common resources, not under any one nation's control. They also advocate a policy of "no harm" — each riparian nation has the right to "equitable utilization" of a shared water supply, and a nation's water use should not damage its neighbors' water needs. Prior appropriation claims are not allowed, and countries are called on to share accurate information on water resources.[93]

Before fair water-use policies can be expected, governments must consider the needs of the poor and politically weak, whose water needs are usually greatest, says water expert Sandra Postel, director of the Global Water Policy Project in Massachusetts. That means "adding seats around the table," she says.[94] For example, Ghana successfully expanded its water and sanitation services in recent years after water policy was decentralized, and village and district water councils were formed. The result: improved planning and more reasonable priorities for water funding, according to the U.N.[95]

Misusing Water

In Mumbai's Dharavi slum, which lies between the international airport and the city's financial center, an estimated 1 million Indians live in huts and shanties. With only one toilet for every 1,440 people, gutters overflow with waste in the rainy season, turning the streets into open sewers.[96]

Such unsanitary conditions in developing countries contribute to a plague of diarrhea that not only kills an estimated 1.8 million children across the globe each year but also repeatedly sickens many times that number, leaving them malnourished and vulnerable to other diseases and keeping them from school.[97]

Trachoma, spread by a fly that breeds in human feces, afflicts nearly 6 million people worldwide, causing widespread blindness. The disease "is a passport to poverty," says the U.N.'s "Human Development Report," because it prevents victims from working.[98]

"At the start of the 21st century one in five people living in the developing world — some 1.1 billion people in all — lack access to clean water," and nearly half the developing world has no access to adequate sanitation.[99]

Some of the same conditions existed in Europe and the United States during most of the 19th century, as farm families migrated to vast urban slums. During the summer in 1858, the stench of untreated sewage in the Thames River (called the "Great Stink" by the *London Times*) forced the Parliament to close temporarily.[100] In the 1890s Britain's infant mortality rate was about the same as Nigeria's today.

Water-treatment legislation in mid-19th-century Britain mandated creation of municipal water companies, followed by an expansion of sanitation services after 1880. By 1910, the country's rate of infant mortality had fallen by nearly 40 percent. The critical factor for change, according to some experts, was an extension of voting rights in Britain beyond property-owning classes to those who lacked clean water and sanitation, creating a political constituency for reforms.[101]

But the cost of expanding sanitation services in the developing world today would be immense. A study led by former International Monetary Fund President Michael Camdessus estimates that closing the sanitation services gap could cost $87 billion over the next two decades.[102]

Experts today debate which must come first in the developing world: good governance or solutions to water and sanitation needs. In *The World's Water 2006-2007*, the authors conclude that "eradicating corruption and political interference and ensuring the participation of all stakeholders will be critical to the successful governance of water."[103] The 1,320-km (820 miles) Rhine River — long called "the sewer of Europe" — was cleaned up after a 1986 industrial fire in Basel, Switzerland, allowed more than 30 tons of pesticides, dyes, mercury and other poisons to spill into the river. Millions of fish were killed, and major cities had to close their municipal water intakes. German Chancellor Angela Merkel, a former environmental minister, has called the "rebirth of the Rhine . . . one of the great environmental success stories of the century."[104]

AFP/Getty Images/Tony Mwanki

A Masai herdsman in Kenya's Rift Valley tends to a dying sheep in January 2006. Today 850 million people live in areas where adequate food supplies are at risk because of drought — two-thirds of them in South Asia and sub-Saharan Africa, where the impact of climate change on food production is expected to be worst.

But to the east, the blighted Danube testifies to the damage caused by selfish, beggar-thy-neighbor policies by the nations along its 1,770-mile course. Efforts to

Water Schemes Range From Monumental to Zany

Many are costly and controversial.

After wildfires devastated parts of Southern California and dry winds parched the Southwest last summer, New Mexico's Gov. Bill Richardson, a Democratic candidate for president, made a startling proposal.

"States like Wisconsin are awash in water," Richardson told the *Las Vegas Sun*, proposing that water from the Great Lakes be piped to his state. With nearly 20 percent of the world's fresh water, the five vast lakes are an irresistible target to promoters, politicians — and potentially — corporate water suppliers.

"You're going to see increasing pressure to gain access to this supply," said Aaron Packman, a professor of civil and environmental engineering at Northwestern University. "Clearly, it's a case of different regional interests competing for this water."[1]

In 1985, Quebec provincial officials floated a plan to sell Canadian river water to the high plains states. The Great Replenishment and Northern Development Canal (GRAND) envisioned pumping river water from Quebec into a reservoir in Ontario. From there the water could travel by aqueduct to the Great Lakes and then by canal to the American plains. Nothing came of it.

Even grander was the North American Water and Power Alliance in the 1960s, which proposed to dam dozens of north-flowing rivers in Canada's western provinces, channeling their waters into a new reservoir 500 miles long — about the distance from Pittsburgh to Chicago — to irrigate the high plains and refill the Colorado River's flows to California. But the half-trillion-dollar price tag sank the proposal. And its environmental cost would have been "ungraspable," says Canadian journalist Marq de Villiers, author of *Water: The Fate of Our Most Precious Resource.*[2]

The idea still seems to stir anxieties in Canada. An offhand remark by President George W. Bush in 2001 about the benefits of Canadian water exports to the United States caused a brief uproar, and last year Canada's Liberal Party Leader Stephane Dion accused the government in Ottawa of trying to put the matter back on the U.S.-Canada agenda — a claim both governments denied.[3]

Mega-project dreams still survive in China, however, which is planning a series of canals to carry Yangtze River water thousands of miles to the Yellow River and on to the huge cities of Beijing and Tianjin.[4]

And in 2004, Israel agreed to purchase the equivalent of 35 million gallons of freshwater per day from Turkey's Manavgat River, to be shipped aboard tankers. Turkish water exports to Cyprus and other water-short destinations were also under consideration. The agreement was put on hold in 2006 after higher oil prices made tanker transportation uneconomical, according to both countries.[5]

AP Photo/California Dept. of Water Resources/Dale Kolke

The monumental California Aqueduct brings vitally needed water 444 miles from Northern to Southern California farmers and residents.

And then there are the slightly zany ideas, such as Calgary entrepreneur James Cran's plan to move water by sea inside floating 5,000-ton plastic bags, or towing Arctic icebergs to distant metropolises.[6]

Most monumental water-moving schemes, however, trigger intense opposition. Gov. Richardson's proposal, for instance, is opposed by eight Great Lakes-area states and two Canadian provinces, and drew a terse, unequivocal "No" from Michigan's Democratic Gov. Jennifer Granholm.[7]

---

[1] Tim Jones, "Great Lakes key front in water wars," *The Chicago Tribune*, Oct. 28, 2007, www.chicagotribune.com/news/local/chi-water_bdoct28,1,5145249.story.

[2] Marq de Villiers, *Water: The Fate of Our Most Precious Resource* (1999), p. 260.

[3] Launce Rake, "Canadians fearful of U.S. water grab," *Las Vegas Sun*, May 28, 2006. See also Bruce Campion-Smith and Susan Delacourt, "Secret talks underway, Dion claims," *The Toronto Star*, Aug. 18, 2007, p. 18.

[4] Diane Raines Ward, *Water Wars: Drought, Flood, Folly and the Politics of Thirst* (2002), p. 171.

[5] Josef Federman, "Israel, Turkey put landmark water agreement into deep freeze," The Associated Press, April 5, 2006

[6] de Villiers, *op. cit.*, p. 277.

[7] Jones, *op. cit.*

reengineer the river began in the 16th century with projects to steer its annual floods into canals or trap them behind huge dams. Historically, vast amounts of untreated human wastes and toxic industrial effluents were also dumped into the river, a situation that worsened during the Cold War. Soviet-era bosses had no scruples about flushing wastes into rivers, and Moscow pushed Hungarian and Czech governments to divert the Danube into man-made waterways in order to speed Russian barge traffic. Parts of the project were begun, but before it went very far, the Soviet Union collapsed.

In the 1990s, a third of the Danube's flow was being taken for human use — an extraction rate that researchers warned would be unsustainable if the vast region served by the river faced continued growth and a prolonged drought.[105]

Today the Danube nations are working toward the river's recovery, and the European Union has pledged $3.3 billion to help.[106]

Ocean Waters

As a last resort, some wealthy nations and cities facing serious shortages of freshwater — including the Persian Gulf states, Israel, Singapore and a handful of cities in California, Florida and Australia — have turned to desalination of the oceans' limitless resources.

More than 10,000 desalting plants were in operation or contracted for construction in January 2005, with a total capacity of 9.6 billion gallons per day. At present, however, desalination plants have the capability to provide just three one-thousandths of daily global freshwater consumption.[107]

Governments usually subsidize up to a third of the consumer cost for desalinated water because it costs many times more than typical urban water service.[108] Improved technology and engineering dropped average desalination costs from $1.60 per 264 gallons in 1990 to about 60 cents in newer plants by 2002. But construction costs have risen recently due to higher steel prices, and operating costs have climbed sharply as energy prices have risen. (Energy costs account for one-third to more than one-half of the expense of desalinating water.) The safe disposal of the brine residue from desalination remains an environmental issue that is still not well researched, according to "The World's Water" report.[109]

Some experts believe desalination will begin to grow at double-digit rates as water becomes scarce and prices for conventional water rise.[110] For example, California had 20 desalination plants in the construction pipeline in 2006, which could increase California's desalination capacity 100-fold, providing about 7 percent of the freshwater the state used in 2000.

CURRENT SITUATION

Melting Snows

The deep snowpack covering the world's mountains in winter is a renewable gift of nature — melting in spring to restock rivers, lakes, reservoirs, aquifers and eventually flowing back into the ocean. Then evaporating ocean water turns into snowfall in the mountains, repeating the cycle. But the snowpacks have been shrinking — and melting earlier — over the past half-century, upsetting crucial seasonal water flows.[111]

In parts of the Western United States, for example, the snowpack is down to 40 percent of normal. While short-term climate conditions like El Niño are partly to blame, Earth's predicted warming trend is expected to cause dramatic changes in the future. The U.S. Department of Energy's Pacific Northwest National Laboratory has forecast, for instance, that by century's end South America's Andes Mountains will have lost half of their winter snow cover, and ranges in Europe and the U.S. West nearly half.[112] (*See figure, p. 209.*)

"Our main reservoir is snow, and it's going away," says Phillip Mote, a professor of atmospheric sciences at the University of Washington in Seattle.[113]

The early melting is seen as an indication that climate change is already affecting water scarcity. "Some of what's happening with the early snow melts could be due to variations based on ocean circulation," said Gregg Garfin, project manager of the University of Arizona's Institute for the Study of Planet Earth. "But there's a pretty large fraction that can't be explained that way, and we think that's due to increasing temperatures."[114]

The amount of snow melting into the Colorado River Basin has declined by 10 to 30 percent over the last 30 years, according to Brad Udall, director of the University of Colorado's Western Water Assessment.[115]

Earlier melting has caused unseasonal spring flooding in parts of the West,[116] while a decade of drought has left forests more vulnerable to fires and beetle infestations,

AP Photo/Reed Saxon

Wildfires destroyed hundreds of homes in Malibu, Calif., last October during a severe drought, reigniting the perennial national debate about the folly of building homes in water-scarce areas.

said Tom Swetnam, director of the University of Arizona's Laboratory of Tree-Ring Research. "Lots of people think climate change and the ecological responses are 50 to 100 years away," he said. "But it's not. It's happening now."[117]

In the American Southwest — as in other arid regions of the world — drought is the biggest, most persistent enemy, but scientists are divided over how much of the current drought is due to long-term climate change.

A report by scientists at the Met Office Hadley Centre for Climate Prediction and Research — Britain's weather office — cites evidence that rising emissions of greenhouse gases have exacerbated drought conditions during the past half-century. Greenhouse gases — the carbon dioxide, methane, nitrous oxide and ozone produced from burning fossil fuels — are causing the Earth's temperature to rise by helping to trap the sun's heat, creating a greenhouse effect, according to the Intergovernmental Panel on Climate Change.

"Further research is required," said the Hadley Centre report, noting "the potential seriousness of future climate change impacts if CO_2 emissions continue to increase substantially."[118]

These judgments are still hedged. "It is quite possible that . . . climate change may be having an impact on droughts, not only in the U.S. but around the world," says Michael J. Hayes, director of the National Drought Mitigation Center at the University of Nebraska, Lincoln. But that's not clear yet. "I don't think we can use what is happening today as an argument for climate change. It should open our eyes to the potential impacts that might occur."

Looking further ahead into the century, scientists warn that drought is likely to persist over longer periods, hitting hardest at the world's most-vulnerable arid regions.[119]

A trend toward extreme weather events, ranging from drought and high temperature to violent storms and flooding, is already evident, according to the National Center for Atmospheric Research.[120] Global warming is likely to fuel even more extreme weather, center researchers said. "There's a two-third's chance there will be a disaster," says Nobel laureate Steven Chu, director of the Lawrence Berkeley National Laboratory, "and that's in the best scenario."[121]

The Southwestern United States and other regions appear headed, by mid-century, to a condition of permanent drought caused by global warming, concluded Columbia University's Lamont-Doherty Earth Observatory, after surveying recent studies. "[G]lobal warming not only causes water shortage through early snow melt, which leads to significant water shortage in the summer over the Southwest, but it also aggregates the problem by reducing precipitation," said Mingfang Ting, senior research scientist at Lamont-Doherty and co-author of the survey.[122]

Wasted Water

Although Atlantans worry that falling levels in Lake Lanier are jeopardizing their drinking water, they might be surprised to learn that up to 18 percent of the city's water is being lost through leaky pipes and wastefulness.[123] In London, the mayor asked the Thames Water company to stanch the 238 million gallons per day being lost through old, leaky water pipes rather than build a costly desalination plant to purify Thames River water. Regulators have since approved the project because of the urgency of the shortages.[124]

U.S. water systems lose an estimated 15 percent to 25 percent of their water through leakage, and older or poorly maintained networks around the world lose more than 40 percent. However, notes American water conservation consultant Amy L. Vickers, water leakage is "chronically underestimated, ignored, or treated as a tired 'Unsolved Mystery,' " by utilities.[125]

AT ISSUE

Should water be privatized?

YES

Terry L. Anderson
Executive Director, PERC,
Senior Fellow, Hoover Institution

Written for *CQ Global Researcher* February, 2008

"No one washes a rental car" is a truism that suggests that ownership is crucial to stewardship. We also might say, "No one conserves water" for the same reason — too often it's not clear who benefits from conserving water because it's unclear who owns the water. As long as water's cheap, why fix the leaky faucet or switch to an efficient irrigation system?

Making the ownership link is relatively easy, because water is already claimed by someone — either a municipality, individual farmers or a government agency.

In practice, however, claims compete with one another, especially when water is scarce. Miners and farmers on the Western frontier in the 19th century devised the prior-appropriation system, whereby water owners were allowed to resolve conflicts by moving water to higher-valued uses, and trades between farmers have gone on for a century.

The recent drought in the Southeast has raised a red flag about scarcity. The best mechanism for allocating water is to clarify ownership among municipal, agricultural, industrial and environmental users and allow trades. If Atlanta must buy water from lower-valued agricultural users, farmers will have an incentive to save water and sell it, and municipal consumers will face a higher price and thus an incentive to conserve.

Some worry that water markets will put undue burden on the poor while the rich continue enjoying their country club lawns. But the poor could be issued water stamps, akin to food stamps, for buying water. Or suppliers could charge less for minimum amounts of water needed for necessities and increase the price of water for luxuries.

When water rights are allocated through political processes, the poor usually do not get many of the initial rights, forcing them to purchase water if they are to get any. And data from the Chilean water markets suggest that the poor don't fare much better when water is traded on the open market. Perhaps there should be some guaranteed survival quantity of water that is a basic human right.

The problem is not a failure of water markets, but a failure of political allocation, which will not be rectified by preventing water markets from delivering water at a profit to all, regardless of income.

As water scarcity increases in the 21st century, water bureaucracies will bring more conflict, while water markets will foster more cooperation. With this choice, it will be impossible to keep a good water market down.

NO

Wenonah Hauter
Executive Director, Food & Water Watch

Written for *CQ Global Researcher* February, 2008

In the early 1990s, multinational corporations began to view water services as an important, new profit center — especially in the United States, where 85 percent of water utilities are public. With 1.2 billion people in the developing world lacking access to safe drinking water, the corporations lobbied the World Bank to condition its loans for water services on privatization.

Since then, numerous failed ventures have proven that the cost of privatizing water is too high. It was certainly too high for Tanzania, which terminated a 10-year contract with Biwater after two years of poor management left the government short $3.25 million and the poorest citizens of Dar es Salaam without water. Likewise, massive rate hikes and poor management led Bolivia to end a 40-year contract with Bechtel after only a few months. Similar ventures in Argentina, the Philippines, Indonesia, South Africa and the United Kingdom also have proven unworkable.

In the United States, many municipalities have considered privatization to upgrade their aging systems, but the ventures have been plagued by corruption, high rates, poor service and public outrage. Atlanta terminated a 20-year contract with United Water 16 years early due to bungled emergency responses, boil-water alerts, discolored water and billing difficulties. In 2002, a coalition of citizens' organizations in New Orleans defeated what would have been the largest water-privatization initiative in the United States. Meanwhile, residents of Stockton, Calif., sued the city for failing to perform a proper environmental review of the city's water-privatization contract.

Given this abysmal track record, new solutions are necessary to meet water needs. For example, some U.S. cities have cut costs by improving internal management. Phoenix saved $77 million by working with a labor management team to optimize staffing, organize self-directed work teams and utilize new technology. Similarly, San Diego saved $37 million by developing a more cost-conscious management system.

Safeguarding our water systems is a vital public responsibility. Yet, shockingly, the Environmental Protection Agency estimates that each year we fall $22 billion short of our water infrastructure spending needs. To address this funding gap, we must ensure that public utilities can upgrade and maintain their systems without turning to privatization.

At Food & Water Watch, we support a Clean Water Trust Fund to help ensure that the future of America's water lies in publicly accountable management and secure, clean, affordable water for all.

In coastal cities, vast amounts of rainwater and melting snow are "basically lost," flowing into storm drains that flow out to sea, says the U.S. Geological Survey's Hirsch. "The urban design is to get rid of it as fast as you can: get it off the roof, off the street, into the storm sewers and rush it off into the ocean, never used by anybody." Extravagant water consumption continues in wealthy residential areas and in farming regions where inefficient surface and sprinkler irrigation systems waste up to 25 percent of the water they use.[126] Efficient "drip" irrigation systems — which deliver water directly onto the crops, reducing evaporation to only 5 percent — are used on less than 1 percent of irrigated lands worldwide, largely because of higher equipment costs.[127]

But according to Vickers and other experts, a conservation ethic is beginning to emerge, particularly where water supplies are threatened by drought. For example, aggressive conservation strategies in Boston and Albuquerque, N.M., are reducing systemwide demand by 25 and 18 percent, respectively. "A few other systems, such as New York City, have also realized substantial water savings and wastewater volume reductions that have allowed them to avert major infrastructure expansions," Vickers notes.[128]

In the United States, some states have begun requiring cities to use reclaimed wastewater ("graywater") to irrigate parks and golf courses. Illinois, Florida, California, Arizona and Ohio reported the largest increases. The U.S. Geological Survey estimated that the amount of graywater used more than doubled between the 1970s and 1995.[129]

Water conservation also is expanding in the construction field. In the United States, Canada, Brazil, India and three-dozen other nations, water-saving green architecture for commercial and government buildings is growing in popularity, but the large-scale use of water-conservation practices by water utilities is still "very rare," says Vickers.[130]

Hirsch says policymakers must recognize that rivers and lakes need sustained flows of water to maintain their long-term environmental viability — and their full range of usefulness. Although this movement is "still in its infancy," at least 70 nations have begun programs to conserve or restore water flows in rivers.[131] For example, a $10 billion project in Florida aims to restore the natural flow of the Kissimmee River, and programs in Australia, Israel, Finland, Thailand, South Africa and Zambia would release flood waters from dams to move sediments downstream and expand plant and animal habitats.

"When given a chance, rivers often heal," write the Global Water Policy Project's Postel and Brian Richter, a staff director at the Nature Conservancy, in *Rivers for Life.*[132]

"If 12 jumbo jets [full of children] were crashing every day, the world would want to do something about it. They would want to find out why it was happening."

— U.N. water expert Brian Appleton, commenting on the deaths each day of 5,000 children due to lack of access to clean water.

OUTLOOK

Thirst and Hunger

The world's population, now about 6 billion, is likely to jump by more than a third by 2050, reaching nearly 9 billion, according to the U.N.[133] Such a large increase will cause not only thirst but also hunger, says the International Water Management Insttute. The average European uses about 13 gallons of water a day for drinking, cooking and sanitation. But the food an individual consumes in a typical day requires 800 to 900 gallons to grow.[134]

"The world needs roughly 70 times more water to produce food than it needs for cities," says Rijsberman, former director of the International Water Management Institute in Sri Lanka.[135]

Since 1950, water withdrawals for human use have tripled and irrigated cropland doubled. Today, despite important increases in farming productivity, 850 million people live in areas where adequate food supplies are at risk — two-thirds of them in South Asia and sub-Saharan Africa, where the impact of climate change on food production is expected to be worst.[136]

The productivity of irrigated cropland has increased dramatically in the past half-century, according to the World Bank. The production of rice and wheat, for instance, increased 100 percent and 160 percent in that period, respectively, with no increase in water use per bushel. "However, in many (river) basins, water productivity remains startlingly low," the bank reports. Without greater agricultural productivity or major shifts in farming locations, the amount of water needed for farming will jump 70 to 90 percent by 2050, according to the assessment.[137]

As food requirements continue to rise, the increase in irrigation has slowed as underground water levels have begun to recede. Farmers also face growing competition for water from industry.[138]

Rijsberman predicts the average price of water used in agriculture worldwide could increase by two to three times in the coming decades, inflating global food prices. In addition, industries and power producers can outbid farmers for scarce water. If irrigated harvests are cut back through a lack of water or because water is diverted to industrial use, world grain prices will rise even more.[139]

Policymakers still must resolve a major question about water pricing: Should it be priced competitively, according to its value, like wheat, rice and other food commodities grown with water? A handful of governments have done just that: Chile allows landowners with water on or under their property to trade water rights to the highest bidders. Mexico, several Australian states and California also have water-trading programs.[140] In Texas, the flamboyant oil trader T. Boone Pickens has created a company, Mesa Water, to buy water from landowners above the Ogallala aquifer, to sell to water-short Texas cities.[141]

But many experts think trading water as a commodity is a non-starter for most governments. "There is no movement in the real world, with elected officials," says U.S. water-law expert Robert Glennon. "Water pricing is the third rail of water politics."

Another option, supported by the World Bank and others, is trading "virtual" water. That occurs when a country with scarce water or poor agricultural land concentrates on developing export goods to earn the money needed to import food from water-rich nations with productive, low-cost food producers. Such trades, which would require a lowering of agricultural trade barriers, could bring down food production costs in water-poor countries and help reduce global water consumption, according to a World Bank report. Wheat grown in India, for example, consumes four times more water than wheat grown in France. By importing maize rather than growing it, Egypt reduces its national water consumption by 5 percent.[142]

But importing "virtual" water also has a downside. "In Morocco, for example, one study showed that while the nation as a whole would benefit from agricultural trade liberalization, those benefits would be concentrated on the urban population; farmers — particularly poor farmers — stood to lose," said a World Bank report.[143] For that reason, critics of expanded international trade oppose the "virtual" approach.

AP Photo/Carlos Osorio

National Geographic/Getty Images/James L. Stanfield

Spraying vs. Dripping

Due to evaporation, irrigation systems like this one in Lakefield Township, Mich. (top), waste up to 25 percent of the water they distribute. More expensive drip irrigation systems, like this one in Israel (bottom), lose only about 5 percent to evaporation but are used on less than 1 percent of irrigated lands worldwide.

Other advocates call for greater reliance on rain-fed farming. Just over half of the world's food, by value, is produced using rainfall, but this sector — dominated by poor rural farmers — has traditionally been ignored by food producers and governments in favor of major irrigation strategies.

"Upgrading rain-fed areas has high potential both for food production and for poverty alleviation," says the International Water Management Institute. Increasing small-scale rainwater storage with supplemental irrigation and better land management could produce quick output gains in these areas.[144]

If farmers continue to depend on irrigation for 40 percent of their water, producing an acceptable diet for 2.4 billion more people in the next 30 years would require another 20 Nile Rivers or 97 Colorado Rivers, says water expert Postel. "It is not at all clear where this water is to come from."[145]

NOTES

1. Charles C. Mann, "The Rise of Big Water," *Vanity Fair*, May 2007; Reuters, "China drought threatens water supply for millions," March 28, 2007.
2. Xinhua News Agency, "Drought leaves nearly 250,000 short of drinking water in Guangdong," *People's Daily Online*, Dec. 13, 2007; http://english.people.com.cn/90001/90776/6320617.html.
3. Jonathan Watts, "Dry, Polluted, Plagued by Rats: The Crisis in China's Greatest Yangtze River," *The Guardian* (Britain), Jan. 17, 2008; http://chinaview.wordpress.com/category/environment/drought/.
4. Xinhua News Agency, "Climate change blamed as drought hits 100,000 at China's largest freshwater lake," *People's Daily Online*, Dec. 14, 2007; http://english.people.com.cn/90001/90776/6321329.html.
5. Chris O'Brien, "Global Warming Hits China," Forbes.com, Jan. 6, 2008; www.forbes.com/opinions/2008/01/04/poyang-lake-china-oped-cx_cob_0106poyang.html.
6. Peter H. Gleick, "Time to Rethink Large International Water Meetings," *The World's Water 2006-2007*, Island Press, p. 182; www.worldwater.org/.
7. David Molden, ed.; "Summary," *Water for Food, Water for Life: A Comprehensive Assessment of Water Management in Agriculture*, International Water Management Institute, p. 10; www.iwmi.cgiar.org/assessment/files_new/synthesis/Summary_SynthesisBook.pdf.
8. See "Summary, Human Development Report 2006: Beyond scarcity: Power, poverty and the global water crisis," United Nations Development Programme, p. 26, http:// hdr.undp.org/en/media/hdr2006_english_summary.pdf.
9. Carmen Revenga, *et al.*, "Executive Summary, Pilot Analysis of Global Ecosystems: Freshwater Systems," World Resources Institute, 2000, pp. 4, 26; www.wri.org/publication/pilot-analysis-global-ecosystems-freshwater-systems.
10. Stacy Shelton, "Lake Lanier hits lowest point since its construction," *The Atlanta-Journal Constitution*, Nov. 19, 2007; www.ajc.com/metro/content/metro/stories/2007/11/19/lanierlowweb_1120.html?cxntlid=homepage_tab_newstab. For background, see Mary H. Cooper, "Water Shortages," *CQ Researcher*, Aug. 1, 2003, pp. 649-672.
11. M. Falkenmark, *et al.*, "On the Verge of a New Water Scarcity: A call for good governance and human ingenuity," Stockholm International Water Institute (SIWI) Policy Brief, 2007, p. 17. For background, see Colin Woodard, "Curbing Climate Change," *CQ Global Researcher*, February 2007, pp. 27-50.
12. "Water and Terrorism," *The World's Water 2006-2007, op. cit.*, p. 1.
13. Environmental Protection Agency, "Water Sentinel Initiative," www.epa.gov/watersecurity/pubs/water_sentinel_factsheet.pdf.
14. Met Office Hadley Centre, "Effects of climate change in developing countries," November 2006, pp. 2-3, www.metoffice.gov.uk/research/hadleycentre/pubs/brochures/COP12.pdf; Michael McCarthy, "The Century of Drought," *The Independent* (London), Oct. 4, 2006, p. 1.
15. McCarthy, *ibid.*, p. 1.
16. World Water Council.

17. Quoted in "Billions without clean water," March 14, 2000, BBC, http://news.bbc.co.uk/2/hi/676064.stm.

18. David Katz, "Going with the Flow," *The World's Water 2006-2007, op. cit.*, pp. 30-39.

19. Data Table 5, Access to Water Supply and Sanitation by Region, *The World's Water 2006-2007, op. cit.*, p. 258.

20. "Synthesis of the 4th World Water Forum," August 2006, p. 23-24, www.worldwaterforum4.org.mx/files/report/SynthesisoftheForum.pdf. For background on Millennium Development Goals, see www.un.org/millenniumgoals and "U.N. Fact Sheet on Water and Sanitation," 2006, www.un.org/waterforlifedecade/factsheet.html.

21. "Human Development Report 2006," *op. cit.*, p. 8; http://hdr.undp.org/en/reports/global/hdr2006/.

22. Australian Broadcasting Corp., "Issues in Science and Technology," transcript, Sept. 22, 2007.

23. Frank Rijsberman, Charlotte Fraiture and David Molden, "Water scarcity: the food factor," *Issues in Science and Technology*, June 22, 2007.

24. *Ibid.*

25. Sharon P. Nappier, Robert S. Lawrence, Kellogg J. Schwab, "Dangerous Waters," *Natural History*, November 2007, p. 48.

26. Marq de Villiers, *Water: The Fate of Our Most Precious Resource* (1999), p. 267.

27. "World hit by water shortage," *Birmingham Post*, Aug. 21, 2006, p. 10; http://icbirmingham.icnetwork.co.uk/birminghampost/news/tm_method=full%26objectid=17597105%26siteid=50002-name_page.html.

28. "Water Resources Sector Strategy, Strategic Directions for World Bank Engagement," World Bank, 2004, p. 5, www-wds.worldbank.org/external/default/WDSContentServer/WDSP/IB/2004/06/01/000090341_20040601150257/Rendered/PDF/28114.pdf.

29. de Villiers, *op. cit.*, pp. 176-177.

30. Frank R. Rijsberman, "1st Asia-Pacific Water Summit," MaximsNews Network, Oct. 8, 2007; ww.abc.net.au/7.30/content/2006/s1716766.htm.

31. Diane Raines Ward, *Water Wars: Drought, Flood, Folly and the Politics of Thirst* (2002), p. 171.

32. Nappier, *et al.*, *op. cit.*

33. "Human Development Report," *op. cit.*, p. 176. Also see Meena Palaniappan, Emily Lee and Andrea Samulon, "Environmental Justice and Water," *The World's Water 2006-2007, op. cit.*, p. 125.

34. "Human Development Report," *ibid.*

35. Palaniappan, *et al.*, *op. cit.*

36. Marc Reisner, *Cadillac Desert, the American West and its Disappearing Water* (1986), p. 10.

37. *Ibid.*, p. 437.

38. *Ibid.*, pp. 10-11; also see Robin Clarke and Jannet King, *The Water Atlas* (2004).

39. "Approaches to Private Participation in Water Services," World Bank, 2006, p. 213.

40. Daniel Yergin and Joseph Stanislaw, *Commanding Heights: The Battle for the World Economy* (2004).

41. Juan Forero, "Multinational Is Ousted, but Local Ills Persist," *The New York Times*, Dec. 15, 2005, p. 1; also, Public Citizen, "Water Privatization Case Study: Cochabamba, Bolivia," pp. 1-2, www.tradewatch.org/documents/Bolivia_(PDF).PDF; and Bechtel Corp. statement, "Cochabamba and the Aquas del Tunari Consortium," www.bechtel.com/assets/files/PDF/Cochabambafacts0305.pdf.

42. "European environment giant Veolia to increase investment in China to $2.5 billion by 2013," Xinhua News Agency, Nov. 1, 2007.

43. *Pinsent Masons Water Yearbook 2007-08*, p. xii, www.pinsentmasons.com/media/1976627452.pdf.

44. Quoted in Jeff Fleischer, "Blue Gold: An Interview with Maude Barlow," *Mother Jones*, Jan. 14, 2005, www.motherjones.com/news/qa/2005/01/maude_barlow.html.

45. "Economic Failures of Private Water Systems," Food & Water Watch, Dec. 2007, www.foodandwaterwatch.org/water/waterprivatization/usa/Public_vs_Private.pdf.

46. Scott Wallsten and Katrina Kosec, "Public or Private Drinking Water?" AEI-Brookings Joint Center for Regulatory Studies, March 2005, pp. 2, 7;

www.reg-markets.org/publications/abstract.php?pid=919.

47. Felipe Barrera-Osorio and Mauricio Olivera, "Does Society Win or Lose as a Result of Privatization?" Inter-American Development Bank, Research Network Working Paper #R-525, March 2007, p. 19.
48. *Ibid.*, p. 21.
49. Ward, *op. cit.*, pp. 206-207.
50. *Pinsent Masons Water Yearbook*, *op. cit.*, p. 3.
51. *Ibid.*, p. 5.
52. Paul Constance, "The Day that Water Ran Uphill," *IDB America*, Inter-American Development Bank, Dec. 9, 2007, www.iadb.org/idbamerica/index.cfm?thisid=3909&lanid=1.
53. "Human Development Report," *op. cit.*, p. 92.
54. *Ibid.*, p. 179; Ward, *op. cit.*, p. 210.
55. Malcolm Scully, "The Politics of Running Out of Water," *The Chronicle of Higher Education*, Nov. 17, 2000.
56. Peter H. Gleick, "Environment and Security," *The World's Water 2006-2007*, *op. cit.*, p. 189.
57. "Human Development Report," *op. cit.*, p. 221.
58. Benny Morris, *Righteous Victims* (2001), pp. 303-304.
59. Ward, *op. cit.*, p. 174.
60. *Ibid.*, p. 85.
61. *Ibid.*, p. 192.
62. Undala Alam, letter to the *Financial Times*, April 1, 2006, p. 6. Also see www.transboundarywaters.orst.edu/publications/related_research/Alam1998.pdf.
63. Gleick, "Environment and Security," *op. cit.*, p. 189.
64. *Security and the Threat of Climate Change* (2007), CNA Corp., p. 3; http://securityandclimate.cna.org/.
65. *Ibid.*, p. 20.
66. *Ibid.*, p. 22.
67. "Human Development Report," *op. cit.*, p. 216; Clarke and King, *op. cit.*, p. 79.
68. *Ibid.*, p. 47.
69. "Human Development Report," *op. cit.*, p. 218.
70. CNA, *op. cit.*, p. 14.
71. "Dams and Development: A New Framework for Decision Making," World Commission on Dams, Nov. 16, 2000, p. 8; www.dams.org/report/wcd_overview.htm.
72. Xinhua News Agency, "China's Grand Canal Queues for World Heritage Status," July 6, 2004, www.china.org.cn/english/culture/100401.htm.
73. Terry S. Reynolds, *Stronger Than a Hundred Men: A History of the Vertical Water Wheel* (1932), pp. 32, 142.
74. Jill Jonnes, *Empires of Light: Edison, Tesla, Westinghouse, and the Race to Electrify the World* (2004).
75. Revenga, *et al.*, *op. cit.*, p. 12.
76. World Commission on Dams, *op. cit.*, p. 9.
77. *Ibid.*, p. ii.
78. Ward, *op. cit.*, p. 51.
79. *Ibid.*, p. 46.
80. Lin Yang, "China's Three Gorges' Dam Under Fire," *Time*, Oct. 12, 2007, www.time.com/time/world/article/0,8599,1671000,00.html. Also see Bruce Kennedy, "China's Three Gorges Dam," CNN.com, 2001, www.cnn.com/SPECIALS/1999/china.50/asian.superpower/three.gorges/.
81. Jonathan Watts, "Three Georges Dam risk to environment, says China," *The Guardian*, Sept. 27, 2007.
82. Xinhua Financial News, "Chinese Government Fights Back in Defense of Three Gorges Dam," Nov. 27, 2007; Jim Yardley, "China vigorously defends the Three Gorges Dam project," *The International Herald Tribune*, Nov. 28, 2007, p. 3.
83. Revenga, *et al.*, *op. cit.*, p. 28.
84. "Synthesis of the 4th World Water Forum," *op. cit.*
85. Ward, *op. cit.*, p. 47.
86. *Ibid.*, p. 187.
87. de Villiers, *op. cit.*, p. 59. Also see "Islamic Water Management and the Dublin Statement," The International Development Research Center, Canada, www.idrc.ca/en/ev-93949-201-1-DO_TOPIC.html.
88. Katz, *op. cit.*, p. 37.

89. Robert Glennon, *Water Follies: Groundwater Pumping and the Fate of America's Fresh Waters* (2002), p. 16.
90. *Ibid.*, p. 14.
91. "Human Development Report," *op. cit.*, p. 185.
92. *Ibid.*, p. 214.
93. Ward, *op. cit.*, p. 188.
94. Sandra Postel and Brian Richter, *Rivers for Life, Managing Water for People and Nature* (2003), p. 168.
95. "Human Development Report," *op. cit.*, p. 103.
96. *Ibid.*, p. 37.
97. *Ibid.*, p. 42.
98. *Ibid.*, pp. 45-46.
99. *Ibid.*, p. 33.
100. *Ibid.*, p. 29.
101. *Ibid.*, p. 30, citing Frances Bell and Robert Millward, "Public Health Expenditures and Mortality in England and Wales, 1870-1914," pp. 221-249.
102. Palaniappan, *et al.*, *op. cit.*, p. 131, citing the World Water Council, "Financing Water for All," Global Water Partnership, March 2004.
103. *Ibid.*, p. 139.
104. de Villiers, *op. cit.*, p 171.
105. *Ibid.*, pp. 172-177.
106. *Ibid.*, p. 174; "Human Development Report," *op. cit.*, p. 219; "Future Danube Flood Actions Depend On International Cooperation," Commission for the Protection of the Danube, April 21, 2006; www.icpdr.org/icpdr-pages/pr20060421_danube_flood.htm. For background, see Brian Beary, "The New Europe," *CQ Global Researcher*, August, 2007.
107. Peter H. Gleick, Heather Cooley, Gary Wolff, "With a Grain of Salt: An Update on Seawater Desalination," *The World's Water 2006-2007*, *op. cit.*, p. 55.
108. *Ibid.*, pp. 68-70.
109. *Ibid.*, pp. 78-79.
110. *Ibid.*, p. 161. General Electric Co. projects an annual growth rate of 9 to 14 percent, growing from $4.3 billion in annual desalination expenditures in 2005 to $14 billion in 2014.
111. P. W. Mote, *et al.*, "Declining Mountain Snowpack in Western North America," *Bulletin of the American Meteorological Society 86*, January 2005, pp. 49-48.
112. "New Century of Thirst for World's Mountains," Pacific Northwest National Laboratory, May 18, 2006, www.pnl.gov/news/release.asp?id=158.
113. Eric Bontrager, "West will need to revisit water, land management in light of global warming, experts say," *Land Letter*, Sept. 28. 2006; www.eenews.net/ll/ (subscription required).
114. Shaun McKinnon, "Southwest Could Become Dust Bowl, Study Warns," *The Arizona Republic*, April 6, 2007, p. 1; www.azcentral.com/arizonarepublic/news/articles/0406climate-report0406.html.
115. Bontrager, *op. cit.*
116. *Ibid.*
117. Shaun McKinnon, "Snow runoff: What's at Stake," *The Arizona Republic*, Nov. 25, 2007, p. 8; and Stephen Saunders and Maureen Maxwell, "Less Snow, Less Water: Climate Disruption in the West," The Rocky Mountain Climate Organization, September 2005, pp. 2, 9, 19, www.rockymountainclimate.org/website%20pictures/Less%20Snow%20Less%20Water.pdf.
118. "UK Government: Global drought in the 21st century," M2 Presswire, Oct. 26, 2006; www.continuitycentral.com/news02870.htm.
119. "Fourth Assessment Report — Climate Change 2007: Synthesis Report, Summary for Policymakers," Intergovernmental Panel on Climate Change, Nov. 17, 2007, p. 8; www.ipcc.ch/pdf/assessment-report/ar4/syr/ar4_syr_spm.pdf.
120. Claudie Tebaldi, Katharine Hayhoe, Julie M. Arblaster and Gerald A. Meehle, "Going to Extremes," Institute for the Study of Society and Environment, National Center for Atmospheric Research, 2006, p. 22; www.cgd.ucar.edu/ccr/publications/tebaldi_extremes.pdf.
121. Jon Gertner, "The Future is Drying Up," *New York Times Magazine*, Oct. 21, 2007; www.nytimes.com/2007/10/21/magazine/21water-t.html?_r=1&oref=slogin.

122. "New Study Shows Climate Change Likely to Lead to Periods of Extreme Drought in Southwest North America," Lamont-Doherty Earth Observatory, April 6, 2007, www.ldeo.columbia.edu/news-events/new-study-shows-climate-change-likely-lead-periods-extreme-drought-southwest-north-ameri.
123. "A Review of Water Conservation Planning for the Atlanta, Georgia Region, August 2006, prepared for the Florida Department of Environmental Protection," Pacific Institute, p. 23, www.pacinst.org/reports/atlanta/atlanta_analysis.pdf.
124. "Report to the Secretaries of State for Communities and Local Government and Food and Rural Affairs," *The Planning Inspectorate*, Sept. 29, 2006, p. 7-8, www.communities.gov.uk/documents/planningandbuilding/pdf/319931, and www.thameswater.co.uk/UK/region/en_gb/content/News/News_001394.jsp?SECT=Section_Homepage_000431.
125. Amy L. Vickers, "The Future of Water Conservation: Challenges Ahead," The Universities Council on Water Resources (UCOWR), p. 52, www.ucowr.siu.edu/updates/pdf/V114_A8.pdf. Also see Marcia Clemmitt, "Aging Infrastructure," *CQ Researcher*, Sept. 28, 2007, pp. 793-816.
126. Clarke and King, *op. cit.*, p. 87.
127. "Re-engaging in Agricultural Water Management — Challenges and Options," The International Bank for Reconstruction and Development/The World Bank, 2006, p. 3, web.worldbank.org/WBSITE/EXTERNAL/TOPICS/EXTARD/0,,contentMDK:20858509~pagePK:210058~piPK:210062~theSitePK:336682,00. html.
128. Vickers, *op. cit.*, p. 52.
129. Harriet Emerson and Mohamed Lahlou, "Conservation: It's the Future of Water," National Drinking Water Clearinghouse, www.nesc.wvu.edu/ndwc/ndwc_conservarticlesetc.htm/harrietarticle.html.
130. "Fact Sheet," U.S. Green Building Council, www.usgbc.org/DisplayPage.aspx?CMSPageID=222.
131. Katz, *op. cit.*, p. 32.
132. Postel and Richter, *op. cit.*, p. 201.
133. "World Population Prospects," U.N. Department of Economic and Social Affairs, 2006, http://esa.un.org/unpp/.
134. Molden, *op. cit.*, p. 1; *Birmingham Post*, *op. cit.*, p. 10.
135. Quoted in Kerry O'Brien, "Water scarcity 'due to agriculture,'" Australian Broadcasting Corp. Transcripts, Aug. 16, 2006; www.abc.net.au/7.30/content/2006/s1716766.htm.
136. Molden, *op. cit.*, pp. 7-8.
137. *Ibid.*, p. 14.
138. "Re-engaging in Agricultural Water Management," *op. cit.*, p. 38.
139. Rijsberman, *op. cit.*
140. Postel and Richter, *op. cit.*, pp. 112-117.
141. Jim Getz, "Kaufman County won't vote on Pickens' freshwater district: But Roberts County calls election on Pickens' pitch for freshwater district," *The Dallas Morning News*, Sept. 5, 2007.
142. "Re-engaging in Agricultural Water Management," *op. cit.*, p. 102.
143. *Ibid.*, p 103.
144. International Water Management Institute, *op. cit.*, p. 10.
145. de Villiers, *op. cit.*, p 24.

BIBLIOGRAPHY

Books

Clarke, Robin, and Jannet King, *The Water Atlas*, *The New Press*, 2004.
Editors at the World Meteorological Organization present a visual primer on water scarcity, sanitation shortfalls and climate impact on water resources.

de Villiers, Marq, *Water: The Fate of Our Most Precious Resource*, *Stoddard Publishing Co.*, 1999.
A Canadian journalist provides a global overview of challenges confronting the world's water supplies.

Glennon, Robert, *Water Follies: Groundwater Pumping and the Fate of America's Fresh Waters*, *Island Press*, 2002.

An attorney and water-policy expert advocates new policies to preserve Western U.S. aquifers.

Olivera, Oscar, *Cochabamba! Water Rebellion in Bolivia, South End Press*, 2004.
The leader of the Bolivian protest against water privatization gives his side of the conflict.

Postel, Sandra, and Brian Richter, *Rivers for Life, Managing Water for People and Nature, Island Press*, 2003.
Experts at the Global Water Policy Project in Massachusetts (Postel) and The Nature Conservancy (Richter) chronicle the campaign to restore environmental conditions in threatened rivers.

Reisner, Marc, *Cadillac Desert, the American West and Its Disappearing Water, Penguin Books*, 1986.
This award-winning classic by a former Natural Resources Defense Council expert critiques federal land and irrigation policies and their impact on water use in the West.

Ward, Diane Raines, *Water Wars: Drought, Flood, Folly and the Politics of Thirst, Riverhead Books*, 2002.
An environmental writer reviews controversial global policies affecting dams, water treaties and other water-resource issues.

Articles

Mann, Charles C., "The Rise of Big Water," *Vanity Fair*, May 2007.
A correspondent for *Science* and *The Atlantic Monthly* explores the controversy over privatization programs for water and sanitation worldwide.

Reports and Studies

"Approaches to Private Participation in Water Services: A Tool Kit," *The World Bank*, 2006, http://publications.worldbank.org/ecommerce/catalog/product?item_id=4085442.
The world's major foreign-aid lender provides lessons learned from water-privatization efforts.

"Beyond scarcity: Power, poverty and the global water crisis," *United Nations Development Programme, U.N. Human Development Report* 2006, http://hdr.undp.org/en/reports/global/hdr2006.
This detailed review of worldwide water and sanitation challenges includes case studies of successes and failures.

"Comprehensive Assessment of Water Management in Agriculture: Water for Food, Water for Life," *International Water Management Institute*, 2006, www.fao.org/nr/water/docs/Summary_Synthesis Book.pdf.
A consulting group based in Sri Lanka reports on the impact of water scarcity on global irrigation and food production.

"Dams and Development: A New Framework for Decision Making," *World Commission on Dams*, 2000, www.dams.org/report.
Water experts, educators and government officials assess issues surrounding major dam construction and operations.

"IPCC Fourth Assessment Report," *Intergovernmental Panel on Climate Change*, 2007, www.ipcc.ch/ipccreports/ar4-syr.htm.
A scientific panel sponsored by the World Meteorological Organization and the United Nations Environment Programme issues its most recent outlook on climate change threats.

"National Security and the Threat of Climate Change," *CNA Corp.*, December 2007, http://securityandclimate.cna.org/report/.
A panel of retired U.S. generals and admirals forecasts security issues that will emerge as a result of climate change.

"Synthesis of the 4th World Water Forum, Mexico City," *World Water Council*, 2006, www.worldwatercouncil.org/index.php?id=1386.
An international committee presents a summary of its fourth conference on water-resources issues.

Gleick, Peter H., *et al.*, "The World's Water 2006-2007, The Biennial Report on Freshwater Resources," *The Pacific Institute for Studies in Development, Environment, and Security*, 2006, www.pacinst.org/publications/worlds_water/2006-2007/index.htm.
The institute's latest review of global water-resource issues includes chronologies of water conflicts and analyses of strategies for sustainable freshwater resource management.

For More Information

The CNA Corp., 4825 Mark Center Drive, Alexandria, VA 22311; (703) 824-2000; www.cna.org. A nonprofit research organization that operates the Center for Naval Analyses and the Institute for Public Research, concentrating on security, defense and other government-policy issues.

Food and Water Watch, 1616 P St., N.W., Suite 300, Washington, DC 20036; (202) 683-2500; www.foodandwaterwatch.org. A liberal research and advocacy organization focused on water resources, food security, sanitation and globalization issues.

Intergovernmental Panel on Climate Change, C/O World Meteorological Organization, 7bis Avenue de la Paix, C.P. 2300, CH-1211 Geneva 2, Switzerland; 41-22-730-8208/84; www.ipcc.ch. Intergovernmental research body.

International Water Management Institute, 127, Sunil Mawatha, Pelawatte, Battaramulla, Colombo, Sri Lanka; 94-11 2880000, 2784080; www.iwmi.cgiar.org. Research group supported by 60 governments, private foundations and international organizations.

The Met Office Hadley Centre, Met Office, FitzRoy Road, Exeter, Devon, EX1 3PB, United Kingdom; 44 (0)1392 885680; www.metoffice.gov.uk/research/hadleycentre. Britain's official center for climate-change research.

Pacific Institute, 654 13th St., Preservation Park, Oakland, CA 94612; (510) 251-1600; www.pacinst.org. A nonpartisan think tank studying development, environment and security issues.

Property and Environment Research Center, 2048 Analysis Dr., Suite A, Bozeman, MT 59718; (406) 587-9591; www.perc.org. A pro-market research and advocacy group.

Public Citizen, 1600 20th St., N.W., Washington, DC 20009; (202) 588-1000; www.citizen.org. A liberal consumer-advocacy group.

Stockholm International Water Institute, Drottninggatan 33, SE — 111 51 Stockholm, Sweden; 46 8 522 139 60; www.siwi.org. A research organization affiliated with the Swedish government.

U.N. Human Development Office, 304 E. 45th St., 12th Floor, New York, NY 10017; (212) 906-3661; hdr.undp.org/en/humandev. Publishes an annual report on health, economic and other social conditions.

U.S. Geological Survey, 12201 Sunrise Valley Dr., Reston, VA 20192; (888) 275-8747; www.usgs.gov. The government's mapping agency and research center on water resources, geology, natural hazards and other physical sciences.

World Bank, 1818 H St., N.W., Washington, DC 20433; (202) 473-1000; www.worldbank.org. Provides technical and financial assistance to developing countries.

World Water Council, Espace Gaymard, 2-4 place d'Arvieux, 13002 Marseille, France; 33 491 994100; www.worldwatercouncil.org. An international research and advocacy group of government and international agency officials, academics and corporate executives; sponsors World Water Forum every three years.

9

The Troubled Horn of Africa

Can the War-Torn Region Be Stabilized?

Jason McLure

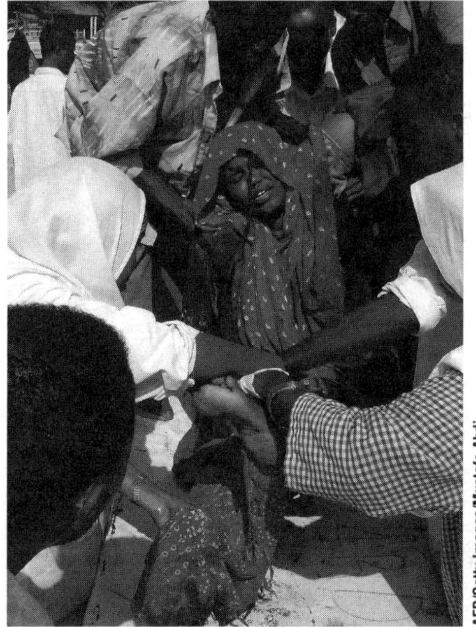

AFP/Getty Images/Mustafa Abdi

A Somali woman wounded in fighting between government soldiers and Islamist insurgents last June is among thousands of civilians killed or wounded in Somalia's 18-year civil war. The conflict has destabilized the entire region, forcing nearly 1.3 million people from their homes and creating a lawless safe haven for pirates and terrorists.

From *CQ Global Researcher*, June 2009.

Halima Warsame's husband and son were killed two years ago after a mortar shell landed on their shop in Mogadishu, the war-torn capital of Somalia. But the impoverished nation's long civil war wasn't finished with her yet.

After living in a camp for people who had fled the fighting, she returned home in April. But in mid-May renewed fighting forced her to return to the camp.

"I thought with the Ethiopian troops gone and the new government [in place] everything would be alright, only it got worse," she says. "I don't see any hope that our situation will ever improve."[1]

Indeed, there is little reason for optimism. During just two weeks in May, at least 67,000 people were driven from their homes in the beleaguered seaside capital by clashes between the country's U.N.-backed transitional government and Islamist extremists. But they are just the latest victims. Somalia's 18-year civil war has killed tens of thousands, forced nearly 1.3 million people from their homes and created a lawless safe haven for pirates and suspected terrorists.[2]

Once a gem of Italian colonial architecture overlooking the Indian Ocean, parts of Mogadishu have been reduced to a moonscape of gutted buildings where warring militias wielding shoulder-fired grenade launchers and AK-47s periodically wreak havoc, sending civilians fleeing to dozens of primitive camps surrounding the city.

The fighting has continued despite more than a dozen attempts to establish a central government — including the latest, in January, when moderate Islamist Sheikh Sharif Sheikh Ahmed became

Grinding Poverty Afflicts Most of Africa's Horn

The four nations in the Horn of Africa cover an arid swathe about three times the size of Texas. More than 100 million people live in the war-torn region — 85.2 million of them in landlocked Ethiopia, Africa's second-most populous country. Tiny Djibouti is the smallest with half a million people. Ethiopia and Eritrea are near the bottom on the U.N.'s 179-nation Human Development Index, which ranks countries by life expectancy and other factors. Somalia doesn't even make the list, since it has no way to collect statistics. Some analysts say the area's poverty and weak or corrupt governments make it a safe haven for Islamic terrorists and pirates.

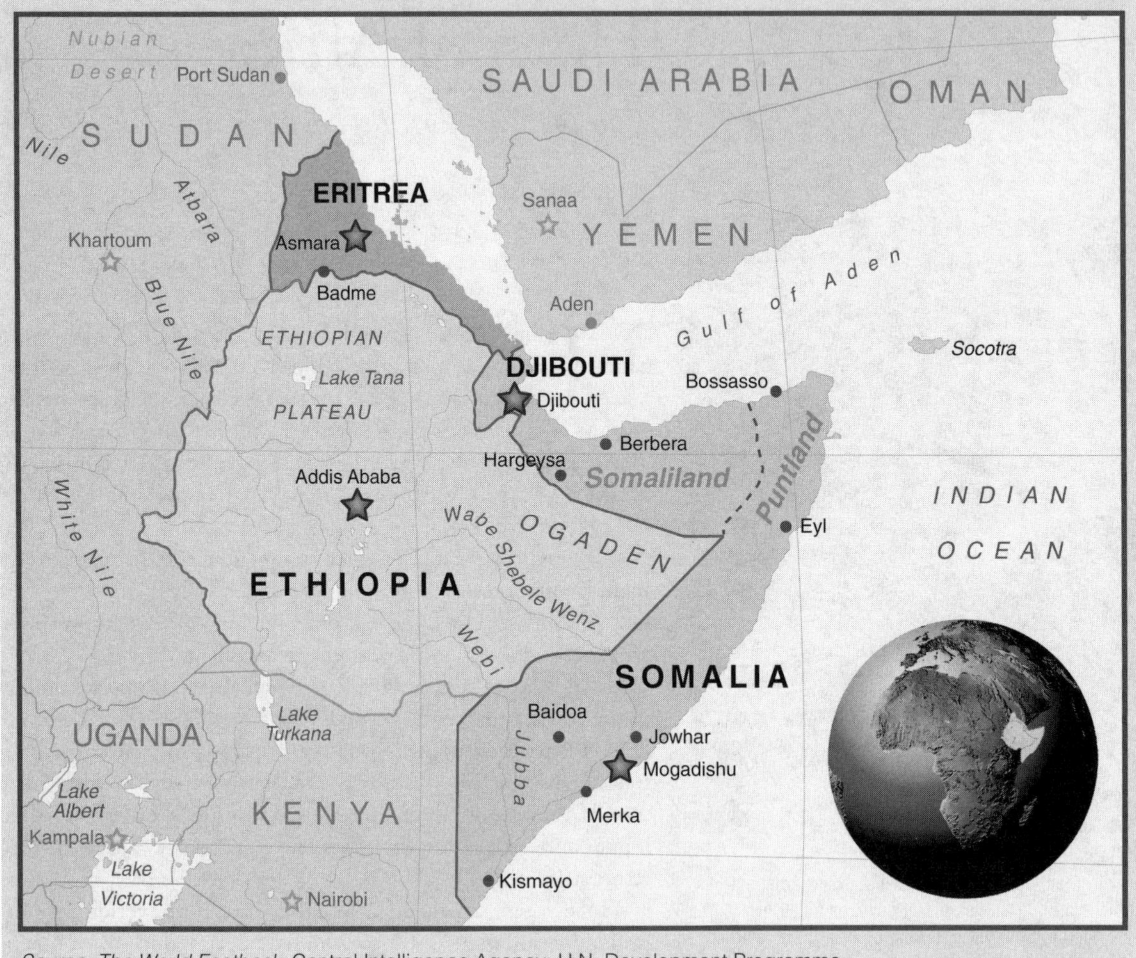

Source: The World Factbook, Central Intelligence Agency; U.N. Development Programme

president. In fact, Ahmed's government is said to have, at best, a tenuous hold on just a few blocks of the capital itself. The ongoing security vacuum has encouraged the clan violence and anarchy that make Somalia a global poster child for a "failed state."

But the fighting in Somalia is only part of an interrelated web of conflicts plaguing the Horn of Africa — one of the most benighted corners of the world's poorest continent. Archrivals Ethiopia and tiny Eritrea have backed factions in Somalia's civil war and continue to arm rebel groups destabilizing the region. And both nations have kept tens of thousands of troops dug in along their mutual border since the end of a 1998-2000 border war that killed 70,000.

In January, Ethiopia ended a two-year occupation of Mogadishu, where it initially succeeded in ousting an Islamist alliance that U.S. officials feared was courting links with the al Qaeda terrorist group. Western nations have showered Ethiopia with billions of dollars in aid and avoided criticizing the regime's recent clamp-down on opposition parties, journalists and human rights activists.

Eritrea, once admired for its self-sufficiency and discipline, has become an isolated dictatorship facing possible international sanctions for having backed the Islamist insurgents in Somalia. Meanwhile Eritrea's effort to build a military counterweight to much-larger Ethiopia has kept more than a third of its productive population serving in the military.[3]

"Eritrea and Ethiopia are battling to determine which will be the dominant power in the region," says Dan Connell, a former adviser to the Eritrean government and author of the book *Against All Odds: A Chronicle of the Eritrean Revolution.* "The border issue is more excuse than cause."

Thus beleaguered by poor governance, conflict and poverty, Ethiopia and Eritrea rank near the bottom on the United Nations' 179-country Human Development Index, which ranks countries by life expectancy, literacy and other factors. Somalia, with no functioning central government to collect statistics, doesn't even make the list.[4] But with 40 percent of the population needing emergency aid, U.N. officials describe Somalia as the world's worst humanitarian and security crisis.[5]

"The region seems to be going backwards fast," says Ioan Lewis, a retired professor at the London School of Economics who has written several books on Somalia. "Whether it can change gear and change course, I really don't know."

The region's human rights record worries the international community as much as its dire economic

Horn of Africa at a Glance

Somalia

Area: 246,201 sq. miles (slightly smaller than Texas)
Population: 9.8 million (July 2009 est.)
GDP per capita: $600 (2008 est.)
Unemployment rate: n/a
UN Human Development Index rank: not included
Religion: Sunni Muslim
Government: Sheikh Sharif Sheikh Ahmed was elected president in January 2009; Somaliland in the north remains autonomous, having declared its own local government in 1991 but has not been recognized internationally. Puntland, in the northeast, declared itself the Puntland State of Somalia in 1998 but has refrained from making a formal bid for independence.

Ethiopia

Area: 435,186 sq. miles (about twice the size of Texas)
Population: 85.2 million (July 2009 est.)
GDP per capita: $800 (2008 est.)
Unemployment rate: n/a
UN Human Development Index rank: 169 (out of 179)
Religion: Christian, 61%; Muslim, 33%; other 6%
Government: Federal republic, bicameral Parliament; Prime Minister Meles Zenawi was elected in 2000.

Eritrea

Area: 46,842 sq. miles (slightly larger than Pennsylvania)
Population: 5.6 million (July 2009 est.)
GDP per capita: $700 (2008 est.)
Unemployment rate: n/a
UN Human Development Index rank: 164 (out of 179)
Religion: Muslim, Coptic Christian, Roman Catholic, Protestant
Government: Provisional government since independence from Ethiopia in 1991, constitutional options presented but none yet implemented; single-party state run by the leftist People's Front for Democracy and Justice; President Isaias Afwerki elected by National Assembly in 1993 in country's only election so far.

Djibouti

Area: 8,880 sq. miles (about the size of New Jersey)
Population: 516,055 (July 2009 est.)
GDP per capita: $3,700 (2008 est.)
Unemployment rate: 59% in urban areas, 83% in rural areas (2007 est.)
UN Human Development Index rank: 151 (out of 179)
Religion: Muslim 94%, Christian 6%
Government: Republic; President Ismail Omar Guelleh has held office since 1999.

Source: The World Factbook, Central Intelligence Agency; U.N. Development Programme

AFP/Getty Images/Mustafa Abdi

AFP/Getty Images/Adrian Dennis

Death and Demonstrations

The remains of Somalis killed during Ethiopia's two-year occupation are recovered near a former Ethiopian military camp in Somalia (top). More than 10,000 people reportedly were killed during the occupation, which ended in January. Ethiopia also has come under international criticism for a recent crackdown on opposition leaders, the press and human rights organizations. Protesters demonstrate against Prime Minister Meles Zenawi during the April meeting of world leaders in London (bottom).

conditions. The European Parliament on Jan. 15 expressed its "great concern" for the state of "human rights, the rule of law, democracy and governance in all countries of the Horn of Africa," where there were "credible reports of arbitrary arrests, forced labour, torture and maltreatment of prisoners, as well as persecution of journalists and political repression."[6]

The chaos has provided refuge to suspected al Qaeda terrorists and allowed pirates to wreak havoc on international shipping. The conflict and poverty have sent millions of refugees fleeing to neighboring countries or to camps in Somalia for internally displaced persons (IDPs) where they depend on international aid agencies for food and shelter — aid that is often blocked by violence, theft or piracy. (*See graph, p. 236.*)[7]

Somalia's civil war has been fuelled in large part by distrust and competition between the country's Byzantine network of clans and subclans and by warlords with a vested interest in instability. A brief flicker of hope accompanied the withdrawal of Ethiopian troops in January and the accession of Sheikh Ahmed to the presidency of the country's Transitional Federal Government. But that hope was dimmed by fierce fighting in April and May and the capture of key towns by Islamist insurgents. Even veteran observers of Somalia marvel at the seeming senselessness of the fighting.

"All I can say now is that I have felt it a privilege to observe a people who shot themselves in the foot with such accuracy and tumbled into the abyss in such style," Aidan Hartley, a Kenyan-born Reuters correspondent who covered Somalia in the early 1990s, wrote in a 2003 book.[8]

Such sentiments are still echoed today. "We are all . . . shocked that Somalis keep finding reasons to kill Somalis," said Ahmedou Ould-Abdallah, a Mauritanian diplomat who is the U.N. special envoy to Somalia, during a Feb. 2 press conference.

The four nations of Africa's Horn — Somalia, Ethiopia, Eritrea and the micro-state Djibouti — cover an arid swathe about three times the size of Texas. About 100 million people live in the region — 85.2 million of them in Ethiopia, Africa's second-most populous country after Nigeria. To the north, tiny Eritrea — which split away from Ethiopia in 1993 — maintains Africa's largest army in an effort to deter its southern neighbor from invading.

Conflict is not new to the Horn of Africa, where the predominately Christian highlanders of the Ethiopian plateau have been fighting with the Muslim lowlanders of eastern Ethiopia (known as the Ogaden) and Somalia for centuries. But the region is also periodically plagued by famine, due to a rapidly growing population and increasingly unpredictable rainfall. This year the warfare and drought will force about 15.5 million people in Somalia and Ethiopia to seek humanitarian aid.[9]

And the long-term trends are equally worrying. About 80 percent of Ethiopians and Eritreans are subsistence farmers or herders. Agricultural production per capita has declined in Ethiopia since the 1960s, while the population has more than tripled.[10] Eritrea's government-controlled economy has eliminated nearly all private enterprise, and its farmers don't produce enough food to feed the country, a situation exacerbated by the government's decision not to demobilize tens of thousands of farmers from the military.[11] Somalia, which imports about 60 percent of the grain needed to feed its estimated 8 to 10 million people, has little prospect of feeding itself anytime soon.

"Ethiopia adds to its population between 1.5 to 2 million people a year," says David Shinn, U.S. ambassador to the country from 1996 to 1999. "That is not sustainable for a country that has been unable to feed itself for more than three decades."

While Somalia's humanitarian disaster is the region's most pressing issue, a longer-term question is whether the war-wracked country as presently configured can survive. Its northwestern region, known as Somaliland, has declared independence after building a functional administration and maintaining a comparatively peaceful, democratic existence for the last decade.

"The hard questions have not been asked as to what sort of a nation-state Somalia should look like," says Rashid Abdi, a Nairobi-based analyst for the International Crisis Group, a conflict-resolution think tank. "The focus has been on creating a national government. Unfortunately, in spite of a lot of investment in the last 15 years, we are nowhere near a functioning, credible nation-state."

Western policy in the region has been influenced largely by the perception that Somalia's lawlessness provides a safe haven for al Qaeda. Somalia's radical Islamist al-Shabaab militia, the most powerful group battling the transitional government, has links to al Qaeda and reportedly has been recruiting jihadists in the United States.[12] And while recent reports indicate that hundreds of foreign fighters from the Middle East and Muslim communities in North America and Europe have arrived in Somalia, analysts disagree over whether Somalia's Islamic radicals pose any real threat outside of the Horn.[13] Some blame the George W. Bush administration in particular for fomenting chaos in Somalia by arming warlords whose sole virtues were their willingness to fight Islamic groups.

"Violent extremism and anti-Americanism are now rife in Somalia due in large part to the blowback from policies that focused too narrowly on counterterrorism objectives," writes Kenneth Menkhaus, an American Horn of Africa specialist from Davidson College who worked as a U.N. official in Somalia in the 1990s.[14]

If there is reason for optimism, it is that the new Obama administration in Washington has signaled its willingness to focus more on human rights and stability and less on waging war against radical Islamists and their allies. Such a move would involve both pressing Ethiopia to resolve its border dispute with Eritrea and showing a greater willingness to work with moderate Islamists in Somalia, who many believe are the only force capable of bridging the divide between the country's constantly warring clans.

As analysts and diplomats discuss the Horn of Africa's future, here are some of the questions being debated:

Is there a real threat of international terrorism from Somalia?

When 17-year-old Burhan Hassan didn't come home from school in Minneapolis last Nov. 4, his mother thought he was at a local mosque. Unfortunately he wasn't. Although his family had fled Somalia when he was a toddler, Hassan — it turned out — had embarked that day for the southern Somali port town of Kismayo, a stronghold of al-Shabaab, the military wing of the Islamic Courts Union (ICU) that briefly controlled southern Somalia in 2006 before being ousted by Ethiopian troops.

U.S. law enforcement and counterterrorism officials fear Burhan is one of about 20 young Somali-Americans who may have left the United States since mid-2007 to join the group, which the State Department considers a terrorist organization.[15] The fear is that they may return to the United States or Europe as part of a sleeper cell, sent by a group that is increasingly vociferous about its links to international terrorism. Since 2007 some American generals have considered Somalia a "third front in the war on terror,"[16] and U.S. military planes are a common sight over the nation.[17]*

A spokesman for al-Shabaab said it began seeking links with al Qaeda after it was listed as a terrorist group

* In 2003, the U.S. opened a military base in Djibouti, less than 30 miles from the border of Somalia. Camp Lemonier houses about 2,000 U.S. personnel who monitor suspected terrorists in the Horn of Africa and train the militaries of Ethiopia and other U.S. allies.

AFP/Getty Images/Simon Maina

Newly elected Somalia President Sheikh Sharif Sheikh Ahmed is regarded by many as one of the few men whose clan base and political skills might bring peace to the war-ravaged country. Somalia has had no effective central authority since former president Mohamed Siad Barre was ousted in 1991, touching off an endless cycle of war between rival factions.

by the Bush administration in 2008. Before that, Shabaab "had no official links with al Qaeda," Sheikh Mukhtar Robow, a spokesman for the group, said in 2008. Now, however, "we're looking to have an association with them. Al Qaeda became more powerful after it was added to the list; we hope that it will be the same with us."[18]

Experts differ on whether the links are substantive. Those who worry that Somalia has become a safe haven for terrorists point out that several Somali Islamist leaders were trained in al Qaeda camps in the Afghanistan-Pakistan border regions in the 1990s before returning to Somalia to help form al-Ittihad al-Islamiya, a forerunner of al-Shabaab.

"We face a very serious counterterrorism challenge in Somalia, with extremists affiliated with al Qaeda training and operating in substantial portions of southern Somalia," said Susan Rice, the Obama administration's U.N. ambassador, during confirmation hearings in January. "And that has the potential to pose a serious and direct threat to our own national security."

Those concerned about the terrorism threat from Somalia often cite Gouled Hassan Dourad, a Somali national who was trained in Afghanistan, captured in Somalia in 2004 and held in the CIA's secret prison system before being transferred to Guantánamo Bay in 2006. The United States claims he supported al Qaeda's East Africa cell and was privy to plots to attack an Ethiopian airliner and the U.S. military base in Djibouti in 2003.[19] Likewise, Fazul Abdullah Mohammed — a Comoran national accused of involvement in the 1998 bombings of U.S. embassies in Kenya and Tanzania and suspected in the 2002 truck bombing of the Paradise Hotel in Mombasa that killed 15 — is also thought to have taken refuge in Somalia.[20] A third figure, Hassan al-Turki, is said to run a training camp for Islamist militants in southern Somalia, and, like Mohammed, has been the target of an unsuccessful U.S. air strike in Somalia.[21]

"Definitely you have the al Qaeda East Africa cell that has only been able to function in Somalia with the protection of Somali Islamist movements," says Andre LeSage, an American Horn of Africa specialist at the Pentagon's National Defense University. "Previously, it had been with the protection of al-Ittihad, now it's with the protection of al-Shabaab."

But others say the international terrorism threat from Somalia has been exaggerated, both by al Qaeda and by the United States and its allies. "There is very strong documentation, using declassified al Qaeda documents, indicating that it was in and out of Somalia starting in 1992-1993," says Shinn, the former ambassador to Ethiopia. "They had relatively little success, however. They thought it was going to be relatively easy pickings until they learned Somalis could be just as obstreperous with them as with everyone else. It was very tough sledding.

"Over time they've had increasing success. But I think there is a certain amount of hype here," he says, especially when the West compares al-Shabaab to the ultra-conservative Taliban in Afghanistan. "The idea that the Taliban is moving into Somalia is just utter nonsense."

Indeed, some argue that U.S. support for Ethiopia's 2006 invasion of Somalia and subsequent U.S. air strikes in Somalia that have often mistakenly killed civilians have been counterproductive and have helped to radicalize the population — increasing the terrorism threat. But so far, these analysts point out, no Somali-born citizens have been involved in successful acts of international terrorism.

"The Ethiopian invasion was totally negative," says Lewis, the Somali historian. "The terrorist threat is much more real now than before the interventions."

Coordinated suicide attacks last October on five separate targets in the autonomous Somali regions of Somaliland and Puntland — apparently carried out by

Aid to Ethiopia Spiked Dramatically

The Horn of Africa in 2007 received more than $3 billion in aid from the 30 developed countries that make up the Organization for Economic Cooperation and Development (OECD). Drought-plagued Ethiopia received the most — $2.3 billion — in part because of its consistent support for the West's war on terrorism.

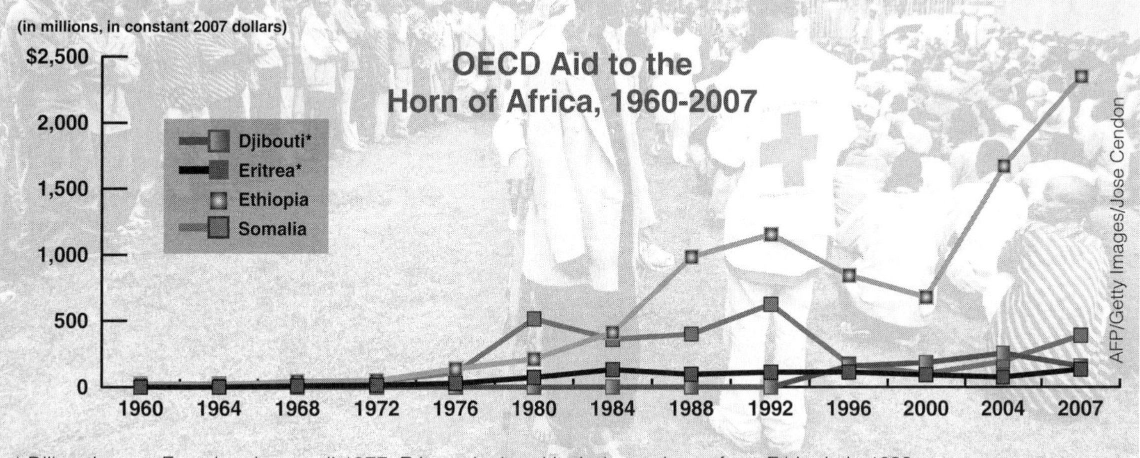

* Djibouti was a French colony until 1977. Eritrea declared its independence from Ethiopia in 1993.

Source: Organization for Economic Cooperation and Development

al-Shabaab — have raised fears the group's capacity for such tactics is growing.[22]

"The suicide bombings in Puntland and Somaliland were clear evidence that these guys have the capacity to work outside their comfort zone," says Menkhaus. "They've also demonstrated their capacity to induce some young men to commit suicide, which is fairly new to Somalia.

"Where will the next threat present itself? Kenya, Ethiopia, Djibouti? Shabaab has every reason to keep this conflict internationalized," he adds.

Is Somalia a viable state?

In the 18 years since the fall of dictator Mohamed Siad Barre, Somalia's foundations have steadily crumbled, with two large northern swathes of the country declaring themselves autonomous or independent entities.

In some ways, the Somalia that existed in the three decades before 1991 — a unified Somalia with a capital in Mogadishu — was an historical anomaly. It never existed previously and has not existed since. Though some analysts express optimism about the newest U.N.-backed Transitional Federal Government (TFG) formed in February, the fact remains that its 14 predecessors since 1991 have all failed.[23]

The TFG struggles to control the port of Mogadishu, which is its main source of revenue, and has authority over just a tiny fraction of Somali territory. Though the current government has 36 cabinet ministers, most of the ministries have no employees and no budget.[24] The situation is so chaotic that businessmen print their own currency, and educated Somalis seek passports from neighboring countries to facilitate international travel.

Despite a string of U.N.-funded peace-and-reconciliation conferences in neighboring countries, a constantly shifting array of militia groups has defied outside attempts at reconciliation. In 2008, World Food Programme convoys bringing aid from Mogadishu to refugee camps 18 miles away needed to pass through more than a dozen checkpoints controlled by different militia groups, according to Peter Smerdon, a spokesman for the program.

"There are too many separate interests on the ground in Somalia," says LeSage, of the National Defense University. "You have so many different power centers there, and each one is being held by a different faction

Somali War Refugees Burden Neighboring States

Nearly a half-million Somalis have fled into neighboring countries to escape the country's 18-year civil war. Most have gone to Kenya and Yemen. Only 10 percent have remained in other Horn of Africa countries.

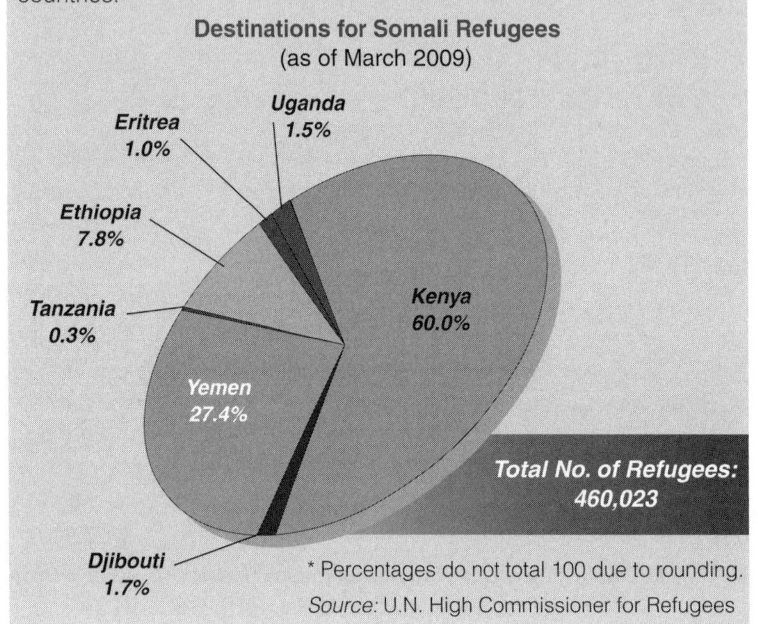

* Percentages do not total 100 due to rounding.
Source: U.N. High Commissioner for Refugees

leader. They don't all share the same agenda for the way forward for the government. . . . You've already got 30-odd political groups just in Mogadishu."

The notable exception is Somaliland, formerly controlled by Britain. It declared independence from Somalia in 1991, ratified a national constitution in 2001 and has remained relatively peaceful since then. Its autonomous government, based in Hargeysa, prints money, operates a police force and issues passports. The region's combination of electoral democracy and clan-based power-sharing has drawn widespread praise, though so far no other government has recognized its independence.

"Somalia hasn't been functioning as a unified state at all, and Somaliland is virtually a separate state that really requires international recognition," says historian Lewis. "I don't think Somalia needs to exist in its present fashion."

Mohamed Hassan, Somaliland's ambassador to Ethiopia, says his homeland's independence was inevitable: "It was a bad marriage, and when a marriage is bad you have to separate.

"We don't know who to talk to now in Somalia," he continues. "There is no central government. They are so fragmented. They have been killing and killing and killing and oppressing. The people of Somaliland have enjoyed peace, security and democracy, and they're confident they can continue."

Because of the lack of international recognition, however, the region has not garnered needed development aid or political support. Many countries are reluctant to recognize break-away states unless it is politically expedient to do so, and there is no coherent international policy for recognizing separatist states.[25]

"There is no way Somaliland will rejoin Somalia, not in my lifetime," says Abdi, the International Crisis Group analyst. "They are dead-set on independence. If we don't reward Somaliland with some form of recognition, they risk sliding back. I think they are the most democratic administration in the Horn of Africa."

Neighboring Puntland also has functioned largely autonomously from both the Islamist militias and the Western-backed transitional government in the south. Dominated by the Majerteyn subclan of Somalia's Darod clan, the region declared itself the Puntland State of Somalia in 1998 but has refrained from making a formal independence bid.[26] That's in part because Abdullahi Yusuf, a native of Puntland, served as president of the TFG in Mogadishu for four years until being pressured to resign in December.

Puntland also has made democratic strides. The regional president was ousted in a parliamentary election in January by Abdirahman Mohamed Farole, a former finance minister.[27] But the area's reputation has been harmed by its status as a launching point for dozens of pirate attacks in 2008 and 2009. In December a U.N. report expressed concern "about the apparent complicity in pirate networks of Puntland administration officials at all levels" — a charge Puntland officials have disputed.[28] (*See sidebar, p. 242.*)

"They are somewhere between secession and union with the rest of Somalia," says Abdi. "Depending on how things evolve in the next few months, Puntland is just hedging its bets. If they think union with Somalia is a dead-end, they will go their own way."

Recognition for either autonomous region would likely have to come first from Ethiopia, the regional power and a close ally of both administrations, or from the African Union (AU). So far both have refrained from doing so. "Those areas are pretty well-secured," Jean Ping, the Gabonese chairman of the African Union Commission, told a Jan. 27 press conference. "But the AU is characterized by respect for the territorial integrity of Somalia."

The United States has said it prefers a unified Somalia. "We will stay in line with the AU; that was the Bush administration's policy," says Jendayi Frazer, the U.S. assistant secretary of state for African affairs from 2005 to 2008. And it's a policy the Obama administration is likely to continue.

Most analysts say a unified Somalia would need a decentralized administrative system in order to be effective. "Our insistence that Somalis remake themselves in our image with ministries of this and this and this isn't realistic," says Menkhaus, the former U.N. official in Somalia. "A state that could emerge in a more organic way is possible. That might include a full array of local Islamic courts, municipalities and hybrid arrangements involving professional groups and clerics."

Should the United States reconsider its policies toward Ethiopia?

Ethiopia's human rights record is among the worst on the continent. But because the predominantly Christian nation — Africa's second-most populous country — cooperates in counterterrorism efforts, the United States and its European allies rarely criticize Prime Minister Meles Zenawi's government.

"There has been full support largely because they view the region through the counterterrorism lens, and Ethiopia has been considered the primary partner in the region," says Leslie Lefkow, a researcher at Human Rights Watch. "This has been problematic because it's ignored the very serious downward trajectory of Ethiopia's human rights record."

Indeed, the Zenawi government has become increasingly repressive in recent years:

- During an ongoing offensive against insurgents in eastern Ethiopia's Somali-speaking Ogaden region, Ethiopian troops have been accused of burning villages, raping women and summarily executing civilians suspected of supporting the separatist Ogaden National Liberation Front.[29]
- Opposition leader Birtukan Mideksa has been held in solitary confinement since December, when she was jailed for life for disputing terms of a pardon agreement that freed her and other opposition leaders from prison in 2007.[30]
- In April 2008, the ruling party and its allies swept to victory in local elections after major opposition parties withdrew, citing government intimidation.
- In January Ethiopia's parliament effectively banned foreign aid agencies from funding groups that promote democracy and human or women's rights.[31]

Lefkow also points out that U.S. support for Ethiopia's invasion of Somalia has not been rewarded by the death or capture of major terrorist suspects. "The small number of people that the U.S. was interested in have not been detained," she says. "The scores of people who were detained in 2007 were either not implicated at all in anything or were very minor people."

Western support for Ethiopia's 2006 invasion of Somalia — as well as Ethiopia's continued occupation of territory awarded to Eritrea in 2002 by the Eritrea-Ethiopia Boundary Commission — have led to growing resentment toward the West among Ethiopia's rivals.

"Sovereign Eritrean territories are still under Ethiopian occupation," Eritrean President Isaias Afwerki said in April 2008.[32] "This is basically the problem of the United States. Ethiopia doesn't have the power to occupy Eritrean territory without the support and encouragement of the U.S. administration. And this is the core of the problem."

"U.S. support for the Ethiopian invasion and pursuit of terrorist targets in Somalia in the name of the war on terrorism have further weakened Washington's credibility in the Horn of Africa and galvanised anti-American feeling among insurgents and the general populace," says a December 2008 report from the International Crisis Group.[33]

Connell, the former adviser to Eritrea, says Ethiopia has manipulated U.S. support to its own ends. "Ethiopia

Ethiopia Takes On Malaria

New effort attacks a deadly foe.

When malaria swept through the green hills of his village in southwest Ethiopia three years ago, Biya Abbafogi was lucky. The 35-year-old coffee farmer and three of his children were stricken with the deadly, mosquito-borne disease, but they all survived. Thirteen neighbors and friends in Merewa didn't.

"We would take one child to the hospital and come back and another one would be sick," he says.

The treatment Abbafogi and his family received was cheap by Western standards — just $40. But that was about a third of his annual coffee earnings, and the bills from the medical clinic — located two hours away by foot — forced Abbafogi to sell one of the oxen he used to plow his small corn field.

But today things are much better for Merewa's 4,335 residents, thanks to two young women trained to treat and prevent malaria and other common ailments. They're not doctors or nurses, and they haven't been to college. But with just one year of training they've cut malaria rates during the infectious season from 15 to 20 new cases per day to one to three.

Merewa's success has been replicated all across Ethiopia, where the government has dispatched an army of up to 30,000 "health extension workers" in the past four years. With money from donors like the Geneva-based Global Fund and the Carter Center in Atlanta, the women have distributed 20 million mosquito-repelling nets and offered basic malaria testing and treatment in isolated villages dozens of miles from the nearest paved road.

Every year 4 million Ethiopians contract malaria, which is particularly deadly for children. As many as one in five youngsters under age 5 who get the disease die from it. In response, Ethiopia is at the forefront of two major public-health initiatives in poor countries. The first, known as task-shifting, trains lower-skilled health professionals — who are cheaper to pay and easier to retain — to provide basic treatments and teach prevention. The second aims to distribute anti-malarial bed nets to 600 million Africans living in mosquito-infested regions by 2011.

Ethiopia's poverty helped drive the new approach. As one of the world's poorest countries, Ethiopia has trouble keeping doctors from moving to better-paying jobs overseas, says Tedros Adhanom, Ethiopia's health minister. "Right now, 50 percent of the doctors Ethiopia trains will emigrate," he says. To compensate, he says, Ethiopia is training more doctors — medical schools admitted 1,000 students in 2008, four times more than in 2007 — and shifting as much work as possible to nurses and health extension workers.

Lower-skilled extension workers don't emigrate, and they're also willing to work for less and to serve in rural areas, Adhanom says. "To tackle our health problems, the solutions are simple," he says. "You don't need highly skilled people to tell you how to prevent malaria."

Health workers learn 16 different health-education and treatment interventions, including midwifery, malaria treatment and hygiene education. They also make sure villagers are vaccinated and organize insecticide spraying to kill malaria-transmitting mosquitoes.

The mosquito net distribution program faces many obstacles in a country where many of the 85 million citizens live miles from paved roads. But improved technology offers hope the new anti-malaria effort will succeed where earlier attempts failed.

Bed nets not only provide a physical barrier against malaria-bearing mosquitoes but also kill the pests with insecticide sprayed on the nets. In the past, bed nets had to be dipped in chemicals annually to retain their potency. But newer nets are treated with long-lasting chemicals that require re-dipping only once every three to four years.

Dipping the older nets every year posed "a huge logistical problem" in rural places, Adhanom says. "Fewer than 40 percent of villagers would show up to have their old nets dipped. That really compromised the whole program."

So far, the combined initiatives seem to be working. Malaria prevalence dropped by 67 percent in Ethiopia between 2001 and 2007, according to a World Health Organization study, while the number of deaths of children under 5 has dropped 56 percent.[1]

---

[1] "Impact of the Scale-Up of Anti-Malarial Interventions Measured Using Health Facility-Based Data in Ethiopia," World Health Organization, Feb. 1, 2008.

is embroiled in a self-interested effort to promote its interests at the expense of its neighbors," he says. "We cannot build relations with so-called anchor states under such circumstances. Tamp down the regional confrontations, however, and the relationship again makes sense from our perspective. Let it fester and we will again and again be drawn into fights that are not of our own making and not in our interests."

Others say the United States won't offend Ethiopia because it has contributed peacekeepers to help monitor the conflicts in Sudan's Darfur region and Burundi and supports the Comprehensive Peace Agreement between north and south Sudan. And despite human rights abuses, Ethiopia's governance looks good in comparison with neighboring Eritrea, Sudan and Somalia.

"What you have is a very difficult balancing act where you try to push Ethiopia to open up on human rights . . . without jeopardizing Ethiopia's help on regional issues," says Shinn, the former ambassador to Ethiopia. "I don't take the opinion that you should just hammer them on human rights and let the other side drop off. On the other hand, I don't think their help in counterterrorism and peacekeeping is so important you ignore human rights."

While some critics of the regime say the United States and other Western countries should cut economic aid to Ethiopia over concerns about rising oppression, others say that would be naïve. (*See "At Issue," p. 249.*)

The Bush administration's top diplomat for Africa agrees. "Obviously, we have a lot of interests in Ethiopia," says Frazer. "Ethiopia has one of the largest, best-trained militaries in Africa. There are many Ethiopians in the United States, and Ethiopia is a major player within the African Union."

The Obama administration is still formulating its policy toward the region but has suggested that democratic reforms will have a higher priority than counterterrorism cooperation.

"It is extremely important that Ethiopia . . . not close down its democratic space, that it allow its political opposition — its civil society — to participate broadly in the political life of that country," Johnnie Carson, Obama's assistant secretary of state for African affairs, told a Senate subcommittee on April 29. "We have our strongest relationships among our democratic partners where we share ideals and values together, rather than where we share common enemies together. A balanced relationship is absolutely essential."

BACKGROUND

Christian Kingdoms

Christianity arrived in Ethiopia in the early 4th century A.D., about 300 years before it arrived in England. According to tradition, two shipwrecked Syrian sailors brought the religion to what the Romans called Abyssinia.[34] A series of Christian kingdoms would rise and fall in the Ethiopian highlands until the 14th century, when feudalism descended over the country.

The dark ages lasted until the 1850s, when central authority was resurrected by the emperors Tewodros II, Yohannes IV and Menelik II. By the 1890s, Italy — a latecomer to the race for colonies in Africa — had conquered much of present-day Eritrea, which had only sporadically been under Ethiopian rule. But Italy's colonial ambitions were checked when Menelik's troops resoundingly beat back an Italian invasion from its Eritrean colony in 1896, ensuring that Ethiopia would remain the lone African nation never colonized by Europeans.

After becoming emperor in 1930, Haile Selassie, a former noble from the eastern city of Harar, barely had time to consolidate his rule before facing another challenge from Italy. In 1935 up to 100,000 Italian troops invaded northern Ethiopia. Selassie appealed to the League of Nations for help, but was rebuffed by France and the United Kingdom. Backed by bombers and tanks, the Italians had conquered most of Ethiopia's main cities by 1936, forcing Selassie into exile in Britain.[35]

But the Fascist Italians never controlled the countryside, and by 1941 a British-backed Ethiopian insurgency had ousted them.[36] Selassie reasserted the country's sovereignty in 1942 and turned to a new patron, the United States, to escape falling into Britain's colonial sphere.[37]

Compared with Ethiopia's rich history of ancient lords and kings ruling over peasant farmers in the cool highlands, Somalia's history is one of desert nomads who appeared in the Horn of Africa relatively late. Newly Islamized Somalis first began expanding south from the coastal area near the modern port of Berbera in northwestern Somalia in the 10th century. Fiercely independent camel and goat herders, Somalis have only rarely been brought under

CHRONOLOGY

1850s-1940s *Britain, France, Italy and Ethiopia divvy up the Horn of Africa, setting the stage for later ethnic disputes.*

1950s-1970s *Emperor Haile Selassie's grip on Ethiopia and Eritrea weakens as Somalia gains independence.*

1952 U.N. panel rules Eritrea should become part of a federation with Ethiopia rather than gain independence.

1960 Somalia gains independence, uniting British Somaliland with Italian Somalia, but not Somali-speaking regions of Kenya, Ethiopia and Djibouti. . . . Eritrean exiles in Egypt found Eritrean Liberation Front to fight for independence, beginning a three-decade-long struggle.

1969 Somalia's democratically elected president is assassinated. Military seizes power under Gen. Siad Barre, who proclaims Somalia a socialist state.

1974 Coup deposes Ethiopia's Selassie. Military group called the Derg takes control under Col. Mengistu Haile Mariam, establishing communist government.

1977-1978 Somalia conquers much of southeastern Ethiopia before Soviet Union enters war on Ethiopia's side. Barre turns away from communist bloc.

1980s-1990s *Civil wars overthrow authoritarian rulers across the Horn, but Somalia fails to recover.*

1983-1985 Drought triggers massive famine in Ethiopia, exacerbated by Mengistu's efforts to block food supplies to northern areas held by Eritrean and Tigray rebels. . . . Up to a million people die.

1991 As Soviet Union collapses, Ethiopia's Derg is overthrown by Eritrean and Tigrayan rebels from the North. Clan militias oust Barre regime in Somalia and then turn on one another. Somalia's civil war begins.

1992-1995 U.N. and U.S. try to help Somalia after up to 300,000 die from famine due to civil war and drought. U.S. withdraws in 1994 after U.S. troops die in "Black Hawk Down" incident.

1993 Eritreans vote for independence.

1998-2000 Ethiopia and Eritrea go to war over economic and border disputes. Ethiopia advances into Eritrea by 2000, capturing disputed town of Badme. U.N. peacekeepers begin patrolling border zone.

2000s *U.S. focus on anti-terrorism in the Horn leads to realigned loyalties.*

2001 Somaliland, which declared independence in 1991, ratifies constitution that endorses independence from southern Somalia, still mired in civil war. . . . Sept. 11 terrorist attacks on U.S. put focus on fighting al Qaeda threats in Somalia. Eritrean President Isaias Afwerki arrests Eritrean dissidents and closes private press.

2002 Eritrea-Ethiopian Boundary Commission awards Badme to Eritrea, but Ethiopia continues occupation.

2005 Ethiopia's first multiparty elections end badly as opposition leaders protest government claims of victory. At least 193 protesters are killed by Ethiopian security forces in Addis Ababa and thousands more injured. Government jails more than 120 opposition leaders, journalists and human rights activists.

2006 Islamic Courts Union (ICU) defeats U.S.-backed warlords in Mogadishu to take control of southern Somalia. Eritrean-armed ICU threatens jihad against Ethiopia.

December 2006 U.S.-backed Ethiopian troops invade Somalia, eventually ousting ICU. Efforts to install U.N.-backed Transitional Federal Government (TFG) amid Islamist insurgency fail due to resentment of Ethiopian occupation and intransigence of TFG President Abdullahi Yusuf.

December 2008-Present Ethiopian troops withdraw from Somalia; Islamist militias still control much of the south. Yusuf resigns. Sheikh Sharif Sheikh Ahmed, former ICU chairman, becomes president of U.N.-backed Somali government. . . . Shabaab and hardline militias declare war on Sheikh Ahmed's new government. Islamists capture additional towns in southern Somalia.

the control of a central state. A notable exception occurred during the holy wars against Ethiopia in the 13th-16th centuries, which culminated in the mid-16th century, when a predominantly Muslim army under Ahmed Gragn — "Ahmed the Left-Handed" — conquered much of the Ethiopian highlands.

The clan is the foundation and defining feature of Somali society. It is also at the root of the nation's problems, fostering factionalism and competition for resources rather than a sense of nationhood. The four major clan groups — Darod, Hawiye, Isaq and Dir — are each divided into sub-clans and sub-sub-clans, defined by shared ancestors going back hundreds of years.[38]

By the 19th century, France, Britain and Italy were competing with the rulers of Zanzibar, Egypt, Oman and Ethiopia for control of Somali lands. By the 1890s, the French had taken control of what is now Djibouti; Britain had established a protectorate in Somaliland; the Italians controlled central and southern Somalia and the Ethiopians ruled the Ogaden — now eastern Ethiopia.[39]

After World War II Italy was given "trusteeship" of its Somali territory, where it had developed banana and mango plantations using forced labor during the colonial era. But as independence movements swept the continent in the 1950s, the U.N. decided to unify British and Italian Somalia into a single independent state.[40] The move dashed nationalists' hopes for a Greater Somalia encompassing Somali-speaking populations in Djibouti, northern Kenya and the Ogaden.

Rise of Dictatorships

In the 1960s Somalia's young, democratically elected government unsuccessfully tried to expand its territory through a brief war with Ethiopia and by sponsoring Somali rebels in Kenya's Somali-speaking Northern Frontier District.[41] The assassination of President Abdirashid Ali Sharmarke in 1969 by one of his bodyguards heralded the end of those aspirations and of the country's nine-year-old democracy.

The army seized power under Gen. Barre, who quickly moved the government toward communism. On the first anniversary of the coup in 1970, Barre announced that his nation of nomadic herders henceforth would pursue "Scientific Socialism," Barre's own strain of Marxism.

"The Big Mouth," as he was known colloquially, soon established internal-security services and security courts to prosecute political crimes and "Victory Pioneers," modeled on China's Red Guards, to defend the revolution.[42] Exerting unprecedented political authority over the people, he tried to quell tribalism by prohibiting citizens from referring to their clan affiliations and by building rural schools and clinics.[43]

Meanwhile, Ethiopia's Selassie won a major diplomatic victory after World War II, when he persuaded the U.N. to unite Eritrea and Ethiopia, dashing the hopes of Eritrea's fledgling independence movement. But by the 1960s, the emperor's reign — backed by the landowners who ruled millions of peasants like medieval serfs — was chafing at the currents of the 20th century. His Amhara-dominated government faced rebellion from Tigrays in Eritrea and Oromos in southern Ethiopia. He also faced war with Somalia, which still sought control of the Ogaden.[44]

By 1973 the imperial regime's denial and botched response to a famine in northern Ethiopia, combined with soaring inflation and pressure from the Somali and Eritrean rebellions, led to a military revolt. The next year, "His Imperial Majesty Haile Selassie I, King of Kings, Lord of Lords, Conquering Lion of the Tribe of Judah, and Elect of God" was ousted.[45]

The new military government — headed by Lt. Col. Mengistu Haile Mariam and calling itself the Derg, the Amharic word for committee — aligned itself with the communist bloc and nationalized all private land, giving each peasant family 10 hectares (25 acres). The aging Selassie mysteriously died the same year. Many Ethiopians believe he was smothered with a pillow by Mengistu himself.

In 1977, the Derg was still struggling to consolidate its rule. To eliminate civilian Marxist rivals, it launched the so-called Red Terror, during which tens of thousands of students, businessmen and intellectuals suspected of disloyalty to the military government were murdered.[46] Meanwhile, with rebellions widening in the southeast and north, Somalia seized the opportunity to invade the Ogaden in hopes of fulfilling the grand dream of a Greater Somalia.

Although the Ogaden War pitted two of the Soviet Union's client states against each other, the U.S.S.R. eventually supported Ethiopia. Reinforced with Cuban troops and Soviet airpower, the Derg's army drove the Somalis out of the Ogaden in early 1978.[47]

Somali Pirate Attacks on the Increase

Sophisticated gangs rake in millions in ransoms, thwart navy patrols.

"I will never go back to sea," 25-year-old seaman Jiang Lichun told the *China Daily* after being held hostage for seven months by Somali pirates in the Gulf of Aden.[1]

During his harrowing 2007 ordeal, a shipmate was murdered after ship owners initially refused to pay a $300,000 ransom. "We heard six gunshots, but no one could believe Chen was dead," he said. Later, when the hostages were allowed up on deck, it was covered with blood.[2]

More recently, American sea captain Richard Phillips did not have to wait seven months to escape the clutches of Somali pirates. After his U.S.-flag ship carrying humanitarian aid for Africa was attacked in April, he gave himself up as a hostage so his shipmates could go free. He spent several days in a lifeboat with the pirates before U.S. Navy snipers killed his captors and freed Phillips.[3] Since then the pirates have seized several more ships with dozens of hostages.

AFP/Getty Images/Pierre Verdy

French soldiers take suspected Somali pirates into custody on the French warship Le Nivose on May 3, 2009. Attacks on commercial ships increased from 20 in 2006 to 111 in 2008. Last fall, a vessel was attacked on average once every other day.

The uptick in piracy in the Gulf of Aden has become the face of the lawlessness that engulfs Somalia. Until recently, the chaos had been largely contained within Somalia's borders. But in recent years what began as the occasional attack by local fishermen, angry at foreign vessels vacuuming their coastal waters, has morphed into one of Somalia's biggest sources of revenue, with sophisticated criminal gangs ramping up the hunt for ransoms.

Attacks on commercial ships off Somalia's coast increased from 20 to 111 between 2006 and 2008. Last fall, a vessel was attacked on average once every other day. Though killings have been rare, about 300 seamen and 18 vessels were being held by Somali pirates in late April. Ransoms paid in 2008 alone amounted to between $50 million and $80 million.[4]

The growth of Somali piracy was an unforeseen consequence of the 2006 U.S.-backed Ethiopian invasion of Somalia. The invasion ousted Somalia's governing Islamic Courts Union (ICU), which had effectively stamped out piracy during its brief reign in 2006. "The Islamic Courts, for some reason known only to themselves, decided to take action against maritime piracy," says Pottengal Mukundan, director of the International Maritime Bureau. "They made a public announcement saying those guilty of piracy would be punished in 2006. During the summer of 2006, there were no attacks at all."

Since the ICU was ousted, piracy has exploded. Armed with rocket launchers and machine guns, Somalia's buccaneers prowl the seas in small vessels that can range as far as 200 miles off shore. Often they'll approach a boat disguised as fishermen or traders, then fire weapons at the bridge and attempt to climb aboard using ropes and grappling hooks. Once aboard there is little foreign militaries can do. The pirates quickly take the crew hostage and steam the hijacked ship back to Eyl and other pirate bases along Somalia's Indian Ocean coast to await ransom payments.

The pirate gangs have become highly organized and intertwined with Somalia's various militias. "They have

Civil Wars

The 1983-1984 famine that would make Ethiopia synonymous with images of emaciated children resulted not just from drought but also from government policies intended to starve rebel-held areas.[48] With the Derg preoccupied with preparations for a lavish 10th anniversary celebration of the communist revolution, up to a million Ethiopians died in the famine as the government

spies," says Gérard Valin, a vice admiral in the French navy, who led a successful raid on pirates in April 2008 after the payment of a ransom to free a French yacht. "They have people in Djibouti, Nairobi and the Gulf giving them intelligence about the good ships to take. It's a business. They have people for taking ships, and they have people for negotiations."

The millions of dollars flowing into Somali fishing villages from piracy have overwhelmed the local economy. Pirates have built luxurious new homes and support hundreds of others who supply food, weapons and khat leaf, a stimulant popular with the pirate gangs. Ilka Ase Mohamed lost his girlfriend to a pirate who wore a black cowboy hat, drove a Land Cruiser and paid a $50,000 dowry to his girlfriend's mother.

"This man was like a small king," the 23-year-old Mohamed told *The Washington Post*. "He was dressed like a president. So many people attended him. I got so angry, I said, 'Why do they accept this situation? You know this is pirate money!' "[5]

The wave of attacks in late 2008 climaxed with the hijacking of the *Sirius Star*, a Saudi supertanker carrying $100 million worth of crude oil. Since then, foreign navies, which had largely ignored the problem, have rallied to the cause. As of late March as many as 30 warships from 23 countries were patrolling the area in a loose anti-pirate alliance that includes the United States, Iran, India and Pakistan.[6] Still, the problem won't be solved at sea, says Valin. Even with two dozen warships on patrol, he says, it's often difficult to distinguish between a fishing boat and a pirate skiff until the pirates are nearly aboard a commercial vessel, and many countries struggle with how to prosecute pirates picked up in international waters.

What's needed, experts say, is a functioning government on land that will shut down pirate safe havens. That's no easy task for either the newly elected Somali government of Sheikh Sharif Sheikh Ahmed — which controls just a few small areas in southern and central Somalia — or the Puntland regional government, which is the nominal authority over the areas where most of the pirates operate. Pirate ransom revenues last year were greater than either government's budget, and a U.N. report in December accused the Puntland administrators of complicity with pirate gangs.[7]

Somali Piracy Up Sharply

The 114 pirate attacks in the Gulf of Aden and Indian Ocean so far this year represent an 11-fold jump over 2004. This year 29 of the attacks were successful, more than twice the 2007 number.

Somali Pirate Attacks, 2004-2009

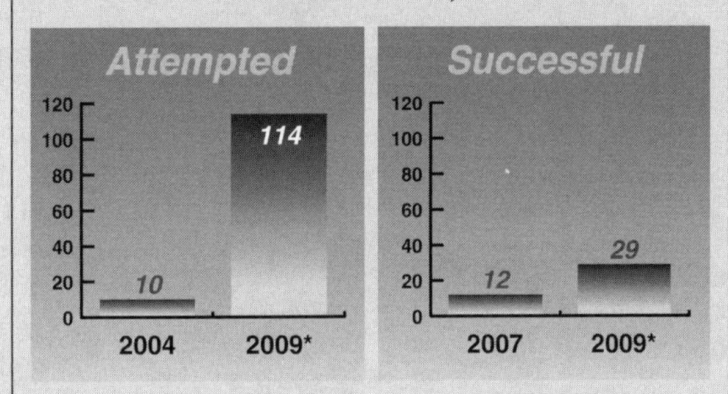

* Through May 12, 2009

Source: International Maritime Bureau

---

[1] "Chinese Sailor Recalls Terror of Somali Kidnapping," Agence France-Presse, Jan. 4, 2009.

[2] *Ibid.*

[3] Josh Meyer, "Snipers kill pirates in dramatic rescue," *Chicago Tribune*, April 13, 2009, p. 1.

[4] "Somalia: Anti-pirate Alliance," *Africa Confidential*, March 20, 2009, p. 8.

[5] Stephanie McCrummen, "Somalia's Godfathers: Ransom-Rich Pirates; Coastal Villagers Find Blessings and Ruin at Hands of Sea Robbers," *The Washington Post*, April 20, 2009, p. A1, www.washingtonpost.com/wp-dyn/content/article/2009/04/19/AR2009041902236.html.

[6] "Somalia: Anti-pirate Alliance," *op. cit.*

[7] "Report of the Monitoring Group on Somalia," United Nations, Dec. 10, 2008, www.un.org/sc/committees/751/mongroup.shtml.

systematically tried to hide images of starving peasants from the outside world while using aid to buttress government control rather than to alleviate suffering.[49] In an effort to undermine support for the rebels, entire regions of Tigray peasants in the north were forcibly moved to government camps — a policy known as villagization.[50]

Meanwhile, the humiliation of the Ogaden War led to an unsuccessful coup attempt in Somalia against Barre,

U.N. Somalia Funding Falls $12 Million Short

The Office of the U.N. High Commissioner for Refugees (UNHCR) says it needs more than $32 million to aid refugees in Somalia but has received only about $20 million from member states.

Funding for UNHCR Operations in Somalia

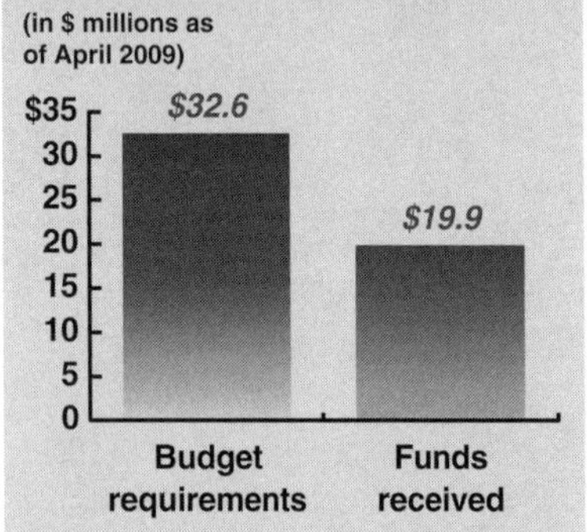

(in $ millions as of April 2009)

	$ millions
Budget requirements	$32.6
Funds received	$19.9

Source: U.N. High Commissioner for Refugees

led by officers from the Darod's Majerteyn sub-clan. From then on Barre maintained power by playing off the clans against each other. After the war, 700,000 Ethiopian Somalis poured across the border into Somalia, swelling the population by up to 20 percent. The collapse of the banana and mango plantations under socialism made Somalia's economy increasingly dependent on foreign aid.

The result was a widening civil war. By 1990, with government control of the countryside collapsing, Barre's enemies referred to him as the "Mayor of Mogadishu." In January 1991 he was chased from Mogadishu by a Habar Gida (a subgroup of the Hawiye clan) militia headed by a former heroin smuggler and police chief, Gen. Muhammad Farah "Aideed," whose nickname means "one who does not take insults lying down."[51] After a long sickness, the Somali state was now dead.

In Ethiopia, Mengistu's demise came the same year. By 1988 the Ethiopian Army was demoralized by the failure to win a military victory or reach political compromise with Isaias Afwerki's Eritrean People's Liberation Front. With Eritrean rebels controlling access to the Red Sea and Zenawi's Tigrayan rebels pushing south into central Ethiopia, Mengistu fled to Zimbabwe, and rebels occupied Asmara and Addis Ababa.[52]

Somalia's Descent

Back in Mogadishu, Barre's 1991 ouster led to an orgy of bloodshed. A period of "ethnic cleansing" ensued, mostly along clan lines. The Darod were especially targeted for their links with the hated Barre. Individual militia groups took control of the port, the airfield and major intersections.

At checkpoints, travelers were asked to recite the names of their ancestors — a Somali ritual that identifies people by clan and sub-clan. Those with the wrong lineage were often shot on the spot.[53] Darod militias retreated south, laying waste to the villages of smaller clans and killing and terrorizing civilians and stealing their grain. The ensuing famine claimed some 300,000; a million more were forced from their homes in search of food.

In reaction, the United States sent 28,000 troops to join 5,000 international peacekeepers under the optimistic banner Operation Restore Hope.[54] Though the mission initially succeeded in delivering aid to tens of thousands, it quickly became bogged down in street battles with militias and efforts to capture Aideed. In October 1993 several U.S. helicopters sent on a mission to arrest two of Aideed's top lieutenants were shot down over Mogadishu. In the ensuing effort to rescue trapped U.S. pilots and commandos, 18 American soldiers were killed and 84 injured in fighting that left hundreds of Somalis dead. Afterwards, the naked bodies of American soldiers were dragged through the streets as residents celebrated.

Immortalized by Mark Bowden's book *Black Hawk Down*, the battle led U.S. forces to withdraw by March 1994 and the remaining U.N. peacekeepers to leave a year later.[55] The stinging humiliation suffered by the U.S. military in Somalia is widely credited with leading to America's hesitancy in 1994 to intervene in a month-long genocidal rampage in Rwanda that left nearly a million people dead.[56]

After the U.S. withdrawal Aideed's militias expanded their control of southern Somalia, allying themselves with Islamists aligned with hard-line Saudi and Egyptian clerics. Aideed declared himself "interim president" but was killed in 1996 in fighting with rival Hawiye militias from the Abgal subclan.[57] Thereafter, the international community largely ignored Somalia until the terrorist attacks on New York and the Pentagon on Sept. 11, 2001, led to a renewed focus on Somalia as a haven for Islamic terrorists.[58]

One-Party Rule

Ethiopia embarked on a new path after 1991. The Derg had been defeated primarily by the separatist Eritrean People's Liberation Front. Zenawi's Tigray People's Liberation Front (TPLF) claimed power in Addis Ababa and agreed that Eritreans should be allowed a national referendum on independence. By 1993, Eritrea was independent, and Afwerki was in power in Asmara.

To expand his base, Zenawi reconstituted the TPLF as the Ethiopian People's Revolutionary Democratic Front (EPRDF) during the last years of the civil war. The party, still dominated by Tigrayans from the north, became the foundation of a one-party state. Opposition parties faced harassment, intimidation and imprisonment while politically favored businessmen were given control of economic assets. Tension over economic disputes soon emerged between former allies Zenawi and Afwerki: Eritrea raised port fees on its landlocked southern neighbor and destabilized the Ethiopian birr, still used by both countries, by establishing its own currency market.[59]

The friction erupted into warfare in 1998 in the town of Badme. An estimated 70,000 were killed and 750,000 displaced by the fighting before the Organization of African Unity helped arrange a cease-fire in 2000. By then Ethiopian troops had conquered Badme, and a 25-kilometer demilitarized buffer zone had been established inside Eritrean territory, patrolled by U.N. peacekeepers.

After the war, Afwerki quashed dissent in Asmara, arresting those who questioned his war strategy and abolishing the private press. Rule by the increasingly isolated Afwerki has evolved into a personality cult, and the economy has stagnated as military conscription decimated the labor force. Although an independent boundary commission awarded Badme to Eritrea in 2002, Ethiopia has never fully accepted the decision, and Eritrea — lacking both diplomatic support and military equipment — lacked the power to enforce it.

Ethiopia then briefly moved toward democracy. During political campaigning in 2005, the opposition Coalition for Unity and Democracy (CUD) debated ruling party officials on state television and was allowed to stage large rallies in several cities.

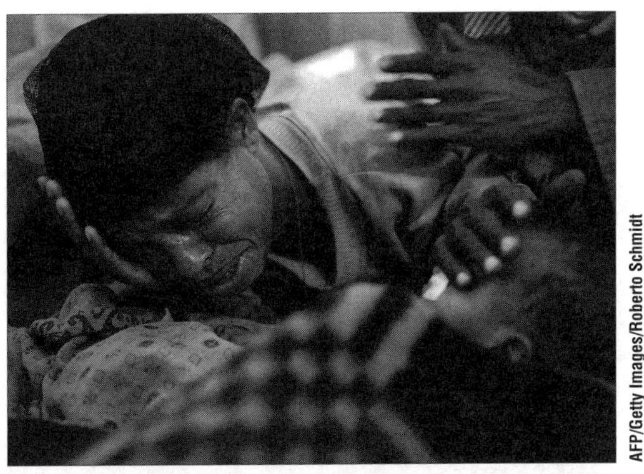

AFP/Getty Images/Roberto Schmidt

A mother in the Ethiopian town of Kuyera grieves over her sick child at a medical center run by Doctors Without Borders on Sept. 3, 2008. Earlier that day two children in nearby beds had died of malnutrition. Food shortages caused by a 2008 drought left at least 75,000 Ethiopian children under age 5 at risk, according to the U.N.'s Office for the Coordination of Humanitarian Affairs.

After the election, the ruling party claimed an outright victory in parliament, but the CUD disputed the claim. In ensuing demonstrations, 193 people were killed by government security forces, and 127 top opposition leaders, journalists and human rights activists were jailed. Since then democratic freedoms in Ethiopia have been steadily scaled back. In 2008 local and parliamentary elections, opposition parties managed to win just three of 3.6 million races.[60]

In Somalia, the roots of the country's latest attempt at governance trace to 2004, when the Transitional Federal Government was formed with Ethiopian support under the leadership of President Abdullahi Yusuf, a Darod warlord from the Puntland semi-autonomous region. Yusuf's government was viewed skeptically from the beginning by many Somalis, who saw it as a puppet of Ethiopia.[61]

The fledgling TFG largely stayed in exile in its initial years, and by 2006 all-out war had erupted in Mogadishu between a group of CIA-backed anti-Islamist warlords calling themselves the Alliance for the Restoration of Peace and Counterterrorism and supporters of the Islamic Courts Union (ICU), a group of Islamists that sought to bring order to the lawless country by settling disputes and

AFP/Getty Images /Khaled Fazaa

The increasingly harsh government of Ethiopian Prime Minister Meles Zenawi has triggered calls for Western governments to withhold aid from the regime. But in part because Ethiopia has staunchly supported the West's anti-terror campaign, international aid to Ethiopia has grown dramatically in recent years.

bringing criminals to trial under Islamic law. By mid-2006 the alliance, widely despised by ordinary Somalis for its corruption and criminality, was defeated and replaced by the ICU — which ended fighting in much of southern Somalia while instituting a strict form of sharia law.[62]

But the ICU, openly supported by Ethiopia's nemesis Eritrea, laid claim to Ethiopia's Ogaden region. By December 2006 it had succeeded in provoking an Ethiopian invasion. The United States, hoping to capture al Qaeda suspects linked to ICU radicals, gave the Ethiopians intelligence and logistical support, and U.S. Special Forces accompanied Ethiopian troops in the invasion.[63]

Ethiopia's technologically superior army quickly smashed the ICU's militia. But it soon found controlling Mogadishu more difficult than invading it. Within weeks remnants of the ICU's military wing — al-Shabaab — had allied with disaffected local clans to begin a bloody guerrilla campaign against the Ethiopian occupation. Ethiopia sought African Union peacekeeping troops to replace its forces in Mogadishu, but less than a quarter of the 8,000 authorized AU troops arrived in the first year after the Ethiopian invasion.[64]

Meanwhile the TFG under Yusuf's leadership proved both corrupt and inept. Reliant on Ethiopian soldiers for security in Mogadishu, it failed to bring functioning schools or clinics to the areas of southern Somalia nominally under its control. As the insurgency grew in Mogadishu, hundreds of thousands of people fled the fighting for makeshift refugee camps west of the city. Members of the government were accused of looting food aid from World Food Programme trucks. Radio stations that broadcast critical news were shuttered, and journalists were arrested.

Two years after Yusuf returned to Mogadishu, a U.N. report found that his government's central bank and finance ministry appeared to exist "in name only" and that Yusuf kept a printing press inside his presidential compound to print Somali shillings.

Ethiopian efforts to train a Somali security force to bolster the TFG failed dramatically. By October 2008, an estimated 14,000 of the 17,000 troops trained by the Ethiopians had deserted.[65] The Islamists recruited hundreds of the armed deserters by paying them $200 a month and playing on resentment of the Ethiopian occupation.[66]

By late 2008 Islamists and other opposition militias controlled most of southern Somalia, including the key ports of Kismayo and Merka. Disillusioned with Yusuf's failure to make peace with moderate Islamists, Ethiopia gave notice that it would withdraw troops even if that meant the Islamists would reclaim control.

Yusuf resigned in December 2008 after neighboring states threatened to freeze his assets. Ethiopian troops headed for the exit within weeks, opening the door for a new attempt at peace in the Horn of Africa.

CURRENT SITUATION

Fledgling Government

On May 24, a suicide bomber driving a Toyota Land Cruiser exploded a bomb at the gates of a TFG military compound in Mogadishu, killing six soldiers and a civilian.[67] The bombing was just the latest incident in a new spasm of violence between the TFG and Shabaab insurgents that has seen the Islamist militants tighten their grip over southern and central Somalia.

It wasn't supposed to be this way. After Ethiopian troops, widely despised by ordinary Somalis, pulled out of Mogadishu in January, Yusuf was replaced as president of the TFG by Sheikh Ahmed, the moderate Islamist who had chaired the Islamic Courts Union before the Ethiopian invasion and, from exile in Djibouti, had opposed both the occupation and Yusuf's corrupt government. Though 14 previous U.N.-backed Somali governments had failed to bring peace and stability to the country, it was hoped that Ahmed, as a Hawiye clan leader with previous links to some of the insurgent groups' leaders, could make peace with the Hawiye and Islamist militias opposed to the TFG.

Instead, bolstered by as many as 300 foreign fighters and arms from Eritrea, al-Shabaab has rejected Ahmed's overtures and moved from strength to strength, capturing Ahmed's hometown of Jowhar and neighboring Mahaday, cutting government links with central Somalia.[68] Ahmed has been forced to take refuge in a compound in Mogadishu, protected by foreign troops from the African Union. The growing chaos has led the TFG's new prime minister, Omar Abdirashid Ali Sharmarke, to all but rule out peace talks with insurgents.

"I don't think there is a chance to just sit with them and discuss issues with these people," Sharmarke told Reuters in late May. "The only way to deal with them that they can understand is to fight, and we are prepared to eradicate them."[69]

As fighting intensified in May, Ethiopia launched an apparent strike into Somalia, raising the specter of a possible re-invasion should the TFG collapse and al-Shabaab take control.[70] "Ahmed and the new TFG face an increasing challenge from al-Shabaab and an allied organization known as Hizbul Islam," says Shinn, the former ambassador to Ethiopia. "Al-Shabaab, although not centrally controlled, is well financed from outside and relying on a growing number of foreign fighters."

"The euphoria with which Sheikh Sharif's government was greeted has evaporated," says Abdi, of the International Crisis Group. "Things are very difficult. Unless something happens to unlock this logjam, this is just one of those cycles of transitions that will end up in a failure."

The TFG's reliance on 4,000 Ugandan and Burundian troops in Mogadishu — operating under the African Union — also hurts the fledgling government's legitimacy. "As foreigners [the AU troops] are also resented," says Shinn. "They are keeping the port and the airport out of the hands of al-Shabaab and protecting the presidency. The TFG probably could not accomplish this on its own."

Additional outside help seems remote. The U.N. has repeatedly declined requests from African nations to send a force to stabilize the country, while the AU has struggled to find more countries willing to contribute to the force. An uptick in attacks on AU peacekeepers last year has raised fears that the mission could end in a debacle as the U.S.-U.N. mission did 15-years ago.

"The AU peacekeepers haven't kept any peace because there is no peace to keep," says historian Lewis. "They're just useless."

Still, al-Shabaab also faces risks, especially since its brand of Islam is more radical than Somalia's traditional Sufi Islam. Among the moves that have provoked public revulsion: the amputation of the hands of accused thieves, public flogging of criminals and desecration of the graves of Sufi saints. Most dramatically, in October Islamist clerics in Kismayo ordered the public stoning of a young woman who may have been as young as 13 for committing adultery. Human rights groups said the woman, who was killed in a stadium in front of as many as 1,000 onlookers, had been raped.[71] More recently, al-Shabaab's decision to continue its war after Ethiopia withdrew has also tarnished its identity as a liberation movement fighting Ethiopian occupiers.

"In Mogadishu, public disappointment towards al-Shabaab militants is growing," says Faizal Mohammed, a Somali columnist for the Addis Ababa-based *Sub-Saharan Informer.* "Hawiye elders and some religious leaders have criticized al-Shabaab's move to continue the war after the Ethiopian withdrawal and to target AU peacekeepers."

The TFG also received a recent boost when Islamist warlord Yusuf Indahaadde, the former ICU defense minister, decided to support Ahmed and the TFG after Ahmed announced his government would implement Islamic law.[72]

"It will be messy and slow and it will be subject to reversals, but there is no reason why the right coalition of political and religious and business interests could not

AFP/Getty Images/Abdirashid Abdulle

Somalis displaced from their homes in war-torn Mogadishu prepare a meal at the Dayniile camp — one of dozens that surround the Somali capital. The ongoing civil war and poverty have sent more than a million refugees fleeing to neighboring countries or to camps inside Somalia, where they depend on international assistance for food and shelter — aid that is often blocked by violence, theft or piracy.

pull something together," says Menkhaus, the former U.N. official. "This new coalition government, it's the type of government that could work."

Meanwhile, the country continues to be a source of terrorism. On March 15 a suicide bomber allegedly trained in Somalia killed four South Korean tourists in Yemen. Three days later a second bomber attempted to kill a group of Koreans investigating the attack.[73]

Some analysts say the U.S. and Ethiopian intervention in Somalia has worsened the threat of terrorism by radicalizing the Islamists. "The problem has grown into a much bigger, hydra-headed problem because of that policy," says Lefkow, of Human Rights Watch. "That was a very ill-judged strategy on the part of both the Ethiopians and the U.S."

Ethiopia has a different view. "Ethiopia successfully neutralized" the Islamic Courts, says Ethiopian Foreign Minister Seyoum Mesfin. "Today there is only al-Shabaab and a few terrorist groups working as small units without any formidable organization. Their military backbone [and] organizational structure have been completely shattered."

Frazer, the former Bush administration diplomat, says the Ethiopian intervention had little effect on the threat. "When Ethiopia wasn't there, they were opening the country to jihadists," she says. "When Ethiopia was there, they were continuing to do it. After Ethiopia left, the country is still open to jihadists."

Standoff Continues

In February Ethiopian state-run television was filled with images of troops parading through Ethiopian cities, celebrating their withdrawal from Somalia. Though the two-year occupation of Somalia began with the ouster of one anti-Ethiopian Islamist group and ended with a more radical anti-Ethiopian group taking control of much of the country's south, Ethiopia's foreign ministry declared "Mission Accomplished."[74]

"We believe a great victory has been secured," Prime Minister Zenawi said on March 19. But the withdrawing troops have not had much time to rest. Despite official denials from Zenawi's government, Somali residents along the border between the two countries have reported repeated Ethiopian incursions since January.[75] In March the Ogaden National Liberation Front — an Eritrean-backed ethnic Somali separatist group in eastern Ethiopia — claimed it killed 24 Ethiopian troops near the town of Degehebur, not far from the Somalia border.[76]

Meanwhile, the standoff between Ethiopia and Eritrea continues to feed regional instability. Throughout 2008 Eritrea delivered up to $500,000 a month to a faction that was battling both Ethiopian troops and TFG security forces inside Somalia. And Eritrea regularly delivers arms and ammunition by small boat to Somali insurgents. It has also supplied arms and funding to the militia of Mohamed Sai'd "Atom," whose Shabaab-affiliated fighters have battled Puntland security forces. Atom's militia was also implicated in the kidnapping of a German aid worker in 2008 and a bombing that killed 20 Ethiopian migrants waiting for transport to Yemen in the Puntland port of Bossasso.[77]

"The Eritreans, under Isaias, are pursuing the same sort of strategy they followed in winning their independence: setting out to weaken Ethiopia from as many directions as possible," says Connell, the former adviser to the Eritrean government. "This results in steady support for all of Ethiopia's enemies, within Ethiopia's borders and without. Hence the support for Islamists in Somalia, whom you might least expect Eritrea to favor."

Eritrea's support of such groups has hindered its diplomatic efforts to get international enforcement for the

AT ISSUE

Should the West cut aid to Ethiopia over human rights concerns?

YES

Berhanu Nega
Exiled former mayor, Addis Ababa
Leader of opposition group Ginbot 7
Professor of economics, Bucknell University

Written for *CQ Global Researcher*, May 2009

The West's policy toward Ethiopia has been a disaster, and President Barack Obama and European leaders must reconsider their support to its government. Ethiopia received more than $1 billion in U.S. aid last year plus generous support from the United Kingdom and European Union. However, the country's human rights record is among the worst on the continent and getting worse by the day.

The possibility of a peaceful transition to democracy vanished in 2005 after Prime Minister Meles Zenawi's security forces killed 193 innocent civilians for peacefully protesting a stolen election and jailed tens of thousands of democracy activists, including 127 opposition leaders, journalists and civil society activists — including me.

Ethiopia is now a totalitarian police state with a human rights record comparable to that of Robert Mugabe's Zimbabwe. Meles and his inner circle have cowed the parliament, the courts and the press. Human rights groups claim the government has killed civilians in several regions. The government held local elections last year with more than 95 percent of the candidates from the ruling party; passed a restrictive new press law; jailed opposition leader Birtukan Mideksa and banned most human rights, democracy and gender-equality organizations.

Why shore up such a brutal dictatorship? Ethiopia is one of the poorest nations in the world, and Western policy makers say aid helps the poor more than the government. But after 18 years in power, Meles' regime still cannot feed its people: Some 14 million Ethiopians required foreign food aid last year. Donors have little control over how aid is delivered, and the government deliberately withholds foreign food aid to punish villages sympathetic to ethnic-Somali rebels.

The West's aid props up an anti-democratic regime and is ineffective in helping the poor. But proponents say Ethiopia — bordered by war-torn Sudan, a belligerent Eritrea and lawless Somalia — needs aid to remain stable in one of the world's toughest neighborhoods. But that's hard to swallow, given that Ethiopia's disastrous, two-year occupation of southern Somalia ended up ejecting a moderate Islamist government while empowering radicals; its nine-year border dispute with Eritrea remains unresolved; and numerous, armed indigenous groups wage domestic attacks with increasing ferocity.

U.S. and European economic pressure could make Meles' government negotiate a peaceful settlement to the country's explosive political problems.

NO

Patrick Gilkes
Adviser to Ethiopia's Ministry of Foreign Affairs; Author, The Dying Lion, Conflict in Somalia and Ethiopia; *and, with Martin Plaut,* Conflict in the Horn: Why Eritrea and Ethiopia Are at War

Written for *CQ Global Researcher*, May 2009

Activists who call for cuts in foreign aid to Ethiopia are seriously misguided. Ethiopia's government is far from perfect, but those who pressure the U.S. Congress and other Western governments to slash assistance to Ethiopia should remember it has averaged economic growth of 11 percent from 2003 to 2008, nearly double Africa as a whole and comparable to that of the Asian "tiger" economies in the 1990s.

The country launched a five-year Sustainable Development and Poverty Reduction Program in 2006 and is devoting about 60 percent of its federal budget to "pro-poor spending," as defined by the World Bank. This is one of the best rates in Africa.

The government has held defense spending to less than 1.5 percent of gross domestic product, even as it has fought a two-year anti-terrorism engagement in Somalia and strives to deter Eritrean aggression. Ethiopia remains a desperately poor nation, but there have been massive investment and major advances in infrastructure, education and health.

Despite the opposition's failure to take up seats in the first multi-party federal elections in 2005 and ensuing violence, local elections took place last year without incident. Ethiopia's federal structure has produced widespread acceptance of self-rule and meaningful fiscal and political devolution. Ethiopia provides a very clear demonstration of the effective use to which aid can and should be put. These must be developments well worth nurturing.

Much has been done in human rights — despite exaggerated opposition claims and poor research by Human Rights Watch and other groups. This includes major training programs for the judiciary, armed forces and police as well as the recent establishment of a government ombudsman and a Human Rights Commission. The recently enacted law regulating nongovernmental organizations (NGOs) has been controversial, but its critics wildly overstate its ramifications. The goal is protection and transparency for NGO humanitarian and development activity.

Ethiopia's long and close relations with the United States and Europe have been enormously important to development. Amidst international financial crisis and climate change, Ethiopia needs support to ensure development efforts don't falter, as it successfully implements its long-term strategy of democratization and poverty reduction. There's still much to do. This is certainly not the time to interrupt the process or threaten regional stability.

AP Photo/Farah Abdi Warsameh

A Somali insurgent holds a rocket-propelled grenade launcher in Mogadishu in January 2009, shortly after Ethiopian troops ended a two-year occupation of parts of Somalia. Some analysts say U.S. support for Ethiopia's 2006 invasion of Somalia radicalized many Somalis and increased the threat of anti-U.S. terrorism from Somalia.

Ethiopia-Eritrea Boundary Commission's 2002 decision awarding Badme to Eritrea.[78] With a strong push from Ethiopia, the African Union's Peace and Security Council in May called for international sanctions against Eritrea for its role in arming Somali militants.

Ethiopia also backs proxies. In May 2008 it hosted a conference of Eritrean rebel groups and opposition parties in Addis Ababa.[79] Last August, Ethiopia delivered 3,000 to 5,000 AK-47 assault rifles to the Puntland semi-autonomous government and has provided weapons and training to at least one other anti-Islamist militia in Somalia.[80]

Tens of thousands of troops from the two armies remain dug in across their shared border, sometimes only meters apart. And without U.N. peacekeepers, who were forced to withdraw in February 2008, the border skirmish could again flare up into all out war.

But many analysts believe such an outcome is unlikely. "Eritrea doesn't have diplomatic might or military strength to challenge the status quo," says Shinn, the former U.S. ambassador to Ethiopia. "It's not in either of their interests to resume that war, and they both know it."

However, both regimes have used the continuing presence of an external threat to sharply reduce democratic freedoms. "The stalemate on the border feeds and in turn is fed by growing authoritarianism in both states," said a June 2008 International Crisis Group report. "The ruling regimes rely on military power and restrictions on civil liberties to retain their dominant positions."[81]

However, it continued, "Both regimes have an interest in keeping the conflict at a low simmer rather than resolving it."

OUTLOOK

Unresolved Conflicts

Few analysts are optimistic that the Horn of Africa's political and economic status will be vastly improved over the next decade.

For the moment, Ethiopia's future looks the brightest. The government says economic growth averaged 11 percent between 2003 and 2008, bolstered by large inflows of aid and debt forgiveness. Some independent economists say the figure is overstated, and that real growth has been around 7 or 8 percent — still a remarkable figure for a land-locked country with no significant oil or mineral reserves.

But, problems abound. The global financial crisis will undoubtedly slow growth. Exports of coffee, Ethiopia's largest foreign-exchange earner, appear likely to decline for the second consecutive year while hospitals and factories face shortages of key supplies. And with dim prospects for a breakthrough with Eritrea, Ethiopia will probably face continuing conflict on at least three fronts: in Somalia, in the Ogaden and along its northern border with Eritrea.

"The future is impossible to predict so long as this simmering confrontation remains unresolved," says former Eritrean adviser Connell. Ethiopia and Eritrea "have enormous potential for growth, but the conflict between them and attendant repression of rights within each country hold both back."

Ethiopia's government, dominated by ethnic Tigrayan Christians from the northern highlands, remains unpopular with the ethnic Amharas and Oromos from central, southern and western Ethiopia, who together make up nearly two-thirds of the population. And the recent crackdown on opposition leaders, the press and human rights groups casts a pall over upcoming 2010 elections.

"I'm not optimistic that 2010 is going to be a breakthrough," says former U.S. Ambassador Shinn. "The tip-off was the local elections in 2008. I think that's a pity."

The government's failure to improve food self-sufficiency also leaves the ongoing threat of drought and famine, which helped trigger the demise of both the communist Derg regime and the Selassie government. "Ethiopia has a relatively high population growth rate," says Shinn. "If you can't feed your people and you're constantly at the mercy of foreign handouts, you've got to do something about it."

In Eritrea the outlook is decidedly dim. The economically and politically isolated government offers few prospects for improving its citizens' lives. "Eritrea is a one-man dictatorship masquerading as a one-party state," says Connell, who formerly worked for the Afwerki government. "The ruling party is little more than a cabal of Isaias Afwerki loyalists, whom he plays off against one another to maintain his iron-fisted rule. The closest analog I can imagine is North Korea." Afwerki's repressive rule, he adds, "is far more effective and all-encompassing than that of, say, [President Robert] Mugabe in Zimbabwe."

In April Human Rights Watch accused Eritrea of becoming a "giant prison" and issued a 95-page report detailing government atrocities against dissidents and evangelical Christians. Thousands of Eritreans risk the government's shoot-to-kill policy to flee to neighboring Sudan and Ethiopia each year, the report said.[82]

"The country is hemorrhaging," said an independent analyst, who asked that his name not be used so that he can continue traveling to Eritrea. "It's largely a police state. I don't see how the regime can survive in the long term. The government has control at the moment, but at some point something will give way."

In Somalia, analysts say probably only an Islamist government can reach across clan divisions to bring a semblance of order to the country's south. "It wouldn't surprise me if an Islamist movement took hold," says the historian Lewis. "How severe it will be and how rigorous is up for grabs."

Unfortunately, he continues, "the radical Islamist movement that they have now developed is particularly poorly educated and poorly informed about the world. It's taking the Somalis really back almost to colonial times."

Rebuilding the country after 18 years of civil war will be a long and difficult task.

"The best-case scenario is that [TFG President] Sharif may succeed in bringing in the hardline groups and — after a bumpy five to six years of transition — we may see a moderate Islamist government take control and become a regional player," says Abdi, of the International Crisis Group. "The worst-case scenario is Sharif's government will collapse, and insurgents will step up their attacks and Ethiopia will invade Somalia again. Somalia is by no means out of the woods."

If the radicals succeed, the threat from terrorism is likely to grow. The recent recruitment of Somali-American jihadis to fight in Somalia raises the question of whether radical Islamists in Somalia might be able to export suicide bombers to Western countries with Somali immigrant communities.

"Would they be able to use U.S. passport holders from places like Minneapolis as sleepers?" asks Menkhaus, the former U.N. official in Somalia. "It's something we need to pay attention to."

The Obama administration should take a more low-key, comprehensive strategy in helping Somalia than the short-term counterterrorism goals followed by the Bush administration, according to Menkhaus. "In fighting terrorism on land and piracy at sea, U.S. national security interests will be better secured if we aligned ourselves more with the interest of most Somalis in better security and effective governance," he writes. "Helping to build the house and using the back door will be much more effective than barging into the front door of a house that has yet to be built."[83]

NOTES

1. "Somalia: Exodus Continues Despite Lull in Mogadishu Fighting," IRIN News, May 21, 2009, www.irinnews.org/report.aspx?Reportid=84483.

2. "Escalating Violence Displaces Somalis," U.N. High Commissioner for Refugees, summary of briefing by spokesman Ron Redmond, May 26, 2009, www.unhcr.org/news/NEWS/4a1bbefb2.html. See also "Some 45,000 Somali Civilians Flee Mogadishu in Past Two Weeks," U.N. High Commissioner for Refugees, May 20, 2009, www.unhcr.org/cgi-bin/texis/vtx/news/opendoc.htm?tbl=NEWS&id=4a140e5b2, May 26, 2009.

3. "Beyond the Fragile Peace Between Ethiopia and Eritrea: Averting New War," International Crisis Group, June 17, 2008, p. 10, www.crisisgroup.org/home/index.cfm?id=5490&l=4.

4. "United Nations Human Development Indices: A Statistical Update 2008," U.N. Development Programme, http://hdr.undp.org/en/statistics.
5. "Consolidated Appeal for Somalia 2009," U.N. Office for the Coordination of Humanitarian Assistance, Nov. 19, 2008, www.relief web.int/rw/dbc.nsf/doc104?OpenForm&rc=1&cc=som. See also "Somalia is Worst Humanitarian Crisis: U.N. Official," Global Policy Forum, Jan. 30, 2008, www.globalpolicy.org/component/content/article/205/39493.html.
6. See "European Parliament resolution of 15 January 2009 on the situation in the Horn of Africa," European Parliament, www.europarl.europa.eu/document/activities/cont/200901/20090122ATT46879/20090122ATT46879EN.pdf.
7. For background, see John Felton, "Aiding Refugees," *CQ Global Researcher*, March 1, 2009, pp. 59-90.
8. Aidan Hartley, *Zanzibar Chest* (2003), p. 187.
9. "Horn of Africa Media Briefing Note," U.N. Development Programme, Feb. 11, 2009, www.reliefweb.int/rw/rwb.nsf/db900sid/EDIS-7P6MR3?OpenDocument. Note: The U.N. does not have statistics for those in need of emergency aid in Eritrea, which evicted most foreign aid organizations following the 1998-2000 Ethiopia-Eritrea war.
10. Derek Byerlee and David Spielman, "Policies to Promote Cereal Intensification in Ethiopia: A Review of Evidence and Experience," International Food Policy Research Institute, June 2007.
11. "Eritrea," *CIA World Fact Book*, Central Intelligence Agency, www.cia.gov/library/publications/the-world-factbook/geos/er.html.
12. Dina Temple-Raston, "Al Qaeda Media Blitz Has Some on Alert," National Public Radio, April 8, 2009, www.npr.org/templates/story/story.php?storyId=102735818.
13. Lolita C. Baldor, "Terrorists Moving from Afghan Border to Africa," The Associated Press, April 28, 2009, http://abcnews.go.com/Politics/wireStory?id=7445461.
14. Ken Menkhaus, "Somalia After the Ethiopian Occupation: First Steps to End the Conflict and Combat Extremism," Enough Project, www.enoughproject.org/publications/somalia-after-ethiopian-occupation-first-steps-end-conflict-and-combat-extremism.
15. Dan Ephron and Mark Hosenball, "Recruited For Jihad?" *Newsweek*, Feb. 2, 2009, www.newsweek.com/id/181408.
16. Alex Perry, "Somalia's War Flares Up Again," *Time*, Nov. 12, 2007, www.time.com/time/world/article/0,8599,1682877,00.html.
17. Scott Johnson, "An Unclenched Fist: Barack Obama Has a Unique Opportunity to Bring Something Resembling Stability to Africa's Horn," *Newsweek*, Feb. 2, 2009, www.newsweek.com/id/181313.
18. Scott Johnson, "Dilemmas of the Horn," *Newsweek*, April 21, 2008, www.newsweek.com/id/131836.
19. "Biographies of High Value Terrorist Detainees Transferred to the U.S. Naval Base at Guantánamo Bay," Office of the Director of National Intelligence, Sept. 6, 2006, www.dni.gov/announcements/content/DetaineeBiographies.pdf.
20. Lloyd de Vries, "Elusive Al Qaeda Suspect Was Real Deal," CBS News, Jan. 10, 2007, www.cbsnews.com/stories/2007/01/10/world/main2347258.shtml.
21. Alisha Ryu, "US Airstrike in Somalia Targets al-Qaida Suspect," Voice of America, March 3, 2008, www.voanews.com/english/archive/2008-03/2008-03-03-voa15.cfm?CFID=141624149&CFTOKEN=26521211&jsessionid=de308dbc94966565a9d81e432739512c471d.
22. Hamsa Omar and Jason McLure, "Somali Breakaway Regions Targeted by Suicide Bombers (Update1)," Bloomberg News, Oct. 29, 2008.
23. Jeffrey Gettleman, "The Most Dangerous Place in the World," *Foreign Policy*, March/April 2009, www.foreignpolicy.com/story/cms.php?story_id=4682.
24. Akwei Thompson, "Somali's New 36-Member Cabinet Larger Than Speculated," Voice of America, Feb. 22, 2009, www.voanews.com/english/Africa/2009-02-22-voa20.cfm, March 14, 2009.
25. For background, see Brian Beary, "Separatist Movements," *CQ Global Researcher*, April 2008, pp. 85-114.
26. I. M. Lewis, *A Modern History of the Somali Nation and State in the Horn of Africa* (2002), p. 289.

27. Alisha Ryu, "New Puntland President Faces Stiff Challenges," Voice of America, Jan. 15, 2009, www.voanews.com/english/archive/2009-01/2009-01-15-voa51.cfm.
28. "Report of the Monitoring Group on Somalia," United Nations, Dec. 10, 2008, www.un.org/sc/committees/751/mongroup.shtml.
29. Jason McLure, "Caught in Ethiopia's War," *Newsweek.com*, Jan. 22, 2008, www.newsweek.com/id/98033. See also Jeffrey Gettleman, "In Ethiopia, Fear and Cries of Army Brutality," *The New York Times*, June 18, 2007, and "Collective Punishment: War Crimes and Crimes Against Humanity in the Ogaden Area of Ethiopia's Somali Retion," Human Rights Watch, June 11, 2008, www.hrw.org/en/node/62175/section/1.
30. Jason McLure, "Ethiopian Police Re-arrest Opposition Leader Mideksa," Bloomberg News, Dec. 29, 2008.
31. "Clean Sweep for Ethiopian Party," BBC News, May 19, 2008, http://news.bbc.co.uk/2/hi/africa/7408185.stm. Also see Jason McLure, "Ethiopian Law Curbs Promotion of Rights, Critics Say," Bloomberg News, Jan. 6, 2009, www.bloomberg.com/apps/news?pid=20601116&sid=ahIahjCUZMz0&refer=africa.
32. "President Isaias Afwerki's Interview with Al-Jazeera Television," Eritrean Ministry of Information, April 24, 2008, www.shabait.com/cgi-bin/staging/exec/view.cgi?archive=17&num=8190.
33. "Somalia: To Move Beyond the Failed State," International Crisis Group, Dec. 23, 2008, p. 26, www.crisisgroup.org/home/index.cfm?id=5836&l=1.
34. Graham Hancock, *The Sign and the Seal* (1992), pp. 12-13.
35. Harold G. Marcus, *A History of Ethiopia* (2002), pp. 99-104, 138-142.
36. Sebastian O'Kelly, *Amedeo: The True Story of an Italian's War in Abyssinia* (2003).
37. Marcus, *op. cit.*, pp. 150-152.
38. Lewis, *op. cit.*, pp. 22-23.
39. *Ibid.*, p. 48.
40. *Ibid.*, p. 181.
41. *Ibid.*, pp. 201-202.
42. Ayaan Hirsi Ali, *Infidel* (2007), p. 55.
43. Lewis, *op. cit.*, pp. 210-212, 224.
44. For a first-person account of the student ferment that led to Haile Selassie's ouster, disillusionment under the succeeding Derg regime and the 1977 Ogaden War, see Nega Mezlekia, *Notes From The Hyena's Belly* (2000).
45. Marcus, *op. cit.*, pp. 173-178, 180.
46. Mezlekia, *op. cit.*, p. 295.
47. John Lewis Gaddis, *The Cold War* (2005), pp. 207-208.
48. See Robert Kaplan, *Surrender or Starve: Travels in Ethiopia, Sudan, Somalia and Eritrea* (2003).
49. See Myles F. Harris, *Breakfast in Hell: A Doctor's Eyewitness Account of the Politics of Hunger in Ethiopia* (1987).
50. Marcus, *op. cit.*, pp. 208-209.
51. Lewis, *op. cit.*, pp. 245-246, 259-263.
52. Michela Wrong, *I Didn't Do It For You: How the World Used and Abused a Small African Nation* (2005), pp. 349-352.
53. Hartley, *op. cit.*, p. 184.
54. Lewis, *op. cit.*, pp. 264-265, 268-269.
55. See Mark Bowden, *Black Hawk Down: A Story of Modern War* (1999).
56. For background, see Sarah Glazer, "Stopping Genocide," *CQ Researcher*, Aug. 27, 2004, pp. 685-708.
57. Lewis, *op. cit.*, p. 280.
58. *Ibid.*, pp. 305-306.
59. Marcus, *op. cit.*, pp. 237, 242, 249-250.
60. "2008 Human Rights Report: Ethiopia," U.S. Department of State, April 24, 2009, www.state.gov/g/drl/rls/hrrpt/2008/af/119001.htm.
61. Ken Menkhaus, "Somalia: A Country in Peril, A Policy Nightmare," Enough Project, Sept. 3, 2008, www.enoughproject.org/files/reports/somalia_rep090308.pdf.
62. *Ibid.*

63. Gettleman, *op. cit.*
64. Jason McLure, "Nigeria Needs Helicopters, Tanks to Send Troops to Somalia," Bloomberg News, June 28, 2008.
65. "Report of the Monitoring Group on Somalia," *op. cit.*
66. "Somalia: To Move Beyond the Failed State," *op. cit.*
67. Mustapha Haji Abdinur, "Suicide Attack on Somali Military Camp Kills Seven," Agence France-Presse, May 25, 2009.
68. Derek Kilner, "Somali Insurgents Take Another Town North of Capital," Voice of America, May 18, 2009, www.voanews.com/english/2009-05-18-voa18.cfm.
69. Abdiaziz Hassan, "Somali PM: Little Hope of Talks with Insurgents," Reuters, May 21, 2009.
70. "Ethiopian Forces Return to Somalia: Witnesses," Agence France-Presse, May 19, 2009.
71. "Stoning Victim 'Begged for Mercy,'" BBC News, Nov. 4, 2008, http://news.bbc.co.uk/2/hi/africa/7708169.stm. See also: "Somali Justice — Islamist Style," BBC News, May 20, 2009, http://news.bbc.co.uk/2/hi/africa/8057179.stm.
72. "Residents: Islamic Insurgents Seize Somalia Town," The Associated Press, May 20, 2009.
73. "Man Blows Himself Up in Failed Yemen Attack," Reuters, March 18, 2009, www.reuters.com/article/latestCrisis/idUSLI290474.
74. Jason McLure, "Ethiopia Quits Somalia, Declares 2-Year 'Mission Accomplished,'" Bloomberg News, Jan. 5, 2009, www.bloomberg.com/apps/news?pid=20601116&sid=aJqblcQ0bUCo.
75. Abdi Sheikh and Abdi Guled, "Ethiopia Denies Its Troops Enter Somalia," Reuters, Feb. 3, 2009. See also: "Ethiopian Forces Return to Somalia: Witnesses," Agence France-Presse, May 19, 2009.
76. Ogaden National Liberation Front Military Communique, March 7, 2009.
77. "Report of the Monitoring Group on Somalia," *op. cit.*, p. 33.
78. "Beyond the Fragile Peace Between Ethiopia and Eritrea: Averting New War," *op. cit.*
79. Jason McLure, "Eritrean Group Calls for 'Popular Uprising' Against Government, Bloomberg News, May 8, 2008.
80. "Report of the Monitoring Group on Somalia," *op. cit.*
81. "Beyond the Fragile Peace Between Ethiopia and Eritrea: Averting New War," *op. cit.*
82. "Service for Life: State Repression and Indefinite Conscription in Eritrea," Human Rights Watch, April 16, 2009. See also Jason McLure, "Eritrea a 'Giant Prison,' Human Rights Watch Says (Update 1)," Bloomberg News, April 16, 2009.
83. Ken Menkhaus, "Beyond Piracy: Next Steps to Stabilize Somalia," Enough Project, www.enough-project.org/publications/beyond-piracy-next-steps-stabilize-somalia.

BIBLIOGRAPHY

Books

Ali, Ayaan Hirsi, *Infidel, Free Press*, 2007.
This coming-of-age tale of a Somali girl living in Somalia, Saudi Arabia, Ethiopia, Kenya, the Netherlands and, finally, the United States explores how Somali culture and Islamic codes subordinate women.

Hartley, Aidan, *The Zanzibar Chest, Harper Perennial*, 2003.
A Reuters correspondent's memoir of covering wars in Somalia, Ethiopia and Rwanda in the early 1990s is interlaced with his family's British colonial history in East Africa and Yemen. Highlights include his eyewitness account of entering Addis Ababa in 1991 with Tigrayan rebels for the fall of the communist Derg regime and witnessing the U.S. military's "Black Hawk" assault on Mogadishu.

Lewis, I. M., *A Modern History of the Somali, James Currey Ltd.*, 2002.
One of the few Western academics to have spent his career studying Somalia, anthropologist Lewis focuses on how clan identities have shaped Somalis' history.

Marcus, Harold G., *A History of Ethiopia, University of California Press*, 2002.
This brief history begins with the famed fossil of Lucy, a human ancestor who roamed eastern Ethiopia 4 million years ago, and ends shortly after the 1998-2000 Ethiopia-Eritrea war.

Mezlekia, Nega, *Notes from the Hyena's Belly: An Ethiopian Boyhood, Picador USA*, 2000.
An Ethiopian writer's memoir of growing up during the 1970s provides a first-person account of the country's communist revolution and the ethnic tensions between Somalis and Ethiopian highlanders that still shape regional politics.

Wrong, Michela, *I Didn't Do It For You: How the World Used and Abused A Small African Nation, Harper Perennial*, 2005.
Mixing history and travelogue, a British journalist traces Eritrea's four-decade battle for independence after World War II. Wrong shows how the stubborn and resourceful Eritrean resistance becomes a pawn of Cold War powers and documents post-independence disillusionment under the dictatorial regime of former rebel leader Isaias Afwerki.

Articles

Ephron, Dan, and Mark Hosenball, "Recruited for Jihad?" *Newsweek*, Feb. 2, 2009, www.newsweek.com/id/181408.
Two Washington journalists uncover efforts by Somali Islamists to recruit fighters from U.S. refugee communities.

Gettleman, Jeffrey, "In Ethiopia Fear and Cries of Army Brutality," *The New York Times*, June 18, 2007, www.nytimes.com/2007/06/18/world/africa/18ethiopia.html.
The only Western journalist to enter Ethiopia's Somali region without being accompanied by Ethiopian security forces in recent years gives an account of atrocities by Ethiopian soldiers. Gettleman was arrested by the Ethiopian government during the trip.

Gettleman, Jeffrey, "The Most Dangerous Place in the World," *Foreign Policy*, March/April 2009, www.foreignpolicy.com/story/cms.php?story_id=4682.
The New York Times East Africa correspondent gives a short history of how Ethiopia and the United States exacerbated Somalia's civil war between 2005 and 2008.

Perry, Alex, "Somalia's War Flares Up Again," *Time*, Nov. 12, 2007, www.time.com/time/world/article/0,8599,1682877,00.html.
Perry outlines the motivations of the various actors in Somalia's civil war, including the transitional government, Islamist militias, Ethiopia and the United States.

Reports and Studies

"Beyond the Fragile Peace Between Ethiopia and Eritrea: Averting New War," *International Crisis Group*, June 17, 2008, www.crisisgroup.org/home/index.cfm?id=1229.
The continuing cold war between Ethiopia and Eritrea after their 1998-2000 war is fueling a host of regional conflicts.

"2008 Human Rights Report: Ethiopia," *U.S. Department of State*, Feb. 25, 2009, www.state.gov/g/drl/rls/hrrpt/2008/af/119001.htm.
Despite its close ties with Ethiopia's government, the U.S. State Department provides one of the most rigorous and detailed reports on human rights violations under Prime Minister Meles Zenawi.

"Report of the Monitoring Group on Somalia," *United Nations*, Dec. 10, 2008, www.un.org/sc/committees/751/mongroup.shtml.
The U.N. team that monitors Somalia's arms embargo describes the various militias and their links to foreign governments, piracy and other illicit activities.

Menkhaus, Kenneth, "Somalia: A Country in Peril: A Policy Nightmare," *Enough Project*, Sept. 3, 2008, www.enoughproject.org/files/reports/somalia_rep090308.pdf.
A former U.N. official in Somalia dissects the missteps by Somali regional and international powers that led Somalia to the brink and suggests how to bring peace to the troubled country.

For More Information

African Union, P.O. Box 3243, Addis Ababa, Ethiopia; (251) 11 551 77 00; www.africa-union.org. Seeks political and economic cooperation among the 53 member nations.

Amnesty International, 1 Easton St., London, WCIX 0DW, United Kingdom; (44) 20 74135500; www.amnesty.org. Advocates for human rights around the globe and publishes periodic reports on abuses.

Council on Foreign Relations, 1779 Massachusetts Ave., N.W., Washington, DC 20036; (202) 518-3400; www.cfr.org. Nonpartisan think tank that offers extensive resources, data and experts on foreign policy issues.

Enough Project, 1225 I St., N.W., Suite 307, Washington, DC 20005; (202) 682-1611; www.enoughproject.org. Lobbies for ending genocide and crimes against humanity.

Human Rights Watch, 350 Fifth Ave., 34th Floor, New York, NY 10118-3299; (212) 290-4700; www.hrw.org. Investigates human rights abuses worldwide with a team of lawyers and researchers.

Institute for Security Studies, P.O. Box 1787, Brooklyn Square, Tshwane (Pretoria) 0075, South Africa; (27) 012 346 9500; www.iss.co.za. African foreign policy think tank that provides a range of views on African issues.

International Crisis Group, 149 Avenue Louise, Level 24, B-1050 Brussels, Belgium; (32) 2 502-9038; www.crisisgroup.org. Provides independent research on international relations and the developing world.

10

Separatist Movements

Should Nations Have a Right to Self-Determination?

Brian Beary

AFP/Getty Images

The American Embassy in Belgrade is set ablaze on Feb. 21 by Serbian nationalists angered by U.S. support for Kosovo's recent secession from Serbia. About 70 separatist movements are under way around the globe, but most are nonviolent. Kosovo is one of seven countries to emerge from the former Yugoslavia and part of a nearly fourfold jump in the number of countries to declare independence since 1945.

From *CQ Global Researcher*, April 2008.

Angry protesters hurling rocks at security forces; hotels, shops and restaurants torched; a city choked by teargas. The violent images that began flashing around the world on March 14 could have been from any number of tense places from Africa to the Balkans. But the scene took place high in the Himalayas, in the ancient Tibetan capital of Lhasa. Known for its red-robed Buddhist monks, the legendary city was the latest flashpoint in Tibetan separatists' ongoing frustration over China's continuing occupation of their homeland.[1]

Weeks earlier, thousands of miles away in Belgrade, Serbia, hundreds of thousands of Serbs took to the streets to vent fury over Kosovo's secession on Feb. 17. Black smoke billowed from the burning U.S. Embassy, set ablaze by Serbs angered by Washington's acceptance of Kosovo's action.[2]

"As long as we live, Kosovo is Serbia," thundered Serbian Prime Minister Vojislav Kostunica at a rally earlier in the day.[3] Kosovo had been in political limbo since a NATO-led military force wrested the region from Serb hands in 1999 and turned it into an international protectorate after Serbia brutally clamped down on ethnic Albanian separatists. Before the split, about 75 percent of Serbia's population was Serbs, who are mostly Orthodox Christian, and 20 percent were ethnic Albanians, who are Muslim.[4]

Meanwhile, war-torn Iraq witnessed its own separatist-related violence on Feb. 22. Turkish forces launched a major military incursion into northern Iraq — the first big ground offensive in nearly a decade — to root out Kurdish separatist rebels known as

Separatist Movements Span the Globe

Nearly two dozen separatist movements are active worldwide, concentrated in Europe and Asia. At least seven are violent and reflect ethnic or religious differences with the mother country.

Selected Separatist Hot Spots

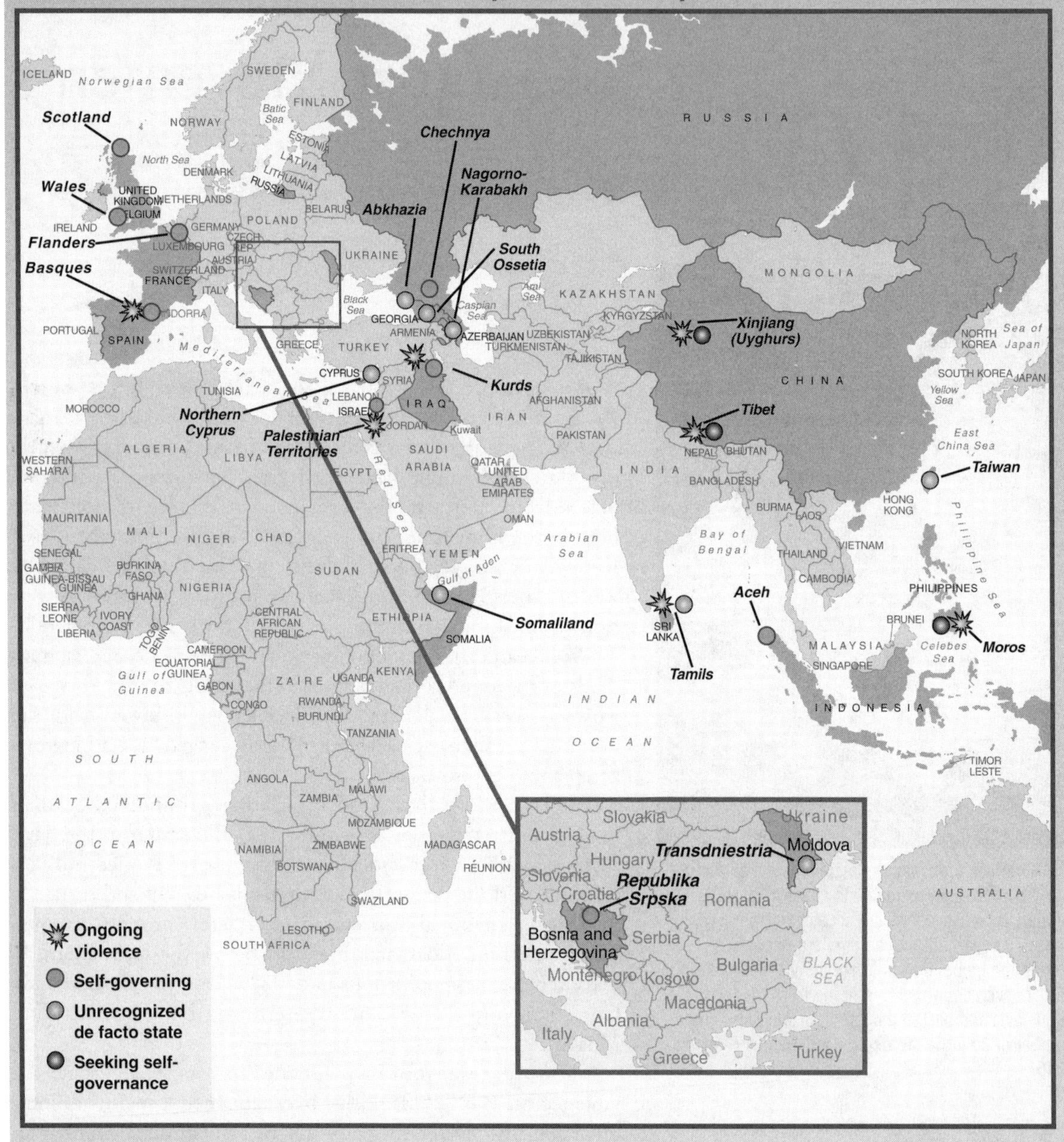

Sources: Unrepresented Nations and People's Organization, www.unpo.org; *Political Handbook of the World 2007*, CQ Press

Ongoing Separatist Movements

Africa

Somaliland — Militants in this northern Somalia territory established an unrecognized de facto state in the 1990s after the government of Somalia collapsed. The area was ruled by the United Kingdom from 1884 to 1960 and then became unified with the former Italian-ruled Somalia from 1960 to 1989.

Asia/Eurasia

Abkhazia — Independent Soviet republic briefly in 1921. Subsequently united with Georgia. Declared independence in 1992; war with Georgia ensued, which the Abkhaz won with Russian support. Since then, a stalemate has persisted. Up to 300,000 Georgians have fled since the 1990s, leaving an estimated 100,000 Abkhaz as the dominant force.

Aceh — One of the first places where Islam was established in Southeast Asia. Indonesia annexed the territory in 1949 upon becoming independent. Aceh was granted autonomy in 1959 and declared independence in 1976, with thousands dying in violence since then. A further 100,000 were killed in the 2004 Indian Ocean tsunami. A peace agreement was signed in 2005 granting autonomy.

Chechnya — A Muslim region in southern Russia, Chechnya was briefly independent in 1922. It declared independence after the collapse of the Soviet Union, but Russia opposed the secession and went to war with Chechnya from 1994-1996 and again in 1999. It became an autonomous Russian republic after a 2003 referendum.

Kurds — The world's largest ethnic group without its own country resides in Iraq, Iran, Turkey and Syria. The Iraqi Kurds have had autonomy since 1991. In Iran and Turkey they have no autonomy but are relatively free to speak Kurdish. The language is banned in Syria.

Moros — Muslims in the southern Philippines who live primarily on the island of Mindanao. Migration by Christian Filipinos from the north has diluted the Moro population. A militant Islamic fundamentalist group, Abu Sayyaf, is fighting the government to create a Moro Muslim state. Malaysia has committed the most international peacekeeping forces to stem the violence.

Nagorno-Karabakh — Declared independence from Azerbaijan in 1991, followed by a three-year war, during which most of the Azeris fled. A ceasefire has existed since 1994. It is now a de facto independent republic — unrecognized by the international community — populated mostly by ethnic Armenians.

Palestinian Territories — Since the largely Jewish state of Israel came into being in 1948, Arabs from the former Palestine have had no country of their own. The Palestinians live mainly in two non-contiguous areas, the Gaza Strip and West Bank, which Israel occupied in 1967 after a war with Egypt, Jordan and Syria. While the Palestinians have their own civilian administration and neither Israel nor neighboring Arab countries claim sovereignty over them, there is no independent Palestinian state yet because the terms cannot be agreed upon. A violent conflict between Israelis and Palestinians has persisted for decades.

South Ossetia — This region, which became part of Georgia in 1922, tried to become autonomous in 1989, but Georgia refused. After a war from 1990 to 1992 it became a de facto independent republic. Referenda in 1992 and 2006 confirming independence have not been recognized by any other country. Ossetian towns are governed by the separatist government; Georgian towns are overseen by Georgia.

Taiwan — The island off China's southeastern coast was established as a rival Chinese government in 1949 following the defeat of Chiang Kai-shek's Nationalists by Mao Tse-tung's communists. Between 1949 and 1971, it was recognized by most countries as the official government of China, but in 1971 mainland China replaced it as China's representative in the United Nations. In the 1990s, the Taiwanese government started a campaign to become a U.N. member again. Politics is polarized between those favoring unification with China — who won two recent elections — and those seeking official independence.

Tamils — Militant separatists known as the Liberation Tigers of Tamil Eelam (LTTE) have run a de facto state in northern Sri Lanka for many years. The LTTE assassinated Indian Prime Minister Rajiv Gandhi in 1991 for helping Sri Lanka crack down on the Tamils and Sri Lankan Prime Minister Ranasinghe Premadasa in 1993. A ceasefire was declared in 2002, but violence resumed in 2005. The Tamils are predominantly Hindu whereas the majority-Sinhalese community is Buddhist.

(Continued)

(Continued)

Asia/Eurasia (*Cont.*)

Tibet — China took over the Buddhist region in western China by force in the 1950s. Tibet's spiritual leader, the Dalai Lama, fled in 1959 and set up a government-in-exile in India. Recent separatist violence has been fueled by resentment over Chinese immigration into the autonomous region and the government's continued refusal to grant independence. The violence has prompted the Dalai Lama to consider resigning as the head of the exiled government.

Xinjiang — Known as East Turkestan or Chinese Turkistan, this vast region on China's northwest border with Central Asia — which comprises one-sixth of China's land mass — was annexed by China in the 18th century. Its 18 million inhabitants include 47 ethnic groups, including the Turkic-speaking Muslim Uyghurs — who once comprised 90 percent of the population. Today the Uyghurs make up only 40 percent of the inhabitants due to government policies that encourage Han Chinese to migrate there. Although the region has been officially autonomous since 1955, ethnic tensions have escalated in recent years. The U.S. State Department complains of serious human rights abuses against the Uyghurs due to Beijing's efforts to forcibly assimilate them and undermine their culture. China says Uyghur separatists are Islamic terrorists.

Europe

Basque Country — Basques in northeast Spain and southwest France have been pushing for greater autonomy or independence for more than a century. The militant separatist group ETA has killed about 1,000 people since 1968. Spain has granted its Basques extensive political and cultural autonomy but France has not.

Flanders — Flemish nationalism has grown in recent decades in Flanders, the northern part of Belgium where 60 percent of the population lives, most of them Dutch-speaking. Flanders, which has grown wealthier than French-speaking Wallonia to the south, already has extensive autonomy, but most Flemings would like more; many favor full independence.

Northern Cyprus — When Cyprus gained independence from British rule in 1960, relations between the Turks and Greeks on the island quickly deteriorated. Turkey's invasion in 1973 led to the Turkish Cypriots creating their own de facto state in the north that is only recognized by Turkey.

Republika Srpska — This self-governing territory within Bosnia, created in 1992, is populated mainly by ethnic Serbs who opposed Bosnia's secession from Yugoslavia. Moves to integrate it with the rest of Bosnia have failed so far.

Scotland and Wales — Demands by Celtic peoples in the northern and western corners of the United Kingdom for greater control over their affairs resulted in a devolution of power in 1999: A parliament was installed in Scotland and an assembly in Wales.

Transdniestria — First became a part of Moldova in 1812 when Russia captured both territories. From 1917 to 1939 it was part of the Soviet Union, while the rest of Moldova was ruled by Romania. From 1945 to 1991 both parts fell under Soviet rule. In 1992, when Moldova became an independent country Transdniestria seceded amid fear that Moldova would unify with Romania. The Moldovan army was repelled with the support of the Russian army. Its secession has not been recognized internationally. The area is dominated by Russian-speakers, with the Russian military also present.

The Americas (not shown on map)

Bolivia — After Evo Morales, Bolivia's first indigenous president, proposed changing the constitution last year to share more of the country's natural resources with the nation's indigenous highlanders, the mainly European-descended lowlanders have been threatening to secede.

Lakota Nation — This Indian nation of eight tribes living in South Dakota and neighboring states signed a treaty with the United States in 1851 granting them land rights. In 1989 they were awarded $40 million for losses incurred based on an 1868 land-rights treaty. In December 2007 a group of dissident Lakota delivered a declaration of independence to the State Department, which did not respond.

Québec — This majority French-speaking province has been threatening to secede from Canada since the 1960s. In two referenda on independence — in 1980 and 1995 — the Québécois voted to remain part of Canada. Today, they have a large degree of regional autonomy.

Sources: Unrepresented Nations and People's Organization, www.unpo.org; *Political Handbook of the World 2007,* CQ Press

the PKK, who have waged a bloody independence campaign against Ankara since 1984.[5]

The three hotspots reflect the same worldwide phenomenon — the almost inevitable conflict caused when a group of people want to separate themselves from a state that refuses to let them go. Despite today's oft-heard mantra that mankind is living in a global community where borders no longer matter, having a homeland of one's own clearly remains a dream for millions.

Out of more than 70 separatist movements around the globe, about two dozen are active, most in Europe and Asia, and seven of them are violent. And since 1990, more than two dozen new countries have emerged from separatist movements, mostly the result of the disintegration of the Soviet Union and the breaking apart of the former Yugoslavia.[6] Almost half of the 25 successful separatist movements were accompanied by some amount of violence, most of it ethnically based. *(See map and chart, pp. 258–260.)*

In fact, the number of independent countries around the globe has waxed and waned over the past 150 years. During the 19th century, the number declined as the European colonial powers gobbled up territories in Asia and Africa. Then after World War II the number mushroomed as those empires disintegrated. The United Nations has grown from 51 members when it was founded in 1945 to 192 members today (not counting Kosovo).[7] *(See graph, p. 269.)*

Among the groups fighting for independence today, the Kurds are the largest, with approximately 25 million dispersed in Turkey, Iraq, Iran and Syria.[8] Other separatist movements are microscopic by comparison: The South Ossetians — who have seceded from Georgia and formed a de facto but as-yet-unrecognized government — number just 70,000, for example. Some movements, like the Québécois in Canada and the Scottish in the United Kingdom, have been peaceful, while others, like the Tamils in Sri Lanka and Palestinians in Israel, have been violent. Indonesia has had two separatist movements with very different destinies: East Timor (Timor Leste) on Indonesia's eastern tip became independent in 1999 — although it is still struggling to fend for itself, relying on international aid to make up for its severe food shortages — while Aceh in the west has opted for autonomy within Indonesia.[9]

Separatism often triggers serious rifts between the world's major powers. In the case of Kosovo, the United

AFP/Getty Images/Vano Shlamov

Protesters at a March rally in Tbilisi, Georgia, want Russia to stop supporting South Ossetia and Abkhazia, two Georgian regions that seceded and formed de facto states. Their placards — which say "Russia! Stop Dealing With the Fates of Small Nations!" — indicate how a separatist movement can become a pawn in a geopolitical tug-of-war. Russia supports the two breakaway states, while most of the international community does not recognize them.

States and its NATO allies — including the United Kingdom, France, Germany, Italy and Turkey — backed the secession. U.S. Assistant Secretary of State Daniel Fried has dubbed it "the last chapter in the dissolution of Yugoslavia," while acknowledging "many things can go wrong and probably will."[10] In stark contrast, Russia steadfastly opposes independence for Kosovo and is standing shoulder-to-shoulder with its historical ally, Serbia.

Outgoing Russian President Vladimir Putin has said, "If someone believes that Kosovo should be granted full independence as a state, then why should we deny it to the Abkhaz and the South Ossetians?" According to Matthew J. Bryza, U.S. deputy assistant secretary of State for European and Eurasian Affairs, Russia is covertly providing material support to South Ossetia and Abkhazia — two de facto states that have emerged from within Russia's political foe, the ex-Soviet Republic of Georgia.[11] The United States and the rest of the international community don't recognize the secession of either state.

Meanwhile, the Chinese government opposes the pro-independence movement among the ethnically

World's Newest Country Remains Divided

Kosovo is struggling to be recognized.

Delaware-size Kosovo grabbed the world's attention on Feb. 17 when its ethnic Albanian-dominated government declared its independence from Serbia, triggering street protests among some Serb citizens.

Because of fierce opposition from Serbs both inside Kosovo and in Serbia, a large international presence with armies from six "framework" nations keeps an uneasy peace: The United States controls the east, Ireland the center, Turkey and Germany the south, Italy the west and France the north.[1]

"Do not trust the apparent calm, it's the main difficulty of this mission," says Captain Noê-Noël Ucheida from the Franco-German brigade of the 16,000-strong NATO force in Kosovo. "It can be calm. But it becomes tense in the morning and ignites in the afternoon."[2]

The spotlight fell on Kosovo in 1999 — several years after the break-up of Yugoslavia — when Serbian leader Slobodan Milosevic's brutal campaign to forcibly remove Kosovar Albanians led to NATO having to step in and take the province out of Serb hands. Now Kosovo's 2 million Albanians seem determined to open a new chapter in their history by implementing a U.N. plan granting them internationally supervised independence. Not for the first time, the world's leading powers are divided over a conflict in the Balkans. The United States, Germany, United Kingdom, France and Italy back independence while Serbia, Russia and China oppose it.

Further complicating the issue are the 100,000 Serbs living in Kosovo, including 40,000 concentrated in a zone north of the Ibar River; the remainder are dispersed throughout the south. Just as Kosovo's Albanians fought tooth and nail to free themselves from Serb rule, so the Serbs in north Kosovo are equally resolved to be free of Albanian rule. "They already run their own de facto state," says Nicolas Gros-Verheyde, a French journalist who toured Kosovo just before the declaration of independence. "They are heavily subsidized by the Serbian government in Belgrade, which tops up the salaries of local police officers and supplies the electricity and mobile phone network."

The Ibar River is fast becoming yet another border in the Balkans. "Cars in the north have different registration plates. When Kosovar Serbs drive south, they remove them to avoid being attacked. Our translator, who was Serbian, would not even get out of the car," says Gros-Verheyde. He notes there was much greater contact between the Serb and Albanian communities during his previous visit to Kosovo in 1990, when the Serbian military patrolled the province. "But 15 years of ethnic conflict has bred mistrust and hatred," says Gros-Verheyde.

Daniel Serwer, vice president of the Center for Post-Conflict Peace and Stability Operations at the United States Institute of Peace (USIP), feels Serbia only has itself to blame for losing Kosovo. It drove the Kosovar Albanians to secede by excluding them from the Serbian government, he argues. "If Kosovars had been included — for example by being offered the presidency of Serbia — it might not have seceded. The Serbs want sovereignty over the territory of Kosovo, but they could not care less about the people," he says.

The economy of Kosovo has suffered terribly from two decades of strife throughout the region. With unemployment

Turkic Uyghur people, who live in the western Chinese autonomous region of Xinjiang. China has tried to stifle separatism in its western provinces by promoting mass migration of ethnic Chinese to both Tibet and Xinjiang to dilute the indigenous population. Critics say China used the Sept. 11, 2001, terrorist attacks in the United States as a pretext for clamping down on the Uyghurs, who are Muslim, by claiming they were linked to Islamic terrorist movements like al Qaeda.[12]

China's separatist woes are an embarrassment just four months before the start of the Summer Olympic Games in Beijing — China's chance to shine on the world stage. The Chinese call the Tibetan protests a "grave violent crime involving beating, smashing, looting and burning" orchestrated by the Dalai Lama, the Tibetan leader-in-exile.[13] But Western leaders are not buying Beijing's line. Nancy Pelosi, Speaker of the U.S. House of Representatives, traveled to India to meet with the Dalai Lama on March 21 and declared the Tibet situation "a challenge to the conscience of the world."[14]

Despite the international condemnation of China's treatment of the Tibetans, however, the international community and the United Nations (U.N.) — which in 1945 enshrined the right to self-determination in its

at 50 percent, thousands have migrated to Western Europe and the United States, sending money back to their families. Much of the country's income is derived from trafficking in drugs, weapons and women, claims Gros-Verheyde. Roads are dilapidated, and electricity is cut off several times a week.

Meanwhile, the international community is ever-present: The mobile phone network for Kosovar Albanians is provided by the principality of Monaco, the euro is the local currency and NATO soldiers' frequent the hotels and restaurants.

"The Albanian part is livelier than the Serbian," says Gros-Verheyde. "The birth rate among the Albanians is very high. They want to increase their population to ensure they are not wiped out."

Kosovo's future remains uncertain. Most of the world's nations have not yet recognized it as an independent country, and many are unlikely to do so, including Spain, Slovakia and Romania, which fear potential secessionist movements of their own.[3] Internally, tensions between the Albanian and Serb communities are unlikely to simply melt away. In fact, relations could further deteriorate over how to divide up the country's mineral resources, most of which lie in the Serb-controlled northern part.

Meanwhile, the world will keep a watchful eye and presence. The European Union (EU) is in the process of deploying a 1,900-strong police and rule-of-law mission to replace a U.N. police force.[4] Indeed, many observers think the EU may hold out the best hope of salvation: Under a plan proposed by the European Commission — and supported virtually across the board in Europe — all Balkan nations would be integrated into the EU, ultimately diminishing the significance of borders and smoothing out ethnic tensions.

AP Photo/Samir Delic

Ethnic Albanians celebrate Kosovo's declaration of independence from Serbia on Feb. 17, 2008. The new state is backed by the United States and key European allies but bitterly contested by Serbia and Russia.

In the meantime, NATO holds the fort with a "high-visibility, low-profile" doctrine. "The soldiers have bullet-proof vests but keep them in the vehicles," says Gros-Verheyde. "They carry machine guns on their back but do not walk through villages with a weapon at their hip. A soldier told me the only exception to this was the American soldiers who have been traumatized by Iraq."

[1] Nicolas Gros-Verheyde, "One eye on Belgrade, the other on Pristina," *Europolitics*, (EU affairs subscription-based news service), Jan. 22, 2008, www.europolitics.info/xg/europolitique/politiquessectorielles/defense/217304?highlight=true&searchlink=true.

[2] Quoted in *ibid.*

[3] Joanna Boguslawska, *Europolitics*, Dec. 14, 2007, www.europolitics.info/xg/europolitique/politiquesexternes/relationsexterieures/215424?highlight=true&searchlink=true.

[4] For details, see Web sites of NATO and U.N. forces, respectively, at www. nato.int/KFOR and www.unmikonline.org.

founding charter — have provided little support to recent separatist movements. Many countries are wary of incurring the wrath of economic giants like China, and international law on separatism is ambiguous, leading to an inconsistent and non-uniform global reaction to separatist movements.

Though several international conventions reaffirm the right to self-determination, they also pledge to uphold the "principle of territorial integrity" — the right of existing states to prevent regions from seceding. "International law grows by practice," says Thomas Grant, a senior fellow and legal scholar at the United States Institute of Peace (USIP), an independent institution established and funded by the U.S. Congress that tries to resolve international conflicts. "The legal situation adapts itself to the factual situation." (*See box, p. 274.*)

Consequently, the international community's response to de facto separatist states varies widely. For example, most of the world refuses to deal with the Turkish Republic of Northern Cyprus, which has been punished with an economic embargo since 1973, when Turkish troops invaded Cyprus and permanently occupied the north, creating a Turkish-dominated de facto state there. Somaliland — which established a de facto state in northwestern Somalia in 1991 after the government in Mogadishu collapsed — has been largely ignored by the world community despite being a relative beacon of stability in the otherwise unstable horn of Africa.[15] The Tamils' campaign to gain independence from Sri Lanka attracts relatively little international diplomatic attention these days, in part, some say, because the area is not considered critical by the major powers.

Meanwhile, the island nation of Taiwan, off the coast of mainland China, is accepted as a global trading partner — the United States alone has 140 trade agreements with the Taiwanese — but not as an independent country. Few countries are willing to challenge Beijing's "one-China" policy, which denies any province the right to secede and sees Taiwan as its 23rd province.[16]

In addition, the world has done nothing — apart from occasionally condemning human rights violations — to prevent Russia from brutally repressing Chechnya's attempt to secede. While separatists there largely succeeded in creating their own state in the 1990s, Moscow has since regained control of it, although an insurgency continues.

The U.N. has no specific unit looking at separatism as a phenomenon. Instead, it usually waits for a conflict to break out and then considers sending a peacekeeping mission to restore law and order.

"U.N. member states are likely to be wary of separatism because of the knock-on effects it can have on themselves," says Jared Kotler, communications officer at the U.N.'s Department of Political Affairs. "Member states are very aware how one movement can encourage another — possibly in their own country."

"Thus far, territorial integrity has always won the debate," says Hurst Hannum, a professor of international law at Tufts University in Medford, Mass., and a specialist in self-determination theory. "This is why Kosovo will be an important precedent despite statements by all concerned that it should not be seen as such."

In Latin America, where most countries won wars of independence in the early 1800s, separatist movements are rare today, although one recently sprang up in Bolivia. Bolivians living in the lowlands, who are mostly of European ancestry, are threatening to secede to prevent the government from redistributing the profits from the nation's oil and gas reserves to the mainly indigenous highlanders. In North America, the United States has not experienced a serious separatist threat since 1861 when 11 Southern states seceded, provoking the Civil War. And while few predict an imminent resurgence of such movements in the United States, diverse secessionist groups are beginning to coordinate their efforts.[17] (*See "At Issue," p. 279.*)

Some separatist movements have been highly successful. For example, since declaring independence from the Soviet Union in 1990, Lithuania has liberalized and grown its economy, consolidated democracy and joined the European Union (EU) and NATO.

Seth D. Kaplan, a foreign policy analyst and author of the forthcoming book *Fixing Fragile States*, has some advice for countries struggling to put out secessionist fires. "Countries that can foster sufficient social cohesion and a common identity while minimizing horizontal inequities are the most likely to stay whole," he says. "Those that don't and have obvious identity cleavages are likely to ignite secessionist movements."

While the world confronts growing separatism, here are some key questions being asked:

Should there be a right of self-determination?

"In principle, yes," says Daniel Serwer, vice president of the Center for Post-Conflict Peace and Stability Operations at the United States Institute of Peace. "But the real question is: What form should self-determination take?"

Self-determination is often interpreted to mean the right to secede and declare independence. But it can take other forms, too, such as local autonomy, similar to what Canada has granted to Québec, or a federal system with a strong central government that protects minority rights.

"In Kosovo, after nine years under U.N. control, young people expected independence," says Serwer. But other minorities have chosen a different path, he adds. For instance, "the Kurds in Iraq were thrown out of their homes" by Saddam Hussein. "They were even gassed. But so far they have not chosen the route of independence."

Gene Martin, executive director of the Philippine Facilitation Project at USIP, notes, "Local autonomy may not be enough for some people, who feel they just do not belong to a country." Plus, he adds, the government's ability or willingness to relinquish its authority also affects whether a minority will push for local autonomy or for full independence. Martin has been involved in brokering peace between the Philippine government and the Moro Islamic Liberation Front, which has for decades fought for an independent state for the Moros, a Muslim people living in southern Philippines.

Marino Busdachin — general secretary of the Hague-based Unrepresented Nations and Peoples Organization (UNPO), which represents 70 nonviolent movements pushing for self-determination — rails against the U.N. for not upholding that right. "Self-determination exists on paper only. It is a trap," he says. "We cannot apply to anyone for it. The U.N. member states block us."

Moreover, he says, seeking self-determination should not be confused with demanding the right to secede. "Ninety percent of our members are not looking for independence," he says.

That's a significant distinction, according to Diane Orentlicher, a professor of international law at American University in Washington, D.C. Although the U.N. has enshrined the right to self-determination, it has never endorsed a right of secession, and no state recognizes such a right. Such a step would be dangerous, she writes, because it would allow minorities to subvert the will of the majority. "Minorities could distort the outcome of political processes by threatening to secede if their views do not prevail," she writes.[18]

Dmitry Rogozin, Russia's ambassador to NATO, shares that view. "If the majority wants to live in a shared state, why does the minority have the right to break away?" he has asked.[19] "Look at Berlin. You could say it's the third-largest Turkish city [because of the large number of people of Turkish origin living there]. If tomorrow the Turks living in Berlin want to create a national state in the city, who can be against it?"

"The challenge for the West in Kosovo," says self-determination legal expert Hannum at Tufts, is to recognize its independence without implicitly recognizing its right to secede — just as "the West pretended that the former Yugoslavia 'dissolved' as opposed to recognizing the secession of its various parts."

The State Department's Bryza, who deals with conflicts in Abkhazia, South Ossetia and Nagorno-Karabakh, a separatist enclave in Azerbaijan, agrees. "It is unreasonable to have self-determination as the only guiding principle," he says. "If we did, the world would live in utter barbarity."

Fixing Fragile States author Kaplan believes separatism makes sense in a few cases, such as Kosovo and

AP Photo/Al Jacinto

The Moro Islamic Liberation Front — which for decades has fought for an independent state for the Moros, a Muslim group living in the south of the predominantly Catholic Philippines — are negotiating with the government to peacefully settle the dispute.

Somaliland. "But, generally, the international community is right to initially oppose separatism," he says.

So when should a group have the right to secede? "When you are deprived of the right to participate in government, and there are serious violations of human rights, such as genocide," says the USIP's Grant. "The bar is placed very high because you want to preserve the state, as that is the mechanism you use to claim your right of secession."

This is why, argues Serwer, ethnic Albanians in Macedonia, which borders Kosovo, do not have the right to secede. "If they called for independence — and I don't think they want this — I would say 'nonsense,' because they have their rights respected. It is only when other forms of self-determination — like local autonomy — are blocked that secession becomes inevitable."

Meto Koloski — the president of United Macedonian Diaspora, which campaigns for the rights of Macedonian minorities in Greece, Bulgaria, Albania, Serbia and

More Than Two Dozen New Nations Since 1990

Since 1990, 26 new countries have declared independence — 15 of them the result of the dissolution of the Soviet Union. Yugoslavia has separated into seven new states, the last one, Kosovo, declaring its independence in February.

Successful Separatist Movements Since 1990

Emerged from Ethiopia (1993)
Eritrea

Emerged from Indonesia (2002)
Timor Leste

Emerged from the Soviet Union (1991)

Armenia	*Kazakhstan*	*Russia*
Azerbaijan	*Kyrgyzstan*	*Tajikistan*
Belarus	*Latvia*	*Turkmenistan*
Estonia	*Lithuania*	*Ukraine*
Georgia	*Moldova*	*Uzbekistan*

Emerged from Czechoslovakia in 1993
Czech Republic
Slovakia

Emerged from Yugoslavia
Bosnia and Herzegovina (1992)
Croatia (1991)
Kosovo (2008, from Serbia)
Macedonia (1991)
*Montenegro (2006)**
*Serbia (2006)**
Slovenia (1991)

* For three years, Serbia and Montenegro existed as a confederation called Serbia & Montenegro, and then split into separate countries.

Sources: Unrepresented Nations and Peoples' Organization, www.unpo.org; *Political Handbook of the World 2007,* CQ Press, 2007; Tibet Government-in-exile, www.tibet.com.

Kosovo — says, "Everyone should have a right to self-determination, their own identity, language and culture but not to their own state."

Secession also is problematic — even if backed by a clear majority of those in the seceding region — because the minority opposed to secession could end up being oppressed. "Secession does not create the homogeneous successor states its proponents often assume," writes Donald Horowitz, a professor of law and political science at Duke University in Durham, N.C. "Guarantees of minority protection in secessionist regions are likely to be illusory; indeed, many secessionist movements have as one of their aims the expulsion or subordination of minorities in the secessionist regions.[20]

"There is an inevitable trade-off between encouraging participation in the undivided state and legitimating exit from it," he continued. "The former will inevitably produce imperfect results, but the latter is downright dangerous."[21]

Some would argue that certain separatist movements have no legal basis because the people concerned already exercised their right of self-determination when their country was first founded. "The whole self-determination theology is very slippery," says a U.S. government official with extensive knowledge of the separatist conflict in Aceh, Indonesia. "We support the territorial integrity of Indonesia. We never concluded that the human rights situation in Aceh was intolerable."

Jerry Hyman, governance advisor at the Center for Strategic and International Studies in Washington, highlights an often-overlooked point: "We have to ask how economically and politically viable are states like Transdniestria? If you apply this [right to secede] to Africa, it could explode. At best, Africa is a stained-glass window." Economic viability tends to be ignored when assessing separatist claims, he says, because the "we're special" argument usually prevails.

"If they are not viable, they will end up like East Timor, relying on the international community financially," he says.

Are globalization and regional integration fueling separatism?

Several organizations and treaties have emerged in recent years to encourage more regional integration and cross-border trade. The EU is the oldest and largest, but newer arrivals include the Association of Southeast Asian Nations (ASEAN), the African Union (AU), the Latin American trading blocks ANDEAN and MERCOSUR and the North American Free Trade Agreement (NAFTA). In addition, the World Trade Organization (WTO) is working to abolish trade barriers globally. Experts differ over whether these organizations promote or discourage separatism.

The Peace Institute's Grant believes they can encourage it. "What are the political impediments to independence?" he asks. The new states are not sustainable as a small unit, he says, adding, "If you reduce the significance of national borders and improve the free movement of people, goods and capital, you remove that impediment."

For instance, the possibility of being part of the EU's single market makes an independent Kosovo a more viable option and has seemingly suppressed Albania's desire to merge with the Albanians in Kosovo to create a Greater Albania. Asked if Albania had a plan to establish a Greater Albania, Foreign Minister Lulzim Basha said, "Yes, we do. It has a blue flag and gold stars on it," describing the EU flag. "Today's only goal is integration into NATO and the EU as soon as possible."[22]

Günter Dauwen, a Flemish nationalist who is director of the European Free Alliance political party in the European Parliament, says the EU fuels separatism by not adequately ensuring respect for regions. Dauwen is campaigning for more autonomy and possibly independence for Flanders, the mostly Dutch-speaking northern half of Belgium that already has a large degree of self-government. "The national capitals control the EU. They decide where funds for regional development go. This creates terrible tension."

Over-centralization of decision-making is particularly acute in Spain, he says, where it has triggered separatism in the region of Catalonia in the northeast and Galicia in the northwest. In addition, France suppresses regionalist parties in Brittany, Savoy and the French Basque country, he says. "When we complain to the EU, its stock answer is that only nation states can devolve power to the regions."

Dauwen points out that the European Court of Human Rights (ECHR) has condemned countries for not respecting the rights of ethnic minorities, but the EU doesn't force its members to comply with those rulings. For instance, he says, the ECHR condemned the Bulgarians for not allowing ethnic Macedonians to form their own political party. But the EU did nothing to force Bulgaria to abide by the ruling, further fueling the desire for separatism.

The State Department's Bryza disagrees. "The opposite works in my experience," he says. "As Hungary and Slovakia have deepened their integration into the EU, the desire of ethnic Hungarians who live in countries neighboring Hungary to become independent is receding. And the possibility for Turkish Cypriots in northern Cyprus [whose de facto state is only recognized by Turkey] to be part of the EU gives them an incentive to rejoin the Greek Cypriot government in the south, which is already in the EU."

AP Photo/Gemunu Amarasinghe

Female Tamil Tiger fighters undergo training at a hideout deep in Tiger-controlled territory northeast of Colombo, Sri Lanka, in 2007. The Tamils, who comprise 18 percent of Sri Lanka's population, began fighting for independence in 1983 — a struggle that has resulted in the deaths of some 70,000 people. Tamils now control large swathes of the country.

Likewise, Ekaterina Pischalnikova — special assistant to the special representative of the secretary-general at the U.N. observer mission in Georgia, which is trying to resolve the Georgia-Abkhaz conflict — says EU regional integration has helped to "mitigate rather than fuel separatist movements."

Busdachin of the Unrepresented Nations and Peoples Organization says the EU "is helping to resolve separatist conflicts in many cases because it has the most advanced regime for protecting minorities." For example, the EU has consistently pressured Turkey, which wants to join the union, to grant the Kurds the right to express their language and culture more freely. Such a move could quell some Kurds' desire for full independence, he says, adding that he would like to see ASEAN, MERCOSUR and other regional organizations follow the EU model.

Author Kaplan — who has lived in Turkey, Nigeria, China and Japan — says regional integration "is only promoting separatism in the EU. Europe is peaceful and prosperous so there is no real need for states. But when you get into the wild jungle, the state is more important." For instance, he explains, "states in Africa and Central America do not want to give up their power, even though they would benefit the most from regionalism."

In Asia, ASEAN has no clearly defined policy on separatism, leaving it up to national governments to decide how to deal with separatist movements. The Shanghai Co-operation Organization (SCO) — set up in 2001 by Russia, China, Kazakhstan, Kyrgyzstan, Uzbekistan and Tajikistan to combat separatism, terrorism and extremism — strongly opposes separatist movements like that of China's Uyghurs.[23]

Ironically, separatism also can fuel regional integration. Many of the countries that have recently joined the EU or intend to do so — Lithuania, Slovakia, Slovenia, Montenegro and Macedonia — were formed from separatist movements. Too small to be economically self-sufficient, they see integration into the EU market as the only way to ensure continued prosperity and stability.

Does separatism lead to more violent conflict?

The recent developments in the Balkans provide strong evidence that separatism can provoke violent conflict — especially when countries divide along ethnic lines, as the former Yugoslavia has done.

Serbia's festering rage over Kosovo's declaration of independence is a prime example. "If this act of secession for ethnic reasons is not a mistake, then nothing is a mistake," said Serbia's Foreign Minister Vuk Jeremic, adding, "Serbia will not go quietly. We will fight, and we will not tolerate this secession."[24]

Serwer at the United States Institute for Peace says, "If you partition a state along ethnic lines, this almost inevitably leads to long-term conflict," especially if the central government resists the separatist movement.

"Secession converts a domestic ethnic dispute into a more dangerous one," according to Duke's Horowitz. "The recurrent temptation to create a multitude of homogeneous mini-states, even if it could be realized, might well increase the sum total of warfare rather than reduce it."[25]

The State Department's Bryza says separatism doesn't have to lead to violence "if leaders of national groups exert wise leadership and temper the ambitions of nationalist groups."

The campaign by Taiwanese separatists to obtain a seat for Taiwan at the U.N. — a March 22 referendum calling for this failed — shows how even nonviolent separatism can trigger conflict. "Bizarre as it may seem, a peaceful referendum in Taiwan may portend war," according to John J. Tkacik, a policy expert at the Heritage Foundation in Washington. He predicted China would invoke a 2005 anti-secession law to justify using "non-peaceful" means to counter Taiwanese separatism.[26] Fear of provoking a war with China is probably the main reason there is so little international support for the Taiwan independence movement.

As former U.S. Deputy Secretary of State Robert B. Zoellick said in 2006, "We want to be supportive of Taiwan, while we are not encouraging those that try to move toward independence. Because I am being very clear: Independence means war. And that means American soldiers."[27]

But independence does not always mean war. With a broadly homogeneous population, its own currency, flag, army, government and airline, Somaliland is an example of how a people can effectively secede without causing chaos and violence. Somaliland's isolation from the international community has not hindered its development — indeed it has helped, argues author Kaplan.

"The dearth of external involvement has kept foreign interference to a minimum while spurring self-reliance and self-belief," he says.

Martin at the Peace Institute points out that since the end of the Cold War, "most wars have been intra-state. Sometimes borders can be shifted to solve the problem and actually prevent war."

But separatist movements also are frequently manipulated by external powers as part of a geopolitical chess game that can become violent. "People want independence because of ethnic hatred and because it is in their economic interests to separate. But outside powers help separatists, too," says Koloski, of the United Macedonian Diaspora. For example, the United States, Britain and France support Kosovo's independence because they believe this will help stabilize the region, while Russia and China support Serbia's opposition because they fear it will encourage separatist movements elsewhere, including in their territories.

In some cases — notably Québec, Flanders, Wales and Scotland — separatist movements have not boiled over into violent conflict. In each, the central government granted some self-rule to the separatist region, preventing the situation from turning violent.[28] In addition, the movements were able to argue their case through elected political representatives in a functioning democratic system, which also reduces the likelihood of violence.

"When a country is too centralized and non-democratic, this produces separatist movements that can become violent," says Busdachin at the Unrepresented Nations and Peoples Organization. "The responsibility is 50-50."

But democracy does not always prevent separatism from escalating into conflict. From the 1960s to the '90s, extreme Irish Catholic nationalists in Northern Ireland waged a violent campaign to secure independence from the U.K., all the while maintaining a political party with elected representatives.

How the global community responds to one separatist movement can affect whether a movement elsewhere triggers a war. "Violence is not inevitable," says Flemish nationalist Dauwen. "But ethnic minorities do get frustrated when they get nowhere through peaceful means, and they see those who use violence — for example the Basque separatist movement ETA in Spain — attracting all the headlines."

As a Tamil activist notes, "Whatever we have achieved so far, we have got by force."

Number of Countries Reaches All-time High

The number of countries in the world has increased sixfold since the 1800s, when European colonization was at its peak. The greatest jump occurred after World War II, when Europe gave up its colonies amid a worldwide movement for independence. The United Nations, which includes nearly all of the world's countries, now has 192 members. The U.N. has not yet recognized Kosovo, which declared its independence in February.

Number of Countries Recognized Worldwide, 1864-2008

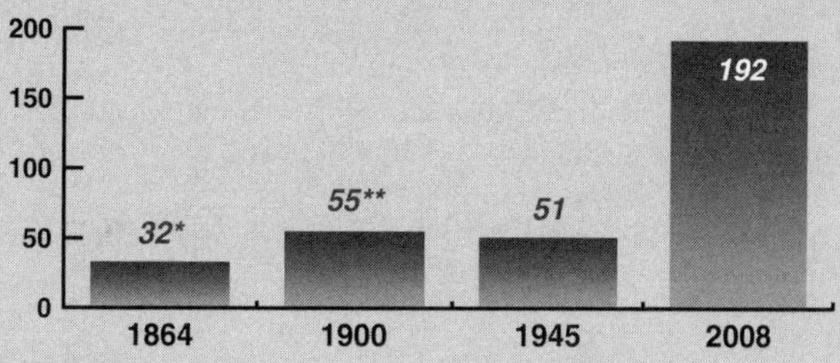

* Includes several states in Australia and New Zealand that were part of the British Empire; Finland and Poland were considered part of Russia; Africa is omitted entirely, since its interior was largely unmapped at that time. Since the U.S. Civil War was in progress, the Confederate States were counted as a separate country.

** The British Empire is counted as a single country, as are the French, German and Dutch empires; Austria-Hungary is considered one country and includes both Liechtenstein and Bosnia-Herzegovina; Finland and several Asian dependencies are counted as part of Russia; Turkey includes five states.

Sources: The Statesman's Year Book, 1864 and 1900; United Nations

BACKGROUND

Emerging Nations

Throughout history separatism has manifested itself in various forms as groups grew dissatisfied with their governments. Even the Roman Empire — which was synonymous with order, peace and civilization in most of its conquered territories — had its Celtic resisters, the Britons and Gauls.[29]

In medieval Europe, the discontented sought to extricate themselves from kingdoms, feudal domains and churches. In the 18th and 19th centuries European colonies in the Americas, Australia and New Zealand began splitting off from the "mother" countries. By the 19th century, with the Hapsburg, Romanov and Ottoman empires on the decline, groups united by ethnicity, language or culture began to cast off their imperial shackles. Then in the late 1800s and early 20th century the major European powers — and the United States — began acquiring and consolidating colonies or territories.

Just three decades after its own war for independence from Great Britain, the United States had to weather its own secessionist storms. In 1814 a handful of New

CHRONOLOGY

1776-1944 *Nation states gradually eclipse multi-ethnic empires as the dominant form of government.*

1776 Britain's American colonies declare independence, triggering war.

Early 1800s Spanish and Portuguese colonies in Latin America become independent.

1861 Eleven Southern U.S. states secede, sparking Civil War. After four years of bitter fighting, the South loses and is reintegrated into the union.

1918 At the end of World War I new European states are created from the ashes of the Hapsburg and Ottoman empires.

1919 U.S. President Woodrow Wilson champions the "right of self-determination" but fails to get it adopted by the League of Nations.

1939 World War II breaks out. Borders shift as Germany, Japan and Italy occupy neighboring countries before being defeated by the Allies.

1945-1989 *More new states emerge as colonies gain independence, but borders are left largely intact.*

1945 U.N. charter includes the right of self-determination.

1949 China invades and occupies Tibet.

1960 U.N. General Assembly proclaims a Declaration on the Granting of Independence to Colonial Countries and Peoples, heralding the end of the colonial era.

1967 Biafra secedes from Nigeria; is reintegrated after a three-year war.

1975 World's leading powers sign the Helsinki Final Act, guaranteeing peoples the right of self-determination.

1984 A new, violent Kurdish separatist revolt breaks out in Turkey.

1990-2008 *Twenty-six new countries are created after the Soviet Union and Yugoslavia break apart.*

1990 Soviet republics begin resisting Moscow's central control. Lithuania on March 11 becomes the first republic to declare its independence, setting off a chain reaction that leads to the dissolution of the U.S.S.R.

1991 Slovenia and Croatia split from Yugoslavia, accompanied by violence, especially in Croatia. . . . New states emerge from the Soviet Union, as do unrecognized breakaway republics in Nagorno-Karabakh, Chechnya, South Ossetia, Abkhazia and Transdniestria. . . . In Africa, Somaliland separates itself from rapidly disintegrating Somalia.

1992 Bosnia splits from Yugoslavia, provoking a three-year war.

1993 Czechoslovakia splits peacefully into the Czech Republic and Slovakia. . . . Eritrea secedes from Ethiopia after a U.N.-monitored referendum.

1995 A referendum in Québec advocating secession from Canada is rejected by 50.6 percent of Québécois.

1999 North Atlantic Treaty Organization seizes Kosovo from Serbia in response to Serbia's persecution of Kosovar Albanians. . . . East Timor declares independence from Indonesia after 25 years of violence.

2004 The separatist region of Aceh is granted autonomy from Indonesia after a devastating Dec. 26 Indian Ocean tsunami creates a feeling of solidarity between Aceh's separatists and the Indonesian authorities.

2005 Chinese authorize use of force to prevent Taiwan from seceding.

2007 Belgium edges closer to disintegration. . . . In Bolivia, people of European descent threaten to secede in response to fears of losing control over the country's gas reserves.

2008 Taiwanese separatists are defeated in parliamentary elections on Jan. 12. . . . Kosovo declares independence from Serbia on Feb. 17, triggering violent protests among Serbs in Belgrade. Separatist protests in Tibet turn violent on March 14; Chinese send in troops to put down the rebellion.

England states opposed to the federal government's anti-foreign-trade policies and the War of 1812 organized a convention in Hartford, Conn., and produced a report spelling out the conditions under which they would remain part of the United States. The U.S. victory against the British in 1815 took the wind out of the initiative's sails, however, and secession negotiations never actually took place.

Then in 1861, largely in response to U.S. government efforts to outlaw slavery, 11 Southern states tried to secede from the union to form their own country. After a bloody, four-year civil war, the South was forcibly reintegrated into the United States in 1865.[30] The U.S. Supreme Court cemented the union with a ruling in 1869 (*Texas v. White*) that effectively barred states from unilaterally seceding.[31]

In 1914 nationalist opposition to imperialist expansionism in Europe sparked World War I. Aggrieved at the Austro-Hungarian Empire's annexation of Bosnia, home to many Serbs, 19-year-old Serbian Gavrilo Princip assassinated Archduke Franz Ferdinand, heir to the imperial throne. Many of the new countries created in the post-war territorial division, such as Lithuania and Poland, were constructed along broadly ethnic lines. At the same time the concept of "self-determination" — the right of a nation to determine how it should be governed — emerged, championed by President Woodrow Wilson.[32]

Wilson's effort to enshrine self-determination in the founding statute of the newly created League of Nations was defeated. The idea of holding a referendum to determine who should govern a disputed territory gained support in this period, too. And when the league set up a commission to determine the status of the Åland Islands (it determined Finnish sovereignty), the concept was developed that a people might have the right to secede when the state they belonged to did not respect their fundamental rights.[33]

One group, the Kurds, fared badly in the post-war territorial settlements. Emerging without a state of their own, Kurds repeatedly staged uprisings in Iraq, Iran and Turkey but were suppressed each time. The most recent and bloody of these has occurred in Turkey, where 40,000 people have been killed in an ongoing conflict that began in 1984. The Kurds in northern Iraq also suffered widespread massacres and expulsions in the late 1980s under Iraqi President Saddam Hussein, but when the United States and its allies defeated Saddam in the 1991 Gulf War, Iraqi Kurds effectively gained self-rule after the U.N. forced Saddam to withdraw from the region.[34]

The Palestinians were also dealt a poor hand in 1948 after their homeland became part of the new state of Israel, populated mainly by Jews fleeing post-war Europe. After winning the Six-Day War in 1967, Israel occupied Palestinian lands on the western bank of the Jordan River and in a narrow strip of land called Gaza. Ever since then, the Palestinians have been fighting to have a country of their own.[35]

Decolonization

The 20th century saw the number of independent countries around the globe more than triple — from the approximately 55 that existed in 1900 to the 192 that make up the United Nations today.[36] Most of the new nations were created in the post-World War II era, as the European powers shed their colonies in Africa and Asia. To ensure that the decolonization process was peaceful and orderly, the United Nations adopted the Declaration on the Granting of Independence to Colonial Countries and Peoples in 1960.[37]

But in practice the emergence of new states was often far from peaceful. Hundreds of thousands of people died in outbreaks of violence during the August 1947 partition of India and Pakistan, which within months went to war with each other over the disputed territory of Kashmir. In 1967 the Igbo people of Biafra tried to secede from Nigeria, triggering a devastating war and famine. Three years later the region was forcefully rejoined to Nigeria. Despite accusations that Nigeria was committing genocide on the Biafrans, the international community did not back Biafra's independence.

The former British colony of Somaliland in the horn of Africa became momentarily independent in 1960 but immediately chose to unite with its fellow Somalis in the newly constituted state of Somalia to the south created from Italy's former colony. When Somalia collapsed into violent anarchy in 1991, Somaliland seceded, and separatist militants installed a civil administration. In northern Ethiopia, Eritrea's 31-year secession struggle finally ended in independence in 1993 after passage of a U.N.-monitored referendum.

In Sri Lanka, which is dominated by Sinhalese people, the minority Tamils — who make up about 18 percent of the population — have been pushing for independence since the 1970s.[38] The Tamils had wielded considerable

Bye-Bye Belgium?

More prosperous Flanders wants autonomy.

Belgium experienced a surreal moment in December 2006 when a spoof news program on a French-speaking TV channel announced that Flanders, the country's Dutch-speaking region, had seceded. Footage of the king and queen of Belgium hastily boarding an airplane interspersed with shocked reactions from politicians convinced many viewers that their country was no more. Some even took to the streets to spontaneously rally for the Belgian cause.

But Dutch-speaking Flemings (as those who live in Flanders are called) were offended at how quickly their francophone compatriots (called the Walloons) believed Flanders had seceded. The incident triggered months of national soul-searching about the future of the country.

Fast-forward to the June 2007 general election, when the separatist-leaning Flemish Christian Democrats won the most seats in parliament and demanded that the constitution be amended to devolve more power to the regions, escalating an ongoing dispute between French and Dutch-speaking parties. The controversy became so fierce it took six months to form a government, and even then, it was only provisional, aimed at keeping the country united until the French- and Dutch-speaking communities could agree on a more long-term program. While a coalition pact was finally approved on March 18, bringing an end to the country's nine-month political limbo, the pact says nothing about devolution of powers, so the real battle has still to be fought.[1]

"If the French do not give us more autonomy, it's bye-bye Belgium," says Flemish nationalist Gunter Dauwen, director of the European Free Alliance, a political group that represents 35 nationalist parties in Europe.

Dauwen's party, Spirit, is demanding that unemployment benefits be paid for by the regional governments rather than the federal government. The jobless rate is higher in French-speaking Wallonia. Under Dauwen's plan, the Flemish would not have to subsidize the unemployed Walloons as they do now.

But such a lack of solidarity irks the Francophones. "We are a small country. We should all get the same benefits," says Raphael Hora, an unemployed Walloon. "You can't have a guy in Charleroi (Wallonia) getting less than a guy in Antwerp (Flanders)."

There is also a growing cultural chasm between Flemings and Walloons, he says. "I speak English, Italian, Spanish, Norwegian, German and Polish — but not Dutch. My father never wanted me to learn it."

Roughly 60 percent of Belgians speak Dutch, 39 percent speak French and the remaining 1 percent speak German. The Belgian constitutional system is Byzantine in its complexity, with powers dispersed between governments organized along municipal, linguistic, provincial, regional and national lines.

Hora, who recently moved to Berlin, sees Belgium's breakup as inevitable: "When it happens, I'll come back to Belgium and campaign for Wallonia to rejoin France. We'll be stronger then."

Dauwen insists independence for Flanders is not the goal for now. "My party is not campaigning for independence yet but for a confederation." Contrary to the widespread perception of Flemings as rampant separatists, Dauwen says, "We are all peaceful and not extreme." Flanders' largest pro-independence party, Vlaams Belang, actually lost support in last June's elections, although it remains a major force, garnering about 20 percent of Flemish voters.

According to Jérémie Rossignon, a landscape gardener from Wallonia living in Brussels, "Belgians are not very proud of being Belgian. They do not boast about their achievements and culture." He feels this is a pity, because Belgium has much to be proud of — from its world-renowned beers, chocolates and restaurants to its sports stars like tennis champ

influence when the island belonged to the British Empire but felt increasingly discriminated against after Sri Lankan independence in 1948. In the late 1970s and early '80s, when Indira Ghandi was India's prime minister, India — which is home to 70 million Tamils — supported the separatist "Tamil Tigers." But in the late 1980s her son and successor, Rajiv Ghandi, dispatched Indian troops to clamp down on the Tigers. He was later assassinated by a female Tamil suicide bomber, Thenmuli Rajaratnam.

Hopes of reconciliation were raised when Sinhalese and Tamil authorities agreed to rebuild areas devastated by the December 2004 Indian Ocean tsunami, which killed some 35,000 Sri Lankans. But the Sri Lankan Supreme Court struck down the agreement.

Justine Henin and the funky fashion designers of Antwerp to the eclectic euro-village that is Brussels.

"There is not much communication between the Francophones and Flemings any more," he continues. "Young Flemings speak English, not French, whereas their parents can speak French."

Meanwhile, he admits, the Francophones "are useless at foreign languages." Foreign-language movies and TV programs are dubbed into French, whereas in Flanders they are subtitled, he notes. The mostly French-speaking monarchy, which is supposed to unify the country, has become another cause of division. Belgium's Italian-born Queen Paola cannot speak Dutch, the language of 60 percent of her subjects, while Crown Prince Philippe has publicly slammed Flemish separatism.

Belgium's predominantly French-speaking capital, Brussels, is located in Flanders, and is seen alternately as a glue holding the country together or an obstacle preventing it from splitting apart. "The Walloons are trying to annex Brussels" by moving to the small strip of land in Flanders that separates Brussels from Wallonia, according to Dauwen. Elected representatives and residents in these municipalities squabble over which language should be used on official documents and street signs. And once a year the Flemings organize a bike ride — known as *Het Gordeel* (the belt) — around Brussels to send a symbolic message that Brussels must not extend itself further into Flanders.

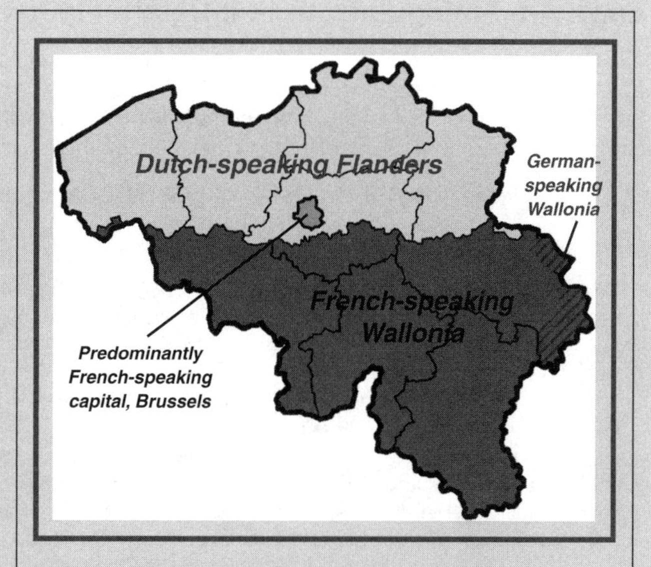

Belgians Speak Three Languages

The Dutch-speaking portion of Belgium is called Flanders. The southern portion, Wallonia, includes both Francophones and German-speaking citizens. French is the predominant language of Brussels, the capital.

The Francophones feel equally passionately. "The Romans conquered Brussels before the Germans did so we should stay French," says Marie-Paul Clarisse, a lifelong Bruxelloise, who works for an EU-affairs newspaper.

One compromise being floated would turn Brussels into Europe's Washington, D.C., and have it run by the EU, which is based in the city. An even wilder solution calls for tiny Luxembourg to annex Brussels and Wallonia.[2] And as if things were not complicated enough, Belgium also has an autonomous German-speaking community living in Wallonia. No one is quite sure what they want.

Even Rossignon, an ardent defender of Belgium, doubts its future: "The separatists will win out," he predicts, and the new government "will regionalize our country even more than it already is."

[1] "New Belgian Coalition Government Reaches Agreement," Agence France-Presse, March 18, 2008, http://afp.google.com/article/ALeqM5jhowUtJkHEsJRfNHhaSlnCb8-Zig.

[2] Laurent Lintermans, "Un Etat federal avec le Luxembourg?" *La Libre Belgique*, Aug. 18, 2007, www.lalibre.be/index.php?view=article&art_id=364931.

Dispersed across a vast plateau in the Himalayan mountains, Tibetans are a mostly Buddhist people with a 2,000-year written history and their own language, Tibetan, which is related to Burmese. China claims ownership of the region based on historical links with Tibetan leaders, which were especially strong in the 18th century. The Tibetans refute this claim and insist the region was never an integral part of China and that from 1913 until 1949 Tibet existed as an independent state.

China invaded Tibet in 1949 and 1950, annexed it in 1951 and in 1965 created the Tibet Autonomous Region — a territory less than half the size of the region Tibetans consider their homeland.

Laws Are Ambiguous on Self-Determination

The right to self-determination — which allows people to secede from a mother state if they so choose — appears in various international conventions, including the founding document of the United Nations. But the international documents are ambiguous, because they also espouse the importance of "territorial integrity"— the right of countries not to have their territory dismembered.

International Texts Dealing with Self-determination and Territorial Integrity

U.N. Founding Charter (Article 1) — 1945

- One purpose of the United Nations is "to develop friendly relations among nations based on respect for the principle of equal rights and self-determination of peoples, and to take other appropriate measures to strengthen universal peace."

U.N. Resolution 2625 — 1970

- "Every State has the duty to refrain from any forcible action which deprives peoples referred to in the elaboration of the principle of equal rights and self-determination of their right to self-determination and freedom and independence."
- "Nothing in the foregoing paragraphs shall be construed as authorizing or encouraging any action which would dismember, or impair, totally or in part, the territorial integrity or political unity of sovereign and independent states conducting themselves in compliance with the principle of equal rights and self-determination of peoples and thus possessed of a government representing the whole people belonging to the territory without distinction to race, creed or color."

African Charter on Human and Peoples' Rights (Article 20) — 1981

- "All peoples shall have . . . the unquestionable and inalienable right to self-determination. They shall freely determine their political status and shall pursue their economic development according to the policy they have freely chosen."

Conference on Security and Co-operation in Europe's Charter of Paris for a New Europe — 1990

- "We affirm that the ethnic, cultural, linguistic and religious identity of national minorities will be protected."
- "We reaffirm the equal rights of peoples and their right to self-determination in conformity with the Charter of the United Nations and with the relevant norms of international law, including those related to territorial integrity of states."

Vienna Declaration and Program of Action adopted by World Conference of Human Rights — 1993

- The conference recognizes "the right of peoples to take any legitimate action, in accordance with the Charter of the U.N., to realize their inalienable right of self-determination."

Sources: Organization for Security and Co-operation in Europe, United Nations, University of Hong Kong, University of New Mexico, Unrepresented Nations and Peoples Organization

Over the past 60 years, according to the Tibetan government-in-exile, China has brutally repressed the Tibetans, killing 87,000 during the 1959 uprising against Chinese rule and destroying or closing down nearly all of the region's 6,259 monasteries by 1962. China unleashed more death and destruction against the Tibetans in 1966 during the Cultural Revolution, the Tibetans claim.[39]

In other regions, movements to allow ethnic minorities to express their cultures and govern their own affairs have flourished since the 1960s. Such efforts have succeeded among the Welsh in Scotland and the Basques in Spain. In Belgium divisions between Dutch-speakers in Flanders, who make up roughly 60 percent of the population, and the French-speakers of Wallonia widened as more power devolved from the central government to the regions. In Canada separatist aspirations among French-speakers, who make up about 80 percent of the population in the province of Québec, culminated in a 1980 referendum on independence that was rejected by 60 percent of the voters. A subsequent referendum in October 1995 failed by a smaller margin, with 50.6 percent voting No and 49.4 percent Yes.[40]

During the Cold War, the United States, the Soviet Union and others signed the Helsinki Final Act of 1975, which established, among other things, the principle of "equal rights and self-determination of peoples." Latvia, Lithuania and Estonia would later use this to justify seceding from the Soviet Union, according to a U.S. government official involved in overseeing implementation of the act. The 1977 Soviet constitution gave the constituent republics the right to leave the U.S.S.R., but the right was not exercised for fear of reprisals from Moscow.[41]

Mikhail Gorbachev — the Soviet leader from 1985 to 1991 whose "glasnost" policy of greater openness to the West proved to be a catalyst for the break-up the U.S.S.R. — had his doubts about self-determination. In his memoirs, he wrote that "the application by a community of its right to self-determination leads regularly to a corresponding attack on the other community. . . . It is obvious that the recognition of the rights of peoples to self-determination should not be absolute."[42]

Yugoslavia Yields Seven New Nations

The former Yugoslavia has broken into seven new countries since 1991, and at least one additional province — the self-governing Republika Srpska in Bosnia and Herzegovina — is threatening to secede. Kosovo, on Serbia's southern border, declared its independence in February. The northern Serbian province of Vojvodina, populated by many Hungarians — is autonomous.

Ethno-centrism Surges

The fall of communism in Eastern Europe in the late 1980s and early '90s unleashed a wave of nationalist sentiment that destroyed the two largest multi-ethnic states in the region — Yugoslavia and the Soviet Union. Lithuania got the ball rolling, declaring independence from the Soviets in March 1990. Within two years, 15 new states had emerged from the former Soviet Union and another four in the former Yugoslavia.[43]

Soon several of the new states were experiencing their own secession movements. Russia fought fiercely and successfully to suppress the independence aspirations of the Chechens, a Muslim people with a long history of resisting subjugation by Moscow. Largely Romanian-speaking Moldova saw its Russian-dominated Transdniestria region morph into a de facto yet unrecognized state with the help of the Russian military. Ethnic Armenians in Azerbaijan's Nagorno-Karabakh region set up their own state in 1991, provoking a three-year war during which thousands of Azeris fled. Two regions — South Ossetia and Abkhazia — seceded from Georgia but have yet to be recognized by the international community.

Yugoslavia was torn asunder — eventually into seven new countries — due to the aggressive policies of nationalist leaders like Serbia's president, Slobodan Milosevic (1989-1997) and Croatia's president, Franjo Tudjman (1990-1999). The republics of Slovenia and Croatia in the northwest seceded in 1991, followed by Macedonia in the south and the triangular-shaped Bosnia and Herzegovina in 1992. The tiny republic of Montenegro seceded from Serbia in 2006. The province of Vojvodina in northern Serbia, populated by a substantial number of Hungarians, is autonomous but still part of Serbia.

Montenegro and Macedonia's splits were bloodless and Slovenia's relatively peaceful, but in Croatia and Bosnia

AP Photo/Yahya Ahmed

In northern Iraq's Qandil Mountains, recruits for a splinter group of the militant Kurdish PKK separatists are training to fight government troops across the border in Iran. Some 16-28 million Kurds are dispersed in Turkey, Iraq, Iran and Syria, making them the world's largest nation without its own country. The PKK wants a single Kurdish state; other Kurds seek either greater autonomy or independence from the countries where they live.

hundreds of thousands were either killed, fled persecution or were expelled, leading to the term "ethnic cleansing." NATO helped to take Kosovo, a province in Serbia whose autonomy was withdrawn in 1989, away from the Serbs in 1999 after Milosevic brutally cracked down on Kosova Albanian separatists. Kosovo remained an international protectorate for the next nine years.

The Yugoslav experience highlighted the danger of using referenda to determine the status of territories. The Serbs living in Bosnia, who made up about a third of the population, did not want to secede from Yugoslavia so they boycotted the 1992 plebiscite. When it passed with the overwhelming support of the Bosnian Muslims and Croats, the Bosnian Serbs violently resisted integration into Bosnia, and a three-year war ensued. The EU had helped to trigger the referendum by imposing a deadline on the Yugoslav republics to request recognition as independent countries.[44]

In 1993, Czechoslovakia split into the Czech and Slovak republics even though no referendum was held, and opinion polls indicated most citizens wanted to keep the country together.[45] The split came about because the leading politicians decided in 1992 that a peaceful divorce was easier than negotiating a new constitution with the Czechs favoring a more centralized state and the Slovaks wanting more autonomy.

In August 1999 East Timor seceded from Indonesia after a U.N.-supervised referendum. East Timor's annexation by Indonesia in 1975 had never been recognized by the U.N., and the East Timorese were Catholic, unlike the predominantly Muslim Indonesians, since the area had been colonized by Portugal.

The path to independence was a bloody one. The Indonesian military supported anti-independence militias who killed some 1,400 Timorese, causing 300,000 to flee, and destroyed much of the country's infrastructure. Australian-led international peacekeepers helped restore order in September 1999, and Timor Leste became a U.N. member on Sept. 27, 2002.[46]

By contrast, the separatist movement in Aceh has never succeeded in gaining independence, despite a decades-long struggle. Instead, the Free Aceh Movement and the Indonesian government signed a peace treaty in 2005, granting Aceh autonomy. The rapprochement was facilitated by a feeling of solidarity that grew out of the December 2004 Indian Ocean tsunami, which killed more than 130,000 people in Aceh.

CURRENT SITUATION

Balkan Pandora's Box

The shock waves emanating from Kosovo's Feb. 17 declaration of independence show that separatism remains an explosive issue. For Prime Minister Hashim Thaçi, a former separatist guerrilla, "independence is everything for our country and our people. We sacrificed, we deserve independence, and independence of Kosovo is our life, it's our future."[47]

The Kosovars waited until Serbia's presidential elections were over before seceding in order to deny the more nationalistic Serb candidate, Tomislav Nikolic, the chance to make political hay out of the declaration. On Feb. 3, Nikolic narrowly lost to his more moderate opponent, Boris Tadiç. Kosovo also deliberately made its declaration before Russia assumed the presidency of the U.N. Security Council on March 1, knowing that Moscow opposes its independence.

At this stage, few expect Serbia to launch a military offensive to take back Kosovo, given the strong NATO presence in the region. The Serbs instead are vowing to diplomatically freeze out any countries that recognize

Kosovo. Russia's ambassador to the EU, Vladimir Chizhov, warned in February that such recognition would be "a thorn in our political dialogue."[48] This has not prevented more than 30 countries so far from endorsing Kosovo's independence, including the United States, Canada, Australia and much of Europe.

Some fear that recognizing Kosovo will open a Pandora's box of ethnically motivated separatism. For example, the ethnic Serbs in Bosnia and Herzegovina, who have already largely separated themselves from the rest of Bosnia by creating Republika Srpska, on Feb. 21 pledged to hold a referendum on secession. But the republic's chances of gaining acceptance as an independent country are slimmer than Kosovo's, because both the EU and the United States firmly oppose it.

Romania and Slovakia worry that their large Hungarian minorities could feel emboldened to demand more autonomy or even unification with Hungary. Hungarians in the Romanian region of Transylvania are already demanding that Romanian law recognize their ethnically based autonomy.[49]

What Is a Nation?

The words nation, state and country are often used — incorrectly — as if they are interchangeable. But international law and usage today make clear distinctions in the concepts, as set out by U.S. lawyer and diplomat Henry Wheaton in his 1836 text Elements of International Law.

A "nation," he wrote, implies "a community of race, which is generally shown by community of language, manners and customs."

A country — or "state" — refers to "the union of a number of individuals in a fixed territory, and under one central authority," Wheaton explained. Thus a state "may be composed of different races of men" while a nation or people "may be subject to several states."

Wheaton noted that in ancient Rome, the philosopher and orator Cicero defined a state as "a body politic, or society of men, united together for the purpose of promoting their mutual safety and advantage by their combined strength."

Source: Henry Wheaton, *Elements of International Law,* 1836.

Frozen Conflicts

Russia's heavy clampdown on separatists in Chechnya serves as a stark warning to other ethnic groups in the region with separatist leanings not to push for independence. The predominantly Muslim Chechens had managed to gain de facto independence from Moscow in their 1994-1996 war, but Russia recaptured the territory in 1999. Tens of thousands have been killed in these conflicts and hundreds of thousands displaced.

Ethnic violence has also spread to other neighboring republics in the North Caucasus like Dagestan, North Ossetia and Ingushetiya, where disparate rebel groups are fighting for more autonomy or independence. To prevent the Balkanization of Russia, the Putin government cracked down hard on the violence.

Meanwhile, the Central Asian republics of Kazakhstan, Tajikistan, Uzbekistan, Turkmenistan and Kyrgyzstan no longer are as economically integrated as they were during the Soviet era, fueling corruption. Reportedly officials routinely demand bribes from traders and workers seeking to move goods or personnel across the new borders.[50] Some of the new states, like Kyrgyzstan, are weak and at risk of fragmenting or being subsumed by their neighbors.[51]

Transdniestria, Nagorno-Karabakh, South Ossetia and Abkhazia remain unrecognized de facto states, since Moldova, Azerbaijan and Georgia all lack the military or economic strength to recapture the four breakaway territories. The long, narrow valley of Transdniestria — which has a population of Russians, Moldovans and Ukrainians — is "like a Brezhnev museum," according to a U.S. government official involved in reconciliation efforts there, referring to the Soviet leader from 1964 to 1982 whose regime was characterized by stagnation and repression. "It is a nasty place: the rulers repress the Moldovan language, and the economy is largely black market." And Georgia's two secessionist regions — South Ossetia and Abkhazia — are egged on by Russia, according to the State Department's Bryza.

These so-called frozen conflicts have produced "an impasse of volatile stability [where] nobody is happy but nobody is terribly unhappy either, and life goes on, as neither central state nor de facto states have collapsed," writes Dov Lynch, author of a book on the conflicts and director of the U.S. Institute for Peace project. Up to a million people have been displaced, standards of living have dropped as economies barely function, organized

AP Photo/Martial Trezzini

Wearing symbolic chains, a Uyghur protester in Geneva demands self-rule for the predominantly Muslim, ethnically Turkic Uyghurs in China's autonomous western region of Xinjiang. He also opposes China's one-child policy, which human rights advocates say forces some pregnant mothers to get abortions. China says recent separatist unrest in Tibet has triggered protests in Xinjiang, where some 500 Uyghurs held a demonstration in Khotan on March 23.

crime flourishes and a "profound sense of psychological isolation" prevails.[52]

In one of those ongoing conflicts, the militant Kurdish separatist organization, the PKK, has stepped up its violent campaign against Turkey, which has responded with a military strike into the PKK's base in northern Iraq.[53] The Kurds in northern Iraq already govern themselves. Some pragmatic Kurdish leaders feel their best solution would be to replicate this model in Iran, Syria and Turkey — where they do not have autonomy — instead of pushing for a single Kurdish state.

Meanwhile, the Israeli-Palestinian conflict seems to be edging towards a "two-state solution" under which the Palestinians would be given a state of their own in the West Bank and Gaza in exchange for acknowledgment of Israel's right to exist. However, the region's ongoing violence makes reaching a final agreement problematic.

In Africa, Somaliland looks to be creeping towards acceptance as a state, too. An African Union mission in 2005 concluded that Somaliland's case for statehood was "unique and self-justified" and not likely to "open a Pandora's box." Nevertheless, its neighbors continue to oppose recognizing it formally.[54]

Asian Disputes

The separatist movement in Sri Lanka remains strong. The Tamil Tigers run a de facto state in the northeast and are fiercely fighting the Sri Lankan government, which wants to regain control of the whole country. On Feb. 4 — the 60th anniversary of the country's independence — Sri Lankan President Mahinda Rajapaksa affirmed his commitment to "go forward as a single, unitary state."[55]

According to a Tamil activist who asked not to be identified, Sri Lanka is squeezing the Tamil-controlled area with an economic embargo and preventing international aid organizations from providing humanitarian supplies. Though Pakistan, India and China are helping the Sri Lankan government, the Tamils are holding onto their territory, he says, with the help of Tamils who have fled the country and are dispersed throughout the world. This "diaspora" community is providing funds for weapons that the guerrillas buy covertly from Asian governments, he says.

In Aceh, the 2005 self-rule pact with Indonesia "is working to some extent," according to a U.S. official in Indonesia. With rising crime, high unemployment, little trade with the outside world and little experience in spending public money, "the challenge for the ex-rebels is to become good governors. They need help from the international community," the official says.

Separatism in Taiwan received a blow in the January 2008 parliamentary and March 2008 presidential elections when the Kuomintang Party, which supports reunification with mainland China, trounced the separatist Democratic Progressive Party (DPP), which seeks U.N. membership for Taiwan.[56]

For its part, the United States continues to sit on the fence, reflecting the international community's ambivalence

AT ISSUE

Could separatism spread to the United States?

YES

Kyle Ellis
Founder, Californians for Independence

Written for *CQ Global Researcher*, March 2008

Asking whether separatism will spread to the United States is a bit of an odd question to pose in a nation founded through an act of secession from the British Empire.

Secession is at the very foundation of what it means to be American, and over the years since the country was founded many secessionist organizations and movements have kept this American tradition alive.

If you think the Civil War ended the question of secession in the United States, any Internet search you run will show just how wrong you are. Dozens of groups in various states are organizing and agitating for secession.

These groups are getting larger, and more serious ones are being founded all the time. As the leader and founder of one of these new organizations, I would like to offer a little insight as to why I believe the idea of secession will become a lot more popular in the years to come.

Here in California, there is much resentment toward the federal government. People don't like how politicians who live thousands of miles away are able to involve themselves in the creation of California's laws and the allocation of local resources, not to mention the billions of tax dollars sent away each year that are never to be seen again.

Other states have other reasons for wanting independence: Vermonters see the federal government as fundamentally out of touch with their way of life; the Southern states believe their unique culture is being systematically destroyed by the actions of the federal government; and Alaska and Hawaii view the circumstances surrounding their admittance into the Union as being suspect, if not downright undemocratic.

All of these groups view the federal government as broken in such a way that it cannot be fixed from within the system — a valid view considering it is run by two political parties that are fundamentally statist in nature. The two-party system is not even democratic (as we know from the 2000 elections), because it effectively disenfranchises millions of third-party voters due to the winner-take-all nature of political contests.

The federal government also continues to encroach upon individual rights and liberties.

It is natural that marginalized and disenfranchised people will seek to break away from a system they are not a part of, just as the founders of the United States sought to break away from Britain.

NO

Seth D. Kaplan
Foreign Policy Analyst and Business Consultant
Author, Fixing Fragile States: A New Paradigm for Development

Written for *CQ Global Researcher*, March 2008

Separatism requires a cohesive minority group that dominates a well-defined geographical area and possesses a strong sense of grievance against the central government. All three of these ingredients were present when the United States had its own encounter with separatism: the Confederacy's bid for independence in the 1860s. Southern whites possessed a unique identity, dominated a contiguous territory and were so aggrieved at the federal government that they were prepared to take up arms.

In recent decades, another disaffected and socioculturally distinct group in North America has waged a potent — but in this case nonviolent — campaign for independence: Canada's Québécois. Within the United States, however, no such groups exist today, and none seems likely to emerge in the foreseeable future. Puerto Rico does have a separatist movement, but Puerto Rico is already semi-autonomous and, more to the point, is only an unincorporated organized territory of the United States — not a full-fledged state. Some argue that California is close to reaching a level of economic self-sufficiency that would enable it to survive as an independent state. However, even if California could afford to be independent, neither its sense of difference nor of grievance seems likely to become strong enough to form the basis for a separatist movement.

Some Native American tribes, discontented with their circumscribed sovereignty, might wish to separate but — even if Washington raised no objections — their small populations, weak economies and unfavorable locations (inland, distant from other markets) would not make them viable as independent states.

The cohesiveness of the United States stands in marked contrast to most of the world's large, populous states. China, India, Indonesia and Pakistan all contend with separatist movements today.

Why has the United States escaped this danger? The answer lies in the impartiality of its institutions, the mobility of its people and the brevity of its history. Its robust and impartial institutions do not provide ethnic or religious groups with a strong enough sense of discrimination to ignite separatist passions. Its citizens migrate within the country at an unprecedented rate, ensuring a constant remixing of its population and tempering any geographically focused sense of difference. And its history as a relatively young, immigrant country — where people focus on the future far more than the past — means that few are fiercely loyal to any particular area.

toward Taiwan. According to Susan Bremner, the State Department's deputy Taiwan coordinating adviser, the United States has "not formally recognized Chinese sovereignty over Taiwan and [has] not made any determination as to Taiwan's political status."[57] In the past, however, the United States has said that if China were to bomb or invade Taiwan, it would help defend the island.[58]

In western China, the Uyghurs continue to see their proportion of the population decline as more ethnic Chinese migrate there. Chinese tourists are flooding in, too, as visiting EU official Fearghas O'Beara recently discovered in Kashgar. "The city was as foreign to the Chinese as it was to me," he said. "At times I felt a bit uneasy as well-to-do Chinese people took copious photos of the 'natives' with their quaint habits and clothing."[59]

Eclipsing all these movements are the newest round of protests by Tibetans that began in March, the 49th anniversary of a failed uprising against Chinese rule in Tibet. Protesters in Lhasa on March 14 burned, vandalized and looted businesses of ethnic Chinese immigrants, venting their seething resentment over the wave of immigration that has turned Tibetans into a minority in their capital city.[60] The Tibetans say 99 people were killed, but the Chinese put the figure at 22.[61] Though the Chinese riot police were initially slow to respond, Beijing is now cracking down hard on the protesters. It also is keeping monks elsewhere confined to their monasteries and forcing them to denounce the Dalai Lama. China accuses the exiled leader of orchestrating the violence — calling him "a vicious devil" and a "beast in human form" — even though he has condemned the violence and advocates autonomy rather than outright independence for Tibet.[62]

Before the outbreak of violence, a Chinese Foreign Ministry spokesman had urged the Dalai Lama to drop his "splittist" efforts to attain "Tibetan independence" and do more for average Tibetans. "The Dalai clique repeatedly talks about Tibetan culture and the environment being ruined. But in fact, the Tibetan society, economy and culture have prospered," said spokesman Qin Gang. "The only thing destroyed was the cruel and dark serfdom rule, which the Dalai clique wanted to restore."[63]

The 72-year-old Dalai Lama, Tibet's leader for 68 years, commands enormous respect around the world, as evidenced by U.S. President George W. Bush's decision to telephone China's President Hu Jintao on March 26 to urge the Chinese government "to engage in substantive dialogue" with the Dalai Lama.[64]

Tension over China's suppression of the Tibetans is mounting as some countries consider calling for a boycott of the Beijing Olympics in August to show solidarity with the Tibetans. European foreign ministers, meeting in Brdo, Slovenia, on March 28-29, came out against an outright boycott of the games, although the leaders of France and the Czech Republic are threatening to boycott the opening ceremony. And on April 1, U.S. House Speaker Nancy Pelosi, D-Calif., urged President Bush to reconsider his plans to attend the opening ceremony if China continues to refuse talks with the Dalai Lama.

But Bush at the time was becoming entangled in yet another separatist controversy. Stopping in Ukraine on his way to a NATO summit in Romania, Bush said he supports Georgia's entry into NATO, which Russia opposes. If Georgia were to join the alliance, the NATO allies could be forced to support any future Georgian military efforts to re-take South Ossetia and Abkhazia — also strongly opposed by Russia. That would put Georgia in the middle of the same geopolitical chess game that Kosovo found itself in.[65]

Secession in the Americas

Across the Americas, separatist movements are scarcer and weaker than in Europe, Africa and Asia. Perhaps the most significant is the recent flare-up in Bolivia, where the mainly European-descended lowlanders are pushing for greater regional autonomy and are even threatening secession.[66] They are wealthier than the mostly indigenous highlanders and fear that the centralization efforts of indigenous President Evo Morales will loosen the lowlanders' grip on Bolivia's natural resources. Already, Morales has proposed amending the constitution so that oil and gas revenues would be shared evenly across the country.[67]

There are also plans to redistribute a huge portion of Bolivia's land — beginning with its forests — to indigenous communities. Vice Minister of Lands Alejandro Almaraz, who is implementing the project, said recently the tension with the lowlanders was "very painful" and warned that "the east of Bolivia is ready to secede and cause a civil war" to thwart the government's redistribution plans.[68]

In the United States, separatism remains a marginal force, though the movement has never been more visible.

"There are 36 secessionist organizations now at work," including in New Hampshire, Vermont, California, Washington state, Oregon and South Carolina, says Kirkpatrick Sale, director of the Middlebury Institute, a think tank on secessionism that he established in 2004.

In Texas, Larry Kilgore — a Christian-orientated secessionist who wants to enact biblical law — won 225,783 votes or 18.5 percent in the March 4 primary for Republican candidate to the U.S. Senate.[69] "If the United States is for Kosovo's independence, there is no reason why we should not be for Vermont's independence," says Sale. "The American Empire is collapsing. It is too big, corrupt and unequal to survive."

Some Native American tribes with limited self-government continue to push for more autonomy. For example, a group of dissident Lakota Indians traveled to Washington in December 2007 to deliver a declaration of independence to the State Department, which did not respond.[70]

OUTLOOK

Ethnocentric Separatism

The growing tendency to construct states along ethnic lines does not necessarily bode well for the future. French philosopher Ernest Renan's warning, delivered in the era of empires and grand alliances, has as much resonance today as it did in 1882: "Be on your guard, for this ethnographic politics is in no way a stable thing and, if today you use it against others, tomorrow you may see it turned against yourselves."[71]

"The Kosovo case is not unique despite the many claims to that effect by European and American diplomats," says Serwer at the United States Institute for Peace. "If people worry about it being a precedent, they should have ensured its future was decided by the U.N. Security Council. That would have created a good precedent for deciding such things."[72]

Though some might support the creation of a U.N. body for assessing separatist claims, U.N. member states would most likely fear it would only serve to give more publicity to separatist causes, writes American University self-determination expert Orentlicher.[73]

The two Western European regions most likely to become independent within the next 10 years are Scotland and Flanders, says Flemish nationalist Dauwen. As for Transdniestria, "the more time that passes, the more likely it will become independent, because the military will resist rejoining Moldova," says a U.S. official working to promote peace in Eastern Europe. The passage of time usually increases the survival odds of unrecognized states, because entrenched elites who profit from their existence fight to preserve them regardless of how politically or economically viable the states are.[74]

The probability of separatist movements morphing into new states also depends on who opposes them. Nagorno-Karabakh, for instance, is more likely to gain independence from Azerbaijan than Chechnya is from Russia because the Azeris are weaker than the Russians.

Political leadership is another factor. When hardliners and extremists rise to power it triggers separatist movements, while the emergence of moderates willing to share power can entice separatist regions to be peacefully and consensually reintegrated into the mother country.

Ethnocentric separatism may also fuel irredentism — annexation of a territory on the basis of common ethnicity. For instance, the Albanians in Macedonia, Kosovo and Albania may push to form a single, unitary state. Ethnic Hungarians living in Romania, Serbia and Slovakia may seek to forge closer links with Hungary; Somalis scattered across Somaliland, Kenya, Ethiopia and Djibouti might decide to form a "Greater Somalia."

"The goal of attaining recognition is the glue holding it together," a State Department official said about Somaliland. "If recognized, I fear that outside powers will interfere more, and it could split."

Likewise, Kurds in Iraq, Turkey, Iran and Syria could rise up and push for a "Greater Kurdistan" encompassing all Kurds. While some countries might support the creation of a Kurdish state in theory, they would be reticent, too, knowing how much it could destabilize the Middle East.

In Southeast Asia, Myanmar (formerly Burma), Thailand and the Philippines are potential separatist hotbeds as tensions persist between the many different ethnic groups, with religious differences further aggravating the situation.[75] "If something moves in the region, it could have a tsunami effect, as happened in Eastern Europe in 1989," says Busdachin at the Unrepresented Nations and Peoples Organization. He adds that most of these groups are seeking autonomy, not independence.

Yet a U.S. official in Indonesia says of Aceh: "I would be very surprised if we would have a new country in 15 years. I don't see that dynamic. Things are moving in the other direction."

And in Taiwan, any push for U.N. membership would worry trading partners like the European Union and the United States, which are keen to maintain good relations with the island but reluctant to anger China.

As for the United States, the strong federal government that emerged during the Great Depression seems to be on the wane as state and local governments increasingly assert their powers. Yet the nation remains well-integrated, and outright secession of a state or group of states seems unlikely. Smaller changes are possible, however, such as the splitting of California into northern and southern states or the evolution of the U.S.-governed Puerto Rico into a new U.S. state or independent country.

In the long term, separatism will fade, author Kaplan believes. "Separatism always appears on the rise when new states are born because such entities do not have the deep loyalties of their people typical of older, successful countries," he says. But as states mature, he notes, the number of separatist movements usually declines.

A starkly different prediction is made by Jerry Z. Muller, history professor at The Catholic University of America in Washington. "Increased urbanization, literacy and political mobilization; differences in the fertility rates and economic performance of various ethnic groups and immigration will challenge the internal structure of states as well as their borders," he wrote. "Whether politically correct or not, ethnonationalism will continue to shape the world in the 21st century." Globalization will lead to greater wealth disparities and deeper social cleavages, he continues, and "wealthier and higher-achieving regions might try to separate themselves from poorer and lower-achieving ones." Rather than fight the separatist trend, Muller argues, "partition may be the most humane lasting solution."[76]

NOTES

1. For detailed accounts of the protests, see *The Economist*, "Trashing the Beijing Road," March 19, 2008, www.economist.com/opinion/displaystory.cfm?story_id=10875823 and Tini Tran, "Tibetan Protests Escalate into Violence," The Associated Press, March 14, 2008, http://news.yahoo.com/s/ap/20080314/ap_on_re_as/china_tibet.
2. Ellie Tzortzi, "US outrage as Serb protesters burn embassy," Reuters, Feb. 21, 2008, www.reuters.com/article/worldNews/idUSL2087155420080221?pageNumber=1&virtualBrandChannel=0.
3. See "In quotes: Kosovo reaction," BBC News, Feb. 17, 2008, http://news.bbc.co.uk/1/hi/world/europe/7249586.stm.
4. See European Commission's Web site for political and economic profiles of Serbia and Kosovo, http://ec.europa.eu/enlargement/potential-candidate-countries/index_en.htm.
5. Selcan Hacaoglu and Christopher Torchi, "Turkey launches ground incursion into Iraq," The Associated Press, Feb. 22, 2008, www.washingtontimes.com/apps/pbcs.dll/article?AID=/20080222/FOREIGN/297026899/1001.
6. For list of current U.N. member states, see the U.N.'s Web site, www.un.org/members/list.shtml.
7. To see growth in U.N. membership, go to www.un.org/members/growth.shtml.
8. See "Kurdistan — Kurdish Conflict," globalsecurity.org, www.globalsecurity.org/military/world/war/kurdistan.htm.
9. Lisa Schlein, "East Timor Facing Food Crisis," June 24, 2007, www.voanews.com/english/archive/2007-06/2007-06-24-voa8.cfm?CFID=213682651&CFTOKEN=33049644.
10. Fried was testifying at a hearing on the Balkans at the U.S. House of Representatives Committee on Foreign Affairs, March 12, 2008. For full testimony go to: http://foreignaffairs.house.gov/testimony.asp?subnav=close.
11. Gary J. Bass, "Independence Daze," *The New York Times*, Jan. 6, 2008, www.nytimes. com/2008/01/06/magazine/06wwln-idealab-t.html?ref=magazine.
12. Several Uyghurs were detained in the U.S. terrorist prison in Guantánamo Bay, Cuba. According to James Millward, history professor at Georgetown University, Washington, D.C., the Uyghurs' detention in Guantánamo became an embarrassment for the United States when it emerged they were pro-U.S. and anti-China. The U.S. administration decided it could not send them back to China because they would probably be mistreated. Although the United States asked more than 100 other countries to

take them, all refused except Albania, where some of the detainees were ultimately expatriated in 2006.

13. Chinese Foreign Ministry spokesperson Qin Gang at press conference, March 18, 2008, www.china-embassy.org/eng/fyrth/t416255.htm.
14. Jay Shankar, "Pelosi Urges Probe of Chinese Claim Dalai Lama Behind Unrest," Bloomberg News, March 21, 2008, www. bloomberg.com/apps/news?pid=20601101&sid=aDLLITUsmrIg&refer=japan.
15. Seth D. Kaplan, "Democratization in Post-Colonial States: The Triumph of a Societal-Based Approach in Somaliland," in *Fixing Fragile States: A new paradigm for development* (scheduled for publication July 2008).
16. Harvey Feldman, fellow in China policy for the Heritage Foundation, speaking at a discussion on Taiwanese elections in Washington, D.C., Jan. 15, 2008.
17. In November 2004, a group of about 50 secessionists, gathered for a conference in Middlebury, Vt., signed a declaration pledging to develop cooperation between the various secessionist groups in the United States, including setting up a think tank, The Middlebury Institute, devoted to studying separatism, secessionism and self-determination. See www.middleburyinstitute.org.
18. Diane Orentlicher, "International Responses to Separatist Claims: Are Democratic Principles Relevant," Chapter 1 of Stephen Macedo and Allen Buchanan, eds., *Secession and Self-Determination* (2003), p. 29.
19. Interview with Nicolas Gros-Verheyde, "Europe should develop its defence policy with Russia," *Europolitics* (EU affairs subscription-based news service), March 4, 2008, www.europolitics.info.
20. Donald L. Horowitz, "A Right to Secede," Chapter 2 of Macedo and Buchanan, *op. cit.*, p. 50.
21. *Ibid.*, p. 73.
22. Basha was speaking at the Center for Strategic and International Studies in Washington, D.C., on May 5, 2007.
23. Lecture on Shanghai Cooperation Organization by Professor Akihiro Iwashita, visiting fellow at the Brookings Institution, delivered at the Woodrow Wilson International Center for Scholars, Feb. 2, 2008.
24. Jeremic was addressing the European Parliament's Foreign Affairs Committee in Strasbourg, Feb. 20, 2008. See the press release at www.europarl.europa.eu/sides/getDoc.do?pubRef=-//EP//TEXT+IM-PRESS+20080219IPR21605+0+DOC+XML+V0//EN&language=EN.
25. Horowitz, *op. cit.*, p. 56.
26. John J. Tkacik, "Dealing with Taiwan's Referendum on the United Nations," Heritage Foundation, Sept. 10, 2007, www.heritage.org/about/staff/JohnTkacikpapers.cfm#2007Research.
27. Zoellick's remark, made at a U.S. congressional hearing on China on May 10, 2006, was quoted in John J. Tkacik, "America's Stake in Taiwan," Heritage Foundation, Jan. 11, 2007, www.heritage.org/Research/AsiaandthePacific/bg1996.cfm.
28. For background, see "Nationalist Movements in Western Europe," *Editorial Research Reports*, April 16, 1969, available at *CQ Researcher Plus Archive*, www.library.cqpress.com.
29. Adapted quote from Ernest Renan, French philosopher and theoretician on statehood and nationalism, in his discourse "What is a nation?" widely viewed as the definitive text on civic nationalism (1882).
30. For more details, see Mark E. Brandon, Chapter 10, "Secession, Constitutionalism and American Experience," Macedo and Buchanan, *op. cit.*, pp. 272-305.
31. The case is 74 U.S. 700 (1868), available at http://caselaw.lp.findlaw.com/scripts/getcase.pl?court=US&vol=74&invol=700.
32. See Patricia Carley, "Self-Determination: Sovereignty, Territorial Integrity, and the Right to Secession," *Peaceworks 7*, March 1996, p. 3, www.usip.org/pubs/peaceworks/pwks7.html.
33. Orentlicher, *op. cit.*, p. 21.
34. For more details, see Washington Kurdish Institute, "The Territorial Status of Kirkuk," position paper, November 2007, http://71.18.173.106/pages/WO-PositionPapers.htm#.
35. For background, see Peter Katel, "Middle East Tensions," *CQ Researcher*, Oct. 27, 2006, pp. 898-903.

36. Figures taken from *The Statesman's Yearbook*, an annual reference book on the states of the world that first appeared in 1864, and from the U.N. Web site, www.un.org/members/list.shtml.

37. For full text of the 1960 U.N. Declaration on the Granting of Independence to Colonial Countries and Peoples, go to www.un.org/Depts/dpi/decolonization/declaration.htm.

38. For background, see "Sri Lanka," *Political Handbook of the World*, CQ Press (2007).

39. According to the Central Tibetan Administration Web site, www.tibet.net/en/diir/chrono.html.

40. For background, see Mary H. Cooper, "Québec Sovereignty," *CQ Researcher*, Oct. 6, 1995, pp. 873-896.

41. Under Article 72 of the 1977 U.S.S.R. Constitution, "Each Union Republic retains the right freely to secede from the U.S.S.R," www.departments.bucknell.edu/russian/const/1977toc.html.

42. Mikhail Gorbachev and Odile Jacob, ed., *Avant Memoires* (1993), p. 30.

43. The 15 ex-Soviet states could have been 16. Karelia, a region now part of western Russia bordering Finland, used to be a separate Soviet republic until 1956 when its status was downgraded to an autonomous republic within Russia.

44. Orentlicher, *op. cit.*, p. 36.

45. *Ibid.*, p. 33.

46. See CIA, *The World Factbook*, https://www.cia.gov/library/publications/the-world-factbook/geos/tt.html.

47. Reported on CNN.com, Jan. 9, 2008, http://edition.cnn.com/2008/WORLD/europe/01/09/kosovo.independence/index.html.

48. Joanna Sopinska, "Russia in last-ditch bid to block Kosovo mission," *Europolitics* (EU affairs subscription-based news service), Feb. 7, 2008, www.europolitics.info.

49. See Medlir Mema, "Kosovo through Central European eyes," Jan. 2, 2008, Center for European Policy Analysis (CEPA), www.cepa.org/digest/kosovo-through-central-european-eyes.php.

50. From lecture by researchers Kathleen Kuehnast and Nora Dudwick at the Woodrow Wilson International Center for Scholars, Nov. 27, 2006.

51. From discussion with Professors Anthony Bowyer, Central Asia and Caucasus Program Manager at IFES, the International Foundation for Election Systems, Eric McGlinchey, associate professor at George Mason University, and Scott Radnitz, assistant professor at the University of Washington, at the School for Advanced International Studies, Dec. 12, 2007.

52. Dov Lynch, *Engaging Eurasia's Separatist States* (2004), pp. 91-93.

53. Al Jazeera, "Toll rises in Turkey-PKK conflict," http://english.aljazeera.net/NR/exeres/3E14DD15-F2D1-4C65-8148-5200DFB3E975.htm.

54. Kaplan, *op. cit.*

55. The president's speech can be viewed in English at www.priu.gov.lk/news_update/Current_Affairs/ca200802/20080204defeat_of_terrorism_is_victory_for_all.htm.

56. See "Opposition's Ma wins Taiwan poll," BBC News, March 22, 2008, http://news.bbc.co.uk/2/hi/asia-pacific/7309113.stm.

57. Letter from Susan Bremner, deputy Taiwan coordinating adviser at the U.S. State Department, June 26, 2007, quoted in article by Tkacik, "Dealing with Taiwan's Referendum on the United Nation," *op. cit.*

58. See Peter Brookes, "US-Taiwan Defense Relations in the Bush administration," Nov. 14, 2003, www.heritage.org/Research/AsiaandthePacific/hl808.cfm.

59. Travel diary of Fearghas O'Beara, media adviser to the president of the European Parliament, who toured the region in August 2007.

60. Jim Yardley, "As Tibet Erupted, China Security Forces Wavered," *The New York Times*, March 24, 2008, www.nytimes.com/2008/03/24/world/asia/24tibet.html?ex=1364097600&en=58a6edae8ae26676&ei=5088&partner=rssnyt&emc=rss.

61. *Ibid.*

62. See "Chinese Crackdown on Tibetan Protests," "The Diane Rehm Show," National Public Radio, March 20, 2008, http://wamu.org/programs/dr/08/03/20.php#19471; also see Pico Iyer, "A Monk's Struggle," *Time*, March 21, 2007, www.time.com/time/world/article/0,8599,1723922,00.html; also see Louisa Lim, "China's Provinces Feel Crush of Tibet Crackdown,"

National Public Radio, March 28, 2008, www.npr.org/templates/story/story.php?storyId=89160575&ft=1&f=1004.

63. "China urges Dalai Lama to drop splittist attempts," Xinhua News Agency, March 11, 2008.
64. See White House press release at www.whitehouse.gov/news/releases/2008/03/20080326-2.html.
65. Joanna Sopinska, "Ministers condemn Tibet crack-down, reject Olympic boycott," *Europolitics*, March 31, 2008, www.europolitics.info. See Peter Baker, "Bush Pushes NATO Membership for Ukraine, Georgia," *The Washington Post*, April 1, 2008.
66. See Kaplan, *op. cit.*, Chapter 9, "Bolivia: Building Representative Institutions in a Divided Country." Also see Roland Flamini, "The New Latin America," *CQ Global Researcher*, March 2008, pp. 57-84.
67. Flamini, *ibid.*, p. 79.
68. Almaraz was giving a presentation on his land reform proposals at the George Washington University in Washington on March 11, 2008.
69. Primary results posted on *The Austin Chronicle's* Web site, www.austinchronicle.com/gyrobase/Issue/story?oid=oid%3A599906.
70. Bill Harlan, "Lakota group secedes from U.S." *Rapid City Journal*, Dec. 21, 2007, www.rapidcityjournal.com/articles/2007/12/21/news/local/doc476a99630633e335271152.txt.
71. Renan, *op. cit.*
72. See Daniel Serwer, "Coming Soon to a Country Near You: Kosovo Sovereignty," *Transatlantic Thinkers*, December 2007, www.usip.org/pubs/usipeace_briefings/2007/1214_kosovo.html.
73. Orentlicher, *op. cit.*, p. 37.
74. Lynch, *op. cit.*, p. 119.
75. See Joseph Chinyong Liow, "Muslim Resistance in Southern Thailand and Southern Philippines: Religion, Ideology and Politics," East-West Center, Washington, 2006, www.eastwestcenter.org/fileadmin/stored/pdfs/PS024.pdf.
76. Jerry Z. Muller, "Us and Them: The Enduring Power of Ethnic Nationalism," *Foreign Affairs*, March/April 2008, www.foreignaffairs.org/20080301faessay87203/jerry-z-muller/us-and-them.html.

BIBLIOGRAPHY

Books

Kaplan, Seth D., *Fixing Fragile States: A New Paradigm for Development, Praeger Security International*, 2008.
A business consultant who has founded successful corporations in Asia, Africa and the Middle East uses various case studies from around the world to analyze what makes states function and why they become dysfunctional.

Lynch, Dov, *Engaging Eurasia's Separatist States — Unresolved Conflicts and De Facto States, United States Institute of Peace Press*, 2004.
The director of a U.S. Institute of Peace project describes the "frozen conflicts" in the breakaway republics of Transdniestra, Nagorno Karabakh, South Ossetia and Abkhazia.

Macedo, Stephen, and Allen Buchanan, *Secession and Self-Determination: Nomos XLV, New York University Press*, 2003.
In a series of essays, different authors debate whether there should be a right to secede and analyze specific secessionist cases, notably Québec and the pre-Civil War Southern U.S. states.

Articles

"The Territorial Status of Kirkuk," *Washington Kurdish Institute*, November 2007, http://71.18.173.106/pages/WO-PositionPapers.htm#.
The institute argues that Kirkuk should be unified with the Kurdish region of northern Iraq.

Mema, Medlir, "Kosovo Through Central European Eyes," *Center for European Policy Analysis*, Jan. 2, 2008, www.cepa.org/digest/kosovo-through-central-european-eyes.php.
A Balkans scholar explains how many of the countries near Kosovo that have sizeable ethnic minorities are wary of the precedent set by an independent Kosovo.

Muller, Jerry Z., "Us and Them: The Enduring Power of Ethnic Nationalism," *Foreign Affairs*, March/April 2008, pp. 18-35.
A professor of history at Catholic University argues in the magazine's cover story that ethnic nationalism will drive global politics for generations.

Ponnambalam, G. G., "Negotiation with Armed Groups: Sri Lanka and Beyond," *Tufts University symposium*, April 6, 2006, http://fletcher.tufts.edu/news/2006/04/ponnambalam.shtml.
An academic paper by a member of the Sri Lankan parliament charts the unsuccessful efforts by the Sri Lankan authorities and Tamil separatists to end their conflict.

Renan, Ernst, "What is a Nation?" March 11, 1882, www.tamilnation.org/selfdetermination/nation/renan.htm.
This classic lecture by a French philosopher and theoretician on statehood and nationalism at the Sorbonne University in Paris is viewed as the definitive text on civic nationalism.

Serwer, Daniel, "Coming Soon to a Country Near You: Kosova Sovereignty," *Bertelsmann Stiftung Transatlantic Thinkers series*, December 2007, www.usip.org/pubs/usipeace_briefings/2007/1214_kosovo.html.
A conflict resolution expert argues for Kosovo's independence.

Tkacik, John J., "Dealing with Taiwan's Referendum on the United Nations," *Heritage Foundation*, Sept. 10, 2007, www.heritage.org/about/staff/JohnTkacikpapers.cfm#2007Research.
A China policy scholar assesses how the international community should respond to the ongoing campaign by Taiwanese separatists to obtain a U.N. seat for Taiwan.

Reports and Studies

Carley, Patricia, "Self-Determination: Sovereignty, Territorial Integrity, and the Right to Secession," *United States Institute of Peace, Peaceworks 7*, March 1996, www.usip.org/pubs/peaceworks/pwks7.html.
A conflict resolution expert outlines the main issues in the self-determination debate, including the uncertainty over what the right entails and who is entitled to claim it.

Gutierrez, Eric, and Saturnino Borras, Jr., "The Moro Conflict: Landlessness and Misdirected State Policies," *East-West Center Washington*, 2004, www.eastwestcenter.org/fileadmin/stored/pdfs/PS008.pdf.
The authors explain how resentment over not having control of their land has fueled separatism among the Muslim Moros in the southern Philippines.

Millward, James, "Violent Separatism in Xinjiang: A critical assessment," *East-West Center Washington*, 2004, www.eastwestcenter.org/fileadmin/stored/pdfs/PS006.pdf.
A history professor at Georgetown University in Washington highlights the plight of the Uyghurs, a Turkic people living in western China, where separatist tensions are simmering.

Schulze, Kirsten E., "The Free Aceh Movement: Anatomy of a Separatist Organization," *East-West Center Washington*, 2004, www.eastwestcenter.org/fileadmin/stored/pdfs/PS002.pdf.
A senior history lecturer at the London School of Economics discusses the history of the separatist movement in the Indonesian province of Aceh since 1976. The paper was published just prior to the brokering of a peace agreement in 2005.

For More Information

Center for Strategic and International Studies, 1800 K St., N.W., Washington, DC 20006; (202) 887-0200; www.csis.org. Think tank focused on regional stability, defense and security.

Centre for the Study of Civil War, P.O. Box 9229, Gronland NO-0134, Oslo, Norway; +47 22 54 77 00; www.prio.no/cscw. An autonomous center within the International Peace Research Institute, Oslo, that studies why civil wars break out, how they are sustained and what it takes to end them.

Commission on Security and Co-operation in Europe (Helsinki Commission), 234 Ford House Office Building, Washington, DC 20515; (202) 225-1901; www.csce.gov. An independent agency of the U.S. government created to promote democracy, human rights and economic development.

European Free Alliance, Woeringenstraat 19, 1000 Brussels, Belgium; +32 (0)2 513-3476; www.e-f-a.org/home.php. A political alliance consisting of regionalist and nationalist parties in Europe seeking greater autonomy for regions and ethnic minorities through peaceful means.

Middlebury Institute, 127 East Mountain Road, Cold Spring, NY 10516; (845) 265-3158; http://middleburyinstitute.org. Studies separatism, self-determination and devolution, with a strong focus on the United States.

United Nations Observer Mission in Georgia, 38 Krtsanisi St., 380060 Tbilisi, Georgia; (+995) 32 926-700; www.un.org/Depts/dpko/missions/unomig. Established by the U.N. in 1993 to verify that the Georgian and Abkhaz authorities are complying with their ceasefire agreement.

United States Institute of Peace, 1200 17th St., N.W., Washington, DC 20036; (202) 457-1700; www.usip.org. An independent agency funded by Congress to prevent and resolve violent international conflicts and to promote post-conflict stability and development.

Unrepresented Nations and Peoples Organization, P.O. Box 85878, 2508CN The Hague, the Netherlands; +31 (0)70 364-6504; www.unpo.org. An umbrella organization that promotes self-determination for various indigenous peoples, occupied nations, ethnic minorities and unrecognized states.

Washington Kurdish Institute, 611 4th St., S.W., Washington, DC 20024; (202) 484-0140; www.kurd.org. Promotes the rights of Kurdish people and awareness of Kurdish issues.

11

Aiding Refugees

Should the U.N. Help More Displaced People?

John Felton

Residents struggle to maintain normalcy in Kenya's Eldoret camp, home to 14,000 Kenyans who fled their homes during post-election rioting in December 2007. But they are the lucky ones. Many of the world's 26 million internally displaced people (IDPs) receive no aid at all or live in crude huts made of sticks and plastic sheeting, without reliable access to food or clean water. The U.N. High Commissioner for Refugees provided aid to some 13.7 million IDPs in 2007.

From *CQ Global Researcher*, March 2009

For more than two decades, the guerrilla group known as the Lord's Resistance Army (LRA) has been terrorizing villagers in Uganda — forcibly recruiting child soldiers and brutally attacking civilians. In recent years, the dreaded group has crossed the border into the Democratic Republic of Congo.

Last October, LRA marauders attacked Tambohe's village in northeastern Congo. They shot and killed her brother-in-law and two others, then torched the houses, even those with people inside.

Tambohe and her surviving family members — five adults and 10 children — fled into the forest, briefly returning five days later to bury the bodies after the raiders had left. The family then walked north for three days until they found safety in a village just across the border in southern Sudan, living with several hundred other Congolese displaced by the LRA.

"We have built a hut, and we live there," the 38-year-old Tambohe later told the medical aid group Doctors Without Borders. "The children sleep badly due to the mosquitoes and because we sleep on the ground. I sleep badly because I dream of the stench of burnt flesh. I dream they [the LRA] come and . . . take us to their camp."[1]

LRA violence is only one aspect of ongoing conflict in Congo that has killed 5 million people in the past decade and forced millions from their homes — including more than 400,000 last year, according to Human Rights Watch.[2]

Many, like Tambohe, fled their homes and crossed into another country, making them legally refugees. Under international law, she and her family should be able to remain in Sudan and receive

Most Displaced People Are in Africa and the Middle East

The U.N. High Commissioner for Refugees (UNHCR) monitors nearly 32 million people around the world who have been uprooted for a variety of reasons, including 25 million who fled their homes to escape war or conflict, mostly in Africa and the Middle East. Among those are 11 million refugees — those who have crossed borders and thus are protected by international law — and nearly 14 million internally displaced people (IDPs) who remain in their home countries. Some critics want the UNHCR to monitor and assist the world's other 12.3 million IDPs now being aided by other agencies.

Displaced Populations Monitored by the UNHCR

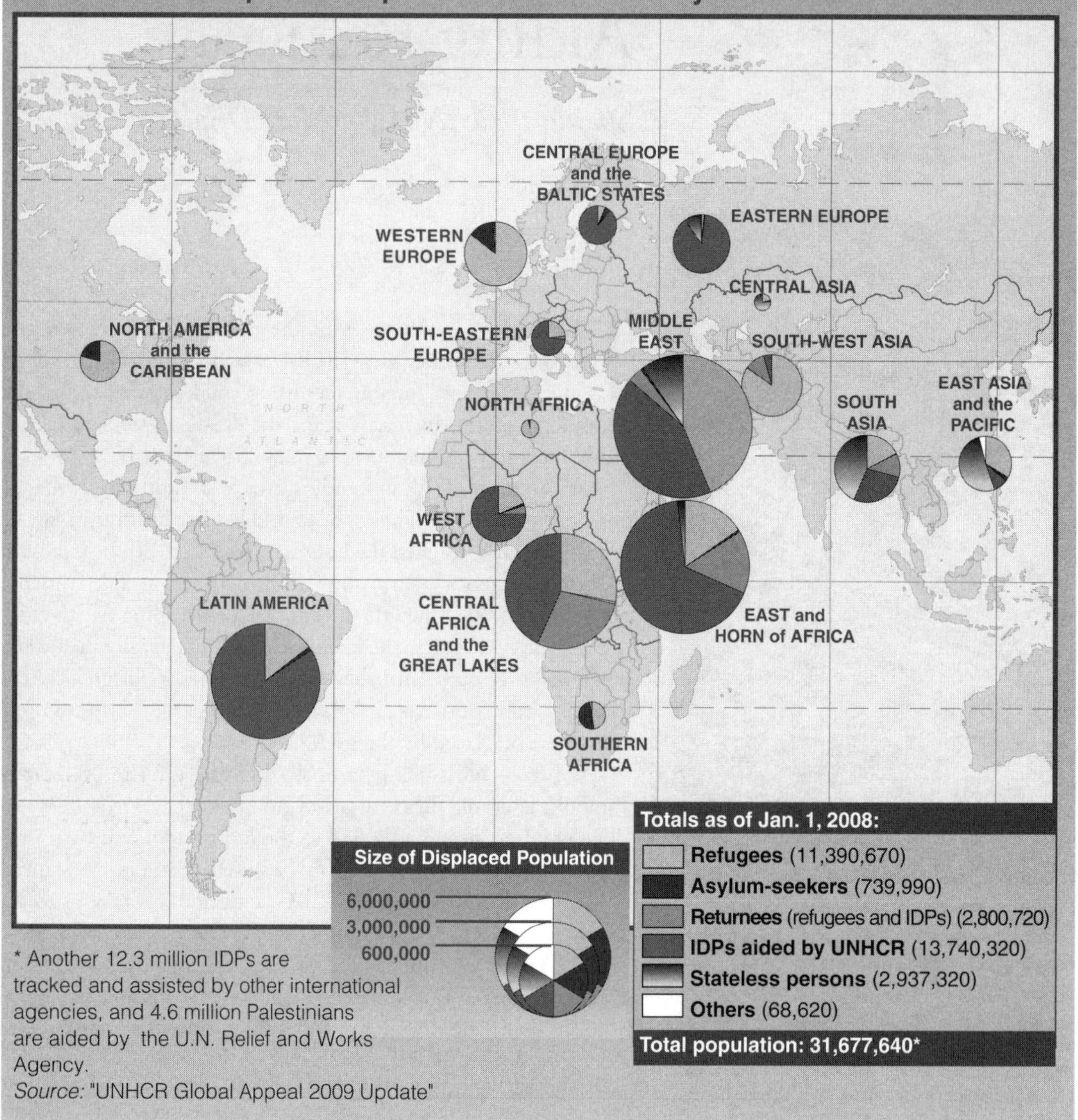

* Another 12.3 million IDPs are tracked and assisted by other international agencies, and 4.6 million Palestinians are aided by the U.N. Relief and Works Agency.

Source: "UNHCR Global Appeal 2009 Update"

humanitarian aid, shelter and protection because they have a "well-founded fear" of persecution if they return home.[3]

If Tambohe had fled her home but remained in Congo, she would have been considered an "internally displaced person" (IDP), and the Congolese government would be legally responsible for aiding and protecting her. But in the Democratic Republic of the Congo and many other countries, international law is little more than a theory. The Kinshasa government is weak, and the army itself has been accused of abusing civilians.[4] So helping the Tambohes of the world falls primarily to the United Nations (U.N.) and nongovernmental aid agencies.

Today, there are more than 90 million refugees, displaced persons and disaster victims around the world. More than 40 million have fled conflict or violence, according to Antonio Guterres, U.N. High Commissioner for Refugees (UNHCR), who leads international efforts to aid the displaced.[5] Of those, about 16 million are refugees (including 4.6 million Palestinians) and 26 million are IDPs. (*See map, p. 290.*) Up to 50 million more people are victims of natural disaster, according to the U.N.'s Office for the Coordination of Humanitarian Affairs. In China's Sichuan Province, for example, many of the 5 million people who lost their homes last May in an earthquake remain homeless, and thousands of Americans are still displaced from Hurricane Katrina, which struck New Orleans in 2005.[6]

Millions of displaced people overseas live in sprawling camps or settlements established by governments or the United Nations, often in harsh desert or jungle environments. A large but unknown number of others, like Tambohe, find their own temporary shelter — sometimes living with friends or relatives but more often building makeshift tents and huts or moving into crowded rental housing in urban slums.

Food insecurity — or even starvation — rank among the most serious consequences of displacement. In Kenya, for example, last year's post-election bloodshed caused so many farmers from key food-producing areas to flee their homes — leaving crops unplanted or unharvested — that an estimated 10 million Kenyans now face starvation.[7]

U.N. Serves About Half the World's Displaced

The U.N. High Commissioner for Refugees (UNHCR) has provided aid to an average of about 5.7 million of the globe's 11 million refugees each year — mostly in developing countries — over the past decade (dark gray lines). Meanwhile, the world's population of internally displaced persons (IDPs) has risen from 19 million in 1998 to 26 million in 2007. Individual governments are responsible for IDPs. But since 2005 the UNHCR has more than doubled the number of IDPs it serves each year — from 6.6 million in 2005 to 13.7 million in 2007 (light gray lines).

Total Refugees and IDPs vs. Those Receiving UNHCR Aid
(1998-2007)

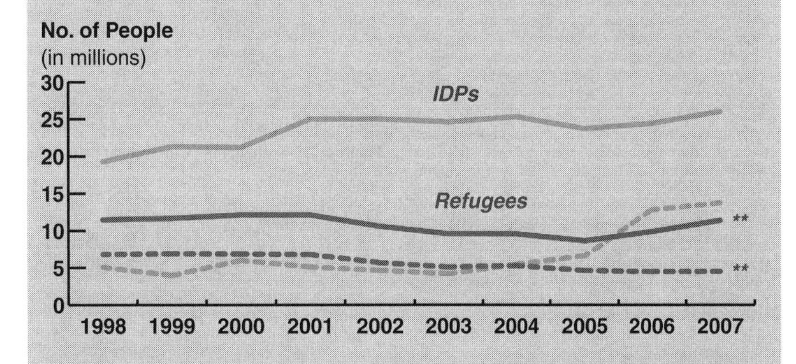

Total Refugees Worldwide*
Refugees Assisted by UNHCR
Total IDPs Worldwide
IDPs Assisted by UNHCR

* Does not include 4.6 million Palestinians assisted by the U.N. Relief and Works Agency in 2007.

** 2007 figures include people "in refugee-like situations" who were not included in previous years and excludes some 822,000 resettled refugees previously included in refugee statistics. Thus the 2007 data are not comparable with previous years.

Sources: 2007 U.N. High Commissioner for Refugees, Statistical Yearbook; "Global IDP Estimates (1990-2007)," Internal Displacement Monitoring Centre

Sudan Hosts Most Displaced People

Of the millions of refugees and internally displaced persons (IDPs) monitored by the U.N. High Commissioner for Refugees, Sudan houses nearly 4 million — more than any other country. Four of the top 10 host countries are in Africa. Most refugees and IDPs come from Iraq, Afghanistan, Colombia and five African countries.

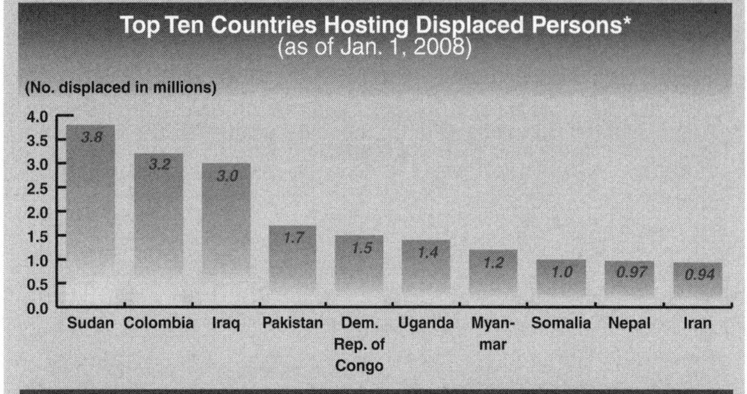

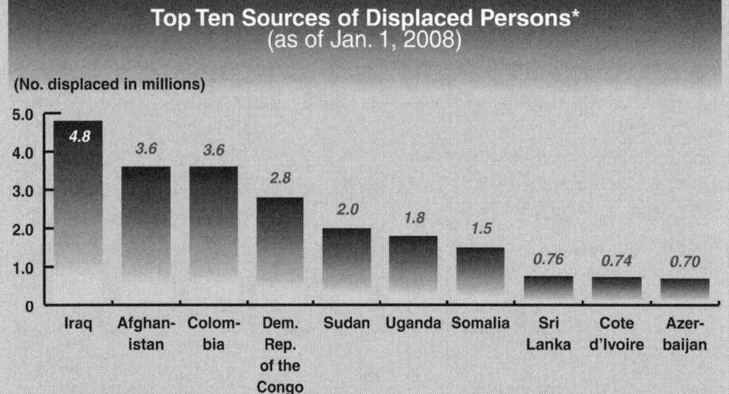

* Does not include 4.6 million Palestinians assisted by the U.N. Relief and Works Agency.

Source: "UNHCR Global Appeal, 2009 Update," U.N. High Commissioner for Refugees, January 2009

Some experts predict the world increasingly will be forced to deal with massive displacements — potentially involving hundreds of millions of people — caused by natural disasters intensified by climate change. Elisabeth Rasmusson, secretary general of the Norwegian Refugee Council, which aids and advocates for the displaced, warned last December that the world faces a potential vicious cycle: As climate change degrades the environment, it triggers more civil conflicts as people fight for access to water and other resources, further damaging the environment — displacing more people at each stage.[8]

Long before concern about climate change, however, international agencies were overwhelmed by the magnitude of conflict-caused displacements, which have been rising dramatically over the past decade.[9] And while the UNHCR's budget has nearly doubled since 2000 — from under $1 billion to $1.8 billion this year — the agency struggles to protect and care for refugees and IDPs in 116 countries around the world. As of Jan. 1, 2008, the agency was aiding 4.5 million of the world's 11.4 million refugees and 13.7 million of the world's 26 million IDPs. (*See graph on p. 291.*) Because the UNHCR and other aid agencies often operate in or near conflict zones, the delivery of humanitarian relief can be dangerous and, at times, impossible. In the Darfur region of western Sudan, for example, aid groups repeatedly have been forced to halt aid shipments because of attacks on relief convoys.[10]

But the lack of security is only one of a daunting litany of challenges faced by the UNHCR and its dozens of partner agencies, including chronic shortages of funds and reliance on "emergency" appeals to wealthy countries, the hostility of local governments, bureaucratic turf battles and indifference among world leaders.

And, despite promises to the contrary, the U.N. Security Council often has been unable or unwilling to take effective action — such as in Rwanda in 1994 and in Darfur since 2003 — to halt horrific death and displacement tolls. In both situations, ill-equipped and undermanned U.N. peacekeepers were unable to prevent what some have called the genocidal slaughter of hundreds of thousands of people. Yet some critics question whether the U.N. is trying to do either too much or too

Refugees Fall into Eight Categories

When people flee their homes and seek aid, they can be assigned to one of eight classifications, each of which conveys unique legal rights or restrictions. For instance, some are entitled under international law to receive humanitarian aid, shelter and protection because they have a "well-founded fear" of persecution if they return home. Here are the key definitions under international law and commonly accepted practice of the various categories of people who are seeking, or in need of, assistance:

Asylum-seeker: A person who has applied (either individually or as part of a group) for legal refugee status under national and international laws. If refugee status is denied, the asylum-seeker must leave the country (and could face expulsion) unless he or she is given permission to stay on humanitarian grounds.

Internally displaced person (IDP): Someone who has been forced to flee his home due to armed conflict, generalized violence, human-rights violations or natural or man-made disasters but has not crossed an international border.

Migrants: In the absence of a universally accepted definition of a migrant, the International Organization on Migration says the term is "usually understood" to cover all cases in which "the decision to migrate is taken freely by the individual concerned for reasons of 'personal convenience' and without intervention of an external compelling factor. An "economic migrant" is someone who leaves his home country in search of better economic opportunities elsewhere.

Persons in "IDP-like" situations: This relatively new term developed by the U.N. High Commissioner for Refugees (UNHCR) describes "groups of persons who are inside their country of nationality or habitual residence and who face protection risks similar to those of IDPs, but who, for practical or other reasons, could not be reported as such." For example, the UNHCR has used the term to describe displaced people in Georgia (including former residents of the breakaway provinces of Abkhazia and South Ossetia) and Russia.

Persons in "refugee-like" situations: Another relatively recent term used by the UNHCR to describe people who are outside their country or territory of origin "who face protection risks similar to those of refugees, but for whom refugee status has, for practical or other reasons, not been ascertained." In many cases, these are refugees who have settled more or less permanently in another country on an informal basis. The largest single population in this group is the estimated 1.1 million Afghans living outside formal refugee camps in Pakistan.

Refugee: Under the 1951 Refugee Convention (as amended in 1967), a refugee is someone who, due to a "well-founded fear of being persecuted for reasons of race, religion, nationality, membership of a particular social group or political opinions," has left his home country and is unable or, owing to fear, "unwilling to avail himself of the protection of that country." A person becomes a refugee by meeting the standards of the Refugee Convention, even before being granted asylum (*see above*), which legally confirms his or her refugee status.

Returnee: A refugee or IDP who has returned to his home — or home country or region.

Stateless person: Anyone who is not recognized as a citizen of any country. Stateless persons lack national or international legal protections and cannot legally cross international borders because they don't have and cannot obtain a valid passport or other identity papers. Between 3 million and 12 million people worldwide are stateless; the wide range results from a lack of information in some countries and conflicting assessments about which groups actually are stateless.

Sources: "Glossary on Migration," International Migration Law, International Organization for Migration, Geneva, Switzerland, www.iom.int/jahia/webdav/site/myjahiasite/shared/shared/mainsite/published_docs/serial_publications/Glossary_eng.pdf; and "Glossary," U.N. High Commissioner for Refugees, Geneva, Switzerland, www.unhcr.org/publ/PUBL/4922d4390.pdf

little, and others say international refugee law needs to be updated to take into account recent trends, such as the rapid increase in IDPs.

Those living in refugee and IDP camps have more immediate concerns, including overcrowded conditions; inadequate housing, food and medical care; and the refusal of local governments to allow them to work (or even to leave the camps). Negash, an Ethiopian who has lived in Kenya's sprawling Kakuma refugee camp for nearly four years, says aid officials often don't understand how their

IRIN/Manoocher Deghati (both)

Camp Life

Tents patched together from scraps of cloth house Afghans living in a camp near Kabul, Afghanistan (top). The government helps Afghans uprooted by decades of war, but many face overcrowded conditions and inadequate housing, food and medical care. Typically, internally displaced persons cannot work for wages in order to preserve jobs for local residents, so some set up their own small businesses inside the camps, such as a Kenyan seamstress at the Eldoret camp in Kenya (bottom).

decisions affect the camp's 50,000 residents every day. "There are people who work for agencies here that don't know what is happening in the camp," he says. "They live in their own compounds and don't really communicate with the refugees to find out what is happening to them."

The United Nations began reforming its humanitarian system in 2005, partly to address concerns about its inability to deliver timely and effective aid to internally displaced people. Jeff Crisp, director of policy and evaluations for UNHCR, says the U.N.'s reforms are having "a solid and positive impact" on the lives of displaced people even though revamping such a large-scale system of delivering aid "clearly is a work in progress."

The rise in refugees and IDPs is the direct result of dozens of small wars between rebels and government soldiers during the last 50 years, particularly in Africa and Asia. Some have dragged on for decades, creating generations of displaced families. For instance, Sudan's 20-year-long civil war displaced 400,000 people, but at least 130,000 remain in neighboring countries, according to the U.N.[11] Colombia's ongoing civil conflict has displaced nearly 10 percent of the country's population.[12]

Even when the wars end, civilians often remain displaced because they fear returning home, their homes have been destroyed or they have become settled elsewhere. In Afghanistan, for example, more than 5 million Afghan refugees have returned home since the United States ousted the Taliban regime seven years ago, but some 3 million remain in neighboring Pakistan and Iran — a large number of whom probably never will go back.[13]

The Afghan refugees represent what experts call a "protracted situation," which is defined as when at least 25,000 people are displaced from their homes for five years or more. (*See sidebar, p. 304.*) More than 30 protracted situations exist around the world, according to Elizabeth Ferris, director of the Brookings-Bern Project on Internal Displacement, run by the Brookings Institution in Washington, D.C., and the University of Bern (Switzerland) School of Law.

As governments, international agencies and specialists in the field seek better ways to protect and aid refugees and internally displaced people, here are some of the questions being debated:

Is the U.N. meeting refugees' needs?

Since its founding in 1951, the UNHCR has been the world's frontline agency for aiding and protecting refugees. Working with other U.N. agencies and nongovernmental agencies — such as CARE and the International Federation of Red Cross and Red Crescent Societies — the Geneva, Switzerland-based agency is spending $1.8 billion this year to provide housing, food, medical care and protection for millions of refugees and displaced persons in 116 countries.[14] The agency also decides the legal status of refugees in 75 countries that can't, or won't, make those determinations themselves. In 2007, the UNHCR determined the status of 48,745 people.[15]

Both critics and its defenders, however, say the agency often falls short of its official mandate to safeguard "the rights and well-being of refugees."[16] Barbara Harrell-Bond, the founder and former director of the Refugee Studies Center at Oxford University and a harsh critic of the UNHCR, says one of her biggest concerns is how aid programs are funded.

"The funds . . . always come from emergency budgets and are allocated to UNHCR by governments at their discretion," she says. As a result, agency programs are "at the mercy of the whims of international politics."

If world leaders become fixated on a particular crisis that is making headlines in Western countries — such as the situation in Sudan's Darfur region — refugees elsewhere suffer, Harrell-Bond says. In addition, education and job training programs designed to help refugees lead dignified lives once they leave the camps are considered "development" programs, she says, which "come from a completely different budget . . . and never the twain shall meet."

Moreover, local governments rarely receive international aid for hosting refugees and usually are anxious for refugees to go home, she says, so they have little incentive to improve camp conditions. As a consequence, refugees are "just warehoused" in camps for years and years. Furthermore, she adds, the UNHCR and its partner agencies routinely deny refugees' basic rights, including the right to leave the camps. Most host governments want refugees to be contained in camps, and the U.N. complies "by putting them in what amounts to gigantic cages," Harrell-Bond says.

In her 2005 book, *Rights in Exile: Janus Faced Humanitarianism*, Harrell-Bond and a co-author argue that "the rights of refugees cannot be protected in camps and settlements." They harshly criticize the UNHCR for not protecting refugees' rights, based on extensive research into the treatment of Kenyan and Ugandan refugees during the late 1990s — treatment the authors say continues today in many refugee camps.

For instance, refugees usually are not allowed to leave the camps and are not allowed to work. Harrell-Bond says the UNHCR should push governments harder to accept refugees into the local community. "Refugees can contribute to the societies where they have taken refuge and not simply live on handouts from the U.N.," she says, citing examples in Uganda and Zambia where so-called "local integration" has worked.

UNHCR Policy Director Crisp acknowledges the agency sometimes fails to meet refugees' needs but says decisions to "warehouse" refugees are made by the host countries. "In many cases, refugees are admitted to countries on strict condition that they be accommodated in camps and provided with their basic needs by UNHCR and other agencies," he says. UNHCR tries to get governments to improve refugees' situations, "but this is not always possible."

Despite such constraints, Crisp says the UNHCR is trying new approaches, particularly for those trapped in

Most Refugees Flee to Neighboring Countries

Contrary to the perception that refugees are flooding into developed countries in Europe and other regions, most find asylum in neighboring countries and remain there. Only between 10 percent and 17 percent leave the countries where they were granted asylum.

Refugees Remaining in or Leaving Their Asylum Regions
(As of December 2007)

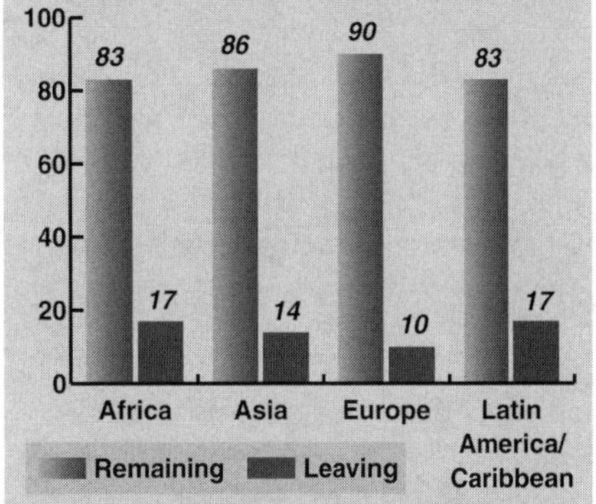

	Remaining	Leaving
Africa	83	17
Asia	86	14
Europe	90	10
Latin America/ Caribbean	83	17

Source: "2007 Global Trends: Refugees, Asylum-seekers, Returnees, Internally Displaced and Stateless Persons," U.N. High Commissioner for Refugees, June 2008

Chaos in Somalia Puts Nation at Risk

Humanitarian aid feeds nearly half the population

Mohamed Abdi, his wife, and five children fled the never-ending violence in Somalia's capital city of Mogadishu last October, finding safety — but not much more — in the breakaway region of Somaliland to the north. The trip took nine days, and all along the way they feared being attacked by the opposing sides in the most recent round of conflict in Somalia.

Once they reached Somaliland, Abdi and his family found very little in the way of services, but the local government welcomed them as refugees. "We don't have much, and we depend on the kindness of these people; some days we eat, some we don't," he told the United Nations' IRIN news service in October. "But at least we have peace and security. That is what we want and the chance to make a living for our families without being afraid of being killed."[1]

Displaced people like Abdi never have it easy, often living in crude shelters and on starvation rations. But the situation is especially grave in Somalia — the only country in the world that for nearly two decades has been without even a functioning government — where a fatal combination of internal conflict and natural disaster has generated hundreds of thousands of refugees, migrants and internally displaced people (IDPs).

Ever since the last real government — a harsh dictatorship — was overthrown in 1991, hundreds of thousands of refugees settled in Kenya and other neighboring countries. Thousands of others have crossed the dangerous Gulf of Aden to equally impoverished Yemen.

Meanwhile, an estimated 1.3 million Somalis have become IDPs — displaced but living within their own country.[2] Most had fled Mogadishu, decimated by years of fighting among warlords, rebel groups, failed temporary governments and the Ethiopian army, which invaded in late 2006 and withdrew in January.

But IDPs escaping violence are not the only Somalis suffering. The U.N. Food and Agriculture Organization reported in October 2008 that 3.2 million people — 43 percent of the population — regularly need humanitarian assistance to survive.[3] While armed conflict has created most of the dislocations among Somalis, frequent droughts and floods have also caused recurrent famines that sent rural families fleeing to urban areas, often to be displaced by fighting.

Waves of conflict and displacement have swept over Somalia ever since the military dictatorship of Major General Mohamed Siad Barre was pushed from power in 1991. The most severe recent displacement occurred in August 2007, just eight months after Ethiopia invaded Somalia to oust a short-lived Islamist regime. Some 400,000 people were displaced by fighting in Mogadishu; most of them ended up in one of 200 camps that cropped up along a nine-mile stretch of the main road outside of the capital — "the most congested IDP nexus in the world," according to a refugee official.[4]

The U.N. High Commissioner for Refugees (UNHCR) and other aid groups provide limited food and medical aid to the camps, but little in the way of shelter. Patrick Duplat, an advocate for Refugees International who visited the camps twice in 2008, describes them as "mostly a sprawl of makeshift shelters — twigs and cloth, and sometimes plastic sheeting, whatever people are able to find."

Since Ethiopia withdrew its army in January, some 40,000 IDPs have returned to several Mogadishu neighborhoods, apparently with the intention of staying, according to the UNHCR.[5] Even so, continued fighting in the city has displaced an unknown number of others. The UNHCR said on Feb. 27 it is still discouraging IDPs from returning to what would be "ruined homes and livelihoods."[6]

In recent years nearly 500,000 people have fled Somalia to neighboring countries, but they have encountered daunting hazards along the way, including bandits, security forces

protracted situations. For instance, in 2008 the high commissioner set deadlines for getting people out of five specific protracted situations:

- Afghan refugees in Iran and Pakistan;
- Bosnian and Croatian refugees in Serbia;
- Eritrean refugees in eastern Sudan;
- Burundians in Tanzania; and
- Members of Myanmar's Rohingya minority who fled to Bangladesh.[17]

More broadly, as part of its 2005 reform program, the U.N. established clear guidelines for which U.N. agency should provide services in specific situations.[18] The

demanding bribes and even possible death on the high seas.[7] Those who avoid violence and persecution may be eligible for refugee status and entitled to return home someday; others probably would be considered migrants because they are searching for economic opportunities overseas.

Thousands of Somalis have risked crossing the Gulf of Aden or the Red Sea by boat to reach Yemen. On Feb. 28, 45 Somalis drowned when their boat capsized as they were crossing the gulf. Those who arrive safely generally are given *de jure* refugee status, even though many might be considered migrants because they never plan to return to their homes. About 82,000 Somalis were registered as refugees in Yemen in late 2008, but the UNHCR said the total could be closer to 150,000.[8]

AFP/Getty Images/Radu Sigheti

An estimated 1.3 million people have been uprooted by the ongoing conflict in Somalia but are still living inside the country. Persistent violence, drought and flooding have created one of the world's longest ongoing humanitarian crises.

Most Somali refugees, however, have fled into neighboring Kenya, even though it closed its borders to Somalis in 2007. According to the U.N., some 250,000 Somali refugees are in Kenya, including at least 45,000 who entered in 2008.[9]

At the border, would-be refugees often set out on foot to the U.N.'s official transit camps at Dadaab, 50 miles inside Kenya, frequently traveling at night to evade Kenyan police. As of late January the camps held 244,127 people — nearly triple their capacity. "Trying to squeeze 200,000-plus people into an area intended for 90,000 is inviting trouble," said Craig Johnstone, deputy U.N. high commissioner for refugees, after visiting on Feb. 5.[10] The UNHCR has been trying to raise $92 million from international donors to build two new camps for 60,000 more refugees.[11]

Human Rights Watch researcher Gerry Simpson, who visited the camps in late 2008, said many people told him they had tried to register as refugees but had given up because of the lack of space in the camps. "After risking their lives to flee appalling violence in Somalia and make it to the relative safety of Kenya, they end up with nothing: no food, no shelter, and incredibly difficult access to water and health care," Simpson said.[12]

---

[1] "Fleeing from the frying pan into the fire," IRIN news service, Oct. 29, 2008, www.irinnews.org/Report.aspx?ReportId=81164.

[2] "Displaced Populations Report," U.N. Office for the Coordination of Humanitarian Affairs, Regional Office for Central and East Africa, July-December 2008, p. 5.

[3] "Poor rains intensify human suffering and deprivation — report," IRIN news service, Oct. 17, 2008, www.irinnews.org/Report.aspx?ReportId=80971.

[4] "Somalia: To Move Beyond the Failed State," International Crisis Group, Dec. 23, 2008, pp. 12, 18.

[5] "Thousands of Somalis Return to Mogadishu Despite Renewed Fighting," U.N. High Commissioner for Refugees, Feb. 27, 2009, www.unhcr.org/news/NEWS/49a7d8bb2.html.

[6] *Ibid.*

[7] "Somalia Complex Emergency: Situation Report," Jan. 15, 2009, U.S. Agency for International Development, www.usaid.gov/our_work/humanitarian_assistance/disaster_assistance/countries/somalia/template/fs_sr/fy2009/somalia _ce_sr04_01-15-2009.pdf.

[8] "2009 Global Update for Yemen," U.N. High Commissioner for Refugees, p. 1, www.unhcr.org/publ/PUBL/4922d4240.pdf.

[9] "Displaced Populations Report," *op. cit.*, p. 6.

[10] "Camp resources stretched by influx of Somali refugees," IRIN news service, Feb. 6, 2009, www.irinnews.org/Report.spx?ReportId=82792.

[11] "Somali refugees suffer as Dadaab camp populations swell to 230,000," UNHCR, www.unhcr.org/news/NEWS/4950ef401.html.

[12] "Kenya: Protect Somali Refugees. Government and Donors Should Urgently Address Refugee Crisis," Human Rights Watch, Nov. 13, 2008, www.hrw.org/en/news/2008/11/13/kenya-protect-somali-refugees.

---

so-called cluster approach made the UNHCR responsible for managing camps for IDPs displaced by natural disasters and providing emergency shelter and protection for IDPs displaced by conflict.[19]

A 2007 evaluation found the new approach had improved humanitarian responses in Chad, the Democratic Republic of the Congo, Somalia and Uganda.[20] Ramesh Rajasingham, head of the Displacement and Protection Support Section for the U.N.'s humanitarian affairs office, says giving UNHCR a "clear leadership" role in managing displacement camps and emergency shelters has fostered "an improved IDP response."

But some non-U.N. experts say the bureaucratic changes have produced only modest benefits. Implementation has

Most Funds Go to Africa, Come From U.S.

More than one-third of U.N. refugee aid in 2009 will go to programs in Africa, more than any other region. In 2007, the United States contributed nearly one-third of the funds for the Office of the U.N. High Commissioner for Refugees (UNHCR) — four times more than No. 2-donor Japan.

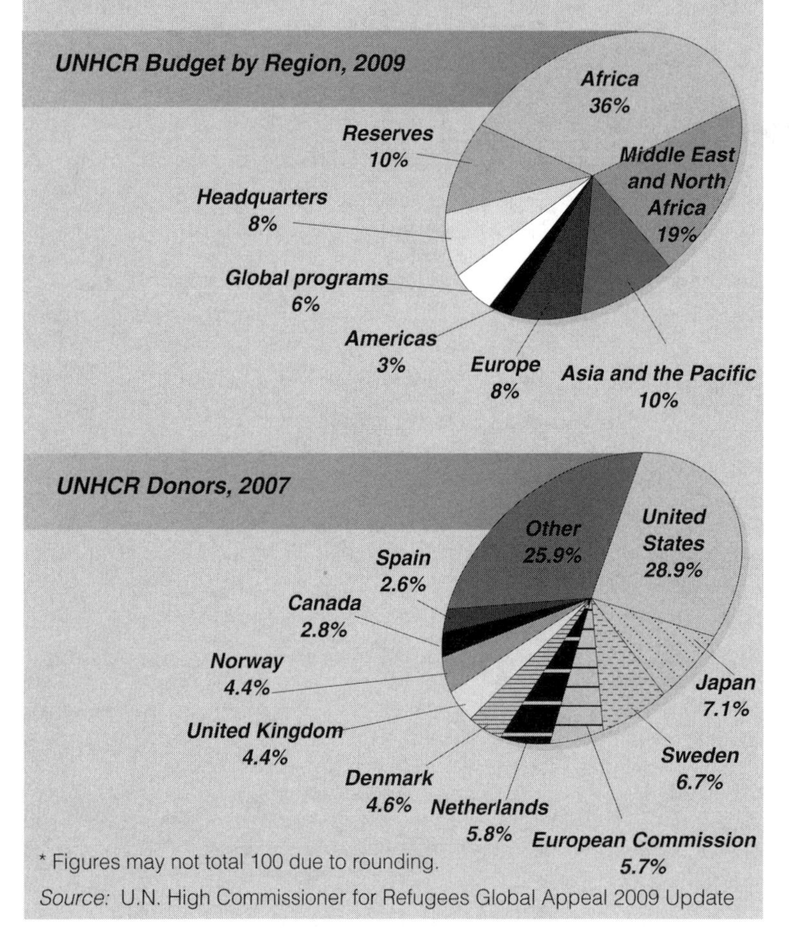

* Figures may not total 100 due to rounding.

Source: U.N. High Commissioner for Refugees Global Appeal 2009 Update

been "half-hearted," especially in protecting IDPs, says Roberta Cohen, a senior fellow at the Brookings Institution and prominent IDP advocate. The UNHCR is not "playing the robust leadership role" she had hoped for in protecting IDPs.

Likewise, Joel Charny, vice president for policy at Refugees International, says the UNHCR's protection of IDPs remains "problematic." Ferris, Cohen's successor at the Brookings-Bern Project on Displacement, recommends a rewards structure that would give agencies and individuals an incentive to better aid and protect displaced persons.

"Agencies need to internalize their work with IDPs and not see it as something separate from their missions or a burden they have to carry," she says.

James Milner, a refugee policy analyst at Carleton University in Ottawa, Ontario, Canada, and former UNHCR consultant, says the agency "does a good job in some places and a bad job in some places." While it has saved millions of lives during civil wars, the agency also ends up "warehousing" refugees for long periods, he says, causing them to abandon hope for better lives and become totally dependent on aid.

Like Harrell-Bond, Milner — who coauthored a 2008 book sympathetic to the agency's successes and failures — traces most of UNHCR's problems to its funding procedures. In effect, he says, industrialized countries that provide the bulk of UNHCR's money "earmark" where they want the money to go.[21]

"The United States, for example, gives funding to emergencies it considers important" but gives less to other situations, Milner says. "When I worked in Cameroon, each October we simply ran out of funding to provide health care for nursing mothers, because that was not a priority for the people in Washington. You can criticize UNHCR for not being more aggressive in some of these situations, but when you recognize the constraints placed on UNHCR, it places the challenges in a broader context."

Should the Refugee Convention be updated?

The 1951 Convention Relating to the Status of Refugees — known as the Refugee Convention — is the basic underpinning of refugee law. Created to protect European refugees during and after World War II, the treaty was amended in 1967 to apply worldwide.

The treaty grants "asylum" to refugees, or groups of them, who can demonstrate a "well-founded fear of being persecuted" because of race, nationality, religion or political beliefs. Those who flee their country because of such a fear are considered refugees. The process of demonstrating that fear and seeking permission to stay in the country of refuge is called seeking asylum. However, in many places — including the United States — asylum seekers may be imprisoned for months or even years while their cases are reviewed. Once asylum is granted, refugees can stay in the host country until it is safe to return home. Refugees who are denied asylum often are deported, usually back to their home countries.

Even with the 1967 amendment, the convention does not apply to the vast majority of people who flee from their homes. For example, IDPs do not have legal protection because they do not cross international borders, nor do those who flee across borders to escape natural disasters.[22] Being covered by the treaty might have little significance for people forced from their homes by violent groups like the Lord's Resistance Army. Even so, some advocates say applying the treaty to IDPs might, in some cases, pressure the governments involved to take better care of their citizens.

The treaty has critics across the ideological spectrum. Some refugee advocates, including Harrell-Bond, complain that it lacks universal standards for granting asylum, so Western countries, in particular, "are free to turn away asylum-seekers on no basis whatsoever."

Some Western officials say the treaty is being misused by "economic migrants" — would-be immigrants from poor countries simply seeking a better life — who claim to be refugees but do not qualify for asylum on the basis of a fear of persecution.

The treaty "is no longer working as its framers intended," then British Home Secretary Jack Straw said in 2001, citing the large increase in displaced people worldwide. "Too much effort and resources are being expended on dealing with unfounded claims for asylum, and not enough on helping those in need of protection."[23] He called for "radical thinking" on a better way to determine who is a refugee and who is not.

Despite such concerns, many experts say the convention will not be amended or updated any time soon. The U.N. treaty-making process is cumbersome and takes years to complete. Moreover, global interest in new treaties has dwindled in recent years, and even IDP advocates aren't willing to risk having the treaty watered down instead of strengthened.

AP Photo/Eranga Jayawardena

More than 250,000 Sri Lankans have been forced from their homes, often repeatedly, in the latest — and possibly final — round of the 26-year war between government forces and separatist Tamil Tiger guerrillas. Above, internally displaced Tamil civilians wait to enter a government shelter near Colombo.

Carleton University's Milner notes the current treaty was negotiated shortly after World War II, "when notions of human justice were quite powerful because of what happened during the war, particularly in Nazi Germany." Nearly six decades later, Western countries — the desired destination for many refugees — are increasingly reluctant to open their borders. "If we reopened the Refugee Convention, we likely would see a race to the lowest common denominator — protecting borders — rather than refugees," Milner says. "That's a risk I'm not willing to take."

Khalid Koser, an analyst specializing in refugee affairs at the Geneva Center for Security Policy, agrees. "At least the current convention has 150-odd signatories, most of whom abide by it," Koser says.

The UNHCR has expressed similar concerns. In a recent paper exploring whether those fleeing natural disasters should be given legal status under the treaty, the agency warned that any attempt to modify the convention could lower refugee-protection standards "and even undermine the international refugee-protection regime altogether."[24]

Meanwhile, Europe is engaged in a spirited debate over implementation of the treaty; since 2001 the European Union (EU) has been developing a common system for granting asylum among its 27 member countries. The European Pact on Immigration and Asylum, adopted by EU leaders on Oct. 16, 2008, promises that EU countries will speed up asylum determinations, eliminating delays that often stretch into months or years.[25] Refugee rights advocates, however, worry the EU is trying to close its doors to legitimate refugees, not just economic migrants who are not entitled to asylum under the treaty.

At Human Rights Watch, refugee policy Director Bill Frelick says the new European pact also does little to relieve unequal burden-sharing. Most migrants and refugees from Africa and the Middle East enter Europe through the poorest countries in southeastern Europe, which have been rejecting refugees at very high rates. For instance, since 2004 Greece has granted asylum to fewer than 1 percent of the refugees from Iraq, Afghanistan and other countries, according to the European Council on Refugees and Exiles, a coalition of 69 nongovernmental organizations.[26] By contrast, some other European countries, particularly in Scandinavia, accept upwards of 90 percent of asylum-seekers, Frelick notes.

"There has been an utter failure to share the refugee burdens," Frelick says. "The richer countries have done an effective job of deflecting the burden off onto the poor countries, which are responding by turning people away, even those who are legitimate refugees."

Should the United States admit more Iraqi refugees?

Fearing that some could be terrorists, the United States has been slow to accept Iraqis who have fled to neighboring countries — notably Syria and Jordan — since the U.S. invasion in 2003.

Through the middle of 2008, the Bush administration accepted only about 10,000 Iraqi refugees out of the 1-2 million who have fled, according to Refugees International and other nongovernmental organizations.[27] But under pressure from Congress and advocacy groups, it stepped up Iraqi admissions last year and admitted more than 13,800 Iraqis as permanent residents — slightly more than the administration's 12,000 annual goal for fiscal 2008, which ended on Oct. 1. The administration's 2009 goal is 17,000 Iraqi admissions.[28]

Several major refugee and human-rights groups want the U.S. quota raised to 105,000 Iraqis in 2009. Among the Iraqi refugees in Syria and Jordan are thousands who worked directly with the U.S. military and other government agencies, American contractors and the news media. Some served as translators or even intelligence operatives, while others filled jobs such as drivers and cooks.

"Their stay in neighboring states remains extremely precarious, and many live in fear of being forcibly returned to Iraq, where they face death threats and further persecution," said a joint statement by Refugees International and a dozen other organizations on July 31, 2008. Helping these Iraqis resettle in the United States "will demonstrate America's dedication to protecting the most vulnerable and our commitment to peace and security in the region."[29]

The U.S. Department of Homeland Security said in September it was "committed to streamlining the process for admitting Iraqi refugees to the U.S. while ensuring the highest level of security."[30] However, the Obama administration has not announced plans for a dramatic increase in admissions. A State Department spokesman said in early February a decision was pending.

A report released in January by the Center for American Progress, a liberal think tank in Washington, D.C., said 30,000 to 100,000 Iraqis have been "affiliated" with the United States in one way or another during the war, and many would be "in imminent danger" of assassination if they returned home.[31]

The group advocates bringing up to 25,000 of those Iraqis and their families to the United States over the next five years. Natalie Ondiak, lead author of the proposal, says the United States "has a moral obligation to the Iraqis who have worked for the government, were loyal to us and now fear for their lives because of the stigma of having been associated with the United States."

However, Ann Corcoran — a Maryland blogger who runs the Refugee Resettlement Watch blog — is a vocal critic of such proposals. She cites cases in which church groups and other agencies bring refugees to the United States but fail to help them adjust to their new lives.

"These organizations are not taking very good care of the refugees who are already here, and they say they don't have the resources to do the job," she says. "So, if we are talking about another 25,000 or 100,000 refugees, where do they think these people will be cared for? Who is going to make sure they have housing and jobs and education for their children? It's just insane."[32]

A better alternative, she says "is to keep them in the region, to keep them comfortable and proceeding with their lives in the Middle East until the situation in Iraq is safe enough for them to return."

Congress in 2006 created a program to speed up admissions for up to 500 Iraqi and Afghan translators per year. In 2008 Congress added another program allowing up to 5,000 Iraqis who worked in various capacities for the U.S. government or contractors to enter the United States in each of the five fiscal years, beginning in 2008. However, Ondiak says only about 600 translators gained admission in 2008.

BACKGROUND

Refugee Rights and Needs

Although the forced displacement of people from their homes is as old as human history, the idea that society has a moral obligation to come to their aid is relatively new.

After World War I, the newly formed League of Nations created the post of High Commissioner for Refugees but gave the office little authority and few resources. The league (the forerunner of the U.N.) also adopted two treaties in the 1930s offering limited legal protection to refugees, but only a handful of countries ratified them.[33]

The displacement of millions of people during World War II finally brought significant action on refugees. As the war was winding down, the United States and its allies created the United Nations Relief and Rehabilitation Agency, which gave emergency aid to 7 million displaced people. After the war, a successor organization, the International Refugee Organization, helped some 1 million dislocated Europeans find new homes.[34]

The modern era of international aid to refugees began in 1950-51, when the United Nations created the office of the U.N. High Commissioner for Refugees and held a special conference in Geneva to draft the treaty that became known as the Refugee Convention. Both the UNHCR and the treaty were aimed at aiding European war refugees or those who fled Eastern Europe after the Soviet Union imposed communist rule across the region. In fact, the treaty applied only to those who had become refugees before Jan. 1, 1951, and the text made clear the drafters had Europeans in mind. Moreover, the U.N. General Assembly gave the UNHCR only a three-year mandate, assuming the refugee problem would be quickly solved.[35]

In 1949, before the UNHCR started work, the U.N. Relief and Works Agency for Palestine Refugees in the Near East (known as UNRWA) was created to assist the 700,000 Palestinians who fled or were driven from their homes in what is now Israel during the 1948 Arab-Israeli war.[36] The UNRWA also was considered short-lived. But nearly 60 years later the ultimate status of the Palestinians remains unresolved, and the UNRWA is still providing food, medical care and other aid to a Palestinian population that has grown to 4.6 million. About 1.4 million Palestinians live in UNRWA camps in Jordan, Lebanon, Syria, the West Bank and Gaza Strip; the rest live on their own.[37]

Conflicts continued across the globe after World War II, some of them widely seen as proxy wars among governments and rebel groups backed by the two Cold War superpowers, the Soviet Union and the United States. In each case, dislocated civilians crossed international borders and created a new generation of refugees.

The U.N. General Assembly officially recognized the new refugee trend in 1967, adopting an amendment, or protocol, to the refugee convention. The Protocol Relating to the Status of Refugees dropped the pre-1951 limitation, giving legal protection to refugees worldwide, not just in Europe.[38] The convention and its protocol are now among the most widely adopted U.N. treaties; each has been ratified by 144 countries.[39]

The collapse of the Soviet Union in 1991 brought new hope for peace. But bloody sectarian conflicts in the Balkans and Africa's Great Lakes region shattered such dreams. Some conflicts dislocated enormous populations, but many people, for one reason or another, stayed in their own countries, where as IDPs they were not covered by the international refugee treaties.

In the 1990s international agencies and human-rights advocates began demanding aid and legal protections for

CHRONOLOGY

1940s-1950s *Newly created United Nations (U.N.) aids refugees after World War II ends.*

1949 U.N. Relief and Works Agency is established to aid Palestinians pushed from their homes during the 1949 Arab-Israeli war.

1950 Office of U.N. High Commissioner for Refugees (UNHCR) is created.

1951 Special U.N. conference adopts Convention Relating to the Status of Refugees (the Refugee Convention) to protect those who fled their countries before Jan. 1, 1951, to escape persecution due to "race, religion, nationality or membership of a particular social group." Generally viewed as applying only to Europeans, the treaty goes into effect in 1954.

1960s-1980s *Cold War conflicts and upheavals create waves of new refugees.*

1967 U.N expands Refugee Convention to cover all refugees fleeing persecution as described in the treaty, not just Europeans who left their home countries before 1951.

1969 Organization of African Unity broadly defines a refugee in Africa as anyone who flees his country because of "external aggression, occupation, foreign domination or events seriously disturbing public order in either part or the whole of his country of origin."

1984 The Colloquium on the International Protection of Refugees in Central America, Mexico and Panama adopts the Cartagena Declaration, defining refugees as anyone fleeing their country because their "lives, safety or freedom" are threatened by "generalized violence, foreign aggression, internal conflicts, massive violation of human rights or other circumstances." Although not official policy, many regional governments adopt the declaration.

1990s-2000s *New wave of civil conflicts forces policy makers to pay more attention to the needs of people displaced within their own borders.*

1992-1995 Civil conflicts in the former Yugoslavia displace several hundred thousand people.

1994 Genocidal rampage in Rwanda kills 800,000 Hutus and Tutsis; hundreds of thousands of others flee their homes, many into neighboring countries.

1997 Government-backed rebels oust longtime dictator Mobutu Sese Seko of Zaire (later the Democratic Republic of the Congo), triggering years of civil war in Africa's Great Lakes region; an estimated 5 million people die, and thousands are displaced during fighting that continues today.

1998 The Guiding Principles on Internal Displacement establish rules for aiding and protecting internally displaced persons (IDPs); the guidelines eventually are incorporated into U.N procedures but are not legally binding.

2002 About 2 million Afghan refugees return home (mostly from Pakistan and Iran) after a U.S.-led invasion topples the Taliban government. Some 6 million had fled during three decades of war — the largest number of refugees generated by any conflict since World War II.

2004 In a landmark decision, Colombia's Constitutional Court orders the government to increase aid to about 2 million people displaced by conflict.

2005 U.N. adopts "responsibility to protect" doctrine, which holds every government responsible for protecting the rights of its citizens and says the international community has a responsibility to intervene if a government abuses its own citizens. . . . U.N. gives UNHCR more responsibility for helping IDPs.

2008 U.N. launches a year-long publicity campaign to focus international attention on the needs of IDPs. . . . UNHCR starts a campaign to help end long-term displacements of those forced from their homes in Afghanistan, the Balkans, Burundi, Eritrea and Myanmar.

2009 African Union is scheduled in April to adopt a treaty recognizing the rights of internally displaced people, based on the 1998 Guiding Principles.

these large groups. In 1992, U.N. Secretary-General Boutros Boutros-Ghali appointed Francis Deng, a former Sudanese diplomat, as the U.N.'s first special representative on internally displaced people.

Deng, who held the post until 2004, was largely responsible for drafting the Guiding Principles on Internal Displacement.[40] Although the document has never been put into international law, U.N. agencies and a dozen countries have incorporated its principles into their laws and policies. (*See box, p. 312.*)

However, says refugee specialist Koser at the Geneva Center for Security Policy, "there is very little political will to formalize [the principles] into a binding convention, and few states would ratify it."

Rising Displacements

U.N. officials and policy experts count more than four dozen countries — most in Africa and Asia — with significant populations displaced by civil wars or other violence. When the consequences of natural disasters are considered, however, the displacement problem becomes nearly universal. Thousands of Gulf Coast residents in the United States remain displaced by Hurricane Katrina in 2006, and millions in China's Sichuan Province are homeless nearly a year after a major earthquake.

Colombia has one of the world's largest IDP populations, and hundreds of thousands of people are still displaced in Chechnya and Georgia in the Caucuses and in Bosnia, Croatia, Kosovo and Serbia as a result of the Balkan wars. Thousands more have been displaced by ongoing conflict and instability in Somalia. (*See sidebar, p. 296.*)

Here are some of the displacements that are high on the international agenda:

Afghanistan — At least 6 million Afghans fled — mostly to Pakistan and Iran — between the Soviet Union's December 1979 invasion and the U.S. ousting of the Taliban government in late 2001. During periods of relative calm in the 1980s and '90s, hundreds of thousands of Afghan refugees returned home, but many fled again when fighting resumed.[41]

Shortly after a new Western-backed government took office in Kabul at the end of 2001, refugees began returning home in large numbers. Between 2002 and late 2008, about 5.6 million refugees returned, of whom nearly 4.4 million received UNHCR aid (the rest returned on their own).[42] Since 2007, thousands of refugees have returned because Pakistan closed some refugee camps, and Iran deported thousands of mostly undocumented Afghan men seeking work.[43]

By late 2008, the UNHCR estimated that about 2 million Afghan refugees were still in Pakistan and nearly 1 million in Iran.[44] Worried about its inability to provide housing, jobs and other services for returning refugees, the Afghan government in 2008 began discouraging large-scale returns. "We don't have the means to provide an encouraging environment for refugees to repatriate," Shir Mohammad Etibari, minister of refugees and returnees, said in September. The U.N. and other international agencies "only make promises but do little."[45]

Another 235,000 Afghans are displaced but still in Afghanistan. Some were forced to return to Afghanistan against their will, only to find that they had no place to live and could find no jobs. Among the most vulnerable are several thousand returnees who were forced out of Pakistan and now live at a camp in the Chemtala desert, about 15 miles west of Jalalabad. Last winter they struggled to survive in mud huts and tents provided by the UNHCR and the Norwegian Refugee Council. "I wish we hadn't left Pakistan," said elderly returnee Golam Shah. "Life was much better there."[46]

A similar complaint came from 18-year-old Wali, who grew up in Pakistan's Jalozai refugee village. Forced out last May, he now lives in a tent in Balkh Province in northern Afghanistan. "I didn't expect to face such problems or to end up in such a place," he said. "There is nothing here — no shelter, not enough water, no trees for firewood, no electricity and no work."[47]

Colombia — A long-running rebel insurgency and the government's aggressive, U.S.-backed war against narcotics cartels have created what the U.N. calls the worst humanitarian crisis in the Western Hemisphere. Up to half a million Colombians have fled to neighboring countries, and thousands have emigrated to the United States. At least 2.8 million mostly rural people are internally displaced in the nation of 45 million.[48]

Since the 1960s the military has brutally suppressed two leftist guerrilla groups claiming to be fighting for land reform and other social causes — the Revolutionary Armed Forces of Colombia (FARC) and the National Liberation Army (ELN). Right-wing paramilitary armies formed by major landowners and elements of the military aided the anti-insurgency campaign.

Millions Remain in Exile for Decades

"Whole generations of kids grow up in refugee camps."

Miljo and Milica Miljic grabbed their two children and fled Tuzla, Bosnia, in 1992, at the beginning of a nearly four-year civil war that tore their country apart. "We didn't take anything with us because we didn't have time," Miljo told a representative of the U.N. High Commissioner for Refugees (UNHCR) this past January. "We had to run for our lives. The only thing that comes to mind in such a situation is to save your children and your own life. You don't think about the photographs, about personal documents, clothes, whatever."[1]

The Miljics are among nearly 97,000 refugees from Bosnia and Croatia who have not returned to their homes, even though the war ended in late 1995. They are still in Serbia, where the refugee population has slowly dwindled down from more than 500,000 in 1996.[2]

The words "refugees" and "displaced persons" conjure up images of short-term emergencies: people fleeing their homes temporarily because of wars, hurricanes or earthquakes, only to return home a few weeks, or at most a few months, later. While many do return home once a crisis has passed, most refugees and internally displaced persons (IDPs) remain displaced long after the emergency is over.

In fact, refugees fleeing conflict end up staying away from their homes an average of 18 years, and many IDPs are displaced for comparable periods. James Milner, a refugee expert at Carleton University in Ottawa, Canada, says some situations last even longer: The Palestinians who fled Israel during the 1948-49 Arab-Israeli war have been in exile ever since.

In recent years experts have begun focusing on "protracted situations" involving refugees and IDPs displaced for at least five years, and numerous conferences have been held to discuss the problem of long-term displacements. U.N. High Commissioner Antonio Guterres said more than 30 situations around the world involve a total of about 6 million refugees who have been living in long-term exile.

"Many are effectively trapped in the camps and communities where they are accommodated," Guterres said. "Their home countries are caught in endless conflict or afflicted by political stalemate or human-rights violations, and most are not allowed to hold jobs, work the land where they live or integrate into the local communities."[3]

Most of the long-term displaced are children and youth, says Elizabeth Ferris, director of the Brookings-Bern Project on Internal Displacement. "You have whole generations of kids who grow up and live in refugee camps, where typically you have a breakdown of normal social institutions," she says.

From 11 million to 17 million people have been displaced for at least five years but are still living inside their own countries, Ferris says. "Unfortunately, the world has paid very little attention to these situations, which are allowed to fester for years and years," she says.

Aside from the Palestinians, perhaps the best-known protracted refugee situation involves the estimated 6 million people who have fled their homes during three decades of warfare in Afghanistan, which began with the Soviet Union's invasion in 1979. Most went to neighboring Iran or Pakistan, where they settled in formal camps or moved into cities. Millions of Afghan refugees returned home after the U.S. invasion in 2001, but nearly 3 million are still refugees.[4]

Many scholars and aid officials worry that another long-term refugee situation is developing among the 2 million or more Iraqis who have fled their homeland. Although the Baghdad government has encouraged some to return, the U.N. and private aid groups say it is still too unsafe, especially for Sunni Muslims or members of other minority groups.[5]

Other protracted refugee situations prioritized by the UNHCR include:

- **Myanmar/Bangladesh.** Some 200,000 Rohingya, a Muslim ethnic group in North Rakhine state in Myanmar, fled to neighboring Bangladesh in 1991 to escape persecution by the military junta in Myanmar. Thousands have since returned to Myanmar, but the majority remain in Bangladesh and are classified by the U.N. as "stateless" persons because Myanmar no longer considers them as citizens.[6]
- **Eritrea/Sudan.** Some 90,000 Eritreans are long-term refugees in eastern Sudan, many since the late 1960s when Eritrean rebels launched a 30-year-long war against Ethiopia. (Eritrea gained its independence in 1993, but the two countries fought another bloody war from 1998 until 2000.) Additional Eritrean refugees continue to arrive in Sudan, joined by refugees from Ethiopia and Somalia. Most live in camps and lack any rights or protections but have increasingly begun to move into Khartoum and other Sudanese cities, over the government's objection.[7]
- **The Balkans.** Like the Miljics, hundreds of thousands of people dislocated by war in the former Yugoslavia during the 1990s have not returned to their home regions. Some 200,000 refugees, mostly ethnic Serbs, became naturalized citizens in Serbia rather than return to Bosnia or Croatia, where Serbs are in the minority.[8]
- **Burundi/Tanzania.** Violent civil conflict in Burundi in 1972 forced thousands to flee into neighboring Tanzania, where the government created three

settlements in central and western Tanzania and provided land and other services for them. In 2007, about 218,000 refugees were still in the settlements. Under an agreement that many experts consider historic, Burundi and Tanzania decided in 2008 to resolve the status of these so-called "old settlement" refugees from 1972. Tanzania agreed to grant citizenship to, and fully integrate into local communities, some 176,000 of the remaining refugees. Those wanting to return to Burundi were to be allowed to do so by September 2009.[9]

AFP/Getty Images/Mohammed Abed

The U.N. Relief and Works Agency, which for 60 years has aided Palestinian refugees, was stretched thin during prolonged Israeli military strikes earlier this year. More than 1,000 Palestinians were killed and many homes were destroyed, such as this woman's house in the Jabalia refugee camp in northern Gaza.

Protracted IDP Situations

Globally, about half of the estimated 26 million IDPs displaced by violence are stuck in protracted situations, according to Neill Wright, the UNHCR's senior coordinator for IDPs. And some who were forced from their homes by natural disasters also remain displaced after five years.

Both types of protracted situations exist in Kenya, where about 350,000 people have been displaced long-term by conflict, unresolved land disputes and natural disasters.[10] Post-election violence displaced another 500,000 Kenyans in late 2007 and early 2008, but about half of those had returned home by late 2008.[11]

Ferris, of the Brookings-Bern project, says at least three-dozen countries have long-term displacement situations, and people are still being displaced in about a dozen others, such as Colombia, the Democratic Republic of the Congo and Somalia. In most other countries, the fighting has ended, but thousands remain displaced because peace agreements were never negotiated or the IDPs there are afraid, or unwilling, to return to their homes for other reasons.

Experts say no single solution will solve the protracted-displacement problem. Even negotiating peace agreements does not guarantee that displaced people can or will return home.

But policy makers have identified several essential elements that would help create "durable solutions" for protracted situations. One element, they say, is recognizing that forcing or encouraging people to return to their original homes may not always be the best solution, particularly when people have been displaced for many years, and they no longer have reasons for returning home.

An alternative to repatriation is "local integration" — allowing displaced people to become part of the local communities where they have taken refuge. This route is often politically difficult because local communities usually don't want to absorb large numbers of outsiders. Milner says he hopes Tanzania's willingness to accept Burundians displaced for nearly four decades as citizens will become a model for other countries.

"This creates a significant strategic opportunity for the international community to demonstrate that local integration can work," he says. "Now, the next step is for the donor community to meet its responsibilities to help countries, like Tanzania, that might be willing to resolve these situations."

The UNHCR also acknowledged in November 2008 that its policy of providing only short-term humanitarian aid to refugees in camps had failed to help them develop personal independence and job skills that would allow them to live on their own. Too often, a UNHCR report said, "refugees were left to live in camps indefinitely, often with restrictions placed on their rights, as well as their ability to support themselves by means of agriculture, trade or employment."[12]

Under the U.N.'s "humanitarian reform" program adopted in late 2005, the agency is changing its approach, says Jeff Crisp, director of UNHCR's policy and evaluation service.

---

[1] "The continuing struggle of Europe's forgotten refugees," U.N. High Commissioner for Refugees, Jan. 12, 2009, www.unhcr.org/news/NEWS/496b6ad12.html..

[2] *Ibid.*

[3] "Protracted Refugee Situations: High Commissioner's Initiative," U.N. High Commissioner for Refugees, December 2008, p. 2, www.unhcr.org/protect/PROTECTION/4937de6f2.pdf.

[4] "Protracted Refugee Situations: Revisiting The Problem," U.N. High Commissioner for Refugees, June 2, 2008, pp. 5-6, www.unhcr.org/excom/EXCOM/484514c12.pdf.

[5] "NGOs warn against encouraging large-scale refugee returns," IRIN news service, Nov. 3, 2008, www.irinnews.org/Report.aspx?ReportId=81258.

[6] "Protracted Refugee Situations: The High Commissioner's Initiative," *op. cit.*, pp. 9-11.

[7] *Ibid.*, p. 14.

[8] *Ibid.*, p. 32.

[9] *Ibid.*, pp. 25-29.

[10] "Frequently Asked Questions on IDPs," U.N. Office for the Coordination of Humanitarian Affairs, Dec. 4, 2008, p. 4.

[11] *Ibid.*, p. 2.

[12] "Protracted Refugee Situations: A discussion paper prepared for the High Commissioner's Dialogue on Protection Challenges," Nov. 20, 2008, p. 13, www.unhcr.org/protect/PROTECTION/492ad3782.pdf.

AFP/Getty Images/Alejandra Vega

Colombia's long-running rebel insurgency and the government's aggressive, U.S.-backed war against narcotics cartels have created the worst humanitarian crisis in the Western Hemisphere, according to the U.N. This family living in a tent in a Bogotá park is among at least 2.8 million displaced Colombians.

Both the guerrillas and paramilitaries eventually became deeply involved in the drug trade, turning an ideological war over land reform and other social issues into a battle for control of illegal cocaine production. The government's war against cocaine — most of which is consumed in the United States — has been funded largely by Washington.

Colombia is now the hemisphere's major source of refugees, most of whom have fled to Ecuador and Venezuela; others sought refuge in Brazil, Panama and Costa Rica.[49] About 460,000 Colombians are in "refugee-like situations" — they've fled Colombia but are not officially considered refugees and receive little if any official aid.[50] The flow of refugees has worsened Colombia's relations with left-leaning Ecuador and Venezuela.

Colombia estimates it has 2.8 million registered IDPs — among the world's highest for an individual country.[51] But nongovernmental agencies say the real number is much higher. The Catholic Church-affiliated Consultancy for Human Rights and Displacement puts the number at more than 4.3 million.[52] Many displaced people do not register for fear of retaliation or being forced to return to unsafe areas. The displacement rate has escalated in recent years, according to both the government and private agencies: About 300,000 people were displaced in 2007, but 270,000 were displaced in just the first six months of 2008.[53]

Colombia's IDPs have received serious attention since the country's Constitutional Court in 2004 ordered the government to provide aid — one of the few instances where an activist court has significantly helped IDPs.

Andrea Lari, a senior advocate at Refugees International, says the government helps IDPs survive on a daily basis but does virtually nothing to enable them to escape from urban shantytowns. The government provides "too much social welfare and not enough . . . job training or education beyond primary schools — the help needed to sustain themselves where they now live," he says. Going home "is not a serious option" for most because they have lost their land and are afraid to return.

Democratic Republic of the Congo — Hundreds of thousands of civilians continue to suffer from fighting in the eastern provinces of Africa's second-largest country — a war that officially ended more than five years ago. At least 400,000 Congolese were displaced in 2008 and early this year by continuing violence, bringing the total displaced to about 1.25 million.[54]

Two major wars — involving five other African countries at one point — raged in Congo from 1997 until peace agreements hammered out in 2002-03 ended most of the fighting and led to elections in 2006. More than 5 million people may have died during the wars — the largest toll by far of any post-World War II conflict, according to the International Rescue Committee.[55]

Lingering conflicts still plague several areas, including North Kivu Province on the borders with Rwanda and Uganda. There, remnants of the Hutu extremist forces responsible for Rwanda's genocide in 1994 have battled a rebel force claiming to support the Congolese Tutsis, members of the same ethnic group targeted by the Hutus in the Rwandan genocide. Until recently, the Congolese army had not curbed either faction.

In January, however, the Congolese and Rwandan armies launched an unusual joint military operation targeting both the Hutu and Tutsi forces in North Kivu. And in a potential step toward peace, the Rwandan army on Jan. 22 arrested the self-styled Tutsi general Laurent Nkunda, whose rebels had wreaked havoc in the region.[56] The arrest — coming on the heels of a related international campaign against the Lord's Resistance Army — offered the first tangible hope in many years that the region's troubles might some day come to an end.[57]

Online Newspaper Fights for Refugees in Kenya

'We need to be able to help ourselves'

Problems with the water supply, inadequate health inspections of food suppliers, indifferent officials. Such issues would be the meat-and-potatoes of any local newspaper. But who draws attention to such concerns in a refugee camp as big as a mid-size city?

Most refugee camps have community organizations that present residents' concerns to camp officials, but they rarely receive wide attention locally. Since last December, however, the problems faced by the 50,000 refugees at the Kakuma camp in northwest Kenya have been exposed not only to local residents but to people around the world via the camp's Internet newspaper, *Kanere* (KAkuma NEws REflector).

The paper (http://kakuma.wordpress.com) is run by staff of volunteer journalists aided by Bethany Ojalehto, a 2008 Cornell University graduate who is studying the rights of refugees at the camp on a Fulbright research scholarship. She says several refugees interested in starting a newspaper approached her for help when she arrived at the camp last October, and she agreed because their interests and her research "blended seamlessly and have now been channeled into this project."

So far *Kanere* is published only in English, which is a common language for many of the camp's residents, who can read it at computer stations in several locations. The paper's editors say they hope to expand into other languages once they get more help.

Twenty-four-year-old Qabaata, one of the paper's editors, says he fled Ethiopia in 2003 after being targeted by government security forces for writing an article supporting a student strike. A journalism student at the time, he went with other students to Kakuma after being arrested and released by authorities in Addis Ababa, Ethiopia's capital. He is seeking asylum status from the UNHCR because he says he cannot return to Ethiopia. "It is not safe for me there," he says. He hopes to win a scholarship to finish his journalism studies but has no immediate prospects for attaining that goal.

Kakuma has one of the most diverse camp populations in Africa. Opened in 1992 to aid refugees from the long civil war in southern Sudan, Kakuma now houses about 25,000 Sudanese, 18,000 Somalis, 4,500 Ethiopians and 1,800 other Africans.[1] Since mid-2008 the U.N. High Commissioner for Refugees (UNHCR) has transferred thousands of Somali refugees to Kakuma from three overcrowded camps at Dadaab, Kenya, about 700 miles to the east. (*See Somalia box, p. 296.*)

Qabaata says *Kanere* provides a unique opportunity to share concerns across the camp's different ethnic and national communities and to voice grievances to camp officials. "The refugees here don't have access to the people who are governing them," he says. "They only have access through their community leaders, but even their leaders do not always have access."

Negash, another Ethiopian refugee who works on *Kanere*, notes that one crucial issue is water. All water for the camp comes from underground aquifers and is rationed at about 20 liters per refugee per day. And some refugees have to walk long distances to get it. The paper's first issue, in December 2008, pointed out that refugees in one section of the camp had recently gone without adequate water for three days while a broken pump was being fixed. Why is water rationed for refugees, the paper asked, while U.N. and other aid agencies' staff members living nearby "are given unlimited water?"

Kanere also deals with UNHCR budget cutbacks, long food-distribution lines, the lack of job opportunities, low pay for refugees compared to local Kenyans and the "poor performance" of the camp's 14 primary and two secondary schools.

Above all, say Qabaata and Negash, *Kanere* advocates on behalf of refugees' basic human rights. "As refugees, we are told we have rights, but in reality we have no rights here in the camp," Negash says. "We hope *Kanere* will empower the refugee community, help it to be self-reliant. As it is, the humanitarian community is just making us dependent, reliant on them. We need to be able to help ourselves."

---

[1] "Kenya: Population of Concern to UNHCR," November 2008, p. 6, www.unhcr.org/partners/PARTNERS/4951ef9d2.pdf.

Permanent Solutions Sought for the Displaced

Aid agencies turning away from short-term solutions

In the past, the U.N. High Commissioner for Refugees (UNHCR) and other aid agencies have focused primarily on short-term fixes — such as providing emergency food, medical care and other aid — for those displaced by war, conflict or natural disaster. They also generally assumed that displaced people wanted to return to their homes, and encouraging them to do so was easier than resettling them elsewhere.

But in recent years aid agencies have begun paying more attention to moving displaced people out of camps and makeshift shelters and back into normal lives.

Three so-called durable solutions have been proposed for refugees as well as internally displaced persons (IDPs), or those still living in their own countries:

- **Return or repatriation** — Returning either to their past residence or to their home neighborhood or region.
- **Local integration** — Settling permanently in the locality or country where the person has sought temporary refuge.
- **Resettlement elsewhere** — For refugees, moving to a willing third country; for IDPs, moving to a different part or region of their home countries.

In the absence of universally accepted standards for deciding when an IDP is no longer displaced, the Brookings-Bern Project on Internal Displacement in 2007 created a "Framework for Durable Solutions" for IDPs, which has been officially "welcomed" by the U.N.[1] It says IDPs' displacement should be considered ended when one of the three durable solutions occurs, and they "no longer have needs specifically related to their displacement." Although former IDPs may still have humanitarian needs, at this point "their needs are basically the same as other people in the local population, and it's the government's responsibility to help them," says project director Elizabeth Ferris.

In 2007, about 2 million IDPs and 731,000 refugees returned to their home countries, their actual homes or to their home regions, according to the UNHCR.[2] About half were in the Democratic Republic of the Congo, although conflict displaced another 500,000 Congolese that same year.[3] More than half of the returning refugees — some 374,000 — were Afghans.[4]

Barbara Harrell-Bond, a veteran advocate for refugees and leading critic of the UNHCR, faults the agency for continuing to focus on repatriation for refugees, because she says integration in asylum countries "often is the only solution." UNHCR officials, however, say local integration and resettlement are difficult because host countries are not inclined to accept refugees and displaced people on a permanent basis.

But resettlement efforts are occurring, albeit on a small scale, say the UNHCR and refugee advocacy groups. In 2007, the UNHCR recommended 99,000 refugees for resettlement in third countries, nearly double the previous year, but only 70,000 were able to resettle — less than 1 percent of the total refugees.[5] Historically, the United States has accepted more refugees than any other country; in 2006, the last year for which comparative figures are

Iraq — The 1991 Persian Gulf War and sectarian violence following the 2003 U.S. invasion of Iraq have swelled the ranks of displaced Iraqis to between 3 million and 5 million — out of a total population of around 28 million. Most have remained in the country but fled their home regions, usually to escape sectarian violence.[58]

Many of the Iraqi IDPs live with friends or relatives and receive government food rations. For those who cannot get rations, the World Food Program on Jan. 3 announced a one-year program to aid about 750,000 Iraqis inside Iraq and 360,000 in Syria.[59]

Many IDPs live in informal camps inside Iraq. The Iraqi government early in 2008 had announced an ambitious plan to build IDP housing, but falling oil prices have forced budget cuts that endanger the effort.[60] Then in late 2008 the government moved to close some of the camps by giving families one-time $4,250 stipends to return to their homes or find new places to live.[61] The UNHCR plans to help about 400,000 Iraqi IDPs this year.[62]

Some 300,000 displaced Iraqis have returned home, and nearly two-thirds of those still displaced want to return to their original home regions, according to a

available, the United States accepted 41,300 refugees — more than half of the 71,700 resettlements that occurred that year.[6]

Local integration sometimes occurs informally, particularly when displaced people are not confined to official camps or settlements. For instance, in Pakistan, many of the estimated 1.8 million remaining Afghan refugees have established new lives in Peshawar, Quetta and other cities. Many had been refugees for more than 20 years, and more than half were born outside Afghanistan; a substantial number were ethnic Pashtuns, which also is the dominant ethnic group in the border areas of Pakistan. As a result, remaining in Pakistan has been a natural solution for them.[7]

AFP/Getty Images/Jaime Reina

Afghan refugees who have just returned from Pakistan wait to register at a transition center in Kabul in June 2008. Aid agencies have begun focusing on moving displaced people out of camps and back into normal lives, often by returning them to their home countries.

In contrast, official agreements allowing large numbers of refugees or IDPs to move permanently from camps into local communities are rare. An exception is Tanzania, where more than 200,000 Burundians have been refugees since 1972. Seeking to resolve a situation that had dragged on so long, and with U.N. help that included limited financial aid, Burundi and Tanzania agreed in 2007 that 172,000 refugees could remain in Tanzania as citizens, while 46,000 would return to Burundi. The agreement is expected to be implemented by late 2009.[8]

James Milner, of Canada's Carleton University, says Tanzania's willingness to accept long-term refugees as permanent refugees "creates a strategic opportunity for the international community to show that there are alternatives to warehousing refugees forever in camps."

The only missing element, he says, is a willingness by the major donor nations to put their money and diplomatic leverage to work to encourage other countries to follow Tanzania's example. "The United States is the hegemon in the global refugee regime," he says. "If the United States were to support more of this kind of action, eventually we could see real solutions for refugees."

[1] "When Displacement Ends: A Framework for Durable Solutions," Brookings-Bern Project on Internal Displacement, June 2007, www.brookings.edu/reports/2007/09displacementends.aspx.

[2] "Note on International Protection," U.N. High Commissioner for Refugees, June 2008, p. 2, www.unhcr.org/publ/PUBL/484807202.pdf.

[3] *Ibid.*, p. 15.

[4] *Ibid.*

[5] *Ibid.*, p. 17.

[6] "Global Trends for 2006: Refugees, Asylum-seekers, Returnees, Internally Displaced and Stateless Persons," U.N. High Commissioner for Refugees, June 2007, p. 8, www.unhcr.org/statistics/STATISTICS/4676a71d4.pdf.

[7] "Afghanistan — The Challenges of Sustaining Returns," U.N. High Commissioner for Refugees, www.unhcr.org/cgi-bin/texis/vtx/afghan?page=intro.

[8] "Protracted Refugee Situations: The High Commissioner's Initiative," U.N. High Commissioner for Refugees, December 2008, pp. 25-29, www.unhcr.org/protect/PROTECTION/4937de6f2.pdf.

survey released on Feb. 22 by the International Organization for Migration.[63]

Since 2003 at least 2 million Iraqis have fled to several neighboring countries: Syria (1.2 million), Jordan (450,000), the Gulf states (150,000), Iran (58,000), Lebanon (50,000) and Egypt (40,000).[64]

Some experts question the government estimates. Amelia Templeton, an analyst at Human Rights First, suggests only about 1 million Iraqi refugees are living in neighboring countries, based on school registrations and the number of refugees receiving UNHCR aid.

In contrast to many other refugee situations, nearly all of the Iraqi refugees live in or near major cities, such as Damascus, Syria, and Amman, Jordan, because Iraq's neighbors don't permit refugee camps. A high proportion of Iraqi refugees are lawyers, doctors, professors and other well-educated professionals.

National Public Radio journalist Deborah Amos tells the stories of Iraqi refugees in Syria and Lebanon in a soon-to-be-published book. She says many of the professionals belonged to the Sunni elite or Christian minority groups (such as Chaldeans), who for centuries were tolerated in

Iraq but suddenly were targeted with violence. Many have spent their life savings during the years in exile and now rely on U.N. handouts. As in much of the world, local governments will not allow the refugees to work, forcing some female refugees in Damascus to turn to prostitution to support their families, Amos writes.

Myanmar — Cyclone Nargis struck on May 2, 2008, killing 140,000 people — mostly by drowning — and forcing up to 800,000 from their homes.[65] Humanitarian agencies pressed the government to allow international aid workers into the vast Irrawaddy Delta, but the secretive generals who run Myanmar resisted the appeals for several weeks until U.N. Secretary-General Ban Ki-moon finally persuaded the top general, Thwan Shwe, to accept outside aid.

Aid agencies and foreign governments donated emergency relief supplies and began helping rebuild homes and communities. But about 500,000 people remained displaced at year's end.[66] Many of those displaced by cyclone-caused floods have faced severe water shortages in recent months due to the recent onset of the dry season and water contamination caused by the cyclone.[67] Full recovery from the cyclone could take three to four years, a senior U.N. aid official said in January.[68]

Meanwhile, members of the Muslim Rohingya minority, from the northern state of Rakhine, are officially stateless. According to Amnesty International, thousands of Rohingyas flee Myanmar each year because of land confiscation, arbitrary taxation, forced eviction and denial of citizenship.[69] Since 1991, more than 250,000 have fled, mostly to neighboring Bangladesh, where the UNHCR runs two camps housing 28,000 refugees; another 200,000 unregistered Rohingyas live outside the camps.[70]

In early 2009, the Thai navy reportedly intercepted boats carrying hundreds of Rohingya trying to cross the Andaman Sea. The action generated international outrage after CNN published a photo purportedly showing armed forces towing refugee boats out to sea and leaving the occupants to die, but the Thai government denied the reports. Some were later rescued off the coasts of India and Indonesia, but many went missing.[71]

In early February actress and U.N. goodwill ambassador Angelina Jolie visited refugee camps in Thailand housing 110,000 Karen and Kareni ethnic refugees from Myanmar. She called on the Thai government to lift its ban on refugees working outside the camps and asked the government to extend hospitality to the Rohingyas.[72]

Prime Minister Abhisit Vejjajiva had said earlier that Thailand would not build a camp for the Rohingyas and will continue to expel them. "They are not refugees," he said. "Our policy is to push them out of the country because they are illegal migrants."[73]

Leaders of the Association of Southeast Asian Nations agreed on March 2 to discuss the status of the Rohingyas at a mid-April summit in Bali. Malaysian Prime Minister, Abdullah Ahmad Badawi said the Rohingya problem "is a regional issue that needs to be resolved regionally."[74]

Sudan — Two major internal conflicts plus other conflicts in central and eastern Africa have displaced millions of Sudanese in the past three decades. At the beginning of 2009, more than 3.5 million were still displaced, including about 130,000 in neighboring countries. Sudan hosts more than 250,000 refugees from nearby countries.[75]

Sudan's two-decade civil war between the government in Khartoum and a separatist army in south Sudan ended with an uneasy peace in January 2005. More than 300,000 refugees who had fled the violence have returned to their home regions, but UNHCR has estimated that about 130,000 remain in Egypt, Ethiopia, Kenya and Uganda.[76] And more conflict could erupt if, as expected, the southerners vote in 2011 for full independence.

Elsewhere in Sudan, a series of inter-related conflicts between the Khartoum government and rebel groups in western Darfur have displaced about 2.7 million people and killed an estimated 300,000.[77] Although Darfur has generally faded from world headlines, the conflict continues, with about 1,000 people fleeing their homes every day.[78] Complicating the refugee crisis, 243,000 Darfuris have fled into Chad, while some 45,000 Chadians have crossed into Darfur to escape a related conflict.[79]

More than 200,000 other refugees also are in Sudan, mostly from Eritrea, having fled the long war between Eritrea and Ethiopia.[80]

CURRENT SITUATION

'Responsibility to Protect'

Since last fall, 26-year-old Kandiah and his family have moved eight times to avoid the long-running civil war

AT ISSUE

Should the U.N. High Commissioner for Refugees help more displaced people?

YES

Joel R. Charny
Vice President for Policy
Refugees International

Written for *CQ Global Researcher*, February 2009

Current efforts to help displaced populations do not reflect the fact that twice as many people displaced by conflict remain inside their own borders rather than crossing an international one, thus failing to become refugees protected under international law. With the U.N. High Commissioner for Refugees (UNHCR) focusing primarily on legal protection for refugees, the current system is outmoded. A bold solution is needed to prevent further unnecessary suffering.

Internally displaced people (IDPs) suffer when their governments don't aid and protect their own citizens. They also suffer from the lack of a dedicated international agency mandated to respond to their needs when their states fail. With IDP numbers growing, expanding the UNHCR's mandate to include IDPs is the best option available to fill this gap.

A dedicated agency would be more effective than the current system, characterized by the "cluster leadership" approach, under which international agencies provide help by sectors, such as health, water and sanitation and shelter. For example, in the 1990s the U.N. secretary-general mandated that UNHCR respond to the needs of IDPs displaced by the civil war in Sri Lanka. Over the years, the agency effectively fulfilled this responsibility with donor support, and the entire U.N. country team — as well as the Sri Lankan government — benefited from the clarity of knowing that the agency was in charge. Moreover, carrying out this exceptional mandate did not undermine either the UNHCR's work with refugees in the region or the right of Tamil Sri Lankans to seek asylum in southern India.

Giving one agency responsibility for an especially vulnerable population is more effective than patching together a response system with multiple independent agencies. Because the circumstances and needs of IDPs are so similar to those of refugees, and because UNHCR has a proven capacity to respond holistically to displacement, it is best suited to take on this responsibility.

Having a formal mandate for IDPs would triple UNHCR's caseload and pose an immense challenge. The agency already has difficulty fulfilling its current mandate and perpetually lacks sufficient funds. Taking the lead on internal displacement would require new thinking, more advocacy work with governments and flexible approaches to programming outside of camp settings. But the alternative is worse: Maintain the status quo and perpetuate the gap in protection and assistance for some of the world's most vulnerable people.

NO

Guglielmo Verdirame
Professor, International Human Rights and Refugee Law, Cambridge University

Co-author, Rights in Exile: Janus-Faced Humanitarianism

Written for *CQ Global Researcher*, February 2009

Forced displacement is a human tragedy even when it occurs within the boundaries of a state. But the test for deciding whether it would be appropriate for the U.N. High Commissioner for Refugees (UNHCR) to add internally displaced people (IDPs) to its current mandate on a permanent basis is not one of comparability of suffering. Rather, the proper test is whether UNHCR is the right institution for dealing with this problem. I think it is not, for several reasons.

First, crossing an international boundary continues to make a difference in today's world. By virtue of being outside their country of nationality, refugees are in a different position than the internally displaced.

Second, the international legal regime for refugees was established as an exception to the sovereign prerogatives enjoyed by states over admission and expulsion of aliens in their territory. While most refugees were the victims of a human-rights violation in their home country, the focus of the refugee legal regime is not on the responsibility of the country of nationality but on the obligations of the country where they take refuge. Because internally displaced persons are still inside their home countries, protecting their rights will require different strategies and methods.

Third, human-rights bodies, including the office of the U.N. High Commissioner for Refugees, are better-placed to deal with what are, in essence, violations of human rights against citizens.

Finally, the rationale for getting the UNHCR involved with IDPs is premised on a distinctly problematic view of the organization as a provider of humanitarian relief rather than as the international protector of refugees. UNHCR's work with refugees has already greatly suffered from the sidelining of the agency's role as legal protector: The warehousing of refugees in camps is just one example. It would not help the internally displaced if the UNHCR's involvement resulted in their being warehoused in camps, as refugees already are.

In a world where asylum is under serious threat, the real challenge for UNHCR is to rediscover its protection mandate, to act as the advocate of refugees and as the institutional overseer of the obligations of states under the 1951 Refugee Convention. It is a difficult enough task as it is.

Legal Protections for Displaced Populations

A 1951 treaty gives refugees the most protection

International law protects some — but not all — refugees who cross international borders, while the nonbinding Guiding Principles on Internal Displacement cover internally displaced people (IDPs), or those forcibly displaced within their home countries.

Here are the main laws protecting refugees and IDPs:

1951 Refugee Convention

The Convention Relating to the Status of Refugees — the basic international treaty concerning refugees — was adopted by a United Nations conference on July 28, 1951, and became effective on April 22, 1954. It defines a refugee as someone who, "owing to well-founded fear of being persecuted for reasons of race, religion, nationality, membership of a particular social group or political opinion, is outside the country of his nationality and is unable or, owing to such fear, is unwilling to avail himself of the protection of that country; or who, not having a nationality and being outside the country of his former habitual residence as a result of such events, is unable or, owing to such fear, is unwilling to return to it."

Excluded are those who flee their countries because of generalized violence (such as a civil war) in which they are not specifically targeted, or those who flee because of natural disasters or for economic reasons, such as a collapsing economy. The convention also prohibits a host country from expelling or returning refugees against their will to a territory where they have a "well-founded" fear of persecution.

The 1967 Protocol

Because the 1951 convention applied only to people who became refugees before Jan. 1, 1951, it was widely considered to apply only to European refugees from World War II. To aid those displaced by subsequent events, the United Nations adopted a new treaty, known as a Protocol, which eliminated the pre-1951 limitation. It took effect on Oct. 4, 1967.[1]

As of October 2008, 144 countries were parties to both the convention and the Protocol, though the two groups are not identical.[2]

Regional Treaties

Two regional documents expanded refugee protections of the convention and Protocol to Africa, Mexico and Central America. The 1969 Convention Governing the Specific

between the Sri Lankan army and rebels known as the Tamil Tigers. By late February they had joined several dozen people sleeping on a classroom floor in Vavuniya, in northern Sri Lanka.

At one point, Kandiah (not his real name) and his family stayed in an area that was supposed to be safe for civilians. For more than a week, he said, "We stayed in the open air with scores of other families . . . but the shelling was intense. There was shelling every day. We barely escaped with our lives."[81]

Kandiah and his family are among more than 250,000 people forced from their homes, often repeatedly, in the latest — and possibly final — round of the 26-year war. Claiming to represent the ethnic Tamil minority, the Tigers have been fighting for independence in the eastern and northern portions of the island.

Although the conflict has been among the world's most violent, international pressure to end it has been modest, at best. The U.N. Security Council, for example, considered it an "internal" affair to be resolved by Sri Lankans themselves, not by the international community and has never even adopted a resolution about it. Norway took the most significant action, mediating a cease-fire in 2002 that lasted nearly three years.

The plight of people like Kandiah illustrates the international community's failure to follow through on promises world leaders made in September 2005. At a summit marking the U.N.'s 60th anniversary, world leaders adopted the "responsibility to protect" philosophy, which holds every government responsible for protecting its own citizens.[82] Moreover, if a government fails to protect its citizens, it cannot prevent the international community

Aspects of Refugee Problems in Africa — adopted by what is now the African Union — defined refugees in Africa, while the 1984 Cartagena Declaration on Refugees is an informal statement of principles drafted by legal experts from Mexico and Central America.[3]

Guiding Principles on Internal Displacement

The U.N. has never adopted a treaty specifically aimed at establishing legal rights for IDPs. However, in 1998 the organization endorsed a set of 30 nonbinding guidelines intended to heighten international awareness of the internally displaced and offer them more legal protection. Known as the Guiding Principles on Internal Displacement, they have been presented to the various U.N. bodies but never formally adopted.

Based on the Universal Declaration of Human Rights and other treaties and agreements, the principles provide legal and practical standards for aiding and protecting displaced people. For example, the first principle states that displaced persons should enjoy "the same rights and freedoms under international and domestic law as do other persons in their country. They shall not be discriminated against . . . on the ground that they are internally displaced."

Regional bodies (including the European Union and the Organization of American States) and numerous nongovernmental organizations have endorsed the principles, and the UNHCR has treated them as official policy since world leaders — meeting at the U.N. in September 2005 — endorsed them. Nearly a dozen countries also have incorporated all or some of the principles into national legislation. In one case, the Colombian Constitutional Court in 2001 placed them into the country's "constitutional block," effectively making them a binding part of national law. Other countries that have adopted the principles into national laws or policies include the Maldives, Mozambique, Turkey and Uganda.

IDP advocates say the most significant potential use of the Guiding Principles is in Africa, where the African Union since 2006 has been working on a plan to incorporate a version of them into a binding regional treaty. This treaty — to be called the Convention for the Prevention of Internal Displacement and the Protection of and Assistance to Internally Displaced Persons in Africa — is expected to be adopted by African leaders at a summit meeting in Kampala, Uganda, in April.[4]

[1] Text of the Convention and Protocol is at www.unhcr.org/protect/PROTECTION/3b66c2aa10.pdf.

[2] "States Parties to the Refugee Convention," U.N. High Commissioner for Refugees, www.unhcr.org/protect/PROTECTION/3b73b0d63.pdf.

[3] Text of Refugee Convention in Africa is at www.unhcr.org/basics/BASICS/45dc1a682.pdf; Text of the Cartegena Declaration is at www.unhcr.org/basics/BASICS/45dc19084.pdf.

[4] Text of the Guiding Principles is at www3.brookings.edu/fp/projects/idp/resources/GPEnglish.pdf.

from intervening on their behalf. World leaders at the summit declared the U.N.'s right to take "collective action, in a decisive and timely manner," when governments failed to protect their own citizens.[83]

The U.N. has not followed through on that ringing declaration, however, usually because of dissension within the Security Council — the only U.N. body authorized to take forceful action. In addition, major countries with large, well-equipped armies — notably the United States and many European countries — have been unwilling to contribute sufficient troops to U.N. peacekeeping forces. The U.N.'s inability to protect displaced people has been most evident in eastern Congo and Darfur, where peacekeeping forces, mainly from African Union countries, are ill-equipped and undermanned.[84]

Early in February, for example, Doctors Without Borders bitterly denounced the U.N. peacekeeping mission in Congo for its "inaction" in response to the recent LRA attacks. Laurence Gaubert, head of mission in Congo for the group, said the U.N. peacekeepers "are just based in their camp, they don't go out of their camp, they don't know what is happening in the area."[85] Gaubert noted that the Security Council last Dec. 22 adopted Resolution 1856 demanding protection for civilians in Congo.[86] "This is something they have signed," she said, "but is not something you can see in the field that they have put in place."[87]

U.N. Under-Secretary-General for Humanitarian Affairs John Holmes acknowledged that the peacekeepers could do more to protect civilians but said the harsh criticism of them was "unreasonable and unjustified."

AFP/Getty Images/Sasa Maricic

Serb refugees stage a demonstration along the Kosovo border in April 2007 to urge the U.N. to return them to their home provinces. Hundreds of thousands of people dislocated by war in the former Yugoslavia during the 1990s have not yet returned to their home regions.

Only 250-300 troops were in the area at the time, he said, and most were engineers, not combat forces.[88]

The U.N. has faced similar hurdles in trying to protect the millions of civilians displaced in Darfur since 2003. African Union peacekeepers began limited operations in Sudan in 2004 but lacked either the mandate or the resources to prevent government-backed militias or rebel groups from attacking civilians in camps and settlements. The Sudanese government agreed in 2006 and 2007 to allow beefed up U.N. peacekeeping missions, but — as in Congo — the U.N. has been unable to deploy adequate forces over such an enormous area. In Sudan, the government dragged its feet in following through on its agreement, and other countries have failed to provide the necessary money and manpower. The UNHCR operates in seven displaced-persons camps in Darfur (and in six camps in eastern Chad) but must rely on the peacekeeping mission for security.[89]

U.N. officials have repeatedly called for more forceful action to protect Darfuri civilians, only to be stymied by the Security Council — largely because of resistance from China, which has economic interests in Sudan — and delaying tactics by Sudan. The Khartoum government on Feb. 17 signed an agreement with the largest Darfur rebel group, the Justice and Equality Movement, calling for negotiation of a formal peace accord within three months.[90] The hurdles to such an accord were evident the very next day, when government forces reportedly bombed some of the rebel group's positions. The future of the peace agreement was further complicated by the International Criminal Court's (ICC) landmark decision on March 4 to issue an arrest warrant for Sudanese President Omar al-Bashir, charging him with directing the mass murder of tens of thousands of Darfuri civilians and "forcibly transferring large numbers of civilians, and pillaging their property." It was the first time the Hague-based court has accused a sitting head of state of war crimes. Unless he leaves Sudan, there is no international mechanism for arresting Bashir, who denies the accusations and does not recognize the court's jurisdiction. Some aid organizations fear the ICC ruling could trigger more violence — and thus more displacements.[91]

Focusing on IDPs

The number of people displaced by violence who remain within their own countries has been averaging more than 20 million per year, according to the Internal Displacement Monitoring Center, an arm of the Norwegian Refugee Council. More than a third of them are in just three countries: Colombia (up to 4.3 million), Sudan (3.5 million) and Iraq (up to 2.8 million).[92] Tens of millions more have been driven from their homes by natural disasters.

In December 2008, to give IDPs more international attention, the U.N.'s Office for the Coordination of Humanitarian Affairs launched a series of events focusing on IDPs, including workshops, panel discussions, a Web site and high-level conferences.

The agency is particularly concerned about displaced people who languish for years without help from their governments. "For millions of IDPs around the world, an end to their years of displacement, discrimination and poverty seems to be of little concern for those in power," said the U.N.'s Holmes. The U.N. also is encouraging governments to adopt the Guiding Principles on Internal

Displacement for dealing with IDPs. And, it is pressing for "more predictable, timely and principled funding" for programs that help IDPs return home or find new homes, he said.[93]

In recent years, displaced people, usually from rural areas, have tended to head for cities. Experts say it is difficult to calculate the number of urban IDPs, but the monitoring center put the 2007 figure at 4 million, and the UNHCR estimated in 2008 that about half of the 11.4 million refugees were in cities.[94]

Urban IDPs and refugees pose logistical problems for local and international agencies charged with helping them. "In a camp, you have all these tents lined up in a row, and so it's easy to know how many people are there, and how much food and medicine you need every day," says Patrick Duplat, an advocate for Refugees International. "In an urban setting, it's much more complicated to reach people. Who is a refugee, who is an IDP and how are they different from the local population?"

U.N. High Commissioner Guterres acknowledged in a speech last October that global efforts to aid and protect urban refugees and IDPs have been "weak."[95] The approximately 2 million Iraqi refugees living in Damascus and Amman represent "a completely new and different challenge in relation to our usual activities in encampment situations," he told a conference in Norway.[96]

Last year the UNHCR tried handing out cash coupons and ATM cards to several thousand Iraqi refugees in Damascus, enabling them to buy food and other goods at local markets. The UNHCR and the World Food Program also gave food baskets or rice, vegetable oil and lentils to Iraqi refugees considered most in need, aiding about 177,000 Iraqis in 2008.[97] But some refugees reportedly were selling their rations to pay for housing and other needs.[98]

A major step toward legally protecting African IDPs could come in April at a planned special African Union (AU) summit meeting in Uganda. Experts have been working for nearly three years on a Convention for the Protection and Assistance of Internally Displaced Persons in Africa. This treaty would incorporate some, but not all, of the 1998 Guiding Principles on Internal Displacement, which sets nonbinding standards for protecting IDPs.[99]

If a treaty is produced, ratified and implemented, it could be an important step in protecting IDPs, because so many are in Africa, says Cohen from Brookings. But she is concerned that the final treaty, which already has been revised several times, might not be as strong in protecting human rights as the voluntary Guiding Principles. "We'll have to wait and see what the leaders agree to, and even if they adopt it," she says.

Guterres strongly endorses the AU's plan for a binding treaty. He also says that because the treaty has been developed by Africans, not imposed by outsiders, it "will not be subject to questions about the legitimacy of its objectives."[100]

OUTLOOK

Environmental Refugees

Environmental deterioration caused by climate change could force up to 1 billion people from their homes in coming decades, according to a paper presented to a high-level U.N. meeting last October.[101] Small island nations, notably the Maldives in the Indian Ocean and Kiribati and Tuvalu in the Pacific, could be inundated — causing mass evacuations — if sea levels rise to the extent predicted by many scientists.[102]

Rising seas also endanger several hundred million people in low-lying coastal regions. Many of these areas are in developing countries — such as Bangladesh and the Philippines — that already are prone to cyclones, floods, earthquakes or volcanic eruptions.[103] Many scientists believe that climate change will increase the severity and frequency of weather-linked disasters, particularly cyclones and floods, thus displacing even more people in the future.

L. Craig Johnstone, deputy U.N. High Commissioner for Refugees, said "conservative" estimates predict that up to 250 million people could be displaced by the middle of the 21st century due to climate change. The minority of scientists who doubt the impact of climate change dismiss such estimates as overblown.[104] But aid officials at the U.N. and other international agencies say they have no choice but to prepare for the worst.

Regardless of the impact of climate change on displacements, experts across the spectrum say it is becoming increasingly important for the international community to decide how long to provide humanitarian aid for displaced people. Decades-long displacements are difficult for both the IDPs and refugees as well as the aid groups and host countries involved. (*See sidebar, p. 308.*)

"When can they stop being vulnerable as a result of their displacement and simply be compared to any other poor person in their country?" asks Koser, at the Geneva Center for Security Policy. He cites the 4.6 million Palestinians still being aided by the United Nations six decades after their original displacement.

UNHCR officials acknowledge that international aid programs are not always equitable but say addressing the vulnerability of the world's poor and ending the causes of displacement depend on the political will of global leaders. In his annual remarks to the Security Council on Jan. 8, High Commissioner Guterres said global displacement issues won't be solved until the conflicts that force people from their homes are ended.

"While it is absolutely vital that the victims of armed conflict be provided with essential protection and assistance, we must also acknowledge the limitations of humanitarian action and its inability to resolve deep-rooted conflicts within and between states," he said. "The solution, as always, can only be political."[105]

NOTES

1. "Only after five days we dared to bury the bodies," Doctors Without Borders, Jan. 19, 2009, www.condition-critical.org/.
2. "Congo Crisis" fact sheet, International Rescue Committee, p. 1, www.theirc.org/resources/2007/congo_onesheet.pdf; also see "World Report 2009," Human Rights Watch, www.hrw.org/en/world-report/2009/democratic-republic-congo-drc.
3. "Convention and Protocol Relating to the Status of Refugees," U.N. High Commissioner for Refugees, www.unhcr.org/protect/PROTECTION/3b66c2aa10.pdf.
4. "World Report 2009," *op. cit.*
5. "Statement by Mr. Antonio Guterres, United Nations High Commissioner for Refugees, to the Security Council, New York," U.N. High Commissioner for Refugees, Jan. 8, 2009, www.unhcr.org/admin/ADMIN/496625484.html.
6. "Internally Displaced People: Exiled in their Homeland," U.N. Office for the Coordination of Humanitarian Affairs, http://ochaonline.un.org/News/InFocus/InternallyDisplacedPeopleIDPs/tabid/5132/language/en-US/Default.aspx; also see "China Earthquake: Facts and Figures," International Federation of Red Cross and Red Crescent Societies, Oct. 31, 2008, www.ifrc.org/Docs/pubs/disasters/sichuan-earthquake/ff311008.pdf.
7. Jeffrey Gettleman, "Starvation And Strife Menace Torn Kenya," *The New York Times*, March 1, 2009, p. 6.
8. "Top UNHCR official warns about displacement from climate change," U.N. High Commissioner for Refugees, Dec. 9, 2008, www.unhcr.org/news/NEWS/493e9bd94.html.
9. "2007 Statistical Yearbook," U.N. High Commissioner for Refugees, p. 23, www.unhcr.org/cgi-bin/texis/vtx/home/opendoc.pdf?id=4981c3252&tbl=STATISTICS; "Statement by Mr. Antonio Guterres," *op. cit.*
10. For background, see Karen Foerstel, "Crisis in Darfur," *CQ Global Researcher*, September 2008, pp. 243-270.
11. "2009 Global Update: Sudan," U.N. High Commissioner for Refugees, pp. 1-3, www.unhcr.org/publ/PUBL/4922d4130.pdf.
12. "Millions of Hectares of Land Secured for Internally Displaced," International Organization for Migration, Jan. 9, 2009, www.iom.int/jahia/Jahia/pbnAM/cache/offonce;jsessionid=29AD6E92A35FDE971CDAB26007A67DB2.worker01?entryId=21044.
13. "Afghanistan — The Challenges of Sustaining Returns," U.N. High Commissioner for Refugees, www.unhcr.org/cgi-bin/texis/vtx/afghan?page=home.
14. See "UNHCR Global Appeal, 2009"; "2009 Global Update, Mission Statement," U.N. High Commissioner for Refugees, www.unhcr.org/publ/PUBL/4922d43f11.pdf; "Statement by Mr. Antonio Guterres," *op. cit.*; "2009 Global Update, Working with the Internally Displaced," U.N. High Commissioner for Refugees, www.unhcr.org/publ/PUBL/4922d44c0.pdf.
15. The Refugee Status Determination (RSD) Unit, U.N. High Commissioner for Refugees, www.unhcr.org/protect/3d3d26004.html.

16. "2009 Global Update, Mission Statement," *op. cit.*
17. "Protracted Refugee Situations: High Commissioner's Initiative," U.N. High Commissioner for Refugees, December 2008, www.unhcr.org/protect/PROTECTION/4937de6f2.pdf.
18. "Humanitarian Reform," United Nations, www.humanitarianreform.org.
19. "The Global Cluster Leads," U.N. Office for the Coordination of Humanitarian Affairs, http://ocha.unog.ch/humanitarianreform/Default.aspx?tabid=217.
20. "Cluster Approach Evaluation 2007," United Nations, www.humanitarianreform.org/Default.aspx?tabid=457.
21. The book Milner co-authored is *The United Nation's High Commissioner for Refugees (UNHCR): The Politics and Practice of Refugee Protection into the 21st Century* (2008).
22. "Convention and Protocol Relating to the Status of Refugees," *op. cit.*
23. "Full Text of Jack Straw's Speech," *The Guardian*, Feb. 6, 2001, www.guardian.co.uk/uk/2001/feb/06/immigration.immigrationandpublicservices3.
24. "Climate change, natural disasters and human displacement: a UNHCR perspective," www.unhcr.org/protect/PROTECTION/4901e81a4.pdf.
25. "European Pact on Immigration and Asylum," www.immigration.gouv.fr/IMG/pdf/Plaquette_EN.pdf.
26. "ECRE calls for suspension of Dublin transfers to Greece," European Council on Refugees and Exiles, April 3, 2008, www.ecre.org/resources/Press_releases/1065.
27. "NGO Statement Addressing the Iraqi Humanitarian Challenge," July 31, 2008, www.refugeesinternational.org/policy/letter/ngo-statement-addressing-iraqi-humanitarian-challenge.
28. "Fact Sheet: USCIS Makes Major Strides During 2008," U.S. Citizenship and Immigration Services, Nov. 6, 2008, www.uscis.gov/portal/site/uscis/menuitem.5af9bb95919f35e66f614176543f6d1a/?vgnextoid=2526ad6f16d6d110VgnVCM1000004718190aRCRD&vgnextchannel=68439c7755cb9010VgnVCM10000045f3d6a1RCRD.
29. "NGO Statement: Addressing the Iraqi Humanitarian Challenge," *op. cit.*
30. "Fact Sheet: Iraqi Refugee Processing," U.S. Citizenship and Immigration Services, Sept. 12, 2008, www.dhs.gov/xnews/releases/pr_1221249274808.shtm.
31. "Operation Safe Haven Iraq 2009," Center for American Progress, www.americanprogress.org/issues/2009/01/iraqi_airlift.html.
32. Her blog site is http://refugeeresettlementwatch.wordpress.com/.
33. "The 1951 Refugee Convention," U.N. High Commissioner for Refugees, www.unhcr.org/1951convention/dev-protect.html.
34. *Ibid.*
35. *Ibid.*
36. "Establishment of UNRWA," www.un.org/unrwa/overview/index.html.
37. "UNRWA Statistics," www.un.org/unrwa/publications/index.html.
38. "A 'Timeless' Treaty Under Attack: A New Phase," U.N. High Commissioner for Refugees, www.unhcr.org/1951convention/new-phase.html.
39. "States Parties to the Convention and the Protocol," U.N. High Commissioner for Refugees, www.unhcr.org/protect/PROTECTION/3b73b0d63.pdf.
40. "Guiding Principles on Internal Displacement," www3.brookings.edu/fp/projects/idp/resources/GPEnglish.pdf.
41. "FMO Research Guide: Afghanistan," Teresa Poppelwell, July 2007, pp. 17-19, www.forcedmigration.org/guides/fmo006/.
42. "Afghanistan — The Challenges of Sustaining Returns," U.N. High Commissioner for Refugees, www.unhcr.org/cgi-bin/texis/vtx/afghan?page=home.
43. "Jalozai camp closed, returnees face difficulties at home," IRIN news service, June 2, 2008, www.irinnews.org/Report.aspx?ReportId=78506; also see "Iran called upon to halt winter deportations," IRIN news service, Dec. 18, 2008, www.irinnews.org/PrintReport.aspx?ReportId=82007.
44. "Afghanistan — The Challenges of Sustaining Returns," *op. cit.*
45. "Minister disputes call to boost refugee returns," IRIN news service, Sept. 10, 2008, www.irinnews.org/Report.aspx?ReportId=80218.

46. "Cold tents for returnees in east," IRIN news service, Jan. 15, 2009, www.irinnews.org/Report.aspx?ReportId=82373.

47. "Afghanistan at the crossroads: Young Afghans return to a homeland they never knew," U.N. High Commissioner for Refugees, Nov. 14, 2008, www.unhcr.org/cgi-bin/texis/vtx/afghan?page=news&id=491d84c64.

48. "2009 Global Update, Colombia situation," U.N. High Commissioner for Refugees, www.unhcr.org/publ/PUBL/4922d43411.pdf.

49. "Colombia Situation," U.N. High Commissioner for Refugees 2008-09 Global Appeal for Colombia, p. 2, www.unhcr.org/home/PUBL/474ac8e814.pdf.

50. *Ibid.*

51. "Millions of Hectares of Land Secured for Internally Displaced," International Organization for Migration, Jan. 9, 2009, www.iom.int.

52. *Ibid.*

53. *Ibid.*

54. "2009 Global Update," Democratic Republic of the Congo, U.N. High Commissioner for Refugees, www.unhcr.org/publ/PUBL/4922d4100.pdf.

55. "Congo Crisis" fact sheet, *op. cit.*

56. "A Congolese Rebel Leader Who Once Seemed Untouchable Is Caught," *The New York Times*, Jan. 24, 2009, www.nytimes.com/2009/01/24/world/africa/24congo.html?_r=1.

57. "An arresting and hopeful surprise," *The Economist*, Jan. 29, 2009, www.economist.com/displayStory.cfm?story_id=13022113. For background, see David Masci, "Aiding Africa," *CQ Researcher*, Aug. 29, 2003, pp. 697-720; John Felton, "Child Soldiers," *CQ Global Researcher*, July 2008.

58. "2009 Global Update: Iraq," U.N. High Commissioner for Refugees, p. 2, www.unhcr.orgpubl/PUBL/4922d4230.pdf.

59. "WFP to help feed one million displaced Iraqis," World Food Program, Jan. 3, 2009, www.wfp.org/English/?ModuleID=137&Key=2732.

60. "Budget cuts threaten IDP housing projects," IRIN news service, Jan. 6, 2009, www.irinnews.org/Report.aspx?ReportId=82209.

61. "IDPs enticed to vacate southern camp," IRIN news service, Dec. 15, 2008, www.irinnews.org/Report.aspx?ReportId=81963.

62. "2009 Global Update: Iraq," *op. cit.*, p. 2.

63. "Three Years of Post-Samarra Displacement in Iraq," International Organization for Migration, Feb. 22, 2009, p. 1, www.iom.int/jahia/webdav/shared/shared/mainsite/published_docs/studies_and_reports/iom_displacement_report_post_samarra.pdf.

64. *Ibid.*

65. "Post-Nargis Periodic Review I," Tripartite Core Group, December 2008, p. 4, www.aseansec.org/22119.pdf.

66. "2009 Global Update: Myanmar," U.N. High Commissioner for Refugees, p. 2, www.unhcr.org/publ/PUBL/4922d42b0.pdf.

67. "Cyclone survivors face water shortages," IRIN news service, Dec. 29, 2008, www.irinnews.org/Report.aspx?ReportId=82129.

68. "Cyclone recovery 'will take up to four years,' " IRIN news service, Jan. 15, 2009, www.IRINnews.org/Report.aspx?ReportId=82383.

69. Michael Heath, "Angelina Jolie, U.N. Envoy, Asks Thailand to Aid Myanmar Refugees," Bloomberg News, www.bloomberg.com/apps/news?pid=20601080&sid=aL5VlfM46aAc&refer=asia#.

70. "2009 Global Update: Bangladesh," U.N. High Commissioner for Refugees, p. 1, www.unhcr.org/publ/PUBL/4922d42818.pdf.

71. "Myanmar Refugees Rescued at Sea," *The New York Times*, Feb. 3, 2009, www.nytimes.com/2009/02/04/world/asia/04indo.html?ref=world.

72. "Angelina Jolie voices support for Myanmar refugees in northern Thailand camps," U.N. High Commissioner for Refugees, Feb. 5, 2009, www.unhcr.org/news/NEWS/498ab65c2.html.

73. *Ibid.*

74. "ASIA: Regional approach to Rohingya boat people," IRIN news service, March 2, 2009, www.irinnews.org/Report.aspx?ReportId=83232.

75. "2009 Global Update: Sudan," U.N. High Commissioner for Refugees, pp. 1-3, www.unhcr.org/publ/PUBL/4922d4130.pdf.

76. "Number of returnees to South Sudan passes the 300,000 mark," U.N. High Commissioner for Refugees, Feb. 10, 2009, www.unhcr.org/news/NEWS/4991a8de2.html; "2009 Global Update," *op. cit.*, p. 1.
77. "Darfur remains tense after recent eruption of fighting, U.N. reports," IRIN news service, Jan. 28, 2009, www.un.org/apps/news/story.asp?NewsID=29699&Cr=darfur&Cr1=.
78. "Report of the Secretary-General on the deployment of the African Union-United Nations Hybrid Operation in Darfur," United Nations, Oct. 17, 2008, p. 11, http://daccessdds.un.org/doc/UNDOC/GEN/N08/553/95/PDF/N0855395.pdf?OpenElement.
79. "2009 Global Update: Sudan," *op. cit.*; "2009 Global Update: Chad," U.N. High Commissioner for Refugees, www.unhcr.org/publ/PUBL/4922d41214.pdf.
80. "2009 Global Update: Sudan," *op. cit.*, p. 3; "World Refugee Survey, 2008," Sudan chapter, U.S. Committee for Refugees and Immigrants, www.refugees.org/countryreports.aspx?id=2171.
81. "Kandiah: 'There was shelling every day. We barely escaped with our lives,' " IRIN news service, Feb. 19, 2009, www.IRINnews.org/Report.aspx?ReportId=83015.
82. For background, see Lee Michael Katz, "World Peacekeeping," *CQ Global Researcher*, April 2007, pp. 75-100.
83. "World Summit Outcome 2005," U.N. General Assembly, Resolution A/RES/60/1, paragraphs 138-139, September 2005, www.un.org/summit2005/documents.html.
84. See Foerstel, *op. cit.*
85. "DRC: MSF denounces the lack of protection for victims of LRA violence in Haut-Uélé," Doctors Without Borders, Feb. 4, 2009, www.msf.org.
86. Security Council Resolution 1856, Dec. 22, 2006, http://daccessdds.un.org/doc/UNDOC/GEN/N08/666/94/PDF/N0866694.pdf?OpenElement.
87. *Ibid.*
88. "Press Conference by Humanitarian Affairs Head on Recent Trip to Democratic Republic of Congo," U.N. Department of Public Information, Feb. 13, 2009, www.un.org/News/briefings/docs/2009/090213_DRC.doc.htm.
89. "2009 Global Update: Sudan," *op. cit.*
90. "Sudan and Darfur Rebel Group Agree to Peace Talks," *The New York Times*, Feb. 18, 2009, www.nytimes.com/2009/02/18/world/africa/18sudan.html?_r=1&ref=todayspaper.
91. "Sudan bombs rebels day after Darfur deal: rebels," Agence France-Presse, Feb. 18, 2009. See Mike Corder, "International court issues warrant for Sudan president on charges of war crimes in Darfur," The Associated Press, March 4, 2009.
92. "2009 Global Update," *op. cit.*; "Global Overview of Trends and Developments: 2007," Internal Displacement Monitoring Centre, Norwegian Refugee Council, p. 12, April 2008, www.internal-displacement.org/idmc/website/resources.nsf/(httpPublications)/0F926CFAF1EADE5EC125742E003B7067?OpenDocument.
93. "UN launches year-long campaign to highlight, and solve, plight of displaced," IRIN news service, Dec. 18, 2009, www.un.org/apps/news/story.asp?NewsID=29358&Cr=IDPs&Cr1.
94. "Addressing Urban Displacement: A Project Description," Internal Displacement Monitoring Centre, Norwegian Refugee Council, 2007, p. 2; also see "2007 Global Trends," U.N. High Commissioner for Refugees, June 2008, p. 2, www.unhcr.org/statistics/STATISTICS/4852366f2.pdf.
95. "Ten years of Guiding Principles on Internal Displacement: Achievements and Future Challenges," statement by Antonio Guterres, Oslo, Oct. 16, 2008, www.unhcr.org/admin/ADMIN/48ff45e12.html.
96. *Ibid.*
97. "WFP to help feed one million displaced Iraqis," World Food Program, Jan. 3, 2008, www.wfp.org/English/?ModuleID=137&Key=2732.
98. "Iraqi refugees selling some of their food rations," IRIN news service, Jan. 28, 2009, http://one.wfp.org/english/?ModuleID=137& Key=2732.
99. "From Voluntary Principles to Binding Standards," *IDP Action*, Jan. 9, 2009, www.idpaction.org/index.php/en/news/16-principles2 standards.

100. "Ten Years of Guiding Principles on Internal Displacement," *op. cit.*
101. "Climate Change, Migration and Displacement: Who will be affected?" Working paper submitted by the informal group on Migration/Displacement and Climate Change of the U.N. Inter-Agency Standing Committee, Oct. 31, 2008, http://unfccc.int/resource/docs/2008/smsn/igo/022.pdf.
102. "Climate Change and Displacement," *Forced Migration Review*, p. 20, October 2008, www.fmreview.org/climatechange.htm; for background see Colin Woodard, "Curbing Climate Change," *CQ Global Researcher*, February 2007, pp. 27-50, and Marcia Clemmitt, "Climate Change," *CQ Researcher*, Jan. 27, 2006, pp. 73-96.
103. "Climate Resilient Cities: A Primer on Reducing Vulnerabilities to Disasters," World Bank, 2009, pp. 5-6.
104. "Top UNHCR official warns about displacement from climate change," *op. cit.*
105. "Statement by Mr. Antonio Guterres," *op. cit.*

BIBLIOGRAPHY

Books

Evans, Gareth, *The Responsibility to Protect: Ending Mass Atrocity Crimes Once and For All*, Brookings Institution Press, 2008.

A former Australian foreign minister and current head of the International Crisis Group offers an impassioned plea for world leaders to follow through on their promises to protect civilians, even those abused by their own governments.

Loescher, Gil, Alexander Betts and James Milner, *The United Nations High Commissioner for Refugees (UNHCR): The Politics and Practice of Refugee Protection Into the 21st Century*, Routledge, 2008.

Academic experts on refugee issues offer a generally sympathetic but often critical assessment of the UNHCR's performance as the world's main protector of refugees.

Verdirame, Guglielmo, and Barbara Harrell-Bond, with Zachary Lomo and Hannah Garry, *Rights in Exile: Janus-Faced Humanitarianism*, Berghahn Books, 2005.

A former director of the Refugee Studies Center at Oxford University (Harrell-Bond) and an expert on refugee rights at Cambridge University offer a blistering critique of the U.N. and nongovernment agencies that protect refugees.

Articles

"Managing the Right of Return," *The Economist*, Aug. 4, 2008.

The practical implications of refugees' legal right to return to their home countries are examined.

Cohen, Roberta, and Francis Deng, "The Genesis and the Challenges," *Forced Migration Review*, December 2008.

This is the keystone article in an issue devoted to the Guiding Principles on Internal Displacement 10 years after their creation. Cohen and Deng were prime movers of the document.

Feyissa, Abebe, with Rebecca Horn, "Traveling Souls: Life in a Refugee Camp, Where Hearts Wander as Minds Deteriorate," *Utne Reader*, September-October 2008, www.utne.com/2008-09-01/GreatWriting/Traveling-Souls.aspx.

An Ethiopian who has lived in northwestern Kenya's Kakuma refugee camp for 16 years writes about life in the camp.

Guterres, Antonio, "Millions Uprooted: Saving Refugees and the Displaced," *Foreign Affairs*, September/October 2008.

The U.N. High Commissioner for Refugees lays out an ambitious agenda of action to aid and protect the displaced.

Harr, Jonathan, "Lives of the Saints: International Hardship Duty in Chad," *The New Yorker*, Jan. 5, 2009, www.newyorker.com/reporting/2009/01/05/090105fa_fact_harr.

A frequent *New Yorker* contributor offers a sympathetic portrait of idealistic aid workers at refugee camps in Chad.

Stevens, Jacob, "Prison of the Stateless: The Derelictions of UNHCR," *New Left Review*, November-December 2006, www.newleftreview.org/?page=article&view=2644.

A review of the memoirs of former High Commissioner Sadako Ogata becomes a strongly worded critique of the U.N. refugee agency. A rebuttal by former UNHCR special envoy Nicholas Morris is at www.unhcr.org/research/RESEARCH/460d131d2.pdf.

Reports and Studies

"2009 Global Update," *U.N. High Commissioner for Refugees*, November 2008, www.unhcr.org/ga09/index.html.
Published in November, this is the most recent summary from the UNHCR of its operations, plans and budget for 2009.

"Future Floods of Refugees: A comment on climate change, conflict and forced migration," *Norwegian Refugee Council*, April 2008, www.nrc.no/arch/_img/9268480.pdf.
The refugee council surveys the debate over whether climate change will worsen natural disasters and force untold millions of people from their homes.

"Protracted Refugee Situations: High Commissioner's Initiative," *U.N. High Commissioner for Refugees*, December 2008, www.unhcr.org/protect/PROTECTION/4937de6f2.pdf.
The UNHCR offers a plan of action for resolving several long-term situations in which refugees have been trapped in camps or settlements for decades.

"When Displacement Ends: A Framework for Durable Solutions," *Brookings-Bern Project on Internal Displacement*, June 2007, www.brookings.edu/reports/2007/09displacementends.aspx.
This detailed blueprint for how international agencies can help IDPs find "durable solutions" to their displacements is the product of conferences and other studies.

Cohen, Roberta, "Listening to the Voices of the Displaced: Lessons Learned," *Brookings-Bern Project on Internal Displacement*, September 2008, www.brookings.edu/reports/2008/09_internal_displacement_cohen.aspx.
The author recommends better ways to aid and protect displaced people around the world, based on interviews with dozens of IDPs.

For More Information

Brookings-Bern Project on Internal Displacement, The Brookings Institution, 1775 Massachusetts Avenue, N.W., Washington, DC, 20036; (202) 797-6168; www.brookings.edu/projects/idp.aspx. A joint project of the Brookings Institution and the University of Bern (Switzerland) School of Law; conducts research and issues reports on policy questions related to internally displaced people (IDPs).

Institute for the Study of International Migration, Georgetown University, Harris Building, Third Floor, 3300 Whitehaven St. N.W., Washington, DC, 20007; (202) 687-2258; www12.georgetown.edu/sfs/isim/index.html. An academic research center focusing on all aspects of international migration, including refugees.

Internal Displacement Monitoring Centre, Chemin de Balexert, 7-9 1219 Chatelaine Geneva, Switzerland; 41-22-799-07 00; www.internal-displacement.org. Provides regular reports on IDPs globally; the major source of information about the numbers of people displaced by conflict.

International Organization for Migration, 17 Route des Morillons, CH-1211, Geneva 19, Switzerland; 41-22-717-9111; www.iom.int. A U.N. partner (not officially within the U.N. system) that aids refugees and migrants and studies migration trends.

Norwegian Refugee Council, P.O. Box 6758, St. Olavs Plass, 0130 Oslo, Norway; 47-23-10 9800; www.nrc.no. A prominent nongovernmental organization that provides aid programs for displaced persons and advocates on their behalf.

Refugee Studies Centre, Queen Elizabeth House, University of Oxford, Mansfield Road, Oxford OX1 3TB, United Kingdom; 44-1865-270-722; www.rsc.ox.ac.uk/index.html?main. A prominent research center on refugees and the displaced. Publishes the *Forced Migration Review,* a quarterly journal written by experts in the field.

Refugees International, 2001 S St., N.W., Suite 700, Washington, DC, 20009; (202) 828-0110; www.refugeesinternational.org. Advocates on behalf of refugees and IDPs and publishes regular reports based on site visits to key countries.

U.N. High Commissioner for Refugees, Case Postale 2500, CH-1211, Geneva 2 Depot, Switzerland; 41-22-739-8111; www.unhcr.org/home.html. The U.N. agency with prime responsibility for aiding and protecting refugees; increasingly has taken on a similar role in regard to IDPs.

U.S. Committee for Refugees and Immigrants, 2231 Crystal Dr., Suite 350, Arlington VA 22202-3711; (703) 310-1130; www.refugees.org. An advocacy group that publishes reports focusing on human-rights abuses and other problems encountered by refugees and immigrants.

12

Child Soldiers

Are More Aggressive Efforts Needed to Protect Children?

John Felton

AFP/Getty Images/Jack Guez

Former child soldier Ishmael Beah addresses a 2007 international conference on child soldiers. His best-selling autobiography about his horrific experiences in Sierra Leone has raised public awareness of the use of children in armed conflicts.

From *CQ Global Researcher*, July 2008.

Ishmael Beah kept on the move in the bush for months with some of his friends to escape the chaos of war-torn Sierra Leone in the early 1990s. Their greatest fear was ending up in the clutches of rebel groups who abducted young boys to join them in fighting against the government and raping, murdering and mutilating civilians. Instead, they wound up in the hands of government soldiers, which wasn't much better.

"We were told that our responsibilities as boys were to fight in this war or we would be killed," he told a U.S. Senate committee last year. "I was 13 years old."[1]

Then, recalling his first day in battle, Beah told the panel that after less than a week of training in how to use AK 47s, M16s, machine guns and rocket-propelled grenades, the adult soldiers led him and his friends into the forest to ambush rebels. "My squad had boys who were as young as 7 . . . dragging guns that were taller than them as we walked to the frontlines."

At first, "I couldn't shoot my gun," he remembered. "But as I lay there watching my friends getting killed . . . I began shooting. Something inside me shifted and I lost compassion for anyone. After that day, killing became as easy as drinking water." For the next two years, Beah said, "all I did was take drugs, fight and kill or be killed."

Children always have been among the first victims of warfare, usually as innocent bystanders. Indeed, in most conflicts, more women and children die — from a combination of disease, starvation or violence — than soldiers. Children also have been pressed into service occasionally as fighters, often as the last, desperate resort of losing armies.[2]

Dozens of Countries Use Child Soldiers

Tens of thousands of children under age 18 — some as young as 5 — serve as soldiers or spies for rebel groups, government-linked paramilitary militias or government armed forces. Most are recruited or conscripted in Africa and Asia. Government armed forces in several industrialized countries induct under-18-year-olds but don't use them in combat.

Countries That Use Child Soldiers
(Between April 2004-October 2007)

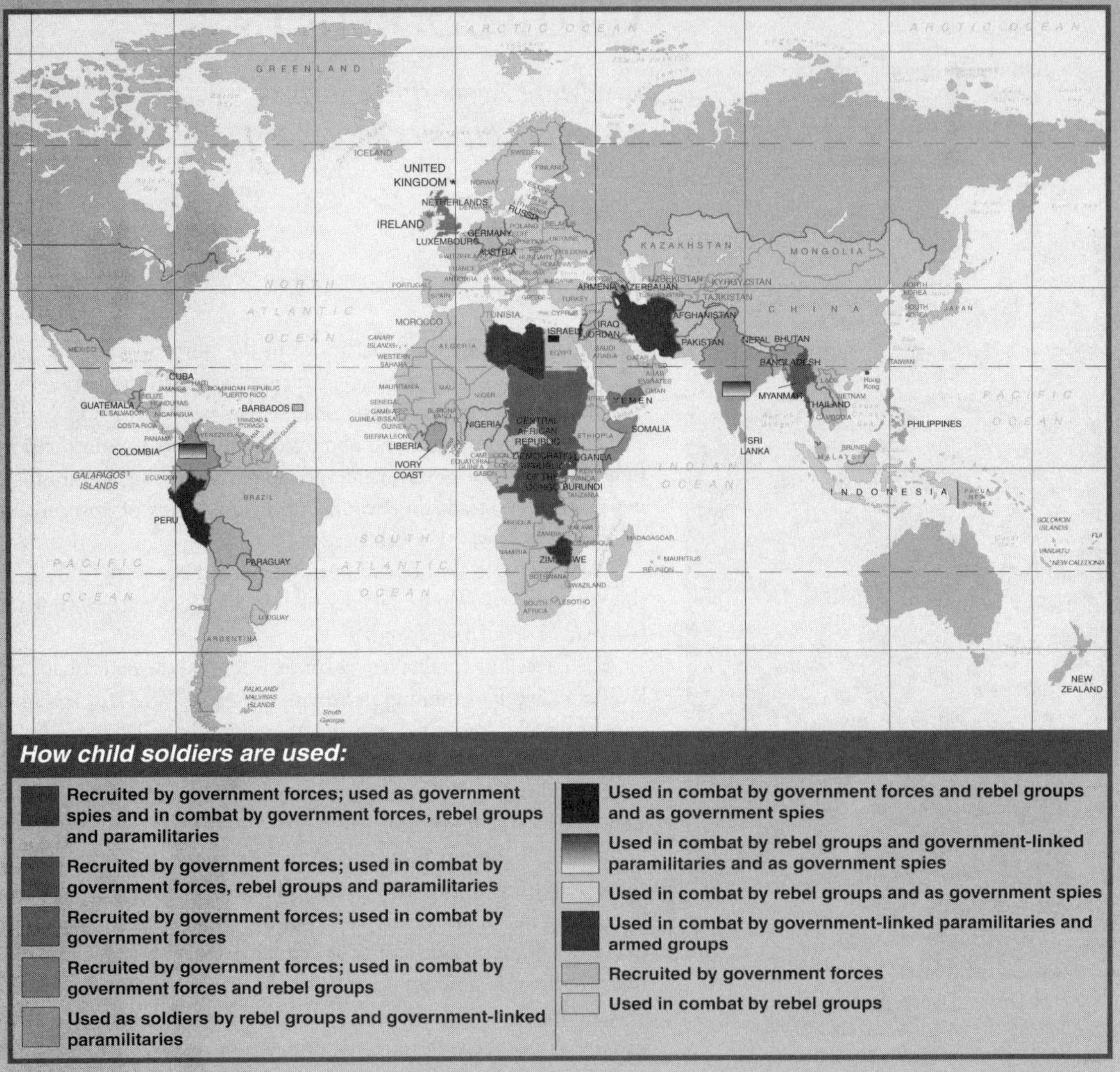

* Deployed children under 18 to Iraq, where they were exposed to risk of hostilities.

Source: "Child Soldiers: Global Report 2008," Coalition to Stop the Use of Child Soldiers

Laws and Resolutions Dealing with Child Soldiers

Several United Nations treaties make it illegal under international law for governments or rebel groups to recruit and use children in warfare, including:

- **Additional Protocols to the Geneva Conventions (1977)** — Establishes age 15 as the minimum for participation in armed combat by government forces or nongovernmental groups; applies both to international and domestic conflicts.
- **Convention on the Rights of the Child (1989)** — Prohibits the recruitment and use of children under 15 by armed groups; a compromise is reached after objection by the United States, Britain and the Netherlands to an 18-year-old standard. The United States and Somalia are the only countries that have not ratified it.[1]
- **Rome Statute (1998)** — Creates the International Criminal Court and defines as a war crime the recruitment or use in combat of children under 15.
- **Worst Forms of Child Labour Convention (1999)** — Adopted by member states of the International Labor Organization; defines a child as anyone under 18 and says child labor includes "forced or compulsory recruitment of children for use in armed conflict."
- **Optional Protocol to the Convention on the Rights of the Child (2000)** — Raises to 18 the minimum age for using children in conflicts, prohibits compulsory recruitment by governments or non-state groups of anyone under 18; allows governments to recruit 16- and 17-year-olds for military service if the recruitment is voluntary and approved by the parents or legal guardians. The United States ratified it in 2002.[2]

Since 1999, the U.N. Security Council has adopted six resolutions pertaining to children in armed conflict:

- **Resolutions 1261 (1999) and 1314 (2000)** — Calls on all parties to respect international law concerning the protection of children, including girls, in armed conflict.
- **Resolution 1379 (2001)** — Asks the U.N. secretary-general to create a blacklist of those who recruit child soldiers.
- **Resolutions 1460 (2003) and 1539 (2004)** — Calls for children to be included in programs designed to help former soldiers disarm, demobilize and reintegrate into society; suggests implementation of country-specific, targeted measures.
- **Resolution 1612 (2005)** — Creates a mechanism for monitoring and disseminating information on six types of child-rights violations; creates a Security Council Working Group to recommend measures on a per-situation basis; urges those using children in conflict to establish action plans for their release and reintegration.

[1] Available at www.unhchr.ch/html/menu2/6/crc/treaties/crc.htm.
[2] Available at www.unhchr.ch/html/menu2/6/crc/treaties/opac.htm.

But in recent times tens of thousands of children like Beah have been actively and regularly used in warfare. Since the closing decades of the 20th century, rebel groups and even government armies routinely have used children in combat or supporting roles throughout Africa, Asia, Europe and Latin America.

Many of these children were forced to participate in or witness acts almost beyond comprehension, including:

- The 1994 genocide in Rwanda during which at least 800,000 people were slaughtered within a few weeks, many hacked to death with machetes;
- Sierra Leone's civil war in which children were forced to kill their parents and cut off the hands and feet of civilians;
- Indiscriminate guerrilla attacks on noncombatants in Colombia and Sri Lanka;
- The forced murders of their own family members and neighbors, perpetrated at the direction of the Lord's Resistance Army (LRA), a rebel group led by fanatical recluse Joseph Kony in northern Uganda and neighboring countries.
- The use of children, in some cases preteens, as suicide bombers by several groups, including the Tamil

19 African Commanders Charged with Using Child Soldiers

A total of 19 former and current commanders — all from Africa — have been charged with enlisting children under age 15 as soldiers. Four are serving time in prison after being convicted. Six are on trial, while six have been charged but never captured. Most were accused of other war crimes as well, including murder, rape, abductions, forced labor and looting. No commanders from other countries have been charged for using child soldiers.

Country	Commander	Military Group*	Status
Democratic Republic of the Congo			
Lubanga	Thomas Lubanga Dyilo	Union of Congolese Patriots	International Criminal Court trial indefinitely suspended 6/2008; his release is pending appeal
Katanga	Germain Katanga	Patriotic Forces of Resistance	ICC pre-trial hearings began 5/27/2008
	Mathieu Ngudjolo Chui	Front for National Integration	ICC pre-trial hearings began 5/27/2008
	Kyungu Mutanga	Mai-Mai	In Congolese custody
	Jean-Pierre Biyoyo	Mudundu 40	Sentenced to 5 years by Congolese military tribunal 3/2006; escaped
	Bosco Ntaganda	Union of Congolese Patriots	ICC warrants issued 8/22/2006
Liberia			
Taylor	Charles Taylor	Former president, Liberia	Trial continues at Special Court of Sierra Leone
Sierra Leone			
	Alex Tamba Brima	Armed Forces Revolutionary Council	Convicted, serving 50 years
	Brima Bazzy Kamara	Armed Forces Revolutionary Council	Convicted, serving 45 years
	Santigie Borbor Kanu	Armed Forces Revolutionary Council	Convicted, serving 50 years
	Allieu Kondewa	Civil Defense Forces	Convicted, 8-year sentence increased to 20 years, 5/2008
	Issa Hassan Sesay	Revolutionary United Front	Joint trial in Special Court of Sierra Leone expected to conclude in August
	Morris Kallon	Revolutionary United Front	
	Augustine Gbao	Revolutionary United Front	
Uganda			
Kony	Joseph Kony	Lord's Resistance Army	ICC warrant issued 7/8/2005
	Vincent Otti	Lord's Resistance Army	Reportedly killed in 2007
	Raska Lukwiya	Lord's Resistance Army	Killed, 2006
Otti	Okot Odiambo	Lord's Resistance Army	ICC warrant issued 7/8/2005
	Dominic Ongwen	Lord's Resistance Army	ICC warrant issued 7/8/2005

* The accused were serving with these groups at the time of their alleged crimes. Some are in other groups now.

Sources: United Nations; Human Rights Watch; Special Court of Sierra Leone, www.sc-sl.org/RUF-Casesummary.html

Tigers in Sri Lanka, the Taliban in Afghanistan and the Palestinian groups Hamas and Islamic Jihad.

Thousands of other children raided and burned villages, shouldered automatic weapons in combat or served as porters, spies or decoys. The girls were often forced to satisfy the sexual appetites of the guerrillas.

The U.N.'s Special Representative for Children and Armed Conflict, Radhika Coomaraswamy, says there are at least 250,000 child soldiers worldwide.[3] But other experts say the nature of civil conflicts makes it difficult to compile accurate records.

"It's absolutely impossible to determine the number of child soldiers with any accuracy," says Victoria Forbes Adam, executive director of the London-based Coalition to Stop the Use of Child Soldiers. "We think it is in the many tens of thousands, but that is a complete guesstimate." Leaders of armed groups, particularly rebels fighting in the bush, generally refuse to open their rosters to international inspection, she explains, and "children come in and out of conflicts, they die of illness, they die of injuries, or they may simply be missing from their communities."

However, many more children are recruited by official national armies than by rebel groups, according to some studies. About 500,000 under-18-year-olds serve at any given time in government armies and paramilitary groups in about 50 countries, according to P.W. Singer, a senior fellow at the Brookings Institution think tank in Washington, D.C., who has written widely on the problem. (*See map, p. 324.*) Most serve in reserve units until they are called into combat, Singer writes.[4]

The United Nations and human rights groups have accused some countries of forcibly recruiting children for their armies. The military government of Myanmar, for example, allegedly rewards recruiters with money and bags of rice for luring children into the army, according to Human Rights Watch (HRW).[5]

The presence of children in combat can make conflicts more persistent because conflicts involving children "are easier to start, more difficult to end, and more likely to resume," says Singer. Children are so readily available, cheap and expendable — from the viewpoint of leaders of armed groups — that using them can be an incentive to start conflicts and keep fighting even if success seems futile, he says.

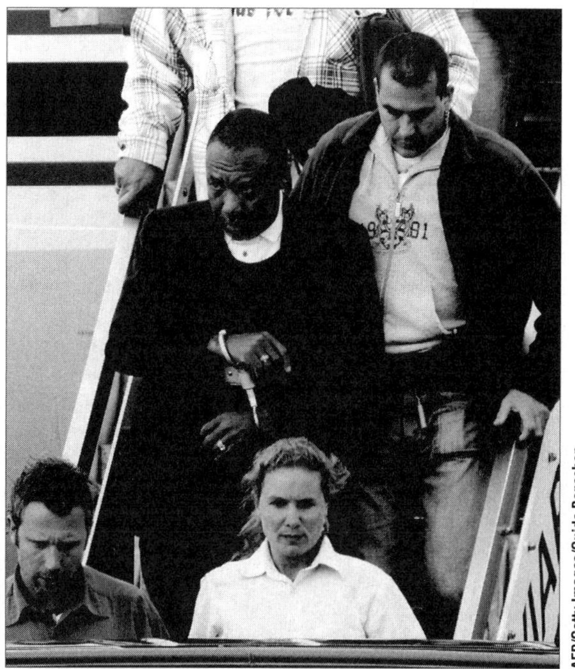

AFP/Getty Images/Guido Benschop

Former Liberian President Charles Taylor, in handcuffs, arrives in the Netherlands in 2006 for his war crimes trial before the Special Court of Sierra Leone in The Hague. Taylor is accused of sponsoring and aiding rebels who carried out murders, sexual slavery, mutilations and the conscription of child soldiers during the civil war in Sierra Leone. The trial continues.

Defining a "child soldier" is a complex issue. Who is a child? And who is a soldier? As set out in several U.N. treaties since World War II, a child is anyone under 18. The most recent legal definition is contained in the 2000 Optional Protocol to the Convention on the Rights of the Child on the Involvement of Children in Armed Conflict — known as the "Optional Protocol." It allows governments to recruit 16- and 17-year-olds but prohibits them from serving in combat. The United States and 25 other countries recruit under-18-year-olds into their armed services, according to the Coalition to Stop the Use of Child Soldiers.[6] Under the Optional Protocol, "non-state actors" such as rebel groups, may not recruit anyone under 18.

But many rebel leaders around the world either ignore the prohibition or claim not to know the ages of their recruits. "They say, 'The children come to us without any birth certificates, so how are we to know how old they are?'" says U.N. Special Representative Coomaraswamy,

Former Girl Soldiers Get Little Aid

Many programs often ignore their needs

When she was 12 years old, Lucy Aol was abducted by the Lord's Resistance Army (LRA), a rebel group in northern Uganda. They made her walk several hundred miles to a hideout in southern Sudan.

"We were used like slaves," she recently recalled. "We used to work in the fields or collect firewood from 7 in the morning until 5 in the evening, and we were given no food. If you made a mistake or refused, they would beat us," she said. "The three girls who were taken from my village with me were beaten to death."

A year after she was abducted, Aol was forced to become the "wife" of a rebel commander. She and her "husband" later fled the rebel group together, but he was killed, and she discovered she was pregnant, and at age 16 she gave birth to a daughter. Now 21, Aol is studying environmental health at a college in Uganda.[1]

Similar stories could be told by thousands of girls in recent decades. Up to 40 percent of the children serving in some armed groups are girls.[2] A 2004 study found that girls served in 38 regional conflicts between 1990 and 2003 and were fighters in all but four.[3] Yet, the plight of young girls forced to join armed groups still isn't on the radar screens of many governments and world leaders — or even those working to reintegrate former male child soldiers into society.

Only in the last few years have aid programs taken girls' needs into consideration, and they still are not being given as much attention or help as the boys. Many girls also avoid official postwar reintegration programs for fear of being stigmatized.

"Boys might be called rebels, but girls are not just rebels. They may have been raped, they may feel spiritually polluted or unclean, and if they are mothers they may be called the mothers of rebel children, and so they are isolated," says Michael Wessells, a professor of psychology at Randolph-Macon College in Virginia who has aided former child soldiers in Africa and Asia for three decades. "But all they want is to be like other children."

"In many parts of the world, if you are female and you're not a virgin, you are not marriageable," says Neil Boothy, a professor at Columbia University who has developed and studied aid programs for former child soldiers for two decades. "And marriage remains the economic pathway for most women in most societies."

Only a few postwar integration programs, however, provide vocational training for both girls and boys. One exception is a program in northern Uganda run by local organizations supported by the Anglican Church. It allows both girls and boys who had been in armed groups to attend a technical school where they learn basic business skills and agricultural trades, such as beekeeping.

who has negotiated with many rebel leaders in Africa and Asia.

Perhaps the most precise definition of a child soldier was produced at a conference of scholars and representatives of various child-protection agencies, organized in 1997 by the United Nations Children's Fund (UNICEF). Convening in Cape Town, South Africa, the group developed the so-called Cape Town Principles, which define a child soldier as anyone under 18 "who is part of any kind of regular or irregular armed force" in any capacity, including cooks, porters, messengers and non-family members accompanying such groups. Also included were girls recruited for sexual purposes and those forced into marriage.[7]

However, David M. Rosen, a professor of anthropology and law at Fairleigh Dickinson University in Madison, New Jersey, argues that the age "when the young are fit to be warriors" varies from culture to culture.[8] In some societies, he wrote in a provocative 2005 book, "young people are deliberately socialized into highly aggressive behavior, and both individual and collective violence are highly esteemed." Other societies, he added, put more emphasis "on peaceful resolution of disputes." Rosen contends the United Nations and international humanitarian organizations have used the subject of child soldiers to advance their own agendas, including, in his view, protecting post-colonial governments in Africa and Asia against internal rebellion and denouncing Israel for its attacks on

A recent study of former LRA girl soldiers focused on several thousand girls and young women who had been forced to "marry" rebel commanders.[4] The study said the presence of forced wives in rebel units "served to bolster fighter morale and support the systems which perpetuate cycles of raiding, looting, killing, and abduction." Thus, says study co-author Dyan Mazurana, forcing girls to become commanders' wives is an integral part of how many armed groups conduct their business — not an incidental factor that can be ignored by governments and aid groups in their postwar negotiations with rebels.

The leaders of local communities often argue that the best way to deal with the forced wives of rebels after a war "is for them to stay with their captors," she continues. But the young women overwhelmingly reject that idea.

Grace Akallo — abducted by the LRA in 1996 but who escaped after seven months — says she "can't imagine" any girl wanting to stay with her captors. "We were all so anxious to get away from them, we would do anything to get away from them," says Akallo, now a college student in the United States.

Complicating the situation, says Wessells, are girls who joined armed groups voluntarily to avoid abusive parents, to escape arranged marriages or in hopes of finding a better life. These girls are often more reluctant than abducted girls to return to their communities after the war, so they are unlikely to seek help from official aid programs, Wessells says.

Reuters/Ahmed Jadallah

A Palestinian policeman teaches a girl how to use an AK-47 assault rifle in a Gaza refugee camp in southern Gaza Strip. Palestinian extremist groups reportedly have used children as suicide bombers.

[1] "In the Tragedy of Child-soldiering in Africa, a Girl's Story Finds a Happy Ending," The Associated Press, Aug. 25, 2007.

[2] Hilde F. Johnson, deputy executive director, UNICEF, address to the Ministerial Meeting on Children and Armed Conflict, Oct. 1, 2007, a follow-up to the Paris Principles and Paris Commitments, formulated in February 2007, www.unicef.org/protection/files/Final-Paris-Principles-1Oct07-HFJ-speech.pdf.

[3] Susan McKay and Dyan Mazurana, "Where are the Girls? Girls in Fighting Forces in Northern Uganda, Sierra Leone, and Mozambique. Their Lives During and After War," International Centre for Human Rights and Democracy, Montreal, 2004, pp. 22, 25.

[4] Kristopher Carlson and Dyan Mazurana, "Forced Marriage within the Lord's Resistance Army, Uganda," Feinstein International Center, Tufts University, May 2008.

Palestinians while ignoring terrorist attacks perpetrated by Palestinian child soldiers.

Children end up in armies and rebel groups for a variety of reasons, depending on the circumstances. All too often, children are abducted from their villages or displaced-person camps or — like Beah — are swept up by government armies. Leaders of armed groups often use narcotics to dull the fears of their child soldiers or to stimulate them for combat. Beah's experiences were similar to those of Albert, a former child soldier who told Amnesty International he was forced to join a rebel group in the Democratic Republic of the Congo when he was 15.

"[T]hey would give us 'chanvre' [cannabis] and force us to kill people to toughen us up," he recalled. "Sometimes they brought us women and girls to rape. . . . They would beat us if we refused."[9]

Many young children join armed groups voluntarily because their families can't support them, or they're lured by the prospect of carrying a gun and wearing a snazzy uniform. Others are enticed by recruiters who make extravagant promises to the children and their families that they have no intention of keeping.

The child soldier problem has captured the world's attention intermittently over the past two decades — most often when children are found to engage in atrocities. Conflicts in the West African nations of Liberia and Sierra Leone during the 1990s seemed to represent the quintessential use of child soldiers in brutal circumstances.

Abducting Girls Is Most Widespread in Africa

Girls were abducted into either official armed forces or non-state armed groups in 28 countries between 1990 and 2003 — 11 of them in Africa.

Countries Where Girls Were Abducted into Armed Groups
(1990-2003)

Africa	Americas	Sri Lanka, Timor-Leste; Europe; Middle East
Angola	Colombia	Sri Lanka
Burundi	El Salvador	Timor-Leste
Democratic Republic of the Congo	Guatemala	**Europe**
Ethiopia	Peru	Federal Republic of Yugoslavia
Liberia	**Asia**	Germany
Mozambique	Myanmar	Northern Ireland
Rwanda	Cambodia	**Middle East**
Sierra Leone	India	Iraq
Somalia	Indonesia	Turkey
Sudan	Nepal	
Uganda	Philippines	

Source: Susan McKay and Dyan Mazurana, "Where are the girls?" Rights & Democracy, March 2004

Besides being an appealing advocate for child soldiers, Beah, now in his late-20s, shows that child soldiers can return to a normal life once they're removed from conflict and receive appropriate assistance from groups specializing in protecting children. Admittedly, as a ward of the U.N. system for several years, Beah had opportunities few other former soldiers enjoy. Even so, child-protection experts emphasize that even after committing heinous acts or suffering deep psychological or physical injuries, former child soldiers can be rehabilitated.

As governments and international organizations around the globe wrestle with the problem of child soldiers, here are some of the questions being addressed:

Does "naming and shaming" help prevent the use of child soldiers?

In his most recent report on children and armed conflict, released in January, United Nations Secretary-General Ban Ki-moon identified 40 governments or rebel groups, in 13 conflicts, that recruited and used child soldiers.[11] This report was a key component of the U.N.'s policy of publicly identifying those who recruit and use child soldiers — and condemning them for it. The U.N. has been in the "naming and shaming" business since November 2001, when the Security Council adopted Resolution 1379, asking the secretary-general to identify governments and groups that engaged in the practice.[12]

Secretary-General Kofi Annan submitted his first such report in 2002, and subsequent reports have been filed each year.

Human-rights advocacy groups, such as Amnesty International and HRW, also have made naming and shaming an important part of their campaigns to draw attention to the use and abuse of child soldiers. These groups issue their own reports on specific conflicts, and a collaboration of such groups, the Coalition to Stop the Use of Child soldiers, periodically publishes a

In Liberia, Charles Taylor rose to power at the head of a rebel army composed substantially of young fighters whom he sent out to rape, pillage and murder. In neighboring Sierra Leone, the Revolutionary United Front (RUF) — a rebel group armed and supported by Taylor — forced its child soldiers to mutilate victims in one of the most depraved civil conflicts in modern times. These wars spawned other conflicts in the region, notably in Guinea and the Côte d'Ivoire, sometimes involving child soldiers who crossed borders to keep fighting because it was the only life they knew.

Beah, who was fortunate enough to be removed from the Sierra Leone conflict by UNICEF, recounted his story in the gripping 2007 bestseller, *A Long Way Gone: Memoirs of a Boy Soldier.*[10] The book, and Beah's engaging media appearances, quickly drew more public attention to the child soldier issue than stacks of U.N. reports and resolutions had done.

comprehensive assessment of the use of child soldiers worldwide. The coalition's most recent report, "Child Soldiers Global Report 2008," was published in May.[13]

In his 2007 report, Secretary-General Ban said naming offending parties "has proven to have a deterrent effect" and has allowed the U.N. and other agencies to maintain political pressure and take action against those who are "persistent violators of child rights."[14]

U.N. Special Representative Coomaraswamy says it's also significant that the child soldier problem is the only "thematic issue" regularly addressed by the Security Council — as opposed to specific crises in individual countries. The council has established a "working group" that meets every two months to discuss the secretary-general's reports. On behalf of the Security Council, the working group condemns those who continue using child soldiers and praises those who agree to stop the practice.

"People do listen to the Security Council," Coomaraswamy says. "They may not always act in ways we wish they would, but they do listen, and this should not be dismissed."

Jo Becker, child rights advocacy director of HRW, agrees naming and shaming has had some impact, but mostly on governments. For example, she notes, governments in Chad, the Democratic Republic of the Congo and Myanmar have pledged to stop using child soldiers due to international pressure. And while these and other governments haven't always kept their promises, at least they have taken the first step of forswearing their use, she says.

Some rebels have responded to international pressure, such as the Tamil Tigers of Sri Lanka, who "promote themselves as a reputable group and rely very heavily on contributions from the international diaspora of Tamils," Becker points out. According to the U.N., the group has released some child soldiers — but certainly not all of them — and continued recruiting children well into 2007, although in lower numbers than in previous years.[15]

However, leaders of many other groups — such as Kony, of the Lord's Resistance Army — appear to have little or no regard for how they are seen internationally and are not swayed by having their names published in U.N. reports. "Kony's name was already mud and could hardly get any worse," says Christopher Blattman, an assistant professor of political science and economics at Yale University who has done extensive research on Kony.

An even more skeptical view comes from Singer at Brookings, who says most of those who use child soldiers see it as a purely pragmatic rather than a moral issue. "You can't shame the shameless," Singer says, "but you can create some sense of accountability by figuring out what their interests are, what drives their calculations and how you can alter their calculations." Prosecuting and imposing sanctions are more effective parts of a "cost structure" that can be imposed on those who use child soldiers, Singer says.

Some experts argue that naming and shaming can be useful in some cases but counterproductive in others. "If you are . . . trying to use communication and negotiations channels [with rebels] to get the release of child soldiers, it can be undermined by strident or hostile criticism of the group," says Michael Wessells, a professor of psychology at Randolph-Macon College in Virginia, who has worked with programs to aid child soldiers for nearly three decades. "The door closes, and the lives of children are damaged even further."

For instance, Blattman says pending International Criminal Court (ICC) indictments of Kony and four of his commanders may have helped persuade Kony to authorize aides to enter into peace negotiations with the Ugandan government in hopes the indictments would be lifted. But the court's insistence on maintaining the indictments "could now be an impediment to peace because it doesn't offer them [Kony and his commanders] much of an option," Blattman says. If Kony faces a choice of prison or lifetime exile, he probably will choose exile and continued conflict, Blattman adds, prolonging his two-decade-long war well into the future.

Nevertheless, Wessells says, it is "profoundly important to make clear that it is not OK for leaders of armed groups to say they can do whatever they want." Reflecting concerns about the potential negative consequences of naming and shaming, an international forum of experts on child soldiers, meeting in Switzerland in 2006, called for more research on the effectiveness of naming and shaming.[16]

Should the United States prosecute alleged child soldiers detained at Guantánamo Bay?

An alleged terrorist captured in Afghanistan when he was 15 could be the first person tried for war crimes

AFP/Getty Images/Ravi Manandhar

Girl soldiers serve with Maoist rebels near Kathmandu. According to a recent U.N. report, the group refuses to release its child soldiers on a regular basis despite signing an historic peace pact with the Nepalese government.

committed as a child. Omar Ahmed Khadr, now 21, is facing trial by a military commission after spending nearly six years in prison at the U.S. military base at Guantánamo Bay, Cuba.

The son of a financier for the al Qaeda Islamic terrorist group, Khadr is charged with murder, spying against the United States and other crimes. He allegedly threw a grenade that killed a U.S. soldier and injured others in Afghanistan on July 27, 2002.[17] Khadr was seriously wounded during the fighting and was transferred to Guantánamo in November 2002, where he was placed under the jurisdiction of the U.S. military commission created after the Sept. 11, 2001, terrorist attacks.

The commission in late 2007 and early 2008 rejected several motions filed by Khadr's attorneys challenging the proceedings, including one contending Khadr had been illegally recruited by his father into working as a translator at al Qaeda training camps in Afghanistan. Col. Peter Brownback, the commission's judge, dismissed that motion on April 30 on the grounds that Congress did not set a minimum age for defendants when it authorized the military commissions in 2006.[18] Khadr's trial is scheduled to begin in October.

HRW and other groups have denounced the government's handling of Khadr, noting that he was treated as an adult despite his age when he allegedly committed the crimes and has been held in "prolonged" periods of solitary confinement for more than five years.[19] In an *amicus curiae* brief submitted to the commission on Jan. 18 on behalf of 23 members of Canada's parliament and 55 legal scholars from Canada, Sarah H. Paoletti, clinical supervisor and lecturer at the Transnational Legal Clinic at the University of Pennsylvania School of Law, argued that Khadr's prosecution "is in stark opposition to longstanding and well-established precedent under international law protecting the rights of children unlawfully recruited into armed conflict."[20]

Paoletti's brief said recent treaties and agreements suggest that former child soldiers should be offered rehabilitation and reintegration back into their communities rather than prosecution. For instance, the 1998 Rome Statute, which created the ICC, denied the court jurisdiction over anyone younger than 18 at the time of the alleged crime. This ban does not apply to courts or tribunals established by national governments.[21]

Similarly, a set of "principles" negotiated by representatives of countries and nongovernmental organizations in Paris last year suggested that former child soldiers should not be prosecuted but rather treated as "victims of offences against international law, not only as perpetrators. They must be treated in accordance with international law in a framework of restorative justice and social rehabilitation, consistent with international law, which offers children special protection through numerous agreements and principles."[22]

David M. Crane, former chief prosecutor at the U.N.-backed Special Tribunal for Sierra Leone, is one of the most prominent opponents of Khadr's prosecution. He says he decided not to prosecute child soldiers — even those who had committed "horrendous crimes" — because adults were the responsible parties. "Even if a child willingly goes along, he really has no choice in the matter, and this certainly appears to be true in the case of Khadr," who was under the influence of his father, Crane says.

The U.N.'s Coomaraswamy has appealed to the United States to halt the prosecution, saying "children should not be prosecuted for war crimes." She is pleased that Khadr's military lawyers are fighting the prosecution "tooth and nail."

The Pentagon has defended its prosecution on the grounds that none of the international treaties dealing with children and armed conflict expressly forbid a national government from prosecuting alleged child soldiers. In fact, a prosecution motion in the case argued that the Optional Protocol obligated the government to take legal action against Khadr. Al Qaeda itself violated that treaty by recruiting Khadr, the prosecution said, so dismissing the charges against him — as his defense lawyers argued — "would effectively condone that alleged violation by allowing Khadr to escape all liability for his actions and would further incentivize such actions."[23]

In another government defense of the Khadr case, the Pentagon official in charge of detention policy, Sandra L. Hodgkinson, told a U.N. committee on May 22 that the U.S. detention of Khadr and other juveniles in Afghanistan and Iraq reduces the threat that they will be used to carry out suicide bombings and other attacks. "If there is a sense that juveniles cannot be removed from the battlefield, there is a valid concern that the tactic of recruiting children will be further utilized against coalition forces and innocent civilians in Iraq and Afghanistan," she said.[24]

Although Khadr is a Canadian citizen by birth, Canada has refused to intervene on the grounds that he has been charged with a serious crime. Even so, the Canadian Supreme Court on May 23 denounced the early stages of the U.S. handling of his case. In a unanimous opinion, the court said U.S. legal processes at Guantánamo in 2002-03 "constituted a clear violation of fundamental human rights protected by international law." Moreover, the court said the Canadian government erred in turning over to U.S. authorities information about interviews with Khadr conducted by the Canadian intelligence service in 2003; Khadr's defense lawyers were entitled to see some of these documents, the court said.[25]

In a follow-up to that decision, a lower-court judge in Canada ruled on June 25 that Khadr's lawyers could be given a document and recordings describing alleged mistreatment of him by U.S. officials at the Guantánamo prison in 2004.

Another alleged child soldier held at Guantánamo, Mohammed Jawad, was captured in Afghanistan in December 2002 when he was either 16 or 17 and charged last January with attempted murder and intentionally causing bodily harm. The military alleges he threw a hand grenade into a vehicle carrying two U.S. soldiers and their Afghan interpreter.[26] Jawad's case is still in the early stages of consideration by a military commission at Guantánamo.

Hearings on both the Khadr and Jawad cases continued in mid-June despite a major Supreme Court ruling on June 12 that Guantánamo prisoners could challenge their detentions in U.S. federal court. The decision didn't directly go to the actions of the military commissions, but defense lawyers already have said they will use it to challenge a broad range of government actions concerning the detainees.

Should Congress pass legislation to combat the use of child soldiers overseas?

The child soldier issue has reached the U.S. Congress, which is considering two bills intended to put some force behind American criticisms of the use of child soldiers. The House-passed Child Soldier Prevention Act would bar U.S. military aid or arms sales to governments that recruit or use child soldiers (defined as children under 16 voluntarily recruited into an official army or under 18 forced to join an army). The U.S. president could waive the ban by declaring that it is in America's national interest to provide aid or sell weapons to governments that use child soldiers.

The Senate, meanwhile, passed the Child Soldiers Accountability Act, which would make it a crime under U.S. law for anyone, anywhere, to recruit a child under 15 into an armed group or use a child in combat. The measure also prohibits entry into the United States of anyone who recruits or uses child soldiers under 15.

Sen. Richard L. Durbin, D-Ill., one of the bill's sponsors, said it would help "ensure that the war criminals who recruit or use children as soldiers will not find safe haven in our country and will allow the U.S. government to hold these individuals accountable for their actions."[27] Senate aides say there has been no active opposition so far to either measure.

The House-passed measure potentially could prove controversial, however, because the national police force in Afghanistan — a key U.S. ally — has been accused of forcibly recruiting children under 18. The State Department cited the allegations in its 2007 human rights report on the country.[28]

Afghanistan was scheduled to receive about $8 million in military aid in fiscal 2008, according to the Center for Defense Information, a liberal think tank in Washington.

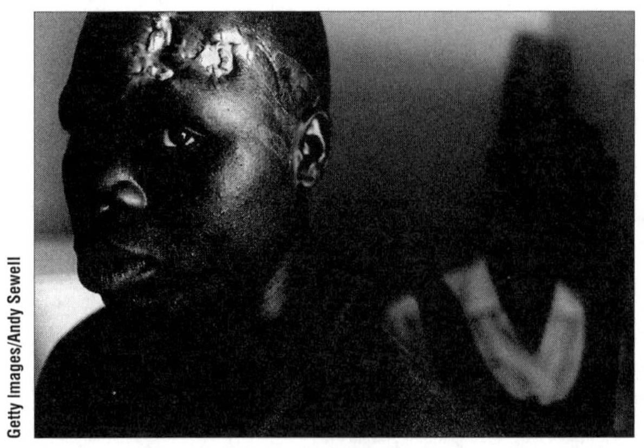

Getty Images/Andy Sewell

Simon, now 19, spent eight years as a child soldier with the Lord's Resistance Army (LRA) after being abducted from his home in northern Uganda. During that time he saw hundreds of people killed, including some who were hacked to death in front of him, and he was forced to kill other child abductees who tried to escape. Besides his psychological wounds, he is struggling to recover form a head wound received during combat. The LRA is led by Joseph Kony, a notorious, self-styled prophet who was indicted by the International Criminal Court in 2005 but remains at large.

The center said the bill could affect military aid to six other countries unless the president waived the provisions. The center compared the State Department's 2007 human rights reports — which dealt with child soldiers for the first time — and the administration's allocations of military aid as well as its arms sales to foreign countries. The six other countries that used child soldiers in some official capacity while receiving U.S. military aid were Chad, the Democratic Republic of the Congo, Somalia, Sri Lanka, Sudan and Uganda. Most of the aid programs were small and included only military training — generally considered the stepping stone to a broader relationship between the U.S. and foreign militaries.[29]

Sen. Durbin said the bill "would ensure that U.S. taxpayer dollars are not used to support this abhorrent practice by government or government-sanctioned military and paramilitary organizations." The United States could continue military aid if the president chose to do so, Durbin added, "but it would be used only to remedy the problem by helping countries successfully demobilize their child soldiers and professionalize their forces."[30]

Neither of the two measures has encountered any formal opposition in either chamber of Congress. Although the Bush administration has taken no formal position on either bill, congressional aides and lobbyists favoring the proposals say they expect the White House to oppose them as a matter of course because legislation limiting a president's flexibility in foreign policy is generally resisted.

BACKGROUND

Child Armies Proliferate

An explosion of civil conflicts around the globe during the last half of the 20th century was accompanied by several developments that ensured children would bear much of the burden of war. Chief among them was the invention of simple-to-use, lightweight weapons — especially automatic rifles and rocket launchers. Even a 10-year-old can carry and use the world's most ubiquitous weapon: the Kalashnikov assault rifle, or AK-47.

After the collapse of communism in Eastern Europe and the Soviet Union between 1989-91, millions of Kalashnikovs and other Soviet weapons fell into the hands of unscrupulous arms dealers, who sold them to rebel leaders and warlords around the world. They often paid with narcotics, diamonds or other resources plundered from their own countries.

Rebels claiming to be fighting for social justice or a host of other causes found they could easily fill their ranks with children. An official of the Chadian military explained their advantages: "Child soldiers are ideal because they don't complain, they don't expect to be paid and if you tell them to kill, they kill."[31]

Children also are easy to abduct or force into military service, especially if they live in unprotected villages or communal facilities, such as refugee camps, where they are often protected only by mothers and unarmed humanitarian workers. "All the boys in the village were asked to join the army," a former child soldier told author Singer. "There was no way out. If I left the village I would get killed by the rebels who would think that I was a spy. On the other hand, if I stayed in the village and refused to join the army, I wouldn't be given any food and would eventually be thrown out, which was as good as being dead."[32]

Social and economic conditions in many poor countries, such as poverty and lack of educational and job opportunities, make children susceptible to the call of combat. "Demagogues, warlords, criminals and others

CHRONOLOGY

1980s *Civil conflicts in Africa and Asia begin to use children in combat.*

1983 Tamil Tiger insurgency erupts in Sri Lanka. The group later gains notoriety for its use of suicide bombers and thousands of child soldiers.

1987 Joseph Kony's Lord's Resistance Army in Uganda begins abducting children for use as soldiers.

1989 U.N. General Assembly adopts Convention on the Rights of the Child, which establishes 15 as the minimum age for recruiting children into armed forces. Eventually, 190 countries ratify the treaty; the United States refuses to ratify it.

1990s *Genocide in Rwanda focuses global attention on child soldiers.*

1994 Thousands of children take part in Rwandan genocide.

1996 UNICEF's Landmark "Impact of Armed Conflict on Children" report focuses international attention on child soldiers.

1997 Zaire's dictator Mobutu Sese Seko is ousted by Laurent Kabila's rebel group, which uses several thousand child soldiers. Kabila's backers in Rwanda and Uganda later turn against him, setting off a war using tens of thousands of child soldiers. . . . Ugandan diplomat Olara Otunu becomes the U.N.'s first Special Representative for Children and Armed Conflict.

1998 Human-rights organizations form Coalition to Stop the Use of Child Soldiers.

1999 First U.N. resolution on child soldiers, Resolution 1261, condemns abduction and recruitment of children for combat.

2000s *U.N. steps up efforts to combat use of child soldiers.*

2000 U.N. "Optional Protocol" sets 18 as the minimum age for children in combat and bars non-state armed groups from recruiting or using children under 18.

2001 U.N. Security Council asks secretary-general to identify parties recruiting or using children in armed conflicts.

2002 U.S. Senate ratifies Optional Protocol.

2003 U.N. Secretary-General Kofi Annan submits first report listing groups recruiting and using children in armed conflicts. Security Council asks secretary-general to report on actions being taken by armed groups cited in his report to stop the use of children.

2004 Security Council calls for "action plans" to stop use of child soldiers.

2005 Security Council establishes monitoring and reporting mechanism on children and armed conflict. . . . International Criminal Court (ICC) issues war crimes arrest warrants for Lord's Resistance Army leader Kony and four commanders for forced recruitment and use of child soldiers in Uganda.

2006 ICC charges Thomas Lubanga Dyilo, leader of the rebel Union of Congolese Patriots, with using child soldiers.

2007 UNICEF and the French government sponsor a conference in Paris on preventing the use of child soldiers and aiding children in post-conflict situations. . . . *A Long Way Gone: Memoirs of a Boy Soldier*, by Ishmael Beah, becomes worldwide bestseller and focuses new attention on child soldiers. . . . Four former militia leaders are convicted by a U.N.-backed special tribunal on charges that they recruited and used child soldiers during the war in Sierra Leone — the first time an international court has addressed the use of child soldiers. . . . Former Liberian President Charles Taylor goes on trial at the Special Court of Sierra Leone (at The Hague) on 11 charges of war crimes and crimes against humanity, including conscripting children into the armed forces and using them in combat.

2008 Cease-fire agreement signed in January offers a potential end to fighting in eastern Congo, where the use of child soldiers is common. . . . ICC temporarily halts its first-ever case, against Congolese rebel leader Lubanga because of a dispute over the handling of confidential evidence.

Former Child Soldiers Can Become Good Citizens

But reintegration must be handled carefully by aid agencies

"My parents ran away when they saw me. I had to follow them; they thought I would abduct them."

— Former girl child soldier, 15[1]

"We feel different because of the way other children look at us; it seems as if we are not children born from this land. They view us as though we come from a different place."

— Former boy child soldier, 17[2]

For many child soldiers, the end of a war can be nearly as traumatic as the conflict itself. Some cannot remember anything but warfare and have little concept of what normal civilian life is like. Others suffered serious physical wounds, and most endure at least short-term psychological problems, and sometimes drug addiction.

Returning child soldiers often find that one or both parents have been killed or may have moved elsewhere. Parents also are sometimes reluctant to accept a returning child whom they no longer know or understand, especially if the child was forced to commit atrocities — sometimes even against his own family.

Because their schooling has been interrupted, most former child soldiers have few job skills appropriate to civilian society. Governments and international aid agencies often include provisions for child soldiers in official programs to disarm, demobilize and reintegrate rebel fighters. But several experts in the field say many of these so-called DDR programs are underfunded, badly managed or lack appropriate resources to meet the special needs of children.

Many researchers consider economic opportunity as the greatest need faced by former child soldiers. "When they go home, their struggles are going to be largely economic — as much, if not more so, than mental health or some other concerns," says Neil Boothby, director of the Program on Forced Migration and Health at Columbia University. "They need to learn how to make a living in a peaceful and useful way. Their fights will be against poverty as much as to maintain mental health."

Boothby and other experts say research also refutes public perceptions — fostered by some news accounts — that former child soldiers are so deranged they cannot adapt to civilian life. At least two studies have found that former child soldiers tend to be good citizens once they are integrated back into their home communities. A long-term study of nearly 40 former child soldiers in Mozambique — all of them demobilized in 1988 — showed they have "turned out quite well," co-author Boothby says.[3] "They are perceived by their communities to be good neighbors, a high percentage are active in the equivalent of the PTA and many are leaders in their communities. It dispels the notion that there are lost generations" of former child soldiers. "The only time you lose generations is when you don't help them after a crisis."

Another study — of young Ugandans abducted by the notorious Lord's Resistance Army (LRA) — also found "a greater propensity toward engaged citizenry, including voting at higher rates and being more involved with community leadership" than their counterparts.[4] Christopher Blattman, a co-author of that study and an assistant professor from Yale University, says only a small minority of youth abducted by the LRA were so traumatized they could no longer function in society.

Grace Akallo, who was abducted at 15, says her personal experience demonstrates that children can overcome their past so long as they get help. "I suffered a lot in the LRA, but I went back to school and my family, and I am fine now. So long as a child gets an opportunity for a future, that child can be OK."

Experts who have assisted or studied former child soldiers say several important lessons have been learned during recent post-conflict experiences, including:

- Governments and aid agencies administering post-war reintegration programs should be cautious about making cash payments to former child soldiers. Giving returnees clothing, food, job training, medical aid and psychological counseling is appropriate, experts say, but in many circumstances giving them cash is not. "We know from many different contexts that when young people in these situations are given cash, bad things happen," says Michael Wessells, a psychology professor from Randolph-Macon College in Virginia, who has helped and studied child soldiers in Africa and Asia. "Commanders sometimes grab the cash and use it to recruit other children, so it runs counter to the intended purpose." A cash payment also can be seen as a reward for serving in an armed group, which is counterproductive, he says. On the other hand, Boothby says cash payments can help in some circumstances if they are carefully monitored to ensure the money benefits the children.

- Girls who have served with armed groups have different needs from boys, particularly if they return from the bush with children. Child soldier aid programs recently have begun to consider girls' special needs, such as child care, assistance with reproductive health matters and psychological aid to deal with the potential stigmatization in their home communities, where the girls are considered "unclean" because of their forced sexual relationships with rebel commanders.
- Reintegration programs should consider the needs of local communities, and community members should be involved in the process. Programs designed by officials in aid agencies or even by government officials in the conflict country often fail because they ignore local situations.
- Donor countries and aid agencies that fund reintegration programs should commit for the long haul. In several recent cases, money ran out before the bulk of former fighters returned from the bush, leaving thousands of youths feeling angry and betrayed. U.N. officials say that after the long war in the Democratic Republic of the Congo, for example, only about half of former child and adult fighters received assistance.[5]
- Targeting aid exclusively or primarily to former members of armed groups risks stigmatizing them and fostering jealousy among their neighbors. Thus, aid programs should be directed at entire communities, not just individuals, Wessells says. Moreover, all children who have served with armed groups — whether as porters, spies or as "wives" of commanders — should be eligible for reintegration aid, not just the fighters, experts say.

AFP/Getty Images/Sena Vidanagama

Former Sri Lankan Tamil Tiger fighters Velayutham Chuti, 18, (left) and 14-year-old Pulidha Logini (right) celebrate with their families after being released by a rival rebel group. The Hindu Tamil Tigers reportedly have used thousands of children in their long battle against the predominantly Buddhist government, making the Tigers one of the world's most persistent users of child soldiers.

[1] "Returning Home: Children's Perspectives on Reintegration: A Case Study of Children Abducted by the Lord's Resistance Army in Teso, Eastern Uganda," Coalition to Stop the Use of Child Soldiers, February 2008, p. 14.

[2] *Ibid.*, p. 16.

[3] N. Boothby, J. Crawford and J. Halperin, "Mozambique Child Soldier Life Outcome Study: Lessons Learned in Rehabilitation and Reintegration," *Global Public Health*, February 2006.

[4] "Making Reintegration Work for Youth in Northern Uganda," The Survey of War Affected Youth, www.sway-uganda.org.

[5] "Report of the Secretary General on Children and Armed Conflict in the Democratic Republic of the Congo," June 28, 2007, pp. 14-15.

Congo Reintegrates the Most Child Soldiers

More than 104,000 child soldiers have been demobilized and reintegrated into society worldwide, including 27,000 in the Democratic Republic of the Congo — more than any other country. UNICEF estimates up to 33,000 children were involved in the long-running Congolese war — the biggest and deadliest since World War II. Uganda, where the Lord's Resistance Army notoriously relied on abducting children, has reintegrated 20,000 former child soldiers into their communities. Outside Africa, Sri Lanka has reintegrated more child soldiers than any other country.

Number of Child Soldiers Reintegrated Into Society
(since 1998)

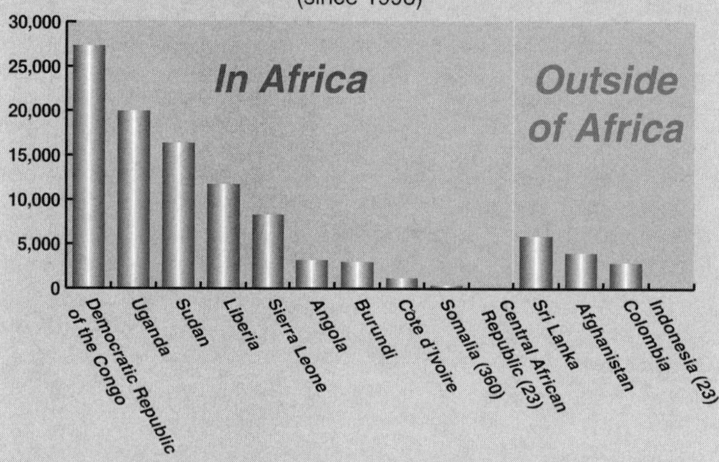

Source: U.N. Integrated Disarmament, Demoblisation and Reintegration System; UNICEF

find it easier to recruit when a large population of angry, listless young men fill the street," Singer said.[33]

Impressionable children also can find military life alluring. When a recruiter from the army or a rebel group shows up and offers an impoverished child the opportunity to wear a uniform and make himself feel powerful by carrying a gun, the sales pitch is often difficult to resist.

U.N. Roles

The task of curtailing the use of under-age fighters has fallen largely to the United Nations, which has had only limited success. The U.N. has taken a two-pronged approach: getting a treaty enacted making it illegal for governments and armed groups to use children under 18 in combat and establishing a system for identifying armed groups that recruit and use child soldiers. The Security Council has threatened to sanction more than a dozen persistent violators of the law but has taken that step only once, in Côte d'Ivoire in West Africa.

Several treaties and regulations adopted by the U.N. after World War II created a legal structure offering theoretical protection to children and discouraging their use in warfare, including the 1948 Universal Declaration of Human Rights, the Geneva Conventions of 1949 and Additional Protocols to those conventions adopted in 1977 and the 1989 Convention on the Rights of the Child. These treaties were strengthened substantially in 2000 with adoption of the Optional Protocol, which specifically barred non-state armed groups from recruiting or using any children under 18 but allowed governments to recruit children 16 or 17 as long as they weren't used in combat until they turned 18. In essence, the treaty made it illegal under international law for anyone to use a child under 18 in combat. In addition, the 1998 Rome Statute — which went into effect in 2002 and created the International Criminal Court — defined as a "war crime" the conscription or use in war of any child under 15.

Since 1996 the Security Council also has adopted six resolutions dealing specifically with children and armed conflict. The last four of these (Resolution 1379 adopted in 2001, Resolution 1460 adopted in 2003, Resolution 1539 adopted in 2004, and Resolution 1612 adopted in 2005) created a system under which U.N. officials monitor the impact of armed conflicts on children and publicly identify countries and groups that illegally recruit and use children in combat.

In some cases, when confronted by the U.N. with solid evidence about their use of child soldiers, warlords have promised to release them. Some have kept their promises, notably the leaders of three groups in Côte d'Ivoire who were subjected to Security Council sanctions in 2006.[34] Most others broke their promises. In Somalia, for example, the Union of Islamic Courts, which briefly held power in 2006, told U.N. officials they would stop using child soldiers, but didn't.[35]

Children at War

The United Nations, nongovernmental groups and academic experts have identified nearly 50 civil conflicts since World War II that have involved children, mostly in sub-Saharan Africa. The following examples are representative of recent or ongoing conflicts involving heavy use of child soldiers:

Colombia — The long-running, multifaceted civil conflict in Colombia has featured the most extensive use of child soldiers in the Americas. According to various estimates, 11,000 to 14,000 Colombians under 18 have been recruited into the country's armed groups.[36] Most are members of the two leftist guerrilla factions, the Revolutionary Armed Forces of Colombia (FARC) and the National Liberation Army (ELN). Several thousand underage fighters also have been associated with right-wing paramilitary groups aligned with the government, the military and major landowners; the largest paramilitary force is the United Self-Defense Forces of Colombia (AUC).[37]

The Colombian army also used under-18-year-olds as fighters until 2000, when it reportedly halted the practice after domestic and international protests. But there have been reports about the army's continued use of children. American journalist Jimmie Briggs said the army still recruits soldiers under 18 but assigns them to noncombat duty until they turn 18.[38] In its "2008 Global Report," the Coalition to Stop the Use of Child Soldiers cited the army for using captured children for intelligence-gathering.[39]

Significantly, since 1999 more than 3,300 former child soldiers (mostly from the FARC) have gone through the government-sponsored demobilization, disarmament and reintegration process — one of the few major demobilization efforts ever conducted during an ongoing conflict.[40]

Democratic Republic of the Congo — The Congolese war — the biggest and deadliest since World War II — took place in the former Zaire from about 1998 until 2003. It involved more than a dozen guerrilla groups and, at various points, the armies or paramilitary groups from Angola, Burundi, Rwanda, Uganda and Zimbabwe. The International Rescue Committee has estimated that up to 5.5 million people — about one-tenth of the Congo's population — may have died as a result of the conflict.[41]

Many of the armed groups used children as fighters or in support roles. In 2002, as part of the war was ending, UNICEF estimated that about 33,000 children were involved in the fighting — or 20 percent of active combatants.[42] In June 2007, U.N. Secretary-General Ban told the U.N. Security Council that 29,291 children had been released by armed groups during the previous three years under a U.N.-sponsored demobilization program. However, due to alleged mismanagement of the program and a failure by donor nations to fulfill their funding pledges, only about half of the former child soldiers had received aid to reintegrate into their communities, the report found.[43]

Although peace agreements were signed in 2002 and 2003, fighting has continued in parts of eastern Congo, where renegade Tutsi commander Laurent Nkunda leads a militia in fighting the Congolese army. Nkunda claims his group is protecting Congo's minority Tutsi population — an ethnic group that was slaughtered by the hundreds of thousands during the 1994 genocide in Rwanda.

The U.N. has accused Nkunda of forcibly recruiting hundreds, and possibly several thousand, children.[44] Nkunda, along with other rebels, signed a cease-fire agreement on Jan. 23, 2008, pledging to end the fighting.[45] Reports since then have suggested the cease-fire merely reduced the level of fighting rather than stopping it.[46] Government security forces also used child soldiers, at least through 2007, according to the U.S. State Department.[47]

Liberia — From the early 1990s until President Charles Taylor was ousted from power in 2003, Liberia was a focal point for several civil conflicts in West Africa, all involving child soldiers. During the early 1990s, Taylor led a rebel army, composed in large part of children, which controlled much of Liberia. After he became president in 1997, he also backed rebel groups in neighboring Côte d'Ivoire, Guinea and Sierra Leone.

AFP/Getty Images/Esdras Ndikumana

Former child soldiers at a demobilization camp in Burundi wait to be reintegrated back into society. About 104,000 children worldwide have been reintegrated into their communities after serving in various rebel or government armed forces.

Taylor's support for the notorious Revolutionary United Front in Sierra Leone — in exchange for access to diamonds and other natural resources in rebel-controlled areas — was the basis for his indictment on 11 war-crimes charges by a U.N.-sponsored tribunal. His trial, which began in July 2007, is still under way. The regional impact of the war in Liberia and Taylor's sponsorship of neighboring rebel armies continued at least until 2005. According to the Coalition to Stop the Use of Child Soldiers, rebel groups in Guinea and Côte d'Ivoire were still recruiting child soldiers (and former child soldiers who had reached age 18) from Liberia.[48]

Myanmar — The U.N., HRW and other organizations say the secretive military government of Myanmar (formerly Burma) makes widespread use of children in its army even though the minimum recruitment age is 18.[49] According to HRW, government recruiters force boys under 18 to lie about their ages or falsify induction forms to meet quotas.[50] The government began recruiting children extensively in the 1990s, when it more than doubled the size of the army — from 200,000 to 500,000 — to combat an upsurge in a decades-old separatist insurgency in Karen state in southeastern Myanmar, the group said.[51]

Responding partly to pressure from the U.N., the government in 2004 created a committee to prevent the military recruitment of under-18-year-olds. Since then, government representatives have insisted the army has no under-age soldiers. However, Secretary-General Ban wrote in a November 2007 report that recruitment continued unabated, with recruiters still rewarded with cash and a bag of rice for each new solider they produced, regardless of his age.[52]

U.N. and HRW officials do not know how many children now serve in the Myanmar military because the government severely restricts international access to the country. However, the HRW report quoted several former soldiers as estimating that 20 to 50 percent of the soldiers in their units had been underage.[53]

Many of the country's non-state military groups also use underage soldiers, but the extent is unknown, according to both the U.N. and HRW.[54]

Sri Lanka — The Liberation Tigers of Tamil Eelam (LTTE), better known as the Tamil Tigers, reportedly has used thousands of children in the Hindu group's long battle against the majority Sinhalese (mostly Buddhist) government, making it one of the world's most persistent users of child soldiers. A breakaway rebel faction, known as the Karuna group, which in recent years has been aligned with the government, also reportedly has used child soldiers.[55] A cease-fire negotiated by Norwegian diplomats in February 2002 helped reduce violence for more than three years, but several incidents in 2005 and 2006 led to an escalation of fighting, particularly in the north, which continues today. The cease-fire essentially collapsed in 2006, and the government formally withdrew from it in mid-January 2008. The U.N. had estimated a year earlier that at least 67,000 people had died in the quarter-century of conflict.[56]

The total number of children caught up in the conflict is unknown. However, a UNICEF database showed that between 2002 and 2007 the Tigers recruited 6,248 children, and up to 453 children were recruited by the Karuna group during the last three years of that period. UNICEF said these figures most likely understate the actual use of child soldiers, because the agency relies on voluntary reporting by parents and community leaders, who often withhold information because they fear retaliation.[57] Whatever the actual total, the Tamil Tigers have used children actively in fighting, including as suicide bombers — a technique the group introduced to the world in the 1980s.

U.N. officials and human rights groups have accused the government of complicity in the Karuna group's use of child soldiers and even allowing the group to recruit or abduct children in government-controlled areas. In some cases army units allegedly have participated actively in forcibly recruiting children.[58] The government has denied these accusations.

The Tamil Tigers pledged in 2007 to stop recruiting child soldiers and release all of those in its custody by the end of that year. As of January 2008, however, UNICEF listed 1,429 cases in which a recruited child soldier had not been released, including at least 168 children who were still under 18.[59]

Sudan — Africa's largest country has experienced two major conflicts and several smaller ones in recent years — all involving child soldiers. Secretary-General Ban reported in 2007 that more than 30 armed groups operated in Sudan.[60]

Ban's report and independent human rights groups have found that children have been recruited and used as soldiers by the government's Sudan Armed Forces, by the pro-government militias known as the Janjaweed (which operate in the western region of Darfur), by the main Darfur rebel groups — the Justice and Equality Movement (JEM) and the Sudan Liberation Army (SLA), which have both splintered into factions — and by armed groups in southern Sudan, including the region's main rebel group, the Sudan People's Liberation Army (SPLA).[61]

The Security Council's Working Group on Children and Armed Conflict has repeatedly — most recently in February 2008 — condemned the "continuous recruitment and use of children" by the government and armed groups in Sudan and demanded that the children be released so they could be reintegrated into their families and communities.[62]

In southern Sudan, the government and the SPLA signed a peace agreement in January 2005 ending a 20-year conflict. The agreement called for creation of a "government of national unity," but real unity has been elusive, as the Khartoum government and the former rebels continue to bicker about many of the same issues that fueled the war, including control over oil production in the region.[63]

Between 2001 and early 2006 the SPLA demobilized about 20,000 former child soldiers, but the Coalition to Stop the Use of Child Soldiers reported that as of late 2007 about 2,000 children remained under the militia's control.[64] Secretary-General Ban reported in August 2007 that the SPLA had made "significant progress" by releasing at least 47 children in one of its units, but two armed groups associated with the government's army had not fulfilled their promises to release children.[65]

AFP/Getty Images/Sonia Rolley

The use of child soldiers, like these, by the Chadian military was officially prohibited in May 2007, but as a government official explained, using children is "ideal" because "they don't complain, they don't expect to be paid and if you tell them to kill, they kill."

In Darfur, the fighting remains well below the peak of the conflict in 2002-03, but serious violence continues despite the presence of a U.N. peacekeeping mission. Ban's report found that nearly all armed groups in Darfur, including the Sudanese army and its related militias, continued to recruit and use children as fighters.[66]

The conflict in Darfur also has spilled into neighboring conflicts in Chad and the Central African Republic, where government armies and rebel groups (some supported by the Sudanese government) have recruited and used child soldiers. The Chadian government, in turn, reportedly participated in the forced recruitment in 2006 of nearly 5,000 Sudanese refugees, including several hundred children, by one of the Darfur rebel groups.[67]

Uganda — As in Sierra Leone, the use and abuse of child soldiers has reached a depraved level in Uganda, largely due to the fanatical Kony's Lord's Resistance Army. The United Nations has estimated that Kony, a violent, self-styled prophet, abducted or forced nearly 25,000 children into his army between 1986 and 2005.[68] However, independent experts have said the U.N. estimate counts only former LRA members who later turned themselves into Ugandan government reception centers. Researchers at Tufts University in Boston estimate that the LRA abducted at least 60,000 boys and girls, and that 15-20 percent of the boys and 5 percent of the girls died during the war, said Yale's Blattman, one of the researchers.

Human rights groups say the LRA continues to abduct children, although in lower numbers than earlier.[69] Blattman says his team believes the LRA now has fewer than 1,000 people — adults or children — in its ranks. The International Criminal Court in July 2005 issued arrest warrants for Kony and four of his aides, charging them with war crimes, including the use of child soldiers; at least one of the aides reportedly has since died.[70]

The LRA was one of several Ugandan groups that took up arms in 1986 against the new government of Yoweri Museveni, himself a former rebel leader who had used large numbers of child soldiers during a five-year war against President Milton Obote. Kony claimed to be fighting on behalf of his own ethnic group in northern Uganda, the Acholi people, but ultimately the Acholi became the principal victims in the two-decade-long war between the LRA and the government.[71] Kony reportedly claims his fight is ordained by God. At a 2006 meeting with Ugandan officials, Kony denied that his forces had committed atrocities and insisted "the tragedy that was taking place in Uganda was done by the Uganda government."[72]

The war developed a critical international dimension in the mid-1990s, when Sudan armed Kony's forces to help in its own war against the SPLA in southern Sudan. Kony used southern Sudan as a base from which to launch attacks against both the SPLA and the Ugandan army. He later established bases in the Democratic Republic of the Congo and the Central African Republic.[73]

The conflict in northern Uganda peaked after March 2002, when the Ugandan government launched an offensive against the LRA, which responded by targeting civilians as well as government forces. Over the next two years Kony increased the pace of abductions of children, forcing many of them to endure beatings and to carry out atrocities against each other and against civilians, sometimes even members of their own families. Girls were forced into virtual slavery, the youngest ones as servants and the older ones as "wives" of LRA commanders, says Grace Akallo, who was abducted at 15 and held for seven months until she escaped. Fearing such abductions, thousands of children living in rural villages trudged long distances every evening to sleep in larger towns considered safe. Known as "night commuters," the children became the most visible symbols to the outside world of the horrors in northern Uganda.[74] Despite denials, the Ugandan government also recruited children into its army and local pro-government militias called the UPDF, according to U.N. officials and human rights groups.[75]

The fighting slowed significantly in 2005, when Sudan signed a peace accord with the rebels in southern Sudan and, reportedly, ended much of its support for Kony — a development that led to efforts to end the war in northern Uganda. Peace talks between Uganda and LRA representatives began in Juba, southern Sudan, in 2006. A cease-fire signed in August that year generally has held, resulting in the longest sustained period of peace in northern Uganda in more than two decades.[76] Although the LRA is no longer operating in northern Uganda, it is still present in the Central African Republic, Congo and Sudan and reportedly has continued abducting children well into 2008, according to a June 23 report by Secretary-General Ban.[77]

A diplomat negotiating on Kony's behalf initialed a peace agreement in February 2008, but Kony himself failed to show up for much-publicized signing ceremonies in April and May, reportedly fearing he might be arrested to face war crimes charges.[78] Uganda has offered to request that the charges against Kony be dropped so he could be tried in a local tribunal, but so far this has not been enough incentive for him to turn himself in.

CURRENT SITUATION

"Empty Threats"

United Nations officials and independent human rights groups say the U.N. Security Council risks losing credibility because of its failure to follow through on repeated threats to impose sanctions against governments and armed groups that persist in recruiting and using child soldiers.

In its last two resolutions on child soldiers — Resolution 1539 in 2004 and Resolution 1612 in 2005 — the Security Council threatened to impose "targeted measures" (primarily sanctions) against armed groups that defy international demands to stop using children in combat, but so far it has not taken any action. The council "needs to show that the threats they make are not empty threats," says Becker, of Human Rights Watch.

Top U.N. officials in recent months also have called on the council to follow through on its threats to punish those who use child soldiers. In his annual report on children and armed conflict, published in January, Secretary-General Ban suggested the council impose various measures, including banning the export or supplying of weapons, banning military assistance, imposing travel restrictions on government officials or leaders of armed groups, preventing armed groups and their leaders from accessing the international financial system and referring violators to the ICC for possible war-crimes punishment.[79]

And on Feb. 12, Special Representative Coomaraswamy confronted the council directly on the issue, pointing out that U.N. reports over the past five years had identified 16 "persistent violators" of international law, some of whom were "making efforts" to comply with the law, while others "remain in contempt of the council and its resolutions."[80]

She doubts the council will impose sanctions anytime soon, however, which she finds frustrating. "You have to realize that [imposing sanctions] is the most extreme action the Security Council can take in any context," she says. "And this is the Security Council, where there are always strong political considerations, and they are very cautious, so I think it will be some time down the road before they agree on sanctions."

Her comments reflect the fact that all actions by the Security Council require extensive compromise among countries with often-conflicting viewpoints, and the council cannot act unless there is unanimous agreement among all five of its permanent, veto-wielding members (Britain, China, France, Russia and the United States). In recent years China and Russia have been the most reluctant of the so-called "permanent five" to intervene in what they consider the domestic affairs of member states.

On the same day Coomaraswamy called for Security Council action, the council said it was "gravely concerned by the persistent disregard of its resolutions on children and armed conflict by parties to armed conflict." The council also said it "reaffirms its intention to make use of all the tools" provided in its previous resolutions. However, it did not mention sanctions nor did it take any specific action — either then or in subsequent months.[81]

AFP/Getty Images/Simon Maina

A young Congolese Patriotic Union soldier totes his rifle in the Democratic Republic of the Congo. In addition to rebel groups, Congo's government also uses child soldiers. Congo is one of seven countries — including Afghanistan, Chad, Somalia, Sri Lanka, Sudan and Uganda — that have used child soldiers while receiving U.S. military aid. Legislation pending before Congress would bar military aid to any country that uses child soldiers.

As Becker's comments suggest, independent human-rights groups are equally frustrated with the Security Council's lack of action. In two reports last January, the Watchlist on Children and Armed Conflict (a coalition of human rights groups) detailed several cases in which the council suggested it would act against violators but did not.[82] Becker says the council's reluctance to act

AT ISSUE

Should the U.S. prosecute alleged child soldiers at Guantánamo?

YES

David B. Rivkin, Jr.
Partner, Baker Hostetler LLP, Washington, D.C.
Former Justice Department official and associate White House counsel during the Reagan and George H.W. Bush administrations

Written for *CQ Global Researcher*, June 2008

In a challenge to the laws of war employed by the United States since 9/11, critics claim the military commission prosecution of Omar Ahmed Khadr is illegitimate. A Canadian national, Khadr is accused of committing war crimes while fighting with al Qaeda in Afghanistan when he was 15. His lawyers argue he is a "child soldier" and thus immune from liability. These claims have no legal or policy merit.

Although the Optional Protocol to the Convention on the Rights of the Child bars recruitment and use of juveniles for combat, terrorist groups are not likely to comply with the protocol or worry about potential liability for their non-compliance. But this is irrelevant to Khadr's liability.

As presiding Judge Peter Brownback has properly ruled, the Military Commissions Act of 2006 gave the commission jurisdiction to try war-related offenses committed by juveniles, and nothing in U.S. law or the Constitution contradicts that. He also has properly concluded that no international treaty, convention or customary law norm establishes age as a bar to war-crimes prosecutions. Indeed, Khadr's lawyers have not cited any international law supporting their extraordinary claim of legal immunity.

This leaves the United States with a choice of whether to continue with Khadr's prosecution or exercise prosecutorial discretion and dismiss all charges against him — even if his prosecution is legally permissible. But first one must ask whether prosecuting him makes policy sense or is fair and just. Would we not be better served by sending Khadr home to be reunited with his family?

The answer is no. The gravity of the alleged offenses and the fact that he chose to join al Qaeda, an unlawful enemy entity, strongly mitigate against granting him immunity. Plus, he performed these actions at 15 — an age old enough to assess the moral and legal implications of his behavior.

Moreover, proponents of immunity fail to see that it would only further incentivize the continued recruitment of child soldiers and the use of children in the commission of war crimes. This result would neither benefit juveniles involved nor help their victims, who usually are civilians.

More broadly, granting him immunity would further debase international laws against war crimes — laws that have taken centuries to develop and are absolutely necessary if 21st-century warfare is not to descend into unbridled barbarism and carnage, to the detriment of the civilized world.

NO

Jo Becker
Advocacy director, Children's Rights Division, Human Rights Watch;
Founding chairman, Coalition to Stop the Use of Child Soldiers

Written for *CQ Global Researcher*, June 2008

Since 2002 the United States has held at least 23 detainees who were under 18 at the U.S. military base at Guantánamo Bay, Cuba. Two of them, Omar Khadr and Mohammad Jawad, are being prosecuted before U.S. military commissions for allegedly throwing grenades at American soldiers in Afghanistan. Khadr was 15 when he reportedly killed U.S. Army Sgt. First Class Christopher Speer and injured other soldiers in a July 2002 firefight. Jawad was 16 or 17 in December 2002 when he allegedly tossed a grenade into a military vehicle and injured two U.S. soldiers and an Afghan translator.

During the more than five years that Khadr and Jawad have been detained at Guantánamo, the United States has ignored their juvenile status. In violation of international juvenile-justice standards, the two have been incarcerated with adult detainees, subjected to prolonged solitary confinement, denied direct contact with their families and refused educational opportunities or rehabilitation.

Under juvenile-justice standards and international guidelines for the treatment of former child soldiers, children should be treated according to their unique vulnerability, lower degree of culpability and capacity for rehabilitation. Although international law does not preclude prosecution of child soldiers for serious crimes, their rehabilitation and reintegration into society must be paramount.

America's treatment of Jawad and Khadr cannot be construed as rehabilitative. They are confined in small cells for 22 hours a day, with little more than a mattress, the Koran and toilet paper. Their attorneys say Jawad and Khadr have been tortured. Khadr says his interrogators shackled him in painful positions, threatened him with rape and used him as a "human mop" after he urinated on the floor during one interrogation session. Jawad was moved from cell to cell and deprived of sleep. Eleven months after arriving at Guantánamo, Jawad tried to hang himself with his shirt collar. His lawyer says he suffers from severe depression and appears to have lost touch with reality.

Under juvenile-justice principles, cases involving children must be resolved quickly and their detention be as short as possible. But Khadr and Jawad were held for more than three years before even being charged. Now, five years after their apprehension, there is no foreseeable end to their ordeal.

Guantánamo, with its flawed military commissions, is no place for children. The United States should either transfer their cases to U.S. federal court and apply fundamental standards of juvenile justice, or release them for rehabilitation.

means that "as long as governments and commanders of these groups know they can recruit and use child soldiers without serious consequences, in particular to them personally, they will do it. But if their visas are denied or their assets are frozen or they suffer some real penalties, they will at least think twice about it."

U.N. officials say they repeatedly have confronted government officials and leaders of armed groups with evidence of their use of child soldiers, often to be greeted with outright denials or with vague pledges to stop the practice. "Their justification is, 'We don't go out and recruit,' which of course is not true," says Coomaraswamy, who often meets with leaders of armed groups using child soldiers. "They say, 'The children are hanging out at the gates, they want to join, many of them are orphans, how can I send them away?' This is usually the line, along with, 'We give them food, they are so happy,' that kind of thing."

Prosecuting Violators

The international community has another, stronger weapon against government leaders and military commanders who use child soldiers: Prosecution for war crimes. So far 19 commanders — all from Africa — have faced charges or prosecution either at the International Criminal Court or in special war crimes tribunals. Five have been convicted; the others are either on trial, awaiting trial, still at large or have reportedly died.

Four of the five convictions were handed down by the U.N.-supported special tribunal on war crimes committed during the brutal civil war in Sierra Leone, which raged from 1991 to 2002. The Hague-based Special Court for Sierra Leone in June 2007 convicted and sentenced three members of the Armed Forces Revolutionary Council — Alex Tamba Brima, Brima Bazzy Kamara and Santigie Borbor Kanu — on charges the rebel group committed war crimes and recruited and used child soldiers. It was the first time an international tribunal had ruled on the recruitment of child soldiers. "These convictions are a ground-breaking step toward ending impunity for commanders who exploit hundreds of thousands of children as soldiers in conflicts worldwide," Human Rights Watch said at the time.[83] The three men were sentenced to prison terms ranging from 45 to 50 years, and those sentences were affirmed in February by the court's appellate division.

A fourth man, Allieu Kondewa, a member of the Civil Defense Forces militia, was convicted in August 2007 on several charges, including recruitment of child soldiers.[84] He was sentenced to eight years in prison, which has since been increased to 20 years.[85]

Crane, the Syracuse University law professor who was the first prosecutor at the Sierra Leone court, says those convictions established important precedents. "This tells the leaders of these kinds of groups all over the world, 'If you are committing international crimes like abducting children and making them kill people, you can be convicted and sent to prison for the rest of your life.' "

A tribunal in the Democratic Republic of the Congo in March 2006 convicted Jean-Pierre Biyoyo, former commander of the Mudundu 40 armed group, on charges of recruiting and using child soldiers. Although he was sentenced to death, the sentence was reduced to five years' imprisonment.[86] Three months later he escaped from prison and eventually joined rebel leader Nkunda in North Kivu province, according to the U.S. State Department.[87]

Among the dozen other officials and warlords charged with war crimes for using child soldiers, the most prominent defendant is Taylor of Liberia, who currently is on trial before the Special Court for Sierra Leone on 11 charges of war crimes and crimes against humanity, including the use child soldiers.[88]

The International Criminal Court has charged three former Congolese guerrilla leaders with various war crimes, including the use of child soldiers. Thomas Lubanga Dyilo, leader of the Union of Congolese Patriots, had been scheduled to be the first person ever tried by the court. He was charged in 2006 with enlisting, recruiting and using child soldiers during the long and bloody fighting in Ituri region in eastern Democratic Republic of the Congo.[89]

However, the case appeared on the verge of collapse in early July as the result of a dispute between the U.N. and the ICC judges over U.N. documents that the prosecution had used to develop its charges. The U.N. had given the documents to the prosecution on a confidential basis. The court's judges indefinitely halted the Lubanga case on June 13 because the documents contain "exculpatory material" that should have been made available to the defense. An initial attempt to work out a compromise failed, and the trial judges on July 2 ordered Lubanga's eventual release as the "logical consequence" of the earlier decision. The prosecution appealed the decision to halt the case, and the ICC's appellate chamber said on July 7 that Lubanga should remain in prison until it had ruled on that appeal. News reports said ICC officials were still hoping for a compromise on the documents issue.

Human Rights Watch expressed disappointment over the legal wrangling, saying the failure of the case would deny justice to the alleged victims of Lubanga's actions. "The victims are the ones who suffer as a result of these embarrassing legal difficulties at the ICC," HRW counsel Param-Preet Singh says. Even so, she adds, denying Lubanga a fair trial "would also be an injustice, and the ICC cannot afford that, either."[90]

The possible collapse of the Lubanga case also came as a disappointment to the U.N., which had expected the case to establish legal doctrines on punishing those who recruit and use child soldiers. In a statement after the June 13 decision to halt the trial, U.N. Special Representative Coomaraswamy urged that the trial "not be compromised for technical reasons" and noted that the case "is considered a major milestone in international attempts" to eradicate the practice of using child soldiers."

U.S. Legislation

Both of the U.S. bills concerning child soldiers have made some progress but are still pending, with time running out for action during an election year. The House approved the Child Soldier Prevention Act — which would bar military aid and arms sales to countries using child soldiers — on Dec. 4, 2007. It was included in a measure to reauthorize a 2000 anti-human-trafficking law.[91] The vote on the underlying bill was 405-2, with no opposition to the child soldier provisions. The Senate, by contrast, has passed the Child Soldiers Accountability Act, which criminalizes the use of child soldiers and bars entry into the United States by anyone using child soldiers. The measure was approved by unanimous consent on Dec. 18, 2007.

Senate sponsors combined both bills into one measure, the Child Soldier Accountability and Prevention Act of 2008 (S 3061), introduced on May 22 by Joseph R. Biden, D-Del., and Sam Brownback, R-Kan. The measure is pending before the Senate Judiciary Committee, after markup was delayed on June 26 by an unnamed Republican senator who put a hold on the bill.

OUTLOOK

Child Terrorists?

Some of the recent conflicts that have involved the most widespread and notorious use of child soldiers have ended with formal peace agreements or dwindled into low-level, sporadic fighting. Among them were the inter-related conflicts in West Africa; the huge, pan-African war in the Democratic Republic of the Congo; and civil wars in the Balkans, El Salvador and Indonesia. The latest global survey by the Coalition to Stop the Use of Child Soldiers said the number of countries where children were directly involved in conflicts declined from 27 in 2004 (when the group issued its previous report) to 17 by the end of 2007.[92]

Becker, of Human Rights Watch, says the decline is good news but does not mean the child-soldier problem has disappeared. "Some conflicts are ending, but that does not mean that children are no longer being used in war," she says. "When armed conflicts occur, children are almost inevitably involved." As examples, Becker cites new, or newly revived conflicts in the past two years in the Central African Republic, Chad and Somalia — all involving extensive use of children.

Moreover, new conflicts can be expected because the underlying conditions that led to most of the world's civil conflicts remain unresolved. "It's not like we have fewer poor kids today, fewer orphans who can be recruited by warlords," says Singer of the Brookings Institution. "You still have these problems on a global scale."

Specialists in the field, as well as government officials worldwide are particularly concerned about what appears to be the increasing use of children as terrorists, including as suicide bombers. The Tamil Tigers developed the tactic two decades ago, even fashioning suicide bomb vests in small sizes for children, according to some sources.[93]

Suicide bombing as a terrorist tactic has spread in recent years to other parts of South and Central Asia — including Afghanistan, India and Pakistan — to Colombia and to the Middle East, including extremist Palestinian factions, and Iraq.[94] Children in their early- and mid-teens have carried out, or attempted, suicide attacks in nearly all these places, sometimes causing large-scale fatalities. In Iraq, U.S military officials have said insurgents often use children to place the roadside bombs, known as "improvised explosive devices," that typically kill American troops.

Singer does not expect terrorism and the use of children by terrorists to diminish anytime soon, despite the efforts of the U.S. "war" against terrorism. In fact, he says, "we could see the use of children as terrorists globally, if you put yourself in the position of the planners of these attacks and how they might be looking to expand their operations."

As for combating the more conventional use of children in civil conflicts, the U.N.'s Coomaraswamy is optimistic the world is ready to act more decisively. "This is an issue on which you have a near-global consensus on the need for action, not just rhetoric," she says. "Not that we will be able to stop all recruitment and use of child solders, but I think we can lessen it quite a bit in the next decade."

She and other experts had hoped that the two most prominent cases involving use of child soldiers — the ongoing Taylor tribunal and the ICC case against Lubanga — would produce ground-breaking convictions demonstrating that the use of children in war will be punished.

The dismissal of the Lubanga case could give added importance to the Taylor trial, where Crane, the former special prosecutor in Sierra Leone, expects a guilty verdict. "That will have an incredible ripple effect, particularly on the dictators and warlords of the world," he says. "It says that the lives of their citizens matter. In particular, it shows Africans themselves that their lives matter."

NOTES

1. Testimony of Ishmael Beah, Senate Judiciary Subcommittee on Human Rights and the Law, hearing on "Casualties of War: Child Soldiers and the Law," April 24, 2007, http://judiciary.senate.gov/testimony.cfm?id=2712&wit_id=6387.
2. P. W. Singer, *Children at War* (2006), p. 23.
3. "Some 250,000 children worldwide recruited to fight in wars — UN official," United Nations Department of Public Information, Jan. 30, 2008, www.un.org/apps/news/story.asp?NewsID=25450&Cr=children&Cr1=conflict#.
4. Singer, *op. cit.*, p. 30.
5. "Sold to be Soldiers: The Recruitment and Use of Child Soldiers in Burma," Human Rights Watch, October 2007, www.hrw.org/reports/2007/burma1007/burma1007web.pdf.
6. "Child Soldiers Global Report 2008," Coalition to Stop the Use of Child Solders, p. 29, www.childsoldiersglobalreport.org/files/country_pdfs/FINAL_2008_Global_Report.pdf.
7. "Cape Town Principles and Best Practices," April 1997, UNICEF, p. 8, www.unicef.org/emerg/files/Cape_Town_Principles(1).
8. David M. Rosen, *Armies of the Young: Child Soldiers in War and Terrorism* (2005), p. 4.
9. "Childhood Denied: Child Soldiers in Africa," Amnesty International, available online under the title "Democratic Republic of Congo: Children at War," on p. 7, at www.amnesty.org/en/library/asset/AFR62/034/2003/en/dom-AFR620342003en.pdf.
10. Ishmael Beah, *A Long Way Gone: Memoirs of a Boy Soldier* (2007).
11. "Children and Armed Conflict, Report of the Secretary General," Dec. 21, 2007, pp. 40-45.
12. U.N. Security Council Resolution 1379, www.securitycouncilreport.org/atf/cf/{65BFCF9B-6D27-4E9C-8CD3-CF6E4FF96FF9}/CAC%20SRES%201379.pdf.
13. "Child Soldiers Global Report 2008," *op. cit.*
14. "Children and Armed Conflict," *op. cit.*, p. 33.
15. "Report of the Secretary General on Children and Armed Conflict in Sri Lanka," Dec. 21, 2007, pp. 3-7.
16. "International Forum on Armed Groups and the Involvement of Children in Armed Conflict: Summary of Themes and Discussion," Coalition to Stop the Use of Child Soldiers, August 2007, p. 16, www.child-soldiers.org/childsoldiers/Armed_groups_forum_report_August_ 2007_revision_0ct07.pdf.
17. "Military Commission Charges Referred," U.S. Department of Defense news release, April 24 2007, www.defenselink.mil/releases/release.aspx?releaseid=10779. For background, see David Masci and Kenneth Jost, "War on Terrorism," *CQ Researcher*, Oct. 12, 2001, pp. 817-848; also see Peter Katel and

Kenneth Jost, "Treatment of Detainees," *CQ Researcher*, Aug. 25, 2006, pp. 673-696.

18. "Ruling on Defense Motion for Dismissal Due to Lack of Jurisdiction Under the MCA in Regard to Juvenile Crimes of a Child Soldier," *United States of America v. Omar Ahmed Khadr*, April 30, 2008, www.defenselink.mil/news/d20080430Motion.pdf.
19. "Letter to U.S. Secretary of Defense Robert Gates on Omar Khadr," Human Rights Watch, April 2, 2008, www.hrw.org/english/docs/2008/02/01/usint17956.htm.
20. *Amicus curiae* brief contained in the April 30 ruling, note 19 above, pp. 108-146.
21. Rome Statute of the International Criminal Court, United Nations Doc. A/CONF.183/9, July 17, 1998.
22. "The Paris Principles: Principles and Guidelines on Children Associated with Armed Forces or Armed Groups," February 2007, section 3.6, www.diplomatie.gouv.fr/en/IMG/pdf/Paris_Conference_Principles_English _31_January.pdf.
23. "Government's Response to the Defense's Motion for Dismissal Due to Lack of Jurisdiction under the MCA in Regard to Juvenile Crimes of a Child Soldier," Jan. 25, 2008. p. 9, footnote 3.
24. Deputy Assistant Secretary of Defense Sandra L. Hodgkinson, testimony to the U.N. Committee on the Rights of the Child Concerning U.S. Implementation of the Optional Protocol on Children in Armed Conflict, May 22, 2008, p. 26, www2.ohchr.org/english/bodies/crc/docs/statements/48USA Opening_Statements.pdf.
25. Randall Palmer, "Top Court Says Canada Complicit in Guantánamo Base," Reuters, May 23, 2008.
26. "Military Commission Charges Referred," U.S. Department of Defense, Jan. 31, 2008, www.defenselink.mil/releases/release.aspx?releaseid=11655.
27. *Congressional Record*, Dec. 18, 2007, p. S15941.
28. "Country Reports on Human Rights Practices: Afghanistan," U.S. State Department, March 11, 2008. www.state.gov/g/drl/rls/hrrpt/2007/100611.htm.
29. "U.S. Military Assistance to Governments and Government-Supported Armed Groups Using Child Soldiers, 2002-2008," Center for Defense Information, April 2, 2008, p. 1, www.cdi.org/PDFs/CS_MilAssist08.pdf.
30. "Casualties Of War: Child Soldiers and The Law," Sen. Dick Durbin, April 24, 2007, http://durbin.senate.gov/showRelease.cfm?releaseId=280883.
31. "Report of the Secretary General on Children and Armed Conflict in Chad," United Nations, July 3, 2007, p. 7; also see "Early to War: Child Soldiers in the Chad Conflict," Human Rights Watch, July 2007, www.hrw.org/reports/2007/chad0707/.
32. Singer, *op. cit.*, p. 63.
33. *Ibid.*, p. 41.
34. "Security Council committee concerning Côte d'Ivoire issues list of individuals subject to measures imposed by Resolution 1572 (2004)," SC/8631, U.N. Department of Public Information, Feb. 7, 2006.
35. "Report of the Secretary General on Children and Armed Conflict in Somalia," May 7, 2007, p. 13, www.unhcr.org/cgi-bin/texis/vtx/refworld/rwmain?docid=4850fe4e2.
36. Jimmie Briggs, *Innocents Lost: When Child Soldiers Go to War* (2005), p. 41.
37. "Child Soldiers Global Report 2008," *op. cit.*, pp. 101-103; "Overcoming Lost Childhoods: Lessons Learned from the Rehabilitation and Reintegration of Former Child Soldiers in Colombia," YCare International, 2007, p. 4; "You'll Learn Not to Cry: Child Combatants in Colombia," Human Rights Watch, September 2003, www.hrw.org/reports/2003/colombia0903/.
38. Briggs, *op. cit.*, p. 56.
39. "Child Soldiers Global Report 2008," *op. cit.*, p. 101.
40. *Ibid.*, p. 102.
41. "Mortality in the DRC: An Ongoing Crisis," International Rescue Committee, January 2008, www.theirc.org/media/www/congo-crisis-fast-facts.html.
42. "Child soldier recruitment continues," United Nations Integrated Regional Information Network, Feb. 19, 2007.
43. "Report of the Secretary General on Children and Armed Conflict in the Democratic Republic of the Congo," June 28, 2007, pp. 14-15, http://daccessdds.un.org/doc/UNDOC/GEN/N07/390/16/PDF/N0739016.pdf?OpenElement.

44. *Ibid.*, pp. 3-6.
45. "MONUC welcomes the success of the Goma conference and the signing of its acts of engagement," United Nations Mission in the Democratic Republic of the Congo, Jan. 23, 2008, www.monuc.org/News.aspx?newsId=16531.
46. "After two key deals, what progress towards peace in North Kivu?" United Nations Integrated Regional Information Network, May 14, 2008, www.reliefweb.int/rw/rwb.nsf/db900sid/KKAA-7EN5EQ?OpenDocument&rc=1&cc =cod.
47. "Report on Human Rights, Democratic Republic of the Congo, 2007," U.S. Department of State, www.state.gov/g/drl/rls/hrrpt/2007/100475.htm.
48. "Child Soldiers Global Report," *op. cit.*, p. 212.
49. "Report of the Secretary General on Children and Armed Conflict in Myanmar," Nov. 16, 2007, pp. 4-5.
50. "Sold to be Soldiers," *op. cit.*
51. *Ibid.*, pp. 25-26.
52. "Report of the Secretary General on Children and Armed Conflict in Myanmar," *op. cit.*, pp. 5-6.
53. "Sold to be Soldiers," *op. cit.*, p. 60.
54. *Ibid.*, p. 94.
55. "Report of the Secretary General on Children and Armed Conflict in Sri Lanka," Dec. 21, 2007.
56. "United Nations Concerned by Civilian Deaths in Sri Lanka," U.N. Department of Public Information, Jan. 2, 2007, www.un.org/News/Press/docs/2007/iha1248.doc.htm.
57. "No Safety, No Escape: Children and the Escalating Armed Conflict in Sri Lanka," Watchlist on Children and Armed Conflict, April 2008, p. 5.
58. "Complicit in Crime: State Collusion in Abductions and Child Recruitment by the Karuna Group," Human Rights Watch, January 2007, www.hrw.org/reports/2007/srilanka0107/.
59. "Press Conference on Children and Armed Conflict in Sri Lanka," U.N. Department of Public Information, April 14, 2008, www.un.org/News/briefings/docs/2008/080414_Children.doc.htm.
60. "Report of the Secretary General on Children and Armed Conflict in the Sudan," Aug. 29, 2007, p. 4, www.cfr.org/publication/11358/report_of_the_secretary general_on_children_and_armed_conflict_in_the_sudan.html.
61. *Ibid.*, pp. 5-6.
62. "Conclusions on Parties in the Armed Conflict in the Sudan," Working Group on Children and Armed Conflict, U.N. Security Council, Feb. 5, 2008, p. 1.
63. "Report of the Secretary General on the Sudan," Jan. 31, 2008, p. 2.
64. "Child Soldiers Global Report 2008," *op. cit.*, p. 319.
65. "Report of the Secretary General on Children and Armed Conflict in the Sudan," *op. cit.*, pp. 2, 5.
66. *Ibid.*, p. 6.
67. "Child Soldiers Global Report 2008", *op. cit.*, pp. 89, 93.
68. "Report of the Secretary-General on Children and Armed Conflict in Uganda," May 7, 2007, p. 3.
69. "Child Soldiers Global Report 2008," *op. cit.*, p. 347; "Uganda: LRA Regional Atrocities Demand Action," Human Rights Watch, May 19, 2008, www.hrw.org/english/docs/2008/05/19/uganda18863.htm.
70. "Report of the Secretary-General on Children and Armed Conflict in Uganda," *op. cit.*, p. 4.
71. "Child Soldiers Global Report 2008," *op. cit.*, p. 347.
72. "The Shadows of Peace: Life after the LRA," IRIN news service, Sept. 18, 2006.
73. "Optimism prevails despite setback in peace talks," IRIN news service, April 18, 2008.
74. "Stolen Children: Abduction and Recruitment in Northern Uganda," Human Rights Watch, March 2003, www.hrw.org/reports/2003/uganda0303/.
75. "Report of the Secretary-General on Children and Armed Conflict in Uganda," *op. cit.*, pp. 2, 5.
76. "Living with the LRA: The Juba Initiative," IRIN news service, May 1, 2008.
77. "Additional report of the Secretary-General on children and armed conflict in Uganda," United Nations, p. 3, June 23, 2008, http://daccess-ods.un.org/access.nsf/Get?OpenAgent&DS=s/2008/409&Lang=E.
78. Charles Mpagi Mwanguhya, "Peace Deal Dissolves," Institute for War and Peace Reporting, May 19, 2008, www.iwpr.net/?p=acr&s=f&o=344708&apc_state=henh.

79. "Report of the Secretary-General on Children and Armed Conflict," Dec. 21, 2007, p. 37.

80. "Statement in the Security Council by Special Representative of the Secretary General for Children and Armed Conflict Radhika Coomaraswamy," Feb. 12, 2008.

81. "Statement by the President of the Security Council," Feb. 12, 2008, http://daccess-ods.un.org/access.nsf/Get?Open&DS=S/PRST/2008/6&Lang=E&Area=UNDOC.

82. "Getting it Done and Doing It Right: A Global Study on the United Nations-led Monitoring and Reporting Mechanism on Children and Armed Conflict," Watchlist on Children and Armed Conflict, January 2008, www.watchlist.org/reports/pdf/global-v8-web.pdf; and "The Security Council and Children and Armed Conflicts: Next Steps towards Ending Violations Against Children," Watchlist on Children and Armed Conflict, January 2008.

83. Christo Johnson, "Sierra Leone tribunal issues historic verdicts," *The Independent* (London), June 21, 2007.

84. "Report of the Special Representative of the Secretary General for Children and Armed Conflict," Aug. 13, 2007, p. 5; Coalition to Stop the Use of Child Soldiers, www.child-soldiers.org/childsoldiers/legal-framework.

85. See www.sc-sl.org/CDF-Timeline.html.

86. "Report of the Secretary General on Children and Armed Conflict in the Democratic Republic of the Congo," *op. cit.*, p. 27.

87. "Report on Human Rights, Democratic Republic of the Congo, 2007," U.S. State Department, www.state.gov/g/drl/rls/hrrpt/2007/100475.htm.

88. "Report of the Special Representative of the Secretary General for Children and Armed Conflict," *op. cit.*

89. "The Prosecutor v. Thomas Lubanga Dyilo," International Criminal Court, www.icc-cpi.int/cases/RDC/c0106/c0106_doc.html.

90. "International Criminal Court's Trial of Thomas Lubanga 'Stayed,' " Human Rights Watch, http://hrw.org/english/docs/2008/06/19/congo19163.htm.

91. For background, see David Masci, "Human Trafficking and Slavery," *CQ Researcher*, March 26, 2004, pp. 273-296.

92. "Child Soldiers Global Report 2008," *op. cit.*, p. 12.

93. Singer, *op. cit.*, p. 118.

94. *Ibid.*, pp. 117-119.

BIBLIOGRAPHY

Books

Beah, Ishmael, *A Long Way Gone: Memoirs of a Boy Soldier*, *Sarah Chrichton Books*, 2007.
A former child soldier tells his compelling story of being recruited into one of Sierra Leone's rebel groups at age 13.

Briggs, Jimmie, *Innocents Lost: When Child Soldiers Go to War*, *Basic Books*, 2005.
A New York journalist provides first-hand reports about child soldiers in Afghanistan, Colombia, Sri Lanka and Uganda.

Rosen, David M., *Armies of the Young: Child Soldiers in War and Terrorism*, *Rutgers University Press*, 2006.
An American anthropologist examines legal and political issues surrounding the use of child soldiers.

Singer, P. W., *Children at War*, *University of California Press*, 2006.
A senior fellow at the Brookings Institution provides a comprehensive overview of the use of child soldiers.

Wessells, Michael, *Child Soldiers: From Violence to Protection*, *Harvard University Press*, 2006.
A professor of psychology at Randolph-Macon College examines issues involving child soldiers, drawing on his own three decades of experiences reintegrating former child soldiers into their former communities.

Articles

Boustany, Nora, "Report: Brokers Supply Child Soldiers to Burma," *The Washington Post*, Oct. 31, 2007, p. A16.
Burma's military government has been forcibly recruiting child soldiers through brokers who buy and sell boys to help the army deal with personnel shortages, according to a detailed report by Human Rights Watch.

Pownall, Katy, "In the Tragedy of Child-Soldiering in Africa, a Girl's Story Finds a Happy Ending," *The Associated Press*, Aug. 25, 2007.
A former female child soldier in Uganda is now studying environmental health at a university.

Reports and Studies

"Child Soldiers: Global Report 2008," *Coalition to Stop the Use of Child Soldiers*, May 2008, www.childsoldiersglobalreport.org/.
A nongovernmental organization offers its latest report on the use of child soldiers, including assessments of how well the United Nations and others are combating the problem.

"Children in Conflict: Eradicating the Child Soldier Doctrine," *The Carr Center for Human Rights Policy, Kennedy School of Government, Harvard University*, www.hks.harvard.edu/cchrp/pdf/ChildSoldierReport.pdf.
The center recommends international action to combat the use of child soldiers.

"Getting it Done and Doing It Right: A Global Study on the United Nations-led Monitoring and Reporting Mechanism on Children and Armed Conflict," *Watchlist on Children and Armed Conflict*, January 2008, www.watchlist.org/news/reports/pdf/global-v8-web.pdf.
A watchdog group critiques the U.N. Security Council's system of monitoring the impact of armed conflict on children, including child soldiers.

"Making Reintegration Work for Youth in Northern Uganda," *The Survey of War Affected Youth*, November 2007, www.sway-uganda.org/SWAY.ResearchBrief.Reintegration.pdf.
This report summarizes two phases of a long-term study of the economic, educational, social and other needs of former child soldiers in the Lord's Resistance Army in northern Uganda.

"The Security Council and Children and Armed Conflicts: Next Steps towards Ending Violations Against Children," *Watchlist on Children and Armed Conflict*, January 2008, http://watchlist.org/docs/Next_Steps_for_Security_Council_-_Child_Soldiers_Coalition_and_Watchlist_-_January_2008.pdf.
The watchdog group recommends that the U.N. Security Council take tougher measures against those who continue to use child soldiers.

"Soldiers of Misfortune: Abusive U.S. Military Recruitment and Failure to Protect Child Soldiers," American Civil Liberties Union, May 2008, www.aclu.org/intlhumanrights/gen/35245pub20080513.html.
A civil rights organization critiques U.S. policies toward the use of child soldiers, including voluntary recruitment of teenagers under 18 and detention of under-18-year-old alleged terrorists by the military.

U.N. Reports

"Children and armed conflict: Report of the Secretary-General," *U.N. Security Council*, Dec. 21, 2007, http://daccessdds.un.org/doc/UNDOC/GEN/N07/656/04/PDF/N0765604.pdf?OpenElement.
In his latest annual report to the U.N. Security Council, Secretary-General Ban Ki-moon listed 40 groups in 13 countries around the world that continue to use child soldiers. A complete list of other U.N. reports on conflicts affecting children is at www.un.org/children/conflict/english/reports.html.

For More Information

Amnesty International, 1 Easton St., London WC1X 0DW, United Kingdom; 44-20-7413-5500; http://web.amnesty.org. Actively advocates on a wide range of human rights issues, including child soldiers.

Child Rights Information Network, c/o Save the Children, 1 St. John's Lane, London EC1M 4AR, United Kingdom; 44-20-7012-6866; www.crin.org. Advocates for enforcement of international legal standards protecting children; associated with Save the Children-UK.

Coalition to Stop the Use of Child Soldiers, 4th Floor, 9 Marshalsea Road, London SE1 1EP, United Kingdom; 44-20-7367-4110/4129; www.child-soldiers.org. A coalition of international human rights groups that sponsors conferences and issues regular reports on child soldiers in armed conflicts.

Human Rights Watch, 350 Fifth Ave., 34th Floor, New York, NY 10118-3299; (212) 290-4700; http://hrw.org/campaigns/crp/index.htm. One of the most active international groups pushing governments, the United Nations and other agencies to stop using child soldiers.

International Committee of the Red Cross, 19 avenue de la Paix, CH 1202 Geneva, Switzerland; 41-22-734-6001; www.icrc.org/web/eng/siteeng0.nsf/html/children!Open. Advocates on behalf of all victims of war, including child soldiers.

United Nations Children's Fund (UNICEF), UNICEF House, 3 United Nations Plaza, New York, NY 10017; (212) 325-7000; www.unicef.org. Monitors the impact of war on children, including the recruitment and use of child soldiers.

United Nations Special Representative of the Secretary-General for Children and Armed Conflict, United Nations S-3161, New York, NY 10017; (212) 963-3178; www.un.org/children/conflict/english/home6.html. The primary U.N. official dealing with children and armed conflict; works with governments and armed groups to develop action plans for releasing child soldiers and easing the burden of children in conflict; issues regular reports on the world's most serious conflicts.

Watchlist on Children and Armed Conflict, c/o Women's Commission for Refugee Women and Children, 122 East 42nd St., 12th Floor, New York, NY 10168-1289; (212) 551-3111; www.watchlist.org. Publishes studies and advocates strong international action to aid children caught up in armed conflict.

War Child International, 401 Richmond St. West, Suite 204, Toronto, Ontario, Canada M5V3A8; (416) 971-7474; www.warchild.org/index.html. A coalition of groups advocating on behalf of children caught in armed conflicts.